The Struggle for Economic Development

THE STRUGGLE FOR ECONOMIC DEVELOPMENT

Readings in Problems and Policies

Edited by **Michael P. Todaro**

Longman

New York & London

THE STRUGGLE FOR ECONOMIC DEVELOPMENT
Readings in Problems and Policies

Longman Inc., 1560 Broadway, New York, N.Y. 10036
Associated companies, branches, and representatives
throughout the world.

Developmental Editor: Irving E. Rockwood
Editorial and Design Supervisor: Ferne Y. Kawahara
Manufacturing Supervisor: Marion Hess

Library of Congress Cataloging in Publication Data
Main entry under title:

The Struggle for economic development.

    Intended to be used with: Economic development
in the Third World / Michael P. Todaro. 2nd ed.
    Includes bibliographies.
    1. Economic development – Addresses, essays,
lectures. 2. Underdeveloped areas – Addresses,
essays, lectures. I. Todaro, Michael P.
HD82.S8458   338.9′009172′4   82–7229
ISBN 0-582-28384-1 (pbk.)   AACR2

Manufactured in the United States of America
Printing: 9 8 7 6 5 4 3   Year: 92 91 90 98 88 87 86

For Annette Todaro
and the memory of
George J. Todaro, Sr.

Contents

Preface

This book of readings has been compiled with two major objectives in mind. First, I wanted to respond to the numerous requests that I have received from instructors in universities throughout the world that I provide a set of contemporary articles and essays as a supplement to my widely used text, *Economic Development in the Third World* (2nd ed., Longman, 1981). Together, these two books should provide all that is needed for a thorough, in-depth undergraduate (and, in many cases, graduate) course in economic development. Second, I wanted to compile a comprehensive collection of problem-focused, policy-oriented readings for those instructors who do not use a main text. Knowing firsthand the difficulties that students have in securing access to articles in professional journals, chapters from scholarly books, and publications of international development organizations, I felt that such a collection of contemporary readings, with frequent updating, would prove invaluable in helping them to understand the many significant, yet complex, issues of Third World development. As in my text, the readings in this collection have been organized along problem-oriented themes, such as economic growth, poverty and income distribution, population growth, unemployment, urbanization, rural development, education, trade and finance, private foreign investment, foreign aid, development planning, and public policy.

The book is divided into four parts with each part and its component chapters corresponding to the parts and chapters of my text (see p. xix for details of this correspondence). *Part I: Understanding Underdevelopment* introduces students to the reality of underdevelopment, the competing paradigms of economic development, and the lessons or nonlessons of the historical experience of economic growth in Western nations. *Part II: Development Problems and Policies: Domestic*, which contains the major block of readings, examines in detail the critical and, for the most part, chronic domestic problems that confront contemporary Third World nations in their quest for economic and social development. As noted above, the issues explored include the relationship between economic growth, poverty and income distribution; the linkages between population growth and development; the relationship between output, employment, and technological choice; the phenomenon of rapid urbanization in connection with unprecedented rates of rural-urban migration; the dilemma of agricultural transformation and rural development; and the problems of accelerating education and human resource development in the context of competing demands on the public and private purse.

In *Part III: Development Problems and Policies: International* the focus shifts to the international components of development problems, with an examination of trade theory as applied to the structural context of the world economy of the 1980s, the use and misuse of commercial policies (import substitution, export promotion, exchange rate manipulations, etc.) to promote domestic industrialization, and the past experience of, and future prospects for, increased private foreign investment (mainly through multinational corporations) and foreign aid. Finally, *Part IV: Possibilities and Prospects* explores ways for promoting more rapid development both internally through planning and public policy and externally through either a modification or a radical restructuring of the international economic order in recognition of the growing economic and political interdependence of the world's economies.

Because the field of economic development is in such a constant and exciting state of evolution and flux, a book of readings should seek to satisfy two criteria. First, it should provide the latest analytical and factual information regarding the major and persistent issues of the day. Second, it should provide the student with a solid conceptual and empirical foundation for understanding development issues as well as an exposure to the range of ideological controversies that dominate the contemporary debate. Students should then be able to reach a more informed judgment regarding not only the particular problems covered in this book but also those related issues that may arise now and in the future.

To meet the above criteria, I have chosen to focus primarily on what I believe to be the most significant writings of the 1970s and early 1980s rather than to attempt to collect the "classic" (i.e., 1950s and 1960s!) articles in the field. Other well-known books of readings that contain these pieces are available for the interested student or instructor. To broaden the coverage, I have included readings not only from professional journals and scholarly books but also from significant World Bank and United Nations publications. Every reasonable effort has been made to try to provide a balanced coverage of the competing perspectives on the nature and possible resolution of various development problems as reflected, for example, in the writings of traditional neoclassical economists, economic structuralists and the dependencia schools of thought. Also, rather than attempting to condense a great number of substantial essays into two- or three-page extracts to fit the limited space available, I felt that students would be better served and less subject to superficial analysis by reading a smaller set of mostly unedited writings. Finally, because development economics, more than any other field of economics, incorporates insights from the other social sciences, I have included in this collection a few writings by political scientists, anthropologists, political philosophers, social and economic demographers, educational specialists, and national political leaders, even though the vast majority of works are by leading development economists. The very positive response by teachers and students to my text, *Economic Development in the Third World*, convinces me of the merits of this more broadened approach.

Many people, too many to mention without fear of inadvertently leaving some out, have directly or indirectly helped in the preparation of this book. I am particularly indebted to those many instructors both at home and abroad who encouraged me to put together a book of readings to supplement my development text. Their prodding finally overcame my resistance, and I am delighted that they prevailed. I hope that they are equally pleased with the outcome. I have been ably assisted in preparing the manuscript by Lydia Maruszko and Kate Venet, and my editor, Irving Rockwood, has been a continuing source of advice and encouragement.

Finally, once again, no identification of those who have influenced and encouraged my efforts would be complete without mention of the most important one, my wonderful wife, Donna Renée, who understands, as few can, what it is all about.

Michael P. Todaro

Acknowledgments

"The Shock of Underdevelopment" from Denis Goulet, *The Cruel Choice: A New Concept in the Theory of Development*. Copyright © 1971 by Denis Goulet (New York: Atheneum, 1971). Reprinted with the permission of Atheneum Publishers.

"Dimensions of Development," reprinted from *North-South: A Program for Survival*, Report of the Independent Commission on International Development Issues under the Chairmanship of Willy Brandt, by permission of The MIT Press, Cambridge, Massachusetts. © The Independent Commission on International Development Issues, 1980.

"Economic Development Theory: The Current Search for a Mirage," by Gus Papanek reprinted from Manning Nash (ed.), *Essays on Economic Development and Cultural Change in Honor of Bert F. Hoselitz*, by permission of The University of Chicago Press. © 1977 by The University of Chicago Press. All rights reserved.

"Development Alternatives: Problems, Strategies and Values" by Peter J. Henriot reprinted from Daniel Callahan and Phillip G. Clark (eds.), *Ethical Issues of Population Aid: Culture, Economics and International Assistance* by permission of Irvington Press.

"Conventional Development Strategies and Basic Needs Fulfillment," by Franklyn Lisk reprinted from *International Labour Review* 115, March/April 1977, by permission of International Labour Office, Geneva.

"Modern Economic Growth: Findings and Reflections," by Simon Kuznets reprinted from *American Economic Review* 63, June 1973, by permission of American Economic Association, Nashville.

"The Structure of Dependence," by Theotonio Dos Santos reprinted from *American Economic Review* 60, May 1970, by permission of American Economic Association, Nashville.

"Poverty, Growth and Human Development," from *World Development Report, 1980*. Copyright © 1980 by the International Bank for Reconstruction and Development/The World Bank. Published by Oxford University Press, Inc. and reprinted by permission of the Press and The World Bank.

"Poverty and Progress: Choices for the Developing World," by Hollis Chenery reprinted from *Finance and Development*, June 1980.

"Is There a Tradeoff Between Growth and Basic Needs," by Norman L. Hicks reprinted from *Finance and Development*, June 1980.

"Policy Choices and Income Distribution in Less Developed Countries," by Charles R. Frank and Richard C. Webb reprinted from *Development Digest* 16, 1978. Originally published in *Income Distribution and Growth in LDCs*. © 1977 by the Brookings Institution. Reprinted with permission.

"Population Growth: Current Issues and Strategies," by Geoffrey McNicoll and Moni Nag reprinted from *Population and Development Review* 8, June 1982, by permission of The Population Council, New York.

"Analytical Approaches to the Relationship of Population Growth and Development" by Nancy Birdsall abridged and reprinted from *Population and Development Review* 3, March/June 1977 by permission of The Population Council, New York.

"Employment and Basic Needs: An Overview," by Assefa Bequele and David H. Freedman reprinted from *International Labour Review* 118, May/June 1979, by permission of International Labour Office, Geneva.

"Conflicts between Output and Employment Objectives in Developing Countries" by Frances Stewart and Paul Streeten reprinted from *Oxford Economic Papers* 23, July 1971, by permission of Oxford University Press.

"Policies to Encourage the Use of Intermediate Technology," by Howard Pack reprinted from *Development Digest* 14, October 1976, by permission of National Planning Association, Washington, D.C.

"The Urbanization Dilemma," by Michael P. Todaro with Jerry Stilkind reprinted from *City Bias and Rural Neglect: The Dilemma of Urban Development*, Public Issues Paper #4, 1981, by permission of The Population Council, New York.

"Migration, Unemployment and Development: A Two-Sector Analysis," by John R. Harris and Michael P. Todaro reprinted from *American Economic Review* 60, March 1970, by permission of American Economic Association, Nashville.

"A Review and Evaluation of Attempts to Constrain Migration to Selected Urban Centres and Regions," by Alan B. Simmons reprinted from *Population Distribution Policies in Development Planning*, United Nations Population Studies, No. 75, 1981, United Nations Publication Sales No. 81.XIII.5 by permission of United Nations.

"Risk, Uncertainty, and the Subsistence Farmer," by Clifton R. Wharton reprinted from *Development Digest* 7, 1969, by permission of National Planning Association, Washington, D.C.

"Agricultural Pricing Policies in Developing Countries," by Gilbert T. Brown reprinted from Theodore W. Schultz, (ed.), *Distortions of Agricultural Incentives*, 1978, by permission of Indiana University Press.

"Rural Development," by The World Bank reprinted from *The Assault on World Poverty*, 1975, by permission of The Johns Hopkins University Press.

"Human Development Issues and Policies: Education," reprinted from *World Development Report, 1980*. Copyright © 1980 by the International Bank for Reconstruction and Development/The World Bank. Published by Oxford University Press, Inc. and reprinted by permission of the Press and The World Bank.

"Education for Development, Reconsidered," by John Simmons reprinted from *World Development* 7, November/December 1979, by permission of Pergamon Press, Inc.

"Financing Education for Income Distribution," by Jean-Pierre Jallade, reprinted from *Finance and Development* 16, March 1979.

"Three Stories About Trade and Poor Economies," by Sheila Smith and John Toye reprinted from *Journal of Development Studies* 15, April 1979, by permission of Frank Cass & Co. Ltd., London.

"Import Substitution and Industrialization in Latin America: Experiences and Interpretations," by Werner Baer reprinted from *Latin American Research Review* 7, Spring 1972, by permission of Latin American Research Review.

"Trade Policy for Developing Countries," by Donald Keesing, reprinted from *World Bank Staff Working Paper*, #53, August 1979, by permission of The World Bank.

"Multinational Corporations in World Development," by United Nations Department of International Economic and Social Affairs, extracted and reprinted in *Development Digest* 12, January 1974, reprinted by permission of United Nations.

"Development Finance: Unmet Needs," reprinted from *North-South: A Program for Survival*, Report of the Independent Commission on International Development Issues under the Chairmanship of Willy Brandt, by permission of The MIT Press, Cambridge, Massachusetts. © The Independent Commission on International Development Issues, 1980.

"The Possibilities of Development Planning," by Tony Killick reprinted from *Oxford Economic Papers* 41, October 1976, by permission of Oxford University Press.

"Towards a Free Market Economy: Chile 1974–1979," by Alejandro Foxley reprinted from *Journal of Development Economics* 10, February 1982, by permission of North-Holland Publishing Company, Amsterdam.

"A View from the South: The Second Phase of the North-South Dialogue," by Mahbub ul Haq reprinted from M. McLaughlin et al. (eds.), *The United States and World Development: Agenda 1979*, by permission of Overseas Development Council, Washington, D.C.

"Can the North Prosper Without Growth and Progress in the South?" by John W. Sewell reprinted from M. McLaughlin et al. (eds.), *The United States and World Development: Agenda 1979*, by permission of Overseas Development Council, Washington, D.C.

Correspondence between chapters from
*Economic Development in the Third
World, 2nd Edition* and *The Struggle
for Economic Development:
Readings in Problems and Policies*

Text Chapter	Reading Numbers
1	1
2	2
3	3, 4, 5
4	6, 7
5	8, 9, 10, 11
6	12
7	13
8	14, 15, 16
9	17, 18, 19
10	20, 21, 22
11	23, 24, 25
12	26
13	27, 28
14	29, 30
15	31
16	32
17	33, 34

Part I

Understanding Underdevelopment

One of the most difficult problems in teaching an undergraduate economic development course for students who have never visited or lived in a Third World country is to somehow convey what life is really like in an economically underdeveloped nation. Thus, our first reading is by a philosopher/political scientist, Denis Goulet, in which the author argues that statistics and abstract models cannot convey to the reader the "shock of underdevelopment"—the conditions of abject poverty and the helplessness and vulnerability that pervade life in poor nations. Although Goulet argues that one cannot understand underdevelopment without having experienced it firsthand, one can at least begin to appreciate the magnitude and dimensions of the problem by reading his forceful essay. An exerpt from the well-known and widely acclaimed Brandt Commission Report follows the Goulet essay. In this report, underdevelopment is described in broader strokes, with emphasis on poverty, ill health, and lack of adequate housing and educational opportunities as well as with other pertinent "dimensions of development." Together, these two readings provide the real-world background for the readings that follow.

Chapter 2 explores the competing paradigms of economic development from the perspective of two economists, Gustav F. Papanek and Franklyn Lisk and a political scientist, Peter J. A. Henriot. Each author describes some of the alternative approaches to conceptualizing the problem of underdevelopment and each reviews traditional and contemporary theories in an attempt to derive implications for development strategies and policies.

In Chapter 3, we look at the historical experience of economic growth in Western nations and the lessons that may or may not apply to contemporary Third World countries through the eyes of Nobel Laureate Simon Kuznets. His "Modern Economic Growth: Findings and Reflections" is in fact his Nobel lecture and represents the synthesis of a lifetime of empirical research on the sources of economic growth. Kuznets's paper is followed by a different, more radical view of the historical experience by a well-known and widely quoted Latin American dependencia theorist, Theotonio Dos Santos. Dos Santos, although not fundamentally disagreeing with Kuznets's finding —that the spread of modern economic growth to other industrialized nations helped their development while having a limited impact on the growth of Third World nations—nevertheless argues that this international outreach by the more developed countries is one of the principal reasons for the continued underdevelopment of Latin America (and, by inference, the rest of the Third World).

1

The Reality of
Underdevelopment

1. The Shock of Underdevelopment*

Denis Goulet

Underdevelopment is shocking: the squalor, disease, unnecessary deaths, and hopelessness of it all! No man understands if underdevelopment remains for him a mere statistic reflecting low income, poor housing, premature mortality, or underemployment. The most empathetic observer can speak objectively about underdevelopment only after undergoing, personally or vicariously, the "shock of underdevelopment." This unique culture shock comes to one as he is initiated to the emotions which prevail in the "culture of poverty." The reverse shock is felt by those living in destitution when a new self-understanding reveals to them that their life is neither human nor inevitable. But why must those who are not destitute experience the reality of dehumanizing existence? Because the prevalent emotion of underdevelopment is a sense of personal and societal impotence in the face of disease and death, of confusion and ignorance as one gropes to understand change, of servility toward men whose decisions govern the course of events, of hopelessness before hunger and natural catastrophe. Chronic poverty is a cruel

kind of hell; and one cannot understand how cruel that hell is merely by gazing upon poverty as an object. Unless the observer gains entry into the inner sanctum of these emotions and feels them himself, he will not understand the condition he seeks to abolish.

The dominant emotions of a development scholar, a technical expert, or an educator are totally opposed to those of his "subjects." They are fragile, he is strong; he has knowledge, but they are ignorant. He understands how decisions are made, while they suffer the consequences of decisions they have not reached. The "developed" man does not fear bad health unduly because he knows it can be cured. Hence, would-be developers must cross the threshold separating rationalist self-sufficiency from vulnerability if they are to comprehend underdevelopment as it truly is. They need to discover—by experiencing impotence and vulnerability—that what appears normal is abnormal, and that what appears aberrant is the lot of the common man. They must also learn that weakness is not something others have and strength something they have. They must discover that developed and underdeveloped men alike are imbued with strength and weakness.

In 1961 I spent three months in Rondônia, a

---

* From Denis Goulet, *The Cruel Choice: A New Concept in the Theory of Development*. Atheneum, New York, 1971, pp. 23–32.

federally administered territory in Brazil's sparsely populated Amazon region. This tropical zone was inhabited largely by *seringueros*—men living in virtual serfdom, whose occupation was gathering latex from wild rubber trees. One of their few pastimes was river fishing. *Seringueros* believed that mermaid-like creatures surfaced in the waters at dusk, and that fishermen should avoid them if they did not wish to be cursed. Although inclined to ridicule such superstition, I once found myself in a rowboat with a *seringuero* out fishing after sunset. As the latter hooked a mermaid, he emitted a shriek of unfeigned horror. I liked to think of myself as a cool-headed observer. Nevertheless, I had just spent several weeks of total isolation in the jungle. As I listened in alarm to the strange sounds of the Amazonian evening, for one compellingly real hour in my life I became *absolutely convinced* of the existence of the mythical creature and of the real danger confronting me and my companion. Because I believed and experienced genuine fear, I was able to help the uncritical and "superstitious" *seringuero* disengage his fishing line. The lesson is simple: emotions which are real for those who experience them are not real for those who merely observe them.

The central emotions of "underdeveloped" men are of this kind. To evoke Gabriel Marcel's well-known distinction, underdevelopment is more of a "mystery" than a "problem." A problem is a difficulty one encounters along his way; he can step back from it, measure it, devise solutions, and perhaps overcome it. In mystery, on the other hand, it is impossible to situate oneself outside the dilemma; a problematic element is present, but the viewer himself is part of the problem. Indeed, the developed viewer is a large part of the underdevelopment problem. Therefore, if he chooses to treat the matter as a mere problem extrinsic to himself, he is condemned to misunderstand it and not solve it. He needs to be shocked into discovering the falsity of the certitudes he brought with him into the "prob-

lem arena." He must make the dramatic discovery that there exists an inherent structural paternalism in the very relationship between him as helper and the other as helpee, between him as "developed" and the other as "underdeveloped." The very existence of such nomenclature is evidence of cultural paternalism. To awaken to it experientially is to undergo the "shock of underdevelopment."

This revelation is no mere adventure of the spirit, however—some kind of transcendent empathy which humbles the sensitive man's soul but bears no consequences for his actions. The very opposite is true: this psychic transformation can revolutionize his technical and political dealings. If indeed relationships between developed and underdeveloped are structurally paternalistic, programs conducted within the boundaries of these relationships necessarily breed paternalism and domination. It is not the policies alone which are deficient but the attitudes as well. Nevertheless, attitudes also determine policies. But I contend that attitudes can be sound only if both parties to the relationship experience the shock of underdevelopment. In order to understand the importance of this shock, we must reflect on the prevailing state of unconsciousness which precedes it and on its consequences.

INERTIA AND COMPLACENCY

Men in backward and advanced societies alike labor under serious misconceptions. Until they are deeply shaken by outside demonstration effects and by impact strategies critical of their ordinary world view, underdeveloped populations ignore the existence of a state of "development" as possible *for them*. It is not that they have no notion of "development," but the notion is not relevant to their aspirations. With the new awareness that accompanies the shock, however, they no longer view themselves as men without culture, because now culture has been redefined in their minds in terms other than the mere possession of reading or writing skills. Moreover, they no longer view themselves as powerless because they can begin to think of themselves as potential agents of their own destiny. They stop regarding themselves as *naturally* poor, illiterate, badly housed, having ill health or poor employment chances, and begin to imagine themselves as possibly less poor and better housed, fed, and clothed. Once they have been shocked into considering their "normal" state of affairs as aberrant and reversible, men are psychically ready to begin playing political roles in society: they have become organizable.

The number of peasants, shepherds, fishermen, and poor urban workers who have undergone this shock is admittedly small. Were it larger, development would encounter both greater ease and greater difficulty in being accepted. Greater ease because more people would demand the goods promised by development, greater difficulty because they would perceive that these goods were being offered to them paternalistically. It is no accident, therefore, that effective pedagogies for awakening consciousness arouse the suspicions of political establishments. Indeed, such awakening augurs a veritable cultural revolution whose structural effects are monumental.

The shock of underdevelopment triggers a recognition in both parties to the relationship that subordinates have been stigmatized by superiors. According to one American black leader, the poor have largely subscribed to the prevailing man's view that "if you are nobody economically you are nobody, period." Recognition that one is "underdeveloped" is, upon analysis, the recognition that: (a) the terms of reference "developed" and "underdeveloped" have been defined by the stronger partner to the relationship; (b) one could be developed; (c) one should be developed. Underdevelopment is a humiliating condition because it reveals weakness or failure, lowers self-esteem in the face of the obvious triumph of the other, and leaves unanswered the question *why?*

Neither is the developed man who experiences the shock immune to disturbing emotions. Is it "right" for him to be developed while the other is underdeveloped? Does any causal link exist between his own development and the other's underdevelopment? Is he in any sense responsible or guilty for the other's underdevelopment? Is it correct to designate the other "underdeveloped" simply because he has fewer material possessions and lacks certain skills? What relationship, if any, is there between "having riches" and "being humanly rich"? Which institutions and interests does the developed man serve? What net effect do these institutions and interests have on the underdevelopment of the other? Must the developed man foster the active interests of the other even if this undermines his own privilege? Such thoughts are disturbing precisely because most development thinkers have uncritically assumed that underdevelopment can be treated as a "problem" to be solved. It turns out, however, that the problem" transcends the limits of mere difficulties to be overcome and raises critical questions regarding the interactions at work. A realistic look at underdevelopment places developed and underdeveloped men alike in a common arena in which the values vital to both are radically challenged. Not only personal values but societal values as well are contested. Consequently, the shock of underdevelopment, once experienced, affects institutions and policies, not merely sensibilities. Thus, if "aid" is revealed to be a means of "domesticating" the other's development, it follows that no aid technician or administrator can continue to approve the fundamental premises upon which his programs rest. If one understands that his technological superiority is but a relative benefit and that a man who is materially poor and technologically inferior may be humanly, esthetically, and spiritually superior to him, he may feel compelled to question the value priorities of his own society and contest the legitimacy of his own institutions.

Since most people engaged in "development work" have not experienced this shock, they remain ill-prepared to understand underdevelopment at its deepest level and to devise appropriate policies for eliminating it. The position here defended clearly thrusts empathy to the forefront of analysis; it then becomes not only a psycho-biological disposition, but a conceptual tool as well. Predictably, individuals and societies resort to all kinds of defense mechanisms to avoid undergoing the shock of underdevelopment. This is true of the needy poor and of the helping rich, since both risk losing much by accepting reality. The experience disenchants a man, destroys his confidence in the familiar images he has of underdevelopment. An Indian villager, for example, may have grown accustomed to identifying acquisitiveness with greed, a trait he is taught to reprimand in moral terms. It is deeply upsetting for him to learn that "greed" may at times prove to be quite an effective, perhaps even a praiseworthy, motor of human and social improvement. Conversely, it is discomforting for a sophisticated technical expert from a rich country to learn that men who live on the margin of subsistence and daily flirt with death and insecurity are sometimes capable of greater happiness, wisdom, and human communion than he is, notwithstanding his knowledge, wealth, and technical superiority. At the very least, the shock alerts men to the massive ethnocentrism latent in their "normal" views of life.

THE RUDE AWAKENING

Development has become a matter of survival for the Third World and a problem of conscience for rich nations. Three important consequences follow from the generalized emergence of a new consciousness.

1. *The poor demand rapid development.* Whatever their prior state, poor nations now demand rapid development. Although illiterate masses are still largely indifferent to the prospect of change, leaders have condemned inertia and committed their societies to the pursuit of development. Velleities usually originate among intellectuals, labor leaders, budding politicians, nationalist entrepreneurs, and civil servants. But the masses are accustomed to acquiesce in decisions taken by leaders. And since they are unfamiliar with the complex mechanisms of modern decision-making, they cannot veto the elite's commitment to development on their behalf. Without a doubt, most leaders want development now.

In 1956 Nehru declared: "We are not going to spend the next hundred years in arriving gradually, step by step, at the stage of development which the developed countries have reached today. Our pace and tempo of progress has to be much faster."[1] And Raúl Prebisch speaks as a typical Latin American when he asserts that "profound transformations of our economic and social structure are necessary to facilitate the appearance of means suited to accelerating the rhythm of economic and social development...these transformations are urgent."[2]

Realistic or not, declarations made by Third World leaders are deeply voluntaristic. They *will* development and believe their act of will can help them obtain it. Among them widespread admiration exists for the development achieved by the Soviet Union within forty years: a huge feudal society has become a world economic, industrial, scientific, military, and political power. The Soviet performance has made them think that rapid success is possible. It is but an imperceptible step for them to conclude that no country, including their own, need evolve slowly over a century or two in order to become industrialized.

In reality, rapid development is impossible for many low-income countries. Their demographic increase, limited resource base, insufficient capital, shortage of skilled managerial, entrepreneurial, and technical personnel, and limited maneuvering room in the world political arena constitute obstacles to rapid gains. Investment capabilities are often so limited, and initial levels of living so low, that even heroic efforts over the next twenty-five years would not raise conditions to levels presently enjoyed by advanced countries. Heilbroner asserts "that economic development over the next decade or two cannot substantially better the lot of the world's *misérables*. . . . It is only self-deception which pictures economic development leading *within our lifetime* to any large and continuous human betterment. That lies still in the distant future. In the meantime this generation of the backward lands will have no alternative but to bear the burdens of the past as they labor for a future they will not live to enjoy."[3]

National planners sometimes recognize this limitation and try to persuade their countrymen that the goals of national efforts, even over the long term, cannot be to reach the affluence now enjoyed by rich countries, but must be simply to abolish mass poverty. Nonetheless, most Third World spokesmen are impatient and do not resign themselves to development's "slow unhurried pace." This impatience is not confined to political leaders and technical experts; it extends to the people at large. Increasingly, peasant leaders, union organizers, adult educators, religious spokesmen, community mobilizers, and other influential men tell their people that change is needed rapidly! Thus, Brazilian Archbishop Helder Câmara exhorts the youth of his country "to accelerate the march of history, for it is necessary that your generation lead the Third World to sit, not as a beggar but as a brother, at the world's round-table where dialogue finally becomes possible."[4]

2. *The poor blame the rich for their own poverty*. Because of development's exasperatingly slow pace, there is a growing tendency on the part of the poor to blame rich classes and nations for their own backwardness. There is not always an explicit accusation of guilt for past exploitation, but rather a stress on the interference of rich nations with the poor's present efforts to overcome underdevelopment. Myrdal summarizes this state of affairs as follows: "(i) the peoples in the underdeveloped countries are becoming increasingly aware of these huge international inequalities and the danger that they will continue to grow; and (ii) these peoples and their spokesmen show an inclination to put part of the blame for their poverty on the rest of the world and, in particular, on the countries which are better off—or, rather, they attribute the inequalities to the world economic system which keeps them so poor while other nations are so rich and becoming richer."[5]

One need not endorse any simplistic "scapegoat" theory of underdevelopment to accord some plausibility to this interpretation. Development writers in growing numbers now attribute the *perpetuation* (if not the creation) of underdevelopment to the voracious nature of the "development" of those already wealthy.[6] Similarly, the notion of "internal colonialism," in which the maintenance of privilege explains the continuation of misery within national borders, is gaining credence.[7] Causal analyses of past development no longer rely solely on technological innovation and entrepreneurial activity as explanatory categories, but appeal to such dominant structures as: privileged access to raw materials, freedom for industrializing nation to "impose" their products on fragile Third World markets, the power of strong countries to control world market mechanisms to their advantage, their ability to disrupt internal efforts at industrialization by poor countries through dumping and other means,[8] and their capacity to attract trained personnel away from the underdeveloped world.

What is germane to this discussion is not some judgment of the rightness or wrongness of these sentiments, but the recognition of their existence and influence. Quite generally and at present levels of consciousness in the world, representatives of underdeveloped nations attribute their own unsatisfactory state, at least in part, to the way rich countries behave. On these grounds the seventy-seven signatories of the Charter of Algiers have pleaded for non-parity treatment, and Fidel

Castro has sought to justify expropriation without indemnization, alleging redress for past "exploitation." On similar grounds other Third World spokesmen argue their "right" to receive assistance from the rich world, independently of the latter's inclination to be "generous" or not. One cannot understand the tensions operative in the present world, therefore, without adverting to this by-product of heightened consciousness: the poor, by and large, hold the rich responsible for their underdevelopment.

3. *The rich world discovers its own under-development*. A third consequence of growth in consciousness is the discovery by the rich world that it too is "underdeveloped." I do not refer primarily to the acknowledgment by advanced countries of the existence of poverty within their own borders. What is more important is that the values of "developed" countries are now being challenged in the light of quite different values observed in "backward" countries. To illustrate, large numbers of Peace Corps volunteers, upon returning to the United States, have examined their own society with critical new eyes. After their experience in Africa, Asia, or Latin America, they can compare the treatment accorded old people in the United States with that dispensed to the aged in societies where the extended family provides satisfying roles for grandparents. Not surprisingly, many judge treatment of the aged in the U.S. to be cruel: "like throwing obsolete people on the junk heap." A similar reappraisal occurs in attitudes toward leisure. As American society automates more fully and creates ever more "spare hours" for large numbers, it becomes painfully evident that neither the educational system of the United States, its mass media, nor other instruments of socialization have prepared people to make joyful use of leisure. Comparisons are inevitable between the United States and "underdeveloped" African or Latin American societies where group rejoicing and celebration are ingrained traditions. Likewise, in the face of increasing bureaucra-

tization of life in "developed countries," there is a growing readiness to entertain the possibility at least that rich countries are emotionally, esthetically, communally, and spiritually underdeveloped. The rebirth of pride in indigenous history taking place in countries now asserting their national identity has awakened men in "developed" countries to values obscured by the ethnocentrism implicit in the use of terms such as "developed" and "underdeveloped." Especially for educators, technicians, and administrators who have "experienced the shock of underdevelopment," growth in awareness poses fundamental challenges to the values of all civilizations and the quality of life. The issue is no longer "making good" in the sense of "getting more goods."[9] Throughout the world and in all domains of human endeavor, it is now true, as one Indian specialist writes, that "the problem is not merely one of developing resources in a narrow technical sense but of improving the quality of human life and of building up an institutional framework adequate to the wider ends in view."[10]

The shock of underdevelopment has shattered the apathy of people who had been resigned to their own secular poverty, and the complacency of those who had judged themselves to be superior because they were wealthier than others. Knowledge about the developed world has made the Third World painfully aware of its own "underdevelopment." Conversely, probes into the deeper meaning of the economic and technical backwardness of the Third World have led developed peoples to suspect that they too are "underdeveloped" in certain basic human dimensions. This common disenchantment gives rise to the further suspicion that the "development" of both rich and poor may well require that the entire world alter its values.

1. Cited in Gunnar Myrdal, *Asian Drama* (Pantheon, 1968), II, 716. On the same page Myrdal also quotes U Nu, then prime minister of Burma: "We have been in a hurry. . . . We have waited

for a long time and we feel we must accomplish a great deal in a short time."

2. Raúl Prebisch, "Aspectos Econômicos da Aliança Para o Progresso" in *A Aliança Para o Progresso*, ed. John C. Dreier (Rio de Janeiro: Editora Fundo de Cultura, 1962), p. 55.

3. Robert L. Heilbroner, *The Great Ascent* (Harper Torchbooks, 1963), pp. 120–121.

4. Helder Câmara, "Carta a los Jovenes," in Centro Intercultural de Documentación (Doc. 68/99), Cuernavaca, Mexico, p. 2.

5. Gunnar Myrdal, *Economic Theory and Under-Developed Regions* (London: Duckworth, 1959), p. 7.

6. For a detailed review of these theories, cf. Jacques Freyssinet, *Le Concept de Sous-Développement* (Paris: Mouton, 1966), pp. 177–242.

7. The concept of "internal colonialism" is analyzed in Rodolfo Stavenhagen, "Seven Fallacies About Latin America," in *Latin America, Reform or Revolution?* ed. James Petras and Maurice Zeitlin (A Fawcett Premier Book, 1968), pp. 13–32.

8. The disruptive effects of U.S. aid to Vietnam, for instance, are described in J. M. Albertini, *Le Programme de Sécurité Mutuelle et le Développement du Sud Viet-Nam*, unpublished Ph.D. thesis, Université de Grenoble, January 1965, pp. 244–270.

9. Barbara Ward, *The Rich Nations and the Poor Nations* (Canadian Broadcasting Corporation, 1964), p. 21.

10. Baljit Singh, "Institutional Approach to Planning," in B. Singh, ed., *Frontiers of Social Science* (London: Macmillan [no date]), p. 369. Cited by Myrdal, *Asian Drama*, II, 711.

2. Dimensions of Development*

Brandt Commission

THE NATURE OF POVERTY

Few people in the North have any detailed conception of the extent of poverty in the Third World or of the forms that it takes. Many hundreds of millions of people in the poorer countries are preoccupied solely with survival and elementary needs. For them work is frequently not available or, when it is, pay is very low and conditions often barely tolerable. Homes are constructed of impermanent materials and have neither piped water nor sanitation. Electricity is a luxury. Health services are thinly spread and in rural areas only rarely within walking distance. Primary schools, where they exist, may be free and not too far away, but children are needed for work and cannot easily be spared for schooling. Permanent insecurity is the condition of the poor. There are no public systems of social security in the event of unemployment, sickness or death of a wage-earner in the family. Flood, drought or disease affecting people or livestock can destroy livelihoods without hope of compensation. In the North, ordinary men and women face genuine economic problems—uncertainty, inflation, the fear if not the reality of unemployment. But they rarely face anything resembling the total deprivation found in the South. Ordinary people in the South would not find it credible that the societies of the North regard themselves as anything other than wealthy.

The poorest people in the world will remain for some time to come outside the reach of normal trade and communications. The combination of malnutrition, illiteracy, disease, high birth rates, underemployment and low

---

* From Brandt Commission Report, *North-South: A Program for Survival*. MIT Press, Cambridge, Mass., 1980, pp. 49–59.

income closes off the avenues of escape; and while other groups are increasingly vocal, the poor and illiterate are usually and conveniently silent. It is a condition of life so limited as to be, in the words of the President of the World Bank, 'below any rational definition of human decency'. No concept of development can be accepted which continues to condemn hundreds of millions of people to starvation and despair.

EIGHT HUNDRED MILLION DESTITUTE

Precisely how many people in the Third World live in such conditions of poverty, no one can say. The International Labour Office estimated the number of destitute at 700 million in the early 1970s. World Bank estimates today put them at 800 million. This suggests that almost 40 per cent of the people in the South are surviving—but only barely surviving—in the kind of poverty we have been describing, with incomes judged insufficient to secure the basic necessities of life.

Mass poverty remains overwhelmingly a rural affliction, and it is rural poverty that seems so harshly intractable. The mass urban poverty of Kinshasa, Mexico City or Cairo is a relatively modern phenomenon. For all its squalor, it is one step up from rural deprivation. To some extent, that is why these cities have grown. But the poor in India, Bangladesh, Pakistan, Indonesia and nearly all of Africa, are still, to the extent of 70 per cent or more of the total population, in the rural villages.

DIFFERING CONDITIONS OF POVERTY

People are poor in two kinds of circumstances: in countries which have reached relatively high average levels of income, where this income is not well distributed; and in countries which have low levels of income where there is little to distribute. Poverty in the North is entirely of the first kind. There are pockets of poverty, and deficiencies in

housing and other services, all the less defensible for existing in the midst of what several commentators have called 'overdevelopment'. In the South, the great majority of the 800 million poor live in the low-income countries of sub-Saharan Africa and South Asia, though many better-off countries have large layers of acute poverty which show that the benefits of growth have not trickled down to the poorest. This does not necessarily mean that these governments are indifferent to their poor or lack the political will to improve their lot. But some of the richer ones, especially in Latin America, could do much more: the growth performance of Latin America in the 1970s (of about 7 per cent per annum), if sustained, could enable them to solve their problems of extreme poverty. In Latin America as a whole, the absolute poor number about 100 million; in twelve out of twenty-three countries where reliable estimates exist, over one-half of the population has incomes insufficient to buy a basket of goods and services deemed essential for a minimum level of welfare.

The experience of some countries confirms that, where assets are distributed more fairly in the first place, sustained economic growth can provide jobs and better conditions for the poor. The better-off countries have sufficient resources to mitigate extreme forms of poverty; if they can maintain high growth rates, they can eliminate it. But for the elimination of poverty in the world as a whole the outlook is bleak. Recent World Bank projections (which contain fairly optimistic assumptions about economic growth, but do not incorporate any major changes in international or national development efforts) suggest that there will still be 600 million absolute poor in the countries of the South by the year 2000.

LOW-INCOME COUNTRIES

For most developing countries of Africa and Asia, the seeming failure to distribute wealth is a symptom of a deeper distress which many of them do not have the resources to tackle. Their rate of growth in the past two decades —less than 3 per cent per year—has not been enough to make much difference to the poor. Their total resources, even if they were equally divided, are insufficient to support their populations. These countries, with a GNP per head of less than $250, had a combined population of 1215 million in 1976. More than half this number live in absolute poverty. Four large countries of Asia—Bangladesh, India, Indonesia and Pakistan—contain about two-thirds of the world's poor. Another third is made up of countries that have been defined by the United Nations as 'least developed' (including Bangladesh). These countries have very different resources and economic structures. India, Indonesia and Pakistan, for example, are major producers of manufactures, including textiles, shoes and electronics; they have a developed infrastructure, with sophisticated commercial and financial services, scientists, engineers and managers; and they will be better able to help the poor if they can sell more exports, with access to the markets of the industrial countries. But virtually all these countries have two-thirds or more of their workers in agriculture, and all of them rely heavily on exporting raw materials. These are among the chief economic causes of their slow growth.

Half or more of the total product of these countries comes from agriculture; and this is part of their problem, since a higher rate of growth in agriculture depends both on mastering the vagaries of nature and on adapting social institutions. In many African countries food output has grown more slowly than population, which has worsened the conditions for the ever-growing number who earn their living by farming. In Asia also there has been a disappointing record, though there are some more promising experiences. In a number of countries, including India and the Philippines, the new crop varieties of the 'Green Revolution' produced substantial agricultural growth, at least from the mid-1960s to the mid-1970s. The expansion of food production

and agricultural employment in the low-income countries is crucial. Historical evidence shows that the absolute number of people dependent on rural employment declines only in the later stages of development, when manufacturing has taken over as the leading sector in growth. Even in the early stages agricultural progress is linked to overall development as it needs markets both in and outside agriculture.

The international environment has not been particularly favourable to the poor countries. Prices of the commodities on which they depend heavily for export earnings have fluctuated erratically and have over long periods deteriorated in relation to the prices of their imports, especially capital goods and oil. In the long run the only effective solutions to these difficulties are diversification, greater flexibility and overall development. But the possibilities of diversification are circumscribed by limited access to the markets of industrial countries which are in numerous cases highly protected against processed products. Moreover, stabilized and remunerative prices of their commodities which can promote greater flexibility for their economies can only result from a better framework for commodity trade as a whole. International agreements on relevant commodities (in particular cotton, hard fibres, tea, oil-seeds and coffee), finance for national stocks and diversification measures are of particular importance to many of the poorest countries.

With a more favourable international economic environment some of the low-income countries would gradually become able to reduce their dependence on concessional assistance. But for the poorest countries, aid for promoting necessary structural transformation will continue to be essential well into the next century.

NEWLY INDUSTRIALIZING COUNTRIES

It would be highly misleading to present the Third World as an unchanging picture of widespread poverty. Even among the low-income countries progress is occurring, the beginnings—and in some cases much more than beginnings—of structural transformation. In a number of developing countries, moreover, there have been truly remarkable advances. In terms of sheer economic growth rates, the most striking cases have been the 'newly industrializing countries', which have been thrusting ahead with manufacturing growth. The Latin American ones—Argentina, Brazil, Mexico—have a quite old-established industrial base, which has increased rapidly in the postwar decades. A spectacular example is Brazil, whose economy at current growth rates will by the year 2000 rival in size that of the Federal Republic of Germany. It is also an important trading partner and thus a stimulus to growth for other countries in the South. Several of what used to be called 'peripheral' countries are now becoming significant nerve centres of industrial production.

Other smaller industrializing countries illustrate how fast the economic map of the world is shifting. They have been able to take advantage of the international division of labour in highly competitive world markets. Many of them are in South East Asia—Republic of Korea, Hong Kong, Malaysia, Singapore, Taiwan—but they also include Yugoslavia, with its different social system. Their economies as a whole have been sustaining an average growth from 5 to 9 per cent over a decade and a half. There are other countries which have begun relatively recently to penetrate export markets with their manufactures: Colombia, the Philippines, Thailand.

Already the names of these 'NICs' have become more familiar to consumers in the North, since they first noticed a few years ago that their sports shoes were made in Korea, their camera in Singapore, or their television set in Taiwan. The future progress of these countries depends considerably on the trade and financial policies of the North. They may suffer new setbacks with the development of micro-processors, which could reduce some of their advantages. While they owe much of their expansion and technology to the multinational corporations, they remain very vulnerable to the corporations' trading practices. And their debts pose serious problems ... Can the dynamism of these countries be integrated in an era of world economic expansion in the 1980s? Or will it be repressed through protectionism and the failure of global economic management? On this question depends not only their own future, but the hopes of many other countries looking towards industrialization.

OIL EXPORTERS

Another group, the oil-exporting developing countries, has become rapidly richer in the last few years. The three with the highest *per capita* incomes—Kuwait, Qatar and the United Arab Emirates—are all special cases with very small populations. Indonesia and Nigeria, on the other hand, are far from wealthy; between them they have over 200 million people, and huge development problems for which oil revenues provide only a partial solution.

But whether rich or poor, almost all oil producers still have serious economic difficulties. The better-off (Gabon, Iran, Iraq, Libya, Saudi Arabia, Trinidad and Tobago and Venezuela) depend heavily on oil and most of them lack the infrastructure and amenities of countries which have been prosperous for longer. With the proceeds of today's oil they need to create a balanced productive economy to sustain their populations in the future when there will be little oil left.

ELEMENTARY NEEDS: HEALTH

The overall features of development take on their human character when we consider the satisfaction of elementary needs. We look first at the three major areas: health, housing and education. In health, there is some cause for hope as well as concern. Most people in the Third World are living much longer today than they were only two decades ago. In sub-Saharan Africa, it is true, life expectancy is still very low: the average is only about 45 years. But in large parts of South and East Asia, in North Africa and the Middle East, people can expect to live 10 to 15 years longer. Much of this has been achieved by controlling communicable diseases, including cholera and malaria. (The latter has unfortunately recently increased, though causing fewer deaths, after being almost under control in the 1960s.) The elimination of smallpox—achieved by the World Health Organization and collaborating countries—was one of the triumphs of the 1970s.

But poor health is still the likely fate of much of the Third World. The population censuses of 1970–71 showed that death rates were not declining as fast as expected. Health authorities were running into the more intractable conditions of poverty and malnutrition, poor hygiene and sanitation, all in turn contributing to high infant and child mortality. There are still countries in Africa where one child in four does not survive until its first birthday. Blindness afflicts 30 to 40 million people in the Third World and threatens many tens of millions more—whether from river-blindness, vitamin A deficiency or water-borne infections. No one knows how many people are undernourished and hungry, but much evidence suggests that the number could be more than one-fifth of the whole Third World, or 500–600 million people; some estimates put it at one billion.

Lack of safe water is a major cause of ill-health; in virtually half the world water supplies are uncertain. Four out of five people living in the rural areas of developing countries do not have reasonable access to even relatively unpolluted water. Even in towns with a public water supply one out of four do not have access to it and, of those that do, more than half receive intermittent and unsafe supplies. In the countryside women often have to

cross long distances to secure their minimum requirements of water for the family. Sanitation is an even worse problem causing numerous water-borne diseases, to which children are particularly susceptible. Between 20 and 25 million children below the age of five die every year in developing countries, and a third of these deaths are from diarrhoea caught from polluted water. All these deaths cannot be eliminated just by providing safe water and sanitation; but there can be no lasting improvement of public health without them. In 1977 the UN Water Conference of Mar-del-Plata in Argentina set an ambitious goal: safe drinking water and hygienic conditions for all by 1990. So far over 100 countries have undertaken (with the help of WHO) self-critical surveys to determine the extent of outstanding needs, and of required external support. To attain the Mar-del-Plata goals, it is estimated that the current rate of investment must be almost doubled in towns and cities, and increased fourfold in rural areas.

Improving health requires efforts far beyond medical care; it is closely linked with food and nutrition, with employment and income distribution and with the international economy. But there are a number of priorities within the health sector itself. In 1978 the WHO held a conference in Alma-Ata, in the Soviet Union, on Primary Health Care. This set a target for governments and the world community, to attain for all people by the year 2000 'a level of health that will permit them to lead a socially and economically productive life'. Primary health care was the key to attaining the target; the conference also asked the governments to link health care to other sectors. The WHO has, in addition, backed an important Action Programme to give developing countries greater opportunities to obtain and produce medical drugs, and to make special provisions for the poorest countries to obtain essential drugs. And the WHO among its health activities has initiated a major programme to control and prevent blindness.

The costs of raising health services to an acceptable level are in themselves relatively small. The WHO estimates that $3 per child would be sufficient to immunize every new-born child in the developing world against the six most common childhood diseases. With present birth rates this amounts to $0.12 per person per year spread over the total population of those countries. To provide primary health care for all might, on the basis of pilot studies, be estimated to cost some $2.50–$4 per person annually. Clean water and sanitation, on the other hand, do require considerable investments, especially in urban areas. Typical costs for simple standpipes or wells can be roughly estimated at $10 per person for water in rural areas; the costs for house connections rise to $75 in rural areas and twice that in urban areas. For sanitation, typical costs are $5 per person in rural areas and $15 to $200 in towns, depending on whether sewerage is included.

Not only more resources, but greater political determination is needed to reform orthodox medical systems and to encourage cooperative community activities for the improvement of primary health care. But clean water and sanitation will remain an unattainable objective in poor countries without development aid. The 1980s have been designated as a Decade for Drinking Water and Sanitation; in order to remedy an intolerable situation, we call for its aims to be fully supported.

ELEMENTARY NEEDS: HOUSING

The need for housing is fundamental. But most developing countries have not been able to give it priority, and the individual is commonly left to fend for himself. The results may not be known statistically, but they are familiar to anyone travelling through the Third World. One recent study showed that one-third to two-thirds of all families in Ahmadabad, Bogota, Hong Kong, Madras, Mexico City and Nairobi could not afford the cheapest new housing currently being built. The rush to the towns has created the same kind of misery as existed in the nineteenth-century cities of Europe and America. But industrialization in those days was labour-intensive, so that the cities grew as the jobs expanded; the migration in today's developing world is often due to the lack of opportunity in the countryside —it is 'rural push' as much as 'urban pull.' The consequences of high birth rates and rapid migration are all too visible in many cities of the Third World, with abysmal living conditions and very high unemployment or underemployment. The strains on families, whose members are often separated, are very heavy. In São Paulo in Brazil, the population was growing at around 6–7 per cent annually in the late sixties and early seventies, in such appalling conditions that infant mortality was actually increasing. The fact that people still migrate to these cities only underlines the desperate situation which they have left behind.

Many lessons are to be learnt from rehousing schemes undertaken in recent years in different parts of the world. The kind of housing required obviously depends on the climate and environment and no one pattern can be offered as a global model. It is relevant that most of the developing countries where the needs are greatest lie in warm climatic zones. Experience shows that, apart from the need to keep down costs and rents, the key factors are the supply of minimal essential services by public authorities, security of tenure in relation to local land laws, and proximity to work places and other social facilities. But it will be many years before even these essentials are universally available.

ELEMENTARY NEEDS: EDUCATION

In education, which is the key to much achievement in other fields, there has been comparatively consistent progress. Spending on schools and teachers has gone up faster than the growth of population nearly everywhere, with many more enrolments to primary and secondary schools in the 1960s, and this progress has continued in the early 1970s: primary enrolment went up by over ten percent a year between 1970 and 1973 in a fifth of African and a third of Asian countries. But there has been much less success in bringing more girls into the schools: they formed less than forty percent of primary school enrollees in 27 out of 34 African countries in 1970, and in 9 out of 37 other developing countries for which information is available. Only in 17 was the proportion forty-eight percent or higher. Secondary enrolment has grown much more rapidly than primary, but from lower levels: only in one-third of Asian countries, and in two-fifths of the countries of Latin America and the Caribbean, have more than forty percent of the relevant age groups been enrolled in secondary schools. In many countries children are needed to work on farms or otherwise earn some income, as was the case in the North not too long ago. In poor families there is often a conflict between the need of the young for education and the need of the family as a whole to enlist children as supplementary producers or earners of income. A report on child labour in the Third World, produced by the ILO in 1979, gave shocking evidence of the numbers of children working long hours for negligible wages—conditions which show once again to what lengths families are driven by painful necessity.

Literacy in general has made varied progress. About one-third of adults in developing countries were literate in 1950; only a little over one half were literate in 1975. Literacy in Latin America rose from 65 percent in 1960 to 75 percent in 1970; in Asia, from 45 to 53 percent; and in Africa from 20 to 26 percent. But there are still 34 countries, according to the UN, where over 80 percent of the population are illiterate. In contrast, higher education has often expanded too fast in relation to many countries' ability to employ graduates, and has sometimes taken a disproportionate share of educational budgets. Almost every country has begun to worry about the problem of 'educated unemployment', and to ask the question: are schools and universities teaching the right subjects to the right people?

Neither illiteracy nor other deficiencies in education will be easily overcome. UNESCO and other international agencies have embarked on extensive programmes, which deserve full support, to reduce illiteracy and to provide education for all. But, as with health, education ramifies into the economy, politics and society, reflecting inequalities and entrenched interests as well as the absence of skilled people and materials.

NEEDS CANNOT BE SEPARATED

These different needs, for health, housing or education, as well as the most fundamental need for food, all provide a clear and practical challenge both to the countries themselves, and to the industrialized nations without whose help the poorer countries can hardly succeed. But the idea that these problems are quite separate, and can be solved by specific initiatives, can no longer be believed. Whatever may be accomplished by medical aid, housing drives or school grants, the only way to achieve major improvements in these areas is to help the economies of these countries to grow and industrialize so that they will increasingly be in a position to help themselves; and this can only be brought about through a change in the international economic environment; through more purposeful collaboration between North and South, and much more systematic assistance from the North.

Further Readings

1. Social Aspects of Development

Adelman, Irma, and Morris, Cynthia Taft. *Society, Politics and Economic Development: A Quantitative Approach*. Baltimore: Johns Hopkins University Press, 1967.

Goldthorpe, J. E. *The Sociology of the Third World: Disparity and Involvement*. New York: Cambridge University Press, 1975.

Hunt, Chester L. *Social Aspects of Economic Development*. New York, London, Toronto, and Sydney: McGraw-Hill, 1966.

Kunkel, John H. *Society and Economic Growth: A Behavioral Perspective of Social Change*. New York, Oxford University Press, 1970.

Weber, Max. *The Protestant Ethic and the Spirit of Capitalism*. Translated by Talcott Parsons. New York: Scribner's, 1958.

2. Africa

Achaya, S. W. "Perspectives and Problems of Development in Sub-Saharan Africa." *World Development*, 9 (1981).

Adams, J. "The Economic Development of African Pastoral Societies: A Model." *Kyklos* 28, no. 4 (1975).

deWalle, Etienne van. "Trends and Prospects of Population in Tropical Africa." *Annals* 432 (July 1977).

Duignan, Peter, and Gann, Lewis H., eds. *Colonialism in Africa 1870–1960*, vol. 4, *The Economics of Colonialism*. New York: Cambridge University Press, 1975.

Gale Research Co. *Africa South of the Sahara, 1978–79*, 8th ed. Detroit: Europa Publication, 1978.

Gugler, Josef, and Flanagan, William. *Urbanization and Social Change in West Africa*. New York: Cambridge University Press. 1978.

Harris, Richard, ed. *The Political Economy of Africa*. Cambridge: Schenkmen, 1975. Distributed by Halsted Press in New York.

International Monetary Fund. *Surveys of African Countries* (7 vols.). Vol. 1: Cameroon, Central Africa Republic, Chad, Congo, Brazzaville, Gabon (1968); Vol. 2: Kenya, Tanzania, Uganda, Somalia (1969); Vol. 3: Benin, Ivory Coast, Mauretania, Niger, Senegal, Togo, Upper Volta (1970); Vol. 4: Zaire, Malagasy Republic, Mala-

wi, Mauritius, Zambia (1973); Vol. 5: Botswana, Lesotho, Swaziland, Burundi, Equatorial Guinea, Rwanda (1973); Vol. 6: Gambia, Ghana, Liberia, Nigeria, Sierra Leone (1975); Vol. 7; Algeria, Mali, Morocco, Tunisia (1977). Washington, D.C.: IMF, 1968–77.

Kamarck, Andrew M. *The Economics of African Development*. Foreword by Pierre Moussa. Rev. ed. New York: Praeger, 1971.

Kamarck, Andrew M. *The Tropics and Economic Development: A Provocative Inquiry into the Poverty of Nations*. Baltimore and London: Johns Hopkins University Press for the World Bank, 1976.

World Bank. *Accelerated Development in Sub-Saharan Africa*. Washington, D.C.: World Bank, 1981.

3. Asia

Asian Development Bank. *Rural Asia: Challenge and Opportunity*. New York: Praeger, 1978.

Maxwell, Neville, ed. *China's Road to Development*, 2nd ed. Oxford, England: Pergamon Press, 1979.

Myrdal, Gunnar. *Asian Drama: An Inquiry into the Poverty of Nations* (3 vols.). New York: Pantheon, 1968.

4. Latin America

Betancourt, Roger R., Sheehey, Edmund J., and Vogel, Robert C. "The Dynamics of Inflation in Latin America." *American Economic Review* 66, no. 4 (September 1976).

Furtado, Celso. *Economic Development of Latin America: Historical Background and Contemporary Problems*, 2nd ed. (Cambridge Latin American Studies, no. 8) New York: Cambridge University Press, 1976.

Grunwald, Joseph, ed. *Latin America and World Economy: A Changing International Order*. Beverly Hills: Sage Publications for the Center for Inter-American Relations, 1978.

Hunter, John M., and Foley, James W. *Economic Problems of Latin America*. Boston: Houghton Mifflin, 1975.

Wynia, Gary W. *The Politics of Latin American Development*. New York: Cambridge University Press, 1978.

2

Competing Paradigms of Development

3. Economic Development Theory: The Earnest Search for a Mirage*

Gustav F. Papanek

For the 20 years that economic development has been a fashionable field for economists many have searched for the key, the crucial factor which explains why some countries achieve rapid economic growth while others stagnate. More recently, concern has shifted to such questions as causal factors in income distribution. This paper is concerned with the more traditional attempts to explain economic growth.

When economists discovered the less developed countries, regions of the world previously the domain of geographers and anthropologists, they quickly discarded climate and culture as major explanatory variables. Cynics might suggest that we were influenced by the obvious fact that economists had very little to say about either. In addition, both explanations left too many cases unexplained. Preindustrial economic growth had not been concentrated in temperate climates, there were no convincing reasons why modern growth should be limited to the temperate zone and there were, in fact, a number of temperate zone countries among the less developed. "Culture" as an explanation of economic growth was a slippery concept. There was no correlation between modern economic growth and the contribution of societies to art or literature. Explanations in terms of the

Protestant ethic seemed strained if they were to accommodate Japan, the Soviet Union, and several Catholic countries.

Among development economists and fellow-traveling social scientists, three broad strands can be identified among those who sought a crucial variable in economic growth: the capital and savings theorists, the human-factor advocates, and those who suggest that sociopolitical causes are paramount. Under each of these broad rubrics a variety of factors were identified as the principal cause of economic growth, or its absence. In each case critics were quick to point out the failure of each theory to explain particular instances of growth or stagnation.

At the same time another group of economists and social scientists avoided identifying a single causal variable as crucial but discerned patterns that were near universal or at

---

* From Manning Nash, ed., *Essays on Economic Development and Cultural Change in honor of Bert F. Hoselitz*. University of Chicago Press, Chicago, 1977, pp. 270–281.

I am grateful for comments and suggestions made by my colleagues Robert Lucas, Michael Manove, and Daniel Schydlowsky.

least very widespread. They saw most countries as following similar paths.

SINGLE CRUCIAL VARIABLE THEORIES[1]

Those who identified a single crucial variable did not argue that only one factor was important in determining economic growth, only that a single factor was of overwhelming importance. Not unexpectedly the crucial variable most often identified by economists was *the rate of investment*. But there were at least three schools of thought on why the rate of investment was inadequate in less developed countries.

One group saw the capacity to save as the problem. The poor majority in less developed countries do not have a margin above subsistence sufficient to permit savings; the rich, affected by the "demonstration effect" of the consumption habits in developed countries, use their surplus for conspicuous consumption.[2] What little savings does take place is just enough, when invested, to keep output increasing at the same rate as population; countries are in a "low-level equilibrium trap."[3]

Others identified not the capacity to save but the incentive to invest as the critical problem. The markets of less developed countries are too small to permit profitable investments in many activities. The incentive to save in order to invest profitably is, therefore, lacking.[4] The problem of limited markets could be overcome by international trade, but here technology and politics interfered. Technology reduces the need for the raw materials produced by the less developed countries, and political pressures cause the erection of barriers against their exports of manufactured products.[5]

Both groups saw the problem compounded by the nature of modern technology which requires large units, that is, large investments, for efficiency. The limited amount of savings

which the less developed countries are capable of generating and the limited markets which they can offer mean that plants would necessarily be small and in many cases, therefore, inefficient.

To overcome the simultaneous problems of inadequate savings, inadequate incentives to invest and the need for large units to obtain economies of scale led to the contention that there was a "critical minimum effort" to escape the low-level equilibrium trap. The solution was simultaneous large-scale investment in several industries. For many countries such a "big push" was possible only with massive foreign aid.[6]

A third group, just a handful, recently has identified inadequate and inefficient intermediation as the principal obstacle to growth in many cases. The machinery to channel savings from those who perform them to investors is feeble, thus discouraging both savings and investment.[7] The failure of intermediation is the result, in large part, of excessive and inappropriate government intervention in the market, intervention which has widespread and negative effects on the whole economy.

Critics could provide empirical evidence that casts doubts on all these theories, although to do so is considered a nasty trick by some social scientists. But there is both historic and contemporary evidence of substantial savings by poor people, from the great cathedrals and pyramids of an earlier age to savings in the form of gold and jewelry in contemporary South Asia. More important, when there have been strong incentives to invest in productive wells or land reclamation even the poor peasants of South Asia have shown a remarkable capacity to save in order to acquire water or land.[8] Moreover, large groups in some less developed countries are substantially above subsistence: the middle-income peasants, the artisans, professionals, small businessmen, and industrialists. Finally, the demonstration effect and its influence on the savings of the rich are not ordained. There are examples of rates of savings for the rich, for instance among the Muslim businessmen of Pakistan, that rival those supposedly motivated by the Protestant ethic. They saved because incentives to invest were strong, consumption was made unattractive by government policies, and a general atmosphere of austerity prevailed.[9]

The argument that the problem is the limited incentive to invest can also be countered by a reference to empirical material. At least a dozen less developed countries have rapidly increased manufactured exports, despite import restrictions in the developed world. For at least some primary products—oil, natural gas, food grains—the terms of trade have clearly not deteriorated. Most important, for most less developed countries the internal market has been sufficiently large to permit the establishment of efficient import-substituting activities in a number of sectors. The problem of market size might be serious for Gambia, Liberia, or Honduras but not for India, Brazil, Argentina, Indonesia, or Nigeria.

That lack of financial intermediaries was a crucial obstacle could be countered by the example of countries that developed efficient financial intermediaries serving the private sector. In other countries government played the same role and in still others much of the saving was in the hands of the same individuals or companies doing the investing, so that the whole significance of financial intermediation was greatly reduced.

The critics of the crucial role of investment could also point to the fact that a number of countries benefiting from a massive infusion of capital from abroad, primarily in the form of foreign aid, showed a rather low rate of economic growth.[10]

With financial resources and investment in physical capital somewhat discredited as the principal obstacle to economic development, attention shifted to *human resources and human capital*. Here again there were three strands: educated and skilled manpower, entrepreneurs, or public decision makers.

A modern economy obviously requires trained and skilled manpower, and indeed levels of education and economic development are highly correlated. It was even argued that while machines would have a hard time training the people needed to run them, educated and trained people would find a way of developing the machines they needed.[11]

Another argument was that the really scarce resource was entrepreneurs, primarily in the private sector—individuals who would seek out new economic opportunities and put together the economic resources needed to take advantage of them.[12] Savings could always be found, workers could always be trained, or both could be imported if ventures were likely to be profitable, and it was the entrepreneurs' role to seek out the profitable opportunities. Theories emphasizing entrepreneurship were generally quite discouraging, since they concluded that little could be done to increase the supply of entrepreneurs. The number of entrepreneurs depended on psychological and social factors, such as child-rearing practices or the loss of status by a previously prestigious community, which were accidents of history and otherwise not subject to influence by social policy.

Another argument was that the really scarce resource was decision makers, primarily in the public sector.[13] Inadequate infrastructure made for inefficiencies, raised costs throughout the economy, and made a good deal of otherwise promising private investment infeasible. For social, cultural, administrative, and political reasons the public decision-making process was constipated, with infrastructure bottlenecks the result. Fortunately, a process of unbalanced growth in which productive capacity was built ahead of infrastructure would create pressures on the public sector to expand the infrastructure and at the same time would increase its decision-making capacity through a learning-by-doing process, so this was a temporary obstacle.

The critics of the human-resources arguments, like the critics of financial-resources theories, were able to cite concrete instances which contradicted the basic contention that scarce human resources were a principal constraint on growth. A number of Latin American countries with very high levels of education since the beginning of the twentieth century have been among those with the lowest growth rates in the less developed world (Argentina, Uruguay, Chile). There was little or no evidence that a high level of education resulted subsequently in a high rate of growth.[14] That levels of education and income were correlated was simply another example of the "Scotch fallacy"—a high level of income is also correlated with a high consumption of Scotch whiskey, but not even the producers of that beverage have argued for a causal relationship.

A number of studies show that entrepreneurial behavior emerged rather quickly under favorable economic circumstances and incentives with respect to industry as well as to agriculture.[15] These studies again raised the question of whether entrepreneurship caused economic growth or the incentive effects of growth caused entrepreneurship. Doubts could also be raised whether it was likely that large countries with a diversity of communities would have no group with the requisite social or psychological background for entrepreneurial behavior. Was a lack of entrepreneurs likely to be a problem only for relatively small and homogeneous societies?

The response to the argument that decision makers were crucial was simple. If the ability to make decisions is the result of unbalanced growth which creates bottlenecks, then there should be a few countries suffering from a major inadequacy in this respect, since the existence of bottlenecks is well-nigh universal.

The concern with human factors in economic growth led quite naturally, and is related to, an emphasis on the *nature of societies* as the crucial obstacle.[16] It was also natural that a number of the theories stressing this factor should be attributable to social scientists who are not economists.

One strand of the argument is that less developed countries are "soft states" whose governments are incapable of dealing with the rigidities of the society that hold back economic development: communalism, superstition, and ignorance. To overcome them requires firm government action.[17] Another argument is that poor and backward societies cannot develop the large-scale organizations required for a modern economy. Such organizations depend on a minimum of cooperation, impossible when everyone is trying to maximize the short-run interest of the family.[18] A more important and widespread argument is that underdevelopment was in fact developed over time by exploitation, dependency, and the backwash effects suffered by less developed countries in their relationship with the developed world. These effects result from imperialism, colonialism, and neocolonialism, which drain the human and financial resources from the less developed countries.[19]

These theories are less clearly defined, and their proponents have advanced less empirical material to support them, so the criticism is also somewhat vague. If one compares countries within the same region, however, it is not clear that forceful governments have achieved higher growth rates. Studies of peasants in less developed countries uniformly have shown that many respond to economic incentives, with little regard to superstition. It is difficult to think of many instances of countries where large-scale organization was made impossible by the inability of people to cooperate. The evidence on the effect of dependency and exploitation is also mixed at best. In fact, many countries most heavily tied to the world market and the world capitalist system have grown rapidly (Korea, Taiwan, Singapore, Hong Kong, Brazil, Venezuela, Nigeria), while some of those that have most closed themselves off from the world system have stagnated (Burma, India, Uganda). Evidently, the relationship between developed and less developed countries affects the latter not only through backwash but also through spread effects, communicating impulses to growth as well as retarding influences.

STANDARD PATTERN THEORIES

So much for theories that stress a single crucial obstacle to economic growth. There is another group of theories which emphasize standard patterns of development.

One such theory assumes that several factors must exist simultaneously, such as a suitable social and political framework and an increase in the rate of saving and investment.[20] Another argues that there is a single crucial causal variable but it differs from region to region, with capital being the problem in South Asia, human resources in Africa, and social and political systems in Latin America.[21]

Another explanation stresses the mechanism of transformation itself. The essential element in economic growth is the transfer of labor from activities, such as agriculture, in which its productivity in social terms is low or even zero to other activities, such as industry, where productivity is substantially higher. This transfer generates savings as output increases substantially while wages remain unchanged until all the unemployed are absorbed. The process also encourages technological change.[22] Finally, there is the recently developed and influential notion that there are a limited number of different patterns of growth, depending on the size of the internal market, the natural resource endowment, aid flows, and perhaps other factors.[23]

A major criticism of most of these theories is that they emphasize description rather than causality. Those that identify several factors as important in economic growth do not identify which are necessary and which are sufficient. More important, the direction of causality is often not clear—does a high rate of savings cause or is it the result of high growth, for instance. Theories which describe the mechanism of growth also have problems with causal-

ity. How does the transfer of labor to high productivity activities get started and what determines its speed? Theories which discern different patterns of development and different development strategies are more plausible, although they have so far not included in the analysis why some countries following a particular pattern or strategy had a high rate of growth while others had a low one.

THE VANISHING OBSTACLES

One other approach is worth mentioning. It is a typically imaginative and broad-ranging effort to include social and political as well as economic factors in the analysis.[24] Some of the factors which other analysts have seen as crucial obstacles can, under a different set of circumstances, turn into assets, or at least vanish as obstacles.

The extended-family system, for instance, can stifle initiative if the more energetic and daring family members are forced to use any increase in income to support lazy or risk-averse relatives. It has, therefore, been seen as an obstacle by most analysts. But if the extended family pools its financial and human resources it can become an asset, giving the brightest, ablest, most innovative members command over more assets than would be the case in a society with nuclear families.

The analysis of obstacles/assets is further complicated by the likelihood that while attitudes affect behavior, behavior can also lead to changes in attitudes. A society which fosters a reluctance to take risks will have fewer effective innovative decision makers. On the other hand, if innovative decisions are forced on many individuals by the need to break bottlenecks, risk-taking attitudes will be encouraged and become more widespread.

Again, this description of reality is plausible but leaves one with a very unsatisfactory state of affairs: each time and place seems to be unique, no generalizations seem possible.

AN ALTERNATIVE APPROACH

It should be fruitful to pursue further the notions of Chenery that there are identifiable patterns of development influenced by identifiable variables and of Hirschman that obstacles and assets depend on circumstances and attitudes can change with behavior. These approaches are much more consonant with the usual economic analysis than either the identification of a single crucial variable or of a standard set of variables.

The single crucial variable theories all say in effect that "economic growth is a complex process influenced by many factors, but one is of predominant importance and explains most of the differences in growth rates which exist. Moreover, over a very wide range there is no decline in the marginal productivity of that factor." In terms of a multiple-regression analysis all independent variables except one have very low explanatory power. Figure 1 gives two examples of graphing single crucial variable theories. Some of the standard pattern theories, on the other hand, say in effect that "several factors must change simultaneously if rapid economic growth is to take place." In terms of production-function analysis growth is the result of several significant variables, but they operate in essentially fixed proportions. In graphic terms the economic growth possibility frontier approximates a right angle (as in fig. 2).

On other issues economists normally think in terms of factors or goods that are substitutable for each other, with declining productivity or utility. There really is no a priori plausible reason why substitutability should not apply as well with respect to economic growth. In other words, a given growth rate can be the result of a country having an abundance of one factor (say capital) and a limited supply of another (say skilled manpower), while another country has the same growth rate with the opposite relative factor availabilities. Alternatively, differences in growth rates can be due to differences in the abundance of a variety of different factors. In graphic terms, what one would then have is a multi-dimensional growth possibility frontier, convex to the origin, with each dimension representing a different factor important in explaining growth. Limiting the graph to the standard two-dimensional, two-factor, representation, one has the usual picture of economics textbooks (fig. 3).

In other words, there is no single crucial factor which largely determines the rate of growth. A severe shortage of capital, for instance, need not prevent a rapid rate of growth, need not be a crucial obstacle, if other factors are present in abundance.[25] On the other hand, an economy with an abundance of capital from aid will grow slowly if skilled labor, decision makers, and entrepreneurs are scarce, government is weak and corrupt, and natural resources are absent. Yet another example: educated manpower may, *ceteris paribus*, make for higher growth. But if a great deal of it is available and combined with very little capital, its marginal contribution to growth will be low and may even become zero

Figure 1. Growth in terms of theories identifying investment and education as crucial.

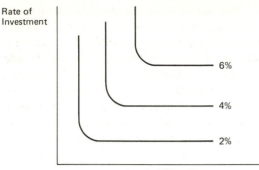

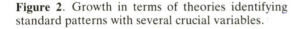

Figure 2. Growth in terms of theories identifying standard patterns with several crucial variables.

or negative. It obviously would not be surprising that it is difficult to find simple correlations between a single independent variable (e.g., investment) and economic growth if multiple, nonlinear correlations are involved.

Curiously enough, analysis of growth in the developed countries has also been in terms of several factors, substitutable at declining marginal productivities.[26] Substitutability is also standard microeconomic theory. It is only in dealing with less developed countries that theories have assumed single causal variables or fixed relationships among variables.

Analyses of both developed and less developed countries have generally postulated essentially static relationships among factors in economic growth. However, it is likely that different factors in growth affect each other over time, even in a private-enterprise economy. That is, the abundance of some factors and the scarcity of others can set up tensions and pressures to increase the supply of the scarce factors. Again this is quite in line with standard economic theory: the rate of return on scarce factors will be high, providing incentives to increase imports, to invest in production, to put potential supplies to use, and to use existing supplies more efficiently. In a planned economy the "annihilation of scarcity" is an obvious and important objective of planning: any plan worthy of its name will call for policies and programs to increase the supply of scarce factors.

For instance, if there is a large inflow of foreign capital, aid, or private investment in a country with few skilled workers or technicians, investment will be used inefficiently. The few people with skills and training will obtain high wages. As a result, incentives will exist for foreign technicians to be brought in, for on-the-job training to increase, for schools to spring up, and for families to find the funds to send their brightest members to learn the skills which command such high incomes. Moreover, planners will allocate resources to increase the supply of those who constitute the most severe bottleneck.

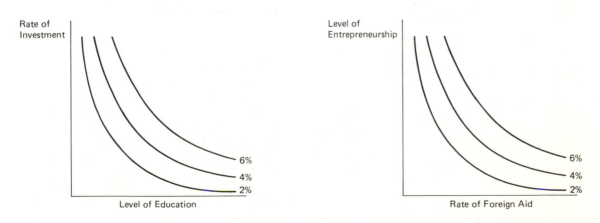

Figure 3. Growth in terms of substitutable factors.

A MODEL OF ECONOMIC DEVELOPMENT

If the foregoing discussion of factors in economic growth is a valid description of the situation, a model which accurately describes growth becomes quite complex. Even in a particular country the role of different factors in explaining growth will, of course, vary.

For instance, in the 1950s Korea may have had few entrepreneurs or experienced decision makers, an unskilled labor force, little natural resources, and an ineffective government but a high rate of investment, financed by foreign aid. The rate of growth would be relatively low in relation to investment. From a simple correlation it would appear that investment is not a major factor in growth. In fact, capital would be responsible for much of the growth taking place, substituting for the other scarce factors but quite naturally doing so at a low rate of productivity or return. With a lot of money to be made by the enterprising and the skilled, both entrepreneurship and training would be fostered. Initially entrepreneurs, quite correctly, would use their ingenuity in various semilegal and illegal activities and in extracting favors from government, both activities affording the highest profits. However, even these activities would develop in entrepreneurs habits of innovating, of looking for high return, of dealing with large enterprises. The changing attitudes which would result in turn would lead in another decade to more conventional entrepreneurial behavior, as Korean businessmen become exporters of skills and management and investors in foreign countries.[27]

Analyzing such a story with the traditional theories or models as tools might lead to the conclusion that investment or capital was not a major factor in Korean growth, that it was strong government or the shift of labor from agriculture to industry that was the explanatory variable. After all, when capital was available during the first period growth was slow. During the second period domestic savings rose but largely substituted for foreign aid, so the higher growth rate cannot be explained, it might be suggested, by greater investment. Indeed, during the second decade the continued low wages of the transferred workers, the effectiveness of government policy, and the enterprise of some businessmen probably generated the savings that made continued growth with less aid possible. But the whole process might never have started without the initial infusion of foreign capital.

What this example is meant to suggest is the complexity of the growth process if (a) a variety of factors, social and political as well as economic, can contribute to economic growth or can be obstacles to such growth; (b) these factors are substitutable, with declining productivity for any factor as it becomes more abundant relative to other factors (that is, any factor's productivity is a function also of the availability of other factors); (c) the factors also have a dynamic effect, with scarcity creating pressures to increase the supply of scarce factors; (d) there are lags and feedbacks involved in the dynamic relationships, lags that may differ in length; (e) most factors are difficult to quantify and some are, at least for now, unquantifiable. Under the circumstances to model growth for one country becomes difficult; for a hundred less developed countries a really satisfactory model that includes ultimate social, psychological and political factors would be complex indeed.

1. A brief discussion of these theories, from a somewhat different point of view is in P. Streeten, *The Frontiers of Development Studies* (New York: John Wiley & Sons, 1972), chap. 2.

2. W. A. Lewis, *The Theory of Economic Growth*, 4th ed. (London: George Allen & Unwin, 1960), pp. 26, 37–38, 232; B. Higgins, *Economic Development*, rev. ed. (London: Constable & Co., 1968), p. 504.

3. R. R. Nelson, "A Theory of the Low-Level Equilibrium Trap," *American Economic Review* 46 (December 1956): 894–908.

4. R. Nurkse, "Some International Aspects of

the Problem of Economic Development," *American Economic Review* 42 (May 1952): 571–83; reprinted in *Economics of Underdevelopment*," ed. A. N. Agarwala and S. P. Singh (New York: Oxford University Press, 1958), pp. 256–77; and *Problems of Capital Formation in Underdeveloped Countries* (Oxford: Basil Blackwell & Mott, 1953).

5. R. Prebisch, "External Bottlenecks Obstructing Development," in *Leading Issues in Economic Development*, ed. Gerald M. Meier, 2d ed. (New York: Oxford University Press, 1970), pp. 484–92, or in *Towards a New Trade Policy for Development*, ed. UN Conference on Trade and Development (New York: United Nations, 1964), pp. 11–16, 107–8, 124.

6. P. N. Rosenstein-Rodan, "Notes on Theory of Big Push," in *Economic Development for Latin America*, ed. Howard S. Ellis (New York: St. Martin's Press, 1961), pp. 57–66; and "Problems of Industrialization of Eastern and South-Eastern Europe," *Economic Journal* 53 (June–September 1943): 202–11, reprinted in Agarwala and Singh, pp. 245–55; Max Millikan and D. L. M. Blackmer, eds., *The Emerging Nations* (Boston: Little, Brown & Co., 1961), chap. 3.

7. E. S. Shaw, *Financial Deepening in Economic Development* (New York: Oxford University Press, 1973), chap. 3; R. I. McKinnon, *Money and Capital in Economic Development* (Washington, D.C.: Brookings Institution, 1973), chap. 6.

8. G. F. Papanek, *Pakistan's Development: Social Goals and Private Incentives* (Cambridge, Mass.: Harvard University Press, 1967), chaps. 7 and 8; W. P. Falcon and C. H. Gotsch, *Agricultural Price Policy and the Development of West Pakistan* (Cambridge, Mass.: Organization for Social and Technological Innovation, 1970).

9. Papanek, chaps. 2 and 8.

10. K. B. Griffin and J. L. Enos, "Foreign Assistance: Objectives and Consequences," *Economic Development and Cultural Change* 18 (April 1970): 317–27; T. Weisskopf, "The Impact of Foreign Capital Inflow on Domestic Savings in Underdeveloped Countries," *Journal of International Economics* 2 (February 1972): 25–38.

11. J. K. Galbraith, "The Causes of Poverty," in *Economics: Peace and Laughter* (Boston: Houghton Mifflin Co., 1971), pp. 228–42 and chap. 6; T. W. Schultz, "Investment in Human Capital in Poor Countries," in *Foreign Trade and Human Capital*, ed. Paul D. Zook (Dallas: South-

ern Methodist University Press, 1962), pp. 7–14.

12. D. C. McClelland, *The Achieving Society* (Princeton, N.J.: D. Van Nostrand Co., 1961); E. E. Hagen, *The Economics of Development*, Irwin Series (Homewood, Ill.: Richard D. Irwin, Inc., 1968); P. Kilby, "Hunting the Heffalump," in *Entrepreneurship and Economic Development* (New York: Free Press, 1971), pp. 1–40.

13. A. Hirschman, *The Strategy of Economic Development* (New Haven, Conn.: Yale University Press, 1958).

14. G. F. Papanek, "Aid, Foreign Private Investment, Savings and Growth in Less Developed Countries," *Journal of Political Economy* 81 (January/February 1973): 12–30.

15. Falcon and Gotsch; Papanek, *Pakistan's Development*, chaps. 2 and 8; Kilby.

16. B. F. Hoselitz, *Sociological Aspects of Economic Growth* (New York: Free Press, 1960).

17. G. Myrdal, *Asian Drama* (New York: Pantheon Books, 1968), vol. 2.

18. E. C. Banfield, *The Moral Basis of a Backward Society* (New York: Free Press, 1958).

19. G. Frank, "The Development of Underdevelopment," in *Imperialism and Underdevelopment*, ed. R. I. Rhodes (New York: Monthly Review Press, 1970), pp. 4–16.

20. W. W. Rostow, "The Take-Off into Self-sustained Growth," *Economic Journal* 66 (March 1956): 25–48, reprinted in Agarwala and Singh, pp. 154–86.

21. Galbraith.

22. W. A. Lewis, "Economic Development with Unlimited Supplies of Labour," in Agarwala and Singh, pp. 400–449; G. Ranis and J. C. H. Fei, "A Theory of Economic Development," *American Economic Review* 51 (September 1961): 533–65.

23. H. B. Chenery and M. Syrguin, *Patterns of Development 1950–70* (London: Oxford University Press, 1975); H. B. Chenery, "Alternative Strategies for Development," Bank Staff Working Paper no. 165 (IBRD, Washington, D.C., 1973), pp. 1–30.

24. A. O. Hirschman, "Obstacles to Development," *Economic Development and Cultural Change* 13 (July 1965): 385–93.

25. Paul Streeten (n. 2 above) has a similar approach, but uses a different classification scheme from that given below.

26. See R. M. Solow, "A Contribution to the

Theory of Economic Growth," *Quarterly Journal of Economics* 70 (1956): 65–94. There is of course a vast literature on the theory of economic growth. The most recent summary (R. Britto, "Some Recent Developments in the Theory of Economic Growth: An Interpretation," *Journal of Economic Literature* 11 [December 1973]: 1343–66) explains that "growth in developing countries [has] been ... considered in a separate category for ... reasons that it is unnecessary to spell out." M. L. Weitzman analyzed rates of factor substitution for the Soviet Union ("Soviet Postwar Economic Growth and Capital-Labor Substitution," *American Economic Review* 60 [September 1970]: 676–92). It is curious that theories for Western and Soviet-type economies should be considered quite separate from those for less developed countries and that work on the latter should have so largely ignored the former.

27. Quite analogous developments, in less extreme form, are described for Pakistan in Papanek, *Pakistan's Development.*

4. Development Alternatives: Problems, Strategies, and Values*

Peter J. A. Henriot

INTRODUCTION

To speak of "development" today is to undertake an especially difficult task. In recent years, the entire field of development has been in considerable disarray, both theoretical and practical. The "conventional wisdom" of the 1960s has by and large been discredited, as theories which were expected to guide dramatic improvements in the lot of the world's poor have proved ineffective or even counterproductive. The "success stories" of several developing countries have turned out over a longer period of time and under more stringent analysis to be less than successful in human terms. And the nations of Latin America, Asia, and Africa—the so-called "Third World"—have posed increasingly serious challenges to the industrialized nations. The "North/South" confrontation has replaced the "East/West" confrontation as the most dangerous threat to world peace—and the meaning and implications of development are a major key to that confrontation. ...

It is ... critical that we have a better understanding of precisely what we mean when we speak of development. It is to this task that the current paper addresses itself. Because the author of this paper is a political scientist and not an economist, the emphasis here will be more on a policy analysis of the meaning of development than on a strictly economic analysis of models and theories. The approach to be taken here will be to explore a series of alternative ways of approaching the topic. "Alternatives" must be spoken of, because there is no "one way" of explaining what is meant by development. The focus of this paper, then, will be on three questions:

1. What are the alternatives to defining the *problems* faced in development?
2. What are the alternatives to proposing the *strategies* faced in development?
3. What are the alternatives to specifying the *values* guiding development?

* From: Daniel Callahan and Phillip G. Clark (eds.), *Ethical Issues of Population Aid: Culture, Economics and International Assistance.* Irvington Publishers, Inc., New York: 1981, pp. 207–238.

No effort is made to be exhaustive in examining alternatives, but simply to offer a few approaches in hopes of clarifying the overall topic.

I.   ALTERNATIVES: THE PROBLEMS FACED

It is clear that the manner in which a problem is defined has much to do with the possible solutions which can be suggested. In the alternative definitions suggested in what follows, it is not possible to make any completely exclusive distinctions since the various definitions overlap. Rather what is being pointed to is the *emphasis* made in each way of defining the problem. This emphasis—whether on what will be called here "capitalization," "marginality," or "dependency"—determines the priorities given certain programs and policies over others, the measurements of success employed, and the relationship of individual nations to the international order among nations.

A. "Capitalization" and the First Development Decade

In the first alternative definition of the problem faced in development, focus is upon the standard measurement of gross national product per capita (GNP/capita). This represents the total economic worth of goods and services produced, divided by the number of people in the country. The standard measurement utilized by the World Bank for dividing the world into sectors is GNP/capita. In general, those nations with a GNP/capita of more than $1,000 are considered "developed" countries, while those below that figure are "less developed" countries (LDCs). Some exceptions to this division do occur, however, notably in the instance of several of the nations which make up the OPEC bloc (Organization of Petroleum Exporting Countries).

When the degree of development is measured primarily in terms of GNP/capita, then the goal of increasing development—i.e., moving from a "less developed" to a "developed" stage—must be stimulation of the growth in GNP. The traditional theories of economic development relate increases in GNP growth to four major factors: capital accumulation, new resources (and/or new "frontiers"), technological progress, and population growth. The primary key to growth is seen to be capital accumulation, which permits increasing production through facilitating patterns of investment. In fact a cyclic pattern is used to describe the development process:

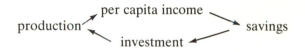

Essential to a healthy "development cycle" is the level of net savings and investment. Higgins describes the phenomenon as follows:

In the now advanced countries, net savings and investment during the periods of rapid growth averaged between 10 and 20 per cent of national income. In most, but not all the now underdeveloped countries net savings and investment run between 5 and 10 per cent of the national income. Here is one of the many vicious circles encountered in any study of the problem of economic development. A high level of national income results in a high level of savings and investment, and consequently, in a rapid rate of economic growth. Underdeveloped countries in general have such low incomes that any substantial volume of savings and investment out of existing income is extremely difficult. To a large degree, the problem of economic growth is a problem of "getting over the hump" to the point where levels of per capita income are high enough to permit sufficient net savings and investment to guarantee continued expansion.[1]

Another way of describing the development process according to this strictly "economic model" has been offered by Rostow in his historical account of development in the industrialized West.[2] When *The Stages of Economic Growth* appeared in 1960, it presented an interpretation of the stages through which modern societies have evolved to their present levels. Rostow outlined five stages:

1. *Traditional society*—productivity limited because of insufficiently developed economic techniques.
2. *The preconditions for take-off*—development of a "leading sector" in the economy which positively influences other sectors; increase in agricultural productivity to support leading-sector activities; improvements in transportation and other forms of social overhead capital.
3. *The take-off*—interval when the old blocks and resistances to steady growth are finally overcome and growth becomes normal condition for all sectors of society; main feature is increase in ratio of savings and investment to national income of 5 percent or less to 10 percent or more; also emergence of political, social, and institutional framework to facilitate impulses toward expansion.
4. *The drive to maturity*—long interval of sustained if fluctuating progress, with 10 to 20 percent of the national income steadily invested; new leading sectors supporting older ones.
5. *Age of high mass-consumption*—structural change no longer takes place at a rapid rate; leading sectors shift toward consumer goods and services.

Central to Rostow's "take-off" theory is the capital accumulation made possible by an increasing level of savings and investment.

Guided by the "conventional wisdom" underlying this economic model of development, great efforts were made in the 1960s to meet the problem of insufficient capitalization. The United Nations' First Development Decade (1960–1970) set a quantities target of a 5 percent annual increase of GNP in the developing countries. Heavy industrialization was the instrument for achieving this growth rate, and large hydroelectric dams, steel mills, factories, etc., were promoted on a grand scale. In order to mount this effort, capital assistance from the rich countries was a necessity. Foreign aid was expected to fill the gap between the capital requirements for a take-off into sustained growth and the domestic capabilities for savings and investment. Hence, bi-lateral and multi-lateral programs and institutions for transfer of capital were strongly pushed during the 1960s, such as the U.S. Agency for International Development, the Alliance for Progress, the International Bank for Reconstruction and Development (World Bank), and the United Nations Development Program.

During the First Development Decade, a target was set for a transfer of public and private capital to developing countries equal to 1 percent of the GNP of the developed countries. Such a target was not met during the 1960s. In fact, the net flow of official development assistance from the industrialized countries declined from a total of 0.52 percent of GNP in 1960 to 0.34 percent in 1970, and continued slipping to 0.29 percent in 1975. (The comparable figures for the United States are 0.53, 0.31, and 0.20.)[3] Nevertheless, significant infusions of capital into the developing countries did take place.

It is important to note that in describing this particular definition of the problem of development, which emphasizes capitalization, the nations which are developing are viewed more or less in isolation. Their difficulties are seen to be primarily internal, the results of local structures inadequate to the task of increasing GNP/capita. In a sense, their history of relationships—primarily colonial—with the industrialized Western nations is forgotten and the present-day implications of that history neglected.

B. "Marginality" and the Second Development Decade

Seen in historical perspective, the overall economic growth rate which has been experienced in the developing nations has been truly remarkable. "The 5 percent annual increase in gross national product achieved as a Third World average during the 1960s, and which was the quantitive target for the United Nations' First Development Decade, is roughly double the rate of economic growth achieved in nineteenth century Western Europe and North America."[4] In classical economic terms, such an outstanding increase could not help but be seen as an indication of significant "development." Yet by the end of the 1960s, it became more and more obvious that the "development" measured by per capita increase in GNP was not reaching the lives of ordinary people in terms of jobs, income distribution, and basic alleviation of critical poverty.

One development economist put the issue in the following way:

The questions to ask about a country's development are therefore: What has been happening to poverty? What has been happening to unemployment? What has been happening to inequality? If all three of these have declined from high levels, then beyond doubt this has been a period of development for the country concerned. If one or two these central problems have been growing worse, especially if all three have it would be strange to call the result "development," even if per capita income doubled.[5]

Stirred by questions such as these, another view of how to define the problem of development began to emerge. According to this view, the problem of development was not the degree of capitalization but the relationship any increase of GNP had to the poor—especially those poorest 40 percent of the population in the developing countries. These poorest 40 percent are the "marginals," people who neither contribute to the productivity of the nation nor share in the benefits of increased productivity. The arguments traditionally advanced to counter objections to growth models of development which do not directly benefit the poor have concentrated on the "trickle down" theory. Given sufficient prosperity in the upper sectors of society—in particular among those who directly benefit from increased GNP growth—it is to be expected that benefits will flow to the lower classes because of increased employment, some redistributive tax measures, and the general health and stability of the economy. But as a matter of fact this benefit flow was not occurring in the developing countries during the 1960s. Quite the contrary was occurring, especially in the so-called "success stories" of Brazil, Mexico and India, which had experienced very high rates of GNP growth during the 1960s. As Adelman notes, "Not only is there no automatic trickle-down of the benefits of development; on the contrary, the development process leads typically to a trickle-up in favor of the middle classes and the rich."[6]

The problem of the "marginals," exacerbated by development models which aimed chiefly at GNP/capita increase and which ignored distributive characteristics, was addressed directly by Robert McNamara before the Board of Governors of the World Bank Group meeting in Nairobi in 1973:

The basic problem of poverty and growth in the developing world can be stated very simply. The growth is not equitably reaching the poor. And the poor are not significantly contributing to growth.

Despite a decade of unprecedented increase in the gross national product of the developing countries, the poorest segments of their population have received relatively little benefit. Nearly 800 million individuals—40% out of a total of two billion—survive on incomes estimated (in U.S. purchasing power) at 30 cents per day in conditions of malnutrition, illiteracy, and squalor. They are suffering poverty in the absolute sense.

Although the collection of statistics on income distribution in the developing world is a relatively recent effort, and is still quite incomplete, the data point to what is happening. Among 40 developing countries for which data are available, the upper 20% of the population receives 55% of national income in the typical country, while the lowest 20% of the population receives 5%. That is a very severe degree of inequality—considerably greater than in most of the advanced countries.

The data suggest that the decade of rapid growth has been accompanied by greater maldistribution of income in many developing countries, and that the problem is most severe in the countryside. There has been an increase in the output of mining, industry, and government—and in the incomes of the people dependent on these sectors—but the productivity and income of the small farmer have stagnated.

One can conclude, that policies aimed primarily at accelerating economic growth, in most developing countries, have benefitted mainly the upper 40% of the population and the allocation of public services and investment funds has tended to strengthen rather than to offset this trend.[7]

Recognition of the need to attend more closely to the social consequences of development has been assisted in recent years by what is called the "social indicators movement." This comprises efforts to devise non-economic measurements of the quality of life—such as education, health, housing, crime, social mobility, etc., as well as the utilization of economic measurements which indicate more distributive characteristics—such as income distribution, employment ratios, etc. The United Nations had devoted considerable research to these "social indicators" in recent years in comparative studies of developed and developing countries.[8]

When the strategy for the Second Development Decade of the United Nations (1970–1980) was devised, therefore, social goals were given explicit attention. These goals focused on the infrastructures of education, medical care, nutrition, and housing, as well as income distribution, land reform, and community organization. The repeated emphasis of the speeches of World Bank President McNamara has been on the social goals, and a "rethinking" of development has also influenced the direction of the U.S. Agency for International Development. The latter, for example, has been mandated, under the Foreign Assistance Act of 1973, to concentrate on assistance for agriculture, rural development,

nutrition, health and population planning, education, and human resource development.[9]

This second definition of the problem of development, emphasizing "marginality," is similar to the first definition which emphasizes "capitalization," in that it also locates the problem primarily as *internal* to the developing countries. No effort is made in the analysis—or in the consequent policy response recommended—to place the problem in any kind of international context.

C. "Dependency" and the New International Economic Order

The first two alternatives in defining the problem of development look at the less developed country primarily in terms of its own internal structures. A growing number of analysts, however, particularly those from developing countries, prefer a definition of the problem which is more historical in its emphasis upon the evolving relationships between developed and developing countries. They see the focus of the problem not located principally within the developing world. For this group of development analysts, at issue is not so much the *quantity of economic growth* (according to the first alternative), or even the *quantity of social growth* (according to the second alternative), but the *quality of the process* by which the growth is achieved.[10]

Economic and social development is important. But the key question to be asked, according to the third alternative, is: Who is controlling the development? To apply Paulo Freire's terminology of the educational process[11] to the international economic process, are the countries *objects* of development—at someone else's hands, or are they *subjects* of development—in control of their own destiny? Answers to this basic question gives rise to the theories of "dependency" and of "underdevelopment." In one form or another these theories have become increasingly influential in Latin America and other Third World areas.

"Dependency" means that the major decisions which affect socioeconomic progress within less developed areas—decisions, for example, about commodity prices, investment patterns, monetary relationships—are made by individuals and institutions outside those countries. It is a situation "in which the economy of certain countries is conditioned by the development and expansion of another economy to which the former is subjected.... The concept of dependence permits us to see the internal situation of these countries as part of world economy."[12]

"Underdevelopment" is seen as the flip-side of the coin of "development."[13] It refers to the process whereby a country, characterized by subsistence agriculture and domestic production, progressively becomes integrated as a dependency into the world market through patterns of trade and/or investment. The production of that country thus becomes geared primarily to the demands of the world market, in particular the demands dictated by the industrialized nations, with a consequent lack of integration within the country between the various parts of its own domestic economy.

These theories of dependency and underdevelopment have been sketched in studies by Celso Furtado, Andre Gunder Frank, Theotonio Dos Santos, Fernando Henrique Cardoso, and others. All of them take seriously the colonial relationships which have historically marked the growth of the countries of Latin America, Africa and Asia. They argue that outside of an explicit recognition of the consequences of that relationship no accurate understanding of the present situation of these countries is possible. For example, Furtado suggests three historical stages in the process of underdevelopment,[14] which can be summarized as follows:

1. *Comparative advantages*.—During the period following the industrial revolution when the system of the international division of labor was being created and a world economy was being structured, the industrialized countries by and large specialized in activities marked by a high degree of widespread technical progress. In other countries, however, domestic and international investment was either in sectors with minimum technology in the productive process (e.g., agricultural plantations oriented toward "cash crops") or in sectors wherein technical progress was isolated (e.g., in the "enclaves" controlled from outside which operated the mineral extractive industries). In both instances, there was little or no technological advance throughout the nation and the income benefits went mainly to a tiny minority. What resulted was the creating of a primary commodity exporting economy.

2. *Import substitution*.—The formation of a small privileged social group within the underdeveloped nation gives rise to the necessity of importing numerous goods to meet the patterns of consumption which this group has adopted in imitation of the rich nations. But poor balance of payments and restrictive trade policies then in turn give rise to local manufacture of the same goods previously imported for consumption. Thus the production of consumer goods becomes strongly skewed toward the needs of the rich minority, income distribution patterns are affected because of the needs for heavy capital accumulation, and there evolves a dependency on imports for the means of production (technology, parts, etc.). In this way the ability of certain rich countries to control technical progress and to impose consumption patterns becomes the decisive factor in structuring the productive apparatus of other countries—those which have become "dependent."

3. *Multinational corporations*.—The rise of the multinational corporation (MNC) has become the most important phenomenon in the international economic order, as internal transactions of MNCs have replaced ordinary market operations. In-

vestment in the manufacturing sector of the poor countries tends to be with capital-intensive, labor saving technologies which accentuate unemployment problems and the maldistribution of income. The MNCs are dominant in the innovative sectors of durable consumer goods, machinery and equipment, electronics, computers, chemicals, and drugs. A precondition for keeping the process of industrialization going, then, becomes dependent cooperation with their particular model of development.

A fourth element in the process of underdevelopment, mentioned by Cardozo and others, is the reinforcement of local domestic elites in the LDCs by international elites.[15] A class analysis shows that leadership in many LDCs—particularly those countries most integrated into the world market economy—is supported by the fabric of business, educational, social and political relationships built up over the years with leadership in developed countries. Thus it is understandable why many of the Third World elites view with displeasure a development process which would challenge these relationships.

The dependency-underdevelopment theories are not without their critics. Many development analysts believe that the case is overdrawn and the history sometimes distorted. But the fact remains that these theories enjoy considerable influence in developing countries today. Therefore the reason for sketching in some detail the elements of the theories is to provide a context for the evolving understandings of development which find expression in the call for a "New International Economic Order" (NIEO). More and more of the developing nations have urged that the problem of development is not to be defined merely in terms internal to their own situation but in terms of the environment within which they must function. There is a call for a new set of "rules of the game" regarding trade, aid, investment

patterns, monetary relationships, decision-making, etc. Power to back this call is found in the formation of producer cartels (e.g., OPEC, bauxite nations, etc.) and is manifested in demands for indexation of commodity prices to combat inflation of manufactured goods, in requests for increased representation in major international monetary and funding agencies such as the International Monetary Fund, and in increased aggressiveness regarding expropriation and nationalization of foreign investments.

In April, 1974, the Sixth Special Session of the General Assembly of the United Nations passed—over the reservations of the United States and other industralized nations—a Declaration on the Establishment of a New International Economic Order.[16] Among other things, the NIEO document calls for respect for the sovereign equality of all nations, sovereign rights over natural resources, the regulation and supervision of MNCs, and preferential trade agreements. In December, 1974, the United Nations General Assembly passed the Charter of Economic Rights and Duties of Nations, repeating the thrust of a call for an NIEO. The UN Seventh Special Session, September, 1975, began the hard bargaining necessary to implement the elements of the NIEO.

What is emphasized, therefore, in this third alternative to defining development is the problem of the international economic order, the structured relationships between rich and poor nations. "What is at stake," writes an African political scientist, "is indeed the belated but still sorely needed transition from an interdependence based on hierarchy and Western charity to an interdependence based on symmetry and mutual accountability."[17]

II.   ALTERNATIVES: THE STRATEGIES FOLLOWED

As would be expected, definitions of problems tend themselves to offer at least initial directions toward solutions. And so it is in considering the alternative ways to define problems faced in development. For this reason, the strategies to be followed in development efforts will depend very much on what is considered to be the key issue. In presenting here a survey of alternative strategies, no effort is made to parallel precisely the definition of problems as outlined in the previous section, but certain patterns of relationships will be obvious.

A. Economic Growth

The most widely accepted strategy for development today continues to be one which "focuses upon the creation of conditions for self-sustained growth in per capita GNP and the requisite modernization of economic, social, and political structures implicit in the achievement of this goal.[18] This strategy rests upon a reading of the historical experience of Western Europe, North America, and the Soviet Union—a partial reading at that—and suggests that this experience should provide the model for LDCs today.

In its emphasis upon the engines of investment, production, and consumption, this strategy tends toward a dualistic development pattern. The industrial sector is given prime consideration in plans and programs. This is usually concentrated in cities and hence the nation experiences rapid urbanization. Factories are constructed for the production of domestic consumer goods and for the manufacture of export goods. An industrial infrastructure is built up which includes power plants, modern transportation systems and skilled technical training. Capital-intensive, labor-saving technology is emphasized as the most efficient approach to increasing production output.

While the industrial sector is thus being promoted, this strategy by-passes or ignores the more traditional sector (e.g., cottage industries) and subordinates the agricultural sector. Agriculture is seen principally in two

ways: (1) a source for improvement of balance of trade through the sale of cash crops (cotton, sugar, cocoa, coffee, etc.) and (2) a support for the needs of urban dwellers engaged in the industrial sector. Full-scale incorporation of the agricultural sector into development plans is frequently neglected in the strategies concentrating on economic growth.

In the strategy of promoting economic growth, the question of income distribution is postponed. Until sufficient economic growth has occurred, it is considered harmful to focus on distributive effects. Policies aimed directly at promoting more equitable income distribution are thought to hamper economic growth by (1) reducing entrepreneurial incentives through curtailing profits, (2) lowering the rate of savings of those most likely to invest, and (3) delimiting the choice of efficient technologies through favoring of labor-intensive production. It is expected that an ever-increasing output of goods and services will in fact mean a prosperity which through a "trickle-down" process will improve the lot of the masses.

B. Growth with Distribution

Despite the significant effects of concentrated efforts to increase GNP growth, there has been a growing dissatisfaction with a "grow first, distribute later" strategy. This dissatisfaction has been heightened by the marked failure of such a strategy to achieve real human progress in terms of a decrease in poverty, increase in employment, and promotion of more equitable income distribution. Grant sums up the empirical evidence for this failure by citing the case of Mexico.

The experience of most developing countries over the past decade indicates that a rising GNP growth rate alone is no guarantee against worsening poverty. Mexico, for example, has been very successful by traditional standards: its GNP has risen by 6 or 7 percent annually for the past 15 years. Yet, at the same time, unemployment in Mexico has been increasing, and the income disparity between the rich and the poor has clearly been widening. This is not only because of Mexico's very rapid population growth, which has been far greater than that experienced by any presently industrialized country, including Japan. It is also because government policies have bypassed the small, labor-intensive producers throughout Mexico and encouraged production primarily through large farms and urban-based factories. Four-fifths of the increase in production has been coming from the less than 5 percent of farms employing only one-sixth of the farm labor force. Half of Mexico's industrial production has been located in its capital city. In addition, the jobs, housing, education, and health facilities provided by the government have generally favored higher income groups. In the early 1950s, the total income of the top fifth of the Mexican population was 10 times that of the lowest fifth; by 1969, it was 16 times as great.[19]

Similar cases have led to a challenge of the economic growth approach and prompted considerable "rethinking" of development strategies within recent years. One of the most public efforts at this "rethinking" can be found in recent addresses by World Bank President Robert McNamara. In 1971, McNamara spoke of the need to attend to agriculture and rural development and to promote jobs through labor-intensive industrialization which aims at production for foreign markets.[20] In his 1972 address to the Board of Governors of the World Bank Group, he told his audience:

> If government policy were directed towards promoting a price structure which reflected the scarcity values of labor and capital more realistically, the technological choice would be different. The result would be greater employment, broader income distribution, and more competitive patterns of production of precisely those labor-intensive goods which labor-scarce affluent countries need, but cannot themselves produce inexpensively.[21]

As noted earlier in this paper, McNamara issued a strong and specific call in 1973 for the need to reorient development strategies in order to provide a more equitable distribution of the benefits of economic growth. He challenged the approach which would consider it to be "wiser to concentrate on the modern sector [rather than on increasing the productivity of small-scale subsistence agriculture] in the hope that its high rate of growth would filter down to the rural poor."[22] He admitted that the World Bank itself had paid very little attention to subsistence agriculture in its 25 years of operation, devoting to it less than $1 billion out of a total of $25 billion of lending.[23]

According to McNamara, the strategy for increasing the productivity of small-holder agriculture includes as essential elements: (1) an acceleration in the rate of land and tenancy reform—meaning, of course, shifts in power structures; (2) better access to credit, with significant restructuring of interest rates; (3) assured availability of water through irrigation projects which actually reach the small farmer; (4) expanded extension facilities backed up by intensified agricultural research which gives priority to low-risk, inexpensive technology that can be put to immediate use; (5) great access to the public services of transportation, education, health care, electrification, etc.; and (6) "most critical of all: new forms of rural institutions and organizations that will give as much attention to promoting the inherent potential and productivity of the poor as is generally given to protecting the power of the privileged."[24]

In emphasizing the rural sector, this strategy does not neglect industrialization. But the criteria for evaluating the success of efforts to industrialize are not simply the rates of increase in GNP/capita. Rather the patterns of industrialization should attend especially to the creation of jobs, the use of intermediate technology, the production of basic necessities for the majority of the population rather than the provision of luxury items for the elite, decentralization of industrial sites away from urban concentrations, and the development of industry to service the agricultural sector. It seems clear, for example, that if the purchasing power of the poor, mainly rural majority is increased, greater mass markets will result for labor-intensive products such as hand tools, textiles, and shoes.

An analysis of development strategies which supports the "growth with distribution" approach can be found in an influential study published in 1972, *Development Reconsidered*. Owens and Shaw distinguish between *dual* and *modernizing* societies:

The basic distinction lies in the way in which these societies view the relationship between government and people. This relationship in *dual* societies is an extension of the ruler-ruled relationship of traditional societies in which decisions are essentially made at the top and passed down to the people. In *modernizing* societies there are explicit efforts to involve the populace in planning their own futures.[25]

Dual society governments encourage economic growth but do not attempt to reach the mass of people. Both investments and profits are concentrated in the hands of a few that are considered to possess more of the necessary expertise and initiative. Modernizing governments, on the other hand, attempt to bridge the gap between traditional elites and the masses, particularly by establishing and strengthening local institutions and systems in which the people work out solutions to their own local problems. The strategy by Owens and Shaw aims to integrate the elements of local participation, national organization, increased employment, focus on small farmers, emphasis on non-formal education, and provision of public services.

This "growth with distribution" strategy has been utilized in several nations in the past decade, with some significant instances of success. One particular variant of the strategy stresses integration of the developing country's economy into the international market through export production. Five nations are repeatedly cited as examples of this approach: Israel, Japan, South Korea, Singapore, and Taiwan. Adelman has described three stages

of a "dynamic sequence of strategies which characterize this approach."

Stage I: Radical asset redistribution, focusing primarily on land, but also imposing (at the very minimum) curbs upon the use and further accumulation of financial capital. This stage may involve negative growth rates, but is necessary to set the economic and political conditions to ensure that subsequent economic growth is not highly unequalizing.

Stage II: Massive accumulation of human capital, far in excess of current demand for skills. In this stage ownership of human capital is redistributed, the human resource base is vastly enlarged, and both the economic opportunities and the political pressures for the next stage are generated. In all five countries, this stage was accompanied by relatively slow rates of economic growth and, at later times, by political instability, social tension, and unrest.

Stage III: Rapid, human-resource-intensive growth. After the investment in human resources has been made, continuing depauperization requires that subsequent increases in growth rate be achieved through strategies that stress rapid labor-intensive growth. This implies that sufficient attention must be paid to the formulation of economic policy. In the smaller nations development will have to be oriented towards export markets. In large countries, on the other hand, industrialization can be oriented more towards satisfying domestic demand, particularly when a more equitable growth pattern generates a mass consumer market and when a more appropriate import-substitution technology is found.[26]

Adelman notes that the five nations taken as examples all have been aided by unusually large per capita infusions of foreign capital. For this reason, and because all are also small nations with nonrepresentative cultural traditions and attitudes, and have been subjected to exceptional challenges that legitimized their governments and made economic viability a major condition for national survival, some economists tend to dismiss these success stories as special cases. Whether or not their unique experience can be repeated elsewhere is questioned. "Special cases they may be," writes Adelman, "but five successful cases are certainly more encouraging than none, and the consistency of their experiences surely weakens the 'uniqueness' argument."[27]

C. Self-Reliant Development

A development strategy which is closely related to the "growth with distribution" strategy, but has notably different *organizational* and *motivational* patterns, is that followed by the People's Republic of China. In some senses it can be said to be a variant of the strategy discussed above in that it emphasizes rural development, promotes labor-intensive technology, relies on decentralized patterns of local control, and takes seriously the input of ordinary citizens into decision-making processes.

But one significant organizational difference is immediately obvious in viewing China as compared with Taiwan, South Korea, or Singapore. Whereas these latter nations are integrated into the international economic order through strong reliance on export-oriented production, China has stressed self-reliance with little or no integration. What integration does occur takes place on that nation's own terms. Mass-produced consumer goods are oriented towards satisfying domestic demands.

Another aspect of China's self-reliance is its independence from the influence of foreign investment. Weisskopf notes that as a matter of policy the Chinese have deliberately pursued conservative international financial policies to avoid long-term indebtedness after the 1960s. They allocated more resources and efforts to the development of indigenous technological capacities rather than relying on imported technologies introduced by foreign private enterprise. The turning point in this strategy, of course, was "the termination of Soviet aid to China in the late 1950's and the lack of aid opportunities from other sources."[28]

Recent events on the international scene do raise questions about future developments in China's strategy of self-reliance. Since the visit of President Nixon to China in 1972, new linkages with the international economic order are probable—but, again, on China's terms. Lin observes:

It remains to point out that Chinese self-reliance, while ruling out acceptance of conditional aid, does not preclude normal trade and international cooperation as accessory stimulants to development. As China rapidly expands her foreign trade, she is also ensuring that it reinforces rather than distorts her own pattern of development and that the basic domestic economy is insulated from any disruptive effects of linkage with the world market. My own conjecture is that China will move logically towards setting up a complete export economy (including production facilities) parallel to the domestic, targeted at not too high a ratio to total national income, which would be geared to the competitive international market. The domestic market would draw on the proceeds but would not be caught in the crippling trap of fluctuations in the world market.[29]

The motivational differences between China's development strategy and strategies followed by other nations should also be noted. That particular articulation of Marxist-Leninist thought found in the directives of Mao-Tse-tung provides a set of motivations which deeply influence the patterns of "growth with distribution." This value-orientation will be explored in detail in the next section of this study. But one example can be pointed to here in noting that Maoist ideology discourages consumption and encourages saving and investment. It thereby promotes the growth of capital stock—a development factor which appears to belong to that core of development theory acceptable both to proponents of a free-market strategy and of a socialist strategy. The values espoused in China promote this by preventing the rise of a "middle class" which is marked by high consumption patterns, and by fostering the virtues of plain living and aiding others rather than promoting a privileged status based on accumulation.[30]

Another effort at self-reliant development

is that being made by Tanzania. President Julius Nyerere has emphasized a pattern of growth which focuses on the village—the "ujamaa" program. And he has made a tremendous effort to maintain independence in relating to outside investments and trade. Terrible poverty conditions heightened by drought and famine situations have crippled this effort in many ways, however, and Tanzania must presently rely heavily on outside assistance. This assistance does not always come without conditions, many of which bring into question the future viability of this distinct African development strategy.

III. ALTERNATIVES: THE VALUES GUIDING

As should be clear from the analysis being offered in this paper, no development strategy is "value-free." Hence, a survey of development alternatives must make some effort to explicate the value presuppositions which guide particular approaches. For our purposes here, two sets of value-systems will be discussed, one clustering around the dominance of technology and the other relating to a coherent ideological position.

A. Technology

The role of technology in development strategies is critical. In almost all cases, modernization has meant a commitment to technology. This at least implies a systematic approach to control of production through labor-saving techniques and a sophistication of communication and transportation operations. Although technology is but one element in overall development strategies, its influence is massive. And it is not simply a neutral instrument. The choice to emphasize technology involves the acceptance of certain societal structures and orientations. As a result, the introduction of technology into a developing country brings with it certain values and endangers other values already present.

Goulet, who has done some of the most important research in the area of technology and values in a development context, suggests three values that are embedded in Western technology and are transmitted in a technological development process:[31]

1. *A particular approach to rationality*. The technological mind wants to treat any phenomenon as something to be broken down into component parts, put together again, and verified. There is consequently a tendency to change things, to extract more out of nature, to organize human efforts so as to get results. In the process, Western technology shows less appreciation of myth and symbol, of the power of the mysterious.
2. *A cult of efficiency*. Technology goes after efficiency and expresses its goal in industrial terms of productivity. The final output is all-important. A cost-benefit analysis is vigorously applied to determine what is esteemed and sought after in the development process.
3. *A predilection for problem-solving*. Technologists do not view nature so as to discover a harmony with it. Rather the effort is to manipulate and dominate nature. Problem-solving thus has a tendency to distort reality, because it reduces reality only to those dimensions which can be treated as mere difficulties to be solved.

When technology is transferred from a developed country to a developing country—most frequently through the operations of MNCs—certain tensions frequently arise. Goulet outlines five of these, in noting the value conflict areas.[32] First, there is a difference in how technology is viewed: as a marketable commodity (the consequence of proprietary knowledge) or as a free good, something to be as freely available as scientific information or public statistics. Second, does technology reinforce the consumption patterns of the upper classes or does it benefit the poor? In short, what is the relationship of technological processes to inequalities among social classes? Third, there is a tension between the repeated demand of developing countries for autonomy and independence and the prohibitive costs of importing technology. This cost, it is frequently argued, is the compelling reason why poor countries must rely on (depend on?) technological assistance from developed countries.

Fourth, more advanced ("high") technology has a tendency to standardize for the sake of efficiency, economies of scale, and avoidance of duplication costs in research and development. This standardizing emphasis conflicts with the values of cultural diversity and pluralistic social patterns of work. Fifth, tensions arise over the search for intermediate technology (which is inexpensive, labor-intensive, small-scale and requires low skill levels and unsophisticated local materials) and the drive for the status of more expensive and wasteful "high" technology which appears more "modern" and "first rate."

These tensions, of course, are not completely inevitable when commitments are made to modernization. What needs to be emphasized here, however, is that the values of technology can be determinative of the values of development. They need to be made explicit, if choices are to be made on the basis of values desired and not simply of availability of technologies.

B. Ideology

An ideological position can also be a dominant force in guiding national development. Such a position is a complexus of values—either explicit or implicit—and sets the goals to be pursued relating to the overall transformation of society. It touches the attitudes, motivations and behavior patterns of all the people. The People's Republic of China provides an important example of this guidance of development by ideology.

In analyzing the guiding values that ener-gize China's transformation and development, Lin distinguishes between "development values" and "superordinate goals"—"the former representing the policy norms as well as values in themselves, and the latter representing the ultimate ends of development."[33] The former can be seen as instrumental values for the attainment of the latter. Three principal development values are suggested by Lin.

1. *Power to the People, with its corollary, Reliance on the People*. A people-oriented development strategy requires that political power be held in the hands of the producer classes (peasants and workers) by every institutional means, formal and informal. This has certain policy derivatives, including: the choice of leaders for their identity with the people and their adherence to strategies and policies reflecting the peoples' interest (hence, the great importance of the Cultural Revolution which helped both to re-educate leaders and reassert the influence of the masses); mass activation, or reliance on the people to emancipate themselves, which emphasizes that even technical innovation (or "R and D" efforts) must utilize "three-in-one" (administrator-technician-worker) teams in order to tap the resources of full worker participation; and participatory management, with direct representation from the basic, working level and avoidance of bureaucratic hindrances in order to bring initiative from below into full play.

2. *The Serve-the-People Ethic*. This value aims at rooting-out the individualistic spirit and any self-serving policies. It becomes a premise in planning and developing both production and distribution, both industrialization and environmental protection. "To keep this value operational at all levels, Mao-Tse-tung has laid special emphasis on the constant reidentification and re-merging of cadres with the masses."[34] Institutional means to promote

this, for example, have been such efforts as the May 7th Cadre Schools and the mass movement of high school graduates to settle in the countryside to help build up the rural areas (where 80 percent of the people live and work).

3. *Self-Reliance and Autonomy in Development*. This value—already referred to in our earlier discussion of a self-reliant strategy—requires the optimal use of all available human, natural, and technological resources throughout the country. A balanced, congruent development is necessary especially in the relationships between industry and agriculture. (China's astounding ability to feed its people attests to at least some success in its endeavor to place priority emphasis—as a human value—on agriculture.) Also necessary is a dual approaching of "walking on two legs"—i.e., utilizing "both indigenous and advanced technologies; both smaller, low-investment, quickly built plants and big industrial complexes; both mechanized and semi-mechanized technologies"[35] Serious attention is also paid to the avoidance of waste, to large-scale recycling efforts, and to patterns of austerity.

These three sets of development values provide the possibility, according to Lin, of achieving in China what he calls the "end" values (or "superordinate goals") of development. These "end" values can be grouped under four headings:

1. Social justice based on freedom from exploitation with human relations of egalitarianism, cooperation, and respect for work.
2. Economic welfare for all in a society of abundance, with special attention to raising the level of life of marginalised groups (such as women and national minorities) and regions that have been resource-poor or historically oppressed.

3. Maximum cultural and esthetic fulfilment. This includes full popular participation in the production of culture.
4. An esthetically and ecologically sound environment. This value is not posed *against* growth, but as *part of* development, fulfilling the same purpose of service to the people as growth.[36]

In citing China as an example here, no more is intended than to illustrate the organizing and motivating power of a coherent ideology. What appears to an increasing number of outside observers as a truly remarkable instance of development success (not without shortcomings, of course) can at least partially be explained as the consequence of what Goulet refers to as the creation of a shared value system based on solidarity, revolutionary consciousness, and the primacy of moral over material incentives. "The Chinese lesson is that values command politics (the primary value is to construct revolutionary consciousness); politics (which includes ethics) commands economics; and economics commands technique."[37]

NOTES

1. Benjamin Higgins, *Economic Development: Problems, Principles, and Policies* (revised edition; New York: W. W. Norton, 1968), p. 189.
2. W. W. Rostow, *The Stages of Economic Growth: A Non-Communist Manifesto* (Cambridge: Cambridge University Press, 1960).
3. See the statistical data presented in James W. Howe, ed., *The U.S. and World Development: Agenda for Action, 1975* (New York: Praeger Publishers, 1975), p. 258.
4. Edgar Owens and Robert Shaw, *Developments Reconsidered: Bridging the Gap Between Government and People* (Lexington, Massachusetts: Lexington Books, 1972), p. 1.
5. Dudley Seers, "The Meaning of Development," in Charles K. Wilber, ed., *The Political Economy of Development and Underdevelopment* (New York: Random House, 1973), p. 7.
6. Irma Adelman, "Development Economics:

A Reassessment of Goals," *American Economic Review* 65 (May 1975), p. 302.

7. Robert S. McNamara, "Address to the Board of Governors," Nairobi, Kenya, September 24, 1973, World Bank reprint, pp. 10–11.

8. See Donald V. McGranahan, *Contents and Measurements of Socio-Economic Development* (New York: Praeger Publishers, 1972).

9. See, for example, "'New Directions' in Development Assistance: Implementation in Four Latin American Countries," report to the Committee on International Relations, U.S. House of Representatives, August 31, 1975.

10. See Denis Goulet, "'Development'. . . or Liberation?" in Wilber, *op. cit.*, pp. 354–361.

11. Paulo Freire, *Pedagogy of the Oppressed*, translated by Myra Bergman Ramos, (New York: Herder and Herder, 1970).

12. Theotonio Dos Santos, "The Structure of Dependence," in Wilber, *op. cit.*, p. 109.

13. See André Gunder Frank, "The Development of Underdevelopment," in James D. Cockcroft *et al.*, eds., *Dependence and Underdevelopment: Latin America's Political Economy* (Garden City, N.Y.: Anchor Books, 1972), pp. 3–18.

14. Celso Furtado, "The Concept of External Dependence in the Study of Underdevelopment," in Wilber, *op. cit.*, pp. 118–123.

15. Fernando Henrique Cardoso and Enzo Faletto, *Dependencia y desarrollo en América Latina* (Santiago: ILPES, 1967).

16. United Nations General Assembly, "Declaration on the Establishment of a New International Economic Order," May 1, 1974, CEST. E21.

17. Ali A. Mazrui, "The New Interdependence: From Hierarchy to Symmetry," in Howe, *op cit.*, p. 134

18. Adelman, *op cit.*, p. 306.

19. James P. Grant, "Growth from Below: A People-Oriented Strategy," Development Paper 16, December, 1973 (Washington, D.C.: Overseas Development Council), p. 7.

20. Robert S. McNamara, "Address to the Board of Governors," Washington D.C., September 27, 1971, World Bank reprint.

21. Robert S. McNamara, "Address to the Board of Governors," Washington, D.C., September 25, 1972, World Bank reprint, p. 14.

22. Robert S. McNamara, "Address to the Board of Governors," Nairobi, Kenya, September 24, 1973, World Bank reprint, p. 13.

23. *Ibid.*, p. 14.

24. *Ibid.*, p. 17.

25. Owens and Shaw, *op. cit.*, p. 4.

26. Adelman, *op. cit.*, p. 308.

27. *Ibid.*, p. 309.

28. Thomas E. Weisskopf, "China and India: Contrasting Experiences in Economic Development," *American Economic Review* 65 (May 1975), p. 361.

29. Paul T. K. Lin, "Development Guided by Values: Comments on China's Road and Its Implications," in Saul H. Mendlovitz, ed., *On the Creation of a Just World Order: Preferred Worlds for the 1990's* (New York: The Free Press), p. 272.

30. John W. Gurley, "Maoist Economic Development: The New Man in the New China," in Wilber, *op cit.*, p. 318.

31. Denis Goulet, "On the Ethics of Development Planning," address at the University of California at Los Angeles, March 6, 1975 (mimeo), pp. 13–15.

32. Denis Goulet, "The Paradox of Technology Transfer," *Bulletin of the Atomic Scientists* 31 (June 1975), pp. 39–46.

33. Lin, *op. cit.*, p. 267.

34. *Ibid.*, p. 269.

35. *Ibid.*, p. 271.

36. *Ibid.*, p. 272.

37. Goulet, "On the Ethics . . .," *op. cit.*, p. 23.

5. Conventional Development Strategies and Basic-Needs Fulfilment*

Franklyn Lisk

INTRODUCTION

It has become increasingly clear that the development strategies of the 1950s and 1960s have not led to significant improvements in the welfare of the masses in the majority of developing countries. In some cases relatively impressive growth performances have been accompanied by increased unemployment and poverty.[1] This article uses a simple classification of the main types of development strategy to examine their general characteristics. The aim is to identify weaknesses which may have contributed to the failure of past and current strategies, for if ever a way is to be found of attaining simultaneously the objectives of growth, full employment and the eradication of poverty, it is essential to see what lessons can be learned from the mistakes of the past quarter of a century. An alternative approach based on the concept of "basic needs" is then considered, together with possible policy guidelines for significantly improving, within a tolerable period, the social and economic conditions under which the majority of people in the developing countries live and work.

A CLASSIFICATION OF DEVELOPMENT STRATEGIES

On the basis of differences and similarities in objectives and policy emphases it is possible to distinguish three approaches to development;[2] these are commonly referred to as growth-oriented, employment-oriented and poverty-oriented.[3] Although each represents a different (though not unrelated) view of the mechanics of development, the differences are more of degree than of kind; for example, all three recognise the need for economic growth. For this reason our typology also roughly indicates the different weights each type gives to the various objectives.

The Growth-oriented Approach

Objectives. The primary objective of this kind of strategy is to increase the rate of output within an economy over a period of time mainly by increasing the rate of capital formation. The growth rate is presented as a function of increase in capital stock, and emphasis is placed on the mobilisation of savings and investment. It is assumed that rapid growth of GNP suffices to bring about higher standards of living through its beneficial influence on other economic and social parameters.

Among growth-oriented strategies there are two major theoretical variants, namely balanced and unbalanced growth. The former calls for massive capital investment on all fronts simultaneously in order to reach the stage when an increased rate of aggregate growth can be generated. This implies the need to overcome obstacles to rapid growth of output and often produces a bias towards capital-intensive projects and a desire for rapid industrialisation.[4] An important assumption in this approach is that technical and commercial complementarities exist between the new industries at different stages of production and in different sectors of the economy—corresponding in some ways to the external economies of large-scale production.

The unbalanced growth doctrine places similar reliance on the forward and backward linkage effects between industries at different

* From *International Labour Review*, Vol. 115, No. 2 (March–April 1977), pp. 175–191.

stages of production to provide the impetus for growth. Instead of all-out investment, however, the proponents of this theory recommended a selective approach concentrating on key sectors or industries where complementarities or linkage effects are supposed to be strongest.[5]

The inadequacy of rapid GNP growth as the sole objective of development can best be illustrated by the trend in some developing countries where in recent years significant growth rates have actually resulted in a decrease in the share of income accruing to the poorest groups. In some cases the relative decrease has even been sufficiently pronounced to result in declines in the absolute incomes of the poor.[6] This proves the fallacy of the argument that improvements in the living standards of a developing country's population will follow automatically from high rates of GNP growth. The events of the past ten years have shown the effects of the "trickle-down" process to be overrated.

The fact is that significant improvements in overall standards of living and social welfare cannot be achieved within an acceptable period solely by increasing the rate of physical capital formation and neglecting necessary structural changes. Increased investment in physical capital is only part of, and dependent upon, what happens in the economy as a whole. We cannot generalise from changes in one set of factors to the entire system.[7] While the capital accumulation concept may be valid in relatively developed countries, it is certainly less so in ones that are faced with structural constraints such as scarcity of managerial and technical skills, low motivation of the workforce, insufficient capacity to absorb new knowledge and apply it effectively, and the problem of resource allocation between basic consumer and capital goods. For countries of the latter sort development should mean not only aggregate economic growth but also significant changes in the living standards of individuals and progress in the social system as a whole.

Policies. In general, growth-oriented strategies focus on investment projects in the modern sector, where technical and commercial linkages between industries are likely to be strongest.[8] Policies designed to secure a more equitable distribution of income are far from welcome, largely because it is thought that such redistribution would jeopardise the attainment of higher rates of capital accumulation. Employment promotion is never an overriding issue of policy, since production relies heavily on capital-intensive technology; whatever amount of labour is required for industrialisation in the modern sector is considered to be automatically forthcoming from an unlimited supply of surplus or underemployed labour in the traditional sectors.[9]

The validity of the argument that a more equitable initial distribution of incomes is inimical to faster capital accumulation hinges on the assumption that in general a higher proportion of profit than of wages is saved. As Stewart and Streeten have pointed out [see Reading 15], however, this is a questionable assumption. "All profits are not saved," they write, "and it may not even be warranted to assume that a higher proportion of profits is saved than of other incomes. Profits remitted and retained overseas, even if saved, will not add to the investible resources of the developing economy."[10] By basing the causal link between savings and economic growth on higher profit yields, growth-oriented development strategies have mainly benefited those earning high incomes and profits in the modern sector. In view of the general absence of political will to redistribute wealth and the ineffectiveness of the redistribution machinery (traditional monetary and fiscal devices) in most developing countries, it could hardly be otherwise. Similarly, the failure of growth-oriented strategies to formulate policies explicitly promoting employment creation—relying instead on high-productivity nuclei in the modern sector to provide secondary stimuli—has left little scope for the trickle-down process because of the bias towards capital-intensive methods of production. The result is that far from trickling down to the rest of the economy, modern sector gains are being withheld from the traditional sector which provides a livelihood for the majority of the population.

Growth-oriented policies also play down the role of current consumption in fostering development. This again seems to derive from the view that redistribution of purchasing power in favour of low-income groups may jeopardise growth by reducing savings and investments. However, this view fails to take into account the possibility of both consumption and investment rising as a result of redistribution, provided some of the investible resources of the economy are directed to supplying the goods and services consumers desire.[11] Moreover, the redirection of productive resources towards higher output of mass-consumption goods and services is likely to promote employment, since the technology mix of the economy will be shifted towards more labour-intensive production methods. Increased consumption of essential goods and services, particularly among lower income groups, is useful in reducing poverty through its influence on individuals' living standards. For these reasons it is perhaps a mistake to draw too sharp a dividing line between consumption and investment in low-income economies.

The limited contribution made to development by growth-oriented strategies explains their failure to cope with the problems of unemployment and poverty in the Third World. An important lesson to be drawn from this is the need for broad-based development objectives and policies that take into account the whole range of socio-political and institutional factors which both determine and are determined by the process of economic and social development. Inasmuch as rapid expansion of GNP is vital to the development process, it is evident that if growth is to be sustained and if its benefits are to be spread widely, development goals must include a significant change in the composition of output through altera-tions in resource allocation and the technology mix of the economy.

The Employment-oriented Approach

Objectives. The objectives of employment-oriented strategies reflect a wider definition of development that includes improvement in the living conditions of individuals in addition to economic growth. Employment promotion is viewed as the principal means of spreading the benefits of economic growth more evenly throughout the economy. Accordingly, the growth objective is modified so as to maximise not only output but the rate of labour absorption. Implicit in this change in the pattern of growth is the need for reallocation of resources in favour of disadvantaged sectors and groups. Thus redistribution of incomes and productive assets receives some attention through emphasis on the central objective of reducing unemployment and under-employment.[12]

While not entirely discounting the possibility of conflicts between the output and employment objectives, employment-oriented strategies stress that simultaneous increases in output and employment can be achieved through direct substitution of labour for capital in the production process. This has often resulted in the setting of employment targets contingent on higher rates of GNP growth than may be feasible. For example, the report of the ILO Comprehensive Employment Mission to Kenya postulated that an over-all annual growth rate of 7 percent was necessary in order to achieve a significant improvement in the level of employment.[13] In view of the existence of certain constraints on output and employment growth in many developing countries, the possibility of achieving gains in both cannot be taken for granted.

While it may be possible in theory to achieve gains in both current output and employment by substituting labour for capital, there is abundant evidence in the literature that they may be hard to come by in practice.[14] Apart from the question of sacrificing current for future gains in one or both objectives, empirical evidence suggests that conflicts are likely to occur if different production techniques are used simultaneously. Two studies by Bhalla in the mid-1960s indicated that a conflict may arise because the more labour-intensive method (in the sense of a lower capital-labour ratio) actually involves more capital per unit of output than the capital-intensive method.[15] Similarly, a recent inter-country study by Pack on the relationship between output and employment growth in six different industries yielded results which indicate that differences in efficiency between similar industries and firms operating in different countries over the same period were mainly attributable to the use of different production techniques.[16]

It is clear from all this that in a developing country gains in both output and employment can be achieved only under certain conditions. First, it must be feasible to substitute labour for capital, which implies the existence of a relatively high degree of technical and managerial efficiency.[17] Second, the prices of factors must be established at realistic levels in relation to their costs in order to avoid the adoption of inefficient and inappropriate technology. Given that these conditions are not common in developing countries, output and employment objectives should be reconciled by reference to what is feasible in terms of labour-capital substitution rather than to what GNP growth rate is needed to achieve a substantial increase in the level of employment.

Policies. Generally speaking, employment-oriented policies reflect the desire to reconcile economic growth with the broader distribution of incomes through increases in the level of productive employment. Thus the key requirement is to restructure domestic demand and production towards a higher level of relatively labour-intensive output, mainly by reducing the capital intensity of modern sector activities and by providing a supply of capital commensurate with the need for increased rates of labour absorption and output growth in the unorganised sector.

As a rule, policies are formulated for critical sectors or areas identified according to the nature of the employment problem in a given situation. Although these identifications are often based on the conventional "rural-urban" or "traditional-modern" division of the economy, there are instances where the nature and causes of unemployment lead to the identification of critical areas that do not conform strictly to such conventional classification. To the extent that various causes may be common to several critical areas within the economy, policies are also formulated on a cross-sectoral basis. Sectoral measures are designed to increase the demand for and productivity of labour within the sector; typical examples are rural public works projects (such as feeder roads, irrigation and land reclamation) or the promotion of small-scale rural and urban activities. Cross-sectoral policies also include measures to facilitate the access of unemployed persons and low-income groups to productive assets such as land, education, production technology and credit facilities, or to control the birth rate as a way of reducing the number of future entrants into the labour force.

As mentioned earlier, employment-oriented strategies sometimes include separate employment-stimulating policies for the modern and traditional sectors of the economy. However, largely because of the need to earn foreign currency, some of the measures to promote employment are also designed to encourage production for export of goods other than the traditional export commodities. Hence the recommendation to expand manufacturing in the modern sector in some cases.[18] The danger here is that, though intended primarily to increase employment, the expansion of manufacturing for export will call for international levels of efficiency which may not be compatible with labour-intensive methods of production in a developing country. Furthermore, diversifying towards manufactured exports could lead to a decline in the production of wage goods. Thus the likely effects of this type of policy are first, a tendency towards capital-intensive production in the modern sector with the threat to the employment objective that this implies; second, a short-fall in production for local consumption relative to higher effective demand over time, leading to price inflation or balance of payments problems; and third, perpetuation of an unbalanced, dualistic pattern of development in a situation crying out for integration of the traditional and modern sectors.[19]

The Anti-poverty Approach

Objectives. Fairly recently it has begun to be realised that efforts to effect redistribution of income through greater access to productive employment still exclude the principal poverty groups in most developing countries. This has led to a certain reorientation of development policy towards the eradication of poverty defined in absolute terms. As might be expected, the poor are mainly outside the "organised" sectors of the economy—self-employed peasant farmers in rural areas and members of the rapidly growing urban informal sector who cannot find adequately remunerative work.[20] Such people often have very little hope of increasing their purchasing power within the foreseeable future. Accordingly, the main objective of poverty-oriented development strategies is to raise per capita incomes above a predetermined "poverty line"[21] as quickly as possible, with the related aim of reducing income and social inequalities.

On the assumption that household income is derived from access to productive assets and employment, the range of objectives is broadened to include the transformation of social structures, including a progressive redistribution of income in favour of the poor. Though growth of GNP is not left out of account it no longer receives top priority, inasmuch as it is assumed that a redirection of consumption and investment in favour of the

poor will probably lead to some reduction in savings and investment by the rich and hence to a lower rate of capital accumulation during the transitional period. In other words, growth of output is pursued only to the extent that it is complementary to the reduction of economic and social inequalities which may have been accentuated by the growth process itself.

In so far as the objectives of poverty-oriented strategies derive from a desire to increase the purchasing power of the underprivileged they represent a major reorientation of development efforts towards those who suffer most from deficiencies in their living standards. However, because the main goal is defined in terms of per capita income, this approach permits only a partial solution to the problem of poverty as it currently exists in many developing countries.

The credibility of the minimum income objective in poverty-oriented strategies appears to depend on the assumption that there are enough adequately remunerated work opportunities to employ all the poor. In many instances this is manifestly not the case as far as the poorest and most disadvantaged of the poor are concerned, for whom the only available employment is hard and virtually unpaid work on the family or communal farm or long periods of "apprenticeship" with kinsmen established in urban areas. For the income objective to be of relevance to these categories, they must first be included in the target groups for whom remunerative job opportunities are to be provided.

As stated above, poverty-oriented strategies pursue economic growth only to the extent that it is compatible with improved incomes for the poor. Consequently targets are defined in terms of higher production and productivity rates among the poor, with the implication that the thrust for aggregate growth is to come mainly from the effects of investment and consumption transfers to them. In practice, however, it is likely that in the context of mixed-economy developing countries a transfer of investible resources from the rich to the poor would lead to an initial slowing-down of economic activity in private enterprises in key areas of production. In such a situation a fall in the rate of aggregate growth or even stagnation becomes a real possibility—given that it may be difficult for the majority of developing countries to raise the level of public investment significantly or to increase production capacity among the poor in the short run. For reasons explained below, a slowing-down of aggregate economic growth is likely to affect the income-earning opportunities and hence the living standards of the poor more seriously than those of the rest of the population. What is required, therefore, is for poverty-oriented strategies to define growth targets in terms of higher aggregate growth rates rather than explicitly in terms of higher rates of productivity and output among the poorer sections of the population, since the possibilities of significantly raising and sustaining the income levels of the poor above the line of absolute poverty are inextricably linked with continuous aggregate growth of the economy. Put another way, in most developing countries poverty cannot be eliminated without, among other things, an acceleration of economic growth.

Policies. Generally speaking, poverty-oriented policies are aimed at the redistribution of wealth, assets and output, mainly through the reallocation of productive resources in favour of explicitly defined poverty groups. Since the criteria used to define these groups often reflect the causes rather than the symptoms of poverty, remedial measures are chiefly directed towards overcoming certain institutional handicaps (e.g. lack of or insufficient access to productive assets, especially land and the right type of technology, and educational and health facilities) that are thought to be responsible for keeping the incomes of the poor at low levels. Following the identification of target groups in an economy, it is common practice to design separate ac-

tion programmes for each. Each programme is made up of "policy packages" designed to remedy specific causes of poverty. On the whole this approach is eclectic rather than doctrinaire, in the sense that the packages are complementary but separate, each containing measures aimed at raising incomes above a specified minimum subsistence level.

As regards content, there is much similarity between anti-poverty and employment-oriented strategies. Like the latter, anti-poverty policy packages include measures designed to change the pattern of land ownership and tenure; to improve access to basic education, vocational training, health facilities, development finance and other productive assets; to foster the development of small-scale farms and businesses; and to reduce the birth rate. However, anti-poverty policies are intended to benefit specific groups exclusively, whereas employment-oriented strategies seek to raise the level of aggregate employment.

In pursuance of their main objective of raising incomes above the minimum subsistence level, poverty-oriented strategies seek to correct distortions in both factor and product prices. For example, the elimination of disparities in relative product prices between rural and urban areas is seen as a precondition for raising rural incomes to the levels prevailing in the urban formal sector, which in turn is considered vital to reducing rural-urban migration. In the urban sector, changes in relative product and factor prices are recommended in order to make the sector more responsive to the opportunity cost of labour and capital, and thereby bring about a shift towards more labour-intensive products and processes and a functional redistribution of income in favour of the lowest income groups.

Complementary to policies implying investment transfers in favour of poverty groups are consumption transfers—in the form of food subsidies, supplementary benefits and other forms of welfare payment—to the seriously poor, however defined. The purpose of consumption transfers is to provide temporary support to those most in need until such time as they attain adequate levels of income.

The foregoing may give the impression that it is possible to increase the per capita incomes of the poor faster than those of more prosperous sections of the population following an initial redistribution of productive assets. This rather heroic assumption can be challenged on at least two grounds. First, with respect to wage employment, any attempt to improve income-earning opportunities among the unskilled and semi-skilled unemployed or underemployed will also at first call for the services of technical and managerial personnel earning above-average incomes, so that some of the benefits are likely to find their way to the better-off sections of the population. Second, since institutional arrangements in the majority of developing countries are biased in favour of the rich and middle-income groups, it may not be feasible to prevent the more affluent from benefiting to some extent from investment and consumption policies designed to help the poor exclusively. Even in the apparently straightforward case of food subsidies for the poorest households, we cannot discount the possibility of a suboptimal effect due to a combination of corruption and inefficiency.[22]

Thus, for anti-poverty policies to be effective in a given situation, they should be worked out after careful consideration of the socio-institutional consequences for different groups of society.[23] It is no good planning to eradicate poverty on the basis of an analytical framework that assumes total receptivity to proposed change if the prevailing political and social structures are characterised by contending factions and interest groups which stand to gain or lose from the proposed policies and the changes they entail in socio-economic status and political influence. From the failures of the past it is important to learn the lesson that development strategies must not be narrowly technical or economic but sufficiently broad-based and value-determined to neutralise conflicts in the socio-institutional matrix.

THE BASIC-NEEDS APPROACH

Concept and Main Characteristics

Underlying the current ILO proposal for an approach to development that will generate satisfying and adequately remunerative employment and reorient growth towards the satisfaction of needs for basic goods and services[24] is the conviction that during the past quarter of a century development strategies have not found an adequate response to the problems of massive unemployment and widespread poverty in the majority of developing countries.

The main objective of the basic-needs approach is to satisfy the essential requirements of each country's population within the time horizon of one generation, or by the year 2000. For this purpose two separate but complementary sets of targets are laid down. The first set mainly concerns personal consumption needs such as food, shelter and clothing, while the second relates to basic public services such as health, sanitation, the provision of safe drinking-water, education, transport and cultural facilities.

In so far as the attainment of an absolute level of satisfaction of basic needs by the entire population of a country approximates to the elimination of absolute poverty, the basic-needs approach is similar to a conventional poverty-oriented strategy. However, there are important conceptual differences. First, whereas conventional anti-poverty programmes are directed at target poverty groups within an economy, the basic-needs approach is founded on the premise that poverty in most developing countries is widespread and that action should therefore be directed at the population as a whole. Second, the basic-needs approach is concerned both with significantly raising the level of aggregate demand and with increasing the supply of basic goods and services as opposed to merely raising the incomes of the poor to a minimum subsistence level. In fact, basic-needs targets are not restricted to the eradication of absolute poverty but extend to the satisfaction of needs over and above the subsistence level as a means of eliminating relative poverty through a continuous process of economic development and social progress. A further difference is that the basic-needs approach strongly emphasises effective mass participation in both the formulation and implementation of policy measures as a way of ensuring that its main objective is not lost sight of.

In a way, the range of objectives of needs-oriented development constitutes a synthesis of the growth, employment and poverty-eradication goals. Growth is envisaged through increased output of basic goods and services; the rapid generation of adequately remunerative and socially satisfying employment is anticipated through the use of technology requiring little capital per worker; and the combination of increases in output and employment levels should enable each worker to meet his and his family's consumption requirements. Closely linked to the growth, employment and anti-poverty objectives are the worker's basic human rights to freely chosen employment and to membership of the organisation of his choice, not only as ends in themselves but as contributing factors to the satisfaction of basic needs.

The basic-needs approach recognises that countries will have different requirements as a result of differences in their economic, social, political and cultural characteristics. Nevertheless, there are certain minimum levels of personal consumption and access to public services that can be regarded as everywhere essential to a decent standard of living, and in these cases it is possible to define targets in physical units on a global basis. For example, minimum targets for food and housing requirements can be defined quantitatively with reference to daily intake of calories and square metres of dwelling space per person. Qualitatively they can be defined in terms of the proportion of protein in food intake and household facilities such as toilets, piped water, electricity and basic furniture. Besides

avoiding the weaknesses inherent in relating diverse human needs to relatively abstract indices such as GNP and monetary values, the advantage of defining targets in terms of the supply of specific goods and services is that it facilitates the identification of individuals whose basic needs have not been satisfied.

Possible Guidelines for Policy Formulation

In view of the limited variety of productive resources and the highly hierarchical socio-economic structures (including unequal distribution of assests) in many developing countries, the satisfaction of basic needs clearly implies far-reaching social and economic changes at both national and international levels. Although national and international policy measures are related, basic-needs targets are likely to be set mainly at the national level in view of the fact that the concept is essentially country-specific. In effect, the primary responsibility for establishing specific targets and formulating policies to fulfil target requirements must and will rest with national authorities.

That said, it may nevertheless be useful to propose some general guidelines for policy formulation. As stated earlier, the basic-needs approach is not one of eschewing economic growth in the name of employment promotion and income distribution; in fact, the acceleration of economic growth is an important condition for the satisfaction of basic needs. However, since in some developing countries high rates of GNP growth have not led to significant improvements in living standards for the majority of the population, it follows that the satisfaction of basic needs will call for measures to orient the pattern of growth more towards the supply and distribution of essential goods and services. This implies structural changes in the allocation and mobilisation of productive resources, including an initial redistribution of assets.

In many developing countries, particularly those of the mixed-economy type, more efficient allocation and utilisation of both local and imported resources for production to meet basic needs could be achieved through a reform of the price system. In this way factor price distortions could be eliminated so as to reflect real costs and thereby make it advantageous to use more capital-saving resources in production. However, the selection and implementation of price-correcting policies will require much caution in view of the fact that the machinery for applying certain kinds of measure, especially of the traditional tax-subsidy type, is likely to be relatively ineffective in developing countries. Generally speaking, carefully planned and timed changes in exchange, interest and tariff rates could serve to correct factor price distortions. At the sectoral level, pricing policies may have to be accompanied by a rural programme focusing on reforms in land ownership and tenure but including improved access to credit, irrigation, fertilisers, extension services and markets.

In order to achieve a faster increase in labour productivity, particularly among the poor, it will be necessary to mobilise more resources for investment in labour-intensive public services and housing projects and for the promotion of small-scale rural and urban activities. This may be achieved partly by progressive income and wealth taxation and partly by selective credit policies, complemented by the above-mentioned pricing policies to encourage greater utilisation of local resources in domestic production. The mobilisation and investment of productive resources in favour of mass-consumption goods and basic services should have a significant redistributional impact on the growth process as well as contributing to greater self-reliance among the lowest income groups.

Changes in pricing policies and investment patterns in support of increased production and consumption of basic goods and services, as indicated above, depend on the utilisation of a more labour-intensive technology mix. Hence the adoption of a capital-saving mix oriented towards basic needs would be an important component of national basic-needs

strategies. Action in this field can be initiated on two broad fronts. The first is research and development—to improve the quality and efficiency of traditional implements and modes of production and to adapt modern technology for use in developing countries. The second is the formulation of policies to prevent the underpricing of capital and other distortions tending to favour capital-intensive technology in lines of production where labour-capital substitution is feasible. However, it should not be the goal of a basic-needs strategy to abandon capital-intensive technology in favour of labour-absorbing methods of production. In general, decisionmakers should be guided by the desire to attain the best combination of efficiency and labour intensity, and as such a country's optimum technology mix may well include varying proportions of capital-intensive and labour-intensive methods of production.

Education is a basic need in the sense that it is—or ought to be—directly related to an individual's chances of obtaining adequately paid employment. At first sight it seems self-evident that spreading educational facilities more widely among a population should contribute to the reduction of unemployment and poverty. However, some developing countries have expanded their educational system in the past two decades significantly without achieving substantial improvements in the living conditions of the masses.[25] Among the explanations advanced for this failure is the well-known mismatch between acquired skills and job opportunities. Thus, while it is necessary to foster equality of access to education, policies to this end should be considered within the context of national macroplanning for socio-economic development so that the educational system can be shaped to the real manpower needs of the economy.

Although high rates of population growth may jeopardise the satisfaction of basic needs, it is clear that the large families typical of low-income countries are more the result than the cause of poverty and underdevelopment.[26]

Accordingly, the basic-needs approach stresses that a population programme must be regarded as an element of national socio-economic planning and formulated in a manner consistent with the culture and the manpower and income distribution targets of each country.[27] The critical factors in formulating national population policies will probably be the availability of resources and the rate of economic growth. In countries where these factors are immediate constraints, rapid population growth may be a major obstacle to needs-oriented development. In such cases comprehensive population control programmes should be introduced.

The basic-needs approach will require mass participation if it is to be successfully applied in a developing economy. In view of the small extent to which the masses currently participate in political and socio-economic decisions in many developing countries—a state of affairs which is itself the result of highly hierarchical social structures—it is essential for a needs-oriented strategy to include measures explicitly aimed at institutional decentralisation of both public and private production, especially among the rural population. In addition to its potential for increasing employment productivity, mass participation is vital for keeping up the momentum of structural reforms in support of basic-needs objectives. It also adds a political dimension which has always been missing from traditional strategies.

The importance of policy at the international level can hardly be overrated. Proponents of the basic-needs approach will therefore support certain changes in international economic relations to help the developing countries meet their national targets. In general, the aim of international reforms should be to achieve a more equitable distribution of the benefits of growth in the world economy. It will be necessary for international agencies and national authorities to co-operate in implementing reforms in international trade and world monetary arrangements and to increase net resource flows to developing countries

which are experiencing severe balance of payments difficulties, including some relief of their debt burden. Finally, with a view to reducing their dependence on aid and concessions from the industrialised countries, the developing countries should take steps to increase economic co-operation among themselves.

1. See I. Adelman and C. T. Morris: *Economic growth and social equity in developing countries* (Stanford (California), University Press, 1973).

2. Since development planning often reflects the political style and ideology of government, it is also possible to classify development strategies in these terms. See, for example, Keith Griffin: "Policy options for rural development," in *Oxford Bulletin of Economics and Statistics*, Nov. 1973, pp. 239–274.

3. More accurately, of course, "anti-poverty-oriented."

4. Among many expositions of this doctrine see, for example, P. N. Rosenstein-Rodan: "Notes on the theory of the 'big push'," in H. S. Ellis (ed.): *Economic development for Latin America* (London, Macmillan, 1961), pp. 57–81; R. Nurske: *Problems of capital formation in underdeveloped countries* (Oxford, Blackwell, 1953); W. A. Lewis: *The theory of economic growth* (London, Allen and Unwin, 1955); H. Leibenstein: *Economic backwardness and economic growth* (New York, Wiley and Sons, 1957); W. Galenson and H. Leibenstein: "Investment criteria, productivity and economic development", in *Quarterly Journal of Economics* (Cambridge (Massachusetts)), Aug. 1955, pp. 343–371; W. W. Rostow: *The stages of economic growth* (Cambridge, University Press, 1960); G. Ranis and J. C. H. Fei: "A theory of economic development", in *American Economic Review* (Menasha (Wisconsin)), Sep. 1961, pp. 533–565; and D. W. Jorgenson: "The development of a dual economy", in *Economic Journal* (London), June 1961, pp. 309–334.

5. See A. O. Hirschman: *The strategy of economic development* (New Haven, Yale University Press, 1958), especially Ch. 4; and P. C. Mahalanobis: "The approach of operational research to planning in India", in *Sankhya* (Calcutta), Dec. 1955, pp. 3–130.

6. See I. Adelman and C. T. Morris: *An anatomy of patterns of income distribution in develop-*

ing nations (Washington, USAID, 1971; mimeographed); and Montek S. Ahluwalia: "Income inequality: some dimensions of the problem," in Hollis Chenery et al.: *Redistribution with growth* (London, Oxford University Press, 1974), pp. 3–37.

7. For a discussion of the limitations to growth based on capital accumulation in developing economies see V. K. R. V. Rao: "Investment, income and the multiplier in an underdeveloped economy," in A. N. Agarwala and S. P. Singh (eds.): *The economics of underdevelopment* (London, Oxford University Press, 1958), pp. 205–218.

8. The relative advantages of the modern over the traditional sectors with regard to investment are obvious in terms of physical infrastructure, public utilities and services. In most developing countries, however, these very advantages are the legacy of colonial rule rather than of factors deeply entrenched in the national socio-economic setting. See Eliezer Brutzkus: "Centralized versus decentralized pattern of urbanization in developing countries: an attempt to elucidate a guideline principle", in *Economic Development and Cultural Change* (Chicago), July 1975, pp. 633–652.

9. See, for example, W. Arthur Lewis: "Economic development with unlimited supplies of labour", in *Manchester School of Economic and Social Studies*, May 1954.

10. Frances Stewart and Paul Streeten: "Conflicts between output and employment objectives in developing countries", in *Oxford Economic Papers*, July 1971, p. 161.

11. For empirical evidence supporting this point see Nicholas R. Lardy: *Regional growth and income distribution: the Chinese experience* (New Haven, Yale University Press, 1975).

12. These being defined in terms of (i) shortage of work opportunities, (ii) inadequate income from work, and (iii) underutilisation of labour. See Erik Thorbecke: "The employment problem: a critical evaluation of four ILO comprehensive country reports," in *International Labour Review*, May 1973, p. 408. Cf. also Jean Mouly: "Some remarks on the concepts of employment, underemployment and unemployment," ibid., Feb. 1972, pp. 155–160.

13. ILO: *Employment, incomes and equality: a strategy for increasing productive employment in Kenya* (Geneva, 1972), p. 12. Similarly, in his evaluation of four of the ILO Comprehensive Employment Mission reports, Thorbecke observed that "the strategies proposed in the reports . . . tend to be associated with . . . higher growth rates of GNP than prevail presently in the four countries" (op. cit., p. 422).

14. See in particular Stewart and Streeten, op. cit.

15. A. S. Bhalla: "Investment allocation and technological choice—a case of cotton spinning techniques," in *Economic Journal*, Sep. 1964, pp. 611–622; and "Choosing techniques: handpounding v. machine-milling of rice: an Indian case," in *Oxford Economic Papers*, Mar. 1965, pp. 147–157.

16. H. Pack: "The employment-output trade-off in LDC's: a microeconomic approach," ibid., Nov. 1974, pp. 388–404.

17. See H. Leibenstein: "Allocative efficiency vs. 'X-efficiency'," in *American Economic Review*, June 1966, pp. 392–415.

18. See, for example, ILO: *Employment, incomes and equality . . .*, op. cit., pp. 185–189; and idem: *Sharing in development: a programme of employment, equity and growth for the Philippines* (Geneva, 1974), pp. 114–117.

19. In the report of the Comprehensive Employment Mission to Kenya one of the four objectives of the proposed strategy is listed as "national integration of the economy". See ILO: *Employment, incomes and equality . . .*, op. cit., p. 12.

20. See, for example, ILO: *Employment, incomes and equality . . .*, op. cit.; idem: *Matching employment opportunities and expectations: a programme of action for Ceylon* (Geneva, 1971); Chenery et al., op. cit.; and Robert S. McNamara: *One hundred countries, two billion people: the dimensions of development* (New York, Praeger, 1973).

21. Determination of the line of absolute poverty in a given situation involves converting essential private and public requirements into money values by applying relevant price indices. For details of the methodology see Montek S. Ahluwalia and Hollis Chenery: "The economic framework" and "A model of distribution and growth", in Chenery et al., op. cit., pp. 38–51 and 209–235.

22. For details on corruption and inefficiency in developing countries see Gunnar Myrdal: *Against the stream: critical essays on economics* (New York, Pantheon Books, 1973), pp. 116–118; idem: "The 'soft State' in underdeveloped countries," in Paul Streeten (ed.): *Unfashionable economics* (London, Weidenfeld and Nicolson, 1970), pp. 227–243; Colin Leys: "What is the problem about corruption?", in *Journal of Modern African Studies* (London),

1965, No. 3, pp. 215–230; and Omotunde E. G. Johnson: "An economic analysis of corrupt government, with special application to less developed countries," in *Kyklos* (Basle), 1975, No. 1, pp. 47–61.

23. For an assessment of some non-economic implications of policy recommendations made by the ILO Comprehensive Employment Mission to Kenya see Warren Ilchman and Norman Uphoff: "Beyond the economics of labour-intensive development: politics and administration", in *Public Policy* (Cambridge (Massachusetts)), Spring 1974.

24. See ILO: *Employment, growth and basic needs: a one-world problem*, Report of the Director-General, Tripartite World Conference on Employment, Income Distribution and Social Progress and the International Division of Labour (Geneva, 1976); and Louis Emmerij and Dharam Ghai: "The World Employment Conference: a preliminary assessment," in *International Labour Review*, Nov.-Dec. 1976, pp. 299–309.

25. In fact there is even evidence of a positive correlation between education and unemployment. See ILO: *Matching employment opportunities and expectations . . .*, op. cit.; Mark Blaug: "Educated unemployment in Asia: a contrast between India and the Philippines", in *Philippine Economic Journal* (Manila), Fall 1972; and Teshome Mulat: *Educated unemployment in the Sudan* (Geneva, ILO, 1975; mimeographed World Employment Programme research working paper; restricted).

26. Because of the need to compensate for the high mortality rate among children and to maximise the economic benefits and security of having more hands to help scratch for a living.

27. This is the position adopted by the 1974 World Population Conference and reiterated in the Programme of Action adopted by the ILO World Employment Conference, Geneva, 4–17 June 1976.

APPENDIX 1. **A three-category classification of conventional development strategies**

Strategy type	Main objectives	Target	Dominant lines of policy	Sectoral emphasis
Growth-oriented	Maximisation of growth of gross national product	Increase in the rate of physical capital formation	Increase in the rates of savings and investment for rapid industrialisation: (*a*) through massive capital-intensive investments simultaneously on all fronts; reliance on technical complementarities between industries at different stages of production (balanced growth); (*b*) through sequential capital-intensive investments in key industries with strong linkage effects (unbalanced growth)	Modern sector
Employment-oriented	1. Maximisation of wage and self-employment, with consequential income redistribution 2. Increase in output to the maximum level that is consistent with 1 above	Increase in the level of productive employment	1. Rural development programmes, including labour-intensive non-agricultural activities, public works 2. Development of urban labour-intensive activities 3. Improved access to land, education, credit facilities, production techniques and public services	1. Modern and urban informal sectors 2. Traditional (rural) sector, mainly organised activities
Poverty-oriented	1. Eradication of absolute poverty 2. Increase in productive employment among the poor 3. Increase in output only in so far as it is compatible with reduction in income and social inequalities	Raising the levels of per capita income of target poverty groups above the absolute poverty line	1. Redistribution of wealth, assets and output in favour of the poor: (*a*) fiscal and credit policies; (*b*) improved access to land, education, health, nutrition; (*c*) re-orientation of production and demand towards labour-intensive, mass consumption goods via changes in relative factor and product prices 2. Marginal reallocation of productive resources in favour of the poor: (*a*) direct and indirect investment transfers; (*b*) direct consumption transfers	1. Traditional (rural) sector, particularly unorganised small farmers and landless labourers 2. Urban informal sector, particularly small industries and unorganised activities

APPENDIX 2. Main characteristics of the basic-needs approach

Main objectives	Target	Dominant lines of policy	Sectoral emphasis
1. Significant improvements in the living conditions of a country's population within one generation 2. Increased output of basic-needs goods and services in the context of accelerated economic growth 3. Promotion of adequately remunerative and socially satisfying employment in support of more equal income distribution	Initially, the satisfaction of an absolute level of basic needs (i.e. minimum requirements of private and public consumption in the form of specific targets) or a minimum standard of living for all households, and later, in a continuing process, the satisfaction of basic-needs targets above the subsistence level	Action on all fronts simultaneously in support of redistribution and growth: 1. Changes in the pattern of growth and the use of productive resources: (*a*) high levels of investment in the production of more labour-intensive basic goods and services; (*b*) introduction of appropriate technology to bring about increased productivity by the working poor; (*c*) greater utilisation of local natural resources in production 2. Changes in the pattern of redistribution: (*a*) mobilisation of the unemployed and underemployed through the provision of sufficient employment opportunities; (*b*) re-orientation of public services in favour of the masses; (*c*) more equal distribution of ownership of or access to land, capital and education 3. Institutional reforms: (*a*) effective mass participation in the decision-making process; (*b*) increased government support for structural reforms 4. Changes in various elements and the pattern of international economic relations in order to facilitate the task of fulfilling national sets of basic needs: (*a*) structural reform of world trade; (*b*) reform of world monetary system; (*c*) increased resource flows in favour of LDCs; (*d*) relief of debt burden; (*e*) increased economic co-operation between LDCs	Country-wide emphasis but focusing mainly on all households below minimum standard of living, irrespective of sector

Further Readings

1. Indicators of Development

Baster, Nancy. *Measuring Development: The Role and Adequacy of Development Indicators*. London: Frank Cass, 1972.

Chenery, Hollis, and Syrquin, Moises. *Patterns of Development, 1950–1970*. New York: Oxford University Press for the World Bank, 1975.

Morris, Morris David. *Measuring the Conditions of the World's Poor: The Physical Quality of Life Index*. New York: Pergamon, 1974.

UNESCO. *The Use of Socio-Economic Indicators in Development Planning*. New York, 1976.

2. Dependency Theory, Imperialism, Marxism

Amin, Samir. *Imperialism and Unequal Development*. New York: Monthly Review Press, 1977.

Baran, Paul A. *The Political Economy of Growth*. New York and London: Modern Reader Paperbacks, 1957.

Frank, Andre Gunder. *On Capitalist Underdevelopment*. Bombay, New York, London, and Hong Kong: Oxford University Press, 1975.

Kahl, Joseph A. *Modernization, Exploitation and Dependency in Latin America*. New Brunswick, N.J.: Transaction, 1976.

Lall, S. "Is Dependence a Useful Concept in Analysing Underdevelopment?" *World Development* 3, nos. 11 and 12 (November/December 1975).

Palma, Gabriel. "Dependency: A Formal Theory of Underdevelopment or a Methodology for the Analysis of Concrete Situations of Underdevelopment." *World Development* 6, nos. 7 and 8 (July/August 1978).

3. Development Goals and Objectives

Adelman, Irma. "Development Economics—A Reassessment of Goals." *American Economic Review* 65, no. 2 (May 1975).

Chenery, Hollis B. "The Structuralist Approach to Development Policy." *American Economic Review* 65, no. 2 (May 1975).

Currie, Lauchlin. "The Objectives of Development." *World Development* 6, no. 1 (January 1978).

Flammang, Robert A. "Economic Growth and Economic Development: Counterparts or Competitors." *Economic Development and Cultural Change* 28, no. 1 (October 1979).

Pugwash Symposium. "The Role of Self-Reliance in Alternative Strategies for Development." *World Development* 5, no. 3 (March 1977).

Singer, H. W. *The Strategy of International Development: Essays in the Economics of Backwardness*. Edited by Sir Alec Cairncross and Mohinder Pari. White Plains, N.Y.; International Arts and Sciences, 1975.

Streeten, Paul, and Burki, Shahid Javed. "Basic Needs: Some Issues." *World Development* 6, no. 3 (March 1978).

Streeten, Paul. "Changing Perceptions of Development." *Finance and Development* 5, no. 3 (September 1977).

4. Theory of Development

Fei, John C. H., and Ranis, Gustav. *Development of the Labor Surplus Economy: Theory and Policy*. New Haven: Yale University Press, 1964.

Hirschman, Albert O. *The Strategy of Economic Development*. New Haven: Yale University Press, 1958.

Nafziger, E. Wayne. "A Critique of Development Economics in the U.S." *Journal of Development Studies* 13, no. 1 (October 1976).

5. Political Development

Almond, Gabriel A., and Coleman, James S., eds. *The Politics of the Developing Areas*. Princeton, N.J.: Princeton University Press, 1960.

Finkle, Jason L., and Gable, Richard W., eds. *Political Development and Social Change*, 2nd ed. New York: Wiley, 1971.

Heeger, Gerald A. *The Politics of Underdevelopment*. New York: St. Martin's Press, 1974.

Huntington, Samuel. *Political Order in Changing Societies*. New Haven: Yale University Press, 1969.

Uphoff, Norman Thomas, and Ilchman, Warren F. *The Political Economy of Change*. Berkeley: University of California Press, 1969.

Van Niekerk, A. E. *Populism and Political Development in Latin America*. Rotterdam: Rotterdam University Press, 1974.

3

Development and Underdevelopment: Historical Interpretations

6. Modern Economic Growth: Findings and Reflections*

Simon Kuznets

I. DEFINITIONS

A country's economic growth may be defined as a long-term rise in capacity to supply increasingly diverse economic goods to its population, this growing capacity based on advancing technology and the institutional and ideological adjustments that it demands. All three components of the definition are important. The sustained rise in the supply of goods is the *result* of economic growth, by which it is identified. Some small countries can provide increasing income to their populations because they happen to possess a resource (minerals, location, etc.) exploitable by more developed nations, that yields a large and increasing rent. Despite intriguing analytical problems that these few fortunate countries raise, we are interested here only in the na-

* *American Economic Review* 63, no. 3 (June 1973), pp. 247–258.

This article is the lecture Simon Kuznets delivered in Stockholm, Sweden, December 1971, when he received the Nobel Prize in Economic Science.

tions that derive abundance by using advanced contemporary technology—not by selling fortuitous gifts of nature to others. Advancing technology is the *permissive* source of economic growth, but it is only a potential, a necessary condition, in itself not sufficient. If technology is to be employed efficiently and widely, and, indeed, if its own progress is to be stimulated by such use, institutional and ideological adjustments must be made to effect the proper use of innovations generated by the advancing stock of human knowledge. To cite examples from modern economic growth: steam and electric power and the large-scale plants needed to exploit them are not compatible with family enterprise, illiteracy, or slavery—all of which prevailed in earlier times over much of even the developed world, and had to be replaced by more appropriate institutions and social views. Nor is modern technology compatible with the rural mode of life, the large and extended family pattern, and veneration of undisturbed nature.

The source of technological progress, the particular production sectors that it affected most, and the pace at which it and economic growth advanced, differed over centuries and among regions of the world; and so did the institutional and ideological adjustments in their interplay with the technological changes introduced into and diffused through the growing economies. The major breakthroughs in the advance of human knowledge, those that constituted dominant sources of sustained growth over long periods and spread to a substantial part of the world, may be termed epochal innovations. And the changing course of economic history can perhaps be subdivided into economic epochs, each identified by the epochal innovation with the distinctive characteristics of growth that it generated.[1] Without considering the feasibility of identifying and dating such economic epochs, we may proceed on the working assumption that modern economic growth represents such a distinct epoch —growth dating back to the late eighteenth century and limited (except in significant *partial* effects) to economically developed countries. These countries, so classified because they have managed to take adequate advantage of the potential of modern technology, include most of Europe, the overseas offshoots of Western Europe, and Japan— barely one quarter of world population.[2] This paper will focus on modern economic growth, but with obviously needed attention to its worldwide impact.

Limitations of space prevent the presentation of a documented summary of the quantitative characteristics commonly observed in the growth of the presently developed countries, characteristics different from those of economic growth in earlier epochs. However, some of them are listed, because they contribute to our understanding of the distinctive problems of economic life in the world today. While the list is selective and is open to charges of omission, it includes those observed and empirically testable characteristics that lead back to some basic factors and conditions, which can only be glimpsed and conjectured, and forward to some implications that have so far eluded measurement.

II. THE SIX CHARACTERISTICS

Six characteristics of modern economic growth have emerged in the analysis based on conventional measures of national product and its components, population, labor force, and the like. First and most obvious are the high rates of growth of per capita product and of population in the developed countries—both large multiples of the previous rates observable in these countries and of those in the rest of the world, at least until the recent decade or two.[3] Second, the rate of rise in productivity, i.e., of output per unit of all inputs, is high, even when we include among inputs other factors in addition to labor, the major productive factor—and here too the rate is a large multiple of the rate in the past.[4] Third, the rate of structural transformation of the economy is high. Major aspects of structural change include the shift away from agriculture to nonagricultural pursuits and, recently, away from industry to services; a change in the scale of productive units, and a related shift from personal enterprise to impersonal organization of economic firms, with a corresponding change in the occupational status of labor.[5] Shifts in several other aspects of economic structure could be added (in the structure of consumption, in the relative shares of domestic and foreign supplies, etc.). Fourth, the closely related and extremely important structures of society and its ideology have also changed rapidly. Urbanization and secularization come easily to mind as components of what sociologists term the process of modernization. Fifth, the economically developed countries, by means of the increased power of technology, particularly in transport and communication (both peaceful and warlike), have the propensity to reach out to the rest of the world—thus making for one world in the sense in which this was not true in any premodern epoch.[6] Sixth, the spread of modern economic growth, despite its worldwide partial effects, is limited in that the economic performance in countries accounting for three-quarters of world population still falls far short of the minimum levels feasible with the potential of modern technology.[7]

This brief summary of two quantitative characteristics of modern economic growth that relate to aggregate rates, two that relate to structural transformation, and two that relate to international spread, supports our working assumption that modern economic growth marks a distinct economic epoch. If the rates of aggregate growth and the speed of structural transformation in the economic, institutional, and perhaps even in the ideological, framework are so much higher than in the past as to represent a revolutionary acceleration, and if the various regions of the world are for the first time in history so closely interrelated as to be one, some new major growth source, some new epochal innovation, must have generated these radically different patterns. And one may argue that this source is the emergence of modern science as the basis of advancing technology—a breakthrough in the evolution of science that produced a potential for technology far greater than existed previously.

Yet modern growth continues many older trends, if in greatly accelerated form. This continuity is important particularly when we find that, except for Japan and possibly Russia, all presently developed countries were well in advance of the rest of the world before their modern growth and industrialization began, enjoying a comparative advantage produced by premodern trends. It is also important because it emphasizes that distinction among economic epochs is a complicated intellectual choice and that the continuation of past trends and their changing patterns over time are subjects deserving the closest attention. Does the acceleration in growth of product and productivity in many developed countries in the last two decades reflect a major change in the potential provided by science-oriented technology, or a major change in the capacity of societies to catch up with that

potential? Is it a way of recouping the loss in standing, relative to such a leader as the United States, that was incurred during the depression of the 1930's and World War II? Or, finally, is it merely a reflection of the temporarily favorable climate of the U.S. international policies? Is the expansion into space a continuation of the old trend of reaching out by the developed countries, or is it a precursor of a new economic epoch? These questions are clearly illustrative, but they hint at broader analytical problems suggested by the observation of modern economic growth as a distinct epoch.

The six characteristics noted are interrelated, and the interrelations among them are most significant. With the rather stable ratio of labor force to total population, a high rate of increase in per capita product means a high rate of increase in product per worker; and, with average hours of work declining, it means still higher growth rates in product per man-hour. Even if we allow for the impressive accumulation of capital, in its widest sense, the growth rate of productivity is high, and, indeed, mirrors the great rise in per capita product and in per capita pure consumption. Since the latter reflects the realized effects of advancing technology, rapid changes in production structure are inevitable—given the differential impact of technological innovations on the several production sectors, the differing income elasticity of domestic demand for various consumer goods, and the changing comparative advantage in foreign trade. As already indicated, advancing technology changes the scale of production plants and the character of the economic enterprise units. Consequently, effective participation in the modern economic system by the labor force necessitates rapid changes in its location and structure, in the relations among occupational status groups, and even in the relations between labor force and total population (the last, however, within narrow overall limits). Thus, not only are high aggregate growth rates associated with rapid changes in economic structure, but the latter are also associated with rapid changes in other aspects of society—in family formation, in urbanization, in man's views on his role and the measure of his achievement in society. The dynamic drives of modern economic growth, in the countries that entered the process ahead of others, meant a reaching out geographically; and the sequential spread of the process, facilitated by major changes in transport and communication, meant a continuous expansion to the less developed areas. At the same time, the difficulty of making the institutional and ideological transformations needed to convert the new large potential of modern technology into economic growth in the relatively short period since the late eighteenth century limited the spread of the system. Moreover, obstacles to such transformation were, and still are being, imposed on the less developed regions by the policies of the developed countries.

If the characteristics of modern economic growth are interrelated, in that one induces another in a cause and effect sequence or all are concurrent effects of a common set of underlying factors, another plausible and significant link should be noted. Mass application of technological innovations, which constitutes much of the distinctive substance of modern economic growth, is closely connected with the further progress of science, in its turn the basis for additional advance in technology. While this topic is still to be studied in depth, it seems fairly clear that mass-uses of technical innovations (many based on recent scientific discoveries) provide a positive feedback. Not only do they provide a larger economic surplus for basic and applied research with long time leads and heavy capital demands, but, more specifically, they permit the development of new efficient tools for scientific use and supply new data on the behavior of natural processes under the stress of modification in economic production. In other words, many production plants in developed countries can be viewed as laboratories for the exploration of natural processes and as centers of research on new tools, both of which are of immense service to basic and applied research in science and technology. It is no accident that the last two centuries were also periods of enormous acceleration in the contribution to the stock of useful knowledge by basic and applied research—which provided additional stimuli to new technological innovations. Thus, modern economic growth reflects an interrelation that sustains the high rate of advance through the feedback from mass applications to further knowledge. And unless some obstacles intervene, it provides a mechanism for self-sustaining technological advance, to which, given the wide expanse of the universe (relative to mankind on this planet), there are no obvious proximate limits.

III. SOME IMPLICATIONS[8]

I turn now to a brief discussion of some social implications, of some effects of modern economic growth on conditions of life of various population groups in the countries affected. Many of these effects are of particular interest, because they are not reflected in the current measures of economic growth; and the increasing realization of this shortcoming of the measures has stimulated lively discussion of the limits and limitations of economic measurement of economic growth.

The effects on conditions of life stem partly from the major role of technological innovations in modern economic growth, and partly from the rapid shifts in the underlying production structure. To begin with the latter, the major effects of which, for example, urbanization, internal migration, shift to employee status and what might be called the merit basis of job choice, have already been noted as characteristics of modern economic growth. Two important groups of effects of this rapid transformation of economic structure deserve explicit reference.

First, the changes in conditions of life suggested by "urbanization" clearly involved a variety of costs and returns that are not now included in economic measurement, and some of which may never be susceptible to measurement. Internal migration, from the countryside to the cities (within a country, and often international) represented substantial costs in the pulling up of roots and the adjustment to the anonymity and higher costs of urban living. The learning of new skills and the declining value of previously acquired skills was clearly a costly process—to both the individuals and to society. But if such costs were omitted from measurement, as they still are in conventional accounts, so were some returns. Urban life, with its denser population, provided amenities and spiritual goods that were not available in the "dull and brutish" life of the countryside; and the new skills, once learned, were often a more adequate basis for a richer life than the old. This comment on the hidden costs and returns involved in the shift toward urban life may apply to many other costs and returns involved in other shifts imposed by economic growth, for example, in the character of participation in economic activity, in the social values, and in the new pressures on deviant members of society.

The second intriguing aspect of structural change is that it represents shifts in the relative shares in the economy of the specific population groups attached to particular production sectors. Since economic engagement represents a dominant influence in the life of people, the shift in the share of a specific sector, with its distinctive characteristics and even mode of life, affects the population group engaged in it. Economic growth perforce brings about a decline in the relative position of one group after another—of farmers, of small scale producers, of landowners—a change not easily accepted, and, in fact, as history teaches us, often resisted. The continuous disturbance of preexisting *relative* position of the several economic groups is pregnant with conflict— despite the rises in absolute income or product common to all groups. In some cases, these

conflicts did break out into overt civil war, the Civil War in the United States being a conspicuous example. Other examples, in the early periods of industrialization among the currently developed countries, or, for that matter, more recently within some less developed countries, are not lacking.

Only if such conflicts are resolved without excessive costs, and certainly without a long-term weakening of the political fabric of the society, is modern economic growth possible. The sovereign state, with authority based on loyalty and on a community of feeling—in short, the modern national state—plays a crucial role in peacefully resolving such growth-induced conflicts. But this and other services of the national state may be costly in various ways, of which intensified nationalism is one and other effects are too familiar to mention. The records of many developed countries reveal examples of resolutions of growth conflicts, of payments for overcoming resistance and obstacles to growth, that left burdensome heritages for the following generations (notably in Germany and Japan). Of course, this is not the only economic function of the state; it can also stimulate growth and structural change. And, to mention a closely related service, it can referee, select, or discard legal and institutional innovations that are proposed in the attempt to organize and channel effectively the new production potentialities. This, too, is a matter that may generate conflicts, since different legal and institutional arrangements may have different effects on the several economic groups in society.

In that modern economic growth has to contend with the resolution of incipient conflicts continuously generated by rapid changes in economic and social structure, it may be described as a process of controlled revolution. The succession of technological innovations characteristic of modern economic growth and the social innovations that provide the needed adjustments are major factors affecting economic and social structure. But these innovations have other effects that deserve explicit mention; and while they are discussed below in terms of effects of technological innovations, the conclusions apply *pari passu* to innovations in legal forms, in institutional structure, and even in ideology.

A technological innovation, particularly one based on a recent major invention, represents a venture into the partly unknown, something not fully known until the mass spread of the innovation reveals the full range of direct and related effects. An invention is a major one if it provides the basis for extensive applications and improvements (for example, the stationary steam engine in the form attributable mostly to James Watt). Its cumulative effects, all new, extend over a long period and result in an enormous transformation of economic production and of production relations. But these new effects can hardly be fully anticipated or properly evaluated in advance (and sometimes not even post facto). This is true also of electric power, the internal combustion engine, atomic energy, the application of short rays to communication and computation, the inventions resulting in such new industrial materials as steel, aluminum, and plastics, and so on through a long list that marked modern economic growth. Even when the technological innovation is an adaptation of a known technique by a follower country, the results may not be fully foreseeable, for they represent the combination of something known, the technology, with something new, an institutional and ideological framework with which it has not previously been combined. Needless to say, the element of the uniquely new, of exploration into the unknown, was also prominent in premodern times, since innovations in knowledge and technology are the prerequisites for any significant growth. But the *rate* of succession of such innovations was clearly more rapid in modern economic growth, and provided the base for a higher rate of aggregate growth.

The effects of such ventures into the new and partly unknown are numerous. Those of most interest here are the *surprises*, the unexpected results, which may be positive or negative. An invention or innovation may prove far more productive, and induce a far wider mass application and many more cumulative improvements that were dreamed of by the inventor and the pioneer group of entrepreneurs. Or the mass application of a major invention may produce unexpected diseconomies of a scale that could hardly be foreseen in the early phases of its diffusion. Examples of both positive and negative surprises abound. Many Schumpeterian entrepreneurs failed to grasp, by a wide margin, the full scope and significance of the innovations that they were promoting and that eventually brought them fame and fortune. And most of us can point at the unexpected negative effects of some technological or social invention that first appeared to be an unlimited blessing.

The significant aspect here is that the surprises cannot be viewed as accidents: they are inherent in the process of technological (and social) innovation in that it contains an element of the unknown. Furthermore, the diffusion of a major innovation is a long and complicated sequence that cannot be accurately forecast, with an initial economic effect that may generate responses in other processes. These will, in turn, change the conditions under which the innovation exercises its effect on human welfare, and raise further problems of adjustment. To illustrate: we can today follow easily the sequence from the introduction of the passenger car as a mass means of transportation, to the growth of the suburbs, to the movement of the more affluent from the city centers, to the concentration of lower income recipients and unemployed immigrants in the slums of the inner city core, to the acute urban problems, financial and other, and to the trend toward metropolitan consolidation. But the nature and implications of this sequence were certainly not apparent in the 1920's, when passenger cars began their mass service function in the United States.

Indeed, to push this speculative line further, one can argue that all economic growth brings *some* unexpected results in its wake, positive as well as negative, with the latter taking on greater importance as the mass effects of major innovations are felt and the needs that they are meant to satisfy are met. If the argument is valid, modern economic growth, with the rapid succession of innovations and shortening period of their mass diffusion, must be accompanied by a relatively high incidence of negative effects. Yet one must not forget that premodern economic growth had similar problems, which, with the weaker technology, may have loomed even larger. Even if we disregard the threatening exhaustion of natural resources, a problem that so concerned Classical (and implicitly even Marxian) economics, and consider only early urbanization, one major negative effect was the significant rise in death rates as population moved from the more salubrious countryside to the infection-prone denser conditions of unsanitary cities. Two points are relevant here. First, the negative effects of growth have never been viewed as so far outweighing its positive contribution as to lead to its renunciation—no matter how crude the underlying calculus may have been. Second, one may assume that once an unexpected negative result of growth emerges, the potential of material and social technology is aimed at its reduction or removal. In many cases these negative results were allowed to accumulate and to become serious technological or social problems because it was so difficult to foresee them early enough in the process to take effective preventive or ameliorative action. Even when such action was initiated, there may have been delay in the effective technological or policy solution. Still, one may justifiably argue, in the light of the history of economic growth, in which a succession of such unexpected negative results has been overcome, that any specific problem so generated will be temporary—although we shall never be free of them, no matter what economic development is attained.

IV. THE LESS DEVELOPED COUNTRIES

Two major groups of factors appear to have limited the spread of modern economic growth. First, as already suggested, such growth demands a stable, but flexible, political and social framework, capable of accommodating rapid structural change and resolving the conflicts that it generates, while encouraging the growth-promoting groups in society. Such a framework is not easily or rapidly attained, as evidenced by the long struggles toward it even in some of the presently developed countries in the nineteenth and early twentieth centuries. Japan is the only nation outside of those rooted in European civilization that has joined the group of developed countries so far. Emergence of a modern framework for economic growth may be especially difficult if it involves elements peculiar to European civilization for which substitutes are not easily found. Second, the increasingly national cast of organization in developed countries made for policies toward other parts of the world that, while introducing some modern economic and social elements, were, in many areas, clearly inhibiting. These policies ranged from the imposition of colonial status to other limitations on political freedom, and, as a result, political independence and removal of the inferior status of the native members of the community, rather than economic advance, were given top priority.

Whatever the weight of the several factors in explaining the failure of the less developed countries to take advantage of the potential of modern economic growth, a topic that, in its range from imperialist exploitation to backwardness of the native economic and social framework, lends itself to passionate and biased polemic, the factual findings are clear. At present, about two-thirds or more of world population is in the economically less developed group. Even more significant is the concentration of the population at the low end of the product per capita range. In 1965, the last year for which we have worldwide comparable product estimates, the per capita GDP (at market prices) of 1.72 billion out of a world total of 3.27 billion, was less than $120, whereas 0.86 billion in economically developed countries had a per capita product of some $1900. Even with this narrow definition of less developed countries, the intermediate group was less than 0.7 billion, or less than 20 percent of world population.[9] The preponderant population was thus divided between the very low and the rather high level of per capita economic performance. Obviously, this aspect of modern economic growth deserves our greatest attention, and the fact that the quantitative data and our knowledge of the institutional structures of the less developed countries are, at the moment, far more limited than our knowledge of the developed areas, is not reason enough for us to ignore it.

Several preliminary findings, or rather plausible impressions, may be noted. First, the group of less developed countries, particularly if we widen it (as we should) to include those with a per capita product somewhat larger than $120 (in 1965 prices), covers an extremely wide range in size, in the relations between population and natural resources, in major inherited institutions, and in the past impact upon them of the developed countries (coming as it did at different times and from different sources). There is a striking contrast, for example, in terms of population size, between the giants like Mainland China and India, on the one hand, and the scores of tiny states in Africa and Latin America; as there is between the timing of direct Western impact on Africa and of that on many countries in Latin America. Furthermore, the remarkable institutions by which the Sinic and East Indian civilizations produced the unified, huge societies that dwarfed in size any that originated in Europe until recently, bore little resemblance to those that structured the American Indian societies or those that fashioned the numerous tribal societies of Africa.

Generalizations about less developed countries must be carefully and critically scrutinized in the light of this wide variety of conditions and institutions. To be sure, their common failure to exploit the potential of modern economic growth means several specific common features: a low per capita product, a large share of agriculture or other extractive industries, a generally small scale of production. But the specific parameters differ widely, and because the obstacles to growth may differ critically in their substance, they may suggest different policy directions.

Second, the growth position of the less developed countries today is significantly different, in many respects, from that of the presently developed countries on the eve of their entry into modern economic growth (with the possible exception of Japan, and one cannot be sure even of that). The less developed areas that account for the largest part of the world population today are at much lower per capita product levels than were the developed countries just before their industrialization; and the latter at that time were economically in advance of the rest of the world, not at the low end of the per capita product range. The very magnitudes, as well as some of the basic conditions, are quite different: no country that entered modern economic growth (except Russia) approached the size of India or China, or even of Pakistan and Indonesia; and no currently developed country had to adjust to the very high rates of natural increase of population that have characterized many less developed countries over the last two or three decades. Particularly before World War I, the older European countries, and to some extent even Japan, relieved some strains of industrialization by substantial emigration of the displaced population to areas with more favorable opportunities—an avenue closed to the populous less developed countries today. Of course, the stock of material and social technology that can be tapped by less developed countries today is enormously larger than that available in the nineteenth and even early twentieth centuries. But it is precisely this combination of greater backwardness and seemingly greater backlog of technology that makes for the significant differences between the growth position of the less developed countries today and that of the developed countries when they were entering the modern economic growth process.

Finally, it may well be that, despite the tremendous accumulation of material and social technology, the stock of innovations most suitable to the needs of the less developed countries is not too abundant. Even if one were to argue that progress in basic science may not be closely tied to the technological needs of the country of origin (and even that may be disputed), unquestionably the applied advances, the inventions and tools, are a response to the specific needs of the country within which they originate. This was certainly true of several major inventions associated with the Industrial Revolution in England, and illustrations abound of necessity as the mother of invention. To the extent that this is true, and that the conditions of production in the developed countries differed greatly from those in the populous less developed countries today, the material technology evolved in the developed countries may not supply the needed innovations. Nor is the social technology that evolved in the developed countries likely to provide models of institutions or arrangements suitable to the diverse institutional and population-size backgrounds of many less developed countries. Thus, modern technology with its emphasis on labor-saving inventions may not be suited to countries with a plethora of labor but a scarcity of other factors, such as land and water; and modern institutions, with their emphasis on personal responsibility and pursuit of economic interest, may not be suited to the more traditional life patterns of the agricultural communities that predominate in many less developed countries. These comments should not be interpreted as denying the value of many transfer-

able parts of modern technology; they are merely intended to stress the possible shortage of material and social tools specifically fitted to the different needs of the less developed countries.

If the observations just made are valid, several implications for the growth problems of the less developed countries follow. I hesitate to formulate them explicitly, since the data and the stock of knowledge on which the observations rest are limited. But at least one implication is sufficiently intriguing, and seems to be illuminating of many recent events in the field, to warrant a brief note. It is that a substantial economic advance in the less developed countries may require modifications in the available stock of material technology, and probably even greater innovations in political and social structure. It will not be a matter of merely borrowing existing tools, material and social; or of directly applying past patterns of growth, merely allowing for the difference in parameters.

The innovational requirements are likely to be particularly great in the social and political structures. The rather violent changes in these structures that occurred in those countries that have forged ahead with highly forced industrialization under Communist auspices, the pioneer entry going back over forty years (beginning with the first Five-Year Plan in the USSR), are conspicuous illustrations of the kind of social invention and innovation that may be involved. And the variants even of Communist organization, let alone those of democracy and of non-Communist authoritarianism, are familiar. It would be an oversimplification to argue that these innovations in the social and political structures were made primarily in response to the strain between economic backwardness and the potential of modern economic growth; or to claim that they were inexorable effects of antecedent history. But to whatever the struggle for political and social organization is a response, once it has been resolved, the results shape significantly the conditions under which economic growth can occur. It seems highly probable that a long period of experimentation and struggle toward a viable political framework compatible with adequate economic growth lies ahead for most less developed countries of today; and this process will become more intensive and acute as the *perceived* gap widens between what has been attained and what is attainable with modern economic growth. While an economist can argue that some aspects of growth must be present because they are indispensable components (i.e., industrialization, large scale of production, etc.), even their parameters are bound to be variable; and many specific characteristics will be so dependent upon the outcome of the social and political innovations that extrapolation from the past is extremely hazardous.

V. CONCLUDING COMMENTS

The aim of the discussion was to sketch the major characteristics of modern economic growth, and to note some of the implications that the empirical study of economic growth of nations suggests. This study goes back to the beginning of our discipline, as indicated by the title of Adam Smith's founding treatise, *Wealth of Nations*, which could as well have been called the Economic Growth of Nations. But the quantitative base and interest in economic growth have widened greatly in the last three to four decades, and the accumulated results of past study of economic history and of past economic analysis could be combined with the richer stock of quantitative data to advance the empirical study of the process. The sketch above draws upon the results of many and widely varied studies in many countries, most of them economically developed; and the discussion reflects a wide collective effort, however individual some of my interpretations may be.

The most distinctive feature of modern economic growth is the combination of a high rate of aggregate growth with disrupting effects and new "problems." The high rate of growth is sustained by the interplay between mass applications of technological innovations based on additions to the stock of knowledge and further additions to that stock. The disrupting effects are those imposed by the rapid rate of change in economic and social structure. The problems are the unexpected and unforeseeable results of the spread of innovations (with emphasis on the new and unknown indicated by that term). Added to this is the range of problems raised by the slow spread of economic growth to the less developed countries, all of which have a long history, separate and relatively isolated from the areas within which modern economic growth originated. Thus, concurrent with the remarkable positive achievements of modern economic growth are unexpected negative results even within the developed countries; while the less developed countries are struggling in the attempt to use the large potential of modern technology in order to assume an adequate role in the one and interdependent world (from which they cannot withdraw even if they wished to do so).

We have stressed the problem aspects of modern economic growth because they indicate the directions of further research in the field. These aspects, the "surprises" and the implicit explanatory "puzzles," are problems not only in the sense of departures from the desirable (that may call for policy amelioration) but also in the sense that our quantitative data and particularly our analytical hypotheses do not provide us with a full view and explanation. As already noted, the conventional measures of national product and its components do not reflect many costs of adjustment in the economic and social structures to the channeling of major technological innovations; and, indeed, also omit some positive returns. The earlier theory that underlies these measures defined the productive factors in a relatively narrow way, and left the rise in productivity as an unexplained gap, as a measure of our ignorance. This shortcoming of the theory in confrontation with the new findings, has led to a lively discussion in the field in recent years, and to attempts to expand the national accounting framework to encompass the so far hidden but clearly important costs, for example, in education as capital investment, in the shift to urban life, or in the pollution and other negative results of mass production. These efforts will also uncover some so far unmeasured positive returns—in the way of greater health and longevity, greater mobility, more leisure, less income inequality, and the like. The related efforts to include the additions to knowledge in the framework of economic analysis, the greater attention to the uses of time and to the household as the focus of economic decision not only on consumption but also on investment, are steps in the same direction. It seems fairly clear that a number of analytical and measurement problems remain in the theory and in the evaluation of economic growth in the developed countries themselves; and that one may look forward to major changes in some aspects of the analysis, in national economic accounting, and in the stock of empirical findings, which will occupy economists in the developed countries in the years ahead.

For the less developed countries the tasks of economic research are somewhat different: the great need is for a wider supply of tested data, which means essentially data that have been scrutinized in the process of use for economic analysis. As already noted, the stock of data and of economic analysis is far poorer for these countries than that for the developed countries—a parallel to the smaller relative supply of material capital. Yet in recent years there has been rapid accumulation of data for many less developed areas, other than those that, like Mainland China, view data as information useful to their enemies (external or internal) and are therefore either not revealed by government or possibly not even collected. The lag has been in the analysis of these data by economists and other social science scholars, because of the scarcity of such scholars

who cannot be spared for research within the less developed countries themselves and because of the natural preoccupation of economists in the developed countries with the problems of their own countries. One may hope, but with limited expectations, that the task of refining analysis and measurement in the developed countries will not be pursued to the exclusion or neglect of badly needed studies of the less developed countries, studies that would deal with the quantitative bases and institutional conditions of their performance, in addition to those concentrating on what appear to be their major bottlenecks and the seemingly optimal policy prescriptions.

1. For a discussion of the economic epoch concept, see Kuznets (1966), pp. 1–16.

2. For a recent classification identifying the non-Communist developed countries, see United Nations *Yearbook*, notes to Table 5, p. 156. These classifications vary from time to time, and differ somewhat from those of other international agencies.

3. For the non-Communist developed countries, the rates of growth per year over the period of modern economic growth, were almost 2 percent for product per capita, 1 percent for population, and 3 percent for total product. These rates—which mean roughly a multiplication over a century by five for product per capita, by three for population, and by more than fifteen for total product—were far greater than premodern rates. The latter can only be conjectured, but reasonable estimates for Western Europe over the long period from the early Middle Ages to the mid-nineteenth century suggest that the modern rate of growth is about ten times as high for product per capita (see Kuznets [1971], pp. 10–27). A similar comparison for population, either for Europe or for the area of European settlement (i.e., Europe, the Americas, and Oceania), relating to 1850–1960, as compared with 1000–1850, suggests a multiple of 4 or 5 to 1 (see Kuznets [1966], Tables 2.1 and 2.2, pp. 35 and 38). The implied acceleration in the growth rate of total product is between forty and fifty times.

4. Using the conventional national economic accounts, we find that the rate of increase in productivity is large enough to account (in the statisti-

cal sense) for almost the entire growth of product per capita. Even with adjustments to allow for hidden costs and inputs, growth in productivity accounts for over half of the growth in product per capita (see Kuznets [1971], pp. 51–75, particularly Table 9, p. 74; and Table 11, p. 93).

5. The rapidity of structural shifts in modern times can be easily illustrated by the changes in the distribution of the labor force between agriculture (and related industries) and the nonagricultural production sectors. In the United States, the share of labor force attached to the agricultural sector was still 53.5 percent in 1870 and declined to less than 7 percent in 1960. In an old European country like Belgium, the share of agriculture in the labor force, 51 percent in 1846, dropped to 12.5 percent in 1947 and further to 7.5 percent in 1961 (see Bairoch et al., Tables D-4 and C-4). Considering that it took centuries for the share of the agricultural sector in the labor force to decline to 50 percent in any sizable country (i.e., excluding small "city enclaves"), a drop of 30 to 40 percentage points in the course of a single century is a strikingly fast structural change.

6. The outward expansion of developed countries, with their European origin, goes back to long before modern economic growth, indeed, back to the Crusades. But the much augmented transportation and communication power of developed countries in the nineteenth century permitted a much greater and more direct political dominance over the colonies, the "opening up" of previously closed areas (such as Japan), and the "partition" of previously undivided areas (such as sub-Saharan Africa).

7. For further discussion see Section IV below, which deals with the less developed countries.

8. Many of the points touched upon in this section are discussed in greater detail in Kuznets (1971), particularly in ch. 2, pp. 75–98, which deals with the nonconventional costs of economic growth, and ch. 7, pp. 314–54, which deals with various interrelations between aggregate change and structural shifts in economic and other aspects of social structure.

9. The underlying data are from Everett Hagen and Oli Hawrylyshyn. These are primarily from United Nations publications, supplemented by some auxiliary sources (mostly for the Communist countries), and use conventional conversion rates to U.S. dollars in 1965. The estimates for the Communist countries have been adjusted to conform to the international GDP concept. The developed countries include most countries with per capita GDP of $1,000 or more and Japan, but exclude those small countries with a high GDP per capita that is due to exceptional natural endowments (for example, Netherlands Antilles, Puerto Rico, Kuwait, and Qatar).

REFERENCES

P. Bairoch et al., *The Working Population and Its Structure, International Historical Statistics*, vol. I, Brussels 1968.

E. E. Hagen and O. Hawrylyshyn, "Analysis of World Income and Growth, 1955–1965," *Econ. Develop. Cult. Change*, Oct. 1969, *18*, Part II, 1–96.

S. Kuznets, *Economic Growth of Nations: Total Output and Production Structure*, Cambridge, Mass. 1971.

——, *Modern Economic Growth: Rate, Structure, and Spread*, New Haven 1966.

United Nations, *Yearbook of National Accounts Statistics, 1969*, vol. II, *International Tables*, New York 1970.

7. The Structure of Dependence*

Theotonio Dos Santos

This paper attempts to demonstrate that the dependence of Latin American countries on other countries cannot be overcome without a qualitative change in their internal structures and external relations. We shall attempt to show that the relations of dependence to which these countries are subjected conform to a type of international and internal structure which leads them to underdevelopment or more precisely to a dependent structure that deepens and aggravates the fundamental problems of their peoples.

I. WHAT IS DEPENDENCE?

By dependence we mean a situation in which the economy of certain countries is conditioned by the development and expansion of another economy to which the former is subjected. The relation of interdependence between two or more economies, and between these and world trade, assumes the form of dependence when some countries (the dominant ones) can expand and can be self-sustaining, while other countries (the dependent ones) can do this only as a reflection of

---

* From *American Economic Review*, 60, no. 2 (May 1970), pp. 231–236.

This work expands on certain preliminary work done in a research project on the relations of dependence in Latin America, directed by the author at the Center for Socio-Economic Studies of the Faculty of Economic Science of the University of Chile. In order to abridge the discussion of various aspects, the author was obliged to cite certain of his earlier works. The author expresses his gratitude to the researcher Orlando Caputo and Roberto Pizarro for some of the data utilized and to Sergio Ramos for his critical comments on the paper.

that expansion, which can have either a positive or a negative effect on their immediate development [7, p. 6].

The concept of dependence permits us to see the internal situation of these countries as part of world economy. In the Marxian tradition, the theory of imperialism has been developed as a study of the process of expansion of the imperialist centers and of their world domination. In the epoch of the revolutionary movement of the Third World, we have to develop the theory of laws of internal development in those countries that are the object of such expansion and are governed by them. This theoretical step transcends the theory of development which seeks to explain the situation of the underdeveloped countries as a product of their slowness or failure to adopt the patterns of efficiency characteristic of developed countries (or to "modernize" or "develop" themselves). Although capitalist development theory admits the existence of an "external" dependence, it is unable to perceive underdevelopment in the way our present theory perceives it, as a consequence and part of the process of the world expansion of capitalism—a part that is necessary to and integrally linked with it.

In analyzing the process of constituting a world economy that integrates the so-called "national economies" in a world market of commodities, capital, and even of labor power, we see that the relations produced by this market are unequal and combined—unequal because development of parts of the system occurs at the expense of other parts. Trade relations are based on monopolistic control of the market, which leads to the transfer of surplus generated in the dependent countries to the dominant countries; financial relations are, from the viewpoint of the dominant powers, based on loans and the export of capital, which permit them to receive interest and profits; thus increasing their domestic surplus and strengthening their control over the economies of the other countries. For the dependent countries these relations represent an export of profits and interest which carries off part of the surplus generated domestically and leads to a loss of control over their productive resources. In order to permit these disadvantageous relations, the dependent countries must generate large surpluses, not in such a way as to create higher levels of technology but rather superexploited manpower. The result is to limit the development of their internal market and their technical and cultural capacity, as well as the moral and physical health of their people. We call this combined development because it is the combination of these inequalities and the transfer of resources from the most backward and dependent sectors to the most advanced and dominant ones which explains the inequality, deepens it, and transforms it into a necessary and structural element of the world economy.

II. HISTORIC FORMS OF DEPENDENCE

Historic forms of dependence are conditioned by: (1) the basic forms of this world economy which has its own laws of development; (2) the type of economic relations dominant in the capitalist centers and the ways in which the latter expand outward; and (3) the types of economic relations existing inside the peripheral countries which are incorporated into the situation of dependence within the network of international economic relations generated by capitalist expansion. It is not within the purview of this paper to study these forms in detail but only to distinguish broad characteristics of development.

Drawing on an earlier study, we may distinguish: (1) Colonial dependence, trade export in nature, in which commercial and financial capital in alliance with the colonialist state

dominated the economic relations of the Europeans and the colonies, by means of a trade monopoly complemented by a colonial monopoly of land, mines, and manpower (serf or slave) in the colonized countries. (2) Financial-industrial dependence which consolidated itself at the end of the nineteenth century, characterized by the domination of big capital in the hegemonic centers, and its expansion abroad through investment in the production of raw materials and agricultural products for consumption in the hegemonic centers. A productive structure grew up in the dependent countries devoted to the export of these products (which Levin labeled export economies [11]; other analysis in other regions [12] [13]), producing what ECLA has called "foreign-oriented development" (*desarrollo hacia afuera*) [4]. (3) In the postwar period a new type of dependence has been consolidated, based on multinational corporations which began to invest in industries geared to the internal market of underdeveloped countries. This form of dependence is basically technological-industrial dependence [6].

Each of these forms of dependence corresponds to a situation which conditioned not only the international relations of these countries but also their internal structures: the orientation of production, the forms of capital accumulation, the reproduction of the economy, and, simultaneously, their social and political structure.

III. THE EXPORT ECONOMIES

In forms (1) and (2) of dependence, production is geared to those products destined for export (gold, silver, and tropical products in the colonial epoch; raw materials and agricultural products in the epoch of industrial-financial dependence); i.e., production is determined by demand from the hegemonic centers. The internal productive structure is characterized by rigid specialization and monoculture in entire regions (the Caribbean, the

Brazilian Northeast, etc.). Alongside these export sectors there grew up certain complementary economic activities (cattle-raising and some manufacturing, for example) which were dependent, in general, on the export sector to which they sell their products. There was a third, subsistence economy which provided manpower for the export sector under favorable conditions and toward which excess population shifted during periods unfavorable to international trade.

Under these conditions, the existing internal market was restricted by four factors: (1) Most of the national income was derived from export, which was used to purchase the inputs required by export production (slaves, for example) or luxury goods consumed by the hacienda- and mine-owners, and by the more prosperous employees. (2) The available manpower was subject to very arduous forms of superexploitation, which limited its consumption. (3) Part of the consumption of these workers was provided by the subsistence economy, which served as a complement to their income and as a refuge during periods of depression. (4) A fourth factor was to be found in those countries in which land and mines were in the hands of foreigners (cases of an enclave economy): a great part of the accumulated surplus was destined to be sent abroad in the form of profits, limiting not only internal consumption but also possibilities of reinvestment [1]. In the case of enclave economies the relations of the foreign companies with the hegemonic center were even more exploitative and were complemented by the fact that purchases by the enclave were made directly abroad.

IV. THE NEW DEPENDENCE

The new form of dependence, (3) above, is in process of developing and is conditioned by the exigencies of the international commodity and capital markets. The possibility of generating new investments depends on the existence of financial resources in foreign currency for the purchase of machinery and processed raw materials not produced domestically. Such purchases are subject to two limitations: the limit of resources generated by the export sector (reflected in the balance of payments, which includes not only trade but also service relations); and the limitations of monopoly on patents which leads monopolistic firms to prefer to transfer their machines in the form of capital rather than as commodities for sale. It is necessary to analyze these relations of dependence if we are to understand the fundamental structural limits they place on the development of these economies.

1. Industrial development is dependent on an export sector for the foreign currency to buy the inputs utilized by the industrial sector. The first consequence of this dependence is the need to preserve the traditional export sector, which limits economically the development of the internal market by the conservation of backward relations of production and signifies, politically, the maintenance of power by traditional decadent oligarchies. In the countries where these sectors are controlled by foreign capital, it signifies the remittance abroad of high profits, and political dependence on those interests. Only in rare instances does foreign capital not control at least the marketing of these products. In response to these limitations, dependent countries in the 1930's and 1940's developed a policy of exchange restrictions and taxes on the national and foreign export sector; today they tend toward the gradual nationalization of production and toward the imposition of certain timid limitations on foreign control of the marketing of exported products. Furthermore, they seek, still somewhat timidly, to obtain better terms for the sale of their products. In recent decades, they have created mechanisms for international price agreements, and today UNCTAD and ECLA press to obtain more favorable tariff conditions for these products on the part of the hegemonic centers. It is important to point out that the industrial de-

velopment of these countries is dependent on the situation of the export sector, the continued existence of which they are obliged to accept.

2. Industrial development is, then, strongly conditioned by fluctuations in the balance of payments. This leads toward deficit due to the relations of dependence themselves. The causes of the deficit are three:

(*a*) Trade relations take place in a highly monopolized international market, which tends to lower the price of raw materials and to raise the prices of industrial products, particularly inputs. In the second place, there is a tendency in modern technology to replace various primary products with synthetic raw materials. Consequently the balance of trade in these countries tends to be less favorable (even though they show a general surplus). The overall Latin American balance of trade from 1946 to 1968 shows a surplus for each of those years. The same thing happens in almost every underdeveloped country. However, the losses due to deterioration of the terms of trade (on the basis of data from ECLA and the International Monetary Fund), excluding Cuba, were $26,383 million for the 1951–66 period, taking 1950 prices as a base. If Cuba and Venezuela are excluded, the total is $15,925 million.

(*b*) For the reasons already given, foreign capital retains control over the most dynamic sectors of the economy and repatriates a high volume of profit; consequently, capital accounts are highly unfavorable to dependent countries. The data show that the amount of capital leaving the country is much greater than the amount entering; this produces an enslaving deficit in capital accounts. To this must be added the deficit in certain services which are virtually under total foreign control —such as freight transport, royalty payments, technical aid, etc. Consequently, an important deficit is produced in the total balance of payments; thus limiting the possibility of importation of inputs for industrialization.

(*c*) The result is that "foreign financing" becomes necessary, in two forms: to cover the existing deficit, and to "finance" development by means of loans for the stimulation of investments and to "supply" an internal economic surplus which was decapitalized to a large extent by the remittance of part of the surplus generated domestically and sent abroad as profits.

Foreign capital and foreign "aid" thus fill up the holes that they themselves created. The real value of this aid, however, is doubtful. If overcharges resulting from the restrictive terms of the aid are subtracted from the total amount of the grants, the average net flow, according to calculations of the Inter-American Economic and Social Council, is approximately 54 percent of the gross flow [5].

If we take account of certain further facts— that a high proportion of aid is paid in local currencies, that Latin American countries make contributions to international financial institutions, and that credits are often "tied" —we find a "real component of foreign aid" of 42.2 percent on a very favorable hypothesis and of 38.3 percent on a more realistic one [5, II–33]. The gravity of the situation becomes even clearer if we consider that these credits are used in large part of finance North American investments, to subsidize foreign imports which compete with national products, to introduce technology not adapted to the needs of underdeveloped countries, and to invest in low-priority sectors of the national economies. The hard truth is that the underdeveloped countries have to pay for all of the "aid" they receive. This situation is generating an enormous protest movement by Latin American governments seeking at least partial relief from such negative relations.

3. Finally, industrial development is strongly conditioned by the technological monopoly exercised by imperialist centers. We have seen that the underdeveloped countries depend on the importation of machinery and raw materials for the development of their industries. However, these goods are not freely available in the international market;

they are patented and usually belong to the big companies. The big companies do not sell machinery and processed raw materials as simple merchandise: they demand either the payment of royalties, etc., for their utilization or, in most cases, they convert these goods into capital and introduce them in the form of their own investments. This is how machinery which is replaced in the hegemonic centers by more advanced technology is sent to dependent countries as capital for the installation of affiliates. Let us pause and examine these relations, in order to understand their oppressive and exploitative character.

The dependent countries do not have sufficient foreign currency, for the reasons given. Local businessmen have financing difficulties, and they must pay for the utilization of certain patented techniques. These factors oblige the national bourgeois governments to facilitate the entry of foreign capital in order to supply the restricted national market, which is strongly protected by high tariffs in order to promote industrialization. Thus, foreign capital enters with all the advantages: in many cases, it is given exemption from exchange controls for the importation of machinery; financing of sites for installation of industries is provided; government financing agencies facilitate industrialization; loans are available from foreign and domestic banks, which prefer such clients; foreign aid often subsidizes such investments and finances complementary public investments; after installation, high profits obtained in such favorable circumstances can be reinvested freely. Thus it is not surprising that the data of the U.S. Department of Commerce reveal that the percentage of capital brought in from abroad by these companies is but a part of the total amount of invested capital. These data show that in the period from 1946 to 1967 the new entries of capital into Latin America for direct investment amounted to $5,415 million, while the sum of reinvested profits was $4,424 million. On the other hand, the transfers of profits from Latin America to the United States amounted to $14,775 million. If we estimate

total profits as approximately equal to transfers plus reinvestments we have the sum of $18,983 million. In spite of enormous transfers of profits to the United States, the book value of the United States' direct investment in Latin America went from $3,045 million in 1946 to $10,213 million in 1967. From these data it is clear that: (1) Of the new investments made by U.S. companies in Latin America for the period 1946–67, 55 percent corresponds to new entries of capital and 45 percent to reinvestment of profits; in recent years, the trend is more marked, with reinvestments between 1960 and 1966 representing more than 60 percent of new investments. (2) Remittances remained at about 10 percent of book value throughout the period. (3) The ratio of remitted capital to new flow is around 2.7 for the period 1946–67; that is, for each dollar that enters $2.70 leaves. In the 1960's this ratio roughly doubled, and in some years was considerably higher.

The *Survey of Current Business* data on sources and uses of funds for direct North American investment in Latin America in the period 1957–64 show that, of the total sources of direct investment in Latin America, only 11.8 percent came from the United States. The remainder is in large part, the result of the activities of North American firms in Latin America (46.4 percent net income, 27.7 percent under the heading of depreciation), and from "sources located abroad" (14.1 percent). It is significant that the funds obtained abroad that are external to the companies are greater than the funds originating in the United States.

V. EFFECTS ON THE PRODUCTIVE STRUCTURE

It is easy to grasp, even if only superficially, the effects that this dependent structure has on the productive system itself in these countries and the role of this structure in determining a specified type of development, characterized by its dependent nature.

The productive system in the underdeveloped countries is essentially determined by these international relations. In the first place, the need to conserve the agrarian or mining export structure generates a combination between more advanced economic centers that extract surplus value from the more backward sectors, and also between internal "metropolitan" centers and internal interdependent "colonial" centers [10]. The unequal and combined character of capitalist development at the international level is reproduced internally in an acute form. In the second place the industrial and technological structure responds more closely to the interests of the multinational corporations than to internal developmental needs (conceived of not only in terms of the overall interests of the population, but also from the point of view of the interests of a national capitalist development). In the third place, the same technological and economic-financial concentration of the hegemonic economies is transferred without substantial alteration to very different economies and societies, giving rise to a highly unequal productive structure, a high concentration of incomes, underutilization of installed capacity, intensive exploitation of existing markets concentrated in large cities, etc.

The accumulation of capital in such circumstances assumes its own characteristics. In the first place, it is characterized by profound differences among domestic wage-levels, in the context of a local cheap labor market, combined with a capital-intensive technology. The result, from the point of view of relative surplus value, is a high rate of exploitation of labor power. (On measurements of forms of exploitation, see [3].)

This exploitation is further aggravated by the high prices of industrial products enforced by protectionism, exemptions and subsidies given by the national governments, and "aid" from hegemonic centers. Furthermore, since dependent accumulation is necessarily tied into the international economy, it is profoundly conditioned by the unequal and combined character of international capitalist economic

relations, by the technological and financial control of the imperialist centers, by the realities of the balance of payments, by the economic policies of the state, etc. The role of the state in the growth of national and foreign capital merits a much fuller analysis than can be made here.

Using the analysis offered here as a point of departure, it is possible to understand the limits that this productive system imposes on the growth of the internal markets of these countries. The survival of traditional relations in the countryside is a serious limitation on the size of the market, since industrialization does not offer hopeful prospects. The productive structure created by dependent industrialization limits the growth of the internal market.

First, it subjects the labor force to highly exploitative relations which limit its purchasing power. Second, in adopting a technology of intensive capital use, it creates very few jobs in comparison with population growth, and limits the generation of new sources of income. These two limitations affect the growth of the consumer goods market. Third, the remittance abroad of profits carries away part of the economic surplus generated within the country. In all these ways limits are put on the possible creation of basic national industries which could provide a market for the capital goods this surplus would make possible if it were not remitted abroad.

From this cursory analysis we see that the alleged backwardness of these economies is not due to a lack of integration with capitalism but that, on the contrary, the most powerful obstacles to their full development come from the way in which they are joined to this international system and its laws of development.

VI. SOME CONCLUSIONS: DEPENDENT REPRODUCTION

In order to understand the system of dependent reproduction and the socioeconomic institutions created by it, we must see it as part of a system of world economic relations based on monopolistic control of large-scale capital, on control of certain economic and financial centers over others, on a monopoly of a complex technology that leads to unequal and combined development at a national and international level. Attempts to analyze backwardness as a failure to assimilate more advanced models of production or to modernize are nothing more than ideology disguised as science. The same is true of the attempts to analyze this international economy in terms of relations among elements in free competition, such as the theory of comparative costs which seeks to justify the inequalities of the world economic system and to conceal the relations of exploitation on which it is based [14].

In reality we can understand what is happening in the underdeveloped countries only when we see that they develop within the framework of a process of dependent production and reproduction. This system is a dependent one because it reproduces a productive system whose development is limited by those world relations which necessarily lead to the development of only certain economic sectors, to trade under unequal conditions [9], to domestic competition with international capital under unequal conditions, to the imposition of relations of superexploitation of the domestic labor force with a view to dividing the economic surplus thus generated between internal and external forces of domination. (On economic surplus and its utilization in the dependent countries, see [1].)

In reproducing such a productive system and such international relations, the development of dependent capitalism reproduces the factors that prevent it from reaching a nationally and internationally advantageous situation; and it thus reproduces backwardness, misery, and social marginalization within its borders. The development that it produces benefits very narrow sectors, encounters unyielding domestic obstacles to its continued economic growth (with respect to both internal and foreign markets), and leads to the progressive accumulation of balance-of-payments deficits, which in turn generate more dependence and more superexploitation.

The political measures proposed by the developmentalists of ECLA, UNCTAD, BID, etc., do not appear to permit destruction of these terrible chains imposed by dependent development. We have examined the alternative forms of development presented for Latin America and the dependent countries under such conditions elsewhere [8]. Everything now indicates that what can be expected is a long process of sharp political and military confrontations and of profound social radicalization which will lead these countries to a dilemma: governments of force which open the way to facism, or popular revolutionary governments, which open the way to socialism. Intermediate solutions have proved to be, in such a contradictory reality, empty and utopian.

REFERENCES

1. Paul Baran, *Political Economy of Growth* (Monthly Review Press, 1967).
2. Thomas Balogh, *Unequal Partners* (Basil Blackwell, 1963).
3. Pablo Gonzalez Casanova, *Sociologia de la explotación,* Siglo 21 (México, 1969).
4. Cepal, *La CEPAL y el análisis del desarrollo Latinoamericano* (1968, Santiago, Chile).
5. Consejo Interamericano Economic Social (CIES) O.A.S., Inter-American Economic and Social Council, External Financing for Development in L.A. *El financiamiento externo para el desarrollo de América Latina* (Pan-American Union, Washington, 1969).
6. Theotonio Dos Santos, *El nuevo carácter de la dependencia*, CESO (Santiago de Chile, 1968).
7. ——, *La crisis de la teoria del desarrollo y las relaciones de dependencia en América Latina*, Boletín del CESO, 3 (Santiago, Chile, 1968).
8. ——, *La dependencia económica y las alternativas de cambio en América Latina*, Ponencia al 9 Congreso Latinoamericano de Sociología (México, Nov., 1969).

9. A. Emmanuel, *L'Echange inégal* (Maspero, Paris, 1969).

10. Andre G. Frank, *Development and Underdevelopment in Latin America* (Monthly Review Press, 1968).

11. I. V. Levin, *The Export Economies* (Harvard University Press, 1964).

12. Gunnar Myrdal, *Asian Drama* (Pantheon, 1968).

13. K. Nkrumah, *Neocolonialismo, última etapa del imperialismo,* Siglo 21 (México, 1966).

14. Cristian Palloix, *Problemes de la croissance en economie ouverte* (Maspero, Paris, 1969).

Further Readings

1. History of Development

Adelman, Irma, and Morris, Cynthia Taft. "Growth and Impoverishment in the Middle of the Nineteenth Century." *World Development* 6, no. 3 (March 1978).

Bairoch, Paul. *The Economic Development of the Third World Since 1900.* Translated from the fourth French edition by Cynthia Postan. Berkeley: University of California Press, 1975.

Bhatt, V. V. "Economic Development: An analytic-Historical Approach." *World Development* 4, no. 7 (July 1976).

Bird, Richard M. "Land Taxation and Economic Development: The Model of Meiji Japan." *Journal of Development Studies* 13, no. 2 (January 1977).

Furtado, Celso. *Economic Development of Latin America: A Survey from Colonial Times to the Cuban Revolution.* Cambridge. At the University Press, 1970.

Gould, John D. *Economic Growth in History: Survey and Analysis.* London: Methuen, 1972.

Hirschman, Albert O. *The Passions and the Interests: Political Arguments for Capitalism Before Its Triumph.* Princeton: Princeton University Press, 1977.

Hughes, J. R. T. "What Difference Did the Beginning Make?" *American Economic Review* 67, no. 1 (February 1977).

Morawetz, David. *Twenty-Five Years of Economic Development: 1950 to 1975.* Washington, D.C.: World Bank, 1977. Distributed by Johns Hopkins University Press, Baltimore.

Rimmer, Douglas. "Have-Not Nations: The Prototype." *Economic Development and Cultural Change* no. 2 (January 1979).

Rostow, W. W. *The Stages of Economic Growth: A Non-Communist Manifesto.* Cambridge. At the University Press, 1961.

Sachs, Ignacy. *The Discovery of the Third World* (English Translation). Cambridge, Mass., and London: MIT Press, 1976.

Smith, Sheila. "Colonialism in Economic Theory: The Experience of Nigeria." *Journal of Development Studies* 15, no. 3 (April 1979).

Part II

Development Problems and Policies: Domestic

The readings in Part II focus in on the most significant and chronic development problems of contemporary Third World nations. In Chapter 4, we explore the nature and dimensions of the poverty and income-distribution problem by looking first at the latest statistics on the magnitude of poverty through the perspective of the World Bank's *World Development Report, 1980*. Then, Hollis B. Chenery summarizes the findings of a major research project on the relationship between economic growth and the extent of absolute poverty that he and some of his colleagues at the World Bank undertook during the 1970s. The notion that development requires, at a minimum, major efforts to provide all people with basic human needs—a notion widely propounded by international development organizations—is then introduced in a paper by Norman L. Hicks. The issue addressed is a critical one both for theory and policy: Is there a necessary tradeoff between the pursuit of rapid economic growth and the provision of basic needs (food, clothing, shelter, health care, security, etc.) for the broad population of a developing country? Finally, Charles R. Frank, Jr., and Richard Webb survey and evaluate the policy choices available to Third World governments in their efforts to modify economically and socially undesirable income distributions.

Chapter 5 examines the major issues and controversies surrounding the question of population growth and its relationship to economic development. The opening article by Geoffrey McNicoll and Moni Nag, an economist/demographer and anthropologist respectively, succinctly and lucidly highlights the contemporary (1980s) world-population situation and focuses on the strategic issues and areas of contention in the population/development literature. Nancy Birdsall's comprehensive review of research findings on the interrelationship between population growth and development prospects provides a valuable survey of what we know (and, mostly, do not know) about the determinants and consequences of demographic change.

In Chapter 6, the problem of unemployment and underemployment and their relation to output growth and technological choice is assessed, beginning with an overview article on employment and basic needs by Assefa Bequele and David H. Freedman of the International Labour Organization (ILO). This is followed by a well-known conceptual paper by Frances Stewart and Paul Streeten that explores the critical question of whether the objectives of maximum-employment creation and maximum-output growth are mutually conflicting or congruent in nature. They conclude that contrary to traditional neoclassical beliefs, the two objectives are more congruent than conflicting. Finally, Howard Pack analytically and empirically examines the issue of factor-price distortions, intermediate technology, and employment creation. He concludes—again contrary to much conventional wisdom —that industries in developing countries can promote more employment opportunities through the substitution of lower-cost, labor-intensive technologies if market prices can be made to more accurately reflect factor scarcities.

The next chapter considers the rapid and historically unprecedented growth of Third World cities. Such growth has resulted in large part from accelerated rural-to-urban migration despite rising levels of urban unemployment and under-employment. The quantitative dimensions of this urbanization dilemma are discussed in an excerpt from Michael P. Todaro's 1981 monograph, *City Bias and Rural Neglect*. This is followed by the widely cited theoretical paper by John R. Harris and Michael P. Todaro that analyzes the relationship between internal migration and urban unemployment, with an evaluation of the welfare implications of alternative public policy responses to excessive migration. Actual policies to redirect migration flows and decentralize the urbanization process in a number of developing countries in the late 1970s are then reviewed and evaluated by sociologist/demographer Alan B. Simmons.

The question of the developmental role of agriculture and the transformation of the rural economy are crucial for any analysis of long-term development prospects. Central to this issue is the need to understand the nature of the risks and uncertainties of subsistence farming—the activity pursued by the majority of people in Third World countries. Clifton R. Wharton, Jr.'s enlightening 1969 essay on this subject remains to this day one of the most concise and informative depictions of the plight of the subsistence farmer. It is, therefore, included as the introductory reading of Chapter 8. Wharton's article is followed by a more recent 1979 piece by Gilbert T. Brown demonstrating how ill-conceived agricultural pricing policies can thwart not only rural but also national development efforts. Conversely, Brown argues that a more appropriate, nondiscriminatory pricing policy can make a major difference in Third World agricultural output. During the 1970s, integrated rural development was widely perceived as a necessary condition for national industrial development, both by international donor agencies, like the World Bank and the U.S. Agency for International Development (USAID), and many governments in Africa, Asia and Latin America. But what is meant by rural development and how might it be achieved? This is the question that is addressed by our last reading in Chapter 8, an extract from the World Bank's rural development sector paper.

The last chapter in Part II, Chapter 9, explores the relationship between education and development by first examining recent trends in schooling opportunities and human-resource growth in an excerpt from the World Bank's *World Development Report, 1980*. This is followed by a more critical evaluation of the development impact of the massive educational expenditures of Third World governments by economist John Simmons. Simmons argues for a reorientation of educational expenditures to better serve the real needs of people in poor countries. Jean-Pierre Jallade, an educational economist, follows with a look at how, if at all, education serves to narrow the distribution of income. He uses data from Brazil and Colombia to demonstrate that, contrary to the accepted wisdom, actual educational expenditures have done little to narrow the gap between the rich and the poor.

4

Growth, Poverty and Income Distribution

8. Poverty, Growth and Human Development*

World Bank Staff

The poor are a mixed group. Some cope reasonably well; others are on the margin of survival. Their well-being can fluctuate widely: the marriages and ceremonies after the harvest are in stark contrast to the hunger and illness that often precede it. A good crop with a new seed, or the chance to work on a nearby road project, may push a poor farm family's income to the point where they can buy a plow with a metal blade or some clothing for their children. But two years of inadequate rain, or a bout of illness, may cost them their land or their livestock—a degree of vulnerability that understandably makes for caution and aversion to risk.

The poor have other things in common, apart from their extremely low incomes. A disproportionate number of them—perhaps two in five—are children under 10, mainly in large families. More than three-quarters of them live in (often very remote) rural areas,

the rest in urban slums—but almost all in very crowded conditions. Many poor families own a small piece of land, some animals or some tools. But both they and other poor people live mainly by working long hours—men, women and children alike—as farmers, vendors and artisans, or hired workers.

As much as four-fifths of their income is consumed as food. The result is a monotonous, limited diet of cereals, yams or cassava —with a few vegetables and in some places a little fish or meat. Many of them are malnourished to the point where their ability to work hard is reduced, the physical and mental development of their children is impaired, and their resistance to infections is low. They are often sick—with tropical diseases, measles and diarrhea, and cuts and scratches that will not heal. Complications of childbirth are a common cause of death. Of every 10 children born to poor parents, two die within a year; another dies before the age of five; only five survive to the age of 40.

The great majority of poor adults are illiterate; their children, though having a much better chance of attending school than in the past, usually do not complete more than a year or two. Unable to read a road sign, let alone a newspaper, their knowledge and understanding remain severely circumscribed.

* *World Development Report, 1980*. Oxford University Press, New York, 1980, pp. 33, 35–37, 39.

Team report led by Paul Isenman and including Nicholas Hope, Timothy King, Peter Knight, Akbar Noman, Rupert Pennant-Rea, and Adrian Wood.

Yet they learn about the possibility of a better life from direct observation, from friends and relatives, and perhaps from small improvements in their own circumstances; and they hope that their children will somehow be able to climb out of poverty.

DIMENSIONS OF POVERTY

It is difficult to measure the extent of poverty. To begin with, absolute poverty means more than low income. It also means malnutrition, poor health and lack of education—and not all of the poor are equally badly off in all respects. There is also room for disagreement about where to draw the line between the poor and the rest, and about the correct way to calculate and compare incomes and living standards at different times and in different places.

To compound these difficulties, the data are inadequate. Household surveys, if they exist, sometimes underrepresent the poor. Very few follow the fortunes of individuals and families through time, or disaggregate the household to examine the well-being of women, children and the elderly. Nor is direct observation necessarily a reliable basis for generalization, especially in the countryside, where many of the poor are beyond the gaze of the casual visitor to villages and rural development projects—away from the roads, away from the markets and project sites, or on the outskirts of the villages.

Despite all this, no one seriously doubts that a very large number of people are extremely poor. Taking as the cutoff a level of income based on detailed studies of poverty in India, the number of people in absolute poverty in developing countries (excluding China and other centrally planned economies) is estimated at around 780 million. In 1975 about 600 million adults in developing countries were illiterate; and only two-fifths of the children in these countries currently complete more than three years of primary school. In 1978, 550 million people lived in countries where the average life expectancy was less than 50 years, 400 million in countries where the average annual death rate of children aged one to four was more than 20 per 1,000—20 times that in the industrialized countries.

Nor is there any serious disagreement about who the poor are. Half of the people in absolute poverty live in South Asia, mainly in India and Bangladesh. A sixth live in East and Southeast Asia, mainly in Indonesia. Another sixth are in Sub-Saharan Africa. The rest—about 100 million people—are divided among Latin America, North Africa and the Middle East. With the partial exception of Latin America (where about 40 percent are in the towns) the poor are primarily rural dwellers, overwhelmingly dependent on agriculture—the majority of them landless (or nearly landless) laborers. Some minority groups—for example, the Indians in Latin America and the scheduled castes in India—are also overrepresented among the poor. And there is a tendency for absolute poverty in particular places, families and social groups to persist from generation to generation.

THREE DECADES OF POVERTY REDUCTION

In aggregate, however, considerable progress has been made in reducing the incidence of poverty over the past 30 years. . . . Progress would have been greater still but for the dramatic growth of population, which has doubled the number of people in the developing world since 1950 and has begun to slow down—though as yet slightly—only since the mid-1960s.

Since 1950 income per person in the developing world has doubled. But in low-income countries, the average increase has been half that, and in both low- and middle-income countries the incomes of the poor have grown more slowly than the average. The *proportion* of people in absolute poverty in developing countries as a group is estimated to have fallen during the past two decades (though probably not in Sub-Saharan Africa in the 1970s). . . . But because population has grown, the *number* of people in absolute poverty has increased.

There has also been progress in education. The proportion of adults in developing countries who are literate is estimated to have increased over the past three decades from about 30 percent to more than 50 percent; the proportion of children of primary-school age enrolled in school rose from 47 percent in 1960 to 64 percent in 1977. These advances have been shared by most countries and regions, including those that initially were furthest behind, such as Sub-Saharan Africa. But the quality of schooling remains low in many countries; and because of population growth, there has been an increase of about 100 million in the absolute number of illiterate adults since 1950.

The most striking advances against poverty have been in health. Average life expectancy in middle-income developing countries has risen nine years over the past three decades. In low-income countries, the increase has been even greater—15 years. But even though infant mortality rates (which are a major determinant of life expectancy) have fallen substantially in developing countries since 1950, there now are so many more children born that the absolute number of infant deaths probably has not declined.

Another way of viewing the progress of the past three decades is to compare the developing with the industrialized countries. The gap in income per person between them has widened, even in proportional terms (though in the case of the middle-income countries only slightly). But the gaps in education and health have narrowed—by 15 percentage points in adult literacy and five years in life expectancy.

POVERTY AND GROWTH

Most poor people live in poor countries. Whether absolute poverty is measured by low income, low life expectancy or illiteracy, there is a strong correlation between the extent of poverty in a country and its GNP per person. . . . This suggests that the solution to poverty is economic growth. There is a great deal of truth in this proposition, but it needs to be carefully qualified.

First, comparing countries, the relation between the extent of their absolute poverty and the level of GNP per person is . . . far from perfect. Because of differences in income distribution, the proportion of the population below the poverty line in 1975 was more than twice as high in Colombia as in South Korea, even though the average incomes of the two countries were close. Sri Lanka is a low-income country, yet the life expectancy of its people approaches that of the industrialized countries. Some middle-income countries, such as Morocco and the Ivory Coast, have literacy rates below those of the average low-income country.

Second, looking at changes over time within particular countries, the connection between growth and poverty reduction over periods of a decade or two appears inexact. There is general agreement that growth, in the very long term, eliminates most absolute poverty; but also that some people may (at least temporarily) be impoverished by development—as when a tenant farmer is displaced by his landlord's tractor or a shoemaker by mass-produced shoes. Because relevant data are sparse and unreliable, however, it remains a matter of dispute how consistently growth over comparatively short periods has reduced the proportion of the population in absolute poverty.

What is clear is that different countries have had different experiences. The proportion below the absolute poverty line apparently has not fallen in some slow-growing countries (including rural India between 1956 and 1974) or in some periods in faster-growing countries. But it appears to have fallen markedly over the past 25 years in several fast-growing countries (including Thailand and Yugoslavia) and in some slower-growing ones (including Costa Rica and Sri Lanka). The association between economic growth and improvements in education and health has also been imperfect.

Third, the connection between economic growth and poverty reduction goes both ways. Few would dispute that the health, education and well-being of the mass of people in industrialized countries are a cause, as well as a result, of national prosperity. Similarly, people who are unskilled and sick make little contribution to a country's economic growth. Development strategies that bypass large numbers of people may not be the most effective way for developing countries to raise their long-run growth rates.

The rest of this chapter looks more closely at some of the elements of absolute poverty and at policies to deal with it. Since economic growth (despite the qualifications) is crucial to reducing poverty, its causes will be considered. The focus then shifts to factors and policies that particularly affect the incomes of the poor. Under both headings the potential contribution of human development is examined.

Economic considerations and policies will predominate. But it is important to stress the contribution (over long periods) of social, political and cultural factors to the poverty of particular countries and particular groups. Nor should this chapter's emphasis on better education and health as a means to raise incomes detract from their tremendous importance as ends in themselves.

SOURCES OF GROWTH

Economic growth comes about in two ways, both of which can be powerfully influenced by government policy. One is building up a larger stock of productive assets and human skills. The other is increasing the productivity of these assets, skills, and the country's natural resources. This involves moving capital and labor between sectors, developing new institutions, inventing and introducing new techniques of production and new products, making better choices among existing techniques, and taking steps to cut costs and eliminate waste. Growth thus involves continuous change—it has aptly been described as a process of perpetual disequilibrium.

Natural Resources

The natural resources of countries are not consistently correlated with either income levels or income growth. Some of the richest and most rapidly growing economies—Austria, Japan and South Korea, for example—have few natural resources; some well-endowed ones—Zaire, for instance—have remained poor.

Nonetheless, no account of the causes of national prosperity and poverty should overlook land, water, minerals, energy and climate. Many countries—among them Argentina, Australia, Saudi Arabia and the Soviet Union—owe a good part of their affluence to natural resources. Nor is it coincidental that most poor countries are in the tropics and, more particularly, that many of the poorest people in the world live in the arid and semi-arid regions of Asia and Africa.

But the link between natural resources and income is affected by population density.... It also depends on the availability of capital and skills and on the development strategy adopted. And it is very much a function of world demand and the state of technology. Malaysia's early progress was founded on tin for plating and rubber for automobile tires. Bangladesh's jute industry suffered from the invention of synthetic fibres (especially because, in contrast to Malaysia, little relevant research was undertaken). A technical breakthrough in "dry" farming would—perhaps more than any other feasible technical advance—transform the prospects of a large proportion of the world's poor.

Investment in Physical Capital

The accumulation of physical capital is a necessary and very important part of economic growth. The productivity of workers in industrialized countries is greater than in developing countries partly because they have more capital to assist them. Similarly, most of the innovations and structural changes that generate growth clearly require substantial physical investment—in roads, machines, inventories, irrigation systems and so on.

Developing countries that have invested a higher proportion of their output have on average grown faster, but the contribution of investment to growth has varied widely. Some, including the fast-growing East Asian countries, have managed to squeeze as much as half an extra unit of annual output from each extra unit of capital. Others, such as Ghana and until recently Uruguay, have invested to much less effect.

Part of the discrepancy is attributable to differences in the share of investment devoted to activities (such as housing) that do not contribute directly to production, but more to variations in the efficiency with which productive investment has been allocated and used. This efficiency has in turn depended on the availability of natural resources and skilled labor and on government policies toward agriculture, industry and foreign trade. . . .

It has sometimes been suggested that income inequality is conducive to higher investment (since the rich save a larger proportion of their incomes than the poor). But in practice this relation is muffled by government and corporate saving and by variation across countries in incentives and attitudes to saving. High investment rates are observed both in countries with relatively unequal income distributions, such as Brazil and Kenya, and in countries with relatively equal distributions, such as China and South Korea. Low investment rates also appear compatible with income distributions that are both more un-

equal, as in Senegal, and less unequal, as in Burma.

Human Resources

It has long been recognized that the qualities of a nation's people have an important influence on its prosperity and growth. This is not simply because better labor adds to output in the passive way that, say, more fertilizer or better machinery does. It is also because human beings are the source of ideas, decisions and actions on investment, innovation and other opportunities.

Technical, scientific and professional skills are clearly essential to producing many modern goods and services. Entrepreneurial and administrative abilities are vital in both public and private sectors. Less immediately obvious, but equally fundamental, are the skills, knowledge and attitudes of the great mass of ordinary workers, including small farmers and traders.

What governs the quality of human resources, and how can it be improved? There is no simple answer, no simple best policy. One important ingredient is practical experience. Another consists of the knowledge and attitudes that children acquire from their parents and from society at large. Then there are the many different kinds of formal education and training: general primary and secondary schooling, technical and vocational schooling, general and specialized higher education—all of which impart specific skills, enhance the ability to learn further and mold attitudes toward work and change.

Partly because measurement is difficult, the evidence is not complete—either on the contribution of human resources to production and growth, or on what determines their quality. But a lot of research has been done on the economic contribution of formal education. In all countries more educated people tend to earn more—to a degree that makes educational spending (especially for primary education and especially in developing countries) often appear an attractive investment. . . .

Studies have also shown that primary schooling can contribute to the productivity of farmers . . . and to industrial productivity. In addition, there is evidence that basic education can contribute to national growth. . . . Developing countries with higher literacy rates have tended to grow faster, even after allowances are made for differences in incomes and physical investment, and they have had higher physical investment rates.

The results of this research reinforce a body of less systematic observations, and some historical evidence, that formal education can aid economic development. The outstanding growth records of Japan and South Korea probably could not have been achieved without their distinctively early mass literacy and numeracy, which (together with land reform, more advanced education and good economic management) contributed to increased agricultural productivity, to the expansion of labor-intensive manufacturing and exports, and to their remarkable ability to adapt to changes in technology and world demand. At the other end of the spectrum, the poor economic performance of the countries of Sub-Saharan Africa is at least partly attributable to extremely low literacy and the scarcity of highly educated and experienced people.

Knowledge, skills and attitudes are not the only aspects of human resources that affect economic performance. A healthy and well-fed labor force is more physically and mentally energetic than one that is sick and hungry, and therefore gets more work done and is more innovative. This is confirmed by a number of experiments and project-level

studies. . . . The aggregate evidence is less clear-cut.

At the same time, however, there are examples that refute any suggestion that education, health and nutrition are in themselves sufficient to induce rapid growth. Burma and Jamaica, for example, with high levels of literacy and life expectancy for their income levels, achieved annual growth rates of only 1.0 and 2.0 percent per person over the period 1960–78. It is also possible (though difficult if economies heavily dependent on petroleum, other minerals or expatriate skilled labor are excluded) to find cases of fairly rapid growth even with low levels of literacy and life expectancy—Pakistan in the 1960s is an example.

The linkage is imperfect partly because literacy and life expectancy are crude indicators of education and health—and are often measured inaccurately as well. But the main reason is that growth also depends on other factors—the availability of natural resources and physical capital and the efficiency with which all resources are used.

Without modern inputs, the right technology and ready access to markets, even educated farmers find it hard to innovate . . . and they can be discouraged from increasing production by low prices. Without rapid accumulation of physical capital, and policies to ensure that this is associated with rapid growth of productive employment opportunities, the earnings of even a healthy and educated labor force will stagnate. Without the right mixture of education and training, shortages of specific skills will hold back growth, while chronic surpluses of other sorts of manpower may emerge.

9. Poverty and Progress—Choices for the Developing World*

Hollis B. Chenery

Concepts of progress in most developing countries are heavily conditioned by their colonial past. Many of them express their objectives in terms of "catching up" with the advanced industrial societies and pattern their economies on this model. This tendency is reinforced by political objectives in countries that wish to acquire military power and influence.

One drawback to the emphasis on growth is that its benefits have usually been concentrated on the modern sectors of the economy, and increasing inequality of incomes has often led to political tensions. An alternative view of progress focuses more on achieving an equitable society and reducing poverty, with growth regarded as a necessary but by no means sufficient condition.

The postwar experience of relatively rapid growth in developing countries has provided a rich body of data on this set of relations that is only now being analyzed. Since there is relatively little established theory to guide this analysis, the collection of data and the formulation of hypotheses have gone hand in hand. Although substantial progress has been made in understanding the economic forces at work, the results to date are largely speculative and fall considerably short of the needs of policymakers. This article explores some of the implications of the prevalent views of progress in developing countries in the light of the information available on the results.

CONCEPTS OF PROGRESS

Catching Up

The material success of the industrialized West has been a powerful incentive to the rest of the world to adopt elements of Western experience that are conducive to accelerated growth. The success of countries with different historical backgrounds and economic and political systems has served to reinforce this objective.

The concept of catching up with the industrial leaders is a product of the industrial revolution and its outward spread from Western Europe. This concept both provides a goal for social action and suggests a means by which this goal can be achieved. The technology and forms of economic organization created by the advanced Western countries have provided the means for accelerated growth for countries in all parts of the world. Nations following this model have differed primarily in their choice of the economic and social elements to be incorporated in their societies.

The prototype of a successful process of catching up is Japan, whose economic structure and income level in 1910 were not significantly different from those of the poor countries of today. Econometric estimates of the sources of Japanese growth suggest that the process of borrowing technology from more advanced countries is now virtually completed and that Japan is likely to attain the income level of the United States by 1990 (Jorgensen and Nishimizu, 1978).

The Japanese example has had a powerful effect on Taiwan, Korea, Singapore, Thailand, and other countries of East Asia. All of these economies are now growing considerably faster than those of the advanced countries, and some may be able to complete the transformation from a state of underdevelopment to one of maturity in less than the 60 years taken by Japan.

Several of these East Asian countries provide modern approximations to the earlier idea of progress as a process in which "good things come in clusters" (Keohane, 1979). Un-

* From *Finance & Development*, 17, no. 2 (June 1980), pp. 12–16.

like most developing countries, the benefits of growth have been widely distributed in Japan, Taiwan, Singapore, and Korea, and the incomes of the poor have grown almost as fast as those of the rich. Postwar governments have been growth minded and authoritarian but not very repressive, and these countries have ranked high on most indicators of social progress. In more typical cases growth has been achieved at the expense of increasing the concentration of wealth and income, however, and the poor have benefited much less.

Equity

Although the more equitable sharing of income features prominently among the political objectives of virtually all governments, it is taken much less seriously in practice than is the objective of rapid growth. Even though widespread government intervention in production and income distribution is justified largely on the grounds of reducing poverty, in fact most studies show that on balance the effects of government revenue collection and expenditure in developing countries favor the upper-income groups rather than the poor.

A few developing countries have, however, gone beyond the endorsement of equitable growth and have adopted policies designed to achieve it. Notable examples include the People's Republic of China, Cuba, India, Israel, Sri Lanka, Tanzania, and Yugoslavia. Although their social goals vary with the form and extent of government control of the economy, there is a common emphasis on providing a minimum level of income to the poorest groups. In the more extreme socialist formulations, greater equality is considered a goal in itself, even if it is achieved with an adverse impact on efficiency—that is, lowering the incomes of the rich rather than raising those of the poor.

A pioneering attempt to reconcile the objectives of growth and the alleviation of poverty in an operational framework was made in 1962 by the Perspective Planning Division of the Indian Planning Commis-

sion (Srinivasan and Bardhan, 1974). This approach was based on a formulation in which the rate of poverty reduction in India was determined by the growth of the national income, while the extent of redistribution considered feasible was based on the experience of other countries. This approach has been refined in the concept of *Redistribution with Growth* (Ahluwalia and Chenery, 1974), which forms the basis of the comparative analysis in the following section. If the idea of a feasible limit to the redistribution that can be achieved with a given set of institutions is accepted, the conflict between growth and distribution is reduced.

A further refinement in the concept of poverty alleviation has been achieved by shifting from the use of income as a measure of poverty to physical estimates of the inputs required to achieve minimum standards of nutrition, health, shelter, education, and other essentials. These indicators of basic needs provide ways of evaluating the effectiveness of any set of policies designed to reduce poverty (Streeten, 1979). The "basic needs" approach focuses particularly on the distribution of education, health, and other public services as a necessary element of policies designed to raise productivity and to alleviate poverty. This is an area in which some of the more effective socialist societies, such as the People's Republic of China, showed marked improvement.

Formulating Social Objectives

The social goals of developing countries—and of international bodies representing them—tend to be stated in political terms that confuse ends and means and ignore the different dimensions of progress. For example, the goal of catching up with more advanced countries is a poor proxy for improving welfare because it often leads to emphasis on heavy industry and other policies that concentrate growth in the modern sectors of the economy. Similarly, many of the goals announced by international agencies, such as the attainment of given levels of nutrition, education, shelter, or industry, are misleading because they ignore the need to achieve a balance among the several dimensions of social progress.

The economist's answer to this problem is to replace a set of separate objectives by a social welfare function that defines the goal of a society in utilitarian terms as the increase in a weighted average of income or consumption of its members over time. Although the national income is one such average, the typical income distribution gives a weight of over 50 percent to the rich (the top 20 percent) and less than 5 percent to the poor (the bottom 20 percent). If the growth of aggregate national income is used as a goal, it therefore implies giving 10 to 20 times as much weight to a 1 percent increase in the incomes of the rich as to a 1 percent increase in those of the poor (Ahluwalia and Chenery, 1974).

In principle, any set of weights could be applied to the income or consumption of different groups to remedy this bias. One possibility is to give equal weight to a given percentage increase in the income of each member of society, which is the equivalent of weighting by the population in each group. A more extreme welfare function, which correponds to the announced goals of a few socialist societies, concentrates entirely on raising the incomes of the poor and gives social value to increasing other incomes only to the extent that they contribute to this objective.

Although there is no scientific way to determine the appropriate welfare function for any given society, the concept is useful in bringing out potential conflicts in the idea of progress and in deriving alternative measures of performance. It will be used for this purpose in the following section.

EXPERIENCE WITH DISTRIBUTION

Perceptions of the nature of progress have evolved considerably as a result of the varied experience of the postwar period. Many of the early postcolonial governments set forth optimistic objectives that now seem highly oversimplified. However, there has also been a notable willingness to learn from experience in countries with varying ideologies. Equity-oriented countries such as the People's Republic of China, Cuba, Sri Lanka, and Tanzania have found it necessary to give greater attention to economic efficiency and growth, while some of the leading exponents of rapid growth—Brazil, Mexico, Thailand, Turkey—are now taking poverty alleviation more seriously.

Although scholarly interest in these relations has expanded rapidly in recent years, the statistical measures needed to test and refine hypotheses are only now becoming available. Twenty-five years ago, Simon Kuznets addressed the question: "Does inequality in the distribution of income increase or decrease in the course of a country's economic growth?" Although his answer was based on evidence for only a handful of countries and was labeled "perhaps 5 percent empirical information and 95 percent speculation," it has provided the starting point for empirical work in this field (Kuznets, 1955). Kuznets hypothesized that the distribution of income tends to worsen in the early phases of development and to improve thereafter. This "U-shaped curve" hypothesis has been subsequently verified in several cross-country studies based on samples of 50 or 60 developing countries (Ahluwalia, 1976).

There are several reasons for the earnings of middle-income and upper-income groups to rise more rapidly than those of the poor in the early stages of growth. Development involves a shift of population from the slow growing agricultural sector to the higher-income, more rapidly growing modern sector. In this process inequality is first accentuated by more rapid population growth in rural areas and ultimately reduced by rising wages produced by more rapid absorption of labor in the modern sector (Frank and Webb, 1977). The more capital-intensive type of development strategy fol-

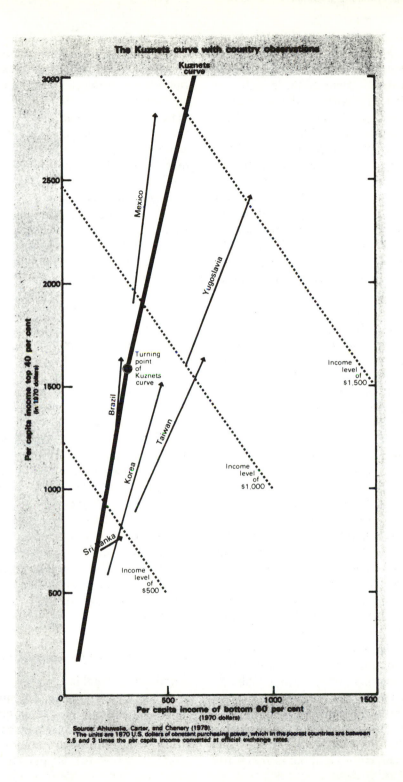

The Kuznets curve with country observations

Source: Ahluwalia, Carter, and Chenery (1979).
¹The units are 1970 U.S. dollars of constant purchasing power, which in the poorest countries are between 2.5 and 3 times the per capita income converted at official exchange rates.

89

lowed by Mexico or Brazil absorbs less labor and produces greater concentration of income, while the more labor-intensive forms of Taiwan and Korea distribute the benefits of modernization more widely. A number of other factors, such as the greater demand for skilled than for unskilled labor and the concentration of public expenditure in urban areas, also contribute to growing inequality in many countries.

My present concern is with the broader aspects of the relations between growth and distribution. How universal is the tendency toward less equal distribution in developing countries? Does it lead to an absolute decline in welfare for some groups? What kinds of policies have served to offset these tendencies? Is social conflict an inevitable concomitant of economic advance? Although none of these questions can be answered with great confidence, the average relationships and the variety of individual experience can be brought out by combining the available cross-country and time-series evidence for the postwar period.

The average relationship between rising income and its distribution is best shown by estimates of the Kuznets curve from data for all countries having comparable measures in some recent period (Ahluwalia, Carter, and Chenery, 1979). Although the variation in income shares was computed separately for each quintile, the general phenomenon is depicted in the chart by considering only two groups, the rich (upper 40 percent) and the poor (lower 60 percent). As national income rises from the lowest observed level to that of the middle-income countries, the share received by the poor declines on average from 32 percent to 23 percent of the total. In a hypothetical country following this average relationship, 80 percent of the increase in income would go to the top 40 percent of recipients.

The relationship between the income growth of different groups and that of the whole society can be brought out more clearly by expressing it in terms of the per capita income of each group. This is done in the chart, which plots the per capita income of the poor against that of the rich. Since the income level "Y" of the society is a weighted average of the two groups "a and b" ($Y = .4Y_a + .6Y_b$), the downward sloping straight lines define given levels of per capita income. Points on these lines indicate different distributions, and a growth process with a constant distribution is represented by a straight line through the origin, as in the case of Yugoslavia. A line deviating toward the vertical axis indicates growing inequality, as in the case of Mexico or Brazil. Growing equality is shown by Sri Lanka and Taiwan.

The Kuznets curve shown in this chart consists of two segments: a phase of worsening distribution up to an income level of about $800 (of constant purchasing power) and a phase of improving distribution thereafter. In the first phase the per capita income of the rich grows from about $300 to $1,600 while that of the poor increases from about $100 to $300. For the poorest 20 percent, the rate of growth is considerably less. Since an increase in national income of this magnitude may take 40 or 50 years even with the relatively rapid growth rates recently experienced in developing countries, in the typical country the very poor cannot look forward to an annual increase of much more than 1 percent—even though the economy is growing at two or three times that rate. Furthermore, there is nothing automatic about the improvement in distribution above $800, as shown by Mexico and Brazil.

Tradeoff Between Growth, Equity

Although acceptable time-series data are only available for a dozen or so countries, they indicate a considerable variation around this average relation. The table gives selected measures of overall growth and of the share going to the lower 60 percent for countries

Changes in Income and Its Distribution

Country	Income Level[†]				Distribution			Growth Rates (In Per Cent)		
		Increments			Percentage Share of Bottom 60 Per Cent					
	Initial Year	Total	Top 40 Per Cent	Bottom 60 Per Cent	Initial Year	Final Year	Increase Incremental	Total	Bottom 60 Per Cent	Ratio of Bottom 60 Per Cent to Total
Good performers										
Taiwan (1964–74)	562	508	758	341	36.9	38.5	39.5	6.6	7.1	1.1
Yugoslavia (1963–73)	1,003	518	822	316	35.7	36.0	36.5	4.2	4.3	1.0
Sri Lanka (1963–73)	388	84	58	101	27.4	35.4	51.3	2.0	4.6	2.3
Korea (1965–76)	362	540	938	275	34.9	32.3	31.1	8.7	7.9	0.9
Costa Rica (1961–71)	825	311	459	212	23.7	28.4	33.6	3.2	5.1	1.6
Intermediate performers										
India (1954–64)	226	58	113	21	31.0	29.2	25.8	2.3	1.6	0.7
Philippines (1961–71)	336	83	155	35	24.7	24.8	25.0	2.2	2.3	1.0
Turkey (1963–73)	566	243	417	128	20.8	24.0	27.9	3.6	5.1	1.4
Colombia (1964–74)	648	232	422	106	19.0	21.2	24.0	3.1	4.3	1.4
Poor performers										
Brazil (1960–70)	615	214	490	31	24.8	20.6	15.5	3.1	1.2	0.4
Mexico (1963–75)	974	446	944	114	21.7	19.7	18.0	3.2	2.4	0.8
Peru (1961–71)	834	212	435	63	17.9	17.9	17.9	2.3	2.3	1.0

Source: Ahluwalia, Carter, and Chenery (1979), Table 5.
† Measured by per capita income expressed in 1970 U.S. dollars of constant purchasing power.

having observations for a decade or more. They are divided into three groups according to the share of the increment in income going to the poor. The five good performers show over 30 percent of the increment going to the bottom 60 percent, while the three poor performers show less than 20 percent. Whether distribution is getting better or worse is indicated by comparing these increments to the initial distribution and by the ratio of the growth of the per capita income of the poor to the national average in the last column.

This information, together with less complete data on other countries, provides a basis for describing the following patterns of growth and distribution observed in the developing world:

- *Growth-oriented pattern*, illustrated by Brazil and Mexico.
- *Equity-oriented, low growth*, illustrated by Sri Lanka.
- *Rapid growth with equity*, illustrated by Taiwan, Yugoslavia, and Korea.

These cases illustrate the main types of deviation from the average pattern that can be observed in the 12 countries of the table; India, Turkey, the Philippines, and Colombia follow the average relations of the Kuznets curve.

These examples suggest the following observations on the relationship between income growth and social welfare in developing countries. First, a small group of countries has achieved rapid growth with considerable equity. In addition to Taiwan, Korea, and Yugoslavia, this group includes Israel, Singapore, and perhaps the People's Republic of China. The policies underlying this successful performance vary from primary reliance on market forces in Taiwan, Korea, and Singapore to substantial income transfers and other forms of intervention in Yugoslavia and Israel. Second, substantial tradeoffs between growth and equity are illustrated by the other cases.

Although Sri Lanka has grown much less rapidly than Mexico or Brazil, the poor have done considerably better in the former case. Cuba presents an even more extreme tradeoff, since the welfare of the poor has risen despite a continuous fall in the nation's per capita income since 1960 (Seers, 1974).

Only in the few cases where economic growth has been both rapid and fairly equitably distributed is it possible to make unambiguous comparisons among countries—or among different development strategies for a single country. In other cases it is necessary to define some properties of a social welfare function to make such comparisons. To take two extreme cases from the table, the incomes of the poor have grown nearly four times as fast over a decade in Sri Lanka as in Brazil, while the opposite is true of the incomes of the rich. Since the latter receive greater weight in the national income, per capita income has grown 50 percent faster in Brazil; conversely a population-weighted index of welfare increases 50 percent faster for Sri Lanka. Even this limited sample therefore demonstrates that judgments about economic progress cannot be separated from social and ethical postulates.

REDUCING WORLD POVERTY

Attempts to extend the concept of material progress to a global scale run up against more acute problems of equity than the national issues described above. Although most governments recognize their national income as one dimension of national welfare, no one has suggested that global income has much relevance to an assessment of global welfare. Instead political and economic efforts of international institutions are increasingly focused on the reduction of poverty and other aspects of equity as objectives that command the support of people of widely varying political views.

In recent years considerable efforts have been made to establish measures of poverty based on standards of nutrition, health, shelter, education, and other essentials. Conservative estimates set the proportion of the world's population that falls below a poverty line based on such minimum standards at between 20 and 25 percent. Although this proportion has declined somewhat in the past 30 years, the overall increase in the world's population has meant that the absolute number of people below this poverty line has continued to grow and is currently of the order of 800 million.

In technical terms the reduction or even elimination of world poverty seems deceptively easy. If resources coould be shifted to satisfying the needs of poverty groups efficiently, it would only require a reallocation of 2 to 3 percent of the world's output per annum from 1980 onward to meet the identifiable costs of eliminating poverty by the year 2000 (Streeten and Burki, 1978). Since three fourths of the world's poor live in very poor countries, however, the annual cost of eliminating poverty in these countries is more meaningfully stated as equal to about 15 percent of their gross national product (GNP), even if expenditures could be designed to serve only the target groups. In the light of the distributional experience outlined in the previous section, the problem is seen to be vastly more difficult.

Some of the principal constraints to a more realistic attempt to reduce global poverty include:

1. The multiple objectives of nation states, among which the alleviation of poverty is usually subordinated to a variety of nationalistic goals.
2. The limited scope for resource transfers in the existing international economic order. Official development assistance from the industrialized countries has declined from 0.50 percent of their GNP in 1960 to 0.35 percent or less since 1970. Transfers from the Organization of Petroleum Exporting Countries (OPEC), while substantial, do not offset the negative effects of higher oil

prices on the growth of the oil importing developing countries.
3. Rapid growth of population, which will double in the next 35 years even though the rate has started to decline.

What are the possibilities of more rapid progress in the face of these and other constraints? In an attempt to compare approaches to poverty alleviation, Ahluwalia, Carter, and Chenery have simulated income growth and the numbers of absolute poor over the next 20 years for a large sample of developing countries (Ahluwalia, Carter, and Chenery, 1979, Tables 3 and 9). If the trends of the past 20 years—a period of relatively rapid growth of income—continue, the number of absolute poor in 2000 would be at about the same level as in 1960. This represents rapid progress in one sense, since the proportion of the poor would fall from 50 percent to 20 percent of the population of developing countries. However, since this result would be achieved only by a reduction in absolute poverty in middle-income countries that offsets the rising numbers in the very poor countries, it is not a long-term solution.

The reduction in poverty will have to come from one of three sources: improved distribution, accelerated growth, or a more rapid decline in population growth. Improved distribution is particularly important in many middle-income countries, such as those in Latin America (where income is quite unequally distributed), but some acceleration of growth is essential in the poor countries of Africa and South Asia. Although there are some short-term tradeoffs between growth and distribution, in the longer term it is more likely that all three types of policy will be mutually reinforcing. Even within restrictive limits to capital transfers, the industrial countries can considerably improve the outcome by giving greater priority to poverty alleviation in allocating aid among countries (Edelman and Chenery, 1977).

These projections lead to the conclusion that although the elimination of poverty is much more difficult than is sometimes suggested, it remains a plausible goal for international policy. One of the principal means to this end would be accomplished if the tendency of the poor to lag behind the higher-income groups in the process of development could be eliminated. There is increasing acceptance of the idea that international efforts should be more directly focused on reducing poverty in order to offset this tendency of the international system. Enough examples of how this result can be accomplished have been cited in economic systems ranging from socialist to free enterprise to suggest that it is a feasible objective.

This conclusion leaves several fundamental issues unresolved. To what extent should poverty alleviation replace the principle of self-help as a guide to international action? To achieve this objective, will it not be necessary to establish enforceable standards of performance to assure that the benefits actually reach the poverty groups? The new emphasis on poverty alleviation does not resolve these old dilemmas in the field of international economic cooperation. It may even accentuate them.

RELATED READING

M. S. Ahluwalia, "Inequality, Poverty and Development," *Journal of Development Economics*, Vol. 3 (September 1976), pp. 307–42.
M. S. Ahluwalia, N. Carter, and H. Chenery, "Growth and Poverty in Developing Countries," Ch. 11 in H. Chenery, *Structural Change and Development Policy* (Oxford, U.K., Oxford University Press, 1979).
M. S. Ahluwalia and H. Chenery, "The Economic Framework," in H. Chenery et al. *Redistribution with Growth* (Oxford, U.K. Oxford University Press, 1974).
J. Edelman and H. Chenery, "Aid and Income Distribution," in *The New International Economic Order: The North-South Debate* edited by J. N. Bhagwati (Cambridge, Mass., M.I.T. Press, 1977).
C. R. Frank and R. C. Webb (Editors) *Income Distribution and Growth in the Less Developed Countries* (Princeton, New Jersey, Princeton University Press, 1977) Ch. 2.
D. Jorgensen and M. Nishimizu, "U.S. and Japanese Economic Growth, 1952–74: An International Comparison," *Economic Journal*, Vol. 88 (December 1978), pp. 707–26.
Nannerl Keohane, "The Idea of Progress Revisited," Stanford University (mimeo), 1979.
Simon Kuznets, "Economic Growth and Income Inequality," *American Economic Review*, Vol. 45 (March 1955), pp. 1–28.
Pitambar Pant, "Perspective of Development (1961–1976): Implications of Planning for a Minimum Level of Living," reprinted in T. N. Srinivasan and P. K. Bardhan, *Poverty and Income Distribution in India*, Statistical Publishing Society (Calcutta, India, 1974).
Dudley Seers, "Cuba" in Chenery *et al., Redistribution with Growth* (Oxford, U.K., Oxford University Press, 1974).
Paul Streeten, "Basic Needs: Premises and Promises," *Journal of Policy Modeling 1* (1979), pp. 136–46.
Paul Streeten and Shahid Javed Burki, "Basic Needs: Some Issues," *World Development*, Vol. 6, (March 1978), pp. 411–21.

10. Is There a Tradeoff Between Growth and Basic Needs?*

Norman L. Hicks

While the developing countries have had substantial increases in output during the past 25 years, it has been widely recognized that this growth has often failed to reduce the level of poverty in their countries. Various alternatives have been proposed to redress this problem—including strategies aimed at increasing employment, at developing rural areas, at redistributing the benefits of growth in favor of low income groups, and at meeting the basic needs of the poor. An approach that concentrates on meeting basic needs emphasizes improvements in health, nutrition, and basic education—especially through improved and redirected public services, such as rural water supplies, sanitation facilities, and primary schools. It has been argued that the direct provision of such goods and services affects poverty more immediately than those approaches that rely on raising the incomes and the productivity of the poor. . . .

The critical question for the individual country is: will the provision of basic goods and services slow down a country's growth rate? In other words, is there a tradeoff between growth and basic needs? From a theoretical standpoint there may be no necessary reason for such a tradeoff; but the evidence is not conclusive. Countries which have emphasized basic needs, such as Burma, Cuba, Sri Lanka, and Tanzania, may be seen to have done so at the cost of lower growth rates of output. On the other hand, one can point to countries such as Taiwan, Korea and Singapore, which have both grown relatively rapidly and made commendable progress in providing social services, reducing poverty, and improving the distribution of income. The issue is complicated by the many factors which affect growth other than the elements emphasized in theory: that is, the allocations of national resources between savings and consumption or between social services and other "productive" sectors. The true impact of an investment program oriented toward basic needs thus becomes very difficult to evaluate.

THE DEBATE

Proponents of a basic needs approach argue that the direct provision of essential goods and services is a more efficient and more rapid way of eliminating poverty than an approach based on hopes that the benefits of increased national growth will eventually reach the poor. While supporting efforts to raise productivity and income, they emphasize that these alone may be neither sufficient nor efficient. Their case rests on their experience that:

• the poor tend not to spend incremental income wisely or efficiently, since they may not be good managers or are not sufficiently knowledgeable about health and nutrition;
• there is serious maldistribution of incomes within households which cannot be overcome by raising family incomes but which can be corrected by the direct provision of goods and services to the neglected members;
• some basic needs—such as water supplies and sanitation—can only be met efficiently through public services; and
• it is difficult to formulate policies or investment strategies to increase the productivity of all of the poor in a uniform way.

The argument against directly providing for basic needs is based on two main contentions.

---

* From *Finance & Development*, vol. 17, no. 2 (June 1980), pp. 17–20.

First, transfers of essential goods and services result in increasing the consumption level of the poor at the cost of eventually reducing the net level of investment and saving in the economy and therefore the welfare of everybody. Second, the poor would be better provided for in the long run through the higher incomes realized by greater overall investment under a more conventional, growth-oriented development strategy. Meeting basic needs is seen as a strategy providing for a temporary consumption transfer to the poor, and not as a transfer of capital resources that would result in a permanent improvement in their condition.

The concept that basic needs can be better met in the long run through increased output appears faulty for two important reasons. First, the basic needs of the poor can be met in ways that have little or no direct effect on national levels of investment and growth—by reducing the consumption expenditures on nonessentials of the poor and the rich or by redirecting the expenditures of the public sector from nonbasic to basic needs activities. Second, it seems quite likely that expenditures on basic needs improve the productivity of human resources, and can therefore be considered a form of long-term investment in human capital. The question then becomes one of identifying the degree to which expenditures on basic needs actually result in permanent improvements in human capital, and whether economic returns to this form of human investment are higher than those from other kinds of investments available to developing countries.

CONFLICTING EVIDENCE

There is a considerable body of literature which attempts to identify the economic returns from improvements in human capital. In developed countries, considerable attention has been given to the concept of "growth accounting." In this approach, the growth of total output (measured by gross national product (GNP) is broken down into components

relating to the growth of factor inputs (land, labor, and capital) and an unexplained "residual" which captures productivity changes of an unidentified origin. While the earliest efforts in growth accounting can be traced back to George Stigler (1947), the definitive work remains that of Edward Denison (1967, 1974, 1979).

Denison's latest estimates show that less than 60 percent of the growth in GNP in the United States can be attributed to the increase in traditional factor inputs—labor and capital primarily—while the remainder is the result of economies of scale, improvements in resource allocation, and a large residual attributed to human capital, which is labeled "advances in knowledge." Education is considered by Denison to be a factor input which alone accounts for 14 percent of the growth of GNP between 1929 and 1976. If education is combined with the residual advances in knowledge, then the contribution of human capital to growth would be about 38 percent. Attempts to apply the same technique to developing countries (Krueger, 1968) tend to show similar results.

There is some question, however, whether the residual can be attributed to improvements in the stock of human capital. It could represent errors in the calculations of other variables, the omission of other important factors, or simply a faulty assumption about the nature of the underlying production function. While growth accounting attributes an important role to human capital in explaining growth, it does not necessarily *prove* that human capital is important. Thus it is not a completely reliable way to measure the contribution of human capital to the growth process.

An alternative way of assessing the impact of improvements in human capital is to measure the rate of return from education. This can be done by estimating the lifetime earnings of people with various levels of education, compared to the private and social costs of education, which include earnings forgone while at school. In general, these kinds of studies have found high rates of return from investment in education particularly from primary education in developing countries. A survey of 17 developing countries by Psacharopoulos (1973) found an average return of 25 percent for primary education. These returns range, however, from a low of 6.6 percent (Singapore, 1966) to a high of 82 percent (Venezuela, 1957).

There are considerable conceptual difficulties in measuring such rates of return on investments in human capital. The returns may be overstated because they capture the "screening" effect of higher education, which means that more highly educated people receive better paying jobs regardless of any true differentials in productivity. The high unemployment rate often found among highly educated people in some developing countries suggests that investments in education may not always raise productivity, particularly in those countries already possessing a large supply of educated persons. Several studies have questioned the utility of education investments in development. For instance, Correa (1970) found in a study of a group of Latin American countries that while health and nutrition were very important factors in GNP, improvements in education appeared to have no impact at all. Nadiri (1972) concluded from a survey of the published literature that education was not very useful in explaining differences in growth rates between developing countries, although it did seem to explain variations in productivity within countries over time. Thus, the evidence on the role of human capital, particularly education, in affecting the growth of output in developing countries is not definitive or measurable. Furthermore, the concept of human capital improvements covers areas (higher education is an example), which are not considered to be as relevant to a basic needs approach, and vice versa.

Another way of measuring the importance of human capital is to look at the statistical correlations between the provision of basic needs and the growth rates in a large number of countries. The problem with simple correlations is that they cannot identify the links between basic needs that have been met and growth. Better provision of basic goods and services is just as likely to be a result of higher incomes, as its cause. At the same time, growth in income is clearly going to be affected by factors other than those related to the provision of basic needs. Thus, one has to isolate the meeting of basic needs from other factors which can be considered important determinants of growth, in order to avoid giving too much weight to the basic needs variables.

MEASUREMENT PROBLEMS

We have no easy measure, however, of progress in meeting basic needs. A variety of social indicators can be used, but using them often presents conceptual problemss. Some indicators reflect results, while others—such as population per doctor and school enrollments —measure inputs. Some indicators measure the average level of social progress for the whole society, while others are based on a "have, "have-not" principle. Thus, the percentage of households with access to clean water can accurately capture the numbers without such service. By contrast, an average of the calories consumed per capita as percent of requirements is quite misleading, since it combines the overconsumption of the rich and the underconsumption of the poor. Likewise, figures on average life expectancy, or average infant mortality, do not give us any idea of the range between the rich and the poor. Two countries with identical average statistics for infant mortality, for instance, could have quite different infant mortality rates for their least favored groups. It would be more useful if social indicators provided data separately for different income groups within a population. There is no reason why we could not construct distribution statistics for social indicators similar to our measures of income distribution.

Until better indicators are produced, however, we are forced to use what we have readily available. It seems appropriate to use life expectancy at birth as one crude measure of the effectiveness of a country's success in providing for basic needs. This single measure can encompass the combined effects on mortality of health care, clean water, nutrition, and sanitation improvements, although it is admittedly an average of country experience with no feel for how well these have been provided for different groups within the population. Progress in meeting needs for primary education can be measured by adult literacy— a better indicator than primary school enrollment, since it is oriented toward effects rather than efforts. These two indicators—life expectancy and adult literacy—give crude but fairly useful measures of progress in meeting basic needs. Both indicators are generally available for most developing countries on a fairly reliable basis, which is not true for some alternative measures, such as infant mortality.

But even if we use these selected social indicators to measure progress in meeting basic needs, the problem of identifying causality remains. Is the progress in meeting basic needs shown by these indicators a result of growth in output, or is it one of the causes? One way to overcome this problem is to look at the data for growth rates of different countries compared to the levels of basic needs at the beginning of a particular period. If past achievements in meeting basic needs now require high levels of consumption expenditures, the data then should show that good basic needs performance has been associated with low growth. On the other hand, if provision of basic needs leads to an improvement in people's productivity, the indicators should show that basic needs are related to higher growth.

COMPARATIVE EVIDENCE

The simplest way of identifying the relationship between the provision of basic needs

and growth is to examine the record of countries that have grown very rapidly in the past and to compare their basic needs performance—measured by life expectancy and adult literacy—with that of the average country. Table 1 presents data for the 12 fastest growing countries between 1960 and 1977 (excluding the oil exporting countries and those with populations of under one million). The average per capita growth rate of these countries—5.7 percent per annum—was substantially higher than the average of all 83 countries in our sample. Further, the populations of this group of countries clearly had above-average life expectancy at the beginning of this period: 61 years, compared with an overall average of 48 years in all 83 countries.

This would seem to demonstrate that improving the provision of basic needs can augment the rate of growth. While this may be true, the data in the table contain a considerable bias. The countries that grew the fastest in the 1960–77 period were also countries which already had above-average levels of income. Since levels of income and life expectancy tend to be closely (but not perfectly) correlated, it is not surprising to find that the statistics for our 12 countries show above-average life expectancy.

To overcome this bias, an equation was established to relate life expectancy to income and to establish the "expected" level of life expectancy for every country. Better than normal performance on life expectancy could then be measured by the deviation between the actual and the expected levels. In a sense, this formula adjusts the level of life expectancy for the level of income. These deviations are shown in the third column of Table 1. The 12 countries in the sample have life expectancies that are, on average, 5.6 years higher than what normally would have been expected on the basis of their relative income level. Consequently, there does seem to be a positive association between life expectancy and growth, even when allowing for the fact that some of the more rapidly growing countries

TABLE 1. Economic Growth, Life Expectancy, and Literacy for Selected Countries

Country	Growth Rate 1960–77[1] (In Percent)	Life Expectancy 1960 (In Years)	Deviation from Expected Levels of Life Expectancy[2] (In Years)	Adult Literacy 1960 (In Percent)	Deviation from Expected Levels of Literacy, 1960[3] (In Percent)
Singapore	7.7	64.0	3.1	—	—
Korea	7.6	54.0	11.1	71.0	43.6
Taiwan	6.5	64.0	15.5	54.0	14.2
Hong Kong	6.3	65.0	6.5	70.0	6.4
Greece	6.1	68.0	5.7	81.0	7.5
Portugal	5.7	62.0	4.7	62.0	1.7
Spain	5.3	68.0	1.8	87.0	1.2
Yugoslavia	5.2	62.0	4.7	77.0	16.7
Brazil	4.9	57.0	3.0	61.0	8.6
Israel	4.6	69.0	2.0	—	—
Thailand	4.5	51.0	9.5	68.0	43.5
Tunisia	4.3	48.0	-0.5	16.0	-23.8
Average top 12 countries	5.7	61.0	5.6	64.7	12.0
Average—all countries[4]	2.4	48.0	-.0	37.6	-.0

Source: World Bank, *World Development Indicators, 1979.*
[1] Growth rate of real per capita GNP.
[2] Deviations from estimated values derived from an equation where life expectancy in 1960 (*LE*) is related to per capita income in 1960 (*Y*) in the following way: $LE = 34.29 + .07679\ Y - .000043\ Y^2\ (R^2 = .66)$.
[3] Deviations from estimated values derived from an equation where literacy in 1960 (*LIT*) is related to per capita income in 1967 (*Y*) in the following way: $LIT = 9.23 + .1595\ Y - .0000658\ Y^2\ (R^2 = .44)$.
[4] Data for average growth rates and life expectancy refer to a sample of 83 countries, while that for literacy covers 63 countries.

are also those at more advanced stages of development.

Adult literacy is another useful measure of a basic needs performance. Table 1 shows that in the rapidly growing countries, about 65 percent of adults were literate in 1960, compared with about 38 percent for the sample of 63 countries. Even when adjusted for income differences, literacy levels in the rapidly growing countries were about 12 percentage points higher than in the other countries at the beginning of the period.

The preceding analysis suggests that meeting basic needs may contribute significantly to growth, but it does not prove that the approach is a sufficient condition for high growth. In Table 2, we turn the question around and look at the 12 countries that have the highest deviation from expected levels of life expectancy. Many of the same countries

TABLE 2. Growth and Life Expectancy, Selected Countries

Country	Deviation from Expected Level of Life Expectancy (in years)	Growth Rate, 1960–77 (in Percent)
Sri Lanka	22.5	1.9
Taiwan	15.5	6.5
Korea	11.1	7.6
Thailand	9.5	4.5
Malaysia	7.3	4.0
Paraguay	6.9	2.4
Philippines	6.8	2.1
Hong Kong	6.5	6.3
Panama	6.1	3.7
Burma	6.0	0.9
Greece	5.7	6.1
Kenya	5.5	2.4
Average, 12 countries	9.1	4.0
Average, all countries	0	2.4

Source: *World Bank, World Development Indicators, 1979.*
Note: For explanation of variables, see Table 1.

shown in Table 1 appear here, namely, Taiwan, Korea, Thailand, Hong Kong, and Greece. In addition, there are a number of other countries which have done well in terms of life expectancy but have not had exceptionally high growth rates during the period, such as Sri Lanka, Paraguay, the Philippines, Burma, and Kenya. Nevertheless, the average growth rate for this second group of 12 countries—4.0 percent per annum—is still considerably higher than the average for the larger group.

One might argue, however, that the simple statistical analysis presented here is inadequate for drawing firm conclusions. The growth performance of countries is dependent on a variety of factors, such as the level of investment, export earnings and capital flows, and the general nature of development policies pursued.

The influence of these factors, as well as the emphasis on basic needs, can be combined and analyzed using multiple regression techniques on the cross-country data. This has been done for the period 1960–73 (see Hicks, 1979), regressing the growth rate of per capita GNP on the investment rate, the growth rate of imports, and the levels of either literacy or life expectancy in 1960. (The growth rate of imports combines the effects of export growth and capital flows.) This analysis concluded that the basic needs variables were significantly related to the growth rate, even after allowing for the influence of the other variables. It was found that countries which had life expectancies ten years higher than expected tended to have per capita growth rates 0.7 to 0.9 percentage points higher. Thus the more sophisticated techniques confirm the simpler ones shown here, which already concluded that those countries which do well in providing for basic needs tend to have better than average performance in terms of economic growth. This would also seem to suggest that a basic needs emphasis in development, far from reducing the rate of growth, can be instrumental in increasing it.

It would appear that economists who formerly focused on human capital may have concentrated too narrowly on one aspect of human capital, namely education. It seems possible that other aspects of a basic needs approach to development, which aim to improve the health and living conditions of the poor, should also be considered as building up a country's human capital. Exactly how health and related basic needs improvements help increase productivity and growth in the economy is difficult to pinpoint. The most obvious relationship is that healthy workers can produce more, work harder and longer, and so on. In addition, healthy students are apt to learn more. Improved health conditions reduce the waste of human and physical resources which results from the bearing and raising children who die before they reach productive ages. The prospect of a short life expectancy reduces the potential gain from long years of schooling. These kinds of gains in productivity from investments in health and education are now being recognized as important as the returns from investments in the more standard forms of physical capital. In other words, investing in people may be a good way to both eliminate the worst aspects of poverty and to increase the growth rate of output.

RELATED READING

M. S. Ahluwalia, and H. B. Chenery, "A Model of Distribution and Growth," in Chenery, *et al. Redistribution with Growth* (Oxford: Oxford University Press, 1974).

Mark Blaug, "Human Capital Theory: A Slightly Jaundiced Survey," *Journal of Economic Literature* Vol. 14 (September, 1976), pp. 827–56.

Héctor Correa, "Sources of Growth in Latin America," *Southern Economic Journal*, Vol. 37 (July 1970), pp. 17–31.

E. F. Denison, *Why Growth Rates Differ: Postwar Experience in Nine Western Countries*, (Washington, D.C.: Brookings Institution, 1967); *Accounting for United States Economic Growth, 1929–1969* (Washington, D.C.: Brookings Institution, 1974); *Accounting for Slower Growth* (Washington, D.C.: Brookings Institution, 1979).

Norman Hicks, "Growth vs. Basic Needs: Is There a Trade-Off?" *World Development*, Vol. 7 (November/December 1979), pp. 985–94.

Norman Hicks, and Paul Streeten, "Indicators of Development: The Search for a Basic Needs Yardstick," *World Development*, Vol. 7 (June 1979), pp. 567–80.

Anne O. Krueger, "Factor Endowments and Per Capita Income," *Economic Journal*, Vol. 78 (September 1968), pp. 641–59.

David Morawetz, *Twenty Five Years of Economic Development* (Washington, D.C.: The World Bank, 1977).

M. Ishaq Nadiri, "International Studies of Factor Imports and Total Factor Productivity: A Brief Survey," *Review of Income and Wealth*, Series 18 (June 1972), pp. 129–54.

George Psacharopoulos, *Returns to Education* (San Francisco/Washington: Jossey-Bass, 1973).

F. Stewart, and Paul Streeten, "New Strategies for Development: Poverty, Income Distribution and Growth," *Oxford Economic Papers*, 28 (1976).

G. J. Stigler, *Trends in Output and Employment* (New York, National Bureau for Economic Research, 1947).

Paul Streeten, "Basic Needs: Premises and Promises," *Journal of Policy Modeling 1*, (1979), pp. 136–46.

Paul Streeten, and S. J. Burki, "Basic Needs: Some Issues," *World Development, 6* (March 1978), pp. 411–21.

11. Policy Choices and Income Distribution in Less Developed Countries*

Charles R. Frank, Jr. and Richard Webb

FACTORS THAT ARE RAISING INCOMES OF THE POOR

The cross-country evidence on income trends for the poor in developing countries presents a picture of rising absolute incomes in a broad variety of economic and political settings, usually, though not always, accompanied by increasing relative inequality. The most striking cases of reduction of poverty are under the socialist economies and in countries with rapid growth rates, notably South Korea and Taiwan. There are various reasons for the good performance on poverty in these countries, some of which have implications for policy in other settings.

(1) First, social services such as education, population control, medical care, sanitation and water supplies, are widely available for the poor as well as the rich. Some socialist countries, such as the Peoples Republic of China, Cuba, North Vietnam, and Tanzania, have a paramedical approach to health care, emphasizing inexpensive and widespread treatment. By contrast, conventional health programs involve highly trained doctors and expensive care in narrowly distributed services. But there are also examples of wide distribution of social services in nonsocialist countries: for example, Taiwan emphasizes services for the rural poor, partly for historical reasons.

(2) A second factor favoring widespread distribution of income in some countries is cultural homogeneity among the population. This, for example, seems to be a significant factor in Korea.

(3) In those countries where society places a high value on education, such as Korea and China, the population can become highly literate and well educated even at low levels of development. Widespread educational attainment prevents the emergence of large wage and salary differentials based on acute shortages of skilled and educated manpower.

(4) In countries with good transportation and communication facilities, regional disparities in income are less marked. Capital, labor, and product markets are more highly integrated. Growth which begins in one region can spread more quickly to others. In contrast, countries with relatively poor transport and communication facilities suffer from increasing regional disparities which exacerbate the national distribution of income.

(5) Another important reason for the even distribution of income is a relatively equal distribution of land, such as occurs in many African and Asian countries. In large sparsely populated parts of Africa the size of a man's holding is often the maximum he can farm with traditional methods. In revolutionary socialist countries such as Cuba, North Vietnam, and North Korea, access to land is widely distributed because of radical land reform. Land reform has also been successful in nonsocialist countries: in South Korea and Taiwan, land reform occurred when a new regime came into power, representing ethnic groups different from those of the landholders.

---

* From *Income Distribution and Growth in LDCs*. Brookings Institution, Washington, D.C., 1977, Chapter 1. Extracted and reprinted in *Development Digest*, vol. 16, no. 3 (July 1978), pp. 95–116.

(6) Finally, trade and industrialization policies seem to be involved in the more satisfactory experience of some countries. An inward-looking, import-substitution strategy often involves protection for the high-income, urbanized, modern sector of the economy at the expense of the urban and rural poor. Controls and quotas on imports and investments create monopoly rents which accrue to the wealthy. Protective tariffs and import controls enable techniques to be used which are highly capital-intensive (though inefficient), and much higher wages can be paid to the highly organized elites in the modern sector. In India, such effects have been reinforced by government policies that have kept the prices of energy, raw materials, and refined metals charged by both public- and private-sector producers comparatively low, in effect subsidizing the modern-sector industrialists.

When tariffs are moderate and not highly variable from sector to sector, however, and export incentives are generally low and used at most to compensate for moderate levels of protection to import-substitution industries, then wage rates in the modern sector are not significantly different from those in urban traditional sectors. The distinction between modern and traditional sectors becomes blurred as their respective labor and capital markets are more integrated. In countries with moderate and equable protection, profit rates tend to be high but reinvestment is also high, growth is rapid, and the absorption of underutilized labor into high-productivity jobs reduces absolute poverty more rapidly.

Some of the causes of relative equality in the distribution of income, such as the cultural and geographical homogeneity, are difficult to promote by deliberate policy changes. Land reform, distribution of social services, building of transportation and communication networks, and setting rules of protection and sub-sidy, however, are government actions that can have great influence on the distribution of income over a period of time far less than a generation.

HOW POLICIES REINFORCE INEQUALITY

We may start with the hypothesis that a developing economy will first experience a worsening and then an improvement in the distribution of income. This pattern, sometimes called the U-shaped effect,...can be attributed to the mechanics of absorption of workers from the traditional sector into the modern sector. However, this pattern, caused by redistribution of population between the two major sectors of the economy, is generally reinforced by government policies. For example, medical facilities tend to be built in the major urban centers. In the initial stages of development, when the degree of urbanization is low, very few segments of the population have access to medical services. Furthermore, since incomes tend to be higher in the urban areas and the political and economic elites are usually located there, the provision of medical services worsens the distribution of income in the early stages of development. Later on, however, as medical facilities spread into rural areas, medical help becomes available to wider segments of the population; and as the proportion of the population living in cities increases, more people gain access to medical facilities.

Education also tends to exacerbate income differentials in the early stages of development. Initial government efforts involve expansion of secondary schools and university education. In Africa, for instance, the departure of former colonial powers left a great need for Africanization of the elite ranks of the civil service and of major firms in the private sector, requiring a large expansion in higher education. In such cases, the provision of educational facilities initially widens disparities because of unequal opportunities for educational advancement. In most countries, however, the urban population has successfully pressed for rapid expansion in secondary and university education irrespective of the degree of social need. As development has taken place, universal primary education has become a more feasible goal, and gradually more education is provided on a universal basis.

Population policy also reinforces the U-shaped effect. Initial demographic changes in a less developed country bring a lowering of the death rate, usually most markedly among the poor. The poor also tend to have higher birth rates. Overall, birth rates tend to fall much more slowly than death rates and only after initial reductions in mortality. Thus poor families tend to have a very much larger family size in the initial stages of the demographic transition. Conversely, the decline in the birth rate seems to occur first among higher income and urbanized segments of the population. For one thing, the desire to limit family size occurs most often among wealthier, urban, more educated population groups, so their demand for population-control services is greater. Moreover, the distribution networks for such services are usually weak in the initial stages of a program, and those who do have access tend to be the more educated and urbanized. Government efforts to promote population control are therefore apt initially to be skewed toward more educated urban and higher-income groups. When wealthier families have much smaller families than poor families, the result is that the per capita distribution of income will worsen relative to a given distribution of income by family. Only in the later stages of a family planning program are techniques devised for distribution of population-control devices and information to the rural poor scattered throughout the countryside. At this stage, the earlier tendency may be reversed.

Public housing projects tend also to go, not to the poorest groups in the population, but to the middle- and upper-income groups. First of all, housing programs tend to be concentrated in urban rather than in rural areas. But even within urban areas the poorest groups are rarely helped. Benefiting relatively poor groups often requires site and service projects, which involve the laying out of streets and sewer lines and provision of some basic minimum services while allowing squatters to construct their own housing on land prepared by government. Even if the resources needed to carry out such projects can be mobilized, there is no way of assuring that access to the facilities is limited to the very poorest segments of the population, who often lack the knowledge and skills to become eligible for inclusions.

GOALS FOR REDISTRIBUTIVE POLICIES

Past discussions of redistributive policy have been clouded by a failure to recognize that redistribution means different things to different people. "Social justice" is in reality an ethical compound made up of several separable goals, such as the desire to alleviate extreme poverty, to increase mobility from lower to higher income levels, to remove excessively high incomes, and/or to reduce income dispersion per se. For many people, some sources of inequality are more acceptable than others. And, obviously, ideas differ regarding the tolerable or optimum degree of inequality. Distributive policy-making has been confused by treating these separate social goals as a single norm, and the practice of measuring and discussing income distribution as a single number, e.g., a Gini coefficient, has reinforced that confusion.

The disaggregation or separate treatment of redistributive goals helps to overcome some of the conceptual and practical difficulties attending the presumed tradeoff between growth and equality. Both the earlier arguments that stressed a conflict between these goals (e.g., because greater productivity at work had to be rewarded to preserve incentives, and because capitalists save more), as well as the more recent counter-arguments that claim complementarities (e.g., because large farms are inefficiently managed, and the rich consume capital- and import-intensive goods), can be unhelpful overgeneralizations once the policy issues are phrased in terms of specific target groups and specific tools of redistribution. Disaggregation permits a more constructive approach that involves searching for particular combinations of policies and target groups that will make best use of potential complementarities, or if these cannot be found will at least minimize tradeoffs.

Disaggregation also brings out into the open what is surely the principal conflict in the design of distributive strategy—that between most aid-givers and foreign observers, who currently tend to emphasize the alleviation of extreme poverty, and governments of most developing countries, which are more likely to favor urban and labor groups that fall outside most definitions of extreme poverty. Both A.I.D. and the World Bank, for instance, define target groups in terms of poverty levels alone. As outsiders, they can more easily assume a position of statistical impersonality, detached from the particular social groups that dominate the distributive discussion in each country. The compelling economic justice of this approach is matched by its apparent maximization of financial feasibility, since it generates the greatest additional welfare for any given amount extracted from the rich: simple calculation shows that relatively small transfers make relatively large improvements possible for the very poor, thanks to the leverage provided by extreme inequalities. There remain, of course, the enormous and, to some, intractable problems of how to deliver that income.

Within developing countries, on the other hand, "economic justice" covers a host of distributive goals among which the attack on extreme poverty has, with few exceptions, been least important. The principal thrust of redistribution has been an attack on extreme wealth, with a redistribution in favor of organized and urban labor groups that are usually in the top quartile or third of the income distribution. This pattern has generally accompanied the transfer of power to middle-class reformist elites. In some countries, e.g., Nigeria and Brazil, rapid growth and/or social mobility has had the self-justifying effect of elevating the goal of economic mobility within the hierarchy of social goals, at least in the eyes of the elites. Finally, regional and communal income differences are in center stage in the distributive battles of almost all countries. As a result of all these factors, the growing concern with extreme poverty among aid-givers today is rejected as a foreign conception in many LDCs—despite the prevalence of minimum wage laws, despite the official attention placed on extreme poverty by a few countries such as India, and even despite the egalitarian current that has flowed from Cuba and China.

The logic of the antipoverty goal misses the strong roots that justice has in the LDCs in the notion of "desert," i.e., that what people deserve, or have a right to, depends on what they have done or on who they are. The particular choice of redistributive targets by LDCs is thus strongly shaped by these conceptions of socially deserved or justified distribution. Social justification, for instance, explains the much stronger attacks on the "unearned" income and usually inherited property of landowners than on the often self-made and seemingly more growth-relevant wealth of industrialists. It helps to explain the much greater strength of demands for redistribution via wage increases and agrarian reform than for the less visibly legitimized sharing associated with fiscal transfers from the richer modern sector as a whole to the rest of the economy. Also relevant to the legitimacy of higher incomes is the question of whether they are believed to have been obtained by "corrupt" methods. While definitions of unacceptable corruption may vary widely among groups, and over time, and such definitions may be inaccurately or inconsistently applied, nevertheless this aspect has considerable influence on the level of tolerance for high incomes. The notion of desert is also a major force underlying the distaste, by LDC policy makers as well as aid donors, for current-income transfers to the poor, except through slow-acting "job-creating" and "productivity-raising" programs. Even the extremely poor must be seen to "earn" their incomes.

Those who deplore the neglect of the very poor by most developing countries note that much of the attention given to competing moral claims is window dressing for political aims; that clumsy policy design and implementation account for some of the neglect, as when regional income differences are used as proxy indicators of poverty; and finally, that much of the current design of redistributive programs—for instance, attacks on the wealthy, and the preoccupation with the highly visible urban poor—reflects the preferences of elites, and not of the poorer majorities. These arguments, however, do not remove the dilemma faced by foreigners offering policy advice or aid to developing countries: to what extent should they accept the distributive goals of LDC governments, or to what extent should the "true" (as assumed by the foreigner) distributive preferences of the poor be respected? This dilemma is most evident, of course, with regard to the desired *degree* of redistribution.

THE SCOPE FOR POLICY

One view of the scope for redistributive policies is that the existing distribution of income (including government benefits) is closely determined by the distribution of political power. There exists what could be described as a "tight fit" between economic and political power. By this view, it is useless to discuss policies that would alter the current situation to the disadvantage of the powerful, who can and will prevent any real change. The repeated frustrations of reformers, who often fail to put across even minor and seemingly almost costless changes, appear to bear out this pessimistic assessment. The implication is, of course, that radical political change must precede any significant improvement in the lot of the poor. Our view is that, despite the weight of existing power and wealth, the relationship between power and income is more complex and fluid than implied by this "tight fit" argument. A better knowledge of the various factors affecting that relationship should, therefore, provide a basis for assessing the opportunities for, and limits to, possible reform.

Political Factors

There is not a strong correlation between the political difficulty of making a given income transfer and the amount involved. The acceptability of any transfer depends also on the mode and purpose of the transfer. This is partly a matter of visibility and partly one of moral legitimacy. It is usually more difficult to extract incomes already received, via direct taxes for instance, than to spirit them away en route to the recipient through a market-price adjustment such as a tariff, a differential exchange rate, or an excise tax.

Perhaps more important is the role of moral legitimacy, particularly in relation to the purpose of a transfer. In general, transfers are more acceptable when destined to raise productivity than to subsidize current consumption. Education has a particularly high degree of legitimacy, perhaps largely because it is associated with productivity—though the right to education seems to have an independent status not enjoyed by any other benefit provided to the poor. A greater moral acceptability of productivity transfers to the poor may often coincide with self-interest on the part of business elites, who benefit from more productive workers and from larger consumer markets. The nationalist motives of elites, particularly the military, can also favor resource transfers to the poor. National strength is built up through the cultural and territorial integration of poor regions (especially in border areas), by upgrading a nation's human resources, and by reducing income disparities that may become a source of internal friction and instability.

The political process can generate more power for the poor than that provided by their scanty private command over economic resources. This can result from competition among elites, chiefly in democratic or quasi-democratic systems where electoral body-counts matter. And it can result from erratic discontinuities and interruptions that upset a class-based political order, such as military coups. If there is a fluid, competitive, pluralistic political regime, for instance, the disadvantaged can be helped by coalitions with middle- or upper-income subgroups who identify or share some interests with the poor. Not all interests are class based: ethnic or regional interest may cut across class; patron-client networks and personal factions are of many kinds. So there may be more fluidity in a political system than a class analysis would allow, and coalitions can be made by varied groups which link different income levels.

The latitude for policy change can increase if political power, like income, spreads out and eventually trickles down to the very poor and disenfranchised. This can happen, for instance, when elite groups look for allies among middle-class and poorer income groups. There are also class renegades, and institutional groups like the military who may look for allies outside the older elite groups. One pattern of change in the configuration of political power has involved the following steps: first, control lies in the hands of a few landed oligarchs, foreign executives of large foreign enterprises plus a small indigenous business elite, or some combination of these. In the next stage, a reform regime emerges which represents new interest groups in the middle- and upper-middle-income brackets. Later, power is seized by organized labor, government civil servants, or military officers.

This pattern is evidenced in the rise to power of Bhutto in Pakistan, the formation of an RPP government in Turkey in 1973, and in the developments that culminated in a military takeover in Peru.

Although the rhetoric of reform seems to be responsive to the needs of the poor, often the policies that are followed help not the poorest groups but the middle-income groups that provide the political backing for the regime. For example, it is widely recognized that the Chilean and Peruvian land reforms mostly benefited the better-off minority of workers on large estates, while small subsistence farmers and landless laborers tended to be hurt by adverse price policies. In the case of Turkey, the first moves of the new RPP reform regime were to raise minimum wages by eighty percent and to increase farm price supports substantially. The former was a way of redistributing income in urban areas, the latter an attempt to help farmers. But increases in minimum wages and salaries for organized labor and civil servants increased demands for food and other consumer goods to the detriment of the very poor self-employed tradesmen or casual workers, and of the rural poor without enough land for their own food needs. Increases in price supports helped the large landholders most. The majority of urban poor, landless laborers, and small landholders were hurt, although the demand for wage labor on the larger farms was increased through the higher price supports.

Although the initial efforts of a reform regime may not be to help the very poor, the loss of power by the very wealthy may be a necessary first step toward the eventual total restructuring of political power. As the middle-class groups gain power, they will in turn come under pressure from poorer groups who begin to organize or be organized and to articulate their needs more effectively. One possible explanation of political trickle-down is a ratchet-effect: many social gains are easier to achieve than to reverse. Once income taxes have been legislated, schools built, unions allowed to operate, and land redistributed, the beneficiaries become more conscious of their benefits, and are more easily mobilized in the defense of those benefits than they would have been for promised benefits at an earlier stage. As a result, successive, though perhaps only occasional, leftward swings of the political pendulum cause a gradual leftward drift in the political center of gravity. Historical trends in labor legislation are good illustrations of this process. The process can be reversed by forceful repression and, perhaps, using time to erode gains that even a strong rightist government cannot afford to attack frontally.

Under some political, cultural, or historical circumstances the process of political trickledown through the middle groups can be bypassed or foreshortened. In Tanzania, for example, the power and prestige of a highly purposed leader, Julius Nyerere, has resulted in programs which help the very poor. Nyerere has suppressed organized labor in urban areas and made conscious attempts to organize a power base among the rural poor. Some compromises had to be made with a powerful civil service to keep it under restraint, but there was no revolution. This pattern of change has been unusual, however.

In some countries there have been conspicuous divergences between economic and political power that led to equalizing policies. For example, in Taiwan the Nationalist Chinese from the mainland has overwhelming political power, yet the native Taiwanese had much greater economic resources in land and capital. The Chinese political elites used the system of government to increase their groups' incomes and access to public services. In East Africa, economic power was largely in the hands of foreign firms and local Asian groups, and with independence the indigenous Africans used their new political power to economic advantage. Foreign firms, foreign executives of local firms, and highly paid foreign civil servants gradually were squeezed out;

Asians have been progressively circumscribed (and in Uganda expelled).

If there are so many potential sources of slippage between political and economic power, and, consequently, of possible gains by the poor, why are incomes distributed so unequally? Why is there so much absolute poverty? The preceding discussion has been deliberately biased toward stressing the possible sources of reform; it is meant to suggest where to look for opportunities for change. The political constraints are more obvious and well known. But the above reasoning also points to an additional conclusion: the constraints on redistribution are not wholly political, and perhaps not even primarily political. The degree of inequality, for instance, and the extent of absolute poverty are not radically less in most countries usually described as socialist or as more egalitarian (though they do appear to be radically less in the Communist regimes of Cuba and China). Part of the explanation of this paradox lies in economic factors that also determine the scope for redistribution.

Economic Factors

Redistribution is easier the more concentrated are: (1) markets and the sources of income or, what often comes to the same thing, the greater the component of economic rent (surplus over direct costs) in income; and (2) the target group of the poor.

(1) *Markets*. Most redistributive instruments involve some form of continuous market interference. Such is the case, for instance, in respect to taxes, price controls, and wage setting. Even once-over transfers, such as property redistribution, create temporary market repercussions. When policy makers decide to interfere in a market for redistributive purposes, they must access the extent of the resultant market disequilibrium between supply and demand. The greater the disequilibrium or "market tension," the greater will be the need for political and administra-

tive resources to implement or enforce that distortion. Since political and administrative resources are limited, the nature of markets must be an important consideration in the choice of redistributive instruments and targets. In general, low elasticities of supply or demand (i.e., smaller responses to changes in price) imply smaller disequilibria and, therefore, easier implementation of policies affecting market prices.

This point is best illustrated by considering two extreme cases. A tax on domestic oil production is extremely easy to administer, and it has minimal market repercussions. Such a tax need entail no sharp fall in supply of the sort that would upset consumers. Nor is it likely to cause quick unemployment of oil industry workers. In short, political costs are low. At the other extreme, a minimum wage for domestic servants is almost impossible to administer. If it *were* implemented, many servants would become unemployed and many houses would be without help. Competitive markets, with large numbers of dispersed buyers and sellers, are a powerful defense against attempts to divert or appropriate income flows originating in those markets. By contrast, it is easier to interfere in markets where production is geographically concentrated, or carried out by few firms and a small number of workers, or in which the rent (from owning a natural resource) or quasi-rent (from long-lived capital investment) is high. An important additional consideration is that international trade creates a powerful mechanism for enforcing taxation by concentrating the flow of products through a few transit points.

The nature of markets is thus a powerful determinant of how much policy-created redistribution occurs, and whom it affects. In a country such as India, with an economy that is predominantly agricultural and oriented to internal markets, there is much less room for political influence on income flows; the income distribution is primarily market determined. The major exception to this is the possibility of land redistribution, which is constrained more by political than by market problems. By contrast, political control has been a major determinant of income distribution in the oil- and mineral-producing countries, as well as in such agricultural exporting countries as Ghana, Nigeria, Argentina, and Uruguay, where export taxes, tariffs, and exchange rate policy have been used by urban groups to appropriate a large share of the income originating in agriculture.

With respect to differences among sectors within countries, it can be seen that the socialist or egalitarian leanings of many developing countries have been powerfully constrained by the dispersed, atomistic nature of their rural and traditional sectors. Socialism in most of these countries is limited to the modern sector. Massive administrative and political resources are required to extend political control to traditional-sector labor, capital, and product markets. The principal exceptions occur when agricultural exports, or concentrated land ownership, provide opportunities for economically easier income redistribution in the traditional sector.

(2) The economic feasibility of redistribution is also affected by the degree of concentration or fragmentation of *target groups of the poor* by regions, occupations, productive sectors, and other groupings that are relevant to the normal coverage of redistributive instruments. Most transfers, be they services such as schools and health or resources such as roads and credit, usually benefit groups rather than individuals. A group can be a village, a district, an occupational class, farmers producing a particular crop, or the consumers of a particular product. The target efficiency of any transfer of money or services, i.e., the proportion of the transfer that actually reaches the target group, depends both on the discriminatory ability of the transfer mechanism and on the degree of concentration of the target group.

In the simplest and cheapest case, the poor

will be concentrated in one region; they will specialize in one occupation or productive activity; and no rich, or nontarget, individuals will live in that region or be dedicated to that activity. Efficient transfers to the poor could then be expected. However, if there are some poor in most villages, in most regions, and in most occupations and activities, it will be far more expensive to make any given income transfer to them. The income available for transfer will be diluted, either because many nonpoor will also benefit (e.g., the rich members of a village to which a road has been built), or because it is administratively expensive to discriminate and ensure that only the poor get the benefit. The clumsiness of most distributive instruments and the relatively dispersed nature of the poor in most countries can greatly magnify the cost of achieving any given increase in welfare for the poor. Policy makers should therefore become acquainted with the coverage of different policy instruments and with the location, sources of income, consumption habits, and other features of the poor.

In sum, we have argued that opportunities for redistribution are not necessarily tightly constrained by the balance of power, and that they are strongly influenced by structural characteristics of the economy. This suggests a great variety of conditions among different countries. Given the variations in distributive goals, in sources of slippage between economic and political power, and in the structural features of different economies, it is hard to conceive a situation in which all of these elements are so aligned that they preclude any possibility of improvement.

POLICY DESIGN

Effective policy design for income distribution requires three elements. First, account must be taken of the broader economic and social policy context, particularly of the way in which other purposes, such as economic growth and stability, are being pursued. Second, policies must make economic sense: taken together, their important direct and indirect economic effects must be of a kind that will have a net favorable result for the poor. Third, political and administrative elements will be critical to the implementation of policies. Commitments to reduce inequality, taken at the highest level of government, may make unrealistic demands on administrative capacities, or they may be subverted because they run counter to the interests and attitudes of bureaucrats, or they may be weakened through the pressure of interest groups working on the bureaucracy.

The Policy Context

Redistribution is rarely an overriding policy concern. Even the more socialist countries are strongly committed to economic growth and stability. Redistribution often becomes paramount immediately after a sharp leftward shift in government. Then the period of intense commitment to reforms, generally involving wage increases, nationalization, and a start toward land reform, is usually followed by a return to the growth objective, and often to some kinds of retrenchment made necessary by the stabilization and growth problems that result from redistributive "excess." Most of the time, and across most of the political spectrum, there is little scope for policies which appear to conflict with growth.

Planning for redistribution, therefore, has much to gain from a joint examination of growth, stability, and distribution policies. A large part of the total policy impact on income distribution will usually consist of byproduct effects of policies aimed principally at growth and stability, so that much of the opportunity for achieving a better income distribution will consist of improvements in the design of policies that are not primarily aimed at distribution. Also, the sensible objective is to attain some degree of *net* redistribution, not to ensure the maximum progressive impact of each policy instrument. Finally, if the principal distributive goal is to reduce absolute poverty rather than to narrow income differentials, then growth, as long as it entails some spillover to the poor, is not an alternative objective; it is itself an instrument, along with redistribution, for reducing poverty.

Indirect Economic Effects

In designing redistribution policies, full account should be taken of the indirect as well as the direct effects. Often policies meant to redistribute income toward the poor do just the reverse because of unanticipated indirect effects. There can be *economic backlash*. It may be partial, or it may completely reverse the intended direction of the policy effort.

Often unintended backlash occurs because of a simple failure to understand the proper relationships of supply and demand. When prices are controlled at low levels, for example, quantities supplied are reduced. If the price of food is kept low through concern for the poor, less food may be available. The poor end up suffering because little food is sold at controlled prices, and they may have to supplement purchases at controlled prices with purchases at high prices in the black market. Similarly, credit policies which encourage low interest rates for small farmers do not provide sufficient returns for lenders to cover their costs. The result is a reduction in the low cost institutional credit available to small farmers, much of which actually flows to large farmers, while the small men must turn to high cost moneylenders.

Another kind of economic backlash occurs whenever quantities are controlled. For example, import controls, whether on such luxury goods as refrigerators and cars or on such essentials as tractors, force up prices. Windfall gains accrue to existing owners and to those lucky enough to obtain import licenses, thus redistributing income toward unintended groups. A third form of economic backlash can occur because of a failure to consider the external sector of the economy. For example, high levels of taxation on incomes encourage emigration by the professional people—doctors, engineers, and university professors—who have significant opportunities to practice outside the country. Likewise, stiff taxes on profits, interest, and other returns to capital may encourage capital to leave the country, both legally and illegally.

Backlash can occur when the long-run effects counteract the favorable short-run effects. The initial effect of public works projects, for example, may be to help the rural poor, particularly by providing employment and raising unskilled wages, but the eventual beneficiaries of public works projects may be more the large landholders, whose incomes rise in response to the building of new access roads and better irrigation facilities. Economic backlash can also occur because the aggregate effects of a policy differ from its micro effects—the famous fallacy of composition. As an example: one small wheat farmer may benefit from rural education and extension programs, cheap capital, and subsidized farm inputs. If the program is expanded on a large scale, however, the resulting decrease in farm prices may be so great that it reduces the income of all small wheat farmers. In addition, backlash can occur because government activities in part of the economy affect expectations and business behavior in other parts. Nationalization of some enterprises may effect the expectations of entrepreneurs elsewhere in the private sector so adversely that investment and profits decline, and government resources available for redistributive purposes are thereby reduced.

Finally, backlash may occur through general equilibrium effects. For example, increases in the wages of civil servants and modern-sector laborers can have a depressive effect on traditional-sector incomes, as noted earlier. Not only is labor absorption from the traditional to the modern sector reduced, but induced migration from rural to urban areas adds to the labor supply in the urban traditional sector, further adding to downward pressure on wages. Within agriculture, the Green Revolution may in many cases have hurt as much as it helped the poor: rising land rents and induced mechanization have often reduced job opportunities for landless laborers and resulted in the eviction of small tenant farmers from land. There can be political backlash effects too. Growing concentration of income and wealth may make future redistribution politically more difficult, even requiring the instruments of coercion. A government may have to face the negative reactions of those who lose out when redistribution means taking from some to give to others. The costs of implementing such a policy may turn out to be greater than anticipated.

A number of approaches to avoid the pitfalls of backlash are possible. For example, a progressive expenditure rather than income tax will mitigate the capital flight caused by steeply progressive income taxes, since savings would be exempted from taxation. A self-assessment approach to land taxation may avoid the incentive to corruption and cheating. (Property owners would be subject to forced sale at the self-assessed value declared for tax purposes.) Charging students for higher education (received largely by children of rich families) will improve the allocation of public funding for education by leaving more money for the schools, and would reduce the problem of underemployment of educated people. In planning public works, feeder roads can be built into areas in which small farmers predominate, small-scale irrigation works can be provided for peasant farmers, or cooperatives formed to take advantage of capital improvements such as tubewells which are normally available only to large farmers.

Policy Implementation

John D. Montgomery has noted that most income-equalizing forms of public intervention are not policies but programs. Questions must therefore be asked about administrative factors. Administrative personnel have their own class-based or ethnic-based predilections; they have professional commitments: and they have constituencies that they service and that pressure them. Thus, for example, some health ministries have been very resistant to paramedical training and development programs. Administrative structures have preferences for different kinds of technological or delivery systems, as well as preferences for substantive goals.

There are often conflicts between different central ministries, between general and specialized administrators, and between agents in the field and personnel working at headquarters. There can be conflicts between agents of local or regional governments and central government agents. The outcome of the interactions between levels and types of bureaucracies cannot be a matter of indifference to those concerned with redistributive policies. The ways that taxes are collected, and whether or not they are actually collected, may depend very much on the agent or extractive channels employed in tax collection. What standards will govern the administrative agents? How can they be held accountable and to whom? Which policies will be administered faithfully, and which will simply be avoided or bent to the "private-regarding" interests of bureaucracies? The first question that a policy maker designing a tax structure might ask in a developing country is not: how will it play politically, but will it go down among the people who are supposed to administer the program? As noted, credit and agricultural extension policies often have chiefly benefited rural elites. This may be because administrators prefer to deal with people more like themselves in values or education, or they may respond to those who can write or otherwise make their voices heard, or they may have more of a professional interest in agricultural innovations than in problems of rural poverty.

Thus, it has to be asked: What levers exist for bending administrative structures in new ways? It is one thing to give civil servants technical knowledge, and another to succeed in changing their practice, giving them new or different skills and making them want to use them. Obviously the strength of structures other than those of civil service matters here. The relationship of party and/or army to civil service will be critical. The supply of administrative or potential administrative personnel will be important too. And just as splits within a political elite give leverage to reform-minded actors, so do splits within and between bureaucracies. It may be possible to appeal to people on a rank and age basis, although this may disrupt civil service lines of command. It may be possible to appeal to administrators to suppport redistributive programs on professional grounds, that is, in terms of efficiency.

In the end, however, it may be necessary to circumvent the formal administrative structure. This is easier to do when the intended social changes can be brought about quickly, as in land seizure or nationalizations, than when redistributions are sought over lengthy periods of time. Indeed, one of the attractions of nonreformist or radical redistribution policies has been that they might be applied not by the normal administrative agents of control but by special ones—e.g., the military in Peru, peasant committees for land reform in various countries, or "shock troop" industrial workers brought to the countryside to help collectivize in the Soviet Union. The dangers of these policies are obvious: deflection from other duties of the agents used; disruption of the functioning of the regular bureaucracy; and turmoil and inefficiency.

THE PROSPECTS FOR BETTER POLICIES

Any redistributive strategy must consider three separate problems: how to take from the rich, how to give to the poor, and how to reduce the need for redistribution by improving the market as a distributive mechanism. The

relative stress placed on each will depend on the social priorities in a country, and on the inequalities of its market distribution of income; the political and technical feasibility of attaining each of these objectives may differ considerably among countries.

Taking from the Rich

There is a tendency to see the problem of taking from the rich as being only a question of political feasibility. But there are economic as well as political problems involved in extracting from the rich. In any case political feasibility, defined broadly to include attitudes and degrees of acceptability, is equally relevant to the design of any policies for reaching the poor and for changing market structures.

Unfortunately, wage increases at the expense of profits are at once the most politically attractive mode of extracting from the rich (short of radical socialization), but the most problematic in the eyes of the economist. Sharing high productivity of modern firms with their workers has a high degree of legitimacy: it favors a clearly identified and vocal set of beneficiaries, and seems easy to implement at no government financial cost. But a limited degree of redistribution via wage increases is possible only for a minority, and usually an already relatively better-off minority, of the labor force working for the larger more modern employers on whom such a policy could be enforced. Outside this sector, market forces are exceedingly powerful constraints on wage policy. And wage increases will almost always hurt the very poor by slowing modern-sector growth and employment expansion.

Income and wealth taxes also strike opposite chords with politicians and economists: their unpopularity with politicians has been matched by their appeal to economists. Redistribution through taxes can in principle minimize market distortions and maximize fairness in both the taking and the giving. But high taxes on earnings open the possibility of migration abroad; and high taxes on capital income reduce both the incentive to save and the capacity to invest. Problems of enforcement are acute. The record of almost all countries where income distribution before and after taxes has been compared indicates that one cannot use taxes to make major inroads into concentrations of income and wealth. However, the fact that taxes cannot make major reductions at the top of the distribution does not imply that government budget expenditures cannot make a large impact at the bottom; small percentages of GNP can make enormous relative improvement if they are transferred (efficiently) to the very poor.

A third way to attack high incomes is via the redistribution of capital. This article does not address itself to the issue of the socialist alternative, which entails virtual elimination of property incomes. Partial redistribution of property, however, is a common feature of market and mixed economies. Land reform is regarded by many as one of the most promising approaches to redistribution. Political resistance can be overcome to some extent through compensation, and the positive production effects of land reform can be sufficiently great that considerable benefits are left to peasants even after ex-owner compensation. Care in land allocation can avoid an inequitable pattern of allocation.

The success of land reform efforts, however, depends more on the configuration of political power than on monetary compensation. The most successful cases of land reform have taken place following sharp political change. In Egypt, Ethiopia, Mexico, and Bolivia, it followed a sudden political upheaval. In South Korea, the Japanese had acquired large land-holdings during their occupation from 1910 to 1945. Under the impetus of the post-World War II American military government, the Korean regime which took over in 1948 expropriated the Japanese landholders and redistributed the land to Korean smallholders. In Taiwan, the Nationalist Chinese expropriated the native Taiwanese in favor of immigrants from the mainland. In Kenya and Alger-

ia, it occurred after a loss of power by foreign groups who had become major landholders. There are, however, other contexts in which land reform might be successful. In Chile, Peru, and Venezuela, for instance, the wealthy landed class have undergone progressive political decline with the rise of reform-minded governments. But allocative problems are important: grants of land, for example, to already better-off peasants or farm workers on the coast of Peru and on larger Chilean farms, as well as the exclusion of most landless from the benefits of land reform in Iran, Egypt, and Algeria reflect more than policy mistakes. The spatial distributions of good land and of peasants rarely overlap closely, and moving peasants is a complicated social and technological task. On the other hand, difficulties of this sort rarely add up to a case *against* land reform; rather, they qualify the expected benefits both with respect to the number of potential beneficiaries and to the size of income gains.

Capital may be redistributed by nationalization of private firms with assets other than land. Unless an entire industry is taken over, there will be negative side-effects of partial nationalization, chiefly through loss of confidence by investors and loss of tax revenues. The beneficiaries of nationalization generally are not the extremely poor, since that result would require that the nationalized surplus be appropriated by the general budget and spent on the very poor; more likely, beneficiaries are clients of the nationalized firm (often, the rich owners of firms that are not nationalized) or workers in the affected firm.

Reaching the Very Poor

There has been a gradual change, amounting almost to a reversal, in the conventional wisdom regarding the redistributive problem. Until recently the difficulty was thought to consist primarily in extracting income from the rich, and this, in turn, was closely identified with the need for major political change. Today, there is a much greater awareness of the difficulties involved in giving to the poor. This "delivery" problem is less a matter of basic power structures or regime types; instead it involves attitudes, perceptions, secondary political structures, administrative behavior, and market complications—distortions and backlash effects that are the inevitable results of attempts to modify market outcomes within a market economy. This lesson has been learned the hard way, through the disappointing experience of numerous reformist and radical governments and the frustrated reform efforts of the aid agencies, over at least the last two decades. Regimes of all types seem to stumble over the same set of delivery problems. The most powerful evidence of such problems is provided by the comparatively feeble rural development programs of such oil- or mineral-rich countries as Iran, Zaire, and Ecuador. And it is evident in the contrast between egalitarian rhetoric and rural neglect in such radical regimes as Algeria, Egypt, and Peru.

These delivery problems are poorly understood. One reason is that awareness of such problems has been largely limited to persons involved in actual implementation, who usually attribute the specific difficulties they encounter to human failings, e.g., ignorance of supply and demand laws, wrong motivations, or insufficient entrepreneurial capacity. Most radicals, in turn, see such failures as proof of the need for major change in power structures, thus implying that there is some minimum critical redistribution of power—not achieved by "reformist" governments—that is a prerequisite for takeoff into an egalitarian society. The recurring and universal nature of most delivery problems suggests that more useful systematic explanations could be found by examining the patterns in (1) the nature of extreme poverty, and (2) the nature of reformist responses.

Many delivery failures can be traced to ignorance regarding who are the very poor. Such ignorance misleads sincere attempts to reach the poor; it also facilitates hypocrisy regarding intended beneficiaries. Examples

range from the gross, such as "low-cost" housing programs that benefit the top quartile and even top decile families, to the less obvious, such as land reforms that give least or nothing to peasants living in areas of marginal farmland where there is no good land to redistribute. Much of the policy literature underestimates the degree of variety among the poor, and that between and within countries—with respect, for instance, to the role of landlessness, unemployment, the health-productivity connection, social discrimination, urban or rural residence, backward regions, and lack of education and skills. The very poor in each country cut across multiple categories, in proportions that may differ considerably among countries, which complicates the job of designing the right policy mix. The scarcity of studies on who are the poor has made it easy for poverty features noted in one country or region to be falsely generalized.

The lack of understanding of market mechanisms outside the modern sector has also hampered many delivery efforts. It has been learned, for instance, that land consolidation and crop diversification programs must allow for the risk-averting advantages of traditional arrangements; that rural credit cooperatives must compete with the flexibility and the marketing and other services provided by traditional moneylenders; that urban job expansion may increase the absolute number of urban poor; and that school lunch programs may produce no net increase in nutritional intake by children. Other types of error resulting from a failure to predict market responses were cited above under the category of "backlash" effects.

What *has* reached the poor? The broad picture is not one of complete stagnation; indeed, for many of the poor, income growth has been rapid. Different types of policy efforts are contributing to this development. One category consists of small-scale, high-quality, and well-targeted programs. They tend to be run by highly motivated and talented individuals; many are sponsored by religious, private, and foreign sources. These programs cover many fields—some specialize in informal training, others in health services, agricultural extension or urban housing. For both philosophical and budgetary reasons the programs stress self-help, and strive to develop motivation and entrepreneurial capacity. With limited budgets, they are oriented more to human resource development and do little in the way of infrastructure. Latin America has been particularly open to such efforts; in Africa they have been curtailed by nationalism; while their largely Western cultural origin has greatly restricted their freedom to operate in the Middle East and in many Asian countries. Some examples of successful programs of this type are the low-cost housing program, Hogar de Cristo, initiated by a Jesuit priest in Chile over 12 years ago, which has become a large-scale, well-organized institution that builds homes that are cheaper than those of official housing programs and yet are highly marketable. Private and Christian Democratic groups in Honduras are responsible for an extensive system of radio-schools providing adult literacy and technical training to a broad audience in remote communities scarcely touched by government rural development efforts.

The critical questions regarding such programs are: how replicable are they, and are they suitable models for larger scale, more bureaucratically managed programs? Many of these efforts have high hidden costs in the form of high-quality managerial inputs; in those programs where managerial costs are not subsidized, costs tend to be very high, as in the case of many programs staffed by UNDP, UNESCO, and other international agency personnel. Their multiplicity and individualism also raise a question regarding replication: Which of the many programs are appropriate models for standardization on a mass scale? The missionary qualities which underlie their success unfortunately also lend themselves to strongly held diverse formulas of techniques for development. Despite a common stress on motivation and a grass-roots approach, their proponents often point to quite different cultural, political, or economic variables as "the key" that will turn vicious circles of poverty into beneficial circles of development.

A second source of benefits to the poor, at the opposite extreme, are the large-scale, usually low-quality and poorly targeted government programs—chiefly schooling, health services, farm extension and credit, and community infrastructure projects. The content of what is delivered through these programs may be poor and is at times dreadful, be it overly academic authoritarian-value-oriented schooling, health services designed to provide curative medicine for local elites rather than preventive public health to rural inhabitants, or agricultural extension agents who are scarcely familiar with the ecology or culture of their assigned regions. Yet, even a program which is full of weakness may be better than none at all. Few would argue against mass primary schooling, even in an ineffective form. There is a strong correlation between countries with high human resource expenditures and more equality: e.g., many would relate the advanced social policies of the state of Kerala in India to its early commitment to mass literacy. And there surely has been some sense to the traditional opposition by landlords to educating peasants; even if ninety-nine of every hundred students return to plough the soil with nothing gained, the community as a whole may gain one literate leader.

Reformists continually shy away from the seemingly hopeless task of improving these service bureaucracies, preferring instead to set up parallel small-scale model programs aimed at inspiring (but usually fated to antagonize) the establishment. But the fact remains that the sheer size of these bureaucracies provides enormous leverage to even the smallest improvement. Judged by cost-benefit standards, they are grossly inefficient, but they must be considered as at least one approach to reducing absolute poverty.

A third source of benefits to the poor is the

spillover or leakage from programs and projects aimed either at better-off groups, or at overall economic growth with no deliberate targeting. Major infrastructure projects fall into this category: a major road linking two industrial centers cannot help but provide access to a large number of rural inhabitants in between. Service innovations, such as government institutions to develop marketing channels for new farm exports, become available to small as well as to large farmers. There is now a widespread tendency to downgrade the potential for income improvement via spillover or trickle-down. This view, supported both by wide evidence of growing dualism and slow employment growth and by a belief in the power of exploitative arrangements, has served to support the more powerful reformist attacks on the rich. However, the additional efforts on behalf of the poor by radical regimes may be more than offset by the loss of modern-sector growth that results from attempts to squeeze, rather than substitute for, the capitalist sector where the gains from spillover from modern-sector growth are large. The potential spillover from such growth consists not only of modern-sector employment expansion but also of both the additional demand for small-scale service jobs in cities, and the leakage of benefits from capital and innovations intended for the modern sector, such as highways and new marketing arrangements. The degree of spillover will depend both on market features and on policy design; and the same is true of how redistribution affects growth. Both growth and redistribution are tools for raising low-end incomes, and the best policy mix for reaching the poor must consider the probable effect of each.

Improving the Market as a Distributive Mechanism

The two elements of a redistributive strategy examined thus far—taking from the rich and giving to the poor—both entail considerable economic and political difficulties. One way to lighten the burden on these forms of redistributive intervention is to adapt the market to produce a more equitable distribution in the first place. In developing countries, this could be done largely by distributing the ownership of physical capital, and by reducing dualism in the productive structure. To what extent are such policies feasible? To what extent are they compatible with growth?

The issue of property redistribution was discussed above under the heading of "taking from the rich." It was argued that there is a substantial difference between the redistribution of land and of other physical property. Land reform has by far a greater redistributive potential for several reasons: it is likely to have broader political and social effects within the countryside that favor the poor; it is a way of reaching very poor groups directly; and often it is complementary and in some conditions perhaps a prerequisite to other policies needed to raise low-end incomes in the rural sector (chiefly measures to raise the productivity of small farms). By contrast, nonagricultural business property can be nationalized, but there is no straightforward way of transferring that property income to the very poor. The poorer rural multitudes cannot be made shareholders or owners of productive modern urban properties in any meaningful sense, i.e., with some ability to control their management. The only political arrangement that is likely to ensure the transfer of such property income to the very poor is a socialist government with the intention and power to prevent workers in the nationalized firms or other groups from appropriating that income.

The second way to reduce market inequalities is to reduce dualism in the productive structure, i.e., to reduce the differences between productivity levels in the modern and traditional sectors. This strategy works through employment creation, since it consists largely of making the modern sector more labor-intensive and thus employing more people in the modern sector with a given stock of capital. Reducing dualism in the productive structure should generate a better income distribution for several reasons. First, wage differentials between the modern and traditional sectors will be smaller for either or both of the following reasons: labor-intensive firms require less highly skilled labor; and they are less vulnerable to unionization and wage pressures. Second, capital ownership is likely to be more evenly spread when firms are labor-intensive because such firms have fewer economies of scale, which leads to easier entry of new firms into the market and to smaller scale production by many firms. Third, to the extent that dualism is *caused* by market distortions, and also, to the extent that dualism—whatever the cause—has *generated* wage distortions, reducing dualism should increase efficiency and growth, and thus enhance market spillover to the traditional sector. Finally, there is the broader argument that income is more easily redistributed within a sector than between (modern and traditional) sectors.

The potential for reducing productivity differentials naturally varies enormously between countries; dualism has become extreme in the oil- and mineral-rich countries. Once the distributive effects of dualism have created vested interests, it is politically more difficult to undo these effects than it would be to prevent them. One major source of dualism consists of factor price distortions, and strong arguments have been advanced by economists that better pricing and allocation policies are likely to produce major long-run benefits in the form of faster growth and lesser inequality. If the short-run effects of such policy corrections on existing vested interest groups could be minimized, e.g., by heavily subsidizing labor-intensive investments (through tax breaks and export bonuses for instance), then large distributive improvements would be brought about over the long run at the price of small, regressive government favors today.

Less commonly noted, however, is a second major source of dualism: the growth of socialism or state capitalism. This is partly an ideological trend, but partly "an act of God": oil and mineral riches are thrusting socialism on many countries, because the enormous revenues from such sources are necessarily appropriated by the public sector. Governments are then strongly biased toward uses of those resources that are highly capital-intensive. The good, and perhaps most powerful, reason for that bias is the scarcity of entrepreneurial talent in government; and large-scale, capital-intensive investments are far cheaper in terms of managerial resources per dollar invested than would be a multitude of small-scale and regionally dispersed investments in labor-intensive enterprises. The bad reasons include corruption, which thrives with the purchase of large-scale capital goods, and the technocratic biases of many bureaucrats. These factors help to explain the paradox of regimes with strong socialist and egalitarian leanings, such as those in Algeria and Peru, which channel the bulk of their investible resources into projects that are highly capital-intensive rather than into the traditional sector or modern activities which employ more people.

The prospects for reducing dualism are therefore highly variable among countries. Where the prospects are good, a potential exists for long-run improvements in income distribution or, at least, for avoiding growing inequality. Even in the best of cases, however, it is an indirect and slow tool for attacking low-end poverty, particularly in such largely agrarian countries as India and Indonesia, and should thus be considered a complement to more direct policies aimed at reducing poverty.

Further Readings

1. Poverty

Ahluwalia, Montek S.; Carter, Nicholas G.; and Chenery, Hollis B. "Growth and Poverty in Developing Countries." *Journal of Development Economics* 6, no. 3 (September 1979).

Balogh, Thomas. *The Economics of Poverty*, 2nd ed., White Plains, N.Y.: International Arts and Sciences, 1974.

Balogh, Thomas. "Failures in Strategy Against Poverty." *World Development* 6, no. 1 (January 1978).

Griffin, Keith, and Khan, Azizur Rahman. "Poverty in the Third World: Ugly Facts and Fancy Models." *World Development* 6, no. 3 (March 1978).

Myrdal, Gunnar. *The Challenge of World Poverty: A World Anti-Poverty Program in Outline*. Foreword by Francis O. Wilcox. New York: Pantheon, 1970.

Papanek, Gustav F. "The Poor of Jakarta." *Economic Development and Cultural Change*. (October 1975).

Rodgers, G. B. "A Conceptualisation of Poverty in Rural India." *World Development* 4, no. 4 (April 1976).

Rondinell, Dennis A., and Ruddle, Kenneth. "Coping with Poverty in International Assistance Policy: An Evaluation of Spatially Integrated Investment Strategies." *World Development* 6, no. 4 (April 1978).

Stamp, Elizabeth. *Growing out of Poverty*. Oxford, England: Oxford University Press, 1977.

Ward, Barbara, et al., eds. *The Widening Gap: Development in the 1970s*. New York: Columbia University Press, 1971.

World Bank. *The Assault on World Poverty: Problems of Rural Development, Education and Health*. Baltimore and London: Johns Hopkins University Press for the World Bank, 1975.

2. Income Distribution: Principles, Concepts, and Policies

Adelman, I. "Growth, Income Distribution and Equity-Oriented Development Strategies." *World Development* 3, nos. 2 and 3 (February–March 1975).

Adelman, Irma, and Morris, Cynthia Taft. *Economic Growth and Social Equity in Developing Countries*. Stanford: Stanford University Press, 1973.

Adelman, I., and Morris, Cynthia Taft. "Distribution and Development: A Comment." *Journal of Development Economics* 1, no. 4 (February 1975).

Adelman, Irma; Morris, Cynthia Taft; and Robinson, Sherman. "Policies for Equitable Growth." *World Development* 4, no. 7 (1976).

Ahluwalia, Montek S. "Inequality, Poverty and Development." *Journal of Development Economics* 3, no. 4 (December 1976).

Atkinson, A. B. *The Economics of Inequality*. New York: Oxford University Press, Clarendon Press, 1975.

Cairncross, Alec, and Puri, Mohinder, eds. *Employment, Income Distribution and Development Strategy: Problems of the Developing Countries, Essays in Honor of H. W. Singer*. New York: Holmes & Meier, 1976.

Chenery, Hollis, et al. *Redistribution with Growth: Policies to Improve Income Distribution in Developing Countries in the Context of Economic Growth*. London and New York: Oxford University Press for the World Bank and the Institute of Development Studies, University of Sussex, 1974.

Cline, W. R. "Distribution and Development: A Survey of Literature." *Journal of Development Economics* no. 4 (February 1975).

Fields, Gary S. "Who Benefits from Economic Development? A Reexamination of Brazilian Growth in the 1960s." *American Economic Review* 67, no. 4 (September 1977).

Fields, Gary S. "A Welfare Economic Approach to Growth and Distribution in the Dual Economy." *Quarterly Journal of Economics* 93, no. 3, (August 1979).

Frank, Charles R., Jr., and Webb, Richard C., eds. *Income Distribution and Growth in the Less Developed Countries*. Washington, D.C.: Brookings Institution, 1977.

Horowitz, Irving, ed. *Equity, Income, and Policy*. New York: Praeger, 1977.

Lal, Deepak. "Distribution and Development: A Review Article." *World Development* 4, no. 9 (September 1976).

Mellor, John W. "Food Price Policy and Income

Distribution in Low Income Countries." *Economic Development and Cultural Change* 27, no. 1 (October 1978).

Pyatt, Graham. "On International Comparisons of Inequality." *American Economic Review* 67, no. 1 (February 1977).

Robinson, Sherman. "Toward an Adequate Long-Run Model of Income Distribution and Economic Development." *American Economic Review* 66, no. 2 (May 1976).

Rothstein, Robert I. "The Political Economy of Redistribution and Self-Reliance." *World Development* 4, no. 7 (July 1976).

Sahota, Gian Singh. "Theories of Personal Income Distribution: A Survey." *Journal of Economic Literature* 16 (March 1978).

Singer, H. W. "Dualism Revisited: A New Approach to the Problems of The Dual Society in Developing Countries." *Journal of Development Studies* 7, no. 1 (October 1970).

Tinbergen, Jan. *Income Distribution: Analysis and Policies*. Amsterdam and Oxford: North-Holland; New York: American Elsevier, 1975.

3. Income Distribution: Statistics and Measurement

Champernowne, D. G. "A Comparison of Measures of Inequality of Income Distribution." *Economic Journal* 84, no. 336 (December 1974).

Cowell. F. A. *Measuring Inequality: Techniques for the Social Sciences*. New York: Wiley. 1977.

Jain, Shail. *Size Distribution of Income: A Compilation of Data*. Washington, D.C.: World Bank, 1975.

Pyatt, Graham. "On the Interpretation and Disaggregation of the Gini Coefficients." Reprinted from the *Economic Journal*, World Bank Reprint Series, no. 38 (June 1976).

Pyatt, Graham. "On International Comparisons of Inequality." *American Economic Review* 67, no. 1 (February 1977).

5

Population and Development

12. Population Growth: Current Issues and Strategies*

Geoffrey McNicoll and Moni Nag

In this essay we attempt a brief review, from first principles, of the nature and scale of the problem of modern population growth and, on the basis of past experience of individual countries, comment on strategic choices for population policy in the future. We start by assembling the latest UN data on the magnitude of current and expected population growth—familiar material to demographers but increasingly ignored in popular discussions of fertility decline. To interpret properly the significance of this growth would call for exploring its intricate ties to social and economic change, a task far beyond the compass of a brief essay. Here we simply note the major claimed benefits and costs of population growth and remark on the balance, as we see it, between them. Public policy in this area, of course, should depend not only on this balance but on the costliness and effectiveness of the policy itself, however roughly that must be judged. While the unique conditions of each country require local analysis of policy alternatives, the experience of countries that have rapidly been moving toward demographic modernity is likely to be the main source of policy insight.

DEMOGRAPHIC PROSPECTS FOR THE NEXT TWO DECADES

Members of the generation born around 1930, who can reasonably hope to outlive the present century, will have witnessed during their lives a trebling of the world's population. From a 1981 total of 4.5 billion, the UN expects the world to reach 6.1 billion inhabitants in 2,000 (in its medium variant assessment made in 1980). The inertia of this growth, built into the age distribution, will carry it forward well into the next century—a population exceeding 9 billion by 2050 would be a plausible forecast.

The regional concentration of population increase is shown in Figure 1, based on the UN medium projections for 1980–2000 (United Nations, 1981). The width of each rectangle in the figure represents the 1980 population of the region; the height, its expected proportional increase; and the area, its expected absolute increase. The contrast between the two extremes, Africa and Europe, is the most dramatic—each starting from about the same size in 1980, but Africa likely to add 13 persons for each one added in Europe. More significant, perhaps, is the contrast between the two regional giants, South Asia (here including the Middle East) and East Asia (excluding Japan), each containing about

* From *Population and Development Review,* 8, no. 1. (March 1982), pp. 121–39.

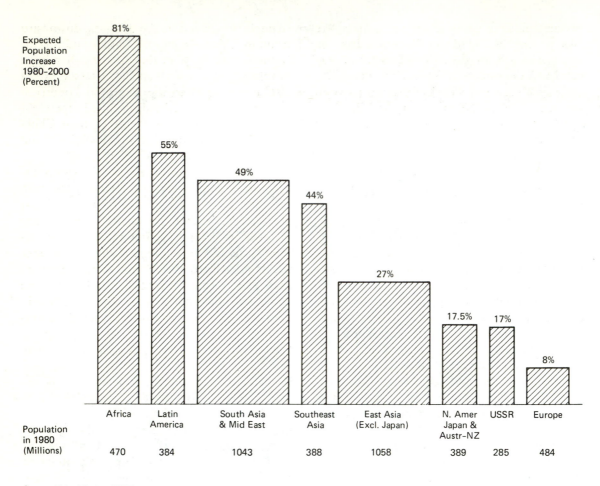

Expected Population Increase 1980-2000 (Percent)

Population in 1980 (Millions)

Africa	Latin America	South Asia & Mid East	Southeast Asia	East Asia (Excl. Japan)	N. Amer Japan & Austr-NZ	USSR	Europe
81%	55%	49%	44%	27%	17.5%	17%	8%
470	384	1043	388	1058	389	285	484

Source: United Nations (1981)

Figure 1. World population in 1980 and expected increase, 1980–2000, by major region.

1 billion people in 1980. South Asia is still clearly in the high-growth category, East Asia not far from the growth rate of the developed world. Dominating this latter contrast are, of course, the differing demographic trends of India and China, which we examine further below.

The UN's most recent assessment of the demographic future does little to buttress the widespread popular belief that population growth is rapidly slowing down, the expansion running out of steam. Overall, the world's growth rate seems to have peaked at about 2.0 percent per year in the 1960s and by now has probably dropped to 1.7 percent. The yearly absolute increase in population is continuing to rise, however. In 1980, some 75 million people were added. In the UN's medium projection, the point of inflexion of the trajectory will not be reached until the late 1990s, when the annual increase will be close to 90 million.

The expectation of a substantial slowdown in population growth, however, is based less on trends in natural increase than on recent evidence of fertility decline. There is a temptation to examine country experience here without weighting by population size, so that a significant decline in, say, Singapore or

Jamaica tends to offset in the public mind the lack of one in Nigeria or Pakistan. But the data, mainly from the 1970–71 round of censuses and the sample surveys of the mid-1970s (in particular, the World Fertility Survey), provide convincing evidence of some decrease in fertility in virtually all the large developing countries.

The latest UN birth rate data for countries with 1980 populations exceeding 50 million (9 developing and 7 industrial countries) are set out in Table 1. The 16 countries make up three-quarters of the world population. The birth rate for the world as a whole, given in the last row of the table, is estimated to have fallen by slightly below 10 percent in the 1960s and slightly above 10 percent in the 1970s, to a level now of about 28 births per thousand population per year. This global average is strongly influenced by the dramatic downward trend in China—somewhat earlier and recently much steeper than that of the other large developing countries—and to a lesser extent also by declines in the industrial countries. The average (unweighted) decline in the eight large developing countries other than China was 4.1 percent from 1955–60 to 1965–70 and 10.5 percent from 1965–70 to 1975–80.

Two significant regional trends in world fertility are not fully evident in Table 1: the birth rate declines spreading in East and Southeast Asia and the recent appearance of quite steep declines in Latin America. In the former region, in addition to China, falling birth rates are being recorded in South Korea, Taiwan, the Philippines, Indonesia, Malaysia, and Thailand; in the latter, most notably in Brazil, Mexico, and Colombia. Identifying the deter-

TABLE 1. Population Size, Birth Rates, and Birth Rate Declines for Countries with 1980 Populations Exceeding 50 Millions

Country	1980 Population (million)	Average Annual Birth Rate (x1000)			Change in Birth Rate (percent)	
		1955–60	1965–70	1975–80	1955–60 to 1965–70	1965–70 to 1975–80
Developing Countries						
China	995	37.6	32.4	21.3	−13.8	−34.3
India	684	44.0	42.0	35.3	− 4.5	−16.0
Indonesia	148	47.1	43.0	33.6	− 8.7	−21.9
Brazil	122	43.1	38.8	33.3	−10.0	−14.2
Bangladesh	88	50.3	49.7	46.8	− 1.2	− 5.8
Pakistan	87	47.2	46.8	43.1	− 0.8	− 7.9
Nigeria	77	52.1	51.0	49.8	− 2.1	− 2.4
Mexico	70	45.7	43.9	38.3	− 3.9	−12.8
Vietnam	54	41.9	41.4	40.1	− 1.2	− 3.1
Industrial Countries						
USSR	265	25.3	17.6	18.3	−30.4	+ 4.0
USA	223	24.8	18.3	16.3	−26.2	−10.9
Japan	117	18.1	17.8	15.1	− 1.7	−15.2
FR Germany	61	16.5	16.6	9.8	+ 0.6	−41.0
Italy	57	18.0	18.3	13.3	+ 2.7	−27.3
UK	56	16.4	17.6	12.0	+ 7.3	−31.8
France	54	18.4	17.1	13.8	− 7.1	−19.3
World Total						
	4,432	36.1	33.1	28.5	− 8.3	−13.9

Source: United Nations (1981).

minants of fertility trends in these two regions is clearly important in making any long-term demographic forecast for the world.

The most visible manifestation of high fertility comes as societies try to absorb successively larger cohorts of young people into their economies. The translation from the economically inert notion of a birth rate to the potentially critical issue of labor force entry is as striking as it is simple. The number of people who will be seeking such entry around the year 2000 is determined essentially by births occurring now—say, over 1980–84. Figure 2 illustrates the consequences of disparate fertility trends in the four largest countries over the past three decades, under the simplifying assumption that the number of potential labor force entrants in a given year is one fifth of the population then in the age group 15–19 years. (The chart therefore ignores such

structural changes as the increase in female labor force participation in the United States or the effects of changing rates of school enrollment.) It shows, for example, that within 20 years India's planners will have to cope with larger pools of labor force entrants than China's—an extraordinary reversal that will occur abruptly in 1990s as China's birth rate decline of the 1970s makes itself felt in the economy. India's situation is, of course, the more typical among developing countries.

Corresponding to a present world birth rate of around 28 per thousand is a death rate of about 11 per thousand—or, in more convenient terms, life expectancy at birth of 58 years. Life expectancy in the developing countries has risen from about 35 years in 1930 to some 56 years in 1980 (51 years in the developing world excluding China). There is wide current concern, however, that the era of

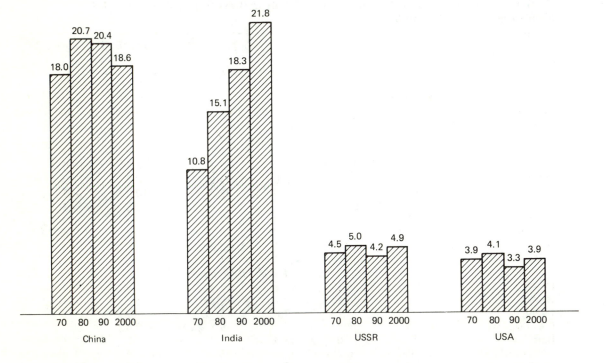

Source: United Nations (1980)

Figure 2. Annual pool of labor force entrants for selected countries, 1970–2000 (in millions), one fifth of estimated population aged 15–19 years in given year

rapid mortality decline may have at least temporarily come to an end. The optimism that led a 1962 UN report to declare "It may not be too much to hope for that, within a decade or two, the vast majority of the world's people will have an expectation of life at birth 65 years or more," was unjustified, and few would now expect such a state to be achieved in the near future. (See Gwatkin, 1980; the UN report referred to is United Nations, 1963.)

The estimates of demographic rates we have been relying on above are by no means incontestable. Between the UN's 1978 and 1980 assessments, for example, China's birth rate figure for 1970–75 was raised from 24.0 to 29.5—an increase of more than 20 million in the implied number of births during this period. In a number of other countries, India and Indonesia among them, early returns from the 1980–81 round of censuses show populations larger than had been expected on the basis of previously estimated birth and death rates; so further adjustments in these estimates are likely to be required.

But even with accurate statistics, demographic prediction is a highly fallible art. What is needed to give scientific substance to assumptions about future trends in fertility and mortality is an understanding of the reasons for observed changes in vital rates in the past. For mortality, the reasons for the most part are cut and dried. The effects of improving economic conditions, better hygiene and sanitation, application of new medical knowledge, and expansion of public health services can, in theory, be separated out and quantified by detailed cause-of-death analysis (see, for example, Preston, 1976). It is the paucity of cause-of-death data, past and present, rather than any fundamental conceptual conflict that accounts for most of the remaining disagreement. In the case of fertility, however, similar efforts to explain past trends lead immediately into some areas of major controversy. Before venturing there, we take up the second suggested basis for the fading con-

cern with population growth—that on balance it does not matter much.

PROS AND CONS OF POPULATION GROWTH

What is the balance of costs and benefits associated with population growth? Any answer must be so hedged about with assumptions and conditions that it is not surprising to find continuing argument on the subject. Costs and benefits to whom? Under whose value premises? Over how long a time period? With what resource endowments? In what kind of institutional and cultural setting? Even the comparatively circumscribed issue of the impact of population growth on a nation's socioeconomic development seems to have few questions that both are settled and effectively remain so—not only because answers generally have to be country-specific and contingent on an agreed content of "development," but also because some important technical questions about population-development interrelations are themselves unresolved.

But there is no justification for an agnostic stance here. The questions, both technical and ideological, are clearly amenable to analysis; orders of magnitude for the relationships at issue can nearly always be found; radical outliers in conclusions either dissolve under analytical scrutiny or can be pushed back to extreme, sometimes bizarre, ethical or ideological positions.

We would summarize the broad conclusions of the majority of researchers on the issue as follows: Under the conditions existing in most poor countries, rapid population growth slows, sometimes drastically, the absorption of the bulk of the population into the modern, high-productivity economy, while any demographic effects in stimulating innovation or investment call at most for a moderate pace of growth; rapid growth hinders the capacity of poor countries to cope effectively with large changes in their natural or economic environments; and, in extreme cases, it constricts what development can hope to achieve for them. It is not the place of this essay to assemble the evidence supporting these statements, but a brief gloss on each is called for.

(1) Rapid population growth imposes obvious costs in investment needed to maintain capital per head. Such investment is at the expense of consumption or of adding to capital per worker and, thus, to labor productivity. At the family level, this effect is compensated by the strong values attaching to children, assuming they are "wanted." Looking just at the economic dimension, the demands of a larger family size provide a strong encouragement to increase family earnings both on the part of parents and by the children themselves. At the aggregate level, however, the net effects on other families—on balance likely to be adverse in most poor-country settings (e.g., through depressed wage rates or overextended infrastructure)—must be added in. Certainly the prospect of continuing large increases in labor force entrants that now confronts so many countries is not counted an economic blessing by the governments affected.

But can such labor force increases act as a stimulus to economic performance, shaking the economy out of an institutional or technological rut? It is often held that population growth induces innovation, stimulates greater private investment, yields scale economies in provision of economic and social infrastructure, and so on. In some cases such benefits may well accrue, but there is nothing to suggest that to capture them requires anything close to the 2–3 percent annual rates of increase common in the contemporary world. (The demographic stimulus seen by North and Thomas, 1973, as contributing to profound economic change in fifteenth century Europe or by Hicks, 1939:302, as a factor behind the Industrial Revolution was in each case below 1 percent per year.) Moreover, these benefits may in fact be more effectively captured by explicit measures entirely outside the demo-

graphic sphere. Since development has become a self-conscious process, governments have acquired all kinds of direct and indirect means of promoting innovation, raising investment rates, or reaping economies of scale, short-cutting the drawn-out historical process. A stranger pronatalist economic argument, newly given popular currency by Simon (1981), is that more people mean more geniuses, more spontaneous creation of useful knowledge, as if the poverty of the Third World was not itself the reason for its technological dependency in the face of already preponderant demographic weight.

The significance of a demographic drag on economic performance depends, of course, on the level of that performance. In the dynamic economies of East Asia, with national incomes increasing by 8–10 percent annually, population growth of 2 percent or so is a comparatively minor issue. But most of the rest of the developing world can take no such comfort. Using the World Bank's categories, per capita income growth in the 1970s was estimated at 2.8 percent per year in the middle-income developing countries, and 1.6 percent in the low-income countries (excluding China). In low-income sub-Saharan Africa, per capita income actually fell over the decade.

(2) In addition to draining off investment to train and equip an expanding labor force, rapid population growth imposes considerable new organizational demands on a society. Social structure is not neutral with respect to scale: doubling population size in a generation, and city size in sometimes a decade, keeps a country's political and administrative apparatus perpetually off-balance. External shocks such as sudden shifts in resource prices, which should elicit concerted public and private sector efforts to redirect technology and manpower in accord with the changed market conditions, may become major economic calamities. Effective actions aimed at halting economically or aesthetically damaging processes of ecological degradation (for example, those making for the impending ex-

tinction of many plant and animal species), which equally call for organizational competence, may be simply beyond reach.

The connections here are complicated by the likelihood (which we discuss below) that weakness in organizational competence is itself part of the reason for continued rapid population growth. Mutual causation of this kind bedevils the analyst's task in the entire field. Moreover, the connections may be disguised: governments typically respond to social disorganization by deploying the technology of political control, providing at least a veneer of stability. It is plausible that rapid demographic change, by threatening social stability, is a not infrequent ccontributory factor behind the emergence of military governments in the contemporary Third World.

Popular discussions of "population pressure" often seek to identify direct adverse effects on economic welfare of worsening population-natural resource ratios or to impute a demographic cause for any unhappy ecological outcome. Nearly always such arguments are slippery, however, since they skirt the critical intermediate issue of how a society organizes itself to respond to resource and ecological problems. The current "firewood crisis" in many poor countries [for example] . . . is best seen not as a simple matter of population-induced deforestation but as a result of the failure of societal arrangements that elsewhere manage to maintain a common resource in the face of competing uses and users. The central issue to be explored is then the demographic contribution, if any, to that failure.

(3) In extreme cases, rapid population growth and the resulting absolute size of population constrict what is achievable by economic development in terms of individual wealth and amenity. Countries that have successfully attained the status of industrial economies are able to set about repairing the worst ravages of the industrialization process and creating the amenities that are increasingly in demand by their expanding middle class-

es. Sheer population density seems comparatively unimportant to the outcome of this endeavor—especially since wealth can buy access to the amenities of the rest of the world. Even if today's brand of international tourism turns out not to be open to the latecomers, simply because of their numbers, amenities less dependent on space and distance can presumably be designed. But it is surely more than mere failure of imagination that we should find it so difficult to foresee the emergence into post-industrial satiety, such as it is, of the massive populations of, say, South Asia or the by-then massive populations of Africa.

If the balance of costs and benefits of population growth is so evident, why is it apparently so easy to call the conclusion into question? Several reasons spring to mind. It may, for one, be a corollary of a belief that, rhetoric aside, there is rather little practical significance to any unweighted summing of numbers of people. To take an extreme case, if a nation's long-run economic policies in reality are designed to benefit a small group within the population, policy achievement is not to be measured by nationwide per capita averages. Less extreme assumptions with certain formal similarities are to be found in neoconservative entitlement theory. (The position has its analogy at the international level. Most countries that have attained a low-mortality, low-fertility regime combine economic strength with comparative demographic puniness—Hong Kong, for instance, has the same gross national product as Pakistan. Their natural interest lies in keeping economic weightings in and population weightings out of the international order.)

A different kind of reason for questioning the existence of substantial net costs of population growth is sometimes drawn from dubious attempts at modeling the economic-demographic system. By dint of constant exposure some analysts may delude themselves into actually believing the assumptions of neoclassical growth theory—an institution-free economic environment in which equilibrium expansion paths pose no maintenance problems and the "steady state" is one of uniform exponential growth of people and product. The disregard of scale effects somehow survives the transition from simple, elegant models in which the stability and efficiency properties of growth paths are explored to attempted depictions of real-world social and economic systems evolving over decades. In one widely publicized simulation exercise (see Simon, 1977), alternative fertility trajectories lead to population sizes after two centuries that differ by a factor of 20. Even if we ignore the hubris entailed in 200-year time horizons, such a difference could not fail to reflect utterly different patterns of socioeconomic institutions, with effects extending far beyond levels of fertility. Yet the same model is assumed to characterize the economy in each case, and from it the conclusion is drawn that per capita income is relatively invariant to fertility. A finding more clearly built into the instrument of analysis is hard to imagine.

The relationships between population growth and socioeconomic change, although at first sight a subject ideally suited to formal simulation, have proved highly resistant to compelling modeling. The number of plausible relationships is very large, their empirical basis often cloudy. A complex model can of course be set down in short order. The problem is that a few "reasonable" adjustments in its assumptions, adding or deleting a feedback loop or two, can lead it to yield entirely different results. For these particular issues, formal modeling merely papers over our ignorance or exaggerates our biases.

Or, perhaps the simplest explanation, the shrill voices from the 1960s of those foreseeing imminent demographic catastrophe, even though now largely silenced, have damaged public hearing for serious analysis of population problems and policies. Presently predicted global population growth (for the moment admittedly rapid, but sure of eventual halting—with reasonable hope, in a century

or so), it seems, can be tolerated and that is all that matters. In this view, possibilities that much lower rates of increase might be attainable and might yield substantial benefits on the development front and in noneconomic spheres, do not warrant investigation.

INDIVIDUAL AND SOCIETAL FERTILITY INTERESTS

We could accept that rapid population growth imposes a whole variety of burdens on a particular society, offset only to a slight degree by its positive features, and yet still conclude that little can or should be done about it. The intractability of population growth to public intervention is perhaps the most important lesson learned over the past several decades of concern with population. It may be that the costs, economic and noneconomic, entailed in any policy action that *would* be effective outweigh the gains to be reaped from its outcome. Such a calculation, quite aside from the intricate distributional judgments it would involve, can only be attempted from a basis of understanding what the feasible options for influencing demographic trends are. With little loss we can restrict a discussion of this to the issue of fertility change.

Over the long haul of human history, societies in a rough sense can be said to organize themselves to support a particular fertility regime appropriate to the resources, technologies, and mortality risks they face. Recruitment of new members, biologically required to be a matter for largely decentralized decision making, is too important a matter to be left wholly up to individual parents. As on virtually any major issue affecting its future welfare, a society intervenes in the demographic behavior of its members to preserve its interests—or the interests of the more powerful groups within it. When an issue such as this must be confronted routinely, routine responses are developed. In other words, some form of control over that particular domain of behavior becomes institutionalized in the society, embodied in the signals conveying social approbation or economic advantage (or their opposites) to individual members. (Realities, of course, do not quite admit of this abstraction of demography from the rest of the social and economic system. But the picture suffices for our purpose.)

What then happens when the situation is suddenly disrupted by new threats and opportunities—new technologies, much larger surviving birth cohorts, a rapidly changing economic and cultural environment? For the society as a whole, the institutional controls that historically governed reproductive behavior have probably become embedded in a broad, more or less coherent sociocultural, legal, and administrative framework and are not readily available for revamping in response to the need for a new demographic regime. So the signals do not change. For individuals and families, as before seeking and acting on their own interests, a variety of demographic outcomes is possible—but only fortuitously an outcome that accords well with the new social interest. In essence, individual and social demographic interests are uncoupled.

Why, it may be asked, did this "uncoupling" not happen historically in the demographic experience of the rich countries? The answer is that it did happen. Community controls over marriage and household establishment broke down under the new economic opportunities and the possibilities for social and demographic mobility they afforded. However, there was no surge in population growth comparable to that in the contemporary Third World because mortality remained high (as it did until well into the present century) and to a lesser extent because emigration was an outlet. Europe's population rose by 7 percent per decade over the nineteenth century, compared to 4.5 percent per decade over 1750–1800 (Durand, 1977). The industrial economy, except at the troughs of its business cycle, was well able to absorb the increase it had precipitated.

The individual fertility interests that were formed by the pattern of industrialization, or were co-formed with it, eventually worked firmly in the direction of smaller families. One facet of the changes that constitute economic development is a steady rise in the cost of children to parents, far outpacing the characteristically tepid efforts of society to subsidize this cost and thus distribute the burden. Children's income-earning opportunities recede; their role as a store of value for their parents' old age or as a hedge against family misfortune is supplanted by new social and economic institutions; educational costs to parents, despite large public expenditures, remain appreciable and become more necessary; the income sacrifice of the time involved in childrearing becomes a large factor in the family economy. More than sufficient reasons can be found in the changing economy and its institutional supports to account for a radical drop in family size.

We do not assume a thoroughgoing material basis for all such changes. Clearly, concomitant cultural developments—particularly in parents' perceptions of children and of the balance of rights and duties between parent and child—have potentially profound import for demographic behavior. Fortunately there is no need to assign precedence between culture and social organization in this explanatory sketch.

With completed industrialization it would be pleasant to report that there is a "recoupling" of social and individual demographic interests at approximately a replacement level of fertility. There is no evidence for this belief, however. Fertility as plausibly will continue to drop far below replacement, with governments scrambling for ways of subsidizing the cost of children to sustain their nations' labor force and tax base. Whether their scarcity will make children again more privately valued, so leading to a fertility rebound, or whether social acceptance of child-lessness and one-child families (and voting power accumulating among the elderly and the childless) will further tip the balance toward very low fertility, cannot as yet be seen.

LESSONS FROM CONTEMPORARY EXPERIENCE

While these low-fertility problems are far removed in scale from the current difficulties of rapid population growth in the Third World, there are important analytical similarities. We shall look briefly at a number of contemporary examples of fertility change, all places where substantial declines have taken place, drawing on the same explanatory apparatus. Brazil, on the one hand, and China, on the other, provide in some respects polar cases. The dynamic East Asian countries (principally, South Korea and Taiwan), and Sri Lanka and the Indian state of Kerala are instructive supplementary cases within these extremes. (In a fuller discussion we would of course be just as interested in why fertility has *not* declined in certain other places.) The statistics cited for the most part are taken from the last two World Development Reports (World Bank, 1980, 1981)—the first of these being used for Taiwan, which thereafter became invisible in UN-system statistics.

Brazil and China

Brazil, the regional giant of Latin America, has shown fairly substantial fertility decline in the last decade. The birth rate has apparently fallen by more than a quarter, to a level below 30 per thousand, over this period, the decline accelerating in the most recent years. (The latest figures are not yet well-confirmed and the 1980 UN data cited in Table 1 only partially reflect them.) In terms of Third World averages, Brazil has a relatively high per capita income: close to US$2,000. This, for comparison, is equivalent in real terms to the level in Japan as recently as the early 1960s—at

which time Japan's birth rate was below 20. It is a highly urbanized country—65 percent of the population lived in urban areas in 1980 (in India, for example, the corresponding figure is 23 percent), and agriculture contributes only some 10 percent of gross domestic product. Manufactured exports have grown rapidly in volume and technological sophistication. Brazil's development strategy has combined vigorous promotion of state and private capitalism, little concern with income distribution, and pronatalist or laissez-faire attitudes toward population growth.

While interpretations of demographic trends must still be highly tentative, Brazil seems to be tracking the classic European pattern of transition from high to low vital rates. Death rates declined sharply in the 1930s, and by the 1960s life expectancy was approaching 60 years. (Today it is around 62.) On average there were four or five surviving children per family at a time when economic changes were making such a size increasingly incompatible with urban industrial life. For the growing middle class, children competed with new-found consumption alternatives; for the poor, with the daily exigencies of scraping for a living and with the possibilities, although slight, of moving up in the world.

By most assessments of the human costs of economic development, the Brazilian pattern is a high-cost route. Its apparent effect, belatedly, in limiting population growth can be seen in part as a reflection of these costs, albeit in the long run a socially beneficial result. But the future pace of fertility decline is by no means assured, while economic difficulties, particularly problems of labor absorption, loom increasingly large. More interventionist policies in the demographic as well as the economic spheres may become more attractive.

The contrast with China's development strategy in the past three decades could hardly be more extreme. If Brazil's experience is reminiscent of Europe's or America's during the turbulent years of early industrialization, China's experience recalls Europe or Japan in the preindustrial period. In essence, China tried to preserve or recreate in a modernizing economy the kinds of community structure and social controls on its population that characterized these traditional societies. The violent Chinese reforms of the 1950s—the killing or dispossessing of the landlords and powerful lineages and the establishment of collectivized agriculture—paradoxically gave new strength and resilience to the rest of the preexisting social system of family, neighborhood ("team"), and village ("brigade"), a strength evidenced by these groups' successful resistance to the later recurrent excesses of Maoist radicalism.

Just as the eighteenth-century English parish or Japanese village had both an economic interest in and the capacity to determine who married or settled in the community, so the post-revolutionary Chinese village gained a similar stake and role—rendered more effective by covering not just household formation but also marital fertility, and rendered more precise by greatly lowered mortality risks and by the modern technology of birth control. The considerable economic autonomy of brigades and even of teams, including assigned obligations to fund most of their own social services, set up local fertility incentives that in large measure coincided with national government interests in slowing population growth. More direct government pressures, through antinatalist and delayed-marriage campaigns, of course, pushed in the same direction, facilitated by an effective health-care system that also provided family planning services. The demographic outcome has been striking indeed: life expectancy rising from below 30 years before the Second World War to 65–68 years today and a halving of the birth rate in less than two decades, to a present level of below 20 per thousand.

The same pattern of social and economic organization that has produced the extraordinary drop in mortality and fertility in China has had altogether less spectacular effects on the economy itself. The sustained surge in labor productivity on Taiwan, for example, finds isolated parallels but no broad counterpart on the mainland. In an effort to establish stronger economic incentives, particularly at the individual level, the present Chinese government has begun a shift away from the collective economy toward reprivatization—a shift that, if it proceeds as it seems to be going, could have large unintended effects on population trends. Both the health system and the local pressures for fertility limitation are intricately dependent on the brigade and team structure, and their course under any weakening of that structure cannot easily be predicted. Selective relaxation of control in the economic but not in the demographic sphere may turn out not to be possible. If so, a consequence of promoting rapid innovation and productivity growth may be, so to speak, to free the fertility genie from the bottle. Concurrent moves in China to introduce draconian economic and administrative measures to achieve one-child families suggest that the government is far from persuaded that a fertility rebound could not occur.

South Korea and Taiwan

If Brazil and China are the extremes of economic-demographic strategy, is it possible to do better somewhere in between—combining rapid economic growth with a pattern of social organization that promotes early mortality and fertility decline and avoids the worst of the human costs of development? If we add to the objectives broad-based political participation, then very likely the problem is overdetermined. Leaving that consideration aside, however, there are a number of countries that seem to have found a successful middle way. Nearly all are in East or Southeast Asia: furthest along are South Korea and Taiwan (Hong Kong and Singapore, the other two members of the so-called Asian "gang of four," are too structurally peculiar for their outstanding success to be relevant here);

Malaysia and possibly Thailand would be in the next tier.

South Korea has averaged 7 percent growth in real per capita income over the past 20 years, during which time life expectancy has risen from 54 to 63 years and the birth rate fallen from 43 to 25 per thousand. The corresponding data for Taiwan, for the period 1960–78, are 6.6 percent average yearly per capita income growth, an increase from 64 to 72 in life expectancy, and a drop from 39 to 21 in the birth rate.

Both countries owe their economic success to extraordinary growth of manufactured exports—admittedly achieved in a favorable international economic environment. Domestically, the result was the product of high entrepreneurial capacity, competent and supportive government economic policies, and a well-trained, energetic labor force. (To say this, of course, does not get us far toward explaining the performance.) Agricultural productivity has also grown steadily. The shift to an industrial economy was achieved without generating a high degree of income inequality among households and without emergence of a very large urban-rural wage differential. Although there is no persuasive evidence that an egalitarian development policy necessarily promotes either economic growth or fertility decline, it does seem that the same factors that led to growth with equity in Korea and Taiwan also speeded demographic transition. These factors included an effective land reform aimed at encouraging small-scale peasant production, supported by a strong agricultural extension program and improvement in rural financial institutions, and rapid expansion of education, health, and family planning services. The development pattern combined the fostering of vigorous private-sector performance in both industry and agriculture, enlightened provision of social services, and stringent government administrative and political control. Unlike China, discouragement of fertility did not become part of this last sphere but remained in the second.

Sri Lanka and Kerala

There are various instances of low rates of mortality and fertility being reached without any apparent stimulus from a dynamic economy and without a strong politico-administrative system. Sri Lanka and the Indian state of Kerala are the best known cases—with life expectancies currently 66 and 60 years, birth rates of 28 and 25 per thousand, yet with per capita incomes in the bottom half of the World Bank's "low income" category. (Kerala is one of the poorer states of India.)

No firm agreement exists about how this "modern" demographic regime emerged in these areas. In certain respects, particularly in the wide availability of education and health services, both places are substantially more advanced than their aggregate production performance would suggest. Such services develop in response to demand as well as in anticipation of it, so they cannot be straightforwardly posited as contributing factors to fertility decline; but in these places government action seems to have come first. A different source of explanation is found in the nature of their labor markets—the extensive pattern of labor commuting from rural to urban areas that has developed in Sri Lanka, the organization of agrarian trade unions in Kerala, and in both (partly in consequence) the relative lack of employment opportunities for children. Modern labor relations and the resulting separation between economic and domestic spheres of life have emerged without the accompaniment of high productivity. Finally, an increasingly heard argument in the case of Kerala (and applicable also to Sri Lanka) is that fertility decline is a response to the diminution of agricultural employment and growing difficulty of finding other work—a situation that widens the gap between aspirations and income and, in turn, makes for a high age at marriage and acceptance of small-family norms. Whatever the reason, Sri Lanka and Kerala have achieved levels of social development and demographic transition somewhat out of line with their extent of economic development—and have done so, in the population case, without substantial government antinatalist pressure.

Economic growth is properly the prime ambition of poor countries, and with little economic success to point to in Sri Lanka or Kerala it can reasonably be asked: What is to be learnt here? The answer hinges on whether or not in these cases the stage has been set for sustained economic advance. Optimistic observers see the beginnings of such an advance under recent liberalization of Sri Lankan economic policies and the prospect, too, that Kerala over the next decade will move substantially ahead in its economic standing among Indian states. Those who instead see a demographic transition induced by poverty or relative deprivation are less sanguine.

Strategic Options

The conclusions we are led to by these and similar examples of recent demographic history are as follows. First, sustained, rapid economic growth creates conditions that make for fertility decline, largely irrespective of government population policy. Second, the timing and pace of fertility decline in these instances, and the social costs of the overall pattern of economic-demographic development, can vary over a wide range, depending on the particular institutional setting of the society—which in turn is in some measure influenced by government policy. Third, there are combinations of patterns of social organization and designs of governmental programs (notably in education, health, family planning, and rural employment) that foster lowered fertility even without much economic growth. Fourth, in these latter cases, it remains an open question in each instance whether or to what degree poor economic performance is linked to these institutional arrangements favoring low fertility. And fifth, if such a link does exist, political or administrative pressure aimed at speeding a decline in fertility may succeed in narrow

terms but at a considerable cost (at least in the short and medium run) in foregone economic growth.

General propositions of this sort need detailing for a specific situation if they are to yield an array of feasible options for economic-demographic strategy. Feasibility is constrained in many ways. Existing institutional arrangements are resilient and cannot be arbitrarily altered except at high cost. (For example, the Chinese land reform of 1950–52 was a fundamental restructuring of rural society, but it was achieved at very high cost; the 1958 campaign to establish communes as the dominant rural social unit was abandoned when the evident costs it would entail in overcoming local opposition were judged unacceptable.) Where there is scope for influencing institutional forms, possible effects on population trends are unlikely to count for much in the choice: both political and economic considerations would inevitably rank ahead of demographic. The feasibility of particular policy directions may change over time as the economy evolves. (For example, massive expansion of urban commuting in poor rural communities—as in Indonesia—made possible by improved transport facilities, erodes the social role of residential groups and thus also the possibility of designing population and development policies that work through those groups.) And, not least, government capacity itself, aside from will, may often be a binding constraint in determining feasibility. (That a government such as Singapore's is able to establish an intricate pattern of antinatalist incentives is of little relevance to the vast majority of Third World governments.)

The desideratum for population policy is that it comprise measures that do not detract from the incentive structure underpinning economic growth, while promoting socially desired demographic ends. A simple division of its content would therefore be into measures that clearly have an economic dimension and thus call for careful meshing with existing incentive patterns, and measures that, in effect, are divorced from the economy and so do not raise the possibility of working at cross purposes.

In the first category the broad object would be the creation of an institutional framework favoring both economic achievement and demographic restraint—getting the incentives right without waiting for this to happen "naturally." In part, such a framework could be an outcome of government routine activities and development programs, where a shift in emphasis or in design may plausibly have a demographic effect. Fertility levels are empirically linked to factors such as literacy and the status of women, and achievements in these areas earlier rather than later in the development process may have some benefits in demographic terms in addition to their other values. Probably in greater part, however, the institutional framework that generates economic and demographic incentives is rooted in the patterns of social organization that exist in the society: labor market, kin group, village community, local government, and so on. Here the objective would be to seek to modify these arrangements so as to bring home to individuals or families more of the social costs of their demographic decisions. This "internalization" of demographic costs could be either at the family level or at the level of some larger social grouping that is in a position to exert social pressure on its members. In many preindustrial societies we noted that rural territorial communities had such a stabilizing demographic role; in the contemporary world, however, creating or sustaining that role during economic development is an altogether more problematic task—as the case of China illustrates. Perhaps more realistic in most cases today is to concede the economic-demographic sovereignty of the family unit. On the kinds of institutional innovation that would act to limit the transfer of demographic costs from the family on to the society at large, no general specifications can be given.

The diverse patterns of demographically related social organization found in countries that are reaching or have attained low fertility offer a rich store of insights to draw on. The unique conditions of each setting where policy is to be made, however, demand a strategy founded on thorough local analysis.

The second policy category, divorced from the economy although not entirely resource-free, covers measures aimed principally at seeking to promote social values associated with low fertility or at easing the translation of such values into practice. The former is an intangible goal and one that is not firmly within the grasp of public policy in any sphere. But cloudiness of outcome permits the policies that seek to direct cultural change to continue to claim efficacy. The latter is where population policy can finally come down to bricks and mortar and management charts. An emerging socioeconomic setting might clearly support a parental interest in low fertility, but one that parents are for some reason inhibited in pursuing. Contraception may, for example, be culturally disfavored; or the means available, unsatisfactory. Here is the rationale for government promotion of family planning—as an exercise in legitimation and in ensuring effective, perhaps subsidized distribution of contraceptive services. (It is not, of course, necessarily a rationale for government itself to operate a family planning program, the direction that action nearly invariably takes: such is the statist orientation of development thinking.)

DEMOGRAPHIC FUTURES

A proper modesty is in order concerning our abilities to predict either economic or demographic futures of nations. In his exemplary review of development experience over 1950–75 David Morawetz (1977) notes that, as late as the early 1960s, the most authoritative forecasts of future world economic growth did not foresee such successes of the next two decades as Brazil or the nations of the East Asian rim. Countries that were predicted to "take off" in that period included India, Burma, Egypt, and Ghana. Around 1950 similarly well-informed observers of Japan foresaw a future for that country of Malthusian stagnation or worse. We can have little confidence in making much better calls today.

The reasons for this uncertainty include our considerable ignorance of the origins of social change and the fact that even well-founded predictions can be upset by events, natural or man made, appearing out of the blue. They also include, however, the degrees of freedom that remain for deliberate choice about the design of social arrangements in any society. Economic development and demographic transition are fundamental, irreversible transformations of these arrangements in which roads not taken are put rapidly out of mind. In retrospect, as a result, the process seems to have an inevitability about it. Failures to accomplish such transformations, which are common enough, similarly seem to have been dealt in the cards. The social scientist, prone to exaggerate the scope of policy choice, in the end gets his comeuppance from the historian, equally, perhaps, prone to diminish it. But the demographic future is indeed in some measure within the domain of social choice, and wise choice here offers potentially large gains in human welfare. We are far from reaching a perfect base of understanding for sound policy action, but that would be a strange reason to turn away from the subject.

REFERENCES

Durand, J. D. 1977. Historical estimates of world population. *Population and Development Review* 3:253–296.

Gwatkin, D. R. 1980. Indications of change in developing country mortality trends: The end of an era? *Population and Development Review* 6:615–644.

Hicks, J. R. 1939. *Value and Capital*. Oxford, England: Clarendon Press.

Morawetz, D. 1977. *Twenty-five Years of Economic Development 1950 to 1975*. Washington, D.C.: World Bank.

North, D. C. and R. P. Thomas. 1973. *The Rise of the Western World: A New Economic History*. Cambridge: Cambridge University Press

Preston, S. H. 1976. *Mortality Patterns in National Populations: With Special Reference to Recorded Causes of Death*. New York: Academic Press.

Simon, J. L. 1977. *The Economics of Population Growth*. Princeton, N.J.: Princeton University Press.

Simon, J. L. 1981. *The Ultimate Resource*. Princeton, N.J.: Princeton University Press.

United Nations. 1963. *Population Bulletin of the United Nations No. 6, 1962, with Special Reference to the Situation and Recent Trends of Mortality in the World*. New York.

United Nations. 1980. *World Population and Its Age-Sex Composition by Country: 1950–2000: Demographic Estimates and Projections as Assessed in 1978*. New York.

United Nations. 1981. *World Population Prospects as Assessed in 1980*. New York.

World Bank. 1980. *World Development Report 1980*. Washington, D.C.

World Bank. 1981. *World Development Report 1981*. Washington, D.C.

13. Analytical Approaches to the Relationship of Population Growth and Development*

Nancy Birdsall

This article reviews the principal analytical approaches to the study of the relationship between population growth and economic development used over the past two decades. The literature relating population to development is vast; no attempt is made here to summarize it. Where earlier reviews are useful, the reader is referred directly to them. The attempt is rather to describe major lines of research on the multiple relationships between population growth and economic development, with special attention to the implications for policy design of the various forms of analysis. The focus is on fertility, on mortality only as it relates to fertility, and not at all on population distribution.

Research in this field can be divided into two, clearly interrelated categories: research on the consequences of fertility and research on the determinants. From a policy perspective, the former might be said to generate interest in the need for a population policy and the latter to contribute to the optimal design of such a policy. Both consequences and determinants research can be further divided into two types: macro and micro. . . .

This classification is useful as a basis for organization of our presentation of the analytical approaches, proceeding from macro- and micro-consequences of population growth and fertility to their macro- and micro-determinants. We begin by discussing the manner in which population growth was included in growth and development models up through the late 1950s and early 1960s; chro-

nologically this type of work on the population-development relationship came first and has significantly influenced both the policies of bilateral and international donors and much of the research on population growth and development that has succeeded it. This work is in the "consequences" school—research and analysis that has focused on the consequences of rapid population growth for the economic development of nations. It can be further categorized as "macro" work, since it uses aggregated economic and demographic factors such as national birth and death rates, the dependency ratio, savings rates, and economy-wide production functions. We also briefly review macro-consequences studies that apply the principles developed in these analyses to particular country economies and/or to particular aspects of economies. In general, these studies conclude that in countries with high fertility rates, the net costs attached to meeting development objectives in such areas as education, health, and employment could be significantly reduced by increasing expenditures on explicit programs to reduce fertility, specifically family planning programs.

Second, we review a body of work on the consequences at the family level—the micro-consequences—of large numbers of children. Much of the relevant research in this area has been done by those in the medical and public health professions and by psychologists and nutritionists. The results of the work have not entered the mainstream of economists' thinking on population-development relationships, although the framework for studies of the loss in human capital exists. Nor has this research had an appreciable effect on policy-formulation.

Third, we consider the extensive and grow-

* From *Population and Development Review*, 3, nos. 1 and 2 (March/June 1977), pp. 63–74, 77–92.

ing literature on the macro- and micro-determinants of fertility. This work has been most fruitful from a theoretical and empirical point of view at the micro-level, with economists analyzing the costs and benefits of children to the "household" or "family" and with sociologists implicitly concentrating more on the woman as the reproductive agent. In considering work on the determinants of fertility, special attention is given to variables that not only affect the parents' cost-benefit calculus regarding children but represent potential areas for policy intervention: reduction of infant mortality, female education and labor force participation, improved distribution of income, and implementation of family planning programs.

It would be logical to assume that research on the *consequences* of rapid population growth has pointed to the need for policies to cope with rapid growth and to slow down such growth; and that, in turn, governments have sought information on how to design effective policies, leading to further research on the *determinants* of growth. In fact, research on the subject has developed in a much more haphazard fashion, and government policies on population have not always evolved logically. Still, it is true that different types of research are more or less important for different countries, depending on their demographic situations, the priority given to population concern, and their general level of development. So this essay includes for each category of research some discussion of its contribution to policy, potential or realized, and of its peculiar relevance to certain countries.

MACRO-CONSEQUENCES OF POPULATION GROWTH

The sustained economic growth of Western Europe and North America during the eighteenth and nineteenth centuries was accompanied by the first steady and sustained increase of population the world had ever known. Kuznets (1966, p. 20) has defined modern economic growth as a sustained increase in population attained without any lowering of per capita product, and some of the theorizing about the relationship between population and economic growth has sought a positive effect of the former on the latter. A growing population has been proffered as a net contributor to economic growth: (a) because of its stimulating effect on demand and its risk-reducing incentive to investment; (b) because it provides for constant improvement of the labor force with better-trained workers; and (c) because population pressure may encourage technological innovation, particularly in agriculture. Moreover, large population size permits economies of scale in production for large markets.

After World War II mortality rates declined dramatically and population growth accelerated in poor countries: if population growth had seemed to be directly related to economic progress in Europe and North America, it now seemed inversely related to the economic prospects of India, China, and Latin America. Population growth is no longer seen as an unequivocal benefit. The situation in the post-war developing world is, of course, different from that of industrializing Europe in a number of significant ways. Governments in the post-war epoch must be more responsive to education, health, and even income standards for their populations. Today's developing countries must achieve growth in the face of the competitive products of another, already-modernized group of countries. Most important, population in today's poor countries is growing at least twice as fast as it was in eighteenth century Europe, at rates of 2 and even 3 percent a year, in contrast to at most 1 percent. The resultant age composition of the developing countries, with as much as half the population in the young, nonproductive ages, is much less favorable to production and proportionately more burdensome with respect to consumption and social overhead investments.

Macro-Economic Models

These unprecedented rates of population growth, implying a doubling of populations every 20–30 years, renewed the attention of economists to the *rate* of population growth. The analytic models of Nelson (1956) and Leibenstein (1954) reintroduced population as an endogenous variable influenced by income. Their models are Malthusian: Increasing income leads to increasing population growth rates; and, as long as population growth exceeds income growth, per capita income falls, resulting in the low-level equilibrium trap.

A seminal contribution to the analysis of the consequences of population growth was the work of Coale and Hoover (1958). Constructing a mathematical model of the economy of India, Coale and Hoover made projections of per capita income for India under low, medium, and high (exogenous) fertility assumptions. They concluded that over a 30-year period, per capita income could be as much as 40 percent lower under the high compared to the low fertility assumption.

Over the years since publication of the Coale-Hoover model, many of the assumptions implicit in their analysis have been challenged. However, their study and the subsequent work on the macro-consequences of rapid population growth that it stimulated, are important in at least three respects: (1) this work reawakened economists and others to the demographic factor as a policy variable, whereas for some time population had been treated as a given in growth models; (2) it alerted those concerned with development to the importance of growth rates as well as absolute size of populations, making population an issue for Latin America and Africa as well as for the crowded countries of Asia; (3) it contributed significantly to the view, especially in the rich countries of the West, that, other things being equal, extremely rapid population growth rates exacerbate development problems in the world's poor countries.

Coale and Hoover's 1958 book generated an industry of economic-demographic simulations. By projecting into the future given population and cost trends, numerous studies have tried to assess the high costs to developing societies of supporting rapidly multiplying numbers of people. Most such studies project public-sector costs associated with provision of, for example, education, health, and job opportunities under alternative assumptions regarding population trends. Few introduce feedback from the changes in expenditures in particular areas or other assumed changes in the economy to changes in population trends. In this regard, the studies adopt the simplifying assumption made by Coale and Hoover that changes in mortality and fertility rates are exogenous to the model, although they can be affected by policies (such as government support for family planning) that are not incorporated into the model. Costs of social services can be projected into the future under alternative assumptions about mortality and fertility; the high cost of high fertility is then easily calculated. These studies for the most part are meant to be illustrative; authors maintain that they are not predicting the future, but illustrating what the future could entail given certain assumptions about rates of population growth.

Although projections of per capita income under different fertility assumptions vary substantially depending on the specific fertility assumptions in the models, they consistently indicate higher per capita income under low fertility assumptions than under high. For example, among seven projections examined, per capita income was 10–15 percent higher after 20 years and 25–40 percent higher after 30 years under low fertility assumptions than under high ones.

In addition to studies that project costs in such specific areas as education, health services, and absorption of labor into the modern sector, work on the macro-consequences of population growth for development includes descriptive essays on the consequences of rapid population growth for the balance of payments, the future supply of food, and the general availability of physical resources. . . .

The principal findings with regard to *clarity* of the presumed effect of population increases on the indicator (i.e., directness of the effect regardless of the roles of other variables) and *strength* of the presumed effect, including lag time before the effect takes hold and the relative importance of population growth compared to other variables, can be summarized as follows:

Education. Rapid population growth has a strong, direct effect on future expenditures on education. High fertility now almost guarantees more children entering the school system five years hence; and while a number of factors including rising wages of teachers and rising enrollment rates may increase educational outlays, an absolute increase in the number of students has been shown to be the single most important factor in increasing educational expenditures. Expenditures can be held down by increasing the teacher-student ratio, decreasing the number of years students are enrolled, or decreasing enrollment ratios, but all these steps involve a decline in a country's per capita stock of human capital.

Health. Population growth similarly increases health costs: More people require more health services. High fertility rates have an immediate effect on costs of health services since obstetric and pediatric needs constitute a substantial proportion of total demand for health services. On the other hand, the contribution of rapid population growth *per se* to the problem of inadequate health care should not be overstated. Where health systems are urban oriented, are essentially curative rather than preventive, and do not serve the poor anyway, reforms in health care delivery (such as the much-discussed barefoot doctor system in China) might provide as much relief and improved health as an immediate reduction in

demand due to lower rates of population growth. And in the long run, demand for health services may not be lower in populations experiencing low rather than high rates of fertility; low-fertility populations have historically enjoyed low mortality rates and have a larger proportion of older persons, placing special demands on health services. Unfortunately, the systematic attempts to demonstrate how lower population growth rates would reduce expenditures on health care . . . have not been matched by analyses of alternative ways to cut costs and maintain health services, so the true opportunity costs of rapid population growth to health care are unclear.

Labor Absorption. Obviously, high fertility leads to rapid growth of the labor force—with a ten-to-fifteen-year lag between new births and new entrants to the labor force. Thirty-year projections for Sri Lanka, Chile, and Brazil indicate a doubling of the size of the labor force, even given "low" fertility, and an increase of as much as two-and-a-half times present size with "high" fertility. Furthermore, assuming a demographic transition to lower fertility rates in ten to fifteen years, labor force size then could be increased not only by the simple addition of today's current births at current rates of labor force participation, but by an increase in the proportion of the population seeking work, as women with fewer births enter the work force at new, higher participation rates. On the other hand, rapid labor force growth leads to unemployment and poverty only under special assumptions: fixed capital-labor ratios in the modern sector combined with insufficient savings and investment and the inability of agriculture and the informal urban sector to absorb labor in socially productive activities. The deleterious effect of rapid population growth on the labor market could be mitigated if appropriate labor-intensive technologies were developed for production in the urban sector, if irrigation and other infrastructures permitting more labor-intensive use of land were created in agricultural areas, and if changes in product mix and general development strategy (such as the light-industry export-led growth of Korea and Taiwan) were available to all developing countries. Short of such adjustments, rapid rates of natural increase condemn a large portion of the labor force to low-productivity, low-wage jobs in agriculture or informal urban services.

Income Distribution. High fertility among the poor in all countries, and in poor countries relative to rich, may exacerbate the problem of improving the distribution of income; however, there is little evidence on this relationship, and historically, improvements in income distribution have been more closely associated with other factors, economic, social, and political. The hypothesis that poverty associated with a skewed distribution of income also contributes to high fertility is discussed in more detail in the section on micro-consequences of high fertility below.

Food, Resources, and Environment. T. W. Schultz's [1971] appraisal of the consequences of population increase for food production is appropriately agnostic; he emphasizes how many questions remain unanswered in this area. Long-range projections of the supply of and demand for food are plagued by such unknowns as income changes, changes in agricultural technology, the heterogeneity of agricultural conditions throughout the world and the political plausibility of redistribution. There is some evidence, however, that the rate of increase of population, if as rapid as in some areas today, increases the likelihood of "population overshoot," the outcome of which is "soil erosion in fields and overgrazed pastures to a degree that native plants cannot reestablish themselves after declining productivity results in abandonment" (Freeman, 1976, p. 41). Analysis of effects of population growth and development on the earth's carrying capacity requires collaboration of development analysts with geographers, ecolo-

gists, and others in the physical sciences; such effects, which will vary greatly by geographic location, are less well explored and understood than the effects of population growth on educational, health, and employment objectives. The indirect negative effects of technology that increases carrying capacity—such as the spread of river blindness and other waterborne diseases associated with the construction of dams for irrigation and power (Freeman, 1976)—are only recently being considered.

Cost-Benefit Analysis

Implicit in those studies that introduce various exogenously determined fertility trends is the assumption that governments can use some form of external intervention to direct fertility trends along the path chosen. In the 1960s this intervention was invariably seen to be the introduction or expansion of publicly subsidized family planning programs. A common approach of macro-consequences studies has been to compare the costs of a family planning program (which causes the lower fertility) to the projected savings realized in health or education costs. Usually the savings in the latter are shown to "pay" for the former in this form of analysis. Such comparisons necessitate a host of assumptions regarding costs of launching family planning programs, acceptor rates, and the relationship between acceptor rates and actual births averted, as well as assumptions about future costs in health, education, or other areas, and about the society's welfare function, which may value children per se in addition to per capita goods.

Among the earliest examples of this approach was the work of Enke [1966], who estimated the value of a "prevented birth" under specific assumptions. He used his estimate to compare the return from traditional development spending to the return from spending on family planning programs and concluded that spending on family planning was 100 to 500 times more effective than spending on other development projects. His micro-analysis thus capped the earlier macro-work; his result was widely disseminated and probably significantly influenced the policies of developed country donors regarding population. Enke's conclusion regarding family planning programs is now widely considered to be exaggerated. Enke's calculation was made before the real costs of providing family planning, and the difficulties of estimating such costs (discussed below) had been seriously considered. Estimation of the benefits of averted births is an even more problematical issue. Estimates of the cost of averting a birth through provision of family planning services range from $1 to $400, being extremely sensitive to, among other things, the selected discount rate. Estimates of the benefits of averted births range from $100 to $900.

The macro-economic models and cost-benefit analyses of the 1960s have come under increasing criticism in recent years, directed both at their underlying assumptions and at the uses to which they have been put. Summarized, their assumptions include:

1. That household savings and public savings are a decreasing function of the dependency burden (ratio of consumers to producers) in the household and in the nation as a whole.
2. That social overhead investment in, for example, education, health, and housing, contributes less to growth in the short run than investment in directly productive activities and tends to occur in greater proportions in societies with higher dependency ratios.
3. That there is little room for adjustment in the capital/labor ratio in modern manufacturing and agroindustrial production, and that capital/output ratios are constant or increasing, so that high-fertility countries are condemned to specialization in labor-intensive products (chiefly agriculture),

which often suffer from poor and deteriorating terms of trade.

A limited amount of research has been conducted to test the assumption that the dependency burden adversely affects savings rates. Leff (1969), in a cross-section study using 1964 data from 74 developed and developing countries, examined the association between savings rates and both the young- and old-age components of the dependency burden. He concluded that the size of the dependency ratio has a significant effect on savings, not only for the countries considered as one group, but also within the two groups of developed and developing countries. But the correlation is apparently reduced if a few demographically atypical countries are excluded. And, of course, at the household level, a single characteristic—such as the propensity to plan—may cause certain families both to save more and to have fewer children. At the public level, governments willing and able to impose higher savings rates through taxation policies or imposition of a non-consumption-oriented industrial pattern, can and have done so, regardless of the dependency burden. Sources of savings in today's developing countries may be less the household sector and more the foreign, corporate, and small business sectors.

Still, short of major structural changes in developing economies, the assumptions regarding savings are probably sound; the possibility of major changes toward more labor-intensive technologies is at best a long-term one; and the political and ethical need to increase the expenditure on social overhead investments in proportion to population growth, irrespective of their impact on productivity, is obvious. As a result the work produced in the 1950s and 1960s on the macro-consequences of rapid population growth for development has not yet been effectively challenged, and has engendered a near-consensus on the excessive social costs of high fertility (with resultant rapid rates of population growth). It should be noted, however, that some critics of the macro-consequences work believe this to be a case in which correct conclusions are sustained by faulty logic and misleading use of modern analytic procedures.

Policy Relevance of Macro-Consequences Studies

Macro-consequences research, beginning with the contribution of Coale and Hoover, has alerted planners to the costs of rapid population growth. The types of analysis discussed in this section have had as a major objective persuasion: convincing governments that population matters. These studies have been most fruitful in those areas in which the relationship between rapid growth of the population and increases in public costs is obvious, and in those areas which are themselves major development concerns: education, health, and labor absorption. Resource and environment problems and inequitable income distribution have less often been linked to rapid population growth. Rapid population growth may not be an important factor in these areas; also the causal links between them and population growth are complex and difficult to analyze.

But countries differ. Creating employment in the cities in Africa is of more immediate concern than exploitation of land resources; the opposite may be true in Bangladesh. Keeping up with educational needs of an expanding population is of high priority in Brazil; in Sri Lanka raising per capita food production is more important. Work on the macro-consequences of population growth must be carried out on a country-specific basis— and, often, focusing on specific areas within the economy, as countries emphasize one or another development program.

Studies conducted in the 1960s normally included projections through the end of the century, with intermediate points in the 1970s, 1980s, and 1990s. Any future studies in this genre may be more effective if they analyze past trends in total costs and costs per capita of population served by health and education services, and compare those empirically derived costs to what might have been under a lower fertility regime. Similarly, expansion of the labor force, already a considerable problem in many countries in the 1970s, might be related to fertility trends since World War II. The use of projections without proper analysis of past trends was sensible at a time when data on those aspects were scarce; but data scarcity has given way to data inundation for many countries. Admittedly, analysis of past trends is almost as thorny a methodological problem as the use of simulation models for projections, but it would inject greater reality into an approach that has to date been plagued by its resort to "illustrative" results.

On balance, it appears that macro-consequences research of the "other-things-being-equal" type is becoming less relevant for the developing world. Its major object is persuasion, and its major intended output is recognition by government planners of the need for population policy. Most of the population of the developing world now lives in countries that have national population policies to reduce fertility. Next steps for these countries include designing effective fertility-reducing programs based on research on the determinants of fertility. . . .

MACRO- AND MICRO-DETERMINANTS OF FERTILITY

The basis for much of the policy directed at reduction of birth rates is the assumption that improved availability of family planning services leads naturally to fewer births. Research on the determinants of fertility (using both macro data, aggregated by country or by regions within a country, and micro data, collected from households or from individuals) has not disputed or refuted this assumption; it has sought to identify other factors besides availability of contraceptives that may influence fertility decisions.

A number of good reviews of the determinants of fertility, with citations to hundreds of studies, already exist. For research up to 1971, a Research Triangle Institute study, *Social and Economic Correlates of Family Fertility: A Survey of the Evidence*, is particularly useful. More recent reviews include Chapter 1, "Some determinants of fertility," in McGreevey and Birdsall [1974], Williams' [1976] essay, "Determinants of Fertility in Developing Countries," and Cochrane (1977). All of these summarize the literature by reviewing findings of the relation between fertility and a series of correlates or determinants of fertility: income, income distribution, education of men and women, female labor-force participation rates, age at marriage, own-family and community infant mortality, knowledge of modern contraceptives, use of contraceptives, availability of family planning services, and so on. . . .

Here attention will be focused on (1) discussion of the macro-determinants approach, with reference to some recent studies that investigate the timing of the relation between fertility and socioeconomic development; (2) discussion of the theory and available data underlying the micro-determinants approach, with reference to several attempts at new types of analysis; and (3) discussion of some recent work on those variables that appear to have a critical effect on fertility and that are potential areas for public policy intervention.

Macro-Determinants Research

In the 1960s and 1970s, curiosity about the exact nature of the relationship between fertility and socioeconomic development has combined with the reduced cost and increased availability of computers to inspire a spate of cross-national studies. These studies use multivariate analysis, an approach that, with the quantitative reach and precision of the computer, permits the researcher to observe simultaneously relationships between a dependent variable and a number of independent variables. In these analyses, some measure of fertility is estimated as a function of some indicators of the degree of a nation's development: the literacy rate, proportion of labor in agriculture, per capita gross national product, the expectation of life at birth, primary and secondary school enrollment ratios, among others. . . .

The traditional explanation of reduced fertility proposed by demographers is that with some lag, reduced fertility follows reduced mortality—the "demographic transition." Cross-national multivariate analyses seek other intervening factors that may have caused fertility to fall. Not surprisingly, certain indicators of advanced development are consistently correlated with low rates of fertility: high rates of literacy, high per capita consumption of energy, high rates of urbanization, low rates of infant mortality, high per capita income. But there are difficulties in the interpretation of such results.

The results of a cross-section analysis, which takes a picture of different countries at one point in time, do not necessarily mirror what has occurred within countries or what will occur over time. In fact, one multivariate analysis that estimated *trends* in fertility as a function of *trends* in several socioeconomic indicators within groups of countries indicated no particular relationship over time between changes in fertility and in the indicators (Janowitz, 1973). And several historical studies of the fertility decline in parts of eighteenth and nineteenth century Europe have led scholars to conclude that no particular indicator or set of indicators was related to changes in birth rates there.

A second difficulty with the macro-determinants approach is that it cannot elucidate the specific mechanisms through which changes in gross indicators over time, or differences in gross indicators across countries, influence the fertility behavior of individuals. Because higher levels of education and greater consumption of energy are associated with lower fertility, we cannot conclude that more classrooms and more lightbulbs will cause lower fertility, nor know, if they do cause lower fertility, exactly how. In this sense, it is actually a misnomer to use the term "determinants" in referring to these studies.

Two recent studies go beyond correlation of socioeconomic indicators with fertility rates, to identify how fertility change fits into the complex of other socioeconomic changes that development entails. Both studies pay special attention to the timing of fertility change, and its association with quantified differences in the other indicators.

In an analysis of the fertility-development relationship for countries of Latin America and the Caribbean, Oeschli and Kirk [1975] explicitly disavow the regression technique, which makes fertility a function of other variables, and construct instead a correspondence system, which is based on the premise that fertility and mortality are part of a holistic development process, the indicators of which cannot be disentangled into cause and effect relationships. The system describes quantitatively the relationships among ten indicators of development plus birth and death rates. From the ten indicators, the authors construct a development index, which can then be related to changes in birth and death rates. They find that countries above a certain level with respect to the development index have experienced rapid fertility decline—about .5 percent a year since 1962, their baseline year for measurement. The values for the Oeschli-Kirk socioeconomic indicators that correspond to the floor value of the development index above which countries experienced this marked fertility decline include: a literacy rate of 78 percent; an expectation of life at birth of 60 years; a primary school enrollment ratio of 65 percent; labor force in nonagricultural occupations of 52 percent; an urbanization rate of 40 percent; and a secondary school enrollment ratio of 22 percent.

These results are generally comparable with another study using 1950 and 1960 data from Latin American countries, in which Gregory and Campbell (1976) estimated the "mod-ernization turning points" for several development indicators, that is, the levels below which improvements generate an increase in fertility, but above which improvements generate a decrease. Using different indicators from Oeschli and Kirk, they find that for changes in per capita income, the infant mortality rate, and the literacy rate, fertility begins to decrease only when the urbanization rate is at 69, 80, and 60 percent respectively. Both studies find the demographic transition occurring at levels of development that exceed those generally found throughout Africa and South Asia, though such levels have been reached in parts of Latin America and Southeast Asia.

Micro-Determinants Research

Better understanding of how individual fertility decisions are affected by environmental changes (which the changes in the gross indicators imply) requires analysis of data collected directly from individuals, that is, micro-determinants research. This research uses census and survey data including information on characteristics of individuals—education, occupation, residence, desired or actual number of children, and so on.

Studies of individuals and households generally follow one of several conceptualizations of the fertility decision: the economic model, the psychological model, or the sociological model. The economic model explains changes in household fertility as a function of changes in the family's economic situation attendant upon socioeconomic development. The objective is to explain by one model both the dramatic growth of populations in developing countries and the equally dramatic large-scale control of fertility in the developed countries.

The "new home economics" of the family treats the child as both a produced (investment) and consumer good. Fertility is the result of rational economic choice within the household. Children, or more properly "child services," are consumed by the household; and because children are assumed to be noninferior goods, increased income increases the demand for them. Child services are also produced in the household, through inputs of parents' time and goods bought in the market, such as housing, formal education, and health services. Children may also be an investment, short-term if they work during their childhood, long-term if they support parents in old age.

If increased income increases the demand for child services, how do the new home economists explain the apparent fact that fewer children are "purchased" by high-income couples in high-income societies? There are two answers. First, though the income effect increases demand for children, the price or substitution effect reduces demand by increasing the price of children relative to other goods, inducing high-income couples to substitute other goods for children. The price effect operates chiefly through the increasing opportunity cost of the mother's time as women increase their educational attainment and employment opportunities. Second, with increasing income, parents opt for "higher quality" children rather than greater quantity, devoting more of their own time and income to children's health and education. Thus the use of the term "child services"; the demand for more child services can be satisfied with fewer but higher quality children.

Economic development increases the costs of children by increasing the value of parents' time and the costs of education, health, housing; at the same time it reduces the benefits of children, as they work less in the market and as institutional forms of old-age insurance substitute for support by children. By this approach the new home economics of the family explains the apparent link between economic growth and the so-called demographic transition.

This economic model thus concludes that for poor families in developing countries, children entail low net costs and, in the extreme case, may actually be a net benefit. (In the extreme case, parents would have as many children as they could and have a finite number of children only because of "supply" constraints: limited fecundity, high fetal and infant mortality.) Complementing the concept in the macro-consequences literature that high fertility entails a high net cost to poor societies, is an explanation in the micro-determinants literature that large family size entails low net costs or even a net benefit to individual poor families. This theoretical gap between the low private and high social costs of children in developing societies has been a principal justification for government policies to reduce fertility. (It has also been a source of some ambivalence in donor attitudes and local policymaker attitudes toward family planning programs, which some interpret as vaguely coercive; if poor families benefit from large numbers of children, why persuade them to limit their fertility?)

Two relatively new streams of research are relevant in this context. The first seeks to broaden the notion of the household as the unit of choice. The new home economics of the family assumes that the household has a common utility function with respect to children. Yet husband and wife are not always in accord regarding children; one analysis, which disaggregated the household decision-making process, found statistically significant differences in the demand for children between certain husbands and wives among Mexican-Americans. Furthermore, even if parents are in agreement in wanting many children, children themselves may prefer few siblings. Parents, who are merely this generation of decision-makers, may be better off with large families because they were able to exploit their children. When the children themselves grow up, the process is repeated.

A second recently evinced concern is to go beyond the household as the unit of choice, and to analyze fertility decisions within the context of the community in which individuals participate or of the clan or other unit that impinges on their behavior. McNicoll (1975) has called attention to the way communities can export the costs of their own rapid population growth through outmigration. Few existing studies address such questions as whether villages with different levels of services—schools, roads, health clinics, family planning services—or different cropping patterns, or different arrangements for the physical security of citizens, or different norms with respect to obtaining jobs for relatives have different patterns or levels of fertility. The apparent success of fertility reduction efforts in the People's Republic of China, where programs are grounded in community-level incentives, partly explains recent interest in examining the effect of community norms. Interest in community structure as well as the characteristics of households or individuals is the basis of recent suggestions that successful fertility-reduction programs be studied by anthropologists at the community level.

Some Critical Variables

Certain variables have emerged as consistently important in their relationship to fertility. A critical few describe characteristics of the socioeconomic environment that can be altered through public policy: infant mortality, female education and labor force participation, availability of family planning services, and, possibly, income distribution. The strength and direction of the effect on fertility of these policy variables is very different for countries at different stages of development and with different cultural environments.

Infant Mortality and Fertility. Almost all studies of the determinants of fertility indicate a positive effect of infant mortality on fertility, that is, countries with high rates of infant mortality on the whole have high rates of fertility. (Infant mortality is an important component of overall mortality, particularly in developing countries.) There is *no* country with high mortality and low fertility, taking high mortality as annual death rates above 15 per thousand and

low fertility as annual bith rates below 30 per thousand.

What is the causal mechanism that links high fertility and high infant mortality? On the one hand, high infant mortality results in high fertility because parents who experience child loss early ultimately may more than replace lost children, and parents in high-mortality communities may insure themselves against future child loss by having more children than they would want. On the other hand, high fertility contributes to high infant (and child) mortality because close spacing of births and many births may deplete the mother's physical resources and reduce the family's per capita financial resources; a commonly noted phenomenon is the death of a child when, on the birth of a subsequent child, the mother ceases breastfeeding the older child.

The major point in the present context is that the relationship between infant mortality and fertility differs by country and by prevailing economic conditions within countries. For example, high fertility is most likely to contribute to high mortality among the poorest groups and is most likely to show up on a country basis in the poorest countries, as indeed it does in Africa. There kwashiorkor is "the disease that kills the child whose mother carries another child in her womb"; it is often related to malnutrition exacerbated by early or sudden weaning.

There is some evidence that the extent to which parents replace lost children may vary with the level of socioeconomic development. Preston (1975, p. 192) suggests that populations at the highest and lowest levels of development exhibit the strongest replacement effects (Bangladesh, France, though by no means is replacement complete even for these), while countries in some intermediate stage exhibit weaker effects (Colombia, Taiwan). Heer and Wu (1975, p. 266) report that in Taiwan, women who suffer child loss are likely to have higher fertility than those who do not, but such women do not fully compensate for their loss; on average, for every child who dies, less than one additional child is born.

Opinion differs as to whether the poorest countries, even with a strong replacement effect, end up with more or fewer people as mortality falls. Studies that have dealt with the timing of the relationship, however, indicate that the response of lower fertility to lower mortality is maximized when the incidence of infant and child mortality is lagged two to four years. This tends to support the opinion that reduced infant mortality will in the long run reduce fertility enough so that the rate of natural increase will go down. This view would be strengthened if studies were better able to incorporate the indirect effect of reduced mortality: lower death probabilities induce parents to invest more in their children, which in turn leads them to lower their desired fertility. They replace a large quantity of children with fewer children of higher quality. In other words, lower mortality not only assists parents to achieve desired family size with fewer births; it may lead parents to reduce their desired family size.

Reduction of infant mortality is an important policy objective on its own merits. Because countries with high average levels of infant and child mortality also have higher levels of fertility, the policy objectives of reducing both mortality and fertility can be mutually reinforcing. (Countries with the highest rates are primarily in Africa and south Asia; most countries of Latin America now have much lower mortality and fertility rates.) Where political and cultural barriers to the advocacy of family planning and other fertility-reduction efforts exist, reducing infant mortality can be expected to lay the groundwork for later efforts concentrating on fertility.

Female Education and Labor Force Participation. Female education bears one of the strongest and most consistent negative relationships to fertility for a variety of reasons: through its effect on raising age of marriage; because it may improve the likelihood that a woman has knowledge of and can use modern contraceptives; and because it has some intangible effect on the woman's ability to plan, her interest in nonfamilial activities, and so on. No need to invoke fertility reduction to justify improving educational opportunities for women: better educated women will be more productive workers, better parents, and better-informed citizens; however, where male/female student ratios indicate that women suffer some schooling disadvantage, fertility effects provide additional justification for rectifying the imbalance. The fertility reducing effect of women's education holds true even for the highest levels of education; women who obtain secondary and higher education marry later, and increasing the age at marriage has a pronounced effect on a country's fertility rate (McGreevey and Birdsall, 1974, pp. 25–28).

But female labor-force participation appears to have an independent effect on fertility only for those women who work in high-prestige, modern-sector jobs. High rates of female labor-force participation, like virtually all other variables, are neither a necessary condition for fertility decline (consider Korea, Turkey) nor a sufficient condition for it (consider countries of West Africa). On the other hand, increasing opportunities for women to work in the modern labor force can accelerate a fertility decline; where women may desire more children than their husbands (as is possible in the Middle East and Pakistan, where custom deprives most women of opportunities in other endeavors), offering women some other avenue of activity than child rearing may reduce family size. Good earnings opportunities, like higher education, can increase the age of marriage for women. Similarly, in countries with high rates of urban migration, allocation of newly created urban jobs to women already residing in cities with working husbands could lower the expected employment rate of prospective new migrants, simultaneously reducing migration and increasing average family income within the cities. With two incomes per family rather than one, the tax and savings base in cities would be higher. (To what extent such benefits are offset by the admitted difficulty of creating jobs for even one member of each family has unfortunately not yet been the subject of any systematic study.)

From the point of view of policy, an important conclusion emerging from these analyses is the highly tentative nature of the effect of "status of women" on fertility. But "status of women" does not define an area where public intervention is possible; education and jobs for women do. Improving women's opportunities for education and for modern jobs, like reducing infant mortality, has its own justification; piggybacking its fertility-reducing benefit onto programs and projects geared to improving women's lives increases the measured benefits of such projects relative to their given costs.

Family Planning Services and Fertility. Do family planning services reduce fertility more efficiently and more effectively than general development programs? The wide range of estimates of the cost of averting a birth ($1–$400) and its benefits ($100–$900) cited above illustrates the difficulty of answering such a question. Estimating the costs of averted births requires estimating the number of births averted because of a family planning program, itself a complicated task; some births might have been averted anyway if some couples are substituting publicly provided contraceptives for private efforts. And "costs per acceptor" is an unreliable measure since acceptors may make repeated visits in different areas, change contraceptives, and otherwise muddy the attendance statistics. Even where the existence of a family planning program is correlated over time with a decline in fertility, assurance that the program itself caused the decline requires the systematic elimination of such other possible causes as increases in income, changes in occupational structure, and increases in education. Few studies of the

effect of programs have adequately controlled for the probable effect of these nonprogram changes on fertility.

Freedman and Berelson (1976) conclude tentatively regarding the effect of family planning programs on fertility: "If the fertility effect of family planning programs were always of overwhelming magnitude it would shine through; if it were always zero the question would not survive. In the middle-ground cases, while problems of data and measurement remain, we find plausible evidence that family planning programs made a difference that matters" (p. 19). Advocates of family planning programs argue that: many programs are still in their infancy and have been poorly run; they have absorbed tiny proportions of national budgets and of foreign aid expenditures; they provide many secondary benefits—improved health for mothers and infants, increased control by women over their own bodies, and greater control by families over their own future. Moreover, support of voluntary family planning programs is one of the few widely accepted direct interventions governments have made to reduce their rates of population growth; the immediate question is not whether support is warranted, but how much and in what form. What is the effectiveness of spending on family planning relative to other expenditures that also have both general development and fertility-reducing effects? Only investigations on a country basis can begin to answer such a question.

The current consensus on family planning programs is that their effects vary by country. Their effects will be more pronounced where they reinforce other factors that would tend to lead to a fertility decline. A series of studies in Taiwan, among the best studies from a methodological point of view, has indicated that the family planning program there has accelerated a fertility decline that was already under way. In a recent analysis Hermalin (1976, p. 11) concludes, using data from 1968 to 1972, that the family planning program in Taiwan had a negative impact on fertility, above and beyond other social, economic, and demographic factors. His result is consistent with Schultz's 1973 analysis showing a negative effect of the family planning program on birth rates, controlling for child mortality and parents' education (Table 4, pp. S259–261). Hermalin shows, moreover, that the rate of decline in fertility is different for rural and urban areas in different periods; in rural areas with initial high fertility, slow declines in the early years of the family planning program were followed by accelerating declines later. Rates of decline are presently lower in urban areas, which have already passed through a period of rapid change. These within-country differences indicate that within countries as across countries, estimates of the cost-effectiveness of a family planning program must take into account differential responses depending on development levels.

Income Distribution and Fertility. Will an improvement in the distribution of income within a country reduce its fertility rate? In an analysis of 1960–65 data on 64 countries, Repetto [1974] reports an elasticity of the general fertility rate with respect to the share of income received by the poorest 40 percent of households of −.36, compared to an elasticity of the general fertility rate with respect to increase in average per capita income of −.20.

Income distribution data are notoriously poor, and Repetto's result suffered in a subsequent estimation in which he omitted several East European countries (which have both low fertility and relatively equal income distributions); the income distribution variable was no longer statistically significant in explaining the fertility variable. Moreover, whether such cross-section results should be used to predict the pattern of a relationship over time is highly questionable.

Though statistically less sophisticated, simple cross-tabulations compiled by Kocher (1973) and Repetto (1974) are more appealing since they utilize time-series data. Repetto took countries (and a region) on which information for at least two points in time was available regarding income distribution and birth rates and grouped them according to changes in the two variables. He was able to show that fertility fell notably more in countries in which the income distribution apparently improved (Costa Rica, Sri Lanka, Taiwan) than in those in which it did not (Brazil, India, Puerto Rico). Kocher, in a similar exercise, found greater declines in crude birth rates for countries (and a region) with fairly equal income distributions (South Korea, Taiwan, West Malaysia) than for countries with less equal income distributions (Philippines, India, Thailand, Mexico, Brazil). His income distribution variable was unfortunately available for one point in time only.

To date no one has adequately distinguished between the *share* of income going to the poorest 40 percent and the average *level* of income of that group, nor has anyone drawn out whatever connection there may be between shares and levels. In fact most of the reasoning behind the apparent link between fertility and "income distribution" actually relies upon a simpler "incomes" sort of argument: once a certain level of economic and social well-being is achieved, fertility will begin to decline. Rich (1973) appeals to this logic in comparing fertility levels across countries with more and less equitable systems of health services and education. Kocher (1976, p. 85) explains his findings, for example, for Sri Lanka, in these terms.

There is thus no real indication that individuals' fertility behavior is affected by their relative income *per se*, over and above their absolute income; the income distribution-fertility link found is more probably the result of a coincidence over the period since World War II between improvements in the level of absolute income of the poorest and increases in their relative share. In any event, insofar as "income distribution" is used to mean some nexus of programs, including income increases, to alleviate the poverty of the poorest, an inverse relationship to fertility seems to hold. Fertility-reducing effects can be added to the other benefits of raising income levels of the poorest groups.

Highlighted above are four areas of public policy intervention. All may contribute to reducing fertility at tolerable cost; all provide benefits in addition to fertility reduction. Careful design of policy in these areas can accelerate the fertility decline that general improvement in standards of living inaugurates.

SUMMARY AND CONCLUSIONS

Research relating population and development demonstrates that extremely rapid population growth rates can exacerbate development problems. Early efforts to include population in growth models include the well-known "trap" and low-level equilibrium concepts; although the assumptions of these and later more elaborated models are often questioned, even sceptics seldom question their basic premise that population growth has implications for capital accumulation, employment levels, income and its distribution, public expenditure on social services, and food availability.

Studies of the consequences of rapid growth of population for education, for health, for labor force absorption, and for progress in other problem areas complement the results of the more general models. These studies have been most useful in those areas in which the relationship between rapid growth of population and increases in public costs is obvious, and in those areas which are themselves major development concerns. Use of this approach must be on a country-specific basis, and often must focus on specific areas within the economy, as countries emphasize one or another program.

Research (mostly in developed countries to date) indicates that children from poor families that are also very large are more likely to suffer from malnutrition and less likely to reach any given level of education than are others in their age groups in the population. The consequences of large families for family welfare provide a rationale for provision of family planning in countries in which fertility reduction *per se* is not an official objective, and in those countries in which fertility reduction is an official objective, but receives little attention.

Within countries, moreover, research indicates that the burden of large families falls most heavily upon the poorest groups. Though data on income distribution are still poor, the weight of logic also suggests that the differential in fertility between the better-off groups and those less fortunate constitutes a drag on efforts to improve the share of income going to the poor.

However, careful analysis of the determinants of household fertility also indicates that high fertility rates are not an inexorable component of underdevelopment—there are policy interventions to reduce fertility that could be, and have been, effective at tolerable cost.

Availability of family planning services appears to have contributed to the speed of fertility decline in some areas. Still, there is considerable room for expansion and improvement of services, even in those countries, including India, Pakistan, Indonesia, the Philippines, and, recently, Mexico, where family planning is well established as a legitimate means to reduce aggregate fertility.

Nor is family planning the only feasible policy intervention. Reduction of infant mortality appears to be a natural prerequisite to reduction of fertility. Research on fertility determinants points to the critical role of female education in reducing fertility. Improvements in opportunities for women to work, under certain conditions, can hasten fertility decline. Any success in increasing incomes of the poorest groups is likely to have fertility-reducing benefits; this includes increasing availability of services in health and education to those groups. No one intervention can be expected to affect fertility in a simple downward direction: the relation between each variable and fertility is complex, as are the relations among these variables and their joint effect on fertility.

This article is based on work the author undertook as a consultant in the World Bank Population and Human Resources Division in collaboration with staff members Rashid Faruqee and Ricardo Moran. She wishes to acknowledge their comments and those of other Bank staff members, especially Timothy King, as well as the contribution of William P. McGreevey. The article does not necessarily represent the views of the World Bank.

REFERENCES

Coale, Ansley J., and Edger M. Hoover. 1958. *Population Growth and Economic Development in Low-Income Countries*. Princeton: Princeton University Press.

Cochrane, Susan H. 1977. "Education and fertility: What do we really know?" Mimeo, World Bank.

Enke, Stephen. 1966. "The economic aspects of slowing population growth." *Economic Journal* 75.

Freedman, Ronald, and Bernard Berelson. 1976. "The record of family planning programs." *Studies in Family Planning* 7, no. 1 (January): 1–40.

Freeman, Peter. 1976. "The environment and large scale water resources projects." Prepared for International Institute for Environment and Development in preparation for United Nations Water Conference, March 1977.

Gregory, Paul, and John M. Campbell, Jr. 1976. "Fertility and economic development." In *Population, Public Policy and Economic Development*, ed. Michael C. Keeley, pp. 160–187. New York: Praeger.

Heer, David M., and Hsin-Ying Wu. 1975. "The effect of infant and child mortality and preference for sons upon fertility and family behavior and attitudes in Taiwan." Pp. 253–379 in *Population and Development in Southeast Asia*, ed. John F. Kantner and Lee McCaffrey. Lexington, Mass.: D. C. Heath.

Hermalin, Albert I. 1976. "Spatial analysis of family planning program effects in Taiwan." Paper presented at Population Seminar, East-West Population Institute, Honolulu, June.

Janowitz, Barbara S. 1973. "An econometric analysis of trends in fertility rates." *Journal of Development Studies* (April): 413–425.

King, Timothy, et al. 1976. *Population Policies and Economic Development*. Baltimore: Johns Hopkins University Press.

Kocher, James E. 1973. *Rural Development, Income Distribution and Fertility Decline*. New York: The Population Council.

———. 1976. *Socioeconomic Development and Fertility Change in Rural Africa*. Harvard Institute for International Development, Discussion Paper no. 16.

Kuznets, Simon. 1966. *Modern Economic Growth*. New Haven: Yale University Press.

Leff, Nathaniel. 1969. "Dependency rates and savings rates." *American Economic Review* 59, no. 5 (December): 886–896.

Leibenstein, Harvey. 1954. *A Theory of Economic-Demographic Development*. Princeton: Princeton University Press.

McGreevey, William P., and Nancy Birdsall. 1974. *The Policy Relevance of Recent Research on Fertility*. Washington, D.C.: The Smithsonian Institution.

McNicoll, Geoffrey. 1975. "Community-level population policy: An exploration." *Population and Development Review* 1, no. 1 (September): 1–22.

Nelson, Richard. 1956. "A theory of the low-level equilibrium trap in underdeveloped economies." *American Economic Review* (December): 894–908.

Oeschli, Frank William, and Dudley Kirk. 1975. "Modernization and the demographic transition in Latin America and the Caribbean." *Economic Development and Cultural Change* 23, no. 3 (April): 391–420.

Preston, Samuel. 1975. "Health programs and population growth." *Population and Development Review* 1, no. 2 (December): 189–199.

Repetto, Robert. 1974. "The interaction of fertility and size distribution of income." Mimeo, Harvard University.

Research Triangle Institute. 1971. *Social and Economic Correlates of Family Fertility: A Survey of the Evidence*. Research Triangle Park, N.C.: Research Triangle Institute.

Rich, William. 1973. *Smaller Families Through Social and Economic Progress*. Washington, D.C.: Overseas Development Council.

Schultz, T. Paul. 1971. "An economic perspective on population growth." In *Rapid Population*

Growth, vol. 2, pp. 148–174. Baltimore: Johns Hopkins University Press.

——. 1973a. "Explanation of birth rate changes over space and time: A study of Taiwan." *Journal of Political Economy* 81, no. 2 (Part II): S238–S274.

——. 1973b. "A preliminary survey of economic analyses of fertility." *American Economic Review* 53, no. 2 (May): 71–78.

Schultz, Theodore W. 1971. "The food supply—Population growth quandary." In *Rapid Population Growth*, vol. 2, pp. 245–272. Baltimore: Johns Hopkins University Press.

Williams, Anne D. 1976. "Review and evaluation of the literature." *In Population Public Policy and Economic Development*, ed. Michael Keeley, pp. 119–159. New York: Praeger.

Further Readings

1. Population and Development

Anker, Richard, and Farooq, Ghazi M. "Population and Socio-Economic Development: The New Perspective." *International Labour Review* 117, no. 2 (March–April 1978).

Berelson, B., et al. "Population: Current Status and Policy Options." Center for Policy Studies, Working Paper No. 44, The Population Council, May 1979.

Cassen, R. H. "Population and Development: A Survey." *World Development* 4, no. 10–11 (October–November 1976).

Coale, Ansley J., ed. *Economic Factors in Population Growth*. New York: Halsted, 1976.

Demeny, Paul. "The Populations of the Underdeveloped Countries." *Scientific American*, September 1974.

Demeny, Paul. "On the End of the Population Explosion." *Population and Development Review* 5, no. 1 (March 1979).

Easterlin, Richard A., ed. *Population and Economic Change in Developing Countries*. Chicago: University of Chicago Press, 1980.

Hawthorn, G., ed. *Population and Development*. London: Frank Cass, 1979.

King. Timothy, ed., *Population Policies and Economic Development*. Baltimore: Johns Hopkins University Press for the World Bank, 1974.

Mauldin, W. Parker. "World Population Situation Problems and Prospects." *World Development* 5, nos. 5–7 (May–July 1977).

McNicoll, Geoffry L. "Community-Level Population Policy: An Exploration." *Population and Development Review* 1, no. 1 (September 1975).

Repetto, Robert. *Economic Equality and Fertility in Developing Countries*. Baltimore: Johns Hopkins University Press, 1979.

Ridker, Ronald G., ed. *Population and Development: The Search for Selective Interventions*. Baltimore: Johns Hopkins University Press, 1976.

Teitelbaum, Michael S. "Population and Development: Is a Consensus Possible?" *Foreign Affairs* 52, no. 4 (July 1974).

Todaro, Michael P. "Development Policy and Population Growth: A Framework for Planners." *Population and Development Review* 3, nos. 1 and 2 (March and June 1977).

6

Employment, Output and Technology

14. Employment and Basic Needs: An Overview*

Assefa Bequele and David H. Freedman

The Programme of Action adopted by the ILO World Employment Conference in 1976 highlighted the importance of employment, as a generator of output and incomes, in a basic-needs strategy. The relationship between employment and basic needs, however, is not uni-directional; rather the linkages between the key variables extend in both directions, with the potential to reinforce one another as part of a cumulative process. As other recent articles in this journal[1] have demonstrated, the satisfaction of minimum requirements in such core areas as food, housing and health care results in qualitative as well as quantitative improvements in a nation's workforce. The purpose of this article is to summarise the major arguments and some of the evidence underpinning the employment-basic needs relationship.

1. EMPLOYMENT, OUTPUT AND INCOMES

The central role of employment rests on two major considerations. First, employment is an end in itself; it provides an individual with the opportunity to participate in society and enhance his sense of worth and dignity. Second-ly, employment provides income and generates output: it is therefore a crucial variable in the analysis of growth, income and levels of living.

Low levels of well-being in developing countries, as reflected in low incomes and the high incidence of malnutrition, illiteracy, disease, etc., are both the result and the cause of serious employment problems in these countries. As ILO and other studies have made clear over the years, open unemployment in developing countries represents only the tip of the proverbial iceberg. The employment problem has to be seen as encompassing underutilisation of labour and jobs that do not provide sufficient income to meet minimum needs. A major objective then is to make employment more productive, remunerative and, one should add, humane.

Employment and Output

In 1977 about 40 million persons or 5.2 percent of the labour force in the developing countries were estimated to be unemployed. A further 291 million or 40 percent of the labour force, predominantly in the rural areas and the urban informal sector, were thought to be underemployed.[2] Employment policy that leads to the full utilisation of this labour in direct production as well as in the construction of infrastructural facilities such as roads,

* From *International Labour Review*, 118, no. 3 (May–June 1979), pp. 315–29.

153

dams, irrigation and soil rehabilitation programmes can result in increased output, capital accumulation and over-all economic growth. The possibilities that employment creation holds in these respects as well as in increasing earnings and in reducing poverty and malnutrition, especially among the poorest members of society, have been documented in various studies, among others those on labour-intensive public works programmes in India, Indonesia, Bangladesh and China.[3]

Since the poor are found mostly in the rural and urban informal sectors and since industry has a limited labour absorptive capacity, the former sectors assume increased importance as sources of employment. Because production in the rural and urban informal sectors is generally geared to food and simple consumer goods respectively, increased employment in these sectors provides greater scope not only for raising total output *per se* but also for raising the production of precisely those goods and services required to meet basic needs.

Job creation for those who are unemployed throughout the year, or parts of it, is only one means of increasing output. The effect on output of rising levels of productivity is also important. For a variety of reasons such as malnutrition and undernutrition, ill-health and lack of skills, productivity in both rural and urban informal sectors is low. The interactions between these factors will be discussed more fully below; suffice it to note here that general or special measures designed to improve the skill, nutritional and health status of the labour force will, by increasing its productivity, contribute to increased output.

Employment and Incomes

Employment facilitates access to essential goods and services in one of two ways: either indirectly through the provision of income in the case of money-earning employment, or directly in the case of production for self-consumption. The latter is of special importance in the developing countries, especially in the rural areas, where a substantial but varying proportion of activity is directed towards the production of food for family or village consumption, or of other basic goods and services that are not bought and sold. This is of course a situation that can be expected to disappear progressively in the course of economic development.

However, where such a situation does exist, productivity-augmenting measures may be a far more effective means of ensuring basic-needs satisfaction than the creation of jobs that provide monetary incomes. For instance, the promotion of employment and production in export-oriented commercial agriculture at the expense of the sector producing food for the home market can lead to nutritional disequilibrium. In such cases, as Mouly rightly points out, "one runs the risk of registering simultaneously an (apparent) increase in employment and no improvement, and possibly even a deterioration of the conditions of life, as the (visible) increase in employment will be accompanied by a reduction in the ... supply of goods and services corresponding to the needs of the population".[4] This underlines the diversity of the employment problem and the need for selectivity in the adoption of policy measures designed to deal with it.

For those who are totally or partially unemployed, however, job creation assumes special importance as a means of obtaining access to basic goods and services. Obviously, unless they have the necessary purchasing power, they cannot obtain the goods they need. But inadequate incomes can also hinder the access of the poor to such services as education and health care even when they are free. Schools may be available but the poor may not be able to send their children because they are needed on the farms. Health centres also may be available but the poor may not utilise them fully, if at all, because they cannot afford the transport to reach them or the medicines prescribed. Income-earning opportunities, therefore, must accompany the provision of basic goods and services.

The labour-intensive public works programmes referred to above are considered to have contributed to the alleviation of poverty by providing the poor with sources of income. At a macro level, Morley reports that the growth in employment in Brazil over the period 1968–73 by 3.24 percent per year, or by 4 million new jobs, led to a 4 percent decline in the proportion of the labour force earning less than the minimum wage.[5] The importance of labour absorption in alleviating poverty has also been documented by Hsia and Chau in their analysis of employment and income distribution in Hong Kong.[6]

There is moreover, as will be made clear later in this article, an important two-way link between improved employment opportunities and the more even distribution of income. The income-equalising effect of an increased demand for labour can be further reinforced by the increased participation of those, especially women workers, who would otherwise not seek work but who, given the opportunity, may take a job to supplement the low earnings of household heads. The labour force participation rates of other household members are in fact inversely related to the earnings of household heads, so that increases in the number of secondary wage earners in a household may be expected to lead to greater income equality among households.

These conclusions are borne out by the Hong Kong experience. The rapid growth of demand for labour in the 1960s brought about a substantial reduction in income inequality by absorbing large numbers of unskilled and semi-skilled persons and by increasing the employment opportunities of female members of households. Consequently, over the period 1966–71, the mean income of the poorest 60 percent of households went up by 69 percent while the mean income of all households rose by 40 percent.[7]

2. GROWTH, BASIC NEEDS AND EMPLOYMENT

Just as increased employment can contribute to growth and the satisfaction of basic needs through higher output and incomes, increased growth in turn provides greater possibilities for rapid employment expansion and basic-needs satisfaction. For many developing countries the growth rate required to absorb the rapidly increasing labour force alone is quite high. Yet the generation of jobs for those who are now unemployed and those who will join the labour force in future years is only one, albeit important, aspect of the development challenge. Equally important is the provision of employment at income levels that are high enough to ensure that basic needs can be met. Looked at in this light, the growth rate required in many parts of the developing world is much higher than that recorded by them over the past 25 years.[8]

Notwithstanding the importance of growth, the extent to which its possibilities are realised depends on its pattern. For growth to benefit the poor it must reach them in the form of goods as well as jobs, and this is not always what happens at present.

A number of studies show that there is no strong or obvious relationship between the rate of economic growth and improvements in the living standards of the poor, whether measured in terms of their share of total income, their absolute level of income or a defined set of basic needs. Adelman and Morris, in their study of 43 developing nations, and the ILO's study of rural poverty in seven Asian countries indicate a deterioration in the relative (and sometimes even in the absolute) income position of the poor.[9] Clearly, therefore, these studies suggest a trickle-up in favour of the small middle class and the very rich rather than a trickle-down to the poor.[10]

While these conclusions are not accepted by everyone, the over-all evidence appears to suggest, as summarised by Morawetz, that

there seems to be no clear relationship between the rate of economic growth and either (a) the degree of inequality at a point in time or (b) the trend of inequality over time. Fast growers include both equal and unequal societies; they also include societies that have been growing more, and less, unequal. The same is true, also, of slow growers.[11]

In addition, there does not seem to be a significant relationship between GNP per capita and its growth rate on the one hand and the level and progress of basic-needs satisfaction on the other.[12]

What all these conclusions suggest is not the unimportance of growth. Indeed, growth is a condition for the alleviation of poverty. Rapid growth generates more output and more employment and hence higher incomes. It also increases resources for investment and thus for the future growth of output and employment. However, its efficacy as an instrument to alleviate poverty depends not only on how much is produced but also on *what* is produced and *how* it is produced.[13] These latter considerations therefore raise two important elements in the intertwined relationship between growth and employment and basic needs, namely the product mix and the factor mix.

The inter- and intra-sectoral flow of investment, and hence the composition of output, is influenced by the pattern of demand, which in turn is a function of the distribution of income. The greater the inequality in income, the more skewed the structure of consumption towards the rich. Moreover, the greater the inequality in consumption expenditure, the higher the proportion of investment and hence of output that will be geared towards "inappropriate" products consumed by the rich. This obviously reduces the supply of goods and services that can meet the basic needs of the poor.

The composition of output not only determines the supply of basic goods and services but also can be crucial in establishing and reinforcing a pattern of sustained and employment-intensive growth. It does this through the differential implications of goods consumed by different income groups for the balance of payments and the factor intensity in production. In respect of the former, the ILO Employment Mission to Colombia found that the products consumed by the rich had a higher import content than those consumed by the poor. Thus the import content of basic industrial consumer goods like clothing, footwear, beverages and furniture was found to be less than 5 percent whereas the coefficient for items such as electrical consumer durables, which were largely bought by the rich, was much higher (about 30 percent).[14] This implies that one of the consequences of a change in the product mix towards goods consumed by the poor would be reduced pressure on the supply of foreign exchange. As the scarcity of foreign exchange has been and will continue to be a major constraint on capital accumulation and hence on growth and output, the Mission argued that all measures, such as income redistribution, which change the structure of consumption and production and, by so doing, "increase the amount of foreign exchange available for the purchase of imported investment goods, permit an acceleration in growth of capital accumulation and therefore also in the rate at which jobs can be created in the longer run".[15]

Important also is the impact on employment of the differential factor intensities that underlie the production of goods consumed by various income groups. Several studies[16] have shown that goods consumed by the rich are generally less labour-intensive than those consumed by the poor. A change in the output mix in favour of products consumed by low-income groups therefore contributes to increased employment. "Hence", as Singer points out, "the emphasis on 'appropriate products' as a precondition for 'appropriate technology' ".[17] We have already noted the close relationship between income distribution and the nature of products and how changes in the former affect changes in the latter. In turn, a "change in the nature of products towards more appropriate products, especially by increasing employment, will help to create and support a more equal income distribution. This offers possibilities of mutually reinforcing policies in the field of income distribution, on the one hand, and products and technology, on the other."[18]

The scope for employment generation as a result of changes in the product mix resulting from changes in income distribution can be significant, as may be deduced from several studies. Paukert et al., for instance, in their study of the employment implications of income distribution in the Philippines, conclude that income redistribution leads to simultaneous increases in employment, gross domestic product and personal income. For example, the most radical income redistribution scenario[19] in their study was found to increase GDP by about 7 percent and employment by about 10 percent. This was due to the resulting shift in the product mix towards more labour-intensive patterns of production. A similar result based on Indian data is reported by Gupta. He estimates that a reduction in income inequality would have increased the annual rate of growth of employment in India by as much as 15 percent largely through its impact on the product mix and, later, on the factor mix.[20]

Sectoral Balance and Linkages

For various historical and structural reasons, development in many countries has been handicapped by the inadequate linkages between sectors. The links between capital-intensive industry and commercial agriculture on the one hand and the urban informal sector and the rest of the rural economy on the other have been tenuous. As a result, one finds significant and sometimes increasing disparities between sectors, regions and social groups in regard to incomes, productivity and the rate of employment creation. These slower growth rates have in turn led to slackened market expansion, thereby constraining growth in general and industrial development in particular.

A shift in the product mix and factor mix towards essential goods and greater employment would be likely to lead to better sectoral balance and linkages than has generally been the case so far, and possibly to increases in over-all output as well.

The stress on appropriate products with simple characteristics would boost domestic production, especially in the urban informal and small-scale industry sectors.[21] These sectors are major suppliers of mass consumption items, and the informal sector especially is known to produce goods consumed primarily by the poor.[22] Both sectors are also characterised by a much lower ratio of capital per worker or a higher ratio of labour per unit of output than are large-scale enterprises. Hence, increased emphasis on appropriate products would provide greater scope for the expansion of the small-scale and informal sectors as well as for the increased absorption of manpower. Furthermore, as enterprises using relatively labour-intensive technologies tend to generate higher rates of surplus in relation to the capital input than more capital-intensive enterprises, and as a higher surplus per unit of capital input leads to higher savings and investment, the promotion of the small-scale and informal sectors would result in a simultaneous increase in the growth rates of output and employment.[23]

The impact on the agricultural sector can also be expected to be favourable. As food is the major item in the consumption basket of the poor, a change in the output mix towards essential goods and the consequent increase in employment are likely to lead to increased demand for food and the expansion of agricultural output. This in turn can lead to higher levels of employment and incomes, restrain rural-urban migration and provide an expanded market and increased supply of raw materials for industry.

Increased growth, coupled with employment expansion and appropriate changes in the product mix, enhances industrial development and harmonises it with the development of other sectors. Economic development is characterised by structural changes in which industry claims an increasing share of total output and employment. This is because, in addition to increasing returns to scale in industry, accelerated industrial expansion is a prerequisite for meeting consumption requirements and supplying other sectors with the intermediate and capital inputs required for sustained and rapid growth. That this is so is readily apparent from both cross-sectional and time series studies, which show that an increase in GDP is generally associated with a more than proportionate increase in manufacturing production.[24] Hence, a higher rate of economic growth, which is a condition for progress in employment expansion and basic-needs satisfaction, and the development of the agricultural and urban informal sectors will both necessitate and make possible the more rapid growth of industry. However, what distinguishes this type of industrialisation from the conventional one is that it lends itself to the direct and indirect satisfaction of basic needs both in terms of the types of consumer and capital goods it produces as well as in terms of the technologies it uses.

In short, a pattern of growth consonant with the income and commodity needs of the poor, who in the Third World form the majority, could lead to a more integrated development of agriculture, industry and—within it—consumer and capital goods industries. The application of appropriate technology to agriculture and the informal sector stimulates over-all increases in productivity, incomes and employment and hence reduces inequalities (regional, sectoral, personal); the increase in employment, along with greater equality in incomes, in turn provides a larger market for over-all development and thereby establishes the base for more sustained growth; the stress on appropriate products geared to local needs and the more effective utilisation of local resources, along with the development of a local capital goods industry conceived within the larger framework of meeting mass needs, reinforce the foundation for higher and sustained rates of growth, employment expansion and basic-needs satisfaction.

3. BASIC-NEEDS SATISFACTION AND IMPROVEMENTS IN PRODUCTIVITY AND EMPLOYMENT

Up to this point we have looked at the employment- and income-generating potential of a pattern of growth oriented towards the satisfaction of basic needs. As noted earlier, the relationship between employment and basic needs is not unidirectional. Just as effective employment policies contribute to basic-needs fulfilment, programmes and policies directed towards meeting the needs of the poor can have a favourable impact on employment in a number of ways. One may begin with the readily apparent linkages between nutrition, health and employment.[25] As Rao Maturu points out, field observations have confirmed that inadequate food consumption and nutritional deficiencies diminish the work capacity of adults and thus their productivity.[26] In many cases malnutrition may be partly the consequence of poor health resulting, for instance, from parasitic infestation or diarrhoeal disease. Yet malnutrition itself increases susceptibility to disease and hence leads to a state of reduced working efficiency. In developing countries, especially in the rural sector where most work still demands considerable physical effort, imbalances between calorie intake and energy requirements will impair individual productivity and impede the growth in national output.

The link between nutritional improvement and higher productivity has been established empirically. Rao Maturu has cited the examples of cane-cutting activities in lowland Guatemala and earth-moving operations in Costa Rica.[27] Other illustrations include the cases of workers on the Pan-American Highway in Brazil who achieved about a threefold increase in daily output, and of rubber plantation workers in Indo-China who increased their output by 50 percent following the provision of better diets.[28]

Malnutrition and poor health affect employment in still other ways. Ill-health can inhibit labour force participation and job search and increase absenteeism. Moreover, as Mach points out, debilitating diseases not only sap workers' vitality, but hamper the fuller utilisation of other resources, such as land. For instance, certain land areas once uninhabitable because of malaria and other parasitic diseases can become cultivable sources of employment and income following successful eradication programmes. In populated endemic areas, malaria epidemics can disable the workforce, thereby greatly impeding the planting and harvesting of crops. The presence of malaria can lead to the recruitment of 30 to 40 percent more workers than required in order to allow for absenteeism due to illness. The elimination of malaria obviates the need for this practice and thereby permits much higher productivity. In the first year following malaria control in Pakistan and Burma, rice production is reported to have increased by 15 percent per acre.[29]

The relationships between nutrition, health and employment take on added significance in the case of women, especially those working and living in rural areas. In addition to performing their roles as housewives and mothers—and frequently also such arduous tasks as carrying water, fuel and other loads over long distances—they often have to work extended hours in the fields.[30] Although such prolonged activity increases their nutritional requirements, they may only get to eat what remains after their husbands and children have been served. Adequate diet combined with the application of appropriate technology would help to relieve some of the strain and drudgery of women's work as well as to raise productivity in sectors where it now tends to be low.

Poor health and nutrition are also related to education and training, which in turn affect both employment opportunities and productivity. The former may prevent regular school attendance and reduce the learning capability of children even when they do attend. This can result in a low level of skill development which in turn has consequences for later employment.[31] Moreover, individuals suffering from ill-health or malnutrition may be slow on-the-job learners with seriously reduced employment prospects. While proper education and training, like good health, cannot ensure employment success, they can make it more likely.

The education and training provided may in any case be inappropriate to a country's occupational and skill requirements, and may even lead to a serious mismatch between job opportunities and employment expectations. The ILO Comprehensive Employment Strategy Mission to Sri Lanka highlighted the problem in the title given to its report: *Matching employment opportunities and expectations*. In nearly every country the job expectations of new labour force entrants are increasingly diverging from the jobs actually available. In Sri Lanka the problem was found to be especially acute. The expansion of the educational system had outrun the economy's capacity to provide the types of jobs that those with secondary school qualifications felt they were entitled to—generally speaking, office jobs.[32]

An alternative educational approach would be to provide certain minimum educational qualifications and preparation for the world of work through a variety of means, both in and out of school, which could be adapted to local conditions and evolving development and employment needs. Examples of efforts to provide more appropriate preparation for the world of work include mobile vocational training schools in Thailand, the village polytechnic movement in Kenya, rural education centres in Upper Volta, the SENA (National Apprenticeship Service) training programmes in Colombia, the production work in crafts undertaken by the students of certain experimental schools in Botswana, and the industrial and agricultural work performed by the students of Chinese schools run by factories or communes.[33]

Adequate shelter is another of the minimum requirements of a family. Although the productivity benefits of good housing generally have not been measured, there appears to be a positive relationship. It is true, as Richards has observed, that it is difficult to separate productivity gains due to improved housing from those resulting from better nutrition, cleaner water, etc.[34] Nevertheless, the individual's housing conditions—the quality of the structure, the shelter and security it provides, the space available per occupant and the availability and adequacy of water supply and sanitation facilities—are a major element in his physical and social environment. They help to shape his behaviour and attitudes towards the larger society, and hence his work capacity and job performance.

4. EMPLOYMENT CREATION IN SECTORS PRODUCING ESSENTIAL GOODS AND SERVICES

As indicated earlier, not only can a basic-needs approach contribute to higher productivity, but its implementation can generate additional jobs. One of the clearest examples is to be found in the housing sector. Studies carried out by Strassmann suggest that construction programmes directed towards poorer groups create more employment per unit of expenditure than those favouring upper income groups. For instance, in Colombia the labour share of construction costs fell from 31.5 percent for single-family one-storey housing to 29.7 percent for 4- to 5-storey dwellings and then to 25.8 percent for 30-storey apartments. Taking account of the more expensive materials used in high-rise buildings, low-rise buildings were found to be cheaper per square metre and more labour-intensive.[35]

Another study, in Mexico, of labour earnings as a share of the structural cost of dwellings showed that while the construction labour content fell from 31–32 percent for low-cost housing to 18 percent for a luxury high-rise apartment, the labour content of construction materials (indirect labour costs) rose from 12–13 percent to 17 percent of structural costs. Nevertheless the total labour share, direct and

indirect, of structural costs declined as housing quality rose. In minimal and low-cost housing the expenditure on labour was 43–45 percent of the total; for good housing it was 39–42 percent; and for luxury housing, only 35–38 percent.[36] At the same time, account needs to be taken of the higher proportion of imported materials often used in the construction of more expensive housing, which reduces the domestic labour content still further.

Health care is another field where an approach more oriented towards meeting the needs of the poor stands to generate additional productive employment while at the same time contributing to the solution of two other serious problems: the steadily rising cost of medical care and the very uneven access to health care services.

The primary health care approach reflects recognition of the fact that highly trained and generally costly doctors and nurses are not required for the performance of many medical procedures and the provision of most preventive services. Primary health care, as defined by the International Conference on Primary Health Care,

is essential health care . . . made universally accessible to individuals and families in the community through their full participation and at a cost that the community and country can afford. . . . It is the first level of contact of individuals, the family and community with the national health system bringing health care as close as possible to where people live and work, and constitutes the first element of a continuing health care process.[37]

With respect to employment there are two points to be stressed. First, given the relatively labour-intensive nature of a primary health care system, especially when compared with more formal medical practice, it may be viewed as a fertile source of training and employment opportunities. The barefoot doctors of China, whose number reached 1.3 million in 1975,[38] offer one of the more striking examples of this fact. Secondly, participation and the fuller utilisation of human resources in one field of activity, when successful, can stimulate greater community participation, self-help and job creation in other areas of development. It is to that subject we now turn.

5. POPULAR PARTICIPATION, EMPLOYMENT AND BASIC NEEDS

The importance of popular participation in a basic-needs-oriented approach to development has already been highlighted in this journal.[39] The present discussion, therefore, will be limited to aspects of participation related to resource mobilisation and employment.

A major facet of participation is the effective involvement of people in the decisions that affect their lives and livelihood. Such involvement in decision-making can act as a powerful inducement to offer labour and skills as well as other resources to development programmes and projects. In situations where money is scarce or labour is otherwise underemployed, initiatives which make effective use of idle resources can contribute substantially to the achievement of development objectives, particularly at the local level. Outputs can take such varied forms as schools, clinics, wells, irrigation channels, land reclamation and road construction, just to give a few examples. In addition to the assets created for the community, there are several important employment and income effects. Opportunities for local participation, especially in self-help activities, can serve as a stimulus to higher productivity. To the extent that the work done is remunerated, primary income is generated and when spent can lead, through the well-known multiplier effect, to further jobs and incomes.

The Rural Access Roads Programme (RARP) in Kenya offers a good example of how local participation and employment creation may be linked, reinforce one another and contribute to the achievement of multiple so-

cial objectives.[40] The RARP, established in October 1974, has as its main objectives (1) making market centres more accessible to agricultural areas with a potentially high productive capacity; (2) providing productive employment opportunities for farm labour during the agricultural slack season; and (3) improving the over-all quality of rural life by facilitating access to planned or existing basic services located in district growth centres.

The RARP features a high level of local participation at all stages of a project. For instance, the choice of the route that a project road will follow is made by the RARP engineers in consultation with local people. Then again, since the access roads are constructed primarily to serve local communities, a feeling of ownership is created. As a result, local people are willing to donate small portions of their land for the construction of project roads.

The programme itself is highly labour-intensive. On-site labour costs alone account for about 55 percent of the total cost, while the strong emphasis placed on the use of locally produced tools and equipment results in off-site employment accounting for still another 15–20 percent of the total. Since 70–75 percent of the total cost can be attributed to on- and off-site wages and salaries, and given the generally high marginal propensity to consume of low-income groups, one may assume that most of the additional income earned from RARP employment is spent on locally produced wage-goods. Moreover, farmers employed during the slack season on RARP projects have more spare cash to invest in agricultural production. This, together with the opening up of agricultural land to market centres by access roads, should lead to the expanded production of staple food and cash crops as well as to the growth of related processing industries. All in all, when the programme reaches its peak in 1980, it will be one of the largest employers of wage labour in Kenya. Already by the end of 1977, when less than 14 percent of the programme had been carried out, labour employed in RARP projects accounted for about 10 percent of total public sector wage-employment.

6. CONCLUSION

Perhaps it is best to conclude this article the way it began, by stressing the strong link between employment and basic needs. A higher level of employment is a necessary condition and a major means for achieving growth in output which, if appropriately composed, will augment the supply of goods and services required to meet basic needs. At the same time, by generating primary income, it provides the poor with the wherewithal to obtain such goods and services.

However, the provision of essential goods and services in turn contributes to increased employment and productivity as well as to improved conditions of life and work. The immense underutilisation of labour, the low work intensity and the poor motivation found in most developing countries are as much the result of malnutrition, ill-health, inadequate housing, etc., as their cause. Even worse, such disabling forms of poverty tend to be cumulative and to affect future generations. For example, where malnutrition is severe and widespread, intelligence and hence creative and productive ability can be seriously or even permanently damaged, with concomitant effects on productivity, technological progress and over-all growth.

In short, therefore, policy efforts directed at the satisfaction of basic needs and the promotion of productive employment are mutually reinforcing and central to the elimination of absolute and relative poverty in the developing world.

1. N. Rao Maturu: "Nutrition and labour productivity", Jan.–Feb. 1979, pp. 1–12; P. J. Richards: "Housing and employment", ibid., pp. 13–26; Richard J. Szal (ed.): "Popular participation, employment and the fulfilment of basic needs", ibid., pp. 27–38: and E. P. Mach:

"Selected issues on health and employment", Mar.–Apr. 1979, pp. 133–145.

2. These are preliminary estimates from the ILO Bureau of Statistics and Special Studies. The "unemployed" are defined as "persons without a job and looking for work", and the "underemployed" as "persons who are in employment of less than normal duration and who are seeking or would accept additional work" and "persons with a job yielding inadequate income". The figures cited do not include China and other Asian countries with planned economies.

3. For analysis and evaluation of the experience acquired in this field see, for example, Emile Costa: *An assessment of the flows of benefits generated by public investment in the Employment Guarantee Scheme of Maharashtra* (Geneva, ILO, 1978; mimeographed World Employment Programme research working paper; restricted); Nguyen Phan-Thuy: *Cost-benefit analysis of labour-intensive public works programmes: a case study of the "Pilot-Intensive Rural Employment Project" (PIREP) in Mangalur Block of Tamil Nadu in India* (Geneva, ILO, 1978; mimeographed World Employment Programme research working paper; restricted); Y. B. de Wit: "The Kabupaten Program", in *Bulletin of Indonesian Economic Studies* (Canberra), Mar. 1973; and John Woodward Thomas: "The Rural Public Works Program in East Pakistan", in Walter P. Falcon and Gustav F. Papanek (eds.): *Development policy II–the Pakistan experience* (Cambridge (Massachusetts), Harvard University Press, 1971), pp. 186–236.

4. Jean Mouly: "Reflections on the role of employment in basic-needs-oriented strategies", in Jean Mouly and S. A. Kuzmin: *Five essays on the basic needs approach* (Geneva, ILO, 1978; mimeographed World Employment Programme research working paper; restricted), p. 3.

5. Samuel A. Morley: *Changes in employment and the distribution of income during the Brazilian "miracle"* (Geneva, ILO, 1976; mimeographed World Employment Programme research working paper; restricted), pp. 1 and 22.

6. Ronald Hsia and Laurence Chau: *Industrialisation, employment and income distribution: a case study of Hong Kong* (London, Croom Helm, 1978), pp. 142–147 and 182–183.

7. As a result, the Gini concentration ratio declined from 0.487 to 0.411 (Hsia and Chau, op. cit., p. 147). The favourable impact of increases in pro-

ductive employment on income distribution could however be dampened by various factors. In Brazil, for example, the vast increase in job creation that took place between 1968 and 1973 was accompanied by a substantial increase in earnings inequality. Thus, although the employed adult labour force grew by 3.24 percent per year, the ratio of the average wage of the top class (i.e., with monthly earnings of over 1,200 cruzeiros) to that of the bottom (monthly earnings of less than 80 cruzeiros) rose from 28.2 in 1969 to 40.4 in 1973. This was because there was a significant widening of the wage structure and new job creation was skewed towards the top of the earnings distribution. Morley, op. cit., pp. 28–39.

8. See M. J. D. Hopkins and O. D. K. Norbye: *Meeting basic human needs: some global estimates* (Geneva, ILO, 1978; mimeographed World Employment Programme research working paper; restricted).

9. I. Adelman and C. T. Morris: *Economic growth and social equity in developing countries* (Stanford, University Press, 1973); and ILO: *Poverty and landlessness in rural Asia* (Geneva, 1977).

10. Michael P. Todaro: *Economics for a developing world* (London, Longman, 1977), p. 153.

11. David Morawetz: *Twenty-five years of economic development, 1950 to 1975* (Washington, World Bank, 1977), p. 41.

12. Glen Sheehan and Mike Hopkins: "Meeting basic needs: an examination of the world situation in 1970", in *International Labour Review*, Sep.–Oct. 1978, pp. 523–541; and Morawetz, op. cit., p. 58.

13. Dudley Seers: "New approaches suggested by the Colombia Employment Programme", in *International Labour Review*, Oct. 1970, p. 386.

14. ILO: *Towards full employment: a programme for Colombia* (Geneva, 1970), p. 147.

15. Ibid., loc. cit.

16. See, for example, ibid.; Felix Paukert, Jiri Skolka and Jef Maton: *Redistribution of income, patterns of consumption and employment: a case study for the Philippines* (Geneva, ILO, 1974; mimeographed World Employment Programme research working paper; restricted); Jeffrey James: *Technology, products and income distribution: a conceptualisation and application to sugar processing in India* (Geneva, ILO, 1977; mimeographed World Employment Programme research working

paper; restricted); and Anand P. Gupta: *Solving India's employment problem: role of fiscal policy* (Geneva, ILO, 1975; mimeographed World Employment Programme research working paper; restricted). The case of construction is considered separately later.

17. Hans Singer: *Technologies for basic needs* (Geneva, ILO, 1977), p. 25.

18. Ibid., loc. cit.

19. This involved the reduction of the Gini coefficient from the 1971 estimate of 0.474 to 0.246. Paukert et al., op. cit., p. 38.

20. This assumed a reduction of the Gini coefficient from 0.32 to about 0.20 over the period 1973–74 to 1978–79. Gupta, op. cit., p. 39.

21. For a more detailed discussion see Singer, op. cit., p. 25; and A. S. Bhalla: *Technologies appropriate for a basic needs strategy* (Geneva, ILO, 1978; mimeographed World Employment Programme research working paper; restricted), p. 19.

22. ILO: *Employment, incomes and equality: a strategy for increasing productive employment in Kenya* (Geneva, 1972), p. 229; idem: *Basic needs objectives and policies in long-term development planning.* Discussion paper for the ACC Task Force on Long-Term Development Objectives (mimeographed, 1978), p. 31.

23. Idem: *Basic needs objectives* . . . , op. cit., p. 29.

24. A study of manufacturing in 50 countries shows that, for any given rate of growth in GDP, the producer goods industries grow faster than the consumer goods ones. See UNCTAD: *Restructuring of world industry: new dimensions for trade cooperation* (New York, 1978), pp. 5–8. See also Ajit Singh: *The "basic needs" approach to development and the significance of Third World industrialisation* (Geneva, ILO, 1979; mimeographed World Employment Programme research working paper; restricted), especially pp. 41–48.

25. For a concise analysis of the linkages, complementarities and trade-offs between the components of basic needs, see Paul Streeten: "The distinctive features of a basic needs approach to development", in *International Development Review* (Washington), 1977, No. 3, pp. 14–15.

26. Rao Maturu, op. cit., pp. 3–4.

27. Ibid., pp. 6–7.

28. Carl M. Stevens: *Health, employment and income distribution* (Geneva, ILO, 1975; mimeo-

graphed World Employment Programme research working paper; restricted), pp. 6–7.

29. Mach, op. cit., pp. 142–143.

30. For a fuller discussion see Iftikhar Ahmed: *Technological change and the condition of rural women: a preliminary assessment* (Geneva, ILO, 1978; mimeographed World Employment Programme research working paper; restricted), pp. 1–8.

31. Richard J. Szal: *Health, employment and development*, Paper prepared for the International Conference on Primary Health Care, Alma-Ata, USSR, 6–12 September 1978 (Geneva, ILO, 1978), p. 9.

32. Dudley Seers: "New light on structural unemployment: lessons of a mission to Ceylon", in *International Labour Review*, Feb. 1972, p. 104.

33. *Education and poverty*. Final report of a preparatory meeting of experts and main working document of the Meeting of Senior Officials of the Ministries of Education of the Twenty-five Least Developed Countries, September 1975 (Paris, UNESCO, Division of Educational Policy and Planning, 1977), pp. 22–23.

34. Richards, op. cit., p. 14.

35. W. Paul Strassmann: *Housing and building technology in developing countries*, MSU International Business and Economic Studies (East Lansing, Michigan State University, 1978), pp. 202 and 208.

36. Ibid., pp. 34–35 and 169. See also Richards, op. cit., pp. 15–17.

37. WHO and UNICEF: *Report of the International Conference on Primary Health Care*, Alma-Ata, USSR, 6–12 September 1978 (doc. ICPHC/ALA/78.10), p. 15.

38. Ng Gek-Boo: *Mass participation and basic needs satisfaction: the Chinese approach* (Geneva, ILO, 1979; mimeographed World Employment Programme research working paper; restricted), p. 22.

39. See Szal: "Popular participation...", op. cit.

40. The discussion of this programme is based upon Franklyn Lisk: *Basic needs activities and poverty alleviation in Kenya*, unpublished manuscript (Geneva, ILO, 1978).

15. Conflicts Between Output and Employment Objectives in Developing Countries*

Frances Stewart and Paul Streeten

* *Oxford Economic Papers*, vol. 36, no. 3 (July 1971), pp. 145–168.

This is a paper presented to a Cambridge conference in Sept. 1970, on 'Prospects of Employment Opportunities in the Nineteen Seventies', sponsored by the Overseas Studies Committee and the Ministry of Overseas Development under the chairmanship of Dr. Ronald Robinson. As the majority of participants were not economists, we tried to be comprehensible to the layman. We are grateful to Mr. Gavan J. Butler, Mr. M. FG. Scott, and Professor H. W. Singer for helpful comments.

Neither of the objectives, maximum output and maximum employment, are unambiguous. The output objective is ambiguous because output at any time consists of a heterogeneous collection of goods. Types of employment, in duration—daily, weekly, and seasonally—in effort and by regions, etc., also differ. In addition, both output and employment occur over time. Current levels of output and employment may influence future levels. Weighting therefore both intra- and inter-temporally is crucial to the *definition* of the objectives. However, we shall begin by ignoring these ambiguities and assume that our sole concern is with current levels of output and employment, and that maximizing current levels automatically leads to achievement of future objectives, or put more formally, that maximizing current levels of output and employment is equivalent to maximizing the present value of the entire streams of output and employment over time. We shall also begin by assuming that there is a single index for output and one for employment.

CONFLICTS RESULTING FROM SCARCE COMPLEMENTARY FACTORS OF PRODUCTION

We can then rephrase the question and ask: Is maximum current production compatible with maximum employment? On the face of it, the answer seems to be an obvious 'yes'. More men must surely be able to produce more. It is hard to picture conditions in which it is impossible to find anything useful to do for extra hands.

At a given time, with a given stock of capital equipment (inherited from the past), the employment of more men on that equipment is likely to increase output, although it could be that, as a result of the reorganization of the work, of less efficient production methods used, of people standing in one another's way or of a fall in efficiency for some other reason, the extra workers do not add to, and may subtract from, production. However, the choice facing a country is not simply a question of employing additional men with the existing capital stock but of the type of new equipment to install, and in this decision about the nature of new investment there can be a conflict between output and employment. Given that the total funds available for new investment are limited, using the funds for equipment to employ people in one way will inevitably mean *not* using the same funds for some other equipment which may involve *less* employ-

ment but might also produce more output. Maximizing output involves using scarce resources as efficiently as possible. If capital is the scarce resource, it involves minimizing the capital/output ratio. The type of production this requires may be, but need not be, consistent with maximizing employment.

Suppose in the textile industry the minimum capital/output ratio is associated with fairly modern-style industry. If £100,000 is available for investment in textiles, if the capital/output ratio is 2:5, and if the capital cost per work place for this type of factory is £1,000 (assuming a given degree of utilization of capacity), then investing all funds in this modern factory will involve extra employment of 100 and extra output of £40,000. An alternative way of investing the funds might be to introduce handspinning. Suppose for this the capital/output ratio was 5:0 and the cost per work place £100; then the extra output resulting from using the funds for handspinning would be £20,000 and the extra employment generated 1,000. In this case there is a fairly dramatic conflict between employment and output maximization. It should be noted that this conflict (which is a fairly realistic one if one examines actual figures for costs. etc., in the textile industry)[1] arises because the more labour-intensive method in the sense of the method which uses a lower capital/labour ratio or shows lower cost per work place, actually involves *more capital per unit of output* than the capital-intensive method. Some theoretical models assume this can never happen. It would be true that it could not, if all techniques of production were invented and developed simultaneously, since the labour-intensive methods which use more capital would never be developed. But in fact methods of production are developed over a historical period with the more labour-intensive methods generally originating from an earlier period. One reason why this sort of situation develops is the existence of economies of scale; as machinery has been adapted for larger-scale production the capital costs in relation to output have tended to fall, so that for large-scale production the later and more capital-intensive methods tend to economize on capital in relation to output. For small-scale production the older machinery may remain efficient.[2]

Implicit in this example is the assumption that there is a specific level of employment associated with each technique, and thus that it is sensible to talk of a 'cost per work place'. In fact, the number of people employed with any given machine may vary. The variation can take the form of using the machine more hours per day, or of employing more workers on the machine, directly or indirectly, at any one time. Since greater utilization of machinery and greater employment arising from using machines more hours per day can normally occur with any type of machine, it does not affect the comparison or conflict. If a machine is used at all there is normally some minimum amount of employment required to operate it (e.g., one man to drive a bulldozer). Above this minimum, employment may be variable. For some types of production output levels may be unaffected by the amount of 'free' or variable labour employed. For others output may be increased—normally by speeding up the pace of operations. But there is almost always an upper limit to the output level attainable as more labour is employed. When the machine is working at maximum pace additional workers may reduce the efforts of other employees rather than increase output. So long as output is responding positively to additional workers the level of employment associated with a given machine may depend partly on the level of wages. Even where output is invariant with respect to employment the actual employment associated with given machinery may depend partly on real wages since managerial effort may be substituted for employment as real wages rise. Thus the employment level associated with any given machine may not be independent of the wage rate. In the examples above some wage level

is implicitly assumed in associating each machine with a unique output and employment level. A range to represent output and employment at different wage levels would have been a more realistic representation. If one assumes that continuous variations in output are associated with continuous variations in employment, for each machine, but that there is diminishing marginal product as employment is increased, one is back in a neo-classical world where there are variable factor proportions and any amount of capital (or any machine) may be associated with any level of employment. In this neo-classical world the limit to employment is set by the real wages workers demand. There can be no conflict between output and employment because every type of machine can be associated with any amount of employment. Thus if the modern factory methods were employed in spinning, the extra 900 workers could be employed in the factory and would each add to output. At least as much employment and more output could result from choice of the factory alternative. We do not believe that this is a realistic assumption. Though some variation in employment is possible with any given machine, there comes a point at which the machine is operating at its maximum pace, when additional workers do not increase output. There is thus a limited range of employment possibilities associated with each machine, which means that there can be a conflict between output and employment. Put in another way, for *any* positive real wage there comes a point at which it is no longer worth while employing extra workers with a particular machine. This point may be reached at a lower employment level and a higher output level for one machine than for another. In this case there is a conflict between output and employment, which is independent of any institutional or other lower limit on the level of real wages.

Just as some economists assume that such a conflict between output and employment cannot arise, others assume not only that it has arisen in the past, but also that it necessarily must arise. The capital-intensive methods of production, it is claimed, will always involve lower capital costs per unit of output (and higher costs per work place) than the labour-intensive methods.[3] This position is as extreme as the other. There is considerable evidence that in many industries, and in many processes, the more labour-intensive methods also save capital per unit of output.[4] In these cases maximizing current levels of employment and output are consistent. Probably of more significance is the possibility of devoting research and development (R and D) efforts to the labour-intensive methods (in the sense of low capital cost per work place) so that they become efficient as compared with capital-intensive methods. Present possibilities reflect the fact that almost all R and D is concentrated on producing methods suitable for the developed world, in which labour is scarce; the labour-intensive methods currently available are generally the products of earlier and less sophisticated science and technology.

The questions at issue can be illustrated diagrammatically (Fig. 1). The neo-classical assumption of substitutability between capital and labour as represented by the continuous convex isoquant excludes the possibility of a conflict between current levels of output and employment. The relative wage level determines the employment associated with a given output level. With a sufficiently low relative wage level, represented by $K'L'$, full employment OA may be achieved. Deficiency of employment opportunities is to be attributed to excessive relative wages. The neo-classical model is sometimes applied only to new investment decisions—with the assumption that there is limited (or no) substitutability between labour and existing machines (the putty-clay model); and sometimes to all capital including existing machines (putty-putty). Clearly freedom of action and possibilities of achieving desired employment levels are greater with the latter type model; for the former the burden of generating desired employment is entirely on new investment.

The alternative view, which produces the conflict between output and employment described above, is that techniques available are limited and opportunities for labour/capital substitution correspondingly narrow. Production possibilities can be more accurately described by a few points on the diagram, than by a continuous curve; some of these points consist of inferior techniques requiring more of both factors, as in Fig. 2. Here a conflict arises between output and employment for any given quantity of capital available. Technique α represents the factory alternative; technique β the handspinning alternative. Output is the same at α and β; β′ is a smaller amount of technique β, involving less output than α. If α and β are the only techniques available and investment resources are limited to, say, OK'', no level of real wages will bring about full employment OA. However, choice of β will increase employment as compared with α, but for the same investment will mean sacrificing output, as at β′.

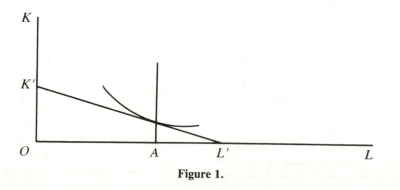

Figure 1.

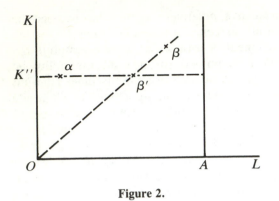

Figure 2.

In the hypothetical example the hand technique involved 900 additional employees compared with the capital-intensive technique. Apart from simply maximizing output, going for the capital-intensive technique and ignoring the employment implications, three possibilities are open. First, there is what we might describe as the Gandhi solution of adopting the hand technique despite halving of output. Second, there is the Nkrumah solution of introducing the modern factories and 'employing' the additional 900 workers in some minor and possibly completely useless capacity in the modern factory. Problems here are first that the extra workers might reduce output as a result of getting in each other's way and diverting administrative personnel (though probably output would not be reduced by as much as if the Gandhi solution were adopted and administrative difficulties might also be less). Secondly, if the modern factories also pay modern (i.e., relatively high) wages, as they generally do, the wage cost may be exorbitant. This has implications for saving and also for the viability of the enterprise if it is in private ownership. The Gandhi solution would probably allow lower wages per head. Thirdly, in a mixed economy it may be impossible to get employers to take on such useless labour. Voluntary agreements to increase employment by as little as 10 per cent have been notoriously short lived. A third solution is to adopt the modern methods and to use some of the extra output to employ the non-employed[5] on public works, etc. The difficulty here is that if any equipment is involved in the public works, employing workers on them will again divert capital equipment from other parts of the economy where the impact on output might have been bigger —in fact we are back at the initial problem.

The dilemma arises from the existence of scarce resources (in the above case capital, but it could have been entrepreneurship, administration, or some other input), which all forms of employment require. Sources of employment which do not use scarce resources will not present this dilemma. If, for example, the non-employed can make their own tools from local materials that are not scarce, and if their employment does not require the diversion of scarce administrative personnel, their employment will increase current output.[6] The same is true of employment which makes fuller use of the existing capital equipment, e.g., shift working, though some scarce resources of organization, administration, skills, etc., are almost always involved.

The aggregate level of organized employment depends not only upon the labour-intensity or capital-intensity of the methods of production adopted, but also on the level of real wages in relation to the consumption goods available to meet these real wages. If real wages in organized employment are higher than the levels of consumption of the non-employed, transferring workers from non-employment to organized employment will involve a net increase in consumption. An upper limit to this process is set by the resources available for the transfer. With a given real wage (and a given distribution between wages and other income) the maximum level of employment is determined by the consumption resources available, which depends on the level of output and the proportion of output saved. The labour-intensive alternative may therefore be ruled out, if the total consumption generated by those additionally employed is greater than available consumption resources. If real wages are flexible downwards or if redistribution is possible this problem does not arise.

REASONS FOR PREFERRING EMPLOYMENT TO OUTPUT

If a conflict between maximizing current output and employment were inevitable, why should we wish to sacrifice output to employment? Four possible answers occur to us, though others might think of additional reasons. First, employment creation and the consequential wage payments may be the only mechanism by which income can be redistributed to those who would otherwise remain unemployed. With an efficient fiscal system, taxation combined with unemployment relief, free social services, and other forms of assistance to the unemployed could be used as an engine of redistribution. In an underdeveloped society, loyalty to the extended family may induce the employed wage earner to share his wages with his often large extended family. But if neither fiscal system nor family provide a systematic channel of redistribution, job creation may have to be used for this purpose. Production will then be sacrificed for better distribution and, as a means to this, greater employment.

Second, unemployment is demoralizing. To feel unwanted, not to be able to make any contribution, lowers a man's morale and makes him lose his self-respect. The preservation of self-respect is worth sacrificing some production. As Barbara Ward has said, 'of all the evils, worklessness is the worst'—clearly not only and even not mainly because it lowers national product. It is worth sacrificing production to reduce this evil.

Third, it might be thought that work is intrinsically good, whatever its impact on morale, self-respect, and other subjective feelings. The Puritan ethic may command job creation as valuable, irrespective of its contribution to production. Puritanism played a valuable part in making desirable the necessary but unpleasant sacrifices which promoted the industrial revolution in Britain. Whether this ethic, where it has been adopted in the developing world (and it is notable that most Puritan-like statements tend to come from expatriates), should be encouraged and where it has not been adopted should be promoted, if it leads to a situation which impedes rather than speeds up growth by requiring the adoption of inefficient techniques to compensate for the masochistic value placed on work, is another question. Other aspects of Puritanism are certainly conducive to development; to the extent that Puritanism is a package deal, this aspect may have to be accepted along with the rest.

Fourth, there are obvious political disadvantages and dangers in widespread unemployment and non-employment. This is an important reason for valuing employment since, in so far as anyone does, it is the politicians who lay down 'the objective function' of society. Political instability resulting from heavy unemployment may, in any case, eventually endanger output levels and growth.

The value placed on employment as such is likely to depend partly on the type of employment. This is not just a question of the pleasantness or unpleasantness of the work, though nobody would value some types of sweated labour. Work which leads to ill health, shortens lives, or breaks spirits may sometimes be a necessary cost of output; it *is* a cost and not a benefit. Besides this aspect the location of work may also be relevant. If it is their failure to deal with the urban unemployment problem that is worrying politicians, urban employment may be valued more than rural. The feeling of worthlessness arising from unemployment is also likely to be more closely tied to long-term urban unemployment than to labour underutilization in the rural areas, which has a long and respectable history. More rapid expansion of urban employment opportunities may have little impact on the number of urban unemployed in so far as the expansion of employment opportunities adds to the flow of migrants from the rural areas seeking employment, and hence leaves the visible pool of unemployment unchanged. None the less, it seems likely that the situation would be less explosive if employment opportunities were expanding at, say, 10 percent per annum, than if they were static, or, as in many countries, actually declining. The desire for employment which is so apparent in many countries cannot be entirely divorced from the desire for higher incomes. Many of those seeking urban employment are looking for work *at the going wages* in the organized industrial sector, where wages are generally considerably higher than incomes obtainable elsewhere. Discussion of the need for rural employment opportunities to reduce the underutilization of labour normally takes place in the context of the need to create opportunities for increasing incomes through fuller labour utilization. Again the need is for incomes as much as for work. It is unlikely that the unemployed, or those scratching a living in the rural areas, would be prepared to suffer some loss in *their* incomes for the sake of more work. What is wanted is increased opportunities to work *and* earn higher incomes. Because both work and higher incomes are required it is difficult to disentangle the two. Clearly, the desire for redistribution of income is of prime importance. To achieve this redistribution, employment opportunities may be needed but the sacrifice, or trade-off, involved may be of the income of the better-off for the sake of that of the worse-off, rather than of output for the sake of employment. However, it can be argued that it is not just a question of income redistribution but of providing a chance to *earn*, not simply receive, the higher incomes.

These are the only reasons we can think of as to why the employment objective might conflict with the output objective, and sacrifice of output to employment, *properly defined*, is justified. But what are the proper definitions? As argued in the first paragraph, objectives are ambiguous. Two types of ambi-

guity are relevant. First, national product consists of a heterogeneous collection of goods, 'of shoes, and ships and sealing wax, of cabbages' (and possibly of the services of kings) and it accrues to different people, in different regions, with varying needs. In putting all these together we must use a system of weighting the different items and different sets of weights may lead to contradictions. One set may give the impression that we are sacrificing product for employment, another may not.

Another ambiguity arises because both production and employment occur in time and stretch into the future. An infinite number of time profiles within any horizon that we care to consider can be drawn up. Any profile for either of our two objectives that lies all the way below another profile of the same objective can be dismissed as inefficient. But in order to choose between those that intersect at some moment of time, we must make additional choices in the light of our policy objectives. What if 5 percent less employment now gives us 15 percent more employment in two years' time? What if a rise of 10 percent in employment now prevents us from employing an additional 5 percent of a vastly larger labour force in ten years and after? We must turn to the problems of *weighting* and *timing*.

WEIGHTING: DISTRIBUTION

Assume a mini-community produces and consumes whisky and milk. Whisky is drunk by the few rich, milk by the many poor. In the first year national income consists of 2 pints of whisky and 5 pints of milk, in the subsequent year of 1 pint of whisky and 10 pints of milk. National income is the sum of whisky and milk, weighted not by pints, but by the appropriate prices. But the relative prices registered in the market are partly the result of income distribution. On the demand side, they depend upon the purchasing power of milk- and whisky-drinkers. The relative prices derived from an *unequal* income distribution are (let us say) 20*s*. per pint of whisky and 2*s*. per pint of milk. With these weights, income has *fallen* between the two years from 50*s*. (20*s*. 2 + 2*s*. 5 = 50*s*.) to 40*s*. (20*s*. + 2*s*. 10 = 40*s*.). A *more equal* income distribution, putting more money into the pockets of milk drinkers relative to whisky drinkers, would give weights for whisky of 10*s*. per pint and for milk of 4*s*. per pint (on the assumption of increasing unit costs with increasing output). The income, weighted by these prices, would have *risen* from 40*s*. (10*s*. 2 + 4*s*. 5 = 40*s*.) to 50*s*. (10*s*. + 4*s*. 10 = 50*s*.).

Let us assume that the second year's production results from employing more men which raises the share of wages relative to profits and hence the demand for milk relative to whisky. A national income accountant, using the first set of weights, would register a fall in national income. People interpreting his statistics would say that we have sacrificed income for the sake of higher employment. But from the point of view of someone using the weights appropriate to the more equal distribution that results from greater employment, income is seen to have risen. There is a conflict between production and employment only if we use the wrong set of weights, assuming we prefer the more egalitarian income distribution.

Weighting other than by market prices should be introduced to reflect the different values of bundles of goods purchased by those at different income levels. Since the marginal utility of income is higher for a poor man than for a better-off man, greater weight should be attached to what goes to the poor than what goes to the better-off. Similar differential weighting might be attached to the expenditure of people in poorer regions within a country.

One difficulty in such an approach concerns the question of what weights to use. In the above example it was suggested that the prices emerging from the more equal income distribution should be used; these involved higher prices (and therefore weights) for the low-

income good—milk—and lower prices and weights for the high-income good. This was only the case because of increasing costs for both goods. With elastic supply and constant unit costs the relative prices would have remained the same. With decreasing costs the relative price of the low-income good would have declined as incomes became more equal. Thus to use the prices emerging from the more equal income distribution is not sufficient to deal with the problem of including the value attributed to income distribution in the measure of income. This may be so even in the case of increasing costs, when the resultant change in prices may not be enough to allow for one's judgement about the distributional implications of the change. The weights attached to the different goods need therefore have no relationship to the pattern of prices that might emerge with the desired income distribution.

Attaching different weights to different goods (e.g., milk and whisky) according to who consumes them is effective as a means of incorporating judgements about the income distribution only if the pattern of consumption differs among consumers of different income levels. At one extreme if all consumers consumed only one good, say maize, and differed only in the amount of that good they consumed, the value attributed to output would not be affected by the distribution of income whatever the weight given to the single good. In this case maize itself must be weighted or valued differently according to who consumes it. This is an unrealistic extreme. But there are many goods that are consumed at all income levels. So long as the pattern (i.e., proportion of income spent on different goods) of consumption differs according to income level a revised weighting system can, in theory, incorporate distributional judgements. Its calculation would be highly complicated, and would change over time as patterns of consumption changed.

An alternative is to attach weights to the income, according to the level of income of the recipient, rather than to goods; this is broadly the system adopted by Marglin[7] where the value attributed to the demand for any good is weighted more heavily the poorer the consumer. For judgements about macro-income changes this approach has much to recommend it in terms of simplicity. It does not, however, rule out ambiguity in real output changes consequent upon changes in relative prices. With such a system 'income' would be increased simply by improving the distribution of income without any change in the output of goods and services.

Weighting according to the value of expenditure to the individuals and groups who benefit from it raises certain philosophical problems. One may not wish to define 'income' and 'growth of income' in such a way as to incorporate all distributional value judgements in the definitions, so that no conflict could ever arise between 'income', its distribution, and employment. A narrower definition is useful, in order to bring out the choices. On the other hand, so long as the conventional definitions are accepted and countries placed in league tables according to them, the arbitrary nature of national income measurement tends to be forgotten and virtue gets associated with movements in this arbitrary figure. Policies as well as value judgements may be influenced by the form of measurement adopted. There is much to be said, therefore, for even a crude and arbitrary adjustment of income measurement in the direction of incorporating judgements about income distribution.

WEIGHTING: TIME

Another serious ambiguity arises from the fact that sacrifices now may yield gains in the future. We must consider two opposite sets of circumstances: first, where less production and more employment now leads to more production later than would otherwise have been possible; second, where less employment and more production now lead to more employment later than would otherwise have been possible.

In order to illustrate the first case, let us return to the situation where men were demoralized by unemployment. We then regarded self-respect and high morale as ends in themselves. But we may also regard them as necessary for the continued employability of men. If men remain unemployed for long, their skills as well as their attitudes deteriorate and they are incapable of producing as much later. This situation cannot be remedied by unemployment assistance, for it is only on the job that ability to work and motivation are maintained. Just as machines sometimes have to be kept going in order to prevent attrition or rust, so workers and teams of workers have to be kept busy to prevent them from becoming rusty or apathetic. Current employment, even where there is nothing to show for it, can be regarded as a form of investment—human maintenance—which prevents future deterioration of productivity. In addition men's productive capacity, their ability to work, their initiative and organizational ability, and their concentration may not merely be maintained but may actually be increased by working. This form of learning by working means that the greater current employment opportunities, the greater is future productive capacity.

The second case works in the opposite direction and is possibly the most important way in which an apparent conflict between employment and output arises. Here we maximize production in the short run, even though it means tolerating more non-employed now, because the extra production enables us to generate more jobs later than would otherwise have been possible. If there is a current conflict between output and employment, it must be remembered that output is useful not only for itself, but can be used to generate more employment.

The inter-temporal 'trade-off' between employment now and employment tomorrow arises because, by tolerating more unemployment now for the sake of producing more, we can provide the men (and their children) with more jobs later. This is only partly a matter of investment, i.e., producing now the machines, or resources with which to buy the machines, that will give jobs tomorrow. A greater volume of food which provides better nutrition for the workers and their children, of health measures and of certain forms of education can also contribute to greater employment (and fuller labour utilization) in the future. The point leads once again to income distribution, but this time not valued independently as desirable, but as instrumental to faster growth. The choice between maximum employment and maximum output reduces to one between jobs now or later, because more output now can promote more, and more effective, employment in the future. To raise employment means sacrificing not only output now (and, on our assumption, the rate of growth of output) but also the rate of growth of employment. This means that at some future date the level of employment will be lower than it would otherwise have been. To go back to the example discussed earlier, suppose in each case, modern factory and handspinning-wheel, 20 percent of income generated is saved. The factory solution will involve £8,000 investment available in the next year, while the hand-wheel alternative will involve £4,000. The divergence will get greater in subsequent years. The factory alternative will lead to an annual growth in income (and assuming the same £1,000 a work place technology is adopted, in employment) of 8 percent per annum while the handspinning-wheel alterna-

tive will lead to 4 percent annual growth in output and employment. (This ignores the impact of extra consumption on growth.) Fig. 3 illustrates the possibilities.

The choice now presents itself as one between different time paths of output and employment. It is thus partly a question of our time preference towards both output and employment: i.e., the basis on which we should make our choice for given possible time paths, as the one illustrated in Fig. 3. But the situation is somewhat more complicated than this because there are other ways in which current choices of output and employment levels may affect the future pattern of both.

As to the right choices, a good deal will depend upon our time horizon and on uncertain future developments. As far as employment is concerned, the life span of one generation and perhaps its children will be relevant, but few would be prepared to tolerate widespread unemployment over two generations to improve the job prospects of their great-grandchildren. This is not only because we show less concern for our great-grandchildren, but also because we may rightly hope that their prospects will improve for other reasons, such as the development of more appropriate technologies, improvements in motivation, administration, education, etc. Within such a time horizon we might argue that, on the one hand, the richer society of tomorrow can look better after its unemployed and to be unemployed then will be a smaller hardship. On the other hand, with present trends of growth of the labour force in less developed countries and likely opportunities for jobs, the total number of un-

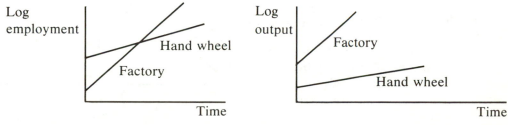

Figure 3.

employed is increasing rapidly. While the lot of a given number of unemployed will therefore be better in the future and the burden of maintaining them lighter, the number to be looked after will be larger. In the more distant future, however, we may assume that population control will have become effective or new scope for migration will have opened up. In view of all this, it seems right to discount future jobs and to give more weight to more jobs now and in the near future.

But, though the discount rate that we should apply to employment should be positive, it may be less than the one we apply to output or to consumption. The main argument for applying a discount rate to output is that the marginal utility of income is less for a richer society. This does not apply in the same way to employment—i.e. the value of extra employment generated does not decline as the level increases—though increasing *incomes* per head may make employment in the future less important as a means of income redistribution. On the other hand, the contrasts between those employed and those not employed and the accompanying resentment may work the other way. Poverty in the midst of affluence is worse than plain poverty widely shared. This, and the question of numbers, suggests that it may be correct to give greater relative weight to future as against current employment, than to future as against current output.

Planners must know not only their preferences between the present and the future, for both output and employment, but also what opportunities there are for trade-offs. Conflicts between current levels and growth rates of output and employment may arise either because growth rates are determined by saving rates (or, more generally, developmental expenditure rates), savings rates by income distribution and income distribution by employment levels, or because growth rates are determined by the allocation of a given savings ratio between sectors and this allocation

influences the level and growth of employment.

It is common to assume in this context that a capital-intensive technique leads to a higher savings ratio for the same income level than a labour-intensive technique. On this assumption, lower employment now can give faster growth of both output and employment. Those who make this assumption[8] assume

(a) that a higher proportion of profits is saved than of wages (at its most extreme the assumption is that all profits are saved, all wages consumed); and that consumption makes no contribution to future growth;
(b) that wage rates do not depend on techniques;
(c) that the government is incapable of securing the savings ratio it desires by taxing wage earners and generating adequate public savings or using inflation to reduce real wages.

Since the growth rate is the product of the savings ratio and the output/capital ratio, the effect on the growth rate of raising the savings ratio by increasing the capital-intensity of technique adopted will depend on the consequences for the output/capital ratio. Fig. 4 illustrates the implications for growth of neoclassical assumptions as the capital-intensity of techniques is increased. With such a production function the most labour-intensive tech-

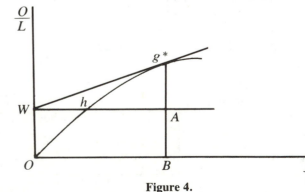

Figure 4.

nique maximizes current employment, for any given capital expenditure. On the diagram, as one approaches the origin, labour requirements per unit of output rise while capital requirements fall. Techniques to the left of *h* involve negative savings and are therefore unlikely to be feasible. But for any given capital-intensity of techniques and in the absence of technical progress (or in the presence of neutral technical progress) the growth of employment is determined by the growth of output. Assuming all wages are consumed and all profits saved, the technique which maximizes the growth of output (and also employment) will depend on the wage level. With wages per employee *OW*, which do not vary according to the technique adopted, the growth rate (s/v) is represented by the slope of the line from *W* to the production function.[9] This is maximized when it is tangential to the production function as at g^* in the diagram. Here there is a conflict between maximizing current employment (which involves choosing the technique nearest to the origin for a given capital stock) and maximizing the growth of output and employment at g^*. However, there is no conflict between maximizing the growth of employment and output, both of which involve the same technique. The conflict between current employment and the growth of employment worsens as the wage level increases, as illus-

trated in Fig. 5. As the wage increases from OW^1 to OW^2, the capital-intensity of the technique which maximizes the growth of output and employment increases (increasing the conflict between current and future employment), while the maximum attainable growth rate declines. If we drop the neo-classical assumption of rising capital/output ratio as the capital-intensity of techniques increases, the most capital-intensive technique available maximizes the growth rate, irrespective of the wage rate.

Additional employment of the kind discussed earlier which is costless in terms of present output since it does not require any scarce resources as additional inputs—neither capital nor administration nor skilled manpower—may impede growth on these assumptions because the extra consumption of those additionally employed will reduce society's propensity to save.

If the rate at which we discount future output is higher than that at which we discount future employment (an assumption which we argued was reasonable), we get the perverse situation that a strategy of optimum employment growth would require greater current unemployment than a strategy aiming at optimum income growth. The former would involve more capital-intensive techniques, higher savings rates, and greater income growth.

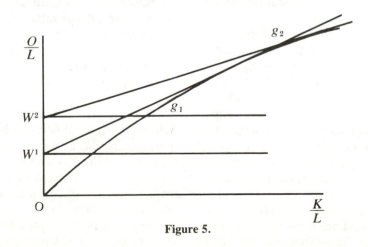

Figure 5.

The assumptions of this model are questionable: first, there is evidence[10] that the wage rate is linked to labour productivity and the choice of technique, so that the more labour-intensive methods involve lower wages per man than the more capital-intensive ones. Secondly, all profits are not saved and it may not even be warranted to assume that a higher proportion of profits is saved than of other incomes. Profits remitted and retained overseas, even if saved, will not add to the investible resources of the developing economy. Thirdly, there is the rather asymmetrical assumption that the government is incapable of enforcing the saving it desires by wages or taxation policy, but is capable of enforcing it through choice of technique, despite the fact that this choice, in a mixed economy, is not directly in its hands in many cases, and involves, if made effective, a lower level of employment. The sacrifice of employment, in this case, is not so much a sacrifice for the sake of future levels of output and employment, but more a sacrifice on the altar of government inability to pursue effective taxation policies.

So far we have focused on the aggregate savings ratio. If it is determined by the distribution of income between wages and profits and if this distribution in turn is determined by the level of employment, a conflict may arise between maximizing current employment and maximizing the growth of employment and income.

Now let us consider the case where a given ratio of savings to income can be invested in either of two sectors:[11] one making capital goods that make capital goods (machine tools), the other making capital goods that make consumer goods (looms). The higher the proportion allocated to the machine tool sector, the faster the rate of growth of total output and the higher consumption at some point in the future and after, though the lower the initial increase in consumption. Assuming employment requirements, in relation to investment, are the same in both sectors, maximum *current* and *future* employment will be achieved by maximizing the proportion of investment allocated to the machine tool sector. This choice also maximizes current and future levels of *output*, but involves the lowest initial increase in consumption, though eventually consumption will be highest with this path. Hence there is no conflict between output and employment, but there may well be conflicts between consumption objectives and employment. If the labour requirements of the machine tool sector are lower than those of the loom sector, a conflict between employment (and current consumption) and growth arises. The proportion allocated to each sector which is optimal from the point of view of income and consumption growth may conflict with the ratio which is optimal from the point of view of employment growth. It should be noted that this two-sector model implicitly assumes that over a period of time the government is able to enforce any savings ratio it likes, and equally any level of real wages per head of the employed. The only limitation on the savings ratio is the productive capacity of the machine sector and not the propensity to save and consume. This is in complete contrast to the earlier model where the government was explicitly assumed incapable of enforcing the savings ratio or real wages per employee that it considered desirable by any of the usual means, and the choice of technique therefore also assumed the role of determinant of the savings ratio. If the same assumption is made for the two-sector model it alters the nature of the choices available since employment can then never rise faster than the output of consumption goods and thus the main source of possible conflict is removed.

This type of two-sector model has been criticized for rigidity of assumptions—particularly the assumption that the capacity of the 'machine tool' industry limits the investment possible, which denies the possibility of expanding investment by increasing imports of machinery. However, the model is more generally applicable than that; it applies to any sector which is holding back development, and which could be expanded by devoting sufficient resources to it. Resources devoted to the bottleneck sector will increase the rate of growth of the whole economy, and ultimately of *all* sectors of the economy at the temporary cost of the development of those sectors from which resources are diverted. Thus conflicts in timing emerge; they may be relevant to the employment question, as suggested above.

TECHNICAL DEVELOPMENTS

Until now we have assumed that the technical choices available remain unchanged, and that output and employment grow at the same rate if a technique of particular capital-intensity is adopted and adhered to over time. In practice the technical possibilities available change over time. Generally technical progress takes a form which involves increasing labour productivity, so that the rate of growth of employment is less than the rate of growth of output. This phenomenon—output increasing faster than employment—has been observed in many developing countries. The increase in labour productivity is partly a question of improved management techniques and greater labour efficiency as a result of learning by doing and the spread of education. In this respect it is probably unrelated to the rate or type of investment (it could be classified as 'disembodied technical progress') and therefore does not affect the choice of technique or the basic comparison between techniques: the technique which maximizes the rate of growth of output will also maximize the rate of growth of employment, though the latter will be lower than the former.

But the increase in labour productivity is also partly due to the installation of new machines (both as net additions to the capital stock and as replacements of old machinery). Technical developments which take the form of new machines and new products may affect the terms of conflict between output and employment. Such developments are likely to affect some techniques more than others. In particular, research, development, and use of techniques in developed countries are virtually confined to techniques of high and *increasing* capital-intensity. For these techniques, labour productivity, and often capital productivity as well, may rise over time, while the more labour-intensive techniques may be unaffected by technical progress. The labour-intensive techniques may therefore become inferior over time and their use may then involve a sacrifice of output as compared with the use of the later, more capital-intensive techniques.

The earlier arguments of this paper might suggest choosing the later more capital-intensive techniques where they result in more output and therefore savings than the labour-intensive techniques on the grounds of maximizing future employment as well as current and future output. (Indeed, if we assume savings are inversely related to employment, for any given output, the more capital-intensive techniques may maximize the rate of growth of employment even where they result in no greater output than the labour-intensive methods.) It might therefore appear that, from the point of view of long-run employment, it would be correct to adopt the output growth maximizing tactic of adopting techniques of successively greater capital-intensity which are developed as time proceeds. But the increasing capital-intensity (defined in terms of capital requirements per worker) means that a given amount of savings generates progressively fewer jobs. If the proportionate increase in the savings available for investment as a result of moving to techniques of greater capital-intensity, which lead to higher output and savings, is less than the increase in capital requirements per worker, then the growth in employment will be *less* with the output-maximizing technique than if the older, more labour-intensive techniques, leading to lower output, were adhered to.[12] In an extreme case, the adoption of successively more capital-intensive techniques, if applied to replacement as well as net investment, might lead to a fall in employment despite rapid and accelerating output growth. In such situations it makes sense to talk of a conflict between output and employment.

There is a paradox here. The later, more capital-intensive techniques, it is postulated, are more efficient (i.e., lead to higher output) and therefore generate more savings. This means that if chosen they would allow greater employment at a subsequent date than the earlier labour-intensive techniques, for any comparable type of employment in terms of capital cost per work place. (E.g., more public-works-type employment would be possible because the savings required to finance such works would be greater.) If our concern is with tomorrow's employment as much as today's we should choose the more capital-intensive technique which will allow potentially more employment tomorrow. But when tomorrow comes the development of techniques extends the choice to yet more capital-intensive techniques. If chosen, these will lead to lower employment levels than if the now inferior techniques previously chosen continue to be adopted. On the grounds of maximizing the surplus available for future employment, the more capital-intensive techniques should again be chosen. This may continue indefinitely. Choice of the later more capital-intensive technique is always justified on grounds of output maximization and future potential employment. But this leads to a persistently lower level of employment than would occur if the capital intensity of methods adopted did not rise continually. The potentially greater employment will be realized in actual employment levels only when this argument is rejected and the accumulated savings or some of them are used for less capital-intensive employment. When they are so used, there will be a sacrifice of output for employment.

The application of this argument can be exaggerated. Only in special circumstances will the use of successively more capital-intensive techniques actually involve a fall in employ-ment. In many cases their use may still maximize the rate of growth of employment. Observations[13] of the relationship between the growth of output, employment, and labour productivity over a large number of countries suggest that generally there is a positive association between the growth of output, employment, and labour productivity. The path which maximizes the growth of output will also maximize the growth of employment but the output growth will be greater than the employment growth.

Greater use of labour-intensive techniques may also bring about various improvements in their costs and performance, including a fall in their cost simply as a result of economies of scale in their production. Labour-intensive techniques may be easier to produce in the developing countries, because they are often of simpler design and more (in number) are required in a particular country so that some of the economies of scale may be exploited. Current relative costs and efficiency of different techniques may therefore fail to reflect potential relative costs after technical progress through use has been realized. They may also fail to take into account the differing possibilities for local production and repair of the different techniques. This means that current possibilities may understate the likely implications for output of labour-intensive techniques; the conflict between employment and output may therefore be less in reality than at first appears.

THE PRODUCT-MIX

So far we have assumed the composition of consumption goods to be determined and have varied only the techniques of producing them and the allocation of investment between sectors. If different consumption goods require different proportions of labour and capital, we can raise the level of employment without varying the techniques of producing any product by enlarging the share of labour-intensive products at the expense of capital-intensive products. If there are opportunities for international trade on favourable terms, this is an obvious solution. If, however, a changing composition involves changing the products consumed at home, the question is whether, with a proper system of weighting, losses in consumers' welfare would arise. If the labour-intensive products are also those largely demanded by the poor, we have already seen that a fall in output may be an optical illusion and that the weights derived from a more equal income distribution might show a rise. There may also be external diseconomies of consumption, or buying as a result of created wants or of habits. If a product is wanted (1) because others buy it or (2) because it was bought in the past or (3) wants are created through advertising, and if these features are peculiar to the capital-intensive product, its elimination may lead to smaller welfare losses (in cases 2 and 3 after a time) than the expenditure values would indicate or it may lead to welfare gains.

The scope for changing the consumers' product-mix in a labour-intensive direction is generally considered somewhat limited, apart from possibilities of international trade, by the need for a reasonable balance in the composition of demand. We cannot expect people to consume all food and no clothes for example, or to have more haircuts at the expense of bicycles. But the conclusions drawn from this, in terms of the narrow scope for product substitution, arise partly from a mistaken definition of product. Any given need may be fulfilled by a number of different products: nylon or cotton shirts fulfil the need for clothing, wooden houses, mud huts, reinforced concrete multi-storey buildings fulfil the need for shelter. While maintaining a reasonable balance in terms of needs (clothing, housing, shelter, etc.), there is considerable scope for substitution towards more labour-intensive products for the fulfilment of each need. The

possibilities of concentrating more on labour-intensive products to fulfil each need may therefore extend the scope for using the product-mix to increase employment opportunities.

CONCLUSION

On examination the possible conflicts between output and employment objectives appear more complex than might be supposed from the increasingly fashionable assertion that 'we must sacrifice output to employment'. The measure of output is itself ambiguous, depending on the weighting attributed to different components of output. Not only current but also future employment levels as well as output must be taken into account. In many cases higher current output levels, and lower employment levels, may lead to higher future levels of employment as well as output. The potential conflict between output and employment is thus likely to be a question of different preferences for an entire time profile of output and employment, with the preferred output path being associated with a rejected employment path. It is unlikely that this conflict could be accurately described as a desire to sacrifice output for employment or vice versa. It is a more complex question of, for example, the weight given to current as against future output being greater than that given to current as against future employment. The terms of a potential conflict of this kind may also be alterable by a shift in the pattern of R and D leading to a shift in the alternatives available; greater government control over the savings potential of the economy would also alter the pattern of conflict.

In this paper we have been concerned to illuminate the conditions under which it is meaningful to talk of a conflict between employment and output. The conclusion we reach is that, in many cases, the path which maximizes the growth in output is also that which maximizes the growth of employment. This might appear to be in strong contrast to the general dissatisfaction currently felt with recent developments in the developing countries, where, it is often argued, output growth has been taken as the overriding objective irrespective of the unfortunate consequences for employment. To some extent (in many Asian countries) recent experience bears out our theoretical contention, that output growth and employment growth are not in conflict as objectives. The dissatisfaction felt appears to have its origin in the unsatisfactory rate of employment creation, in relation to the desire and need for employment, rather than in some sacrifice that has taken place of employment for output. But elsewhere (parts of Latin America, the West Indies, and Africa) it appears that rapid rates of growth of output have been realized with minimal or no increases in employment. Here the increasing capital-intensity of production may have more than offset the additional resources available for investment in their effects on employment creation. In addition the potential savings available from the higher levels of output were not always channelled into investment, as a result of rising real wages, and repatriation of foreign owned profits. The simple model used earlier in the paper assumes that savings are a function of the level of output; in reality who gets the output and how and where it is spent is also of importance. Dissatisfaction with performance in these and other economies is also a reflection of dissatisfaction with the distribution of income, and the meaningfulness therefore, of conventional measures of income and income growth.

1. A. S. Bhalla. 'Investment allocation and technological choice—a case of cotton spinning techniques'. *Economic Journal*, 1964, suggests that the capital/output ratio (including working capital as well as fixed capital) using factory methods in cotton spinning is about three-quarters of that using the hand Ambar Charkha methods. Bhalla's analysis of rice pounding, 'Choosing techniques: hand-pounding *v.* machine milling of rice: an Indian case'. *Oxford Economic Papers*, Mar. 1965, suggests a similar conflict here; the technique which maximizes employment (or has the lowest cost per work place), the pestle and mortar, requires nearly twice the capital per unit of value added compared with the large sheller machine. The latter requires investment per work place about 100 times as great as the former.

2. The importance of scale in determining the efficient range of production possibilities is emphasized by many empirical studies, including G. K. Boon, *Economic Choice of Human and Physical Factors in Production*, North Holland Publishing Co., 1964, and W. P. Strassman, *Technological Change and Economic Development*, Cornell University Press, 1968.

3. See, for example, N. Kaldor in Ronald Robinson (ed.), *Industrialisation in Developing Countries*, published by the C.U.P., Overseas Studies Committee, 1965, pp. 28–9: 'There is no question *from every point of view* of the superiority of the latest and more capitalistic technologies' (our italics). Similar emphasis on the overall superiority of capital-intensive techniques is found in S. Amin, 'Levels of remuneration, factor proportions and income differentials with special reference to developing countries', in *Wage Policy Issues in Economic Development*, ed. A. Smith, Macmillan, 1969, pp. 269–92.

4. A. S. Bhalla, *Economic Journal*, 1964, suggests that the capital/output ratio for traditional spinning methods, as opposed to the Ambar Charkha, may be lower than for factory methods. A. K. Sen, *Choice of Techniques*, Appendix C, suggests that in cotton weaving the capital/output ratio is the lowest for the most labour-intensive technique, the fly-shuttle hand loom, and highest, nearly 2½ times as big, for the automatic power loom (again including working capital). Evidence for the existence of a range of efficient techniques in a number of industries below a certain critical scale of output is also contained in G. K. Boon, op. cit.

5. We use the expression 'non-employed' to distinguish them from Keynesian 'unemployed'.

6. It was this type of employment Nurkse was considering in discussing the under-employment as a source of savings, in *Problems of Capital Formation in Underdeveloped Countries*, Blackwell, 1953.

7. S. A. Marglin, *Public Investment Criteria*, George Allen and Unwin, London, 1967.

8. For example, A. K. Sen, op. cit., and I. M. D. Little and J. Mirrlees, *Manual of Industrial Project Analysis in Developing Countries*, vol. ii, p. 42, Development Centre of the O.E.C.D. (Paris, 1969).

9.
$$s = \frac{g^* A}{g^* B}, \quad \text{where all wages are consumed, all profits saved.}$$

$$v = \frac{OB}{g^* B}.$$

$$\frac{s}{v} = \frac{g^* A}{g^* B} \div \frac{OB}{g^* B} = \frac{g^* A}{OB} = \frac{g^* A}{WA} =$$

slope of line from W to the production function.

10. There is considerable evidence that wages are related to the scale of the enterprise, while the smaller the enterprise the more labour-intensive (in terms of capital per worker) the technique tends to be. See, for example, E. N. Dhar and H. F. Lydall, *The Role of Small Enterprises in Indian Economic Growth*, Delhi, Asia Publishing House, 1961; M. C. Shetty, *Small-scale and Household Industries in a Developing Economy*. Asia Publishing House, 1963; Saburo Okita, 'Choice of techniques: Japan's experience and its implication', in *Economic Development with Special Reference to East Asia*, Ed. K. Berrill, Macmillan, 1964.

11. This is the Feldman model as described by E. Domar, *Essays in the Theory of Economic Growth*, Ch. IX, 'A Soviet Model of Growth'.

12. For the employment generated by new investment is the product of labour per unit of capital invested multiplied by investment ($L = \frac{L}{I} \cdot I$).

13. See 'Wages and Employment', C. St. J. Oherlihy, I.L.O. contribution to the Meeting of Directors of Development Training and Research Institutes, July 1970 (mimeo), Table 2 and Chart II.

16. Policies to Encourage the Use of Intermediate Technology*

Howard Pack

This paper has several purposes: to indicate the policies by which a government may alter the relative costs of capital and labor in industry; to indicate how much is known empirically about the efficacy of such changes; and finally, to consider how a program to undertake such changes can be pursued.

The focus on this kind of policy change for less developed countries (LDCs) assumes that, if factor prices were changed, then methods of production could be introduced which are more labor intensive than those currently in use, and which will be more profitable at the new factor prices than techniques currently in use. This assumption rests on the following research findings.

In a large number of industries a product is producible with a considerable range of alternate ratios of capital to labor. Much of the potential substitution of labor for capital stems from use of labor intensive methods to transport material within the factory, to pack cartons, and store the final product—i.e., in peripheral activities. Evidence is accumulating that the core production process itself also offers efficient possibilities for using less expensive equipment, and more labor per unit of output. Adaption of existing equipment, for example by increasing the normal speed of operation, offers further opportunities to save capital and increase the relative use of labor. Finally, the extensive under-utilization of industrial capacity provides scope for raising effective labor/capital ratios by increased utilization. Some industries, however, seem to offer little possibility for altering the capital/

* *Development Digest*, 14, no. 4 (October 1976), pp. 94–108.

labor ratio from that prevalent in advanced economies; these are typically activities in which most LDCs have no comparative advantage.

THE ROLE OF FACTOR PRICES

Competitive Environment

The ratio of labor to capital costs is usually thought to play a decisive role in determining the ratio of capital to labor used in the production process. This role of relative factor prices, however, requires competition among producers to be effective. There is abundant anecdotal and some numerical evidence which suggests that factor prices have rather little effect in non-competitive environments. A monopolistic firm currently realizing a 30 percent return on its equity capital, though using an inappropriately high ratio of capital to labor, may have little incentive to search for more appropriate methods which may raise its return to 35 percent. If factor prices are to exert pressure toward adopting socially appropriate techniques, some kinds of competitive forces must be present. In some of the small markets in LDCs, such pressures may be best engendered by international competition rather than by a proliferation of large numbers of small domestic companies when none of these are likely to reach economically efficient sizes. In other cases, increased numbers of efficient small producers may be the best solution.

Factor Price "Distortions"

It has become conventional to assert that labor costs in LDCs are "too high," capital costs "too low," and raw materials prices distorted, though not in one direction. What is the precise meaning of these statements? The hiring of a worker entails the payment of a cash wage, and one or more of the following: payments in kind (housing), non-cash fringe benefits (social security), and in some countries such supplements as "thirteenth month" salary. The cost of hiring a worker is "too" high if the value of the cash wage and other benefits exceeds the income which the worker could command elsewhere, given his abilities, both inherited and obtained by education and on-the-job experience. It has long been noted that the typical employee in a modern enterprise, be it a factory, bank office, or government agency, earns considerably more than a worker in small scale artisan shops or in self-employment such as barbering, and certainly more than agricultural workers and small farmers. It is generally believed that the observed income differentials do not represent a reward for greater productive ability, but are artificially high and institutionally supported, reflecting government minimum wage legislation, union bargaining success, and employer aversion to paying lower, more appropriate wages which typify other activities. There have been no studies measuring the extent to which such high wage incomes are the result of greater work-related skills; although recipients of high wages are often unskilled when initially hired, their productivity can increase by learning on the job. But even if some of the observed high wage structure is related to skills, it is likely that union pressure and government minimum wage legislation add to these differentials.

The statement that wages are too high thus refers to the norm of alternate income possibilities for a similarly skilled worker, either in the urban craft sector or in rural activities. It does not imply that these wages are excessive in comparison with those in developed countries, or that such workers are able to afford a luxurious living standard. But high wages accruing to the small group lucky enough to obtain modern sector jobs do imply that production will be undertaken with fewer workers than if wages were lower, thus condemning those not fortunate enough to obtain such jobs to a lower standard of living than would have been possible with a generally lower wage structure. Instead of a million workers employed in the modern sector, each receiving a wage of $500 per annum, 200,000 workers may receive a wage of $900, with the remaining workers earning $150 per annum.

The cost of plant and equipment reflects the purchase price of a factory building or machine, and the costs incurred in financing it. The cost of using plant or equipment is best viewed in terms of a firm's annual expenditure: depreciation of the initial acquisition cost; and a yearly financing charge incurred as the result of a decision to purchase the capital item. The purchase cost of equipment is too low in most LDCs in the sense that the net effect of government foreign trade policies is typically to artificially lower the amount of domestic currency which must be given up to pay for an imported machine. Most LDCs have engaged in a sustained import substitution program, one of whose characteristics is to maintain an overvalued exchange rate, i.e., the domestic currency buys too much foreign currency. This artificial cheapening of foreign goods may be offset by high tariffs on imported goods which compete with domestically produced goods. However, no tariff is imposed on imported equipment, in order to encourage domestic investment. Thus, LDC firms purchasing new equipment pay a lower price than would exist if governments did not discriminate between different types of imported goods. A low purchase price, of course, is reflected in low annual depreciation charges.

The second major cost is the financing charge. Financing of investments may originate either in bank loans or in funds from private sources. The interest charges paid by larger companies in the urban sector is too low as a result of governmentally imposed limitations on bank rates of interest. At these low-ceiling levels of rates, the total demand for loanable funds exceeds the supply, and the existing supply is rationed among competing companies, none of whom are charged more than the legal maximum. Companies which are unsuccessful in this competition are forced to borrow in a private market in which the rates often are three or four times the official

one. The financing charge for new equipment or buildings will clearly be greater for those (usually small) firms which cannot qualify for bank loans. When they are willing to borrow at these rates, this suggests that profitability in their industry is at least equal to this higher rate. Large firms, receiving as it were subsidized loans, pay too low an annual financing charge for the capital which they use.

Apart from low purchase prices and interest rates for many investors, numerous tax regulations further reduce the annual charge for using equipment. For example, investment credits and accelerated depreciation are likely to have adverse effects on the choice of production methods, particularly in view of the already high rates of return being earned by investors who hardly require additional incentives.

The cumulative effect of all these distortions in wages and the cost of capital has presumably been to bias the choice of individual firms toward unnecessarily capital intensive production methods. One indication of this is the discrepancy which has been observed between the growth of output and of employment in the industrial sector. Considering the continuing large flow of new equipment from industrialized countries to LDCs, some of this must be inappropriate given the high wage levels in the former countries for which the equipment is presumably appropriate.

To remove the incentives toward adoption of socially inappropriate equipment, the imperfections in factor markets must be reduced. The following policies would have this effect: (1) Removal of the minimum wage, particularly for new employees, or reducing it to the levels prevailing in the craft sector. (2) Undertaking policies to shift the supply curve of wage goods in order to reduce their price. (3) Limiting the growth of wages paid by the government sector, which often serve as a guidepost for private sector wages. (4) Curtailing the fringe benefits such as social security currently in force. (5) Allowing the official exchange rate to move down towards its equilibrium value and removing tariffs, administrative limits on imports and so on. Alternately, and less desirably, tariffs on imported capital goods could be introduced to raise their cost in domestic currency. (6) Removal of interest rate ceilings. (7) Elimination of tax incentives which reduce the cost of utilizing capital in production. (8) Elimination of the licensing of imported raw materials, a practice which has often been shown to discriminate against small labor intensive enterprises.

It would be difficult to construct a set of policy proposals which would generate more intense opposition among many of the most politically powerful groups who perceive the probability of substantial reductions in income. Highly paid, often unionized workers concentrated in urban areas would be adversely affected. The management of large companies currently enjoying subsidized equipment, low interest rates and access to raw materials would have to contemplate a reduction in windfall profits. Those who would benefit most, the workers and entrepreneurs in the craft and small scale sectors, while surely more numerous, are poorly organized and likely to be less politically active. It is easy to see why such alterations in factor prices, even where the potential overall benefits are understood by the government, may not be attractive to it.

A more immediate question is whether factor price changes will work. Changes in technique are most easily made when new production decisions are taken. Existing equipment usually has limited flexibility, not permitting a decrease in the capital/labor ratio. Will firms facing a changed economic environment actually react in the anticipated direction when expanding their capacity?

First, unless a reasonably competitive environment exists, the rates of return available in highly protected industries may be such that little effort is forthcoming to adjust factor proportions. Small increments to profit resulting from economizing on inputs may not be worth the effort as long as "reasonable" prof-

itability can be maintained. Even assuming a desire to restore or augment profits, managerial time may better be spent cajoling a somewhat higher nominal protection rate for a firm's output, looser quotas on critical inputs, etc., than in adjusting factor proportions. Avenues to increased profitability other than improved productive efficiency must be closed if changes in factor prices are to provide the strongest possible impetus to an exploration of alternate techniques of production.

Secondly, it is possible that despite the objective existence of more labor intensive production methods, this knowledge is not widely diffused among entrepreneurs. Knowledge of appropriate techniques requires familiarity with a number of different kinds of basic production equipment, and with alternate methods for carrying out subsidiary operations such as intraplant movement of material. However, these alternatives are not likely to be advocated by the (large) company's engineer, by the equipment salesman, nor by government agencies.

EVIDENCE ON THE EFFECTS OF CHANGES IN FACTOR PRICES

There have been only a few conscious attempts by LDC governments to alter relative factor prices. The classic success stories of appropriate factor price policies associated with a sustained growth in industrial employment are in South Korea, Taiwan and Singapore. In the first two, the interest rates charged by public and private banks were raised sharply and were maintained much closer to market levels than is usual in LDCs. In Singapore, real wages were held down for some time despite a growing demand for labor; while not precisely a change in price, this does represent a somewhat unusual policy. And there is no question that all three countries have demonstrated a highly successful record of industrial growth. The problem, however, is that of determining what effects are attributable to the factor price policies mentioned.

In Taiwan, interest rates were raised in the early 1950s and kept high through the 1960s. Industrial output grew rapidly, and the growth rate accelerated throughout this period; the increase in employment began more slowly in the 1950s but gradually accelerated to a high level by the late 1960s (Table 1). Although production per employee continued to rise by 7 percent or more per year, it might be said that the maintenance of high interest rates led eventually to factor combinations which provided considerably more employment than would otherwise have occurred. But this would be very hard to prove, given all the other factors influencing these growth rates. Labor intensity also resulted from the export drive focussed on products in which Taiwan's low wages gave it a comparative advantage in world markets.

Korean interest rates were raised only in 1965, so that a short run impact of that change might be easier to find. But the figures in Table 1 do not suggest a shift toward greater labor intensity in industrial growth following that date, since the growth of employment relative to that in production had been larger in the preceding period. The higher interest rates undoubtedly did much to produce the sharp acceleration of growth in both variables after 1965 by mobilizing savings. And Korean industry, like that in Taiwan, appears to be relatively labor intensive in its methods. But here, too, this resulted in part from a drive to export labor intensive products, and the con-

tribution of high interest rates to factor proportions cannot be isolated.

In Singapore, the annual rates of growth from 1968 to 1971 were as follows: industrial output—24.0 percent; industrial employment—17.7 percent; real wages—2.3 percent. Again, there were many influences at work, and the contribution of wage policy to employment growth may be stated in terms of logic but cannot be measured. In all three cases the merits of more appropriate factor pricing seem to be vindicated by the overall results, the more plausibly because these economies were relatively competitive internally along with their open trade policies. But the attribution of results to specific factor price policies remains ambiguous.

EFFECTS OF DIFFERENCES IN FACTOR PRICES FACING FIRMS OF DIFFERENT SIZE

Given the difficulties in interpreting the classical cases of policy-induced changes in factor prices and the possibility that these may be in unusually-entrepreneur or skill-rich nations, are there other empirical bases on which to assess the potential benefits of moving towards a more rational factor price configuration? There is a rapidly accumulating body of evidence whose major implication is that differentials in factor prices faced by firms of different sizes have indeed led to alternative methods of production. The higher wages and the lower interest rates typically paid by large

TABLE 1. Annual Compound Growth Rates in Industry, Taiwan and South Korea (percentages)

| | 1953–58 | | 1958–63 | | 1966–69 | |
	Output	Employment	Output	Employment	Output	Employment
Taiwan	9.0	1.9	13.1	2.8	20.0	13.2
S. Korea	16.1[a]	5.6[b]	10.0	8.3	28.8	13.7

[a] 1954–58
[b] 1955–58

Source: U.N. Growth of World Industry, various issues.

firms appear to have resulted in sharp variations in factor proportions among firms within the same industry in a given country. Such cross sectional evidence suggests that a change in factor-price ratios is likely to be effective if combined with competitive pressures in the output market.

A large number of empirical studies have examined differences which exist among firms of different size as measured by number of employees. Of particular interest is the increase in the capital-labor ratio as the size of firm increases for a given industry such as textiles or food processing. This pattern at least partly represents the increase in the use of equipment, tools, and mechanical conveyors in response to increasing wage levels in the larger firms, it being well documented that the wage per worker is highly correlated with firm size. The earliest demonstration of these now conventional findings appeared in analyses of Japanese manufacturing, and the results have been verified for almost all LDCs which have been investigated, the major exception being Taiwan. Table 2 presents fairly typical wage patterns by firm size for the entire manufac-

turing sector in Mexico in 1965 and Pakistan in 1960. Disaggregation by the two digit classification of industries reveals a similar pattern among firms with similar products.

Thus, even if companies of all sizes paid the same interest rate and had equal access to imported equipment at the same price, such wage differentials provide presumptive evidence that larger firms devote more effort to economizing on labor than do smaller ones. However, equal access to loan finance and equipment are not good descriptions of reality. Typically, small firms finance their expansion from the saving of the entrepreneur or his relatives and close friends, a group likely to have limited resources. If borrowing outside of this primary group occurs, it is usually from non-bank lenders who charge two to four times the going rate charged by commercial banks. On the other hand, commercial banks and governmentally sponsored industrial development banks usually lend to the larger firms at relatively low interest rates. If interest rates of 10 or 12 percent are charged by these large institutions, smaller firms will typically pay 30 to 40 percent.

TABLE 2. Average Wages and Capital/Labor Ratios by Size of Firm, Mexico and Pakistan

Mexico—1965			Pakistan—1960		
Firm Size (number of employees)	Wage Index[a]	Capital per Worker[b]	Firm Size (number of employees)	Wage Index[a]	Capital per Worker[c]
1–5	21	10.5	1–9	58	0.63
6–15	41	31.3	10–19	76	1.96
16–25	55	48.6	20–49	89	2.13
25–50	61	57.5	50–99	96	2.37
51–75	68	62.1	100 and over	100	2.92
76–100	70	63.8			
101–250	78	80.4			
251–500	88	96.2			
over 500	100	104.8			

[a] Index values with 100 for average wage in largest size group.
[b] In thousands of pesos.
[c] In thousands of rupees.

Source: Saul Trejo, *Industrialization and Employment Growth; Mexico 1960–65*, p. 112 (PhD thesis, Yale University, 1971); Gustav Ranis, *Industrial Efficiency and Economic Growth: A case study of Karachi*, p. 33 (Karachi, Institute of Economic Development, 1961).

The pattern of wage and interest differentials must be assumed to play a major role in the pattern of increasing capital intensity by size of firm, as shown in Table 2 for Pakistan and Mexico. This pattern is also typical within industries, though inevitably some exceptions arise. The smallest companies exhibit very low capital-labor ratios, high average product per unit of capital, and usually a somewhat lower average product of labor. As size increases, the capital-labor ratio and output per worker increase and the output per unit of capital declines. Further analysis typically reveals that the smaller firms are at least as efficient as the larger ones in the sense that if both were to face the same socially relevant factor prices (i.e., the wage rate paid by small firms, and an interest rate which measures the rate of return in small scale industry), the average cost of production in smaller firms would be competitive with that of larger firms, indeed often lower.

While features of production other than differences in factor price ratios might explain some of the observed characteristics by firm size, most studies have concluded that they play a major role. Thus, the examination of capital-labor ratios by firm size provides a rich body of data which confirms the likely responsiveness of entrepreneurs to changes in their cost structure. Such studies have been executed for a sufficiently large number of diverse countries so that one may infer such responsiveness is a fairly universal phenomenon in Asia and Latin America, not limited to countries with a particular history or culture. It characterizes both large and small countries, those which are usually thought to be skill-rich and those which are not. In addition to the analysis of census and survey data, a substantial literature based on interviews confirms the strength of the small scale sector and the skilled entrepreneurship which characterizes many craft firms in LDCs. For example, in Pakistan the rate of return on fixed capital was over 18 percent for firms with 20–49 em-

ployees, and less than 12 percent for firms with over 100 employees.

However, it should be noted that neither the presence of abundant entrepreneurship nor many examples of efficient small-scale craft firms have been confirmed in sub-Saharan Africa. The 1972 ILO study of Kenya, despite its emphasis on the potential role of the "informal sector," offers little empirical evidence that craft firms with say 5 to 25 employees exist. Rather, the informal sector consists primarily of self-employed craftsmen such as tailors and carpenters producing products which cannot compete with typical industrial goods, in contrast to the craft firms found in Asia or Latin America. The absence of smaller firms and able entrepreneurs would seem to indicate the need for a different approach to obtaining labor intensive development, as the response to changes in factor prices may not be adequate.

POLICY ADVICE TO LDCs

The Need for LDC Government Agreement

The promotion of a labor intensive development process cannot go very far without the active cooperation of the central government. One might envision, for example, technical assistance on an individual basis from private advisers on small business and technology to a target group of companies in an LDC. However, no more than a few such aid recipients will be able to obtain an increasing share of investible funds unless current policies of artificially low interest rates combined with credit rationing by the banks are changed. While small businesses may exhibit high rates of return and could successfully compete for credit in a competitive capital market, their very smallness and paucity of collateral work against them in a rationed market. Similarly, the extensive use of import licenses in the allocation of both capital and intermediate goods works to their disadvantage as it necessitates substantial managerial time, to say nothing of cash payments, to obtain the requisite licenses. In another vein, unless wage-good output is increased and its price level thus kept low, the growth of nominal wages to both small and large firms will produce strong incentives to rely on increasingly capital intensive techniques. In sum, the requisite changes in the allocation of investment funds, import licenses, and the price of wage goods are beyond the influence of private, non-profit organizations or any other industrial extension agencies which work directly with LDC firms.

It is often argued that extension activities will generate a sufficient number of success stories that the demonstration effect will induce an unwilling government to pursue a labor intensive strategy, including a generalized liberalization of the credit and foreign exchange markets. Unfortunately it is unlikely to work. Although a small number of firms may, with intensive advice, identify new products, purchase appropriate equipment and undertake labor intensive low cost production, it is difficult to understand how this can occur on a sufficiently large scale without a prior change in government policies. Who will lend to large numbers of small enterprises at low (institutional) interest rates given the perceived risks, little collateral, and the disproportionately high administrative costs of small loans? Yet if the "demonstration from below" approach is to be persuasive it is necessary for it to occur simultaneously on a large scale in a number of industries and regions, and thus requires substantial amounts of investment funds.

More generally, this "private–nongovernment" approach is, in a fundamental sense, predicated on a shortage of entrepreneurs. Yet this assumption, for many countries, is counterfactual. The same studies which analyze the characteristics of firms of different sizes also show that large numbers of small firms (say with less than 50 employees) are present in many non-African LDCs in most branches of production, that they have made correct factor choices given the factor prices they face, and that they exhibit high rates of return on their invested capital. These are not the characteristics one would expect if the true bottleneck on expansion of firms using appropriate technology were the absence of entrepreneurial skills. Indeed, they are more suggestive of remarkably adaptive behavior in an economic environment which is skewed to favor large enterprises. There is little reason to doubt that had small businesses been able to obtain access to critical inputs, a faster industrial growth would already have occurred in many countries. My emphasis on the need to change the economic environment does not imply that technical services cannot be beneficial to LDCs, only that by themselves they are unlikely to exert sufficiently large quantitative effects to alter the course of an otherwise capital intensive development policy.

Governments must therefore be convinced of the value of making politically unpopular changes which could assist in the growth of industrial employment. But they may be unaware of the range of choices open to them in pursuing greater employment growth, and of the magnitude of the additional jobs which could be created. Their current policies are not necessarily a result of special interest pressures but rather a response to perceptions which are not accurate descriptions of the reality of their economies. Indeed, many of the most harmful government interventions, undertaken in most cases to effect import-substituting industrialization, were originally advocated by those most concerned with income distribution and unemployment. Important groups in both business and labor are now deriving considerable windfall benefits from the existing system. But there is also extensive evidence of the recognition by many governments of the need to alter current policies if violent change is to be avoided.

Given my premise that changes in technique require government-supported changes in factor prices, it is necessary to follow a two pronged strategy of advice: (1) where governments are insufficiently aware of the employment gains which will result from a change in policy, a demonstration is needed of the aggregate gains; (2) enhancement of the government's ability to achieve the employment goals.

Demonstration of Gains from Change in Policy

An important contribution to generating LDC interest in the possibilities offered by labor intensive techniques can be made by: (1) A systematic cataloguing of those economically efficient techniques by industry which have so far been established. This would include, for each process, specific production alternatives such as the type of core production equipment available, alternate peripheral processes, the sources and costs of relevant equipment. (2) Use of the above information in projecting a plan or set of growth objectives which an LDC government would find plausible and desirable. Such a plan may be the official national plan document, but this is not necessary. Projections for an industry can be made of probable total employment growth without altering current production methods, and also with two or more alternative factor ratio regimes using more labor intensive techniques. The saving in capital obtained by producing

the planned output in a less capital intensive manner should also be calculated, as this is a major benefit that is insufficiently emphasized in most analyses. The output of some projects which were not included in the original plan, but which now become feasible because of the freed investment resources, could also be calculated.

An illustration of this method is presented in Table 3 using data from a study on the choice of technique in textile weaving. Four methods of producing woven shirting material were identified, each exhibiting considerably different labor requirements and capital costs. Columns 1 and 2 indicate the inputs required to produce an additional 100 million square yards of material, an increase well within the goals of some development plans. Column 3 indicates the capital-labor ratio associated with each type of process. Column 4 shows the amount of investible funds saved by adopting the Lancashire loom, the least capital intensive one, rather than each of the others. Column 5 indicates the additional employment which would be generated by investing the funds so saved in an activity whose capital-labor ratio was no greater than that of the Lancashire loom. Finally, column 6 presents the percentage increase in output which could be generated by investing the saved funds in additional weaving capacity. Obviously, other possibilities will be open; the output gain

TABLE 3. Aggregate Effects of Alternate Weaving Techniques

Type of Loom	Requirements Per 100 Million Square Yards Per Annum man-years (1)	investment (2)	Capital/Labor Ratio (2)/(1) (3)	Gains from Using Lancashire Loom Investment Funds Saved (4)	Additional Employment[a] (5)	Increase in Output[a] (6)
Lancashire	2,180	$ 3,582,000	$ 1,645	$ —	—	—
Battery	1,110	7,163,500	6,454	3,581,500	3,247	100%
Airjet	820	7,877,700	9,665	4,295,700	3,971	120
Sulzer	510	15,006,300	29,715	11,424,300	8,615	319

[a] Employment and output from the use of funds saved if these were invested in additional Lancashire looms, or in an activity with the same capital/labor and capital/output ratios.

Source: Underlying data were obtained from *Cotton and Allied Textiles* (Manchester, The Textile Council, 1969).

TABLE 4. Costs of Weaving Shirting Material with Three Methods (dollars per 100 yards)

	Lancashire Loom	Airjet (Elitex)	Sulzer Loom
Space	.198	.093	.152
Power	.385	.385	.291
Weft Waste	.035	.408	.338
Pirning	.472	—	—
Capital Costs[a]	.658	2.167	3.796
Cost of Labor (wage = $832 per year)	1.744	.652	.404
Average Unit Costs	3.493	3.705	4.981

[a] Depreciation and interest charges of 20 percent per annum; includes purchase price plus transport and installation costs equal to 20 percent of the cost of a battery loom.

Source: Cotton and Allied Textiles, Vol. II, p. 83 for lines 1–4. Line 6 calculated from pages 86–90.

calculated here simply provides some orders of magnitude. Table 4 indicates the overall costs of three of these alternatives under representative conditions.

The potential contribution of systematizing information on available techniques and analyzing their implication for a given LDC is obvious. Existing evidence on the benefits to be derived, industry by industry, assure that these are likely to be enormous and such calculations are likely, at the least, to stimulate governments to consider some of the policies necessary to realize them.

Convincing the government of a country of the desirability of changing its economic policies to establish a climate more favorable to labor intensive development is necessary, but may not be sufficient to obtain such development. Although we know that firms of diverse sizes use different techniques, the speed with which changes to appropriate production methods will be made may be accelerated by the presence of good advisory service, especially when there is a demonstrated absence of entrepreneurship.

Technical Assistance to Industry

The services of foreign advisers are likely to be best implemented by those who have been involved in industrial production management over a long period. These managers are likely to have seen the continuous evolution of production methods and are aware that the 1976 method differs considerably from 1956, to say nothing of 1936, and that the latter two were quite viable in their time. Labor intensive methods, particularly in the peripheral processes, characterized American and Western European production until well after World War II. A large pool of westerners exist who have been involved in relevant production management and who could convey both the physical feasibility of labor intensive production as well as some of the organization methods and innovations which surely occurred and increased productivity. By contrast, recent graduate engineers with little production experience are unlikely to be quite so open to alternate production possibilities. They have been exposed to the latest edition of a textbook in food processing and may be unaware that earlier editions showed different equipment. Moreover, most engineering texts and courses concentrate almost exclusively on the technical aspects of production, such as the chemical changes which occur, rather than on costs. Rarely are there discussions of the number of workers used by a machine or the relative costs of different types of equipment. Without exposure to the concepts of costs and the discipline of product prices, engineers are likely to be less open than those with similar training who have had production experience.

In addition to foreign technical assistance, governments should consider their potential for establishing an extension service for small industry within their own ministries, comparable to the advisory service commonly found in agriculture. The problems involved are more complex than those in agricultural extension, and there is less precedent and experience, but the activity merits further exploration.

Tax Policies

Most LDC governments levy some form of business profits tax. The wide variety of tax holidays and accelerated depreciation schemes are directed at reducing these taxes in the hope of generating greater investment, and many of these devices decrease the cost of using capital and thereby encourage capital intensive production methods and should thus be ended. Other ways of reducing the tax burden might be substituted which could encourage the search for labor intensive techniques. For example, reductions in the tax rate applicable to a given level of income could be made contingent on companies presenting a costing of alternate production processes when considering either replacement or expansion. Presentation of detailed cost estimates for at least one more labor intensive process could be

made the standard for being placed in a preferred tax category.

Clearly, all firms could not be required to submit such proposals. Presumably, it would be best to start with the largest companies and then move down through the size distribution. An obvious and important potential role for foreign advice would be a catalogue of alternate processes as well as training for LDC administrators, facilitating their ability to establish the accuracy of the alternatives presented. Compliance with tax provisions could be aided by a national extension service, armed with pertinent information.

Strengthening Ability to Finance Loans

One other important policy area is to strengthen the ability of lending institutions to increase the access of small scale, labor intensive firms to capital. Clearly, not all loan applicants can be accommodated. Some screening must take place along with the high rates of interest which should discourage the less efficient firms from applying. Nevertheless, it would be useful to reconsider bank criteria for credit worthiness (possibly in conjunction with selective guarantees), and to make greater efforts to mobilize savings and time deposits. Higher interest rates would make an additional contribution to industrial growth by attracting more savings, as was shown in South Korea.

Further Readings

1. Employment and Labor

Bairoch, Paul. *Urban Unemployment in Developing Countries: The Nature of the Problem and Proposals for its Solution.* Geneva: International Labour Office, 1976.

Bhagwati, J. "Main Features of the Employment Problem in Developing Countries." *Indian Eco-*

nomic Journal 19, no. 4–5 (April–June 1972).

Cairncross, Alec, and Puri, Mohinder, eds. *Employment, Income Distribution and Development Strategy: Problems of the Developing Countries, Essays in Honour of H. W. Singer.* New York: Holmes & Meier, 1976.

Chakraborty, A. K. "The Causes of Educated Unemployment in India." *Economic Affairs* 20, no. 7 (July 1975).

Edwards, Edgar O. *Employment in Developing Nations: Report on a Ford Foundation Study.* New York and London: Columbia University Press, 1974.

Herve, Michel E. A. "Employment and Industrialization in Developing Countries." *Quarterly Journal of Economics* 80, no. 1 (1966).

ILO. *Employment Growth and Basic Needs: A One-World Problem, Report of the Director-General of the International Labour Office, Tripartite World Conference on Employment, Income Distribution and Social Progress and the International Division of Labour.* Geneva, 1976.

ILO. *Employment in Africa: Some Critical Issues.* Geneva, 1973.

Jolly, Richard, ed. *Third World Employment Problems and Strategy: Selected Readings.* Harmondsworth, England: Penguin, 1973.

Krueger, Anne O. "Alternative Trade Strategies and Employment in LDC's." *American Economic Review* 68, no. 2 (May 1978).

Kuzmin, S. A. "An Integrated Approach to Development and Employment." *International Labour Review* 115, no. 3 (May–June 1977).

Morawetz, D. "Employment Implications of Industrialization in Developing Countries: A Survey," *Economic Journal*, (September 1974).

Ndegwa, Philip, and Powelson, J. P., eds. *Employment in Africa: Some Critical Issues.* Geneva: International Labour Office, 1974.

Pack, H. "The Employment-Output Trade-Off in LDC's: A Microeconomic Approach." *Oxford Economic Papers* 26, no. 3 (November 1974).

Ranis, Gustav. "Employment, Equity and Growth: Lessons from the Philippine Employment Mission." *International Labour Review* 110, no. 1 (July 1974).

Sen, Amartya Kumar. *Employment Technology and Development.* Oxford, England: Clarendon Press, 1975.

Stewart, Frances, ed. *Employment, Income Distribution and Development.* London: Frank Cass, 1975.

Stiglitz, J. G. "Alternative Theories of Wage Determination and Unemployment in LDC's: The Labor Turnover Model." *Quarterly Journal of Economics* 88, no. 2 (May 1974).

Turnham, David, with assistance by Jaeger, Ian. *The Employment Problem in Less Developed Countries: A Review of Evidence.* Paris: Development Centre of the Organization for Economic Co-operation and Development, 1971.

2. Technology

Baer, Werner. "Technology, Employment and Development: Empirical Findings." *World Development* 4, no. 2 (February 1976).

Baron, C. "Appropriate Technology Comes of Age: A Review of Some Recent Literature and Aid Policy Statements." *International Labour Review* 117, no. 5 (September–October 1978).

Bhalla, A. S., ed. *Technology and Employment in Industry: A Case Study Approach.* Geneva: ILO, 1976.

Dunkerley, Harold B. "The Choice of Appropriate Technologies." *Finance and Development* 14, no. 3 (September 1977).

Eckaus, Richard S. *Appropriate Technologies for Developing Countries.* Prepared for the Panel on Appropriate Technologies for Developing Countries. Washington, D.C.: National Academy of Sciences, 1977.

Hawrylyshyn, Oli. "Capital-Intensity Biases in Developing Country Technology Choice." *Journal of Development Economics* 5, no. 3 (September 1978).

James, Jeffrey. "Growth, Technology and the Environment in Less Developed Countries: A Survey." *World Development* 6, no. 718 (July/August 1978).

Pack, H., and Todaro, M. P. "Technology Transfer, Labor Absorption and Economic Development." *Oxford Economic Papers* 21, no. 3 (1969).

Schumacher, E. F. *Small Is Beautiful: Economics as if People Mattered.* New York: Harper & Row, 1974.

Singer, Hans. *Technologies for Basic Needs.* Geneva: ILO, 1977.

Stewart, Frances. *Technology and Underdevelopment.* Boulder, Colo.: Westview Press, 1977.

White, Lawrence J. "The Evidence on Appropriate Factor Proportions for Manufacturing in Less Developed Countries: A Survey." *Economic Development and Cultural Change* 27, no. 1 (October 1978).

7

Urbanization, Rural-Urban Migration and Unemployment

17. The Urbanization Dilemma*

Michael P. Todaro
with Jerry Stilkind

The cities of the developing world are growing at an extremely rapid pace. Millions of people are migrating each year from rural to urban areas, even though many of the largest cities have, for all practical purposes, given up trying to provide more than minimal sanitation, health, housing, and transportation services to their dense populations. Industrial production has expanded, but so too has urban unemployment and underemployment. In the countryside the poorest people are scarcely better off now than they were 15 years ago, and in some areas their situation has worsened.

As large as these cities are today, many are destined to become substantially larger in the years to come. For example, Figure 1 shows that in 1950 about 38 percent of city dwellers lived in the developing world. By 1975, however, about the same number of developing-world people—750 million—lived in cities as those in the developed world. By the year 2000, more than two and a half times that number will populate the urban areas of the developing countries, while the cities of the industrialized world will have increased by less than 50 percent. Whereas only 16 developing-world cities had a population in excess of 4 million in 1975, by the year 2000 there will be 61. The cities of Africa are expected to grow by 336 percent, to almost 250 million population; South Asia by 298 percent, to almost 800 million; Latin America by 235 percent, to more than 450 million; and East Asia by 225 percent, to over 500 million.

In 1950, 11 of the world's largest cities were in the industrialized countries; in 1980 only seven were; by the year 2000, only three will be (see Figure 2). Metropolitan Mexico City will be the largest urban area in the year 2000, with about 31 million people, followed by Sao Paulo, Brazil, with 26 million, Tokyo-Yokohama with more than 24 million, New York with almost 23 million, and Shanghai with a slightly smaller population. Of more significance and alarm, however, are prospects for cities such as Bombay (17.1 million), Calcutta (16.7 million), Jakarta (16.6 million), Cairo (13.1 million), Madras (12.9 million), and Manila (12.3 million) where both urban services and new employment opportunities

* From *City Bias and Rural Neglect: The Dilemma of Urban Development*, Public Issues Paper No. 4, Population Council, New York, 1981, pp. 2–10, 16–19.

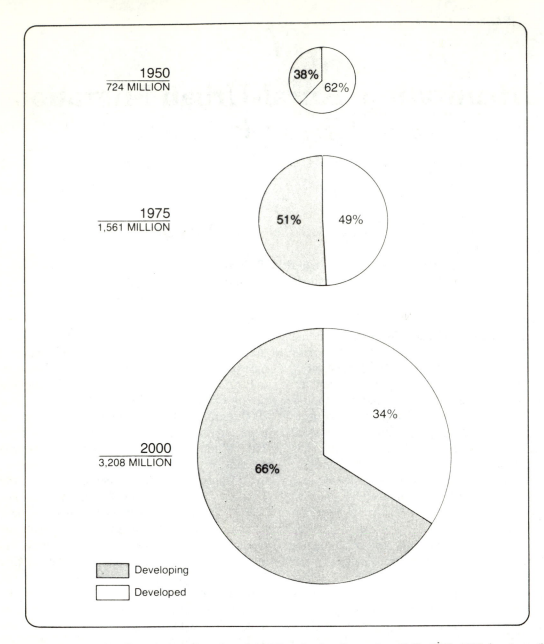

Figure 1. Total Urban Population: Developed and Developing Countries, 1950, 1975, 2000 (projected).

have already fallen far behind population increases.

As a specific illustration of developing-world urban population growth, consider Mexico City. In 1940 the population of Mexico City was slightly in excess of a million and a half inhabitants. This represented only 8 percent of the total Mexican population. Over the next 40 years, however, the situation changed dramatically. Between 1940 and 1950 Mexico City's population almost doubled. Significantly, over 70 percent of this increase—

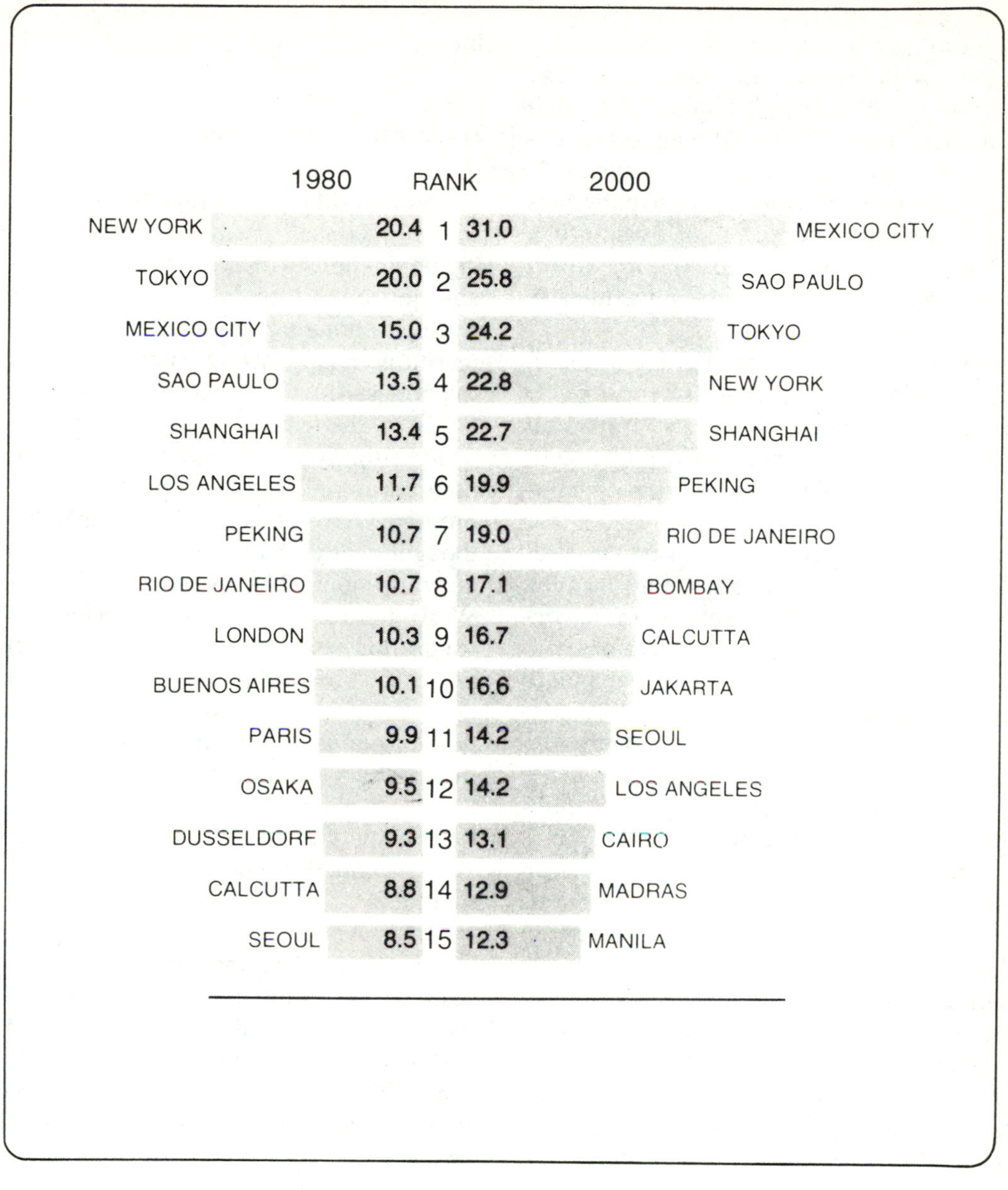

	1980	RANK	2000	
NEW YORK	20.4	1	31.0	MEXICO CITY
TOKYO	20.0	2	25.8	SAO PAULO
MEXICO CITY	15.0	3	24.2	TOKYO
SAO PAULO	13.5	4	22.8	NEW YORK
SHANGHAI	13.4	5	22.7	SHANGHAI
LOS ANGELES	11.7	6	19.9	PEKING
PEKING	10.7	7	19.0	RIO DE JANEIRO
RIO DE JANEIRO	10.7	8	17.1	BOMBAY
LONDON	10.3	9	16.7	CALCUTTA
BUENOS AIRES	10.1	10	16.6	JAKARTA
PARIS	9.9	11	14.2	SEOUL
OSAKA	9.5	12	14.2	LOS ANGELES
DUSSELDORF	9.3	13	13.1	CAIRO
CALCUTTA	8.8	14	12.9	MADRAS
SEOUL	8.5	15	12.3	MANILA

Figure 2. The 15 Largest Metropolitan Areas (UN estimates for 1980 and 2000, in millions).

850,000 people—was due to internal rural-to-urban migration (with minor boundary reclassification) and only 30 percent to natural increase. In the 1950s, the city gained over 1,930,000 new inhabitants, about half of whom were migrants. In the 1960s, the population swelled to over 8.3 million as almost one and a half million new migrants arrived, twice the number of the previous decade. The massive migration into Mexico City during the period 1940–70 also provided the base for the current high level of natural increase. More than half of the city's growth during this period resulted directly or indirectly from heavy internal migration. Demographers estimate that the present Mexico City population is almost 14 million and that by the year 2,000 it will reach 31 million. Although the numbers may be larger than other developing-country cities, as shown in Figure 2, Mexico City's phenomenal growth pattern is shared by a sizable proportion of Asian urban areas, with some of the most rapid growth processes only now gathering momentum in Africa.

It is true, as many observers have noted, that the possibility of earning larger salaries in the cities has been the major stimulus (although numerous noneconomic stimuli also exist) to the mass migration from the countryside. But given the squalid conditions for many in the cities, this migration underscores the dismal life in the rural areas more than the are dealing here with a problem of uncontrolled urbanization, a glaring defect of economies so preoccupied with industrial "modernization" and so biased in their development strategies toward the urban modern sector that they are unable to satisfy even the basic needs of their people in either the cities or the rural areas. Excessive urbanization is also a defect of societies that have not been able to create large enough domestic markets to stimulate both agriculture and industry to produce more (while overseas markets in the developed countries shrink in response to economic policies designed to protect their own local manufactures). For developing nations, the policy of neglecting agriculture, in some cases bleeding it through resource withdrawals, has produced stagnating or inadequate income growth in rural areas, while the policy of importing large-scale, labor-saving technology to achieve instant industrialization has meant that urban job opportunities have not grown as fast as the numbers seeking work. Many thousands of rural peasants deprived of their land by premature mechanization or crowded onto it by rapid population growth have sought their salvation in the rapidly growing cities, only to discover that the reality

rarely reflects the image of a significantly better life.

OVERURBANIZATION

Overurbanization--a situation in which cities cannot adequately provide their rapidly growing populations with basic services and reasonable job opportunities—is not a comfortable concept among economists and planners. One reason is that it was not supposed to happen. Economists in the West and government officials in the countries that gained independence after World War II hastily searched for theoretical guidelines and practical policies to promote development. Unfortunately, they thought they had only one model—industralization. The Soviet Union and the West differed over how to achieve industrialization, but they agreed on its vital importance. The problems of the newly independent countries seemed too severe then and now to permit the luxury of copying the slow evolutionary development of modern capitalism. The planned, forced industrialization of the Soviet Union, without its harshest measures, seemed to be a much more realistic method.

An inevitable part of industrialization is urbanization. The movement of people and resources from the countryside to the city was expected to provide the cheap labor and forced savings to stimulate urban industrialization. Then at some point it was expected that rapid urbanization, like population growth rates, would taper off, resulting in a less populated but more productive agricultural area. Rural people would then be roughly as well off as workers in the industrialized cities. Migration would slow to a trickle because the economic incentive to move would be gone.

With few exceptions industrialization did not become the engine capable of pulling a whole society to a more modern and just platform. The rough balance between the rural and urban sectors seemed as far off as ever, and to a number of economists and government leaders perhaps even impossible to achieve with policies focusing only on the growth of modern industry. By the early 1970s they began to realize that reality was not conforming to theory. Within a few years a new consensus on the most desirable development strategy emerged, emphasizing the role of agriculture and the importance of increasing the incomes of the poorest people in a society. To date, however, the commitment to this strategy has not been strong enough to significantly change the urbanization-industrialization policies of past decades.

Another reason for discomfort among economists and urban planners is that overurbanization cannot be precisely defined. There is no mathematical formula that stipulates a point beyond which cities should not grow. Moreover, optimal city size is a function of a wide range of economic, social, and geographic factors that vary from country to country. Presumably there is no limit to the size of a city as long as it can expand outward and upward and its industry and service sectors grow rapidly enough to absorb large numbers of new workers. In practice, however, the great majority of developing countries lack the financial resources (not to mention the organizational and planning capacity) to pursue policies of unlimited growth. Their leaders are thus deeply concerned about the geographic distribution of their population and increasingly have adopted policies to slow the rate of urbanization. For example, a United Nations survey in 1977 found that 113 of 119 developing countries considered the distribution of their population unacceptable. Some 94 countries on all continents, including South Korea, Indonesia, the Philippines, Kenya, Tanzania, Brazil, Cuba, and Venezuela, reported they had adopted policies to alter the distribution of their peoples, ranging from trying to slow or even reverse migration to the cities to lowering fertility rates. A major finding of the survey was that "the location of population is a more widespread source of

government concern . . . than is natural increase or its components. The former, apparently, is more immediately linked to development means, ends and planning mechanisms than is the latter."[1]

Because of the widespread and growing government concern over rapid urbanization, it is essential that both the population and the development community pay considerably more attention to this critical issue. Much more research is needed, but at this time there would seem to be three clear signs marking cities grown too large to fulfill their historic role in promoting developing-world economic growth. They are:

- The number of unemployed and underemployed is large and growing.
- The proportion of the urban labor force working in industry is scarcely growing and may be declining.
- The sheer numbers of people and the rate of population growth are so great that governments cannot adequately provide more than minimal health, housing, and transportation services.

Research has shown that the rural poor are often simultaneously "pushed" to the cities by stagnating or declining local economic opportunities and "pulled" by expectations of abundant jobs and higher incomes. Discussions of the "pull" of the cities, however, sometimes suggest that it is primarily the bright lights or the good life that successfully lures the peasants in droves. More accurately it is a combination of rural poverty and higher expected incomes in the major cities that simultaneously stimulates rural-to-urban migration. This distinction is not simply semantical. It is made to force researchers and decision makers to focus as much attention on rural poverty as on urban growth. Only then will it be possible to devise policies more in keeping with the need of the whole society. Moreover, it seems increasingly possible that an indirect approach to urban problems, namely through heavy investments in the rural sector, may have more desirable effects on alleviating urban development concerns than the usual urban-directed policies.

Many developing countries have bled agriculture to provide the resources for increasing the pace of industrialization and urbanization. This policy amounts to a significant urban bias that has become ingrained in the economic life of most developing countries. Policies derived from this bias serve to widen the urban-rural expected income gap, ensuring that high rates of migration will continue despite growing urban unemployment. As long as rural incomes remain depressed and urban wages are kept artificially high by government policy and other institutional supports, rural migrants will continue to flood into the cities in search of high-paid but elusive (or illusory) urban modern sector jobs. . . .

Rural-to-Urban Migration

Rural-to-urban migration continues to be a major contributor to the rapid growth of developing-world cities. For example, it is estimated that net migration now accounts for between one-third and three-fourths of the urban population growth in developing countries. Table 1 provides some recent data on the share of urban growth due to migration for a representative group of developing countries. Some writers, however, attribute urban growth mostly to fertility levels among people already in cities. Although this may be correct statistically, it is misleading. Many studies have shown that the vast majority of migrants continue to be men and women in their 20s, the age group most active in forming families. Therefore, their settling in cities pushes up growth due to natural increase. Directly and indirectly, then, the phenomenal growth of most developing-world cities has largely been a result of migration on a historically vast scale.

TABLE 1. **Internal Migration as a Source of Urban Growth: Selected Developing Countries, 1970–75**

Country	Annual Urban Growth (percent)	Share of Growth Due to Migration (percent)
Argentina	2.0	35
Brazil	4.5	36
Colombia	4.9	43
India	3.8	45
Indonesia	4.7	49
Nigeria	7.0	64
Philippines	4.8	42
Sri Lanka	4.3	61
Tanzania	7.5	64
Thailand	5.3	45

Source: K. Newland, *City Limits: Emerging Constraints on Urban Growth*, Worldwatch Paper no. 38, Washington, D.C., August 1980, p. 10.

How rapid has urbanization been? In 1950, 16.7 percent of the developing-world population lived in cities; in 1970, the proportion was 25.8 percent; by the year 2,000, it is expected to be 43.5 percent. But there is a sharp difference in the level of urbanization among regions. In 1970, for example, 22.9 percent of Africans lived in urban areas, 20.5 percent of South Asians, 28.6 percent of East Asians, but 57.4 percent of Latin Americans.

Experts and officials worldwide at first anticipated and welcomed the migration of rural people to the cities of the developing countries, for that was considered a sign that industrialization was taking root. As mentioned above, it was thought that, in time, income growth rates in the cities would level off as the labor market became saturated with migrants. Meanwhile, agricultural growth and the higher earnings of the now relatively scarce labor pool in rural areas would raise incomes to roughly balance those in the cities. This would end the stimulus to migrate. Thus, the responsiveness of labor to changing income-earning opportunities in urban and rural areas was expected to convert what seemed initially an unbalanced growth to a stable, self-correcting process.

As is now evident, this never happened. The principal reasons for the failure are directly and indirectly related to the very industrialization and urbanization policies that were supposed to spur economic growth for all. First, stagnating economic conditions in rural areas ensured that population growth would continue at record high levels. Second, large population increases combined with low incomes forced more and more rural people to look around them for ways to better their condition. Third, the policy of protecting urban industry created higher incomes and more job opportunities in the cities. Other government policies—subsidizing food and legislating modern sector wage and salary scales, for example—further increased urban incomes. The result was a massive movement of people despite high and growing levels of urban unemployment and underemployment. Although some internal migration arises from noneconomic factors, including rural violence, drought, and the desire to break away from traditional role requirements, most researchers agree that the financial motive dominates.

That the growth of cities occurred within the context of an unprecedented population growth rate of 2.1 percent a year was not unexpected. What was unexpected, however, was how very much faster the cities grew in comparison with the overall rate of population increase.

Although urban growth rates have been much higher than rates of increase of rural populations in recent decades, the countryside still contains many more people than the cities. Urban populations increased by an average of 4.3 percent a year between 1950 and 1970, from about 275 million to about 651 million. Rural areas grew at the much slower yearly rate of 1.6 percent during the same period. In absolute terms, however, the rural population increased from 1.4 billion to 1.9 billion. By comparison, urban growth rates in the developed world averaged 2.2 percent a year over the same period, the population increasing from 449 million to 703 million. In rural areas, however, developed-country populations declined an average of 0.2 percent a year between 1950 and 1970, from 406 million to 348 million.

1. United Nations, *Concise Report on the World Population Situation in 1977*. ST/ESA/SER.A/63, New York, 1979, p. 94.

18. Migration, Unemployment and Development: A Two-Sector Analysis*

John R. Harris and Michael P. Todaro

Throughout many less developed economies of the world, especially those of tropical Africa, a curious economic phenomenon is presently taking place. Despite the existence of positive marginal products in agriculture and significant levels of urban unemployment, rural-urban labor migration not only continues to exist, but indeed, appears to be accelerating. Conventional economic models with their singular dependence on the achievement of a full employment equilibrium through appropriate wage and price adjustments are

* From *American Economic Review*, 60, no. 1 (March 1970), pp. 126–138, 141–142.

hard put to provide rational behavioral explanations for these sizable and growing levels of urban unemployment in the absence of absolute labor redundancy in the economy as a whole. Moreover, this lack of an adequate analytical model to account for the unemployment phenomenon often leads to rather amorphous explanations such as the "bright lights" of the city acting as a magnet to lure peasants into urban areas.

In this paper we shall diverge from the usual full employment, flexible wage-price models of economic analysis by formulating a two-sector model of rural-urban migration which, among other things, recognizes the existence of a politically determined minimum urban wage at levels substantially higher than agricultural earnings.[1] We shall then consider the effect of this parametric urban wage on the rural individual's economic behavior when the assumption of no agricultural labor surplus is made, i.e., that the agricultural marginal product is always positive and inversely related to the size of the rural labor force.[2] The distinguishing feature of this model is that migration proceeds in response to urban-rural differences in *expected earnings* (defined below) with the urban employment rate acting as an equilibrating force on such migration.[3] We shall then use the overall model for the following purposes:

(1) to demonstrate that given this politically determined high minimum wage, the continued existence of rural-urban migration in spite of substantial overt urban unemployment represents an economically rational choice on the part of the individual migrant;

(2) to show that economists' standard policy prescription of generating urban employment opportunities through the use of "shadow prices" implemented by means of wage subsidies or direct government hiring will *not* necessarily lead to a welfare improvement and may, in fact, exacerbate the problem of urban unemployment;

(3) to evaluate the welfare implications of alternative policies associated with various back-to-the-land programs when it is recognized that the standard remedy suggested by economic theory—namely, full wage flexibility—is for all practical purposes politically infeasible. Special attention will be given here to the impact of migration cum unemployment on the welfare of the rural sector as a whole which gives rise to intersectoral compensation requirements; and, finally,

(4) to argue that in the absence of wage flexibility, an optimal policy is, in fact, a "policy package" including *both* partial wage subsidies (or direct government employment) and measures to restrict free migration.

I. THE BASIC MODEL

The basic model which we shall employ can be described as a two-sector internal trade model with unemployment. The two sectors are the permanent urban and the rural. For analytical purposes we shall distinguish between sectors from the point of view of production and income. The urban sector specializes in the production of a manufactured good, part of which is exported to the rural sector in exchange for agricultural goods. The rural sector has a choice of either using all available labor to produce a single agricultural good, some of which is exported to the urban sector, *or* using only part of its labor to produce this good while *exporting* the remaining labor to the urban sector in return for wages paid in the form of the manufactured good. We are thus assuming that the typical migrant retains his ties to the rural sector and, therefore, the income that he earns as an urban worker will be considered, from the standpoint of sectoral welfare, as accruing to the rural sector.[4] However, this assumption is not at all necessary for our demonstration of the rationality of migration in the face of significant urban unemployment.

The crucial assumption to be made in our model is that rural-urban migration will continue so long as the *expected* urban real income at the margin exceeds real agricultural product—i.e., prospective rural migrants behave as maximizers of *expected* utility. For analytical purposes, we shall assume that the total urban labor force consists of a permanent urban proletariat without ties to the rural sector plus the available supply of rural migrants. From this combined pool of urban labor, we assume that a periodic *random job selection process* exists whenever the number of available jobs is exceeded by the number of job seekers.[5] Consequently, the expected urban wage will be defined as equal to the fixed minimum wage (expressed in terms of manufactured goods) times the proportion of the urban labor force actually employed (see equation (6)). Finally, we assume perfectly competitive behavior on the part of producers in both sectors with the further simplifying assumption that the price of the agricultural good (defined in terms of manufactured goods) is determined directly by the relative quantities of the two goods produced.

Consider now the following formulation of the model.

Agricultural Production Function:

$$(1) \quad X_A = q\,(N_A, \bar{L}, \bar{K}_A), \quad q' > 0, \quad q'' < 0$$

where

X_A is output of the agricultural good,
N_A is the rural labor used to produce this output,
$\bar{L}$ is the fixed availability of land,
$\bar{K}_A$ is the fixed capital stock,
q' is the derivative of q with respect of N_A, its only variable factor.

Manufacturing Production Function:

$$(2) \quad X_M = f\,(N_M, \bar{K}_M), f' > 0, f'' < 0$$

where

X_M is the output of the manufactured good,

N_M is the total labor (urban and rural migrant) required to produce this output.
$\bar{K}_M$ is fixed capital stock, and
f' is the derivative of f with respect to N_M, its only variable factor.

Price Determination:

$$(3) \quad P = \rho\left(\frac{X_M}{X_A}\right), \quad \rho' > 0$$

where

P, the price of the agricultural good in terms of the manufactured good, (i.e., the terms of trade) is a function of the relative outputs of agricultural and manufactured good when the latter serves as numeraire.[6]

Agricultural Real Wage Determination:

$$(4) \quad W_A = P \cdot q'$$

where

W_A, the agricultural real wage, is equal to the value of labor's marginal product in agriculture expressed in terms of the manufactured good.

Manufacturing Real Wage:

$$(5) \quad W_M = f' \geqq \bar{W}_M.$$

The real wage in manufacturing, expressed in terms of manufactured goods, is equated with the marginal product of labor in manufacturing because of profit maximization on the part of perfectly competitive producers. However, this wage is constrained to be greater than or equal to the fixed minimum urban wage. In our analysis, we shall be dealing only with cases in which $f' = \bar{W}_M$ (i.e., there is never an excess demand for labor at the minimum wage).

Urban Expected Wage:

$$(6) \quad W_u^e = \frac{\bar{W}_M N_M}{N_u}, \quad \frac{N_M}{N_u} < 1,$$

where the *expected* real wage in the urban sector, W_u^e *is equal to the real minimum wage* $\overline{W}_M$ adjusted for the proportion of the total urban labor force (permanent urban plus migrants, denoted as N_u) actually employed, N_M/N_u.[7] Only in the case of full employment in the urban sector ($N_M = N_u$) is the expected wage equal to the minimum wage (i.e., $W_u^e = \overline{W}_M$).

Labor Endowment:

$$(7) \qquad N_A + N_u = \overline{N}_R + \overline{N}_u = \overline{N}$$

There is a *labor constraint* which states that the sum of workers actually employed in the agricultural sector (N_A) plus the total urban labor force (N_u) must equal the sum of initial endowments of rural ($\overline{N}_R$) and permanent urban ($\overline{N}_u$) labor which in turn equals the total labor endowment ($\overline{N}$).

Equilibrium Condition:

$$(8) \qquad W_A = W_u^e$$

Equation (8), an equilibrium condition, is derived from the hypothesis that migration to the urban area is a positive function of the urban-rural *expected* wage differential. This can be written formally as

$$(9) \qquad \dot{N}_u = \psi \left(\frac{\overline{W}_M N_M}{N_u} - P \cdot q' \right),$$

$$\psi' > 0, \quad \psi(0) = 0$$

where $\dot{N}_u$ is a time derivative. Clearly then, migration will cease only when the expected income differential is zero, the condition posited in (8).[8] It is important to note that this assumes that a migrant gives up only his marginal product.[9]

We thus have 8 equations in 8 unknowns X_A, X_M, N_A, N_M, W_A, W_u^e, N_u, and P. Given the production functions and fixed minimum wage $\overline{W}_M$, it is possible to solve for sectoral employment, the equilibrium unemployment rate and, consequently, the equilibrium expected wage, relative output levels and terms of trade. Let us analyze how such an unemployment equilibrium can come about.

The essence of our argument is that in many developing nations the existence of an institutionally determined urban minimum wage at levels substantially higher than that which the free market would allow can, and usually does, lead to an equilibrium with considerable urban unemployment. In our model migration is a disequilibrium phenomenon. In equilibrium $\overline{W}_M N_M/N_u = Pq'$ and migration ceases. ...Now we know from equation (5) that in the competitive urban manufacturing sector, $\overline{W}_M = f'$. We also know from equation (7) that $\overline{N} - N_A = N_u$ and from equation (3) that $P = p\,(X_M/X_A)$. Therefore, we can rewrite our equilibrium condition (8) as

$$(8') \qquad \Phi = p\,(X_M/X_A)q' - \frac{f'\,N_M}{\overline{N} - N_A} = 0.$$

Since X_M and X_A are functions of N_M and N_A respectively, Φ is an implicit function in N_A and N_M which, for any stated minimum wage, can be solved for the equilibrium combination of agricultural and manufacturing employment. From this solution the levels of urban unemployment and commodity outputs can also be determined. There will be a unique equilibrium associated with each possible

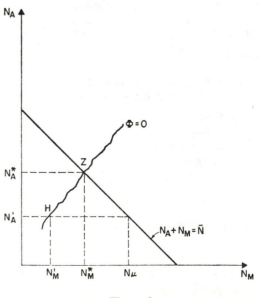

Figure 1.

value of the minimum wage, and the locus of these equilibria is plotted in Figure 1 as the line $\Phi = 0$ in N_A, N_M space.[10] The line $N_A + N_M = \bar{N}$ in Figure 1 is the locus of full-employment points.

Point Z is the only equilibrium full-employment point in Figure 1 at which N^*_M workers would be employed in manufacturing and N^*_A in agriculture. Points on the locus $\Phi = 0$ east of Z are infeasible and will not be considered further, while points to the west of Z are associated with minimum wages higher than the full-employment wage. There is a monotonic mapping such that higher minimum wages are associated with points on $\Phi = 0$ lying farther to the west. Thus we can demonstrate that the setting of a minimum wage above the market-clearing level causes an economy to settle at a point such as H in Figure 1. At H, N'_A workers are employed in agriculture, N'_M in manufacturing, and $N_u - N'_M$ workers are unemployed. It is evident that the minimum wage causes a loss of employment and hence output in both sectors.[11]

It is important to note that even though an equilibrium at point H represents a suboptimum situation for the economy as a whole, it does represent a rational, utility maximizing choice for individual rural migrants given the level of the minimum wage.

One final point might be raised at this juncture. So far we have assumed that the urban minimum wage is fixed in terms of the manufactured good. What if, instead, the minimum wage were fixed in terms of the agricultural good? We would then substitute for equation (5):

(5') $\quad W_M = \dfrac{f'}{P} \gtreqqless \bar{W}_M.$

Substituting (4), (5'), and (6) into (8) we get the equilibrium relationship

(11) $\quad Pq' = \dfrac{\dfrac{f'}{P} \cdot N_M}{N_u}$

We can then imagine an economy starting initially at the point on the production possibili-

ties frontier at which X_M is that for which equation (5') is satisfied and assume that

$$Pq' < \frac{\dfrac{f'}{P} \cdot N_M}{N_u}$$

at that point. The equilibrium point will again be reached through a simultaneous raising of Pq' and lowering of W_u^e in response to migration. As relative agricultural output falls, P will rise. This in turn will cause output of the manufactured good to fall as well, since producers will produce up to the point that $f' = \bar{W}_M P$ which rises in terms of the manufactured good. Note that f' can be raised only through output restriction (since $f'' < 0$). Therefore, in general, we would find that imposition of a minimum wage gives rise to an equilibrium characterized by unemployment and loss of potential output of both goods. A new locus $\Phi' = 0$ will be defined in Figure 1 such that the point on Φ' corresponding to any given minimum wage will be west of the corresponding point on Φ.

Although our initial assumption is a bit easier to handle, the principal conclusion remains unaffected if we make the minimum wage fixed in terms of the agricultural good. Equilibrium is only achievable with unemployment. Actual minimum wage setting is usually done with reference to some general cost of living index, and food is the largest single item in the budget of most urban workers. (See Massell and Heyer, and the Nigeria report.) Hence, the second case may be somewhat more realistic. Note that in the first case the "true" real wage was reduced somewhat by the rising agricultural price, while in the latter case it is increased by the falling relative price of the manufactured good.

III. IMPLICATIONS FOR DEVELOPMENT POLICY

A. Planning in Terms of Shadow Prices

The standard solution to the problem of an institutionally determined wage that is higher than the equilibrium level is to employ labor in the public sector according to a shadow wage and /or to grant a payroll subsidy to private employers that equates private costs with this shadow wage.[12] Two main problems arise with this prescription: first, how can one determine the appropriate shadow wage? and, secondly, what are the implications of executing such a scheme when the institutional wage will continue to be paid to the employed? Our model can shed light on both of these issues.

In a static framework the appropriate shadow wage is the opportunity cost of labor hired by the industrial sector. Hence, if labor is hired to the point that its marginal product in industry is equated with the shadow wage which in turn is equated with the marginal product in agriculture, marginal productivity of labor will be equal in both sectors, a necessary condition for an optimal allocation of resources. Naturally, this assumes a positive marginal product in agriculture and sufficient factor mobility to ensure full employment of labor. The existence of urban unemployment, however, suggests that there may be a pool of labor that can be tapped without sacrificing output. Consequently, it might be suggested that even though agricultural labor is fully employed at peak seasons, the appropriate shadow wage for urban labor is likely to be one that is lower than the marginal product in agriculture. This would be correct if the two labor forces, urban and rural, were separate noncompeting groups. In linear programming terms, there are two labor constraints and each may well have a different associated shadow wage.

Now, the essence of our model is that the two sectors *are* intimately connected through labor migration. If one additional job is created in the industrial sector at the minimum wage, the expected wage will rise and rural-urban migration will be induced. [It can be] shown that more than one agricultural worker will likely migrate in response to the creation of one additional industrial job. Hence, the opportunity cost of an industrial worker will

exceed the marginal product of an agricultural worker. On the other hand, an increase in agricultural income will induce reverse migration with no diminution of industrial output. Thus, the opportunity cost of labor is lower to the agricultural than to the industrial sector!

The literature has been strangely silent for the most part about the full implications of using shadow-wage criteria. In a static context, Stolper has pointed out that financing subsidies or losses of public enterprises gives rise to fiscal problems, but unfortunately this issue has not yet been pursued in sufficient detail.[13] If the problem is considered at all, the analyst usually assumes that a system of nondistorting lump-sum taxes is available. Little, Lefeber, and Little and Mirrlees have pointed out that in a dynamic setting, the extra consumption arising from payment of the institutional wage diverts resources from investment to consumption; thus some of the foregone future consumption should be considered in calculating the shadow wage. In our model, payment of the minimum wage to additional industrial workers will induce more rural-urban migration. Therefore, implementation of a shadow-wage employment criterion will have important effects on the level of agricultural output and on urban unemployment. The argument can be clarified with reference to Figure 2.

The initial equilibrium, given the minimum wage, is at point D with output of the manufactured good restricted to OX_M^*. If individuals did not migrate in response to expected wage differentials, the economy could produce at point E, but migration reduces agricultural output to the level OQ. The theory of shadow pricing suggests that with an appropriate wage subsidy (or public-sector-hiring rule) the economy could move to point L on the production possibilities frontier which, with the posited social indifference map, is the optimum position. Welfare would be increased from a level U_1 to a higher level U_4.

In the context of our model, such a point is unattainable. The effect of implementing a

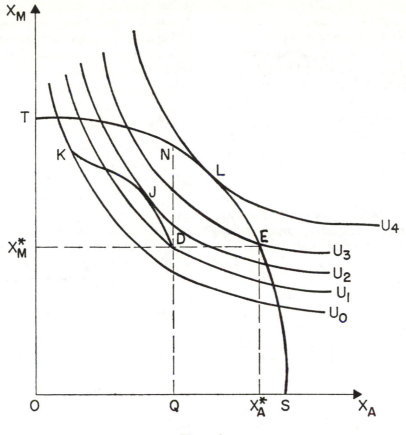

Figure 2.

shadow wage will be to increase production of the manufactured good. But creation of an additional job at the minimum wage will induce some additional migration from the rural sector and therefore agricultural output will fall. Hence, movement from D can only be in a northwest direction. The line DK in Figure 2 is the locus of all such attainable points and it is evident that there is only one point, K, at which there can be full employment of the economy's labor resources. At that point the expected wage will be equal to the minimum wage since there is no urban unemployment. Therefore, the marginal product in agriculture will have to be equal to the minimum wage. But, with the subsidy, the marginal product of labor in manufacturing will be lower than in agriculture, hence K lies inside the production

possibilities frontier. (In the extreme case in which marginal productivity in agriculture can never be as high as the minimum wage, K will coincide with T, the point of complete specialization in manufactures.) This situation will certainly not meet the conditions for a general optimum which can be met only at L. Thus, implementing a shadow wage criterion to the point that urban unemployment is eliminated will not generally be a desirable policy.[14]

However, some level of wage subsidy will usually lead to an improvement. In Figure 2 it is clear that point J, with a welfare level U_2, will be preferable to D. The criterion for welfare maximization . . . is the following:

(12) $$f' = Pq'\left(\frac{dN_u}{dN_M}\right).$$

Note what this means. Creating one additional job in the industrial sector increases output by f' but, since increased employment will raise the expected urban wage, migration will be induced in an amount dN_u/dN_M. The right-hand side of equation (12) states the amount of agricultural output sacrificed because of migration. Thus the shadow wage will be equal to this opportunity cost of an urban job and the amount of subsidy will be $\overline{W}_M - f'$. So long as $f' > Pq' \, (dN_u/dN_M)$, aggregate welfare can be increased by expanding industrial employment through subsidy or public sector hiring. Clearly the more responsive is migration to industrial employment, the higher is the social cost of industrialization and the smaller is the optimal amount of subsidy. In many African economies it is likely that dN_u/dN_M exceeds unity. If so, it will be optimal for the marginal product of labor in industry to be higher than in agriculture and urban unemployment will be a persistent phenomenon so long as minimum wages are set above a market-clearing level.

The discussion so far has ignored two other adverse effects of using a shadow wage. As mentioned earlier, several writers have noted that payment of a subsidized minimum wage to additional workers will increase total consumption, thereby reducing the level of resources available for investment. If foregone future consumption is positively valued, the opportunity cost of industrial labor will be higher than indicated in equation (12) and the shadow wage will be raised correspondingly. Furthermore, wage subsidies or public enterprise losses must be financed and if revenue cannot be raised through costless lump-sum taxes, the opportunity cost of raising taxes must be considered. Both of these effects will reduce the desirable amount of subsidized job creation in the industrial sector.

It is interesting to note that this model implies different opportunity costs of labor to the two sectors. While the creation of an additional job in the urban area reduces agricultural output through induced migration, additional employment can be generated in the agricultural sector without reducing manufacturing output. If this phenomenon is not taken into account, standard application of investment criteria is likely to be biassed in favor of urban projects.

B. Migration Restriction

An alternative approach to the problem of urban unemployment is to physically control migration from the rural areas. Such controls have recently been introduced in Tanzania and have been used for some time in South Africa.[14] Other countries, such as Kenya, are giving serious consideration to instituting such a policy. Although we personally have grave reservations about the ethical issues involved in such a restriction of individual choice and the complexity and arbitrariness of administration, it seems desirable to investigate the economic implications of such a policy.

Looking at Figure 2 it is obvious that with the minimum wage such that industrial output is OX^*_M, prohibition of migration in excess of the labor required to produce that output will allow the economy to produce at point E. The movement from D to E arising from restriction of migration leads to an unambiguous aggregate welfare improvement providing appropriate lump-sum redistribution is effected. Since such compensation is notoriously difficult to carry out in practice, it will be useful to examine the welfare implications of such a move on each of the two sectors in the absence of compensation.

Recall that the two sectors were defined to be a permanent urban group and a rural sector that produces both agricultural goods and exports labor to the urban area in exchange for wages in the form of manufactured goods.[15] In Figure 3 the line $T'S'$ represents production possibilities for the agricultural sector when labor export is allowed. If its entire labor endowment is devoted to agricultural production, it can produce a quantity OS'. However, by exporting its labor, the agricul-

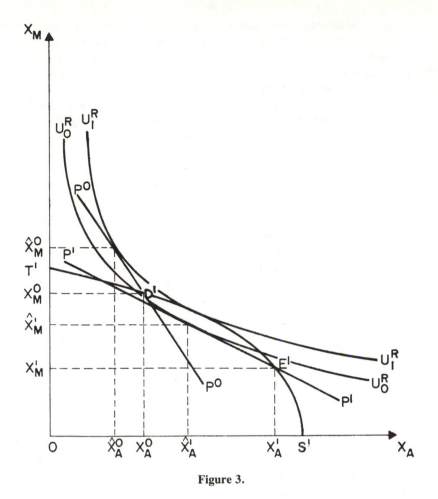

Figure 3.

tural sector can "produce" the manufactured good (wages are paid in the form of this good). Hence this production possibilities frontier depends on market forces (wage levels and unemployment) as well as on purely technological factors. The amount of agricultural output foregone if a unit of labor is to be "exported" is its marginal product; the amount of manufactured goods obtained by the exported labor unit depends on the wage, the amount of employment obtained by the exported unit, and its effect on employment of previously exported units.

In addition to these production possibilities, the rural sector also has the opportunity to trade some of its agricultural output with the permanent urban sector in exchange for manufactured goods. Corresponding to each point on the production possibilities frontier $T'S'$, there is a determinate price of the agricultural good. The manner in which alternative constellations of production and trade affect the sector's welfare can be illustrated by Figure 3.

D' corresponds to the initial unemployment equilibrium D (Figure 2). At that point the rural sector as a whole "produces" X_A^0 and X_M^0 of the two goods. It also has the opportunity to trade at the price P^0. By trading some of its agricultural output to the permanent urban sector for additional manufactured goods, it consumes $\hat{X}_A^0$, $\hat{X}_M^0$ and achieves a welfare level of U_1^R. Restriction of migration results in the sector's producing X_A' X_M'. If it could still trade price P^0, the agricultural sector would clearly be better off. But this is impossible. At E' (which corresponds to E in Figure 2), the price of agricultural good will fall to P' and with trade the best consumption bundle attainable by the sector is $\hat{X}_A$, $\hat{X}_M$ which corresponds to a lower level of welfare U_0^R. (Note that if P' did not cut $T'S'$ there could be no incentive to migrate at E'.)

It can be shown that $Pq'\,(1 - 1/\eta)$ (where η is the price elasticity of demand for the agricultural good) is the amount of the manufactured good sacrificed by the rural sector as a result of removing one worker from producing the agricultural good which could have been exchanged for the manufactured good at the market price $1/P$. This quantity is less than the value of labor's marginal product in agriculture (Pq') since the reduction in output has a favorable terms-of-trade effect. If the demand for the agriculture good is inelastic ($\eta < 1$) we reach the startling conclusion that the sacrifice becomes negative! This is, of course, the familiar proposition that aggregate farm income may be increased by reducing output. The *direct* gain in manufactured goods achieved by the rural sector through exporting an additional unit of labor is $\overline{W}_M N_M/N_u$, the expected urban wage. But additional migration, by increasing unemployment, reduces the earnings of *all* migrants already in the urban labor force by a factor $(1-R)$, where R is the fraction of the total urban labor force supplied by the rural sector.[16]

As long as $Pq'\,(1-\eta) < \overline{W}_M N_M/N_u\,(1-R)$ the welfare of the rural sector will be increased by allowing migration even though unemployment ensues and the economy as a whole sacrifices output. Since Pq' and $\overline{W}_M N_M/N_u$ are always positive and $R\leq1$, additional migration will always benefit the rural sector when $\eta<1$. In general, the lower is Pq', η, or R and the higher is $\overline{W}_M N_M/N_u$, the more will the rural sector benefit from the opportunity to migrate.

From the foregoing, one can conclude that although migration restriction will improve

aggregate welfare of the economy, given plausible values of η and R, substantial compensation to the rural sector will be required if it is not to be made worse off by removing the opportunity for free migration. The permanent urban labor force clearly will be made better off by becoming fully employed at the high minimum wage while also being able to buy food at a lower price. Each unit of labor exported by the rural sector will similarly earn more but this gain will be offset by reduced total labor exports and lower agricultural prices. Whether or not this will be true depends, of course, on the values of the specific parameters of the economy. If η is sufficiently high, the rural sector could be made better off by restricting migration in the absence of compensation, but this seems very unlikely.

C. A Combination of Policies

It has been shown that either a limited wage-subsidy or a migration-restriction policy will lead to a welfare improvement. Which of the two policies will lead to the better position cannot be determined without knowing all the relevant parameters for a particular economy. It is clear, however, that neither policy alone is capable of moving the economy to the optimum that could be achieved with competitive wage determination (point L in Figure 2).

At first sight it may seem strange that with a single market failure, the wage level, a single policy instrument is unable to fully correct the situation.[17] The reason is that the wage performs two functions in this model. It determines *both* the level of employment in the industrial sector *and* the allocation of labor between rural and urban areas. While a subsidy changes the effective wage for determination of industrial employment, so long as the wage actually received by workers exceeds agricultural earnings there will be migration and urban unemployment. Restriction of migration prevents the minimum wage having its effect on unemployment but does nothing to increase the level of industrial employment.

Therefore, if the optimum position is to be achieved, a combination of both instruments will have to be used. In order to reach point L a wage subsidy must be instituted such that industrial employment will increase to the extent that with full employment the marginal product of labor will be equal in manufacturing and agriculture. The subsidy will be positive and equal to the difference between the minimum wage and marginal productivity. At that point $W_u^e = \overline{W}_M$ and $\overline{W}_M > Pq'$. Therefore, individuals would still find it in their interest to migrate and the point will not be attainable unless migration is restricted.

The agricultural sector has to be better off at L than at E since each additional unit of labor exported earns the full minimum wage, marginal productivity in agriculture is less than the minimum wage, and the price of the agricultural good rises. Whether the agricultural sector is better off at L than at D, however, depends again on the parametric values of the model.[18] It can be stated with certainty that the amount of compensation needed to make the rural sector *no worse off* than at D will be less at L than at E, and, furthermore it should be easier to finance since total income is greater.

Even so the fiscal requirements of subsidy (or public enterprise losses) and compensation cannot be taken lightly.[19] A government may find it difficult to find nondistorting taxes capable of raising sufficient revenue. Perhaps a head-tax on all urban residents would be feasible although this too raises the question of how minimum wages are set (unions in tropical Africa have, in some cases, successfully fought to maintain the real after-tax wage). A tax on rural land is ruled out if there must be *net* compensation to the rural sector which, in the absence of pure profits in manufacturing, leaves an urban land tax as the remaining potential ideal tax.

All of the above suggests that altering the minimum wage may avoid the problems of taxation, administration, and interference with individual mobility attendant to the poli-

cy package just discussed. Income and wages policies designed to narrow the rural-urban wage gap have been suggested by D. P. Ghai, and Tanzania has formally adopted such a policy along with migration restriction. In the final analysis, however, the basic issue at stake is really one of political feasibility and it is not at all clear that an incomes policy is any more feasible than the alternatives.

REFERENCES

P. K. Bardhan, "Factor Market Disequilibrium and the Theory of Protection," *Oxford Econ. Pap.* (New Series), Oct. 1964, *16*, 375–88.

E. J. Berg, "Wages Structure in Less Developed Countries," in A. D. Smith, ed., *Wage Policy Issues in Economic Development*, London 1969.

A. Callaway, "From Traditional Crafts to Modern Industries," *ODU: University of Ife Journal of African Studies*, July 1965, *2*.

S. Chakravarty, "The Use of Shadow Prices in Programme Evaluation," in Rosenstein-Rodan, ed., *Capital Formation and Economic Development*, London 1964.

Y. S. Cho, *Disguised Unemployment in Developing Areas, with Special Reference to South Korean Agriculture*, Berkeley 1960.

R. S. Eckaus, "The Factor-Proportions Problem in Underdeveloped Areas," *Amer Econ. Rev.*, Sept. 1955, *45*, 539–65.

J. Erickson, "Wage Employment Relationships in Latin American Industry: A Pilot Study of Argentina, Brazil, and Mexico," International Labour Office, 1969, typescript.

J. Fei and G. Ranis, *Development of the Labor Surplus Economy*, Illinois 1964.

D. P. Ghai, "Incomes Policy in Kenya: Need, Criteria and Machinery," *East Afr. Econ. Rev.*, June 1968, *4*, 19–35.

J. Gugler, "The Impact of Labour Migration on Society and Economy in Sub-Saharan Africa. Empirical Findings and Theoretical Considerations," *African Social Research*, Dec. 1968, *6*, 463–86.

E. E. Hagen, "An Economic Justification of Protectionism," *Quart. J. Econ.*, Nov. 1958, *72*, 496–514.

J. R. Harris and M. P. Todaro, "Urban Unemployment in East Africa: An Economic Analysis of

Policy Alternatives," *East Afr. Econ. Rev.*, Dec. 1968, *4*, 17–36.

——and——, "Wages, Industrial Employment, and Labour Productivity: The Kenyan Experience," *East Afr. Econ. Rev.* (New Series), June 1969, *1*, 29–46.

J. P. Henderson, "Wage Policy in Africa," Paper prepared for delivery at the African Conference on Economics, Temple University, mimeo, April 1968.

C. R. Hutton, "The Causes of Labour Migration," in Gugler, ed., *Urbanization in Sub-Saharan Africa*, Kampala 1969.

C. H. C. Kao, K. R. Anschel, and C. K. Eicher, "Disguised Unemployment in Agriculture: A Survey," in C. K. Eicher and L. W. Witt, eds., *Agriculture in Economic Development*, New York 1964, 129–44.

J. M. Katz, "Verdoorn Effects; Returns to Scale, and the Elasticity of Factor Substitution," *Oxford Econ. Pap.*, Nov. 1968, *20*, 342–52.

L. Lefeber, "Planning in a Surplus Labor Economy," *Amer. Econ. Rev.*, June 1968, *58*, 343–73.

W. A. Lewis, "Economic Development with Unlimited Supplies of Labour," *Manchester Sch. Econ. Soc. Stud.*, May 1954, *22*, 139–91.

I. M. D. Little, "The Real Cost of Labour, and the Choice Between Consumption and Investment," in Nigeria, *Report of the Commission on the Review of Wages, Salary and Conditions of Service of the Junior Employees of the Governments of the Federation and in Private Establishments 1963–64.*

P. N. Rosenstein-Rodan, ed., *Pricing and Fiscal Policies: A Study in Method*, Cambridge 1964, 77–91.

——and J. A. Mirrlees, *Manual of Industrial Project Analysis*, Vol. II. "Social Cost Benefit Analysis," Paris 1969.

B. F. Massell and J. Heyer, "Household Expenditure in Nairobi: A Statistical Analysis of Consumer Behaviour," *Econ. Develop. Cult. Change*, Jan. 1969, *17*, 212–34.

L. G. Reynolds, "Wages and Employment in a Labor-Surplus Economy," *Amer. Econ. Rev.*, Mar. 1965, *55*, 19–39.

W. F. Stolper, *Planning Without Facts: Lessons in Resource Allocation from Nigeria's Development.* Cambridge 1966.

M. P. Todaro, "A Model of Labor Migration and Urban Unemployment in Less Developed Countries," *Amer. Econ. Rev.*, Mar. 1969, *59*, 138–48.

NOTES

1. For some empirical evidence on the magnitude of these real earnings differentials in less developed economies, see Reynolds, Berg, Henderson, and Ghai.

2. We do not make the special assumption of an agricultural labor surplus for the following reasons: Most available empirical evidence to date tends to cast doubt on the labor surplus argument in the context of those economies of Southeast Asia and Latin America where such a surplus would be most likely to exist (see Kao, Anschel, and Eicher). Moreover, few if any economists would seriously argue that general labor surplus exists in tropical Africa, the area to which this paper is most directly related.

3. For a dynamic model of labor migration in which urban unemployment rates and expected incomes play a pivotal role in the migration process, see Todaro. However, unlike the present model which attempts to view the migration process in context of aggregate and intersectoral welfare considerations, Todaro's model was strictly concerned with the formulation of a positive theory of urban unemployment in developing nations. As such, it did not specifically consider the welfare of the rural sector, nor was it concerned with the broader issues of economic policy considered in the present paper.

4. In tropical Africa especially, this notion that migrants retain their ties to the rural sector is quite common and manifested by the phenomenon of the extended family system and the flow of remittances to rural relatives of large proportions of urban earnings. However, the reverse flow, i.e., rural-urban monetary transfers is also quite common in cases where the migrant is temporarily unemployed and, therefore, must be supported by rural relatives. For an excellent discussion of this phenomenon from a sociological point of view, see Gugler (pp. 475–78).

5. The qualitative conclusions of the model do not depend on the precise nature of the selection process. We have assumed random selection not merely for analytic convenience but also because it directly corresponds to an appropriate dynamic construct developed in Todaro's 1969 article. There it is shown that over time expected and actual earnings will converge to a positive number even though the rate of job creation is less than the rate of migration so that unemployment is increasing.

It is interesting to note in this context that sociologist Gugler who has spent considerable time studying labor migration in Africa has recently concluded that rural-urban migration is essentially an economic phenomenon that can be portrayed as a "game of lottery" in which rural migrants come to the city fully aware that their chances of finding a job are low. However, the great disparity between urban and rural wages makes the successful location of an urban salaried job so attractive that unskilled migrants are willing to take a chance (pp. 472–73). See also Hutton.

6. A sufficient , but not necessary, condition for this assumption is that all individuals in the economy have the same homothetic preference map. Again, the assumption is made for analytical convenience. The qualitative conclusions of our analysis will remain unaffected under several plausible assumptions about distribution of income and tastes.

7. This assumes a very particular form of wage expectation, namely that the expected wage is equal to the average urban wage. Although this is a convenient expression to work with, we could be more general and make the expected wage some function of the average urban wage. Indeed, the only restrictions on such a function that are necessary for our results are that, *ceteris paribus*, the expected wage varies directly with the minimum wage and inversely with the unemployment rate.

8. $\psi(0) = 0$ is purely arbitrary. If, instead, we assume $\psi(\alpha) = 0$ where α can take on any value, migration will cease when the urban-rural expected wage differential is equal to α. None of the subsequent analysis is affected qualitatively by specifying $\alpha = 0$. Equation (8) would merely be written as $W_A + \alpha = W_u^e$.

9. Other assumptions could be made. Much of the literature has stressed that in peasant economies producers receive their average product which is higher than their marginal product. Indeed, this is at the heart of the well-known Lewis and Fei-Ranis models. However, these models ignore the migration decision and seem to assume that migrants continue to receive their share of peasant production yet migrate only if jobs are actually available. In much of Africa it appears that migrants continue to receive income from land after migration and commonly hire labor to work on their farms in their absence. There is also a considerable group of landless individuals who work on

farms for wages. Thus it would appear that our assumption is not unreasonable. The analysis could easily be modified to make earnings foregone equal to average product, however.

10. In Figure 1 we have assumed that

$$\frac{d N_A}{d N_M} = -[\Phi N_M / \Phi N_A] > 0$$

although this need not necessarily hold true. Differentiating (8′) partially with respect to N_A we find that

$$\Phi N_A = \frac{-\rho' f q'^2}{q^2} + \rho q'' - \frac{\rho q'}{\overline{N} - N_A}$$

which is unambiguously negative since $q'' < 0$ and $\rho' > 0$. Differentiating (8′) partially with respect to N_M we find that

$$\Phi N_M = \frac{1}{\eta_{LW}} - \eta p \, \frac{f' N_M}{X_M} + 1$$

which is less than, equal to, or greater than zero as

$$-\frac{1}{\eta_{LW}} + \eta P \, \frac{f' N_M}{X_M} \gtreqless 1,$$

where

$$\eta_{LW} = -\frac{d N_M}{d \overline{W}_u} \cdot \frac{\overline{W}_u}{N_M}$$

is the wage elasticity of demand for labor and

$$\eta P = \left(\frac{dP}{d \frac{X_M}{X_A}} \right) \cdot \frac{X_M/X_A}{P}$$

is the elasticity of the terms of trade with respect to a change in relative outputs. It follows, therefore that the slope of the locus of equilibria, dN_A/dN_M depends on the respective employment and price elasticities.

A sufficient condition for Φ_{NM} to be negative (making dN_A/dN_M positive) is for the wage elasticity of employment to be less than one, a situation which recent empirical studies suggest is likely to exist (see Erickson, Harris and Todaro (1969), and Katz). However, even if η_{LW} exceeds unity, dN_A/dN_M can still be positive providing price elasticity is sufficiently high. The logic of these conditions is clear. If η_{LW} is less than one, a decline in the minimum wage will lower the urban wage bill even though employment and output increase. This causes the expected urban wage to decline thereby reducing the expected rural-urban earnings differential which gives rise to reverse migration and increased rural employment and output. If η_{LW} exceeds unity, a fall in the minimum wage is accompanied by an increased urban wage bill and, hence, a higher expected urban wage. However, the expected rural-urban earnings differential can either increase or decrease in this case depending on the movement in terms of trade which raises the value of the marginal product in agriculture. For example, if η_{LW} were 1.5 and the wage share of manufacturing output ($f'N_M/X_M$) were .50, then an agricultural price elasticity greater than 0.67 would be sufficient to make dN_A/dN_M positive.

11. If $dN_A/dN_M < 0$, which we believe to be empirically unlikely, this statement would have to be modified. In such a case, increasing the minimum wage will decrease manufacturing employment but will increase agricultural employment and output. Unemployment will result from the imposition of a minimum wage but we can no longer assert that the level of unemployment will increase concomitantly with the level of the minimum wage.

12. Hagen (p. 498) states, "a subsidy per unit of labor equal to the wage differential [between agriculture and industry] will increase real income further [than a tariff] and if combined with free trade will permit attaining an *optimum optimorum.*" Bardhan (p. 379) similarly adds. "The best remedy for the misallocation caused by a wage differential is . . . an appropriate subsidy to the use of labor in the manufacturing industry." It is important to recall that this argument is dependent on variable proportions production functions. If production coefficients are fixed, a wage subsidy will have no effect in the short run. The classic statement of this case is by Eckaus. Bardhan explores its implications for subsidy in a dynamic context. Both of these papers, however, posit surplus labor in agriculture, an assumption we do not wish to make in an African context.

13. Lefeber assumes that a wage subsidy can be financed by a profits tax, while other writers, e.g., Hagen, Bardhan, and Chakravarty never even consider the problem. Even Little and Mirrlees who present an excellent discussion of how to calculate a shadow wage never mention the fiscal problems of implementation.

14. *DK* is not uniformly convex. Therefore, *K* may be the best attainable point in some cases and the first-order conditions may not ensure optimality. As drawn in Figure 2, moving from *D* to *K* rep-

resents a worsening of welfare, but this clearly is not a necessary conclusion.

14. See Harris and Todaro (1969) for an analysis of the Tanzanian program.

15. In considering the welfare of the rural sector as a whole we are making the tacit assumption that there is redistribution of goods between individuals in this sector. This is a very strong assumption. Yet there is considerable evidence from tropical Africa that employed urban migrants repatriate substantial portions of their earnings to their kinsmen remaining in the rural areas and conversely that income both in cash and kind is received by unemployed migrants from kinsmen remaining on the farm. To the extent that the extended family system does redistribute goods between members, this assumption may be tenable as a first approximation. As Gugler (p. 480) has pointed out, it is appropriate to view the extended family as maximizing its income by allocating its members between agriculture and urban wage employment. Although there is some evidence that growing numbers of urban workers are settling permanently and gradually eliminating rural ties, it will be many years before such ties are completely severed.

16. If the urban unemployment were experienced only by migrants, this term would equal zero since the total amount of earnings through labor export would be constant. It can be positive only because the permanent urban labor force shares in unemployment, thereby reducing its share of the constant wage bill in the manufactured good industry. An interesting extension of the model would be to incorporate different employment probabilities for the permanent urban and migrant rural labor forces and then to check the sensitivity of results with our more simplified assumption of equal probabilities.

17. We wish to thank a referee of this *Review* for drawing this to our attention.

18. As drawn in Figure 2, *L* must represent a higher welfare level than *D* for the rural sector since *P* rises and the sector produces more of both goods. In fact if *L* lies along *TS* north of the ray going through *D* there will be an unambiguous sectoral welfare improvement. However, if *L* lies south of the ray on *TS*, the rural sector could be worse off than at *D* since *P* falls.

19. This argument coincides with the statement by Stolper (p. 195), "It should be noted, however,

that even at best the application of shadow prices leads to the substitution of one problem, the budget, for another one, an imperfect market.''

We would not go as far as Stolper in rejecting out of hand any use of shadow pricing because of the fiscal implications. The general point is valid that one cannot disregard the consequences of implementation of shadow-price criteria if actual prices or wages continue to diverge from the shadow prices or wages.

19. A Review and Evaluation of Attempts to Constrain Migration to Selected Urban Centres and Regions*

Alan B. Simmons

Most developing countries have indicated dissatisfaction with the size and continuing high growth rates of their largest cities.[1] Migration from the countryside and natural population increase in these metropolitan areas have led to an unprecedented rate of population growth and overloaded public services and social infrastructure. The streets are generally congested and noisy, the air and drainage ditches are often polluted, adequate housing is scarce, slums and squatter dwellings abound, sewerage facilities are inadequate; and outlying suburbs may lack water, garbage collection and electricity. The financial resources to solve these problems would take a large part of the national budget and thereby divert resources away from needed development programmes in the countryside and smaller urban centres.

This paper concerns the rather controversial topic of restrictions, regulations, controls, disincentives and other socio-economic measures directed towards slowing and reversing rural-urban migration. Developed market econ-

omies use residential zoning regulations and industrial tax incentives extensively for urban and regional planning; the Eastern European centrally planned economies tend to use residence permits, job assignments and housing allocation programmes.[2] Among the developing countries of the world one finds examples of all the preceeding constraint mechanisms and many cases of even more coercive measures, such as the forced resettlement of urban squatters. It is not the objective in this paper to condone these measures as drastic but possibly necessary solutions; nor is the objective to condemn them as a threat to freedom and economic efficiency. Rather, the paper documents· the varieties of constraints on migration which have been employed in different countries, particularly in developing countries, and assesses their effects on slowing metropolitan growth and on other development goals.

A. SOME PRELIMINARY QUESTIONS

A brief summary of the reasons that cities in developing countries are growing so rapidly and the problems resulting from such growth will establish the context for the review of migration constraint policies.

* From: United Nations Department of International Economic and Social Affairs, *Population Distribution Policies in Development Planning*. Population Studies, No. 75, New York, 1981, pp. 87–100.

Aspects of Urbanization That Cause Problems

Urban growth patterns vary greatly from one developing country to another. Overall levels of urbanization—that is, the proportion of people who live in towns, small cities and large metropolitan areas—are high in Latin America, moderate in Eastern South Asia and East Asia, and low in other regions of South Asia and Africa.[3] In all developing countries, levels of urbanization rise as levels of national income and industrial production rise. From this point of view there is little to be alarmed about: the currently developing countries appear to be following the pattern established earlier by the now developed countries.

The reason for alarm and concern is not the level of urbanization, but rather its rate and concentration. Compared with the currently developed countries when they experienced accelerated urbanization, urban areas in developing countries are growing at historically unprecedented rates, in part because overall rates of natural population growth are exceedingly high in the urban and rural areas of developing countries. Natural growth (births less deaths) constitutes 60 per cent or more of total urban growth in the developing countries.[4] Of course, migrants contribute significantly to this natural increase, since those who move to cities tend to be young adults with high fertility and low mortality. Current rates of migration to urban areas in developing countries appear to be within the range of rates experienced by developed countries. When migration and the fertility of migrant and "nonmigrant" parents are combined, city growth can reach high levels. Although most of the cities in less developed countries are growing in the range of from 4 to 6 percent each year (doubling the city population every 12–16 years), some cities, including several in Africa, are growing from 10 to 12 percent each year (doubling the city population every six or seven years). It is this rate of increase which overburdens urban infrastructure.

In the developing countries, urbanization is concentrated in a relatively few urban centres in each country. Typically, the largest city in a country is many times larger than the second largest. Among the extreme cases, Bangkok is nearly 40 times larger than Chiengmai, the second largest city in Thailand.[5] The social costs of these large "primate" cities and the regional disparities in income associated with their emergence concern planners. Mexico City, for example, now has in excess of 10 million inhabitants, but is still an attractive place for individual investors and migrants seeking to maximize their market and employment opportunities. However, among other problems, Mexico City is running out of water and large areas of the city currently have no water for extensive periods of the year. The cost of bringing in water from new sources is rising to levels that could threaten the national budget.[6] Available water is at lower altitudes, 200 kilometres away and will have to be pumped up—the electricity to pump the required water is estimated at one fifth of the current national electricity production.

Why People Continue to Move to Congested Cities

Unskilled migrants in particular have difficulty obtaining employment, food and housing in metropolitan cities. Their continued migration to cities is therefore a paradox. But the answer is simple and has been confirmed by repeated studies: migrants are actually better off economically in the city than in the countryside.[7] Although life is difficult in an urban slum, it is apparently worse in many rural areas. The reasons behind this fact can be explained by an analysis of historical patterns of investment and economic growth. The specific details vary from one country to another, but the following elements are generally held in common:

(a) Rapid population growth brought about by lower death rates and agricultural development has led to a large landless class and unemployment in rural areas;

(b) Seasonal employment and subsistence agriculture provide exceedingly low levels of income, with the result that rural people tend to drift to urban locations;

(c) Urban centres, particularly the largest cities, offer agglomerative economies attracting private investment, public enterprise and government offices. Investment in rural areas and smaller cities is too small to bring about economic growth or attract migrants;

(d) Employment in government and modern industry in the metropolitan cities provides workers and professionals with wages;

(e) The services demanded by more affluent workers provide the base for a much larger "informal sector" of hawkers, vendors, cabmen, gardeners, maids and other assorted workers. Wages in these occupations are generally low but sufficient to attract rural migrants.

Whether Developing Countries Should Attempt to Slow Metropolitan Growth

Currently, no general answer can be given to the question whether developing countries should attempt to slow metropolitan growth. A specific assessment must be made in each country and unique circumstances (such as the water and energy supply implications of continued growth in Mexico City) must be taken into account. In the decision, a key factor is the cost of population distribution programmes. Some of these costs are direct, associated with specific relocation programmes. Others are "opportunity costs" relating to whether slower or dispersed city growth will be economically less efficient and drag down national economic progress. While the debate on this latter issue continues, there is reason to believe that the hierarchical structure of urbanization (that is, the presence or absence of a single

"primate city" dominating all other urban areas) has been largely unrelated to economic performance in developing countries. Among developing countries with a growing economy some continue to reveal strong primacy patterns (Mexico, Thailand); others, decreasing primacy (Brazil, Malaysia and the Republic of Korea); and, in general, developed countries have much lower rates of primacy. Apparently, policy-makers can assess specific needs in their countries and modify urban structures accordingly without necessarily restricting economic growth.

B. CONSTRAINTS AS POLICY TOOLS

Migration constraints include all administrative, social and economic measures designed to force, channel or restrict population movement. Administrative measures include zoning regulations (on housing or industrial location), legal prohibitions on migration and forced resettlement. Social measures include mass exhortation, education and information campaigns to direct migrants. Economic measures include property taxes, rent and land subsidies and infrastructure inputs (highways, electricity etc.) which influence the location of migrants and firms.

Migration constraints should be viewed as "policy tools". They are not complete policies. Rather, they can be applied selectively to achieve various "policy objectives", such as holding farmers on the land, discouraging migrants from entering select cities, directing population flows towards frontier areas and so on. A complete migration policy would specify both the objectives and the mechanisms.

Constraint mechanisms tend to be controversial primarily because they often emphasize "negative" controls, such as disincentives, prohibitions, bans, fines and penalties intended to direct people away from areas where they currently live or where they would like to live. "Positive" policy tools, in contrast, encourage population movement through incentives, including better housing, working conditions, salaries and so on.

In practice, the distinction between disincentives and incentives is difficult to maintain. The two are often opposite sides of the same coin. Offering subsidized low-cost housing to people who live in location "a", and not subsidizing higher rents in location "b", can be seen either as an incentive to move to "a" or as a disincentive forcing migrants away from "b". It is therefore useful to consider both disincentives and incentives as constraint mechanisms.

Migration policies can be "one-sided" or "two-sided". One sided policies are those which apply measures in one area only without applying complementary measures in other areas. Two-sided policies are those which apply complementary, co-ordinated constraints to destination and origin areas. Two-sided programmes may be based entirely on administrative measures, such as compulsory job placement and housing assignment programmes co-ordinated in both locations. However, they may also include co-ordinated economic incentives and disincentives.

Table 1 gives a classification of several policies designed to slow metropolitan growth and their associated migration constraint mechanisms. The table shows that some policies are inherently one-sided (e.g., "closed-city" policies) while others are often but not always "two-sided" (e.g., agricultural development and growth-pole strategies). Of course, the alternative destinations emphasized in two-sided strategies may be pursued as economic programmes valuable in their own right, without reference to controlling metropolitan growth.

As Table 1 also shows, the complexity of co-ordinating migration constraint mechanisms varies significantly from one policy approach to another. The simplest policies to co-ordinate are those which involve only the metropolitan government (e.g., "closed-city" policy) and require no co-ordination with other levels of government, even though inputs from the latter would serve to strengthen the effort. Dormitory-town and satellite-city policies may be co-ordinated by the city and the provincial or state government where the city is located. Broader national rural development and growth-pole policies are administratively far more complex, as they require co-ordination over at least three levels of government: city; state or provincial; and national.

Next to be considered are examples of the policies designated to slow metropolitan growth and the way in which various constraint mechanisms have been employed in them.

C. CLOSED-CITY AND ANTI-ACCOMMODATION POLICIES

Many municipal governments in developing countries at first reacted to increased migration as if it were an invasion which they had to repel. Towns and cities that had been growing slowly through natural population growth appeared to explode in size overnight when the first waves of migrants arrived. In the process, various municipal zoning regulations, laws and commercial standards were broken. Migrants, for example, squatted on public land.[8] In Latin America, they frequently organized "land invasions" in which several hundred families would creep on to a vacant urban plot at night and quickly erect pre-assembled cardboard and tin shacks.[9] Beggars, vagrants and unemployed were found in increasing numbers on the streets. Land speculators sold tiny, unimproved and unzoned "pirate" lots on the outskirts of town for modest prices. Not surprisingly, the immediate reaction of many local municipal authorities was to crack down on slum-dwellers, vagrants and residents in unorganized suburbs. Bulldozers moved in to crush squatter housing; the military forced relocation; migrants were "bussed" back to their villages; and prohibitions were placed on hawkers and vendors.[10]

TABLE 1. Policies Designed to Slow Metropolitan Growth and Associated Constraint Mechanisms

Policy Objective	Constraint Mechanisms		Administration of Constraints
	Applied in the Metropolitan Area	*Applied in Alternative Destinations*	
'Closed-city policies'' To stop migrants from settling in the metropolitan area	Destruction of squatter housing Forced eviction Identity cards and passports Restrictions on investment in housing and industry Pay return trip home Bans on informal sector occupations (street vendors, etc.)	None	One-sided policy applied in the metropolitan area. These policies can independently be administered by the municipal governments. Other levels of government may assist
Dormitory towns and satellite cities To relocate migrants and others born in the city to towns in the vicinity, separated from the core by "green belts" and connected to the core by commuter transportation	No subsidies for housing Zoning against new housing Freeze on social services Discouragement of industry through higher taxes and property values Job assignments Housing placement Commuter transport "Green-belt" zones around city	Subsidized housing Zoned for new housing Expanded social services Attraction of industry through tax and relocation incentives Job assignments Housing placements Commuter transport	Two-sided policies applied in the metropolitan area and in alternative destination. Both the municipal governments and the authorities in the district immediately surrounding the city must be involved. The national Government may assist.
Intermediate cities and rural development To redirect migrants to alternative destinations which are distant from the city	As given above, but excluding commuter transport Regional and sectoral wage policies	As given above, but excluding commuter transport Regional and sectoral wage policies Infrastructural investments (highways, electricity, etc.) In rural programmes, land settlement and colonization with credit and technical assistance	Two-sided policies involving three levels of government: municipal, regional and national. Strong national co-ordination required.

These repulsions were frequently spontaneous, disorganized and temporary; but in some countries, official "anti-accommodation" and "closed-city" programmes were established on a systematic, continuing basis.

Jakarta

One of the best known attempts to prohibit the entry of migrants to the city is found at Jakarta, the capital of Indonesia. In 1970, the Governor of Jakarta passed a decree whereby migrants to Jakarta were obliged to register with the city government and to deposit a sum equivalent to their return fare to Jakarta.[11] Six months after registration, if migrants could not prove that they were employed and domiciled they were given one-way tickets to their places of origin.

While seemingly straightforward, these regulations were extremely difficult to administer. Violators proved too numerous to control. In one night, for example, city officials and police rounded up as many as 13,000 persons who were vagrants and lacked identification cards.[12] Accordingly, they were taken in trucks to their villages of origin. However, they are reported to have returned to Jakarta almost immediately. Some city government officials later admitted that they recognized from the beginning their incapacity effectively to administer the closed-city scheme; however, they had hoped that the policy announcement and the periodic "deportation of migrants would act as a tool to discourage new migrants.[13] An undesirable side-effect of these regulations was petty corruption. Identification cards and other official papers were clandestinely peddled in Jakarta.

More recently, a strategy of "anti-accomodation" policies has been introduced to limit job opportunities of unskilled workers at Jakarta. A highly visible and common job for new migrants from the countryside is *betjak* driving—that is, pedalling a brightly coloured tricycle "taxi" through downtown streets. The *betjak* was previously the main form of urban transportation at Jakarta. In 1971, there were over 126,000 registered *betjaks* in Jakarta, most working two shifts a day, employing up to 240,000 drivers in all, who, with their families, numbered as many as 700,000 or 800,000 people.[14] The government wants to get *betjaks* off the street and as a first step has introduced *betjak*-free zones. All vehicles must be registered and no new *betjaks* can be built. Reports indicate that from 20,000 to 30,000 *betjaks* have already been removed in *betjak*-free zones and that the Master Plan for Jakarta called for their total elimination by 1980.[15] Over the past several years, the government also attempted to remove unlicensed sidewalk vendors, marginal workers, scavengers and beggars from the city streets. Measures include the confiscation of goods from vendors without licences.

Despite some claims that migration to Jakarta has been drastically reduced, the evidence suggests that the various administrative measures have had only a modest impact. An early account of the experiment noted that "despite registers, control cards, cash deposits and transmigration, the Indonesian capital . . . leaks internal migrants like a sieve".[16] The question, however, is whether it would be growing more rapidly if the "closed-city and anti-accommodation" policies had not been instituted. This may indeed be the case. Unemployment, for example, has increased in surrounding cities, perhaps as a consequence of migrants being deflected away from Jakarta.[17] Also, some statistics show that the number of *betjak* drivers and street vendors in the city has declined, suggesting that people formerly active in these occupations have returned to rural pursuits or migrated elsewhere.[18] As yet, however, there are no conclusive data to indicate how effective the policies have been.

Manila

A less direct but no more successful attempt to discourage the entry of migrants to the city is seen at Manila.[19] In 1963, the newly elected mayor implemented an election promise to provide free education to city residents.

However, this provision applied only to *bona fide* residents of Manila—migrants and commuters had to pay a large fee to enter the school system. Administering the system proved extremely difficult. Claims of residence were supposed to be proven by certificates of tax payments, sworn statements (affidavits) and a residence certificate. Most migrants were too poor to pay taxes, yet they were often willing to pay a lawyer the fee for drawing up an affidavit. Anyone with 60 centavos was able to get a residence certificate, even with a fictitious address. The result was predictable: petty corruption, on the one hand; and the rapid increase in the city school enrolment, on the other. By 1968, the city of Manila was spending more than a third of its budget on education alone.

South Africa

The application of very tight controls, national identification cards and internal passports to control migration has been effective in keeping migrants out of cities in South Africa.[20] The South African pass laws permit black male workers to move to urban areas for employment, while black women and children remain in the towns in the vicinity or in homeland villages. Illegal workers and squatter settlements with families are occasionally "deported". Urban squalor, however, is exported outside city boundaries to "dormitory slums" within commuting distance.

Eastern Europe

The centrally planned economies of Eastern Europe have had mixed success in applying bans on movement to metropolitan cities. Between 1965 and 1970, Poland registered all citizens in allocated housing on a prescribed basis. In order to move, a person was required to have an employment offer in the new locality and approval from local authorities.[21]

Similarly, in Hungary and in the Union of Soviet Socialist Republics, migration to restricted cities is possible only for persons with needed work skills.[22] Such measures would appear to offer complete assurance of policy success in achieving the goal of reduced metropolitan growth. In practice, however, the policies may have limited impact due to conflict between population distribution schemes and industrial planning.

In the Soviet Union, industrial planning has taken priority over territorial and housing concerns. Economists focusing on production have argued for locating firms in larger cities, where scale and agglomeration economies are greater.[23] As a result, restrictions on labour mobility may have been only marginally effective in reducing metropolitan growth. Certainly, cities in the USSR have continued to grow quickly in recent years, although perhaps less quickly than might have been the case without migration constraints.

Of the Eastern European countries, perhaps only Hungary has effectively reduced metropolitan growth. Between 1971 and 1975, the annual rate of net migration to Budapest dropped from 0.97 percent to 0.24 percent per annum.[24] This decline occurred primarily because industrial investment and employment decreased at Budapest and increased in other areas, particularly the Hungarian Plain region. In Hungary, State-owned industrial firms make their own location and investment decisions; hence, their movement to the Plain region occurred not as a result of administrative decree but rather of infrastructural investments on the Plain and zoning restrictions at Budapest. In addition, labour was scarce at Budapest and plentiful on the Plain. Housing investment policy prevented a transfer of labour from the Plain to Budapest; hence, the factories had an additional incentive to shift to the Plain.

China

Among the developing countries of the world, China provides a significant example of direct regulations to control migration. In order to migrate to the city, Chinese citizens must obtain both a "removal certificate" (from authorities in the place of current residence) and an employment offer or a school registration certificate from urban authorities. The migrant also requires approval from the urban agency responsible for population registers.[25] Other disincentives include a food-rationing system for urban non-agricultural workers, restrictions on urban firms from hiring in rural areas and the turning-back of unauthorized migrants at check-points on roads and at omnibus depots and railway terminals.

Evidence on urbanization patterns in China is scanty, but apparently the growth of large cities decreased during the period of controls, although overall urbanization increased due to the movement of farmers into local towns and the growth of smaller administrative cities.[26] The period of strong migration controls in China in the late 1960s was part of an intense rural development effort, with many attempts to create self-sufficient rural communities ("walking on two legs"). Significant resources were directed away from large-scale urban industrial development. The question is what will happen in the large cities of China now that there appears to be a return to national programmes of modern technology and heavy manufacturing. The answer depends upon the industrial location strategy it will pursue.

D. DORMITORY TOWNS AND SATELLITE CITIES

A number of countries have sought to slow the growth of large cities by building, some distance from them, dormitory towns, industrial parks and even satellite cities complete with both housing and industry. If the new peripheral centres are within commuting distance of the existing metropolitan area, then individuals and firms can take advantage of proximity to various services and markets concentrated in the core city (i.e., agglomerative economies are not lost).

Dormitory towns within a commuting radius of a major city and separated from it by a "green belt" have been developed in a number of developed and developing countries with variable success. In Western Europe, for example, Paris has followed the earlier experiment around London by constructing five new towns in the vicinity, each designed to house 500,000 inhabitants. As a result of the application of strict zoning laws on housing, the towns are growing as expected.[27] Similar results have been obtained in some Eastern European countries, such as Hungary and Poland, where restrictions on migration to the major cities and industrial labour shortages in the same cities give rise to extensive commuting from villages in the vicinity.[28]

In developing countries, some efforts to establish urban settlements peripheral to metropolitan cities have resulted in an outright failure. Other attempts have been successful in relocating population, although perhaps not so successful in improving the welfare of the migrant groups. For example, efforts launched in the 1960s by the mayor of Manila to raze shanty towns and to resettle residents 30 kilometres or more from the city centre led to unforeseen problems.[29] Those problems included riots, the hasty return to the city centre of many who were relocated and the eventual acquiescence of civil authorities to squatter demands for land in existing slum areas so that they would have ready access to work and urban services. Mexico City sought to relocate manufacturing in special industrial parks at the edge of the city. The locations, however, were close to the metropolis so that workers commuted to them from existing residential areas. The parks were soon absorbed into the expanding metropolis.[30]

Rio de Janeiro

At Rio de Janeiro policy towards slum-dwellers has fluctuated under different governments. In the late 1960s and early 1970s, the city eradicated *favelas* on hillsides near the centre of the city by means of a "carrot-and-stick" policy. Zoning laws and forced eviction were combined with relocation assistance and low-cost housing just outside the city.[31] But even the low-cost rents were too high for many of the relocated families and as many as 60 percent defaulted on rent payments. A significant number eventually returned to squatting, mostly in peripheral towns, because zoning enforcement against squatting within the city became increasingly forbidden. Many new *favela* settlements are continuing to be established on the northern and western fringes of the city—it was estimated that Rio de Janeiro had 273 *favelas* in 1977, containing 1 million inhabitants or 20 percent of the city population.[32] Work opportunities are concentrated in the city centre and poor transportation is a great drain on the time and incomes of the fringe *favela* dwellers.

The outcome of this *favela* eradication programme may be summarized as follows:

(a) Considering only the three-year period 1969–1971, the population resettlement objectives of the city government were largely achieved. More than 16,000 squatter dwellings were destroyed; and in this manner, valuable land within the city was made available for commerce and accommodations for higher income families;

(b) The housing authority responsible for relocating the squatters suffered a financial collapse, due principally to the high level of default on repayments in the new housing estates;

(c) The economic position of the squatters did not improve and may have deteriorated;

(d) The government abandoned slum eradication programmes and shifted to the organization of housing developments for citizens with adequate resources to pay the mortgage costs.

Dakar and Lima

Among the moderately successful dormitory-city schemes one may include the town of

Pekine, about 8 kilometres outside of Dakar, Senegal; and various *pueblos jovenes* (young communities) in the hills adjacent to Lima, Peru. About 200,000 people live at Pekine, drawn there by strict residential zoning laws at Dakar and certain services, such as communal water taps and electricity, at the dormitory town. Omnibus service to the city is functional (although less than adequate); the town is well designed; and a World Bank "sites and services" project is under way to improve housing and services.[33]

The *pueblos jovenes* around Lima were established primarily to deal with clandestine land invasions and initial squatter-town development which had already taken place in the hills 10–12 miles from the central city. Their establishment included identification of town sites, allocation of lots free of charge, provision of basic services, setting-up of municipal governments and improvement of transportation routes to the city. Everything else, including the building of houses and the establishment of municipal services, was left up to the families and their municipal councils. Over time, they became an important destination for new migrants arriving in the city.[34] Slum eradication programmes and resettlement schemes played only a minor role in the growth of the *pueblos jovenes*.

Under pressure from continuing inmigration, these dormitory towns had grown to house more than 1 million people by 1975, or nearly one quarter of the population in the metropolitan region of Lima. This growth took place despite the fact that the Government of Peru has, since 1969, given priority to investment in rural areas, such that the poor within Lima and in the surrounding towns received little financial help.[35] Pekine and the *pueblos jovenes* reflect the low incomes of their inhabitants. Although they continue to accommodate population migrating towards the metropolitan region, they serve to decongest the principal urban area and to provide access to employment and urban services for their residents.

Hong Kong

Dormitory-city policies that provide significant improvements in the living conditions of their residents are very expensive and beyond the capabilities of most countries. Hong Kong cannot yet be considered "developed", but it has a relatively high level of resources available for urban programmes and provides an interesting example of what can be done if economic and political conditions are favourable.

The population of Hong Kong is currently approaching 5 million, in a total land area of only 404 square miles. Much of the land is unfavourable to urban development due to the prevalence of rocky and precipitous hillside.[36] About 90 percent of the available land is in the New Territories leased from China in 1898 for 99 years. Although Hong Kong is an urban area without a rural hinterland, over the past two decades similar congestion problems have been shared with most less developed countries. Higher income and employment opportunities in Hong Kong have exerted a strong "pull" on Chinese communities in Eastern South Asia. Illegal immigration has been largely controlled in recent years but legal migration continues. In 1973, for example, approximately 90,000 people entered Hong Kong, about 70 percent of them legally.[37] About 40 percent of the total population of Hong Kong was born elsewhere. Fertility rates dropped to rather low levels in the decade after 1963; but as children born in earlier years become adults, the higher population growth prior to that decline is still augmenting the demand for housing.

Since 1955, as a result of previous immigration and high fertility, Hong Kong has struggled with a large deficit in housing and with problems arising from extensive slums. Public housing programmes began in 1953 following a disastrous fire in a squatter area which left 50,000 people homeless.[38] At first, the construction consisted of inexpensive low-rise apartments, each apartment with approximately 120 square feet designed to accommodate a five-person family. Toilets and wash-room facilities were centrally located and communally operated. Since then, standards have improved and upgraded housing programmes have expanded. The programmes are so extensive that by the mid-1980s it is estimated that 57 percent of the entire population will live in public housing estates, generally at rents from 60 to 80 percent less than those in the private housing market.[39]

Because land in the urban areas of Hong Kong is very limited, the city has begun developing towns in the New Territories and on the east coast of the Kowloon Peninsula. Four new towns—Kwun Tong, TsuenWan, Shatin and Tuen Mun—are being built to house an estimated 2.2 million persons or 40 per cent of the projected population of Hong Kong in 1984. The Tsuen Wan site will have an adjoining industrial estate and harbour.[40]

The policies for uran decentralization in Hong Kong are multiple, overlapping and mutually reinforcing. Industrial investment and growth are based on private capital, and land purchase prices reflect market value. Building and use are heavily zoned, however. Housing is increasingly in government hands; hence, in addition to normal zoning regulations on residential constructions, the government has access to a major policy tool. Heavy investments are currently being made in commuter transportation.

Hong Kong has several advantages over other cities with regard to planning dormitory towns and satellite cities:

(a) Because of its status, it does not suffer from the conflict between central and local government, and the related problems of revenue sharing (who will pay for and who will benefit from social services) do not arise;

(b) In contrast to the situation in most developing countries, the land in Hong Kong belongs to the government. Private investors can buy and sell leased land, but the government can readily reclaim land for public purposes;

(c) Although most developing country cities experience one fiscal crisis after another, Hong Kong is an affluent city with good administrative controls and effective taxing bodies. Hence, resources are available for costly public programmes;

(d) The city is heavily industrialized and has no impoverished rural hinterland to develop. Resources can go directly into urban decentralization programmes compatible with economic growth;

(e) The government is stable and effective, and zoning regulations are thoroughly enforced and obeyed.

E. INDUSTRIAL GROWTH POLES

Congestion in metropolitan cities can be relieved if industry and spin-off job opportunities are successfully located in other smaller cities (or even rural areas) and urban workers and new migrants are directed there. The "growth-pole" concept assumes that initial government expenditures in local economic infrastructure—highways, electricity, ports and so on—will lead to self-sustaining economic growth in sparsely settled or previously economically disadvantaged regions. Many national economic plans throughout the developing countries of the world identify potential growth-pole centres and mechanisms to encourage their development.

Industrial growth-pole schemes implemented to date in developing countries have been fraught with unexpected problems.[41] Direct outlays and subsidies for growth-pole ventures have proved extremely expensive and have had a sobering effect on Governments. Skilled workers have been reluctant to leave their homes in the large urban areas even when attracted by high wages. Small industries in particular have been hesi-

tant to move to distant locations because small firms require access to products from other intermediate-sized firms in the metropolis; they also require ongoing contact with their clientele and depend heavily upon urban repair services. Some large firms can overcome these difficulties with purchasing and sale offices in the metropolis, by taking their own maintenance and workers to the growth-pole site and by negotiating with Governments to obtain large subsidies for transportation facilities, town planning, electricity and ports. As a result, successful growth-pole efforts are both few in number and restricted to the activities of larger firms, particularly in such countries as Venezuela and the Republic of Korea, which are at an intermediate stage of economic development.

Ciudad Guayana

An important experiment to create an urban alternative in Latin America is the expansion of Ciudad Guayana in Venezuela. From a small mining town at the confluence of the Orinoco and Caroni rivers, planners and engineers built a city for a population of 300,000 to be reached by 1980.[42] The development authority for the region established a steel mill and expanded ports in the vicinity. Vast investments were made in social overhead and infrastructure. As Gilbert states:

Venezuela had enormous funds from petroleum revenues with which to support the Guayana project; between 1965 and 1975, its income was budgeted at US $3.8 billion, of which US $2.0 billion would come from the national government. The size of this budget can be seen if it is compared to the total government budget of neighbouring Colombia, a country with more than twice as many inhabitants. While the Venezuelan Government spent US $200 million annually on the Guayana project, the Colombians' total budget was a mere five times higher.[43]

This scale of investment at Ciudad Guayana is rarely within the reach of countries that do

not have the oil and mineral wealth of Venezuela. Even with full financial support, however, Ciudad Guayana has had problems. From
the outset, the orderly projections of planners
were upset by migrants flocking to the area
and building their shanties in every section. In
time, the city extended services and amenities
to the poor residential populations.

Republic of Korea

Industrial and urban decentralization programmes in the Republic of Korea appear to
provide a clearly successful case in contrast to
many other experiments in Asia. A major
objective behind these programmes was to reduce the growth of Seoul. Over the period
from 1966 to 1970, the population of Seoul
grew at 9.8 percent per annum, a rate which
would double the population of the city
approximately every seven years, if it were to
continue.[44] Industrial and population concentration in the city created a double problem:
urban congestion; and the danger to national
security of having such a large proportion of
productive capacity close to the border with
the Democratic People's Republic of Korea.
During the early 1970s, the Government introduced tax and credit incentives to industrial
investment in alternative locations. Evaluative
studies report that these policies had a dramatic impact. The growth of Seoul dropped to
around 4.5 percent per annum; smaller cities
around Seoul grew at an impressive rate of
12.7 percent per annum.[45] One comment-
ator[46] takes note that the success of
the Republic of Korea in slowing the growth
of Seoul is "unique" among developing market economies and may be the result of equally unique development circumstances: (a) a
small land area; (b) a homogeneous language
and culture; (c) good health-care delivery and
schooling facilities spread throughout the
country; (d) a stable (authoritarian) Government with high administrative competence; (e)
rapidly declining rural population growth;
and, last but not least, (f) a booming economy

which has encouraged investors to locate in
areas that might not have been their first
choice. Much of the industrial growth and
migration was directed to areas close to Seoul
and Pusan, and hence could take advantage of
support services, supplies and markets in
these large cities.

F. AGRICULTURAL DEVELOPMENT

From the perspective of planners who wish to
slow metropolitan growth, heavy investment
in agricultural development has been viewed
both as a possible panacea and as a potential
danger. It is a possible panacea because it
could increase rural incomes, absorb rural
labour, slow the migration of landless workers
and small farmers to the city and increase the
demand for decentralized commerce and industry in towns and regional cities. It is a
potential danger because rural investment
could rob the city of its resources and skilled
labour force, displace less skilled farm labour
(through mechanization) and provide low returns to investment. In the latter case, one
would solve metropolitan growth problems
and possibly reduce rural-urban income differentials only at the cost of overall economic
growth.

No simple answer to the planner's dilemma
is currently available since the results of agricultural development programmes in different
countries have led to diverse outcomes, depending upon local economic conditions and
programme administration. The following
selected findings are from countries that have
successfully slowed metropolitan growth
through agricultural development and urban-
regional planning. The findings come from
two centrally planned economies (Cuba and
China) and one market economy (Malaysia).

Havana

Although some capital cities in various developing countries have slowed their rate of
growth, Havana is virtually unique in having

reduced its growth to less than that for the country as a whole.[47] Various overlapping policies—agricultural development, new rural communities, urban slum eradication and national job and housing allocation—have contributed to this outcome.

Prior to the revolution, Havana grew to dominate all other urban areas in the country. By 1954, Havana was almost eight times larger than the second most populous city (Santiago de Cuba) and it contained roughly one fifth of the total population of Cuba.[48] The typical contradictions of a developing-country metropolis were evident—some sections were really extensive slums with large numbers of marginally productive and unemployed workers, including many beggars and prostitutes, while other sections resembled the middle-class suburbs and boutique districts of cities in developed countries. Immediately after the revolution, from 1959 to 1963, Havana grew quickly as an inward flow of migrants more than compensated for the persons leaving Cuba.[49] Subsequently, growth declined and may have been as low as 1.3 percent per annum over the period 1970–1974. Average annual population growth over the longer period between 1959 and 1974 was 1.9 percent for Havana and 2.1 percent for the rest of the country,[50] suggesting that net emigration may have occurred. (The slower growth rate of Havana may also have resulted from differential fertility and mortality. Data are not available to evaluate the possible role as slow natural population growth which may have served to reduce the growth rate of Havana to a level below that for the country as a whole.)

The significant decline in the growth rate of Havana was principally achieved by an overall transfer of resources, investment, and employment to other areas of the country, particularly the agricultural sector. The following stages of this transfer are noteworthy:

(a) After an unsuccessful and expensive attempt to induce rapid industrialization in the earlier years of the revolution, Cuba changed directions and intensified agricultural development efforts. The shift was arduous and involved an important political and bureaucratic shuffle and many of those associated with the Ministry of Industry and earlier industrialization policies lost their positions.[51] In 1965, the Ministry of Food Industry was organized;

(b) To increase agricultural production, the Government decided to halt the flight of workers to towns and cities. Accordingly, annual median incomes in agriculture were adjusted steadily upward after 1966; by 1973, they almost equalled those in industry, whereas a few years earlier they had been only half as high (see Table 2);

TABLE 2. Cuba: Agricultural and Industrial Wages, 1962–1973

Year	Median Wages (pesos)		Ratio of Agricultural to Industrial Wages
	Agricultural	Industrial	
1962	954	1 941	0.49
1966	1 059	2 063	0.51
1972	1 301	1 565	0.83
1973	1 416	1 603	0.88

Source: Jorge R. Dominguez, Cuba: Order and Revolution (Cambridge, Massachusetts, and London, The Belknap Press of Harvard University Press, 1978), p. 390.

(c) Throughout the 1960s, other efforts to "urbanize" the countryside were undertaken; these efforts, among others, tended to ruralize access to "urban" services. The number of rural schools more than doubled and teaching personnel in rural areas more than trebled in the 1960s.[52] Rationing of scarce commodities and free health care in rural clinics were also introduced;

(d) The provision of new housing was placed under the Ministry of Construction. There was a clear preference for construction in rural areas where other economic developments with increased labour requirements were being undertaken.[53] By 1975, for example, a total of 296 *comunidades nuevas* were built, each housing around 120 families (150,000 people in total). The volunteer labour of *micro brigadas* was used extensively in order not to disrupt agricultural production and other economic activities:

(e) Havana continued to be a preferred location for specialized industry, advanced training schools and government ministries, but other economic activities were dispersed elsewhere. In addition, new residential zoning laws were established, Havana slums were eradicated and a 32,000-acre area was zoned around the city, and a large number of workers were resettled to dormitory cities. Alamar, for example, located five miles from Havana, is expected to house 150,000 people by the early 1980s;

(f) Residence permits, ration cards and worker identity cards were introduced in Cuba in 1962. There is no evidence that these measures and the registration systems associated with them were directly monitored to control migration into Havana; rather, it appears that the shifting structure of job opportunities, wages and housing benefits were designed to discourage workers from moving to the cities.

The population distribution consequences of policies in Cuba are evident, but the way in which development policies and urbanization trends have affected overall economic performance is difficult to assess. To date, Cuba may be described as a country successful in improving the living conditions of the average citizen, which has taken place primarily through redistribution of economic resources and improved social services. Economic growth, however, has been very low, perhaps even negative—one estimate shows per capita incomes in Cuba declining at an annual rate of 0.06 percent, on average, between 1960 and 1965.[54] This slow growth undoubtedly reflects many factors—the loss of skilled professional workers who went to the United States of America, errors made in early years and perhaps the long period required before investments in the agricultural sector can pay off. Cuba has invested heavily, for example, in fruit-trees, which take many years to mature.

Rustication in China[55]

Very few countries in the world have programmes designed to resettle urban-born families in rural areas. Yet within these countries the programmes are of startling magnitude and have led to the largest planned population shifts in the world. The extremely coercive programme in Democratic Kampuchea over recent years has forced hundreds of thousands of urban residents to rural areas where they have been made to work the land with little more than their bare hands. This programme is, of course, primarily motivated by political and ideological considerations largely independent of careful economic plans. In contrast, China has had for many years a variety of gradual, orderly *hsia-fang* ("sent down to the land") programmes addressing both economic and political objectives.[56]

In China, over the period 1969–1973, somewhere between 10 million and 15 million urban secondary-school graduates were "rusticated", that is, resettled in rural areas.[57] At the same time, administrative controls, including travel permits, access to ration cards etc., were used to prevent or limit the migration of peasants to the cities. These programmes were supported by widespread media propaganda and political action. In addition to minor programmes that were largely political in their goals, the really major programmes appear to have been primarily motivated by national economic considerations. The major goal was to stimulate agricultural production (*hsia-fang* was one of several reforms and efforts in this direction). Although it has not been publicly acknowledged, there is reason to believe that urban unemployment and the question of job placement for the burgeoning supply of second-ary-school graduates beginning to appear in the cities[58] were important considerations.

The Chinese programmes were remarkably successful in transferring population to rural areas. In this way, the embarrassment of visible unemployment and poverty programmes may have been avoided. One reporter states that no beggars are seen in the cities of China; there are no shanty towns and no one sleeps in the streets.[59] This result was largely accomplished by instituting laws and administrative procedures that restrict freedom of movement.

It is difficult to say how much the rustication effort has contributed to rural development. Those reviewing the scattered evidence conclude that the students at first contributed little to production, but later did make economic contributions. In the beginning, they were not welcome in the rural communities where they were placed. Their cultural backgrounds were different. They lacked agricultural skills. Land and capital were in short supply, and extra labour could not always be effectively utilized. The students represented extra mouths to feed. One observer states that the costs of unemployment were not reduced; they were only shifted to rural households and communities.[60] Not surprisingly, many students were reluctant to go to rural areas, and they returned to the cities whenever administrative controls were relaxed. In 1974, a number of social and economic incentives were instituted to placate the rusticated youth. These incentives included improved rations, wages and living conditions; and resettlement in separate "youth points" where they formed their own productive teams rather than being integrated into peasant teams.

It appears that the rusticated students eventually did assimilate into the new communities. Therefore, their low wages and productivity during the initial period could be considered "investments" for future rural development. These conclusions are largely conjectural because accounts of the rustication move-ment are impressionistic and no quantitative data exist to evaluate how many resettled students have stayed, in what rural areas, what kind of work they do nor what their current economic contributions may be. The Chinese example does permit one to conclude, however, that resettlement of urbanities in the countryside is possible, through the use of laws, massive propaganda, widespread social support and effective administrative backing. In order to achieve this kind of resettlement without such supports, the restructuring of the economy to attract urban workers into agriculture would have to be even greater than that which China has been able to achieve. Policy-makers in other countries of Asia have not seriously pursued reverse migration as an economic development strategy.

New Towns and Land Colonization in Malaysia

Malaysia has undertaken a series of programmes over the past 20 years to decentralize economic growth in various regions. Among these programmes is an energetic land development scheme begun in 1956 with the creation of the Federal Land Development Authority (FELDA); by 1977, 21 years later, FELDA had developed no less than 918,000 acres of land in rubber trees, oil-producing palms and sugar-cane.[61] In the process, FELDA settled approximately 41,000 families (3 percent of the current rural population). A number of reports point to the success of the resettlement and the economic viability of the new communities. The investment requirements have been high: about 26,000 Malaysian dollars (approximately $US 12,000) were necessary to settle each family relocated in 1976.[62] This amount covered costs associated with clearing the land, constructing houses, providing fertilizer and tools and maintaining the family in the initial period. A typical FELDA scheme encompasses about 400 families (approximately 2,400 persons). Each settler receives a specific piece of land (about

10 acres) when his "loan" for resettlement costs is repaid; but most of the farming is done collectively, as part of a corporate enterprise.

The FELDA scheme and other resettlement schemes, combined with broader rural development programmes in Malaysia, have been rather successful in increasing rural production and raising rural incomes. The question is whether these measures have also lowered rural-urban migration; the answer is, most likely, yes. Between 1957 and 1970, the urban population of Malaysia grew at the same rate as the rural population: 2.6 percent per annum.[63] As natural population growth was somewhat lower in urban areas, some rural-urban migration obviously took place over the period; but the rate appears to have been extremely low. Kuala Lumpur, the capital and largest city, grew only slightly more rapidly: 2.7 percent per annum, a rate much lower than the metropolitan capitals of other countries of Asia.[64] Migration was directed toward such areas as Penang State, which had the advantage of FELDA financing for resettlement and rural development schemes. In contrast, Kelantan State, which did not utilize federal funds for land development (a party in opposition to the federal Government was in power there), suffered a net loss of migrants.[65] Perhaps as much as 8 percent of all interstate migration in Malaysia in recent years has been a direct consequence of FELDA resettlement and an additional amount was undoubtedly a result of spin-off economic effects induced by FELDA schemes.[66] FELDA resettlement policy gave each new family an income of $M 300 per month, an amount four times the national average. While actual income figures were often much lower, the settlers appear to have gained from their move. A statistical analysis of the determinants of interstate migration reveals that the states that gained the largest numbers of migrants were distinguished primarily by having higher per capita income.[67] Not surprisingly, there is a backlog of applicants for participation in FELDA resettlement schemes.

CONCLUSIONS

It is difficult to draw general conclusions from a review of case studies taken from around the world. The difficulty is compounded when the case studies themselves are assembled from fragmentary research findings. Even if the studies were more systematic and thorough, one would face the problem of generalizing from a small number of cases, each from a given country with unique political, cultural and economic circumstances. The outcome of a particular intervention may have more to do with the specific national context where it was implemented than with the policy chosen. Although it is not possible to reach any firm conclusions or policy guide-lines from this review, the following tentative conclusions may be advanced for future study:

(a) *Developing countries with strong policies are more successful in implementing constraints on metropolitan city growth.* China, Cuba, Hong Kong, Malaysia and the Republic of Korea all have experienced some success in slowing metropolitan growth. They are obviously very different in terms of political orientation, culture, level of development and urbanization. Yet, in relation to many less successful countries (Mexico, Brazil, Indonesia and the Philippines), the successful countries are distinguished in several ways, including a high national priority on solving this problem, a greater allocation of resources and coordination across various levels of government;

(b) *Strong policies to slow city growth emerge when current trends in migration and urban concentration are seen to threaten national development goals.* The countries with strong policies appear to have important objectives in addition to the desire to eliminate slums and urban sprawl. These objectives were different in each country. The Republic of Korea, for example, pursued strong industrial and population de-centralization policies not only to decongest Seoul but to move industrial capacity and human settlements away from its border with the Democratic People's Republic of Korea for reasons of security. China and Cuba instituted strong measures in the context of socialist revolutions, with a high national priority given to rural-urban equity and agricultural development as the basic strategy towards economic growth. In both China and Cuba, the strong shift to agricultural and rural development came after earlier failures in rapid industrialization. Hong Kong, with no natural resources and very little land, urgently required space for factories and for housing its labour force. This need led to an emphasis on spatial planning and heavy investment in satellite towns. In the late 1940s and early 1950s, Malaysia embarked on policies to create new towns in an effort to control insurgents. The plan was to concentrate farmers and residents of scattered rural hamlets in secure towns where they would be protected from hostilities, would be provided with social services; and, significantly, would be unable to help the insurgents. Later land development and new community programmes built upon the success achieved in the earlier programmes;

(c) *Direct prohibition of migration is not necessary to slow metropolitan population growth; indirect controls operating through the distribution of jobs and housing are effective.* Direct controls on migration can be used to control migration even in countries where the advantages of the city are so great that many people would move into them if they could (e.g., South Africa). But this strategy requires a level of policing that is generally neither administratively feasible nor politically acceptable. Attempts to use such controls have often been "half-hearted" because there was not a strong political will to deny

poor rural people access to the city (e.g., Manila and Jakarta). Such controls apparently work better when backed by major shifts in investment to improve life in non-metropolitan areas (China and Hungary). Most important, several countries have shown that direct controls on migration are not necessary, if sufficient resources can be shifted to alternative destinations. Cuba was apparently able effectively to slow the growth of Havana without using the direct administrative controls over migration to which it had access, because national investment and housing policy kept people from moving into the city. Malaysia, to which direct controls were inaccessible, was able to slow the growth of Kuala Lumpur through broad regional planning, zoning and land development;

(d) *Two-sided constraint policies which co-ordinate administrative and economic measures at the urban destination and rural source are most effective.* "Closed-city" policies, such as those applied at Jakarta, are largely ineffective because they are unrelated to policies intended to increase economic opportunity elsewhere. Similarly, growth-pole and rural-development policies that are unrelated to investment strategies in existing metropolitan centres will most likely fail. Unrelated schemes will be more expensive; and without financial support, industry will not be attracted. Both Cuba and the Republic of Korea reduced the growth of their capital cities by applying co-ordinated zoning and investment controls: in Cuba, through administrative decree on investment in agriculture and rural housing; in the Republic of Korea, through incentives and disincentives. Housing allocation and job assignment programmes in China and Hungary were co-ordinated in metropolitan areas and alternative destinations. Although Malaysia has some land allocation and regional programmes administered at the provincial level, the major programmes are administered nationally;

(e) *Centrally administered policies at a country-wide level are more likely to succeed.* The immediate problems of rapid metropolitan growth are probably first noted by municipal officials responsible for urban services, housing, land titles and traffic. They may react by crying for policies to stop migration into the city. Yet, other officials in industrial planning may continue to see the advantages of locating firms and national institutions (universities, military headquarters and so on) in the largest cities and will pay little attention to its future impact on the demand for urban services. If both go ahead with independent programmes, as is often the case (e.g., Indonesia and the Philippines), the programmes that have the greatest impact on employment demand will tend to have the greatest impact on migration patterns. This is true, as previously stated, even in the centrally planned economies, which have the administrative tools to control migration directly. In the Soviet Union, industrial planning led to continued metropolitan growth even when housing and occupational assignment programmes were designed to discourage it. When housing and industrial location policies are congruent, the effect on population movements is significant (Cuba and Hungary). Other countries are often unable to implement policies because of conflict between levels of government concerning who will finance and who will benefit from new programmes. When a decentralization policy is being pursued, the metropolitan area is likely to receive less in terms of investment and government revenues for social services. The Republic of Korea may have been more successful in its programmes because of a strong, stable central Government which could override provincial and metropolitan governments. Hong Kong has had the added advantage

that there is only one level of government.

1. Samuel H. Preston, "Urban growth in developing countries: a demographic reappraisal", *Population and Development Review*, vol. 5, No. 2 (June 1979), p. 195.

2. Roland J. Fuchs and George J. Demko. "Population distribution policies in developed socialist and Western nations: *Population and Development Review*, vol. 5, No. 3 (September 1979), pp. 439–467.

3. Population Reference Bureau, *World Population Reference Sheet* (Washington, D.C., 1979).

4. S. H. Preston, loc. cit., p. 198.

5. Vinyo Vichit-Vadakan, "Land use policy in Thailand with special reference to the Bangkok Metropolitan area", in John Wong, ed., *The Cities of Asia: A Study of Urban Solutions and Urban Finance* (Singapore, Singapore University Press, 1976), pp. 237–246.

6. Wayne A. Cornelius, "Introduction", in Wayne A. Cornelius and Robert V. Kemper, eds., *Metropolitan Latin America: The Challenge and the Response*, Latin American Urban Research Series, vol. 6 (Beverly Hills, California, and London, Sage Publications, 1977), p. 10.

7. For reviews of findings, see Sally Evans Findley, *Planning for Internal Migration: A Review of the Issues and Policies in Developing Countries*. International Statistical Programs Center Research Document, No. 4 (Washington, D.C., United States Bureau of the Census, 1977); Alan Simmons, Sergio Diaz-Briquets and Aprodicio A. Laquian, *Social Change and Internal Migration: A Review of Research Findings from Africa, Asia and Latin America* (Ottawa, International Development Research Centre, 1977); and Michael P. Todaro, *Internal Migration in Developing Countries: A Review of Theory, Evidence, Methodology and Research Priorities* (Geneva, International Labour Office, 1976).

8. John F. Turner, "Uncontrolled urban settlement: problems and policies", in Gerald Breese, ed., *The City in Newly Developed Countries: Readings on Urbanism and Urbanization* (Englewood Cliffs, New Jersey, Prentice-Hall, 1969), pp. 514–516.

9. Elsa Usandizaga and A. Eugene Havens, *Tres barrios de invasion: estudio de nivel de vida y actitudes en Barranquilla* (Bogotà, Facultad de

sociologia de la Universidad Nacional de Colombia/ Ediciones Tercer Mundo, 1966).

10. See examples cited by William A. Hance, "Controlling city size in Africa", in Centre national de la recherche scientifique, *La croissance urbain en Afrique noire et à Madagascar* (Paris, 1972), vol. 2, pp. 656–657; and Aprodicio A. Laquian, *Slums Are for People: the Barrio Magsaysay Pilot Project in Phillippine Urban Community Development* (Honolulu, East-West Center Press, 1971).

11. Richard Critchfield, "The plight of the cities: Djakarta—the first to close", *Journal of World Business*, vol. 6, No. 4 (1971), pp. 89–94.

12. Judy B. Williams, "Sadikin closes Jakarta", *Insight*, February 1973, pp. 16–20.

13. Gerald Krausse, "Economic adjustment of migrants in the city: the Jakarta experience", *International Migration Review*, vol. 13, No. 4 (Spring 1979), p. 49.

14. R. Critchfield, loc. cit.

15. G. Krausse, loc. cit., p. 60.

16. J. Williams, loc. cit.

17. Gavin W. Jones, "What do we know about the labour force in Indonesia?", *Majlah Demografi Indonesia* (Jakarta, IPADI Lembaga Demografi, Facultas Ekonomi, Universitas Indonesia), vol. 2 (December 1974).

18. Gustav F. Papenek, "The poor of Jakarta", *Economic Development and Cultural Change*, vol. 24, No. 1 (October 1975), pp. 1–28; and G. Krausse, loc. cit., p. 60.

19. For sources, see Alan B. Simmons, "Slowing metropolitan city growth in Asia: policies, programs and results", *Population and Development Review*, vol. 5, No. 1 (March 1979), p. 93.

20. T. J. D. Fair and R. J. Davies, "Constrained urbanization: white South Africa and black Africa compared", in Brian J. L. Berry, ed., *Urbanization and Counterurbanization*, Urban Affairs Annual Reviews, vol. 11 (Beverly Hills, California, and London, Sage Publications, 1976), pp. 145–168.

21. Zbigniew M. Fallenbuchl, "Internal migration and economic development under socialism: the case of Poland", in Alan A. Brown and Egon Neuberger, eds., *Internal Migration: A Comparative Perspective* (New York, Academic Press, 1977), pp. 305–327.

22. R. J. Fuchs and G. J. Demko, loc. cit.

23. George A. Huzinec, "The impact of industrial decision-making upon the Soviet urban hierarchy", *Urban Studies*, vol. 15, No. 2 (June 1978), pp. 139–148.

24. George J. Demko, Roland J. Fuchs and Thomas J. Camarco, "Population redistribution policies in Hungary and an assessment of this effectiveness", Columbus, Ohio State University, Department of Geography, 1978 (mimeographed).

25. Thomas P. Bernstein, *Up to the Mountains and Down to the Villages: The Transfer of Youth from Urban to Rural China* (New Haven, Connecticut, Yale University Press, 1977).

26. Cheng-siang Chen, "Population growth and urbanization in China, 1953–1970", *Geographical Review*, vol. 63, No. 1 (1973), pp. 68–72.

27. Niles M. Hansen, *French Regional Planning* (Bloomington, Indiana, Indiana University Press, 1968).

28. Roland J. Fuchs and George J. Demko, "Commuting in Eastern Europe: causes, characteristics, consequences", *East European Quaterly*, vol. 11. No. 4 (1977), pp. 463–475.

29. Aprodicio A. Laquian, *The City in Nation-Building* (Manila, University of the Philippines, School of Public Administration, 1966): and idem, op. cit.

30. W. A. Cornelius, loc. cit.

31. Alejandro Portes, "Housing policy, urban poverty, and the State: the *favelas* of Rio de Janeiro, 1972–1976", *Latin American Research Review*, vol. XIV, No. 2 (1979), pp 3–24.

32. Ibid., p. 19.

33. World Bank, Transportation and Urban Projects Department, *Sites and Services Projects* (Washington, D.C., 1974).

34. Henry A. Dietz, "Metropolitan Lima: urban problem solving under military rule", in Wayne A. Cornelius and Robert V. Kemper, eds., *Metropolitan Latin America, The Challenge and the Response*, Latin American Urban Research Series, vol. 6 (Beverly Hills, California, and London, Sage Publications, 1978), p. 209.

35. Ibid., p. 224.

36. Y. C. Jao, "Land use policy and land taxation in Hong Kong", in John Wong, ed., *The Cities of Asia: A Study of Urban Solutions and Urban Finance* (Singapore, Singapore University Press, 1976), p. 278.

37. Ibid.

38. Ibid., p. 280.

39. Ibid., pp. 282–283.

40. Ibid., pp. 289–290.

41. S. E. Findley, op. cit.; and Louis Lefeber and Mrinal Datta-Chaudhuri, *Regional Development Experiences and Prospects in South and Southeast Asia* (Paris, Mouton, 1971).

42. Lloyd Rodwin, *Nations and Cities: A Comparison of Strategies for Urban Growth* (Boston, Houghton Mifflin Co., 1970).

43. Alan Gilbert, *Latin American Development: A Geographical Perspective* (Harmondsworth, Penguin Books, 1974), p. 265.

44. Koichi Mera, "Population distribution policies in the Republic of Korea", World Bank Staff Working Paper, Washington, D.C., July 1976.

45. Ibid.

46. Joan M. Nelson, "Population redistribution policies and migrant's choices", draft paper prepared for the Seminar on New Conceptual Approaches to Migration in the Contex of Urbanization, organized by the Committee on Urbanization and Population of the International Union for the Scientific Study of Population, Bellagio, Italy, 30 June–4 July 1978, pp. 18–19.

47. Barent Landstreet, "Urbanization and ruralism in Cuba", Toronto, York University, Department of Sociology, 1978, p. 21 (mimeographed).

48. Josef Gugler, "A minimum of urbanism and a maximum of realism: the Cuban experience", paper presented at the Ninth World Congress of Sociology, Uppsala, August 1978, p. 11.

49. B. Landstreet, op. cit., pp. 19–20.

50. Ibid., p. 21.

51. Jorge R. Dominguez, *Cuba: Order and Revolution* (Cambridge, Massachusetts, and London, The Belknap Press of Harvard University Press, 1978), p. 390.

52. Nelson Amaro and Carmelo Mesa Lago, "Inequality and classes", in Carmelo Mesa-Lago, ed., *Revolutionary Change in Cuba* (Pittsburgh, University of Pittsburgh Press, 1971), p. 345.

53. B. Landstreet, op. cit., pp. 22–27.

54. World Bank, *World Bank Atlas: Population, Per Capita Product, and Growth Rates* (Washington, D. C., 1977), p. 20.

55. This section is based on A. B. Simmons, "Slowing metropolitan city growth in Asia: policies, programs and results".

56. T. P. Bernstein, op. cit.

57. Parris H. Chang, "China's rustication movement", *Current History*, vol. 69, No. 408 (September 1975), pp. 85–89.

58. Jan S. Prybyla, "*Hsia-fang*: the economics and politics of rustication in China", *Pacific Affairs*, vol. 48, No. 2 (Summer 1975), pp. 153–172.

59. Ross Munro, "The real China: life in the city is only for the select few", *The Globe and Mail* (Toronto), 10 October 1977, pp. 1–2.

60. P. H. Chang, loc. cit., p. 88.

61. Tunku Shamsul Bahrin and P. D. Perera, *FELDA: 21 Years of Land Development* (Malaysia, Ministry for Land and Regional Development, 1977).

62. Ibid., p. 151.

63. Lee Ying Soon, "An analysis of internal migration in Peninsular Malaysia: dimensions, causes and some policy implications", *The Philippine Economic Journal*, vol. XVI, Nos. 1–2 (1977), table 2.

64. Ibid., table 3.

65. Ibid., p. 18.

66. Ibid.

67. Ibid., table 5.

ADDITIONAL REFERENCES

Chen, Pi-chao. Overurbanization, rustication of urban-educated youths, and politics of rural transformation; the case of China. *Comparative politics* (New York) 4(3): 361–386, April 1972.

Cosmas, Desmond. The discarded people; an account of African resettlement in South Africa. Baltimore, Penguin Books, 1972.

Garza, G. *and* Martha Schteingart. *In* Metropolitan Latin America: the challenge and the response. Wayne A. Cornelius *and* Robert V. Kemper, *eds*. Beverly Hills, California, and London, Sage, 1978, pp. 51–86. (Latin American Urban Research Series, 6)

Hansen, Niles M., *ed*. Growth centers in regional economic development. New York, Free Press, 1972. 298 pp.

Ivory, Paul E. *and* William R. Lavely. Rustication, demographic change, and development in Shanghai. *Asian survey* (Berkeley, California) 17 (5): 440–455, May 1977.

McDonald, Hamish. Death of a village in "closed city". *Far eastern economic review* (Hong Kong) 23 April 1976:29–30.

Mertens, Walter. Jakarta; a country in a city. *Demografi Indonesia* (Jakarta) 6:50–109, 1976.

Rho, Yung-Hee. Greenbelt and urban land use

control in the case of Korea. *In* The cities of Asia a study of urban solutions and urban finance. John Wong, *ed*. Singapore, Singapore University Press, 1976. p. 81–105.

Seybolt, Peter J., *ed*. The rustication of urban youth in China; a social experiment. White Plains, New York, M. E. Sharpe, 1977. 200 pp.

Shaw, R. Paul. On modifying metropolitan migration. *Economic development and cultural change* (Chicago) 26(4):677–692, July 1978.

Stren, Richard E. Urban inequality and housing policy in Tanzania; the problem of squatting. Berkeley, California, Institute of International Studies, 1975. 128 pp. (Research series, 24)

Walton, John. Guadalajara; creating the divided city. *In* Metropolitan Latin America; the challenge and the response. Wayne A. Cornelius *and* Robert V. Kemper, *eds*. Beverly Hills, California, and London, Sage, 1978. p. 25–50.

Further Readings

1. Rural-Urban Migration

Connell, John, et al. *Migration from Rural Areas: The Evidence from Village Studies*. New York, London, and Melbourne: Oxford University Press, 1976.

Fields, G. S. "Rural-Urban Migration, Urban Unemployment and Under-Employment, and Job/Search Activity in LDCS." *Journal of Development Economics* 2, no. 2 (June 1975).

Findlay, Sally, *Planning for Internal Migration*. Washington, D.C., U.S. Department of Commerce, 1977.

Griffin, Keith. "On the Emigration of the Peasantry." *World Development* 4, no. 5 (May 1976).

Mazumdar, Dipak. "The Rural-Urban Wage Gap, Migration, and the Shadow Wage." *Oxford Economic Papers*, (November 1976).

Oberai, A. S. "Migration, Unemployment and the Urban Labor Market." *International Labor Review* 115, no. 2 (March/April 1977).

Peek, P., and Gaude, J. "The Economic Effects of Rural-Urban Migration." *International Labor Review* 114, no. 3 (November/December, 1976).

Todaro, Michael P. "Urban Job Expansion, Induced Migration and Rising Unemployment: A Formulation and Simplified Empirical Test for LDC's." *Journal of Development Economics* 3 no. 3 (September 1975).

Todaro, Michael P. *Internal Migration in Developing Countries: A Review of Theory, Evidence, Methodology and Research Priorities*. Geneva: ILO, 1976.

Todaro, Michael P. "A Model of Labor Migration and Urban Unemployment in Less Developed Countries." *American Economic Review* 59, no. 1 (March 1969).

Yap, Lorene Y. L. "The Attraction of the Cities: A Review of Migration Literature." *Journal of Development Economics* 4 (1977).

2. Urban Development

Andors, Stephen. "Urbanization and Urban Government in China's Development: Toward a Political Economy of Urban Community?" *Economic Development and Cultural Change* 26, no. 3 (April 1978).

Beier, George; Churchill, Anthony; Cohen, Michael; and Renand, Bertrand. "The Task Ahead for the Cities of the Developing Countries." *World Development* 4, no. 5 (May 1976).

Davis, Kingsley. "Asia's Cities: Problems and Options." *Population and Development Review* 1, no. 1 (1976).

Lipton, Michael. *Why Poor People Stay Poor: Urban Bias in World Development*. Cambridge, Mass.: Harvard University Press, 1976.

8

Agricultural Transformation and Rural Development

20. Risk, Uncertainty, and the Subsistence Farmer*

Clifton R. Wharton, Jr.

Village-level economies operate much as self-contained, self-sufficient economic enclaves with communal goals, institutions and processes designed far more for the preservation of human life than for development. Since in its earliest phases, sedentary agriculture is a productive process whose product may be eaten by the producer, there is inevitably a strong attachment by the peasant farmer to the goals, institutions, and processes associated with the economy, society, and polity of the village.

Despite the almost infinite variety of village-level institutions and processes to be found around the world, they have three common characteristics which are pertinent to change: (1) they have historically proven to be successful, i.e., the members have survived; (2) they are relatively static, at least the general pace of change is below that which is considered desirable today; and (3) attempts at change are frequently resisted, both because these institutions and processes have proven dependable and because the various elements constitute something akin to an ecologic unity in the human realm.

THE RESPONSIVENESS OF SUBSISTENCE FARMERS

The earliest characterizations of subsistence or traditional farmers described them as technologically backward, with deficient entrepreneurial ability, and with limited aspirations. The influence of limited aspirations is best summarized in the colonial stereotype of the "lazy natives" who refuse to work for an income beyond what they require for their subsistence. Economists labeled such behavior the "backward bending supply curve of labor." Other social scientists, more culturally sensitive and empathetic, viewed such behavior as merely instances where non-economic variables dominated and swamped economic factors favorable to economic maximization.

Interestingly, these early views of limited or negative peasant responses to economic opportunity were held by many individuals who were witnesses to or participated in instances of massive "response" by subsistence and peasant farmers to improved economic opportunities. During the colonial period, in most instances, the economic opportunity was the dynamic development of new markets in the metropolitan country for the beverages,

---

* From *Development Digest*, 7, no. 2 (April 1969), pp. 3–10.

food and industrial raw materials which could be produced in the colony. Some but not all of the rapid dynamic response in these cases could be explained by the coercion of colonialists, or by the development of infrastructure facilities by the colonial power, or by a crop's promotion by organized interest groups.

More recently, the idea of an economically inert peasantry has been seriously challenged. First, there are those economists led by Professor Jones and Professor T. W. Schultz, who find ample evidence that subsistence farmers *are* economic men who do maximize in the utilization of their available economic resources *given* the available technology. Such farmers may be operating at low absolute levels of production but nonetheless they are optimizing at the ceiling of the available technological possibilities. This group argues that what is fundamentally lacking is improved technology. The obvious solution under such circumstances is to give first priority to the development of new technology to alter the production possibilities.

Second, a large number of economists have been conducting rigorous empirical research to determine whether or not such farmers respond to economic incentives. Despite the varieties of empirical and analytical measures used and crops involved, the overwhelming evidence indicates that subsistence and semi-subsistence farmers do in fact respond to economic incentives. They increase the production of those crops whose relative economic returns have improved, and decrease those which have become disadvantageous. Some of the observable response has come as a result of greater intensification in the use of available resources without any significant alteration in the existing technology; others have come through the adoption of new techniques and practices.

Despite all this new evidence, there is equally ample evidence, usually in semi-anecdotal or case study form, where farmers have seemingly not responded to an "obvious" economic opportunity. Explanations of such cases vary. Some analyses rely upon non-economic explanations—the indigenous culture militated against the new practice; there were serious religious prohibitions which would prevent the adoption of a new technology; higher production would disrupt the fabric of the traditional society. Others find that upon closer examination the economic advantages turned out to be illusory—the landlord secured all the gain; the moneylender skimmed off the cream; the government guaranteed price was not in fact paid; the cost structure made the new innovation unprofitable.

The current pressures of burgeoning population on world food supplies have heightened the need for more rapid economic responsiveness and the more rapid adoption of new technology. Improved understanding of the resistances to adopt or to respond are becoming critical. One set of explanatory variables which deserves more rigorous study is the influence of risk and uncertainty juxtaposed against the subsistence levels of living and production of such farmers. Risk factors are not predominant or exclusive influences in the adoption process; it is merely that their greater specification will facilitate their inclusion with other equally important factors.

THE CAUSES OF RISK AND THE SOURCES OF UNCERTAINTY

A basic distinction relevant for the decision-making framework of the subsistence farmer is between: (1) those future events to which he can assign probabilities based upon past experience or personal knowledge; and (2) those future events to which he cannot assign probabilities, or where the probabilities offered are not derived from his personal experience but are based on external knowledge provided by others.

Even the most illiterate peasant farmer has a knowledge of the probabilities which attach to his current, traditional practices. These relate to three major sources of year to year variability. First, the farmer faces *yield variability*. Actual field or barn yields obtained are a function of a wide range of variables—sunshine, humidity, rainfall and even their incidence and timing during the cropping season; pests such as birds, rats, worms; blights, fungi and viruses; and even the unpredictable acts of God and man such as wars, insurrections, and revolts. Second, there is *cost variability*. Even in subsistence and semi-subsistence type agriculture there are inputs required for production which are purchased—ranging from minor farm tools and fertilizer to oxen rental and hired labor. Whether or not actual cash is employed in the payment process is inconsequential. The critical issue is the variability in the incidence of such costs. The typical farm decision-maker faces expenses which tend to fall into two categories: those which are subject to his decision-making control, and those which are outside his control. In both cases, predictable and unpredictable probabilities are involved, i.e., risk and uncertainty. Family labor is fundamentally subject to the control of the farm decision maker, but its utilization is affected by illness and even the availability of off-farm employment. The costs of farm product processing such as milling, off-farm storage, transport to market and interest on loans are outside his control, although knowing what these costs were in previous years helps him in formulating the probabilities. Third, there is a *product price variability*. Choice of crop and crop combinations as well as intended levels of output are based upon price expectations. The divergence between expected prices when crop choice and planting decisions are made and actual prices after harvest may be considerable, both positively or negatively.

The critical element is that these three variabilities combine in any given crop period to affect the net return to the farm family. The extent to which the farmer can reduce unintended fluctuations in each category is quite limited, but every effort is made to reduce those subject to his control. Historical knowledge on the past variabilities in each does exist, and he takes these into account—whether it is distrust of assured government prices, or fear of a locust cycle.

INTERACTION OF RISK, UNCERTAINTY AND SUBSISTENCE ON TECHNOLOGICAL INNOVATION

Any new technology or practice has associated with it some expected probabilities for yields per acre and consequent income figures. Extension workers or salesmen who are promoting new techniques often present them in terms of average (sometimes maximum) yields obtained at an experiment station. But the typical subsistence farmer has his own subjective rate of discount for such probabilities. He has learned from bitter experience to be wary of new methods which *as he sees them* have been insufficiently adapted and evaluated for his particular situation, and which may not perform in his fields as promised. The farmer, in deciding whether to adopt an innovation, may be seen as making a choice: on the one hand he estimates the most probable yield from a new technique, and the range of variability around this expected figure; on the other hand, he uses as a basis for comparison the expected yield from the familiar method he has been using, and the much narrower range of variability around that expected level. In short, he compares not only the levels of expected net yields, but also the reliability with which these yields can be expected, as he sees it.

Let us assume we are dealing with a subsistence farm family which consumes, say, 80 percent of its production in the average year. This consumption is fairly constant; in good years the farmer may have some surplus produce to sell, and in bad years little or none, but at least his family is fed. Such a consumption level can be regarded as his minimum subsistence level, i.e., a level he will strive not to fall below. This definition of a minimum subsistence level is not purely physiological: the farmer's notion of a minimum is likely to be somewhat above that which will barely sustain life, but below the level of nutrition adequate for maintenance of a desirable standard of physical exertion. Farmers' ideas of minimum tolerable levels may vary quite a bit from place to place, from farmer to farmer, and through time. But, when a farmer's output comes close to what he considers as his minimum standard, then his behavior as a producer is affected.

When the subsistence farmer confronts a possible innovation, he will be concerned with two questions: (1) Will the new method, taking its probable costs into account, produce an expected yield appreciably higher than his old method? (2) Is there a reasonable probability that something will go wrong, and that the new method will result in a net yield below his minimum subsistence level? *Even if the answer to (1) is yes, he will not change his method unless he can also answer (2) in the negative.* Thus, the closer his current output is to his minimum subsistence level, the more conservative he is likely to be. The more unfamiliar the proposed innovation and/or the change agents concerned with it, the more cautious will be the farmer's approach.

However, if he can be convinced that the new method is not only better but reliably so, and that its probable negative variability will still leave him better off than he was before, then he is most likely to make the change. A good illustration of this point may be seen in the table below, where objective figures on variability (cross sectional) are presented: although the farmers' subjective estimates of variability cannot be recorded, the impact of experiences in various places should bring these subjective estimates close to the objective realities.

EXAMPLE OF RICE YIELDS

The recent experience with the new rice varieties from the International Rice Research Institute is perhaps indicative. The rapidity with which the new varieties (especially IR–8 and IR–5) have been spreading in Asia refutes the stereotype of the non-economic peasant. The Philippines has been a rice importer—some 230,000 tons annually from 1961 to 1967. The very rapid adoption of the new high-yielding varieties first introduced in 1966 has already made the Philippines self-sufficient in rice for the first time in recent history.

The statistical variance in yields per hectare associated with the newer varieties is considerably larger than with the traditional varieties. If the average yields for the new and old varieties had been fairly similar, then the average farmer would probably have resisted adoption. What is especially significant in the present case is not merely that the average yields with the new varieties are higher, but that the negative standard deviation for the new varieties is *higher* than the average yields of the old traditional variety.

Average Yields of IR–8 and Local Rice Varieties in the Philippines, Dry and Wet Seasons 1966–67* (metric tons per hectare)

	$-SD_x$	$\overline{X}$	$+SD_x$
Dry Season			
IR–8	3.24	5.86	8.48
Binato	1.51	3.17	4.83
Wet Season			
IR–8	2.59	4.49	6.39
Local	1.00	2.32	3.64

* Data supplied by the International Rice Research Institute, Los Banos, the Philippines.

This helps to explain the startling phenomenon currently taking place with the "Green Revolution"—the rapid adoption of the new high-yielding varieties of wheat and rice.

SOME PUZZLES AND PARADOXES EXPLAINED

The above analysis may help to explain a few puzzles and paradoxes commonly encountered with technological innovation in the developing world.

Differential Adoption Within Same Community

In many agricultural areas, one can find farmers who have adopted a new innovation coexisting with neighboring farmers who have failed to adopt even though the latter see the new technology every day and are aware of it. "Demonstration effects" and "neighbor effects" seem to have no impact.

Food Staple vs. Non-Food Staple Variations

A common experience is a differential resistance to technological adoption between staple and non-staple food crops. Technological innovation tends to move more rapidly among farmers specializing in non-food staples (especially commercial crops) than is true with food staples.

The "Dual Farmer"

One frequently encounters farmers who grow both a food staple and a non-food staple. They are willing to innovate or to employ a new technology with a commerical crop but persist in traditional practices with the food staple.

New Crops vs. Old Crops

Another common observation has been that the introduction of new crops requiring new technology seems to be easier than changing the technology of a traditional, well-established crop.

In each of the four cases, a good deal of the variation in adoption can be attributed to the relationship between subsistence standards of living, and the expected variability in output of the food staple under the new technology. In the first case, for example, the non-adopters are most frequently those farmers who are less commercial (both in product and input) and whose resources relative to their minimum subsistence standard of living are extremely close. Where the proposed innovation and its associated variability exceeds the minimum subsistence level, as was the case with the new rice varieties in the Philippines, then adoption proves to be swift.

Some further implications of this analysis may be outlined. Given a close historical relation between annual food output and a farm family's minimum subsistence level, the degree of risk aversion—and thus the extent of resistance to innovations—will be *reinforced* by five factors:

1. the greater the concentration on food crop(s) in the farm;
2. the lesser the availability of other food sources;
3. the lesser the opportunities for alternative employment of family labor, or of other farm resources;
4. the tighter the capital rationing facing the farmer, and the higher the interest rate he must pay;
5. the closer the value of the family's minimum subsistence level is to the value of the family's net worth (assets minus debts).

PROGRAM AND POLICY IMPLICATIONS

If risk and uncertainty are as important in the content of subsistence as indicated, then certain steps are required to assure a greater rapidity and extent of adoption of new technology.

1. Information on the variability of any new technology is an important as its average performance. Any determination of the economic feasibility of a new practice or technique should pay equal, if not more, attention to the variability in yields, especially the lower deviations as they relate to minimum subsistence standards of living of potential innovating farmers.

2. In developing new technologies, agricultural research organizations should recognize the importance which subsistence farmers attach to the variabilities associated with any possible innovation. Plant breeders, for example, should pay greater attention to those specific characteristics which may help to reduce negative deviation and offer greater dependability.

3. Where only a narrow range covers the minimum subsistence standards, levels of living, and physiologic minima, programs designed to diffuse new technology need to pay much greater attention to methods for "risk insurance" or assuring

the peasant who innovates that failure (i.e., an output falling below his minimum subsistence standard) will not result in a major penalty, viz., loss of life or loss of property or indebtedness. Existing social structures and institutions (viz., extended family) which already provide some degree of "risk insurance" should be recognized as such and wherever possible treated as complementary to any new insurance system.

4. Methods of technological introduction and trial in a peasant community should recognize that in the early stages the typical farmer attaches a subjective variability to the expected yield of the new technology which is considerably wider than the true one. Extension and information measures should concentrate just as much on reducing this subjective variability in the minds of potential innovators as on spreading knowledge about the average or maximum yields. Assurance as to the dependability of the practice or technology may be more important to the peasant farmer than its dramatic output possibilities.

21. Agricultural Pricing Policies in Developing Countries*

Gilbert T. Brown

Most developing countries for the last quarter century have had policies designed to lower the prices of food and other agricultural goods and to increase the prices of manufactured

* From Theodore W. Schultz (ed.), *Distortions of Agricultural Incentives*. Bloomington: Indiana University Press, 1978. Extracted and reprinted in *Development Digest*, 17, no. 2 (April 1979), pp. 25–36.

goods. Trade and foreign-exchange controls have been major instruments of these policies, along with taxes, direct price regulations and other market-control measures. The conventional wisdom supporting this twisting of the terms of trade against agriculture has had four main pillars, based on the assumptions:

(1) that aggregate agricultural production is not very responsive to price changes;

(2) that the chief beneficiaries of higher prices would be the larger-size farmers;

(3) that higher food and other agriculture-related prices such as clothing would most adversely affect low-income consumers; and

(4) that manufacturing provides a more rapid means of growth, and that achieving that growth depends upon large transfers of income (profits) and foreign exchange from agriculture to manufacturing. Thus, policies that depress agricultural prices and increase manufacturing prices have been expected to result in more rapid economic growth and in a more equal distribution of income as well.

Lagging agricultural production and a slowing of economic growth rates in many developing countries that followed such policies, however, have led to increasing concern about measures that reduce farm incomes and incentives. Argentina, Egypt, Kenya, the Ivory Coast, Pakistan, Peru, the Philippines, Thailand, and Uruguay are among the countries which have acted to significantly increase agricultural relative to nonagricultural prices in the 1970s. Greater emphasis in the development literature on rural-development strategies, and on strategies to meet basic needs and to benefit persons in the lowest 40 percent of the income distribution, has also provided new intellectual support for price policies more favorable to agriculture, such as lessened subsidies for capital goods, less overvalued exchange rates and protection for industry, and increased production of foodstuffs and other wage goods.

In contrast to those of the developing countries, price policies in the industrialized countries during this period have been distorted in favor of rather than against the farmer; the typical problem has been overproduction rather than underproduction of agricultural commodities. Moreover, greater agricultural productivity per hectare in industrialized than in developing countries is a phenomenon that has occurred largely since the 1930s, and within the period of differential price policies. In the period 1934–38, grain yields averaged 1.15 tons per hectare in industrial countries, and 1.14 tons (i.e., the same level) in developing countries. By 1975, however, grain yields in industrial countries were more than double those in developing countries, 3.0 tons versus 1.4 tons per hectare. This is not to argue, of course, that the more rapid growth in agricultural yields and production in the industrialized countries is due solely to differences in price policies. A plausible hypothesis is that both the more favorable farm prices and the more rapid growth of farm yields in industrial countries reflect efforts to support farm incomes and increase agricultural productivity, while developing countries have generally been much more concerned about increasing industrial incentives and production, and urban incomes.

The focus of this paper is not on the factors that explain the differences in growth rates between developed and developing countries, however, but on the effects of prevalent pricing policies in today's developing countries. My hypothesis is that agricultural production, income distribution, and economic growth would all benefit from reduction or elimination of "distortions" that reduce agriculture's domestic terms of trade. By distortions, I mean government policies which change prices from what they would be in a free market with no controls. The relations of agriculture's domestic terms of trade to income distribution and economic growth particularly are complex problems too important to neglect.

Several general problems of terminology or analysis should be briefly mentioned. References to "free-market" prices are to those that would exist in the absence of specific controls and policies that now distort the relation of agricultural to nonagricultural prices, including those relationships that magnify differences between domestic and world-market prices. This is not to imply that world-market prices are "free," or that policy should aim to equate domestic and world-market prices or price relatives at all times. Neither is it to imply that "shadow" free-market prices (i.e., those which would be found under perfect market conditions) can be known with exactitude; we are inevitably dealing with a second-best or even third-best world. Rather, the comparison to probable prices "in the absence of controls" reflects only a judgment about approximate price relationships (e.g., too high, or too low). References to changes in prices are to changes from existing distorted price relations. It must be remembered, however, that prices are an incomplete measure of incentives. If agriculture's relative productivity is increasing, it is possible for agricultural incomes and incentives to be growing at the same time that agricultural prices are declining. A fundamental distinction must be made between measures such as price controls, taxes, and subsidies that artificially lower food and agricultural prices, and measures such as on-farm investment, technological advances, and rural infrastructure development (e.g., roads, electricity, and water), that lower prices by lowering the real costs of production. Reductions in real resource costs of production can benefit urban dwellers, farmers, and rural laborers alike.

PRICING POLICIES AND AGRICULTURAL PRODUCTION

Efficient Use of Resources

Higher prices may stimulate agricultural production by causing farmers to use more labor and other variable resource inputs to reach higher output levels with existing methods of production, or by inducing investment and the discovery and adoption of new agricultural technologies that result in new, lower-cost production possibilities.

The usual empirical basis of arguments that agricultural production is not very responsive to price changes rests upon low price elasticities derived from multiple-correlation analysis of the acreage or output of a particular crop in relation to the relative prices of that crop versus others, or to several presumably independent variables such as output price and use of fertilizer, labor, and water. This multiple-correlation methodology can be faulted on several grounds, including the lack of independence between prices, on one hand, and the level of use of fertilizer and other inputs. The use of acreage rather than output in most such studies underestimates the price elasticity of production by not taking account of changes in yields, which for some years have been accounting for more than half the annual growth in world food-grain production. Also, it is doubtful that yearly fluctuations in prices can adequately represent the changes in the longer-run income expectations that determine rates of investment in agriculture and the adoption of new techniques. These decisions appear to depend more upon whether expected profitability is above or below a "threshold" level of acceptability, which may be little affected by yearly price fluctuations unless these cause longer-run expectations of profitability to change. Moreover, incentives are a function of net income and not just prices, so that a new technology may importantly change the incentive effect of a given set of prices—as happened during the Green Revolution in wheat and rice.

Price incentives can cause farmers to use improved seeds, along with more fertilizer, pesticides, and other purchased inputs, to adopt improved cultural practices, and to apply more family or hired labor. All of these ways of increasing the efficiency of resource use may occur at once, for example, if a small farmer decides to reduce or give up his off-farm employment—or a son does not migrate to the city—in order to adopt the more labor-intensive techniques required to reap the benefits of new varieties. Generalities about most small farmers as "subsistence" farmers unaffected by agricultural prices are highly misleading.

Timmer and Falcon found a close rank correlation between unmilled rice prices and rice yields among Asian countries. For 1970, rice yields varied from 5.64 and 4.55 metric tons per hectare in Japan and South Korea to 1.7–2.1 tons per hectare in Indonesia, Thailand, the Philippines, and Burma. At the same time, the ratio of the price of a kilogram of rice to the price of a kilogram of fertilizer nutrients showed a similar wide variation, from 1.43 and 0.96 in Japan and Korea to 0.1–0.4 in the other countries. This pattern of relationships between prices and yields cannot be explained as a short-term response, but reflects long-standing differences in price policies among these countries. It appears to indicate long-run responsiveness of production to incentives. It is noteworthy that the three countries with the highest yields—Japan, South Korea, and Taiwan—have some of the poorest soils among the nine countries studied. The high prices to farmers in these countries appear necessary to cover the costs of achieving these yields under the given climatic, soil and other conditions; the decisions to pay such high prices may have been primarily political. It is interesting to speculate to what levels rice yields and production would fall in Japan if farmers there received the same price as Thai farmers, or conversely the levels to which rice yields and production would climb in Thailand within a few years if Thai farmers faced the same rice and fertilizer prices as Japanese farmers.

Shifts in the Production Function

The most important long-run effects of price incentives on production may be through price-induced shifts in the production function (i.e., development of new technologies) rather than through greater efficiency of resource use with existing production functions (technolo-

gies). These long-run effects depend upon the extent to which the incentive structure has an important effect on scientific research and on adoption of new techniques by farmers, on public and private investment related to agriculture, and on institutional changes such as land reform, extension services, marketing, and distribution facilities.

Clear links have been demonstrated between prices and the timing and nature of new technological discoveries, and also the adoption of these techniques by farmers. Much of the agricultural research initiated since the late-1973 jump in oil prices is "energy saving," with heavy emphasis on reducing fertilizer requirements—for example, through nitrogen fixation, seed treatment, and placing a small amount of fertilizer close to the seed or seedling roots. Studies of the diffusion of new techniques and of new investment in developing countries indicate that where profitability of adopting a new technique or investing, say in a tube well, is very high, that the new techniques will be rapidly adopted and the new investment quickly made. At least there are wealthy individuals who make choices between agricultural and nonfarm investments. A large proportion of upper- and even middle-class individuals in South Asia, for example, reside in cities but own substantial farmland operated by a hired manager, tenant or a relative. For these individuals, as for the small farmer deciding how to divide his time between his own farm and other employment, the choices between farm vs. nonfarm investment and labor are recurring ones. Higher returns to farming certainly attract more labor and more investment into farming—other things being equal. Nearly all studies show high marginal saving rates among even poor farmers. Thus, an important part of the additional income accruing to farmers through higher prices is likely to result in greater savings and investment. In countries where farm yields are low and returns to additional investment in agriculture are high (e.g., where fertilizer use is well below optimal levels), an important part of that saving is likely to be invested in farming. Public investment and institutional changes may also be importantly affected by prices, but research on these topics is in its infancy so the evidence is scarce.

INCOME DISTRIBUTION

Low prices for food and other farm products are politically popular on the theory that they increase real incomes and employment of the urban poor, and that the only losers are large farmers. There is a high cost attached to such low prices, however, if their effect is to retard cost-reducing investment and innovation in agriculture. Competition between farmers and traders assures that most of any decline in unit costs would be passed on to consumers in lower prices, even though farm incomes rise. Moreover, studies of the effects of price distortions and controls in specific countries usually conclude that it is the upper- and middle-income urban groups (including employers) and large farmers who are the chief beneficiaries.

The argument that higher food prices hurt low-income urban consumers who have to buy most of their foodstuffs is usually based on the short-term income effects of higher food prices on the assumption of unchanged incomes. These studies tend to ignore even relatively short-run adjustment processes that reduce the income loss, such as shifts in consumer demand toward substitute foodstuffs, and the fact that in low-income countries urban wages usually respond fairly quickly to the cost of basic foodstuffs. The logic of the common argument in developing countries that food prices must be kept low in order to assure the competitiveness of manufactured exports rests entirely on this relationship between the two. The benefit to employers of below-market agricultural prices is even clearer in the case of nonfoodstuffs: cotton yarn and textile manufacturers in Pakistan, for example, for many years have been able to buy cotton from farmers, many of whom are quite poor, at no more than two-thirds and sometimes half of world market prices because of foreign exchange and export tax controls; but they sell much of their output at world market prices.

Price and production controls that are intended to provide low-cost food to poor urban groups also tend to divert production away from those cheaper food crops. In Peru, low official prices have greatly reduced production of *frijol canario*, a popular bean which has been a major source of protein for low-income urban consumers; the limited output is being channeled through black markets at prices about 60 percent above the official control prices. In Egypt, farmers have increasingly diverted land, fertilizer, and other inputs from growing wheat, maize, rice, and cotton—for which they are given quotas to sell to the government at low, controlled prices—to growing fruits, vegetables, and livestock, which are not price-controlled. This diversion helps assure a supply of these latter foods for upper-income urbanites, but at a high cost in the balance of payments and in massive budget subsidies to lower the retail price of imported wheat. In Kenya, price ceilings on meat and maize transfer income from low-income herdsmen and farmers for the benefit of middle- and upper-income urban dwellers.

Marketing Controls

Most developing-country controls on price margins and marketing between farmers and consumers are supposed to protect consumers against "monopolistic" traders. The few significant studies of such controls, however, suggest that such interventions frequently have very adverse effects on efficiency, production, and income distribution. The most comprehensive Indian study concluded that the private grain market was highly competitive, that traders operated efficiently within government-imposed technological and policy constraints, and that government efforts, rather than being expended in market controls, could have been much more fruitfully directed toward helping to improve the competitive environment, including improved farm-to-market transportation facilities, dissemination of market price and stock information, and managing national support price and buffer stock programs. Periodic threats by the Indian government during the prior twenty-five years to nationalize all trade in grains, and the issuing of new rice-milling licenses primarily to cooperatives and public-sector firms, however, had resulted in very little private investment to improve either storage or milling facilities. Furthermore, government-agency marketing costs are several times as high as those of private traders, who flourish despite government policies.

A study in Peru concluded that marketing measures initiated to eliminate abuses by middlemen represented one of the major constraints limiting agricultural production, and might drive out private marketing talent with no comparable gain in public-sector expertise. Because of stringent laws and penalties against speculation and monopolization, there is little private investment in storage facilities in Peru. This lack of storage facilities results in periodic gluts, scarcities, and excessive price fluctuations as wholesale truckers move products between consumption centers on a day-to-day basis to take advantage of price differences among different areas.

Input Subsidies and Income Distribution

Farm subsidies also benefit primarily middle- and upper-income farmers in low-income countries. Large-scale farmers buy most subsidized inputs. Poorer farmers usually lack the money to buy adequate amounts of fertilizer and pesticides, and are commonly unable to get credit except at near-prohibitive private rates of often 60 to 100 percent per year. In countries with subsidized bank credit for agriculture, rich farmers tend to get most of the credit through open or disguised bribery. Subsidy programs for tractors, tube wells, and other fixed investments also go mostly to the largest and richest farmers. Data from Kenya indicate that about 80 percent of fertilizer, which has been subsidized for many years, has gone to large farmers.

DEVELOPMENT STRATEGY AND AGRICULTURAL PRICING

The ultimate question about agricultural pricing policies is their effect on economic development, including income distribution and social consequences. We are unable to model and quantify adequately an entire economy in a way that measures its complete response to variations in relative prices. We can progress toward that goal, however, by examining the effects of agricultural-pricing policies on government budgets, national saving and investment, and the balance of payments.

Government Budgets

Revenue and expenditure data shed further light on the effect of government actions on farmer incentives and income distribution. We have made calculations of the transfers of resources among producers, consumers, and the government due to the effect of government measures on the prices received by farmers and the prices paid by consumers for wheat in Pakistan in various years between 1966 and 1976. These show a large transfer of income from wheat producers to consumers through lower-than-world-market prices for domestic wheat, including that procured by the government. These transfers are estimated at 348 million rupees in 1966 and 1,540 million rupees in 1976, and they equalled 62 percent of the income received by farmers from marketed wheat in the former year and 52 percent in the latter. At the same time the farmers received budgeted government subsidies on inputs used in producing wheat equal to about 7 percent of the domestic value of marketed wheat at domestic prices in 1966 and 10 percent in 1976. Consumers received transfers from less-than-world prices for their purchases in the private market, and from sales through officially controlled ration shops, of both domestic and imported wheat at substantially less than their cost to the government. The net result of these transactions has been a large income transfer from producers (1,237 million rupees in 1976) equal to 41 percent of the value of marketed wheat at domestic prices, and a large income transfer to consumers (3,280 million rupees in 1976) equal to somewhat more than the total payment to domestic farmers for their entire crop of marketed wheat.

One of the important questions is whether the benefits of these subsidies in providing lower-cost wheat to consumers are as great as their costs. The economic and social costs are increases in taxes and/or government borrowing, or of decreases in other government expenditures—perhaps a combination of these. All consumers are beneficiaries of the system, whether they buy government-rationed and price-controlled wheat or make their purchases in private markets. The cost of these subsidies weighs heavily on small "subsistence-level" farmers. In Pakistan, such farmers sell more than 30 percent of all marketed wheat but receive only a small fraction of the fertilizer, pesticide, tube well, tractor, and other subsidies. The average real income of these small farmers is considerably below the average urban income.

As for cost effectiveness in reaching really poor consumers, many of those in the lowest 40 percent of the income distribution are farmers or rural workers who would benefit from higher farm prices; and some of the poorest urban dwellers would have stayed on or returned to farms if farm prices and incomes had been higher. These facts suggest that low food prices penalize rather than help many of the poor. The 2 billion rupees of government budget subsidies to lower wheat prices in 1976 amounted to one-half the value of all marketed wheat, including imported wheat. Thus, on budgetary grounds alone, ignoring production and other indirect effects, this is an ex-

tremely expensive way to provide low-priced wheat to those who are in real poverty; it could be done at much less expense through a direct food subsidy or other income-supplement program directed to the needy and malnourished.

A typical and in no way exceptional example of the relation of the cost of these budget subsidies to expenditures on agricultural extension, research, education, and statistics is available from Pakistan budget data. For fiscal year 1975, subsidies to consumers for wheat and to farmers for purchased inputs at the provincial and national government levels were budgeted to equal about 60 percent of all other current and capital expenditures on agriculture, irrigation, and water development projects. The cost of subsidies was drastically underestimated, however, and actual payments amounted to about 90 percent of the budgeted level of the type of expenditures noted. Actual wheat subsidies were forty-four times as great as budgeted expenditures on extension services, and fifteen times the total budgeted expenditures on agricultural extension, research, education, and statistics. It seems unlikely that the benefits of wheat subsidies were as great as would have been a near doubling of the real resources devoted to all agriculture and water development programs. It also seems likely that increased expenditures on these latter categories would have done far more than the subsidies to lower food prices, though with a time lag.

Taxation

There is a substantial literature on the economic advantages of direct rather than indirect taxation of agriculture, since land and income taxes do not directly affect either relative product prices, cropping patterns, input/output price ratios, or the output levels from which farmers will realize the maximum levels of income. High levels of land taxation were very successfully used, both to stimulate agricultural output and to transfer resources to the government and to industry, during the modernization of agriculture in Japan and in colonial India. However, the lack of significant levels of such taxation in most developing countries today, and the presumed administrative as well as political difficulties in their imposition, are often cited as reasons for focusing on indirect taxation of agricultural commodities, and particularly on taxation of exports. Changes in taxation would be a budgetary requirement of price and subsidy changes in many countries. A package combining higher output prices with reduced subsidies and increased land taxation could work to everyone's interest, and be more politically acceptable than a change only in prices and subsidies.

Savings and Investment

The effects of pricing policies on national saving are obviously very complex. Budget subsidies to consumers during the high grain prices of the 1970s rose to roughly one-fourth of total government expenditures in some food-deficit countries such as Egypt and Pakistan, and to as much as 5 percent of gross domestic products. These were exceptional years; but such subsidies are typically still a significant drain on saving and hence on resources available to finance investment.

Substantial savings may also be lost through income transfers from agriculture to the rest of the economy through price distortions. Studies of private saving rates among rural and urban groups show higher marginal saving rates in rural than in urban areas. Furthermore, small-farmer marginal saving rates appear to be almost as high as those of large farmers. Farm saving rates might have been further increased if pricing policies had made investment in agriculture more attractive. Thus, the distortion of input and product prices in order to funnel income away from farmers and toward industry may have significantly reduced national rates of saving and, therefore, of investment. Rates of overall economic growth may hence have suffered from

lower rates of saving and investment as well as from misallocation of budget and investment funds. This is just the opposite effect, of course, from that predicted by economists who argued in the 1950s and 1960s, from inadequate empirical data, that marginal saving rates of the urban sector and industrialists were higher than those of farmers.

Observation of the industrial sector in many developing countries suggests that relatively little productive investment may result from the involuntary transfer of income from agriculture to industry. Rates of utilization of physical capital in industry are extremely low in these countries. Moreover, much of the income transferred may not even result in productive investment but may be frittered away in inefficiency and increased consumption, such as in wage increases to already relatively high-income industrial workers, additional unneeded employment of workers (especially in public-sector industry), or increased consumption by managers.

Balance of payments

While the totality of potential effects of relative changes in agricultural prices upon the balance of payments is very complex, spectacular balance of payments changes appear feasible in some countries by reducing price distortions against agriculture. Kenya's move in early 1975 toward world-market prices for both agricultural products and inputs has virtually eliminated previous large expenditures for wheat and sugar imports, both by increasing domestic production of these crops and by cutting demand for each by about 20 percent through substitution of other domestic foodstuffs. Reduction of subsidies on imported farm equipment that have mostly benefited rich farmers and encouraged capital-intensive and import-intensive agricultural production techniques seems to be simultaneously strengthening the balance of payments, increasing wheat production and lowering its cost, and improving incomes and employment among relatively poorer sections of Kenya's rural population. By contrast, declines in rice exports from Burma, and in agricultural exports from Pakistan and Egypt, are only a few examples of the sometimes very substantial declines in export earnings that have resulted from paying farmers much less than the market value of their crops.

Higher agricultural prices closer to market level might also significantly reduce nonfood imports by changing the distribution of income and hence the composition of demand. If less discrimination against agricultural prices shifted income distribution in favor of farmers, there would be changes in the composition as well as the level of demand for both consumption and investment goods. Research indicates that such shifts would tend to increase demand for labor-intensive domestic products and reduce demand for capital-intensive and imported products.

CONCLUSIONS

Analysis of the significance of price policy in general and agricultural price policy in particular has not kept up with practical experience concerning policies affecting prices in developing countries or with changes in development-strategy theories. There are several types of studies that might be especially useful in advancing our knowledge of the responses of farmers and of national economies to price changes. First, detailed case studies of the decision making of individual farmers are badly needed. Much of our "conventional widsom" about farm-level response to changes in agricultural prices, for instance, is based upon aggregative data. Studies have only recently begun on how developing-country farmers of different income levels spend their time and earn their incomes.

Second, detailed case studies of the effect of particular price policies in individual countries are needed. Evidence from various sources has been presented in this paper about some consequences of particular price policies in particular countries. Such material needs to be much more systematically examined and incorporated into the knowledge of development specialists and policy makers; information is available and is too often regarded as interesting anecdotal case material. The problem is too important to neglect. In the process of seeing what can be accomplished with current tools of analysis, new analytical breakthroughs appear likely.

Third, it is important that the overall structure of price policies be studied, along with the place of price policy in overall economic policy. Such studies have generally not been undertaken because they are considered "unwieldy," "vague," and too big to be productive. Nevertheless, the examples cited here of the neglect of agricultural pricing issues suggest that these issues are also too important not to be the subject of some direct work, rather than always working with the pieces. These studies will necessarily be national studies initially. It would also be useful to look at comparative policy structure and growth experiences in different developing countries since perhaps 1950. For example, what were the characteristics of price policy and overall economic policy in countries with rapid overall growth, and how did these policies compare with those of countries which experienced difficulties?

Fourth, the role which developed countries could play in helping to overcome agricultural pricing policy problems in developing countries should be examined. For instance, could foreign aid help to finance a phased adjustment in urban food prices over several years, both to avoid sharp short-term income effects from higher prices and to cover the period between the undertaking of farm-level price increases and the actual achievement of increased and cheaper food-grain supplies? Developed countries could also make an important contribution by managing their own agricultural production and import and export programs so as to minimize disruptions to world markets.

22. Rural Development*

World Bank Staff

Rural development is a strategy designed to improve the economic and social life of a specific group of people—the rural poor. It involves extending the benefits of development to the poorest among those who seek a livelihood in the rural areas. The group includes small-scale farmers, tenants and the landless.

A strategy for rural development must recognize three points. Firstly, the rate of transfer of people out of low productivity agriculture and related activities into more rewarding pursuits has been slow; and, given the relative size of the modern sector in most developing countries, it will remain slow. Secondly, the mass of the people in the rural areas of developing countries face varying degrees of poverty; their position is likely to get worse if population expands at unprecedented rates while limitations continue to be imposed by available resources, technology, and institutions and organizations. Thirdly, rural areas have labor, land and at least some capital which, if mobilized, could reduce poverty and improve the quality of life. This implies fuller development of existing resources, including the construction of infrastructure such as roads and irrigation works, the introduction of new production technology, and the creation of new types of institutions and organizations.

Since rural development is intended to reduce poverty, it must be clearly designed to increase production and raise productivity. Rural development recognizes, however, that improved food supplies and nutrition, together with basic services such as health and education, can not only directly improve the physical well-being and quality of life of the rural poor, but can also indirectly enhance their productivity and their ability to contribute to the national economy. It is concerned with the modernization and monetization of rural society, and with its transition from traditional isolation to integration with the national economy.

The objectives of rural development, therefore, extend beyond any particular sector. They encompass improved productivity, increased employment and thus higher incomes for target groups, as well as minimum acceptable levels of food, shelter, education and health. A national program of rural development should include a mix of activities, including projects to raise agricultural output, create new employment, improve health and education, expand communications and improve housing. Such a program might be made up of single-sector or multisectoral projects, with components implemented concurrently or in sequence. The components and phasing must be formulated both to remove constraints and to support those forces prevailing in the target area which are favorable to development.

The nature and content of any rural development program or project will reflect the political, social and economic circumstances of the particular country or region. Where the scope and need for rural development are not accepted by government leaders, or where the shortage of resources is acute (especially the supply of skilled manpower), initial projects may be experimental in nature or restricted in extent. Where particular needs are pressing, such as in cases of famine or disease, narrowly focused projects may be appropriate.

TARGET POPULATION

Approximately 85% of the 750 million poor in the developing world are considered to be in

* From World Bank, *The Assault on World Poverty*. Baltimore and London: Johns Hopkins University Press, 1975, pp. 3–11.

absolute poverty—based on the arbitrary criterion of an annual per capita income equivalent to $50 or less. The remaining 15% are judged to be in relative poverty—having incomes above the equivalent of $50, but below one-third of the national average per capita income.

Three-fourths of those in absolute poverty are in the developing countries of Asia, reflecting both the low levels of national per capita income and the large size of the rural sector there. As for those in relative poverty, most of them are found in developing countries that are less poor, a large fraction being in Latin America.

Of the population in developing countries considered to be in either absolute or relative poverty, more than 80% are estimated to live in rural areas. Agriculture is the principal occupation for four-fifths of the rural poor. These people are found in roughly equal proportions in densely populated zones (over 300 persons per square kilometer) and sparsely populated zones (less than 150 persons per square kilometer). Thus, poverty is found in the highly productive irrigated areas of Asia, as well as in the adverse conditions of the Sahel, northeast Brazil, the Andean altiplano and the dry zones of India.

The rural poor include small-scale farmers, tenants, sharecroppers, landless workers and their families. There are over 80 million smallholdings of less than two hectares, many of them comprising several small fragments of land, most of which generate incomes below the absolute poverty level. The tenants, sharecroppers and squatters, who represent another 30 million or more families, are often less well-off. While the largest proportion of workers in agriculture is self-employed, the number of landless or near-landless workers is growing—especially in Asian countries. They depend on seasonal work and are among the poorest of the rural community.

Despite high rates of migration from rural to urban areas, the rural population is growing by approximately 2% a year. The consequent worsening of the man-land ratio means that increases in output and income must come primarily from better yields per acre and cultivation of higher value crops. This will require both access to new technology and the capital to utilize it. That, in turn, implies the need for new or improved service systems to support a modern system of agriculture. The new seed-fertilizer-water technology for wheat, rice and maize provides the first major opportunity for extending science-based agriculture to low-income, small-scale producers of traditional crops. Further adaptive research and extension are required to ensure an adequate rate of technological change. Special programs are necessary to help the rural poor to contribute more fully to an increase in output. The programs must include the provision of infrastructure and on-farm improvements.

The need for special intervention to raise rural production and incomes applies also to the provision of social and other services, such as health and education. Poverty is reflected in poor nutrition, inadequate shelter and low health standards. These affect not only the quality of life but also the productivity of rural people. In particular, there is a need for nutrition and preventive health programs, including improved water supplies and sanitation. Better education is an important element, and may also provide an opportunity for the rural young to escape from poverty. In order to remedy both quantitative and qualitative educational deficiencies, increased use of "basic education" is considered imperative.

Compared with urban areas, rural areas have a smaller share of economic infrastructure services, such as domestic water, electricity and waste disposal. Even where the services exist, the poor often do not have access to them because organization is inadequate and the cost is high. A special effort is needed to provide appropriate social and economic infrastructure for the rural poor, and it is important to integrate these components into rural development projects. Without a concerted effort, rural poverty will remain pervasive.

POLICY FRAMEWORK

Experience indicates that a strong commitment to rural development at the national policy level is necessary if the impact is to be effective and broad-based. In many countries, the commitment is lacking. However, most governments are prepared to experiment at the project level and to examine the results. . . .

Often, macroeconomic policies are inconsistent with agricultural and rural development. Price policies that favor manufacturing and processing industries, and those which aim to keep food prices low in urban areas, work againsst rural development. In such cases, subsidies on farm inputs may be justified. Fiscal policies also often militate against the rural poor, who are less well organized and less vociferous than other groups. Thus, public sector spending is heavily skewed in favor of urban dwellers, and in rural areas the rich get favored treatment. Yet the poor often pay considerably more taxes in proportion to income because indirect commodity taxes may be high, while direct taxes are low. In addition, there is often a reluctance to charge those benefiting from publicly financed investments, thus widening the gap between the few who have access to such investments and those who do not. Land policy has obvious implications for the rural poor, given that their incomes depend on the extent to which they control land and its output. In many instances, therefore, land reform is a necessary part of a rural development program.

Policies aimed at ensuring a flow of new, field-tested technical knowledge relevant to smallholder production are essential for the success of rural development. Often the poorest areas are overlooked by such policies, or the subsistence farm is not treated as a system. Where technology is available, it is frequently not applied because extension services, support services, finance and marketing facilities are lacking. Research and demonstration on a local basis to facilitate adoption is required in all these areas.

ORGANIZATION AND PLANNING

Ideally, the planning and implementation of rural development programs involve adequate regional planning, strong central coordination, effective local level organization and the participation of the rural people in the planning and implementation processes. Few countries have been able to come close to this ideal. Regional planning is desirable both because rural development cuts across all sectors and because rural programs need to be framed to meet regional conditions. Such planning necessitates the collection of statistics on a regional rather than a sectoral basis, and the use of regional surveys and resource inventories. Interregional allocations of technical and financial resources must be decided in relation to resource endowments, the domestic and foreign funds available, a balance of equity and growth considerations, and mutually acceptable arrangements for sharing responsibilities between the central and local authorities. All these elements should be brought together into an internally balanced rural development plan. However, the lack of a comprehensive rural development plan should not prevent the evolution of programs on a local level.

Strong coordination at the center is increasingly regarded as essential to the successful implementation of a rural development program. This is a reflection both of the political nature of many of the decisions that must be made and of the need to coordinate the activities of ministries or departments organized along sectoral lines. A special office or unit is favored, having responsibility for definition of target groups, coordination of national and regional efforts, and integration of the activities of national sector agencies. It has also to ensure that all sector policies are commensurate with rural development objectives.

Coordination at the local level is emphasized because of the growing evidence that multisectoral programs can be implemented most effectively through a substantial increase in decentralization. Local control provides the flexibility needed for the proper integration and timing of activities, and for modification of programs in response to changing conditions. Community involvement, which is essential to a sustained development process, is greatly facilitated by local rather than centralized control. One particular advantage is that the problems of the community, as perceived by its residents and those imputed by local officials, tend to be more easily reconciled.

Group arrangements such as cooperatives provide an organized basis for handling many of the problems of providing access to services for large numbers of rural people. They allow a measure of involvement through participation, but also provide a vehicle for collective negotiation of credit, input supplies and delivery of marketable surpluses. Even land management can be organized on a cooperative basis, as in Egypt. Group approaches enjoy widespread support among governments, even though the results have been mixed. They provide an impetus to rural development that is difficult to secure in any other way. In many cases, they build on an established base of mutual aid within the rural population. A major requirement for the successful operation of cooperative groups and for regional and local government is the provision of trained manpower. Thus, training facilities are needed to prepare full-time staff, and to improve the effectiveness of community leaders, school teachers, religious leaders and other agents of change.

PROGRAM DESIGN AND IMPLEMENTATION

Existing rural development projects can be classified for purposes of discussion into three approaches:

1. The minimum package approach, as exemplified by the Bank-supported proj-ects in Ethiopia and the Republic of Korea (seeds).
2. The comprehensive approach, which can be either (a) nationally integrated programs or (b) area development and settlement schemes. Examples of nationally integrated programs are the Joint Commission for Rural Reconstruction in the Republic of China and PIDER in Mexico. Area-specific projects can be either single-product projects such as tea in Kenya, tobacco in Tanzania, cotton in Mali and oil palm in Malaysia; or comprehensive area projects which have more diversified crop and integrated farming systems, such as Comilla in Bangladesh, Lilongwe in Malawi and Caquetá in Colombia.
3. Sector and other special programs, including rural public works, education and training and credit schemes.

A review of these projects points to the many difficult issues in rural development planning, and in project formulation and implementation. Time and again, problems arise from lack of knowledge, incomplete understanding and limited institutional, technical and financial capabilities. It is possible, however, to make a few simple affirmative propositions:

1. Given sound preparatory planning, leadership and the involvement of local people, the small farmer can become an instrument of change to the advantage of the nation as well as of himself.
2. The material resources required for rural development need not be disproportionately large. In many successful schemes, the capital cost per beneficiary has been quite low. Although low capital cost per beneficiary is not by itself a criterion for a good project, it is an important element in designing projects to reach large numbers in the target groups.
3. Rural development schemes benefiting large numbers of people can be as pro-

ductive and economically attractive as schemes of a conventional kind directly benefiting far fewer people.

4. With well-designed programs, offering proper incentives to small farmers, development can be much more rapid than is sometimes believed, and the impact on levels of living following the expansion of cash incomes from a subsistence baseline can be dramatic.

5. Finally, while much remains to be done, conviction of the need for a change in strategy, and commitment to specific actions and programs for rural development, have probably never been greater in developing countries than at the present time. This is an important bridgehead on which new understanding can be built and from which new programs can be launched.

COUNTRY GUIDELINES

The following are desirable characteristics of a framework within which to design and implement rural development programs.

1. *Central leadership and coordination:* Effective rural development planning should be given high priority. Steps to improve planning capacity might include establishing a small but expert unit charged with the development of a national program of action. Such a body should provide leadersip and should have a coordinating role in project identification and preparation and in monitoring ongoing programs. Where nationally integrated rural development programs are desired, the central unit should also be actively involved in project identification and preparation.

2. *Decentralization and participation at the local level:* Provision of an institutional framework at the regional or local level and of good center-local communications and coordination, with appropriate devolution of responsibility to local bodies, are critical. There is no single model for dealing with these problems, but the importance of evolving planning and programming units in both regional-local government institutions and sectoral departments cannot be stressed too strongly. Also important is the need to involve local people in planning, in making decisions and in implementation.

3. *Research:* Expanded technical and economic research into small farm systems, and into crops and techniques generally appropriate for use by the small farmer, should have high priority. A second type of research which is important but neglected relates to the dynamics of traditional rural societies as they begin to enter the modern sector.

4. *Training:* The shortage of trained manpower is perhaps the most serious obstacle to large-scale rural development efforts. An intensified training effort, particularly directed toward the needs of local level institutions, and calling for greater efforts focused on training in the local environments where people work, must also be pursued.

5. *Intermediaries:* The establishment of effective group organizations, such as farmers' associations and cooperatives, should have high priority. They provide the best means of lowering the cost of delivering services and marketing output, so that larger numbers can be reached.

Activities related to rural development planning include the following:

1. *Identification of target groups:* Identification should be in terms of category, number, location and other attributes, with detailed specification of the relationships between these categories and the proposed project actions.

2. *Project design:* Several different kinds of projects may be appropriate:

  (a) Some projects may emphasize specific functional services, such as minimum packages of inputs like fertilizers and seeds, and phasing, so that moderate benefits can be introduced progressively, at low cost per beneficiary, in order to cover a wide cross-section of the rural poor.
  (b) Other more comprehensive projects may involve the integration of related economic and social services in order that full advantage is taken of opportunities to build better balanced and more focused efforts.
  (c) In some cases, sectoral and other special programs may be needed to remove a binding constraint (such as an endemic disease problem) or to meet a special need (such as public works to employ the landless).

In any event, each project must contain the blend of inputs and services necessary to ensure a sustained increase in productivity for the beneficiaries. Particular attention should be given to the appropriate balance between the directly productive and indirectly productive elements in a project. The balance should reflect the levels of services proposed for the sector on a national basis, the most economical means of providing such services, and restrictions on resources that can be used for this purpose.

3. *Implementation:* Items requiring specific attention include:

  (a) Local level training schemes and use of locally available human resources in order to minimize demands on the rest of the economy.
  (b) Adherence to sectoral and regional planning considerations so as to ensure that proper attention is paid to linkages between sectors and regions.
  (c) Establishment of user charges, graduated according to ability to pay, and provision for adequate savings to be drawn from local communities so that funds are available to extend programs on a broader scale.
  (d) Local agricultural research to provide a basis for continuing productivity gains from small-scale agriculture.
  (e) Full use of existing local governmental structures, and assistance in strengthening them for greater subsequent use.
  (f) Promotion of institutional structures which enable the beneficiaries to participate in the running of projects.
  (g) Use of simple monitoring and evaluation systems, both as integral parts of the project management system and as a method of benefiting from experience in designing future projects.

Further Readings

1. Agrarian Reform

Barraclough, Solon, ed. *Agrarian Structure in Latin America.* Lexington, Mass., Toronto, and London: Heath, 1973.

Dorner, Peter. *Land Reform and Economic Development.* Harmondsworth, England: Penguin, 1972.

Griffin, Keith. *Land Concentration and Rural Poverty.* London: Macmillan, 1976.

International Bank for Reconstruction and Development. *Land Reform.* Washington, D.C.: World Bank, 1974.

ILO, *Poverty and Landlessness in Rural Asia.* Geneva, 1977.

United Nations. *Progress in Land Reform.* Sixth Report. New York, 1976.

2. Rural Development

Boscrup, Ester. *Woman's Role in Economic Development.* New York: St. Martin's Press, 1970.

Ghai, D., et al., eds. *Agrarian Systems and Rural Development.* New York: Holms & Meier, 1979.

Johnston, Bruce F., and Meyer, Anthony J. "Nutrition, Health, and Population in Strategies for Rural Development." *Economic Development and Cultural Change* 26, no. 1 (October 1977).

Paine, Suzanne. "Balanced Development: Maoist Conception and Chinese Practice." *World Development* 4, no. 4 (April 1976).

World Bank. *Rural Development.* Sector Policy Paper. Washington. D.C., February 1975.

Yudelman, Montague. "Integrated Rural Development Projects: The Bank's Experience." *Finance and Development* 14, no. 1 (March 1977).

3. Agricultural Development

Berry, R. A., and Cline, W. *Agrarian Structure and Productivity in Developing Countries.* Baltimore and London: Johns Hopkins University Press, 1979.

Clayton, E. S. "A Note on Farm Mechanisation and Employment in Developing Countries." *International Labor Review* 110, no. 1 (July 1974).

Griffin, Keith. *The Political Economy of Agrarian Change.* Cambridge, Mass.: Harvard University Press, 1974.

Hayami, Yujiro, and Ruttan, Vernon W. *Agricultural Development: An International Perspective.* Baltimore: Johns Hopkins University Press, 1971.

Hunter, Guy. *Modernizing Peasant Societies: A Comparative Study in Asia and Africa.* New York and London: Oxford University Press for the Institute of Race Relations, 1969.

Mellor, John W. *The Economics of Agricultural Development.* Ithaca: Cornell University Press, 1966.

Reutlinger, Shlomo. "Malnutrition: A Poverty or a Food Problem." *World Development.* Vol. 5 no. 8 (August 1977).

Schultz, T. W. *Transforming Traditional Agriculture.* New Haven: Yale University Press, 1964.

Schutjer, Wayne A. "Agricultural Development Policy and Demographic Transition." *Journal of Developing Areas* no. 12, no. 3 (April 1978).

Scientific American. "Food and Agriculture." *Scientific American* 235, no. 3 (September 1976).

Simantou, A. "The Role of Developed Countries in World Agricultural Development." *World Development* 5, nos. 5–6 (May/July 1977).

4. Agricultural Credit

Baum, Warren C. "Agricultural Credit and the Small Farmer." *Finance and Development* 13, no. 2 (June 1976).

Donald, Gordon. *Credit for Small Farmers in Developing Countries.* Boulder, Colo.: Westview Press, 1976.

Kato, Yuzuru. "Sources of Loanable Funds of Agricultural Credit Institutions in Asia." *Developing Economies* 10 (1972).

Lele, Uma J. *Role of Credit and Marketing Functions in Agricultural Development.* Washington, D.C.: International Economic Association, September 1972.

9

Education and Development

23. Human Development Issues and Policies: Education*

World Bank Staff

Every individual is born with a collection of abilities and talents. Education, in its many forms, has the potential to help fulfill and apply them. In some societies the economic function of schooling is regarded as minor—since the cultivation of the mind and the spirit, curiosity, contemplation and reasoning have more than economic purposes and justifications. But in the context of this article, it is the role of education in overcoming poverty—increasing incomes, improving health and nutrition, reducing family size—that receives most attention.

A decade or two ago, there was a widespread view that trained people were the key to development. Universal literacy was a political objective in many countries, but money spent on primary schooling was often regarded as diverted from activities that would have contributed more to economic growth. Planners favored the kinds of secondary and higher education that directly met the "manpower requirements" of the modern sector. People who worked with their hands were

thought not to have much need of formal education.

Over the past decade, views have changed substantially. Adequate provision of secondary and higher education and training remains an important priority. But the value of general education at the primary level is now more widely recognized. We now consider some of the evidence that lies behind this change in views, and its implications for development strategy.

Recent Progress

The major educational progress of the past two decades reflects heavy investment by developing countries. Their total public expenditure on education rose in real terms (in 1976 dollars) from about $9 billion in 1960 (2.4 percent of their collective GNP) to $38 billion in 1976 (4.0 percent of GNP). Costs per student vary widely by region—and by type of education (see Table 1). The potential for continued enrollment growth at different levels will, of course, be strongly affected by these costs.

But school attendance in some parts of the world remains low, especially among the poor, in rural areas, and by girls. This is not simply because schools are unavailable—not everyone who has an opportunity for education accepts it. Moreover among those who do

---

* From the *World Development Report, 1980*, Oxford University Press for the World Bank, New York, 1980, pp. 46–53. Team report led by Paul Isenman and including Nicholas Hope, Timothy King, Peter Knight, Akbar Noman, Rupert Pennant-Rea, and Adrian Wood.

255

TABLE 1. Public Expenditures Per Student on Elementary and Higher Education, 1976 (U.S. dollars)

Region	Higher (Post-Secondary) Education	Elementary Education	Ratio of Higher to Elementary Education
Sub-Saharan Africa	3,819	38	100.5
South Asia	117	13	9.0
East Asia	471	54	8.7
Middle East and North Africa	3,106	181	17.2
Latin America and Caribbean	733	91	8.1
Industrialized	2,278	1,157	2.0
USSR and Eastern Europe	957	539	1.8

Note: Figures shown are averages (weighted by enrollment) of costs (in 1976 dollars) in the countries in each region for which data were available.

enroll in developing countries, an average of 40 percent drop out before the fourth year. In Brazil's poor rural Northeast region in 1974, despite an enrollment rate of 46 percent (less than half the national urban average), nearly two-thirds of the students dropped out before the second year—and it is estimated that at most 4 percent completed four years. And the completion statistics conceal the very low quality of some of the schooling provided.

Nonetheless, the very substantial growth in enrollment is a sign of great educational advance. There are several mechanisms through which this has contributed to growth in incomes.

EFFECTS OF EDUCATION ON EARNING POWER

Schooling imparts specific knowledge and develops general reasoning skills (its "cognitive" effects); it also induces changes in beliefs and values, and in attitudes toward work and society ("noncognitive" effects). The relative importance of these is much debated, and poorly understood; both are extremely important.

In the cognitive area, developing a generalized capacity for thinking and learning has been found to be more important than the specific subjects learned. On-the-job training, informal education and vocational training all build on learning abilities acquired earlier. Although literacy and numeracy deteriorate if left unused, the educational experience still generally provides an improved foundation for subsequent learning.

Many of the noncognitive effects of schooling—receptivity to new ideas, competitiveness, and willingness to accept discipline—are directly relevant to productive economic activity. Others—tolerance, self-confidence, social and civic responsibility—are more personal or political in nature, but may also affect individual economic performance.

Some of the evidence on the effects of education rests on attempts to measure attitudes directly. Studies in several countries have shown that "modernity" of outlook toward activities ranging from voting to family planning, saving, and working is more influenced by the level of the individual's schooling than by any other factor. But there are also many studies of the direct effect of schooling on individual productivity and earnings, which are examined here under two heads—those relating to the self-employed and those relating to employees.

The Self-employed

The hypotheses are straightforward: that primary education helps people to obtain and evaluate information about improved techniques and new opportunities, to keep records, and to estimate the returns of past activities and the risks of future ones. More generally, primary schooling is a training in how to learn, an experience in self-discipline and in working for longer-term goals.

Most of the empirical evidence comes from agriculture—studies comparing the productivity, yields and innovative activity of schooled and unschooled farmers. Not all these studies controlled adequately for other influences, particularly wealth; but many did (for example, by including farm size as a proxy for wealth).

The general weight of the evidence (see Table 2) lends strong and consistent support to these hypotheses—and is particularly compelling because the studies measure productivity directly, not through wages. Where the complementary inputs required for improved farming techniques were available, the annual output of a farmer who had completed four years of primary schooling was on average 13.2 percent more than one who had not been to school. As expected, where complementary inputs were not available, the increase in output resulting from additional schooling was on average smaller—but still substantial.

Whether these increases should be regarded as large or small depends on the cost of achieving them. It is thus significant that studies that went on to compare the increase in production resulting from education with the costs of that education (for example, in Korea, Malaysia and Thailand) found rates of return on primary education comparing very favorably with investment in other sectors. It is, of course, impossible to predict which areas will offer scope for improved farming techniques in 10 years' time, when children leave school. In some, effects on farm productivity may be low. But given past progress in agricultural research, it is probable that some places with stagnant technology now will offer greatly improved possibilities. Thus, on growth as well as equity grounds, it would be short-sighted to leave a large part of the next generation of farmers illiterate.

TABLE 2. Farmer Education and Farmer Productivity

Study	Estimated Percentage Increase in Annual Farm Output Due to Four Years of Primary Education Rather Than None
With complementary inputs[a]	
Brazil (Garibaldi), 1970	18.4
Brazil (Resende), 1969	4.0
Brazil (Taquari), 1970	22.1
Brazil (Vicosa), 1969	9.3
Colombia (Chinchina), 1969	−0.8
Colombia (Espinal), 1969	24.4
Kenya, 1971–72	6.9
Malaysia, 1973	20.4
Nepal (wheat), 1968–69	20.4
South Korea, 1973	9.1
Average (unweighted)	13.2
Without complementary inputs	
Brazil (Candelaria), 1970	10.8
Brazil (Conceicao de Castelo), 1969	−3.6
Brazil (Guarani), 1970	6.0
Brazil (Paracatu), 1969	−7.2
Colombia (Malaga), 1969	12.4
Colombia (Moniquira), 1969	12.5
Greece, 1963	25.9
Average (unweighted)	8.1
No information on availability of complementary inputs	
Average of eight studies (unweighted)	6.3

[a] Improved seeds, irrigation, transport to markets and so on.

Employees

The second type of study relates the educational levels of individuals to their wages and salaries. If education affects the capacity to learn, innovate and adapt, its effects should be particularly important for employees doing

TABLE 3. Rates of Return to Education (percentages)

Country Group	Primary	Secondary	Higher	Number of Countries
All developing countries	24.2	15.4	12.3	30
Low income/adult literacy rate under 50 percent[a]	27.3	17.2	12.1	11
Middle income/adult literacy rate over 50 percent	22.2	14.3	12.4	19
Industrialized countries		10.0	9.1	14

Note: In all cases, the figures are "social" rates of return: the costs include forgone earnings (what the students could have earned had they not been in school) as well as both public and private outlays; the benefits are measured by income before tax. (The "private" returns to individuals exclude public costs and taxes, and are usually larger.) The studies refer to various years between 1957 and 1978, mainly in the latter half of the period.

[a] In this sample of 30 developing countries, those countries with low incomes also had literacy rates below 50 percent (at the time the studies were done). All the middle-income countries had literacy rates above 50 percent.

nonroutine or changing tasks. For employees in modern enterprises, primary education also promotes disciplined work habits and responsiveness to further training, as well as offering the advantages of literacy and numeracy.

Studies of the rate of return to education for wage-earners deal mainly with relatively large urban enterprises; but a few have included small businesses and agricultural workers. All find that more schooling leads to higher earnings. And when the extra earnings resulting from primary education are weighed against its costs, high rates of return are consistently found. Similar studies for secondary and higher education find lower, though nonetheless substantial, returns (see Table 3).

INVESTMENT PRIORITIES IN EDUCATION

Primary education is of particular importance in overcoming absolute poverty. But secondary and higher education and training also have major roles to play.

Primary Education

In countries where it is far from universal, the case for increasing the proportion of children who complete primary education is strong. There have been high economic returns in the past. It has been suggested, however, that the rate of return to primary schooling (especially in certain jobs) may decline as the proportion of the labor force with primary education increases. But this may be offset by shifts in the pattern of production toward more skill-intensive goods. In Table 3 the rates of return to primary education in countries with adult literacy rates above 50 percent, while somewhat below those in countries with adult literacy below 50 percent, are still strikingly high. And in the few countries where studies have been done at different periods, rates of return have usually declined, but only mildly.

There are also favorable effects on equity. As primary education becomes more widespread, the additional spending will be increasingly concentrated on backward rural areas, girls, and the poorest urban boys. In general, primary education tends to be redistributive toward the poor (see Table 4). In contrast, public expenditure on secondary and higher education tends to redistribute income from poor to rich, since children of poor parents have comparatively little opportunity to benefit from it.

Primary education of girls has favorable effects on the next generation:

TABLE 4. Public Education Spending Per Household, by Income Group (U.S. dollars)

Income group[a]	Malaysia, 1974[b]		Colombia, 1974[c]	
	Primary	Postsecondary	Primary	University
Poorest 20 percent	135	4	48	1
Richest 20 percent	45	63	9	46

[a] Households ranked by income per person.
[b] Federal costs per household.
[c] Subsidies per household.

In health. Studies in Bangladesh, Kenya and Colombia show that children are less likely to die the more educated their mothers, even allowing for differences in family income.

In nutrition. Among households surveyed in Sao Paulo, Brazil, for any given income level families were better fed the higher the mother's education.

In fertility. Education delays marriage for women, partly by increasing their chances for paid employment; and educated women are more likely to know about, and use, contraceptives.

Finally, it enriches peoples' lives. Many would regard this as sufficient justification for universal primary education, independent of its other benefits.

SECONDARY AND HIGHER EDUCATION

Renewed emphasis on the importance of primary education, and on its high returns relative to secondary and higher education, should not start the pendulum swinging too far in the other direction. High levels of knowledge are necessary for many people who serve the poor, both directly as teachers, health workers and agricultural extension workers, and indirectly as researchers, technicians, managers and administrators. While their skills must be developed to a considerable extent through practical experience and in other ways, there is for some purposes no better or cheaper substitute for the formal disciplines of conventional schooling. Even allowing for doubts about the estimated rates of return to secondary and higher education, and for the existence of some educated unemployment, there are unquestionably severe shortages of skilled people in many developing countries.

More economical ways of producing skilled people need to be found however. Greater reliance on in-career and on-the-job training should be considered, and steps should be taken to reduce the high unit costs of secondary and higher education.

These steps can include reduction in the number of specializations that any one university offers, while there is greater planned differentiation in the specialties offered by universities in a nation, or group of nations. Correspondence courses are another means for decreasing higher educational expenditures. Studies in Kenya, Brazil, South Korea and the Dominican Republic indicate that such courses can effectively teach people in remote areas. Finally, because most postprimary students are from families in a higher than average income bracket, considerably more of the cost could be charged to parents who can pay the charges, while scholarship programs go to students who cannot afford to pay.

The present low cost of secondary and higher education makes it inevitable that in most countries demand for places will exceed supply for the foreseeable future, although some countries, such as South Korea, already have very high enrollment rates. But economic considerations are not the only relevant ones: secondary education often helps in lowering fertility and reducing child mortality (over and above the effects of primary education). All developed countries have found universal free secondary education to be desirable in its own right. The question for developing countries is less "whether" than "when." Higher education clearly also has scientific, cultural and intellectual objectives, as well as economic ones.

IMPLEMENTING EDUCATION FOR THE POOR

The education received by poor children depends on three things. The first is accessibility—are there school places for them within a reasonable distance from home? The second is use—do their parents send them to school, and are they allowed or encouraged to drop out? The third concerns the quality of the education that schools provide.

Accessibility

Financing constraints will often be compounded by difficulties in reaching the poor—distance, low-density populations and poor communications—so that building schools and supplying books, equipment and qualified teachers is a difficult and expensive task. For example, the Nepalese government estimates that it costs more than twice as much to build and equip a school in mountainous regions as it does in the plains; and attracting qualified teachers to remote areas has proved to be extremely difficult.

There is often much that can be accomplished by administrative action with relatively little capital investment. Repetition of classes and early dropout may be the result of excessively high promotion standards. In these circumstances, the flow of students can be accelerated by more automatic promotion—while maintaining quality by correcting some of the causes of repetition or dropout. In

many situations resources can be freed for extending education by raising student-teacher ratios, which are the main determinant of unit costs (given teacher salaries) and are largely determined by class size. Extensive research shows that class size has surprisingly little effect on learning. For example, reducing an elementary-school class from 40 pupils to 15 can be expected to improve average achievement (in a standard test) by only about 5 percentage points. While there may be practical limits to increasing classes much above 50, the research does suggest that, for classes initially below 50, little will be lost if they are increased. It is important to maximize the use of available facilities—by rotating classes, with staggered scheduling and double shifts in areas of high population density. If there are not enough pupils within an acceptable distance from school to fill individual classes, student-teacher ratios and the use of space can be significantly improved by taking new students only in alternate years (as has been done successfully in a project financed by the World Bank in Malaysia) and by teaching more than one grade in a class, as in another World Bank-financed project in El Salvador.

Use

Since most poor parents believe that education would benefit their children—in terms of status and the ability to stand up to officials and merchants, as well as in their incomes—they must have reasons for not sending their children to school where they have the chance. They may question whether they will benefit themselves; they may even regard the school as a threat to their parental authority or traditional way of life; or they may simply believe that social or ethnic barriers are too great, or the quality of the available schooling too low, to make education worth its costs. For poor families, the help of children at home—in animal care, fetching fuel and water, taking care of young children while adults work, and in agricultural work during busy seasons—may conflict with a fixed school schedule. For some families, malnutrition and poor health of children may lead to poor attendance, inattention while in school, repetition of grades and, eventually, dropping out. And there are particular reasons that girls receive less education than boys. Since the mere existence of a school does not automatically mean it is used by all those eligible to attend, special measures may be needed to ensure that the education offered is attractive to the families for whom it is intended.

Changes in school scheduling is one measure. A school calendar may compete unnecessarily with the crop cycle, with important exams held at times when students are most needed by their parents in the fields. Reducing expenditures to the families of poorer students is another measure. Providing free textbooks and uniforms, if required, will reduce the direct costs of school attendance. A further measure is providing information about education so beneficiaries know what to expect. Beyond information and persuasion, compulsory primary education is not uncommon. Using mandatory education laws is sometimes regarded as more unfairly coercive than, say, manipulating costs, since it allows no parental choice at all. However, others argue that compulsory schooling should be viewed more as protecting the rights of children than restricting those of the parents. .

Quality of Education

This is generally low in developing countries, and has been found (for example, in studies undertaken in Thailand, Malaysia and the Philippines) to be lower still for poor and rural pupils. Poor quality public schools may lead the well-to-do to choose private schools for their children, reinforcing social and economic inequality.

Casual observation and small-scale studies have long suggested that poor training of teachers, lack of textbooks, and inadequate school facilities lead to poor educational re-

sults and provide a weak basis for subsequent training. But broad-based evidence to demonstrate the extent of the resulting learning losses has only recently become available—from a large research project, the International Evaluation of Educational Achievement; only four developing countries (Chile, India, Iran and Thailand) were among the 19 countries covered.

While international comparisons of student achievement must be approached gingerly, particularly when different languages or testing styles can affect the results, a clear pattern nonetheless emerges from the study. Differences in average performance of students from the 15 developed countries varied somewhat from subject to subject and country to country; but the differences by and large were small. The developing countries, however, did far less well—in all subjects tested, and at each of the three age levels examined. A typical finding showed the mean score for students in a developing country to be in the bottom 5 to 10 percent of students from a developed country. Some of the handicaps of children in developing countries may be due to lower levels of parental education (which has a substantial impact, particularly in the preschool years) or in some cases to prolonged malnutrition.. But the evidence suggests that they are mainly a reflection of low-quality schooling.

There are a number of promising approaches to improving educational quality in developing countries:

- The curriculum should take into account the linguistic and home backgrounds of students. Materials which are inappropriate only exacerbate tendencies to repeat classes or drop out, particularly for those from poor homes. Whenever possible, subjects should be illustrated with examples that draw on the child's experience.
- The selection and training of teachers should be improved through more training facilities, greater use of in-service training,

and more teachers' guides, advisory services, mass-media programs and bulletins. This takes more resources as well as time, however.

- The design, production and distribution of learning materials should be upgraded. This applies particularly to textbooks, because research indicates that increasing their numbers and availability is the most consistently effective way of raising educational standards. A nationwide textbook project supported by the World Bank in the Philippines significantly increased student learning while increasing costs per student by only 1 percent. When school budgets are squeezed, it is all too easy to cut or defer spending on learning materials. But this is a costly alternative if costs are considered in terms of the education provided rather than simply the expenditures per student in school.

- Properly designed and supported radio projects have potential for improving learning (and in certain cases reducing costs). To take a well-documented example, in Nicaragua regular radio broadcasts achieved dramatic improvements in mathematics for primary students.

Research into these approaches has indicated important potential, but it remains to be seen how much they can improve quality within the constraints of politically feasible budgets. This underlines the importance of finding cheap ways to improve quality if the educational gaps between rich and poor are to be narrowed.

24. Education for Development, Reconsidered*

John Simmons

While education is only one element of the social framework being restructured in the course of economic development, often it is regarded as one of the essential keys for controlling the rate and direction of change within the rest of society. Almost everyone agrees that educational reform is an important priority, but given reforms have often proven ineffective in the face of political and social opposition or subversion. A dilemma has become apparent: educators are expected to take the lead in preparing students for productive, healthy and socially responsible lives, in an environment where typically jobs are scarce, health conditions poor, and social and political structures based on inequitable concentrations of wealth and power. Education may be the key to change, but it sometimes appears to be locked on the other side of the development door.

This article reviews the relationship between education and the achievement of development goals in the world's poorer countries, where peasant farmers and middle class alike have long dreamed of seeing their children attend the university. Citizens at all levels of society have been imbued with the idea that post-primary education is the next generation's passport to a better job, social status for the entire family, and security for themselves in their own old age. For more than 30 years, teachers, education ministries

* From World Development, 7, No. 11/12 (November/December 1979), pp. 1005–1016.

and international civil servants have laboured to make these dreams come true. The extraordinary expansion of school places is a tribute to their efforts. In country after country, education is the only sector in which budget allocations and the construction of new facilities have exceeded the targets of 5-yr plans. In short, there could not be enough investment in formal education. However, the experience of the past 30 years indicates that most education strategies have failed to promote development, if development is conceived primarily as a process for improving the lives of the deprived majority of the world's population. Formal education, which expanded at a fast pace through the 1960s and early 1970s, has usually proved to be expensive, inefficient and inequitable. It no longer holds the same hope for the peasant farmer, the urban middle class or the government planner. That the poor are becoming discouraged is revealed by falling primary-school enrolment rates in countries like Egypt, Nigeria and Pakistan. For the farmer's son or daughter, a little education will no longer guarantee a better job, and a secondary-school degree is usually beyond their means. Scholarships are scarce. The middle class has found that there are not enough university places to go around, or that the bribes required put entry beyond reach. In a few countries that got an early start, the nightmare of rioting students demanding jobs and a new government, or of a third of the school budgets being spent on children who drop out of primary school before reaching the fourth grade has become reality. Moreover, despite the rapid expansion of formal school systems, the number of functionally illiterate will expand to 2 billion in 2000.

Alternatives to formal education have difficulties of their own, but seem to offer special opportunities, particularly for those countries willing to experiment with less traditional approaches to education as part of an overall political commitment to far-reaching social reform.[1]

1. ALTERNATIVES IN EDUCATION

It was long assumed that development was synonymous with the growth of gross national product. As a country's aggregate income increased, the benefits were expected to 'trickle down' to the entire population. Education was expected to contribute significantly to GNP growth, usually by turning out trained managers and skilled workers for a modern industrial sector. Education programmes to fulfill these goals were often based on imitations of programmes in developed countries, with little regard for the distinctive needs of individual developing countries. It has become increasingly evident, however, that when development strategies are intent on maximizing GNP growth, the benefits do not necessarily 'trickle' very far, but rather tend to create a dual economy in which the benefits go to the upper-income elite and urban middle class who are already within the 'developing sector', and in which the majority of the people in the 'undeveloped sector' remain virtually unaffected.[2]

After confronting this trend, observers like Robert McNamara, President of the World Bank, have concluded that 'the poorest countries, then must do everything they can to increase *per capita* income growth, but they must do something else as well. They must fashion ways in which basic human needs can be met *earlier* in the development process'.[3] According to this view, which is now widely accepted by the architects of many international assistance efforts, the ultimate goal of development is to satisfy the real living needs of people: food, safe water, decent shelter, basic health care and basic education. To meet such goals, in a world of scarcity, means focusing on those people whose needs have not even begun to be met, the poorest 40% of the world's population.

Strategies for meeting these development goals put heavy emphasis on raising the productivity of the poor so that they can better meet their own needs, and on redesigning public services to effectively improve their living standards—beginning with the very poorest. Both tacks involve education. A multitude of questions concerning the links between education and development remain to be answered, yet their importance can hardly be doubted.

As a first step towards looking at the lessons learned so far, it is important to distinguish among several different types of education. *Formal education* or *schooling* describes the learning that takes place in schools, uses the traditional academic curriculum and prepares students mainly for urban, modern sector lifestyles, despite the fact that few Third World citizens will be able to enjoy such lifestyles in the foreseeable future.

Learning takes place not only inside the school, however, but also at home, on the street and on the job. This is 'learning by doing', or *informal education*. Disciplines like medicine have long recognized the importance of informal, on-the-job training. The importance of informal learning is also implicitly recognized by most employers, who prefer to hire workers with relevant job experience on the assumption that informal learning in the course of their previous work will have made them more skillful.

Non-formal education is organized learning outside the normal school curriculum. This category includes agricultural training programmes, evening adult literacy classes, radio and mass media campaigns, and vocational training programmes. Compared to bureaucratically dominated formal education, non-formal education has both the proximity and flexibility to respond to employer and community needs, at least in theory.

Education for self-reliance, often called 'problem-posing' education, teaches groups of people how to study together and become aware of the political and economic determinants of their poverty. They learn how to organize themselves to improve their own circumstances, and in that process they learn to build roads, manage water distribution, reduce neighbourhood crime and grow more food. Individual groups select members to be trained as paramedics and teachers. Through cooperative saving, they reduce their dependence on moneylenders. Although Paulo Freire, Julius Nyerere, Saul Alinsky and Adam Curle have popularized the concept recently, Mahatma Gandhi and others preceded them. Mao Tse-tung gave the approach its most comprehensive elaboration and application.[4] Education for self-reliance is a special type of non-formal education.

By contrast with other types of non-formal education, the emphasis here is on full participation of the 'students' in planning and managing, in selecting priorities and projects, and in providing resources. The fundamental principle of education for self-reliance was concisely expressed by Julius Nyerere: 'people cannot be developed, they can only develop themselves. Adult education is the key to development of free men and free societies. . . . Its function is to help men to think for themselves, to make their own decisions, and to execute those decisions for themselves'.[5]

2. FORMAL EDUCATION

Despite sharp increases in education budgets and school enrolments, it has become increasingly evident that formal education in most developing countries has not been meeting the needs of most of the people. Three characteristic problems have appeared:

1. Costly inefficiencies within schools and within educational systems as a whole;
2. Mismatches between what the schools are teaching and what the vast majority of young people need to learn in order to get jobs, raise children, and become effective citizens; and
3. Continuing inadequacy of educational opportunities for the rural and urban poor.

The nature of these problems is graphically demonstrated by a few facts from Pakistan, where:

Unemployment rates appear to be significantly higher among the educated than among the uneducated;

Forty percent of vocational school graduates are unemployed for 2–4 yr after graduation;

Twenty-seven percent of adults tell the census-taker that they can read, but of these, only half (that is, 14% of the entire population) can read and understand a newspaper;

Despite increasing total enrolments, the percentage of each age group which completes primary school is declining;

Nine out of 10 pharmacy graduates leave the country;

Despite the fact that there is only one doctor per 24,200 rural people, an estimated 72% of new MDs are allowed to emigrate. The shortage of nurses is even more dire.[6]

Similar problems are visible in countries as economically and educationally different from Pakistan as Brazil, Tunisia and Liberia, to mention just a few. Cuba and China are the exceptions.

On the global level, aggregate data present a similar picture. Despite rapidly growing enrolments and declining illiteracy rates in most countries, the absolute numbers of children who do not attend school, and of adults who cannot read, are rising simultaneously; in other words, the 'educational gap' is widening. Figure 1 projects the number of adult illiterates for the rest of this century. Optimistically assuming that school enrolments will continue to grow as rapidly as they did in the 1960s, when 9 million new school places were created each year, the high variant projection shows that the number of illiterates will increase until the year 2000, when assumed rates of population and school enrolment

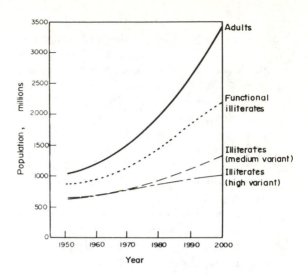

Figure 1. Illiteracy projections.

equalize. The medium variant path is based on a more realistic expansion rate of only 6 million new school places per year, and shows a correspondingly higher number of illiterates.

These projections optimistically assume that all primary school graduates will be literate, when in fact probably less than half of present primary-school graduates are able to read a newspaper (about 30% in Pakistan[7]). The 'functional illiteracy' projection assumes that half of all primary-school graduates are literate, and uses the high variant expansion rate. If the assumption proves correct, between 1975 and 2000 the number of functional illiterates will double, from about 1 to about 2 billion. These projections demonstrate that even if formal education *were* relevant to the needs of most people in developing countries, additional programmes would still be required to fill the educational needs of those who cannot be incorporated into formal education systems due to sheer quantitative limits.

When western experts working in developing countries in the early 1960s stated that economic growth in these countries would be limited by the lack of middle- and high-level manpower, massive efforts were made to reform academic education and supply vocational training. Comprehensive secondary schools and technical institutes proliferated, often with the support of the World Bank and other international assistance agencies. Shortages in middle-level manpower were projected for decades, and the demand for university graduates was not expected to be satisfied in the planners' lifetimes.

However, these predictions of manpower needs proved to be naive. Jobs were not created fast enough to absorb the graduates of middle- and higher-level institutions. Whereas the planners has assumed that jobs could be filled by recent graduates, most positions actually required workers with experience. Many education and manpower analysts failed to realize that a projected demand for 10,000 mechanics did not necessarily mean that employers would actually hire 10,000 vocational-school graduates but rather that there might be 1000 opportunities for unschooled apprentices, 2000 for graduates with or without technical schooling, and 7000 for mechanics with 2–5 yr of previous work experience.

To what extent have the increased numbers of graduates with technical training or post-secondary academic education relieved the manpower constraints on economic growth? The evidence is mixed. In newly independent countries of Africa and Asia, such schooling and training at first helped prepare local citizens to replace the Europeans who left as a result of independence. However, once these jobs were filled, the demand for many of those skills declined. The result was an over-supply of educated workers. Educator-managed institutes and schools had little contact with the labour market. Predictably, their graduates have suffered long unemployment, or were forced to find jobs unrelated to their technical training.

While there is no reason to believe that people cannot be educated in ways which promote economic growth—indeed, examples of success will be given later—formal education seems to have done more to exacerbate than to cure unemployment. The persistently high rate of unemployment among the edu-

cated indicates that developing countries are not currently suffering from shortages of educated manpower but, on the contrary, that they have made some costly over investments in higher levels of education.[8]

As for the impact of schooling on the distribution of income, data have only recently become available but is far from encouraging. The costs of education tend to keep the poor out, and the data consistently show that children of upper-income groups receive more schooling than low-income children. In Tunisia, the number of students receiving higher education whose fathers are of high socio-economic status is 8.8-times higher than one would expect from the proportion of such students in the population.[9] At the University of Karachi in Pakistan, students from upper-income families are over represented by 27 times.[10]

Research conducted in India, Colombia and Brazil leads to the same sobering conclusion: that educational investment has served to increase rather than decrease income inequality.[11] The combined incidence of tax policies and expenditures for education have not only failed to counter disequalizing forces, but in fact support and reinforce them.

Essentially, the system of examinations and school fees excludes all but a tiny proportion of the 40–80% of the population living near the subsistence level from the opportunity to get the credentials of secondary and higher education usually required for upper-income jobs. It is becoming apparent that the slogan of educational opportunity is little more than a mechanism for social control. The 'meritocratic' educational process confirms the status quo, socializing the poor to accept their inferior status. Educators in developing countries have learned what an American educator argued in the 1850s about the importance of introducing the common primary school in Massachusetts. Schools would enable the poor 'to look upon the distinctions of society without envy. . . . They would be taught that they are open to him as well as others and to respect them for this reason'.[12] Schools would promote social control.

Much formal education has been effective for development as defined by the priorities set by the national elites, but it has not been effective for the poor majority, when measured by its effects on improving real incomes and income distribution, accomplishing land reform, or sharing political power.

Even when criteria of efficiency rather than equity are applied to programmes of traditional education, the results have proved disappointing. Recent research suggests that schooling has not been as effective in promoting cognitive achievement, measured by tests, as had been expected. Evidence to this effect in Europe and the United States in the 1960s is paralleled by recent studies in a limited number of developing countries including Brazil, Chile, India, Kenya and Tunisia.[13] Conversely, factors unrelated to schooling, such as parental characteristics, nutrition and peer group experience, have proven to be more important for predicting achievement scores than anyone had anticipated. Expenditure per pupil is usually insignificant in determining differences in test scores. Students in classes of 25 learn no faster than those in classes of 40. Teacher training courses of 2 or 3 years appear to have no more effect on student learning than courses of 1 year. There are some indications that length of teaching experience matters, but the effect is weak. Students who have access to well-stocked libraries and well-equipped laboratories in school do little better than students with poor facilities.

Such information has strong implications for the allocation of scarce education resources, particularly in view of implicit trade-offs among investments in different levels of education. At present, a disproportionate share of public education expenditures goes to higher levels of education. In Pakistan, for example, enrolments and expenditures at different levels are inversely related (see Fig. 2). Nevertheless, trade-offs among levels and types of education have not been seriously considered because it was assumed that the benefits of formal educational investment were unassailable. New evidence regarding the relative ineffectiveness of traditional edu-

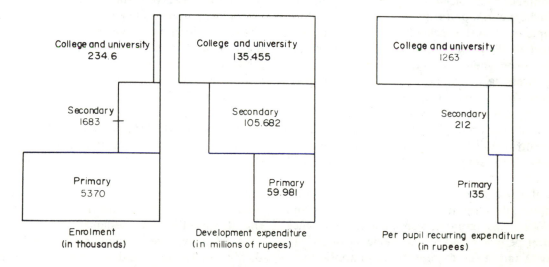

Source: Enrolment and expenditure figures supplied by the Planning Commission Government of Pakistan (1976).
Note: Secondary does not include teacher and technical education.

Figure 2. Pakistan educational pyramids, 1975–1976.

cational inputs, plus pressures within the poorest developing countries to reallocate funds from education to other priorities, make re-examination of old assumptions imperative.

3. NON-FORMAL EDUCATION AND EDUCATION FOR SELF-RELIANCE

Growing awareness of the inadequacy of formal education has led some developing countries to experiment more seriously with some non-traditional approaches which come under the categories of non-formal education and education for self-reliance. In Pakistan, for example, the government is putting increasing faith in the ability of people in the villages and neighbourhoods to study and resolve their own problems. A project in one province has 80 villages selecting their own teachers, managing their school affairs and maintaining the buildings. When faced with the lack of space, several village school councils decided to use their mosques, which were empty most of the day. Teacher attendance has improved as villagers, rather than distant supervisors, have assumed responsibility for selecting of teachers and monitoring their attendance. Students clean the school and maintain the grounds. Top-level support is also important: the government encouraged self-help efforts by stressing the motto 'power to the people.' Even token financial support by the government provides crucial signals to villagers.

Four hundred villages throughout Pakistan are involved in another project which encourages village-level planning and management of community development efforts, including health and education. In contrast to the community development efforts of the 1950s and 1960s, this approach minimizes assistance from people who are not members of the village, and seeks to prevent the imposition of objectives and programmes designed by outsiders.

The underlying assumption of all such projects is that if new approaches to education are to succeed in meeting the real needs of the majority of the people in developing countries, these efforts must focus on groups outside the traditional student population. In this sense, the two groups for which educational investment appears most cost-effective are adults and children under 5 yr of age.

Programmes of self-reliance for low-income adults emphasize three components: developing a critical awareness of the causes and consequences of their poverty through small group discussions, learning the skills of organization and leadership, and extending productive skills. This process encourages peasants to face their problems instead of passively accepting them, in the belief that as fatalism is replaced by hope, real progress can begin. As Paulo Freire wrote after working with the *conscientizacao* approach in Brazil, 'The peasant begins to get courage to overcome his dependence when he realizes that he is dependent. Until then, he goes along with the boss and says, "What can I do? I am only a peasant".'[14] But once people comprehend their situation as an historical reality susceptible to transformation through their own control, Freire observed, they then seek out specific information and begin to apply new skills.

Freire's method, developed while he was the coordinator of the national literacy programme in Brazil, is worth describing.[15] Freire visited the countryside and asked villagers to describe their lives for him, to present their own versions of why things were the way they were. Frequently, the initial response was fatalistic, but Freire persisted in bringing out the contradictions which the respondants themselves had exposed. For example, one group of villagers told how poor their harvest was. When Freire asked why, they replied that it was, 'Because the land is tired.' Freire then asked why some land seemed very productive while other land was not, eliciting the information that rich farmers had fertilizer while the villagers did not. Freire further inquired why that was the case. In the end, a new perspective was formed. As a result the villagers learned to devise alternative ways of analysing and attacking what had always seemed to be insurmountable problems, and finally began organizing to improve their conditions.

The second priority group is pre-school children, from infancy to age 6. Educational psychologists now believe that the single most important influence on school performance is not budget size, class size, teacher experience or training, or physical facilities, but rather the personal characteristics of children at the time they enter school. About half the IQ measured at age 16 has already been developed by age 4. While nutrition and other health conditions are very important, psychologists have found that '...A child's experiences with his adult caretaker during the first 24 months of life are major determinants of the quality of his motivation, expectancy of success, and cognitive abilities during the school years'.[16] Consequently the improvement of a child's early environment—both physical and psychological—appears to be a cost-effective means of enhancing future learning potential.

Because children can be reached primarily through their parents, the strategic priorities of reaching adults and younger children mesh. Adults education can therefore become an effective channel for teaching parents the importance of early learning, about child-rearing practices and about better health and nutrition for children. Pilot projects of this sort are underway in Mauritius, Colombia and Tunisia.

Can such a strategy be implemented on more than an experimental basis? In many countries, social factors have crippled attempts at more widespread educational reform. Is adult education for self-reliance any different, or is it too predicated on political and economic change? The answer to this question is far from simple, for the experience has been mixed. Adult education which stresses participation and self-reliance has been successful under a number of circumstances, but mostly on a relatively small scale. Examples include the Comilla Project in Bangladesh,

the Community Development Programme in India, the Rural Reconstruction Movement in the Philippines and the Cooperative Education System in Tanzania.

In China, on the other hand, where there has been extraordinary political commitment to social reordering, educational reform has been achieved on a massive scale. Although the Chinese acknowledge problems in their education, health and rural development programmes, their efforts in each of these fields come closest to the World Bank's descriptions of ideal development programmes.[17] In China, the school curriculum is relevant to the population's real needs, 10 yr of schooling are almost universally available, and there is a university selection process that minimizes discrimination against the poor. Moreover, all these goals have been attained at low cost within 20 yr. Even countries with five times China's *per capita* income of $250 have not achieved these results.

Case studies from the countries of Sri Lanka, Columbia, China and Senegal illustrate the wide range of forms which education for self-reliance can take.

(a) Sri Lanka: Community Education for Self-reliance

The Sarvodaya Shramadana Movement, founded in 1958, is now the largest non-governmental organization in Sri Lanka.[18] It combines the country's traditional Buddhist social values with local economic development and the provision of basic services for women, children and youth. There is heavy emphasis on full community participation and on a self-reliant approach to development. 'Shramadana' (the mutual sharing of labour) is used both to educate people about their capacity to improve their own standards of living, and to effectively develop the actual physical infrastructure as well. The Sarvodaya organization provides local villages with the skills needed to utilize the resources available, trains community workers drawn from the villages, helps communities form into functional groups, aids in relief from debt, promotes cooperative marketing, launches cottage industries, creates agricultural farms for unemployed youth and supports educational activities ranging from human resources training to instruction about the various available government services.

Sarvodaya has special programmes to meet basic nutritional needs for children up to 6 yr old, as well as for pregnant and nursing mothers. A community kitchen programme was begun in 1973, and by 1976, 450 kitchens were providing over 1 million meals a year—with most of the food being provided by the participants. Malnutrition is viewed not as the result of an insufficient food supply, but rather as the product of inadequate knowledge about nutrition, improper cooking habits, improper diet of infants, children and mothers, illnesses and unequal distribution of existing food supplies. Once nutrition needs are perceived in this light, they can then be approached through self-reliant community educational activities.

When the national school entry age was raised from 5 to 7 in 1972, Sarvodaya began a pre-school education programme which gave special attention to child development needs—such as nutrition, health, love and protection—plus educational psychology. The schools are run by mothers' groups, with one woman selected by the group to attend a Sarvodaya training centre. In 1976, there were 150 pre-schools in operation, with approval, and in some cases funding by government education authorities.

Other programmes include day-care centres for children of working mothers, an extremely popular library service and an extensive health programme. As in the pre-school and community kitchen programmes, the mothers in the community nominate a health worker trainee who takes a 6-month training course before she returns to organize health activities.

Activities of Sarvodaya projects are financed within the communities wherever possible. In poorer villages, financial assistance is provided by the Movement. The Sarvodaya Movement itself was totally self-financed for its first 10 yr, but is now assisted by local and foreign contributions. Sarvodaya expects to become financially self-reliant again by 1985, through the expansion of profitable enterprises.

(b) Colombia: Reaching the Poor by Radio

Mass media campaigns show how low-level modern technology can be adapted to the needs of the rural poor, and can educate large numbers of adults. Like all approaches, it must be used with care to ensure that the chosen media are understood by the poor; that the language, accent and vocabulary are appropriate; that the message is suited to the needs of the rural poor; that the poor have access to the media; and that they are attracted to the message.

The most cost-effective approaches are often based on radio.[19] One highly successful radio campaign is directed by Acción Cultural Popular (ACPO) in Colombia, which runs the country's largest radio network and broadcasts educational programmes to an audience in the hundreds of thousands. The 'radio schools' alone have enrolments of up to 240,000 students and a write-in survey attracted 97,000 responses. In addition to radio, ACPO also uses a weekly newspaper, textbooks, book series, all of which have coordinated contents. Moreover, ACPO has involved local auxiliaries and parish organizations in its programmes, and also coordinates its activities with several national agencies involved in rural development.

Despite its large and still growing budget ($4 million in 1972), ACPO is self-supporting on the basis of earnings from radio advertising and commercial work done by its publishing house. ACPO has a full-time staff of over 300, about 200 field workers who receive small stipends, and more than 20,000 unpaid volunteers. The radio network broadcasts 19 hr/day, including 6 hr/day of structured courses, plus news and various programmes of informal education (practical advice on agriculture and the home, for example). Programmes are oriented to an audience with little or no formal schooling. The language is simple and the general content is relevant to all rural inhabitants.

ACPO demonstrates the possibilities of mass campaigns for reaching large numbers of adults with relevant materials at low cost and with maximum flexibility. Evaluative studies show that ACPO has brought about significant improvements in literacy, general knowledge, participation in community affairs, and behaviour in areas such as child vaccination and nutrition. ACPO's experience highlights the importance of multimedia coordination: radio plus printed matter plus personal contact. It also demonstrates the feasibility and the need for mobilizing large-scale local and voluntary efforts behind a mass educational programme. ACPO's emphasis on motivation and attitude formation is believed to have contributed even more to the programme's broad impact than has the specific information provided. That information, in turn, could be effectively assimilated because it was based on real-life needs, instead of duplicating formal school curriculum. Maintaining a large degree of flexibility allowed ACPO to respond to feedback through research and criticism, and to gear programming to the needs of its target group of small landholders.

(c) China: Barefoot Doctors

A well-known example of how education can be adopted to meet basic health needs is the training of over 1 million 'barefoot doctors' in China since the Cultural Revolution in 1966.[20] Even before the Revolution, Mao Tse-tung had issued guidelines for health care: it should serve the needs of the people, stress prevention, combine western and traditional medicine, and be coordinated into mass medical education campaigns, the barefoot doctors are ordinary peasants, chosen by their communities to receive paramedical training. They provide basic health and medical care at the local level in a country where even a rapid increase in the number of medical schools was unable to fill the demand for health personnel on the scale required for a population of 850 million people.

Barefoot doctors are chosen by their peers on the basis of their interest in helping others, as well as for their desire to study medicine or science. They are initially trained in the commune's medical facilities, or in 1–3 month courses in the hospitals and medical schools of nearby cities or towns. Their training emphasizes the need to maintain ties to their own people, and not to become part of a special elite as is the case in so many other countries. This first stage of medical education includes first aid, diagnosis and treatment of common ailments, giving injections and some common drugs, and acupuncture. The programme enables trainees to become part-time health workers who handle up to 85% of the requests for care. The barefoot doctors also begin assisting and observing trained physicians, gradually assume further responsibility for family planning and vaccination programmes, and later study primary medical care and post-illness follow-up, plus more about diagnosis and referral. After 2 yr, these 'barefoot doctors' have a broad spectrum of training in medicine and public health training. With further study and training, some will eventually become professional physicians.

In a relatively short period of time, China has been able to significantly upgrade its health care capacities with a non-traditional system of health education based on wide-scale non-professional training geared to community needs. By contrast, more typical medical training—highly selective and highly professional—would have produced relatively small numbers of doctors who would have lacked close ties to the needs of China's communities. Not only has the Chinese medical system been able to respond far better to the needs of hundreds of millions of rural people, but a solid foundation for the development of more extensive medical services and better trained personnel has been formed. Furthermore, this has been achieved not as a small pilot project, whose results might not be broadly replicable, but as a nation-wide programme which has actually trained over 1 million new health workers spread across the largest country in the world.

A crucial factor in the programme's success, of course, is China's exceptional political situation, which allowed the commitment to better health care to be implemented without opposition from self-protective groups or professional associations with interests in traditional approaches. Countries without as strong a commitment to overcoming poverty have often tried to implement positive programmes of education for self-reliance, only to have them flounder. *Animation rurale* in Senegal provides such an example.

(d) Building Local Initiative

The *animation rurale* programme in Senegal began in 1959, using a model developed in Morocco.[21] The programme was aimed at 'mobilizing the rural masses', in the hope of reorienting their attitudes and their agricultural methods. Villagers chose representatives from their own communities to be trained outside the village as *animateurs*. The *animateurs* then took extensive courses on civics, cooperative management, and agriculture and animal husbandry before returning to organize their fellow villagers, teach them what they had learned and put these techniques into practice. The *animateurs* returned periodically to the training centres for 4- or 5-day consultation and training sessions. They served both as local leaders for grassroots development, and

as liaisons with outside sources of technical and material assistance.

By 1967, 56 training centres were in operation and 7,000 *animateurs* were in action. But a major weakness had developed. Because *animation rurale* did not follow up the enthusiasm it had generated, failing to coordinate its efforts with various support organizations which could have provided technical advice and practical help, it fell prey to rivalry and competition. The central government of Senegal reorganized its rural development activities and *amination rurale* was pushed aside as a victim of 'rival bureaucratic aggressions'. In 1970, the remnants of *animation* were detached from the Ministry of Rural Economy and reorganized as *promotion humaine*, a cultural and educational programme under the Ministry of Youth and Sport. *Animation rurale* suffered from a lack of resources and a lack of coordination, both internally and in its relations with other rural development activities. Moreover, the efforts of local farmers and *animateurs* were often no match for powerful traditional local leaders. *Animation* is a prime example of the pitfalls that await programmes undertaken without adequate planning or top-level support.

At the same time, the 10 yr since its demise have also exposed the more subtle long-term potential of the participatory approach. It now appears that both the impetus given to local communities and the training of non-traditional leaders have had a slow but very significant impact on the ability of villages to undertake self-initiated development projects and to respond to externally generated opportunities.

4. IMPLICATIONS FOR EDUCATIONAL REFORM

Educational reform has been a popular endeavor throughout the developing world and, in fact, most developing countries have educational reform commissions at work. But while the need for change is clear, experience shows that educational reforms of a genuinely far-reaching nature encounter major obstacles whenever attempts are made to implement them.[22] Reforms must be designed in light of the various practical considerations which will largely determine their actual success or failure. All too often, however, the lack of participation by the intended beneficiaries, along with the political clout of those with vested interests in the status quo, combine to block effective educational reform. Unless the beneficiaries of these changes are themselves enabled to help plan and implement reforms, and until constituencies are formed to counter the inertia of the status quo, the existing inefficiencies and inequities of the educational systems in developing countries are bound to perpetuate themselves.

Some of the problems faced by advocates of reform can be seen in the debate over the expansion of non-formal education. In practice, programmes of non-formal education have often failed because they conflict with perceived interests of both the elites and the poorer classes of many developing countries, support from educational experts and international organizations notwithstanding.

For example, experts frequently urge the expansion of non-formal education as one response to the low employer demand for the kind of training that traditional educational systems supply. In 1974, World Bank authors concluded that formal 'educational systems have been irrelevant to the needs of developing countries for the past two decades', and urged that non-formal and basic vocational education be given precedence over the expansion of formal education at the secondary and university levels.[23] But ministers of education have been cool to such suggestions.

Why? The short answer is that the expansion of non-formal education will cut into the funds allocated for formal education, which is more prestigious and in greater demand. But there is another equally serious problem, which would arise even if all such programmes

were funded by external sources. The expansion of vocational and non-formal education reinforces a dual system of education, with one part of the system training students for manual labour and the other for mental labour; one part for mainly traditional rural employment, the other for modern urban jobs. Unwittingly, the non-formal strategy may work against the poor by destining poorer children for manual jobs from an early age, while reinforcing the social and political status quo—except where the reduction of poverty is the highest national priority, as in China and Cuba.

Each of the examples of education for self-reliance points to other difficulties, fundamentally connected with the difficulties of overall social change. Educational systems are shaped by the political and economic environment. Attempts to improve educational institutions without regard for the broader institutional setting are either shelved or subverted. 'Education, being a sub-system of society, necessarily reflects the main features of that society. It would be vain to hope for a rational, human education in an unjust society.'[24] This reality, more than a lack of knowledge or the limitations of educational planning, constitutes the major reason why educational systems have been so slow to change, as an eminent group of educational planning experts agreed at a recent seminar.[25] As the dependence of education on the surrounding social environment has become more and more clear, 'the mood has swung from the almost euphoric conception of education as the Great Equalizer to that of education as the Great Sieve that sorts and certifies people for their (predetermined) slot in society'.[26] In short, it is difficult to avoid the conclusion that for non-socialist developing countries, further investments of the traditional kind in most aspects of existing educational systems would work *against* the interests of the poor, not for them.

Yet we cannot responsibly conclude that efforts to improve education in Third World countries are futile. The very real difficulties call not for resignation or 'benign neglect', but for renewed and more informed attack. As this paper has argued, the task that lies ahead is two-fold.

Continued efforts to expand and improve existing educational programmes are essential. Countries that are pursuing a development strategy of 'growth with redistribution' need to shift their investment to lower educational levels to better serve the needs of the poor. For countries where a significant proportion of their population lives below subsistence levels, the shift of educational resources to agricultural training could improve employment, efficiency and equity. Vocational training for the modernizing industrial sector must be institutionally tied to the organizations which will employ graduating trainees, to maximize the efficiency of investment in training. Sustained efforts are required to make both the selection of incoming students and the placement of outgoing students more equitable. Curriculum reform and educational innovation need continued support, for although they cannot provide the ultimate solutions to the educational dilemma, each small success means real benefits to the people involved.

But many more people must be reached than can soon, if ever, be enrolled in formal and even non-formal education programmes. New priority must also be given to these citizens for whom full-fledged educational opportunities will not be available. Even if targets of universal education and universal literacy are someday met, a prospect which our projections cast some doubt upon, the educational needs of existing and future generations can be reached only by adopting new strategies. This means adult education linked to other components of community development, and effective use of informal education. Education should be regarded not as a separate component, but rather as an integral element of cooperative, self-reliant activities designed to involve the rural and urban poor in decisions which affect them. Educational

strategies must be part of an overall development strategy, just as an overall development strategy must include the role of education.

These two educational challenges—the improvement of existing programmes, and the development of programmes capable of reaching the most deprived—as well as their possible solutions, are as much political as educational, as preceding studies so clearly demonstrate. The political obstacles come from many sources: from those with a personal stake in existing educational institutions and systems of accreditation, from the elites who rely on the educational system to provide acceptable indicators of social status, from middle-class parents and children who see educational achievement as the road to a 'modern' standard of living like that enjoyed by the developed world, and from the heterogeneous poor, for whom education may symbolize the only hope for the future and who can ill afford any loss of hope.

Thus, even if pilot projects in education for self-reliance could clearly demonstrate real gains, in terms of educational attainment and the satisfaction of real development needs at cost levels that would allow wide-scale replication, substantial political opposition to programmes based on these new models would still remain in most Third-World countries. With lingering memories of the colonialist era, many such nations are reluctant to endorse any forms of organization and technology which appear 'second rate', especially at the prodding of the developed world. Yet it is clear that the poorer countries cannot and probably ought not try to copy the educational systems associated with the developed countries, and that their efforts to do so in Third-World contexts are counterproductive.

Only a few countries have freed themselves from this dilemma. These are the nations which, through political and economic reform, have made strong commitments to progressive social change, have purged themselves of the developmental and educational assumptions which are still accepted in most countries, and have put a trust in the ability of people to determine and meet their own needs. Other countries, if they seek genuine development and expect education to play a key role, will do the same.

1. For the evidence used to support these points, see John Simmons, *The Education Dilemma; Policy Issues in Developing Countries for the 1980s* (Oxford: Pergamon Press, 1979); John Simmons, *Lessons from Education Reform* (Washington, D.C.: World Bank, 1979); F. Champion Ward, *Education and Development Reconsidered: The Bellagio Conference Papers* (New York: Praeger, 1974); 'Special Issue on Education and Development', *Havard Education Review* (May 1975); Martin Carnoy, *Education as Cultural Imperialism* (New York: McKay, 1974); Rolland G. Paulston, *Changing Educational Systems* (Washington, D.C.: World Bank, 1979); and Edgar Faure *et al.*, *Learning to Be* (Paris: UNESCO Harrap, 1972).

2. Hollis Chenery *et al.*, *Redistribution with Growth* (Oxford: Oxford University Press, 1974).

3. Robert McNamara, *Address to the Board of Governors* (Washington, D.C.: World Bank, 1977), pp. 22–23 (emphasis added).

4. Gerald Tannebaum and John Simmons, *The Open Door: Lessons from Education Reform in China* (Washington, D.C.: World Bank, 1977).

5. Julius K. Nyerere, quoted in *Literacy Discussion* VII, Vol. 4 (Winter 1976–1977), pp. iv, ix.

6. John Simmons, 'Can education promote development', *Finance and Development* (March 1978).

7. *Ibid.*

8. See Thomas Balogh and Paul Streeten, 'The coefficient of ignorance', *The Bulletin of the Oxford University Institute of Economics and Statistics* (1963), for an early analysis of a persistent problem.

9. John Simmons, *The Education Dilemma, op. cit.*, Chap. 2.

10. Simmons, 'Can education promote development', *op. cit.*

11. See Asim Dasgupta, 'Education, income distribution and capital accumulation', (Washington, D.C.: World Bank, 1974); Jagdish Bhagwati, 'Education, class structure and income equality', *World Development*, Vol. 1, No. 5 (1973); Jean Pierre Jallade, 'Public expenditures on education and income distribution in Colombia', mimeograph (Washington, D.C.: The World Bank, 1972); and Jean Pierre Jallade, 'Basic education and income inequality in Brazil: the long-term view', mimeograph (Washington, D.C.: The World Bank, 1977).

12. *American Annals of Education and Instruction*, quoted by Merle Curti, *The Social Ideas of American Education*, (Totowa, New Jersey: Littlefield Adams, 1968), p. 93.

13. John Simmons, 'The effectiveness of schooling in promoting learning: a review of the research', Working Paper No. 200 (Washington, D.C.: World Bank, 1974); and Ernesto Schiefelbein and John Simmons, *The Determinants of School Achievement in Developing Countries: A Review of the Research* (Ottawa: International Development Research Centre, 1979).

14. Paulo Freire, *Pedagogy of the Oppressed* (New York: Seabury Press, 1968), p. 47.

15. Based on the account of an ex-priest who worked with Freire, in James Farmer, 'Adult education for transiting', in Stanley Grabowski (ed.), *Paulo Freire: A Revolutionary Dilemma for the Adult Educator* (Syracuse, N.Y.: Syracuse University Press, 1972), p. 1.

16. Professor Jerome Kagan, Harvard University, quoted by M. Selowsky, 'Pre-school age investment in human capital', in J. Simmons, *The Education Dilemma, op. cit.*

17. See the sector papers *Education* (June 1979), *Health* (March 1975), especially pp. 39–40 for discussion of the Chinese model, and *Rural Development* (February 1975).

18. Based on A. T. Ariyaratne, 'A people's movement for self-reliance in Sri Lanka', *Carnets de l'Enfance*, Vol. 39 (1977).

19. See Dean Jamison, Peter Spain and Emile McAnamy *Radio for Education and Development: Case Study* (Washington, D.C.: World Bank, 1977).

20. Based on Gerald Tannenbaum and John Simmons, *The Open Door: Educational Reform in China* mimeograph (Washington, D.C.: World Bank, 1977), pp. 106–111.

21. Based on Philip Coombs and Manzoor Ahmed, *Attacking Rural Poverty: How Non-formal Education Can Help* (Baltimore: Johns Hopkins University Press, 1974), pp. 71–74.

22. For review of the experience of nine countries with major educational reforms, see John Simmons, *Lessons from Educational Reform* (Washington, D.C.: The World Bank, 1979).

23. *Education Sector Working Paper* (Washington, D.C.: World Bank, 1974), p. 3.

24. Edgar Faure *et al., Learning to Be* (Paris: UNESCO, 1972), p. 60.

25. International Institute of Educational Planning, Seminar on New Tasks in Educational Plan-ning, Arc et Senens, France (June 1977).

26. Torsten Husen, 'Problems of securing equal access to higher education: the dilemma between equality and excellence', *Higher Education*, Vol. 5 (1976), p. 411.

25. Financing Education for Income Distribution*

Jean-Pierre Jallade

The belief that the provision of wider opportunities for education has a beneficial effect on the distribution of income holds a strong popular appeal. But in fact, the increased investment in education that has taken place in the Western world over the past decade does not seem to have had the expected impact on the incomes of the poor. The distribution of income in the United States, for instance, has remained practically constant since World War II, in spite of obvious and enormous progress in the distribution of educational opportunities. In other industrialized countries, there seems to be practically no relationship between education inequality and income inequality. In the developing world, the Latin American scene is not very encouraging either—Mexico has experienced a worsening in its income distribution, while achieving considerable progress in the education sphere between 1960 and 1970.

What are the reasons for the seeming lack of impact of expanded education systems on income inequality? Nobody denies that education does provide individuals with extra earning power, but the fact is that the numerous earning functions computed around the world have, so far, failed to give a clear picture of how much extra earning power it is directly responsible for. Controversies over the respective importance of socioeconomic background, native ability, and education on the determination of incomes will be with us for some time to come as economists and other social scientists grapple with how to measure and weigh these variables, and elaborate adequate econometric models. Furthermore, the influences of education and of other variables on incomes probably vary according to the time period under consideration, levels of education, socioeconomic groups, ability, economic environment, and so on. These observations are leading policymakers to realize that education is only one factor among other determinants of income, which need to be combined to achieve social progress. In other words, the spread of education is a necessary, but not a sufficient, condition for greater income equality.

This article will take the experience of the public financing of education in Colombia and Brazil to illustrate three propositions. First, contrary to the often expressed belief of many social reformers, there is no reason why education per se should be an equalizing force in society. Second, government participation in the provision of education cannot bring equity to unequal societies simply through subsidies. It should be financed through progressive taxation. Third, to promote long-term equity, the returns to education should be

* From *Finance & Development*, 16, No. 1 (March 1979), pp. 33–37.

taxed progressively as the incomes of educated individuals rise and the net public subsidies accruing to different socioeconomic groups must be inversely related to incomes.

EDUCATION AND INCOME INEQUALITY

The appropriate, but sometimes overlooked, starting point for a discussion of how education can contribute to a wider distribution of incomes in developing countries is that in most of these countries there exists a situation of income inequality. Unequal incomes result in unequal savings and investments. In order to redress this income inequality through education one and, if possible, two conditions should be fulfilled: low-income groups should be able to invest more in their own education than high-income groups; and/or the rate of return of their investment—that is, their ultimate earning power less the costs of education—should also be at least as high as that of high-income groups.

But a study made of these problems in Brazil and Colombia during the early 1970s shows that low-income groups benefit less than the rich from education, and that government subsidization tends to exacerbate the inequity. For instance, the empirical data collected in Brazil show that adults in the highest income category—that of nonfarm males—earn 13 times as much as their counterparts in the lowest category (farming females with a low socioeconomic background). They are also in a much better position to provide their children with basic education. They have an enrollment ratio of 78 percent as against only 37 percent for the farming females. Moreover, their children can also expect a rate of return on their investment which is usually higher than that expected by their counterparts in the lowest group (see Table 1).

The Brazilian situation, which is probably typical of most Latin American countries, shows that education per se cannot reduce inequality in the long run. To what extent can government policies concerning the financing,

TABLE 1. Brazil: Earnings, Enrollment Ratios, and Rates of Return to Education, in 1972

	Monthly Earnings (In cruzeiros)	Enrollment Ratios in Basic Education	Social Rates of Return (in per cent) to:	
			Primary Education	Lower Secondary Education
Total males–nonfarm	873	78	23.5	13.1
Males with a low socioeconomic background	247	63	22.7	10.5
Total females–nonfarm	380	77	21.2	12.6
Females with a low socioeconomic background[1]	187	64	30.6	11.2
Total males–farm	252	45	21.1	11.0
Males with a low socioeconomic background	91	37	18.5	6.5
Total females–farm	112	45	13.9	10.4
Females with a low socioeconomic background	64	37	15.7	11.5

Source: Tables 1 and 4 in "Basic Education and Income Inequality in Brazil: The Long-Term View" Jean-Pierre Jallade, World Bank, Working Paper No. 268. June 1977.
[1] Having a head of household earning less than 200 cruzeiros a month.

pricing, and taxing of education services affect the impact of education on income distribution? The case for government involvement in education is usually made on two grounds: economic efficiency and social equity. In most developing countries, the subsidization of education is governed by the general and simple rule that everyone is equally entitled to the same amount of public subsidy for a given amount and type of education. In other words, education is subsidized, and, therefore, priced regardless of incomes. This is true for free public education and for fee-paying education as long as fees do not cover the total costs.

Needless to say, this pattern of subsidization has at best a "neutral" effect on incomes. In fact, it probably has an adverse effect because high-income groups tend to remain longer in the education system than low-income groups and therefore receive larger public subsidies. This may be particularly true in many developing countries where the distribution of educational opportunities, and subsidies, is very unequal. In some countries, high-income groups may pay for the education of their children via taxation when the tax system is sufficiently progressive (that is, when tax rates rise with incomes). But this is far from being the case everywhere, especially in the developing world where progressive direct taxation is a much less important source of revenue than indirect taxation, which is not progressive. Thus, the extent to which government involvement in the provision of education affects income inequality depends on the distribution of both taxes and education subsidies among income groups.

A detailed, empirical study of these problems was carried out in Colombia in 1970. The analysis of the distribution of education subsidies showed that in urban Colombia middle-income families (earning annually between 24,000 and 120,000 pesos) received higher subsidies per child enrolled than either very low- or very high-income families (see Table 2). When education subsidies were related to

all children, whether enrolled or not enrolled, in each income group, they definitely appeared to benefit high-income groups more than low-income groups. The picture in rural Colombia was quite similar to that of urban Colombia—with the one big difference that education subsidies were, across the board, much lower in rural than in urban areas.

The extent to which the distribution of taxes across income groups offset the distribution of education subsidies is shown in Table 3. The table shows that, on average, Colombian taxpayers receive 33 pesos worth of education subsidies whenever they pay 100 pesos in taxes and that low-income groups receive back, in the form of education subsidies, a much higher proportion of their taxes than high-income groups. In fact, this proportion

TABLE 2. Colombia: Distribution of Public Subsidies for Education Among Income Groups, 1970

Income Bracket (pesos/year)	Subsidies Per Child Enrolled (pesos)	Subsidies Per Child in Each Income Group (pesos)
Urban Colombia		
0– 6,000	1315	640
6,000– 12,000	1136	490
12,000– 24,000	1357	636
24,000– 60,000	1691	852
60,000–120,000	1521	848
120,000–240,000	1201	784
Over 240,000	986	605
Total	1469	746
Rural Colombia		
0– 6,000	552	83
6,000– 12,000	552	127
12,000– 24,000	554	183
24,000– 60,000	554	276
60,000–120,000	333	333
120,000–240,000	200	200
Over 240,000	100	100
Total	533	125

Source: Tables 3–10, 3–15, and 3–16 in *Public Expenditure on Education and Income Distribution in Colombia*, Jean-Pierre Jallade, World Bank Occasional Papers No. 18, Johns Hopkins University Press, 1974.

TABLE 3. Colombia: Distribution of Taxes and Public Subsidies for Education Among Income Groups, 1970[1]

Income Bracket (pesos year)	Number of Households (in percent)	Subsidies for Education	Subsidies for Primary Education	Subsidies for Secondary Education	Subsidies for Higher Education
			(as percentage of taxes)		
0– 6,000	19.0	117	109	9	0
6,000– 12,000	20.2	83	77	4	2
12,000– 24,000	24.9	72	49	18	5
24,000– 60,000	22.9	55	22	20	14
60,000–120,000	8.8	23	4	7	12
120,000–240,000	3.4	10	1	3	6
Over 240,000	0.8	2	—	1	1
Total	100.0	33	16	9	8

Source: Tables 3.19 and 3.20 in Jallade, *op. cit.*
[1] Education subsidies are computed on the basis of enrollments and public expenditures by level and type (public or private) of education.

decreases regularly from low-income to high-income groups, which shows that not only do high-income groups pay for their education through their taxes but also that government involvement in the provision of education in Colombia contributes to redistribute income from high-income to low-income groups.

However, when each level of education is examined separately, it can be seen that only the public financing of *primary* education has a strong and positive effect on the distribution of income by redistributing income from the 13 percent richer families to the 87 percent poorer families, the cutoff point being 60,000 pesos a year. The redistributive effect is strongly beneficial to the 40 percent poorer families (earning under 12,000 pesos a year), more than three fourths of whom live in rural areas. These families receive 87 percent of their taxes back in the form of public subsidies for primary education.

The picture that emerges from secondary education is quite different: here, the main beneficiaries are two middle-income groups, including about 48 percent of all families. In other words, the public financing of secondary education redistributes income from both the 40 percent poorest and the 13 percent richest

families to a sort of lower middle class, 80 percent of whom are living in urban areas and whose incomes are in the 12,000–60,000 pesos range. The situation for higher education is very similar, except that the two income groups subsidized by both the poor and the rich are higher up in the income scale. Families in these groups represent close to one third of all families, they are almost exclusively urban and earn between 24,000 and 120,000 pesos. Thus a redistribution of income from the poor and the very rich to the upper middle class takes place through the public financing of higher education.

It is clear that the positive effect of the public financing of education on the distribution of income in Colombia is only due to the financing of primary education which strongly benefits the poor. This positive effect is partly but not wholly offset by the negative income distributive effects of the public financing of secondary and higher education which benefit most the lower and upper middle classes respectively.

Whether or not the Colombian case is "typical" of many other Latin American countries is an open question. It is clear, however, that any policy aimed at making a system of finance more equitable should act on either the structure of public subsidies or the structure of taxation.

SCALING SUBSIDIES TO INCOME

To overcome the better ability-to-pay for education of some as compared to others, public subsidies should be inversely related to incomes. No country has ever put this policy into practice, so it is hard to foresee its impact on, say, the demand for education, the quality of education, and the internal and external efficiencies of educational systems. But there exists one important situation—in Colombia —where education is subsidized and, therefore, priced differently for the poor and the rich, and this could yield useful clues about what would happen if subsidies were inversely related to incomes.

In many countries a fully subsidized public education sector coexists with a not-so-heavily subsidized private education sector. On the whole (with some important exceptions, such as Japan), public schools tend to recruit a student body mainly from low-income groups. Conversely, little subsidized, expensive private schools tend to cater to the needs of high-income groups. Thus, it would seem that one way to make sure that education subsidies benefit low-income more than high-income groups would be to foster a private, little subsidized, education sector in which high-income groups can enroll their children.

This is, to a certain extent, shown by Colombia, which has undergone a certain "privatization" of some of the key levels of its education system during the past 30 years. (Only one half of university students were enrolled in public universities in 1970 as against over two thirds in 1940. In the same way, enrollments in public teacher training institutions have decreased from 80 to 70 percent during the same period. Enrollments in private institutions have increased accordingly.)

Although this may promote equity in the short term, it would tend to harm low-income groups in the long term since the "private" education sector would provide a better education and higher ultimate earning capacity than the subsidized system. The existence of private education services for the rich has always faced fierce opposition from many policymakers. Their fear is that, as soon as the full cost—or something sufficiently close to it —of educational services are charged to some groups the quality of the most *common* type of education will deteriorate owing to the lack of a strong political constituency. Those with the highest purchasing power will foster the "best" service, which will yield the highest returns (in the form of examinations passed and, ultimately, earning opportunities), and those with a lower purchasing power will go for cheaper education. Thus, the "privatization" of education may serve to maintain, if not foster, long-term income disparities, especially if the size of the returns to education is positively associated with the importance of the private finance component in educational costs. In this case, the search for equity in the provision of education through an income related pricing system might run against long-term equity.

How far are the fears of these policymakers justified? Is it valid to assert that private education yields higher returns than public education? The only evidence available to support this assertion is circumstantial—rates-of-return calculations have, so far, never been carried out simultaneously and comparatively for public and private education. However, although the situation probably differs from country to country, one has to assume from an economic standpoint that those who seek and gain access to fee-paying schools in spite of sometimes fierce competition and dire financial strain, do so in order to improve on the rate of return which they could get from an equivalent education in a tuition-free school. In Latin American countries, the suspicion that the returns to private education do more than simply offset its higher costs is founded on the above-average ability of private schools to prepare students to gain access to the upper levels of the education system.

So, although the gradual "privatization" of education as income rises may help in promoting short-term equity among taxpayers in the provision of educational services, it still has to be proven that it does not contribute to inequity in the long term.

MORE PROGRESSIVE TAXES

It seems that the only way to introduce more equity into the provision of educational services without the harmful effects of "privatization" is to increase the progressivity of the tax system. In a country like Colombia, this could be achieved through an additional tax on higher incomes, which would be earmarked for the financing of secondary and higher education. Such a tax would help to remove the adverse effects of the public subsidization of those levels of education on the distribution of income by increasing the tax payments of high-income groups. The objective of this tax would be to make sure that the rich will be at least paying for the subsidies which they receive. Of course, the tax rates corresponding to the various income groups could be manipulated in order to achieve any degree of income redistribution. In the long run, their gradual decrease could be geared to the gradual equalization of education subsides across income groups as low-income groups gain access to the higher levels of education, without altering the rest of the tax system.

This Colombian example illustrates some of the issues concerning the impact of government policies on income inequality through the financing of educational services. This is, however, only the short-term aspect of the problem. In the long run, the concern for equity leads to an inquiry into the distribution of the returns to education among socioeconomic groups. Taxation of these returns in a progressive manner may be required in order to achieve a positive impact on income inequality.

A convenient way to assess how the various socioeconomic groups as a whole fare with regard to both the subsidization of education investment and the taxation of the returns to this investment is to adopt the viewpoint of the state, and include the entire population in the assessment. The taxes levied on the returns to education could be interpreted as a way for the government to get back part of the money spent in subsidizing access to education. Taxes would be the benefit stream of government subsidization of education, while the outlays incurred to subsidize individuals to reach a certain level of educational attainment would be the cost stream. The "net" amount of subsidies distributed by the government to each educated person would be assessed by the present value of all the taxes paid on the returns to this education by the educated person during his entire lifetime, minus the subsidies received to reach this level of educational attainment. The "net" subsidy per educated person would then be multiplied by the proportion of people reaching the level of education under consideration in each socioeconomic group to arrive at the comparative costs of education to the government for each group.

Such an analysis was carried out for Brazil at the beginning of the 1970s. The distributive impact of subsidizing (and taxing the returns from) basic education are summarized in Table 4, which compares the situation of the educated from different income groups with the situation of the group as a whole. The table shows that the present values of "net" government subsidies allocated to each educated individual are higher for females and farm workers than for males and nonfarm workers respectively. Educated individuals in the subgroup "with a low socioeconomic background" are also usually getting higher sub-

TABLE 4. Brazil: Allocation of "Net" Government Subsidies for Basic Education Among Socioeconomic Groups

	Enrollment Ratios in Basic Education (*in percent*)	Present Value of "Net" Subsidies Allocated by Government to Each Educated Individual with:			Present value of "Net" Subsidies Allocated by the Government to Each Person in the Group
		Primary Schooling	Lower Secondary Schooling	Total	
		(*in cruzeiros*)			
Total males–nonfarm	78	327[1]	−1,640	−1,313	−1,024
Males with a low socioeconomic background	63	148	−1,820	−1,672	−1,033
Total females–nonfarm	77	− 71	−1,950	−2,021	−1,556
Females with a low socioeconomic background	64	−112	−2,012	−2,124	−1,359
Total males–farm	45	−496	−2,370	−2,866	−1,290
Males with a low socioeconomic background	37	−526	−2,420	−2,946	−1,090
Total females–farm	45	−558	−2,390	−2,948	−1,327
Females with a low socioeconomic background	37	−560	−2,380	−2,940	−1,088

Source: Table 7 in Jallade, *op cit.*
Note: The discount rate to compute the present values is 20 percent
[1] Positive present values means that the taxes recovered on educated individuals' incomes offset the outlays incurred by the government to subsidize this type of education.

sidies than their counterparts in the group as a whole. When the analysis is limited to those participating in education it seems that low-income educated persons are more heavily subsidized by the government than high-income educated persons.

A different picture emerges when all individuals in each group—both educated and uneducated—are included in the analysis. For instance, in spite of their higher incomes, females engaged in nonfarm activities are more subsidized than farming males or females (but also more than their male, better-paid counterparts). In the same way, subgroups including only persons "with a low socioeconomic background" are, on an aver-

age, less subsidized by the government than larger groups in spite of their lower incomes. It seems thus that low-income groups are rather less subsidized than high-income groups—which means that the government is not, through its subsidies and tax policies, oriented toward distributing incomes in a more equitable way.

A more progressive taxing of the returns to education could be achieved through an "education tax" on the incomes of educated individuals. Such a tax would seek to lower the present value of "net" government subsidies accruing to high-income groups and increase this value for low-income groups. As the above analysis has shown, the degree of progressivity of tax payments would be determined on the basis of (1) the present "net" subsidy received by each educated individual in any given group and (2) the enrollment ratio for the same group. Progressivity in tax payments could, of course, vary according to the amount of income redistribution sought.

Progressive taxation of the returns to education through an "education tax" could be most simply achieved by adding or removing a few percentage points in the existing income tax rates of educated individuals in each socioeconomic group. Admittedly, this is not a conceptually perfect solution. The tax base would be absolute income instead of, as it should be, that particular fraction of additional income which is due to additional schooling. However, the advantages of coupling the "education tax" with the income tax would be important from the operational viewpoint. In addition to administrative simplicity, such a tax would probably be more easily accepted if it takes the form of a few additional points in the income tax rate structure without a change in the tax base, rather than if it were a new set of necessarily substantial tax rates applied to a small tax base, namely, additional incomes due to additional schooling. No overhauling of the existing tax system would be necessary and the new rates would be kept flexible in order to take into account changes in the subsidies received and taxes paid by each group.

The proposed "education tax" would also help to shape a pattern of incentives to acquire education that would be conducive to greater equality of educational opportunity, since the private returns from education of high-income groups would be reduced more than the returns of low-income groups. The proceeds of this tax would be used to increase the subsidization of education of low-income groups and improve the availability and quality of educational services available to them.

Nothing so far has been said about the political feasibility of these proposals. Apart from the obvious statement that such feasibility will vary greatly across levels of education within a single country, a possibly good test of a government's willingness to proceed with these proposals and of their likely acceptance by the public is provided by the financing of other public goods in the country. If the financing of such goods as health care, public transportation, and subsidized housing is designed in such a way that its impact on the distribution of incomes goes in the right direction, the case for a progressive system of education finance should be easy to make. If the opposite situation prevails, the chances of education being singled out among other semipublic goods to receive distinctive treatment are weak.

RELATED READING

Mats Hultin and Jean-Pierre Jallade, *Costing and Financing Education in LDCs: Current Issues*, World Bank Staff Working Paper No. 216. May 1975.

Jean-Pierre Jallade, *The Financing of Education: An Examination of Basic Issues*, World Bank Staff Working Paper No. 157. July 1973.

Jean-Pierre Jallade, *Public Expenditures on Education and Income Distribution in Colombia,* World Bank Staff Occasional Papers No. 18. Baltimore and London: The Johns Hopkins University Press, 1974.

Jean-Pierre Jallade, *Student Loans in Developing Countries: An Evaluation of the Colombian Performance,* World Bank Staff Working Paper No. 182. June 1974.

Jean-Pierre Jallade, *Basic Education and Income Inequality in Brazil: The Long-Term View*, World Bank Staff Working Paper No. 268. June 1977.

RATES OF RETURN TO EDUCATION AND INCOME DISTRIBUTION

Conventional "human capital" theory uses two rates of return to education to assess the overall degree of subsidization of education by the government—the private and the social rate. Both rates are computed on the incomes of the educated. The private rate is usually higher than the social rate—the private rate being based on after-tax earnings and private costs (excluding public subsidies), while the social rate is computed on the basis of before-tax earnings and total costs of education (including public subsidies). As a result, the difference between the private and the social rates reflects, on the benefit side, the tax stream paid by educated people and, on the cost side, the public subsidy required to reach the level of education under consideration. A big difference between the two rates means a high level of overall or "net" subsidization (high public subsidies to reach a certain level of education and low taxes afterward) while a small difference means that the subsidies received to reach a certain level of education are nearly offset by the taxes paid afterwards by educated individuals during their active lives.

However, traditional rate of return calculations are of little use for income distribution purposes because they are usually carried out at an aggregate level (using *mean* incomes for each age education group) in order to compare efficiency between education cycles—for instance by showing that the *average* rate of return in primary education is superior to that of secondary education. Such calculations fail to provide any clue about the resulting impact on income inequality. What is needed is a breakdown by socioeconomic groups so that one can compare the subsidies accruing to and taxes paid by the various socioeconomic groups for each level of education.

	Difference Between Private and Social Rates of Return to Primary Education	Difference Between Private and Social Rates of Return to Secondary Education
Total males–nonfarm	1.2	0.8
Males with a low socioeconomic background	1.5	0.9
Total females–non-farm	1.5	1.5
Females with a low socioeconomic background	4.6	1.4
Total males–farm	3.0	1.5
Males with a low socioeconomic background	4.0	1.0
Total females–farm	2.9	3.0
Females with a low socioeconomic background	2.9	3.1

Such a disaggregate analysis was carried out in the case of Brazil (see the table).

The table shows that, by and large, educated people in disadvantaged groups are equally or more subsidized than those of other groups. In the same way people engaged in farming occupations appear to enjoy higher "net" subsidies than those in nonfarming occupations. It does appear, therefore, that government involvement in subsidizing the provision of education and taxing its returns is oriented in the right direction.

A major deficiency of this approach, however, is that it focuses exclusively on the individuals who invest in education, and discounts nonparticipants. And it is not enough for redistributive purposes to know that the few disadvantaged who gain access to a certain level of education are more subsidized than the many coming from privileged groups. One also has to relate the levels of subsidization to the numbers able to take advantage of it. In other words, what is needed is what could be called, for want of a better word, a "redistributive" approach, that seeks to compare the "net" impact of government involvement in the financing and taxing of education across socioeconomic groups as a whole, including those who invest and those who do not invest in education. The discussion of subsidies and taxes in Brazil in the latter part of the article, and the data in Table 4 provides an illustration of this approach.

Further Readings

1. Education

Alatas, Syes Hussein. *Intellectuals in Developing Societies*. London: Frank Cass, 1977.

Blaug, Mark. *Education and the Employment Problem in Developing Countries*. Geneva: International Labor Office, 1974.

Coombs, P. H., with Ahmed, M. *Attacking Rural Poverty: How Nonformal Education Can Help*. Baltimore and London: Johns Hopkins University Press, 1974.

Dore, Ronald P. *The Diploma Disease: Education, Qualification, and Development*. Berkeley: University of California Press, 1976.

Edwards, E. O., and Todaro, M. P. "Educational Demand and Supply in the Context of Growing Unemployment in Less Developed Countries." *World Development* 1, nos. 3–4 (March/April 1973).

Harbison, Frederick H. *Human Resources as the Wealth of Nations*. New York, London, and Toronto: Oxford University Press, 1973.

Psacharopoulos, George. "Schooling, Experience and Earnings: The Case of an LDC." *Journal of Development Economics* 4, no. 1 (March 1977).

Simmons, John, ed. *The Education Dilemma: Policy Issues for Developing Countries in the 1980s*. Oxford: Pergamon, 1980.

World Bank. *Education*. Sector Working Paper. Washington, D.C., December 1974.

Part III

Development Problems and Policies: International

In Part III, we continue our examination of the major problems and policies of development but now with an emphasis on issues that are primarily international in nature. Chapter 10 starts with a survey paper by Sheila Smith and John Toye that focuses on three alternative views of how international trade impacts on the economies of developing countries: the optimistic views of free traders, the skepticism of international structuralists, and the negativism of neo-marxists. Is expanded trade with the more developed nations beneficial for Third World economies as traditional free traders argue or is it potentially harmful as most structuralists and neo-marxists would assert? Smith and Toye have much to say on the subject. Werner Baer follows with a paper that evaluates the impact on Latin American economies of a major component of the rapid industrialization philosophy of development economics in the 1960s—the strategy of import substitution. He finds that the results were far less beneficial than the theoretical arguments in their favor would have implied. In some cases, import-substitution policies may have been actually counterproductive to their expressed goals. Nevertheless, Baer concludes that when compared to the alternatives, import substitution on balance has had many favorable effects. Finally, Donald B. Keesing surveys the range of trade policies available to governments in low-income nations to see to what extent such policies in the context of outward-looking development strategies might serve the interests of promoting rapid industrialization through import substitution and export promotion and diversification. Keesing's analysis is in the neoclassical, "trade-as-beneficial" tradition.

In Chapter 11, we look at the related problems of private foreign investment and foreign aid. Both can play critical roles in the promotion of Third

287

World development, yet each in practice has had a limited positive impact. The major carrier of private foreign investment in the Third World is the multinational corporation (MNCs) and the study prepared by the Department of Economic and Social Affairs of the United Nations Secretariat summarizes the nature of MNCs and the issues surrounding their roles and activities in developing countries. Finally, the Brandt Commission report looks at the recent decline in foreign aid from the developed to the developing world and sets forth a series of recommendations for expanding foreign assistance under conditions more productive to aid recipients and potientially more satisfying to aid givers.

10

Trade Theory, Industrialization and Commercial Policies

26. Three Stories About Trade and Poor Economies*

Sheila Smith and John Toye

1. THREE TYPES OF THEORY AND POLICY

Development economists, when they discuss the role played by international trade in a country's economic development, tend to tell one of three types of story. The first and oldest is a happy story which shows how the welfare of both (and by easy extension, all) countries which engage in trade is increased, even when one country is absolutely very rich and the other is absolutely very poor. The second, of much more recent vintage, is a dull and detailed story about the way in which differences in economic structure between countries bias the gains from trade in favour of the rich, technologically advanced and industrialised economies and against the poor, low-technology agricultural economies. The third story, more recent still, is tragic. It asserts that trade and economic specialisation have actually caused the underdevelopment of the periphery of the world by the very same processes that have developed the capitalist metropolis. The unhappy ending of permanent global polarity could only be rewritten if the international capitalist system were to be superseded.

Each of these types of story usually comes with a ready-made set of policy recommendations. If trade makes both partners better off, obviously all policy makers should promote trade by dismantling tariff and non-tariff barriers to trade (except in a few very exceptional sorts of circumstance). Policy-makers in developing countries should adopt liberal, open, 'outward-looking' commercial policies in order to exploit their comparative advantage in labour-intensive products. If, however, the distribution of the gains from trade is biased against poor, backward economies for structural and institutional reasons, policy-makers should focus their efforts on changing the international economic order in a way that eliminates these biases. But if commercial contact actually *causes* the underdevelopment of the periphery, then the obvious policy is to multiply the barriers to trade until each developing country has withdrawn into national self-sufficiency, or self-insufficiency, as the case may be.

In general, recent trade literature shows the link between each type of theory and policy quite clearly. The massive series of volumes published by the Organisation for Economic Cooperation and Development, summarised by Little, Scitovsky and Scott [*1970*], and for the US National Bureau for Economic Research, presided over by Bhagwati and Kreuger [NBER, *1975*], exemplify the link between

From *Journal of Development Studies*, 15, no. 3 (April 1979), pp. 1–18.

the theory of comparative advantage and the advocacy of trade liberalisation. The work of Singer, [*1950; 1974*] and to a lesser extent Prebisch [*1959*], illustrates the link between theories of structural differences and asymmetric trade gains, on the one hand, and policies for reforming the international economic order, via ECLA, UNCTAD and now the North-South dialogue, on the other. Finally, Samir Amin shows the characteristic link between 'underdevelopment' theorists and the policy of autarchy, at least as a prelude to international socialist cooperation [*1974; 1976; 1977*].

One should not exaggerate the rigidity with which each set of policies is linked to each type of story about the role of trade in development. Utilitarian marginalism is a fairly flexible system of thought, and one is not wanting to say that, in principle, it *could* not be made to reproduce the pessimistic conclusions of dependency theory, by altering a function here and a time-lag there: only that it usually does not. Again, the structuralists and the dependency theorists are sometimes seen embracing each other's policies; but this must surely be attributable either to opportunism or to confusion, or to the fact that they share, in some cases, common intellectual origins.

To a regrettable degree, even professional economists seem to choose one or other of these three broad policy attitudes on grounds of interest and inclination, and then operate *within* the fundamental assumptions of the appropriate type of theory. A more rational approach is to reexamine some of these assumptions in order to find out why the types of theory are mutually incompatible; and then to ask which assumptions are to be preferred as the more reasonable ones.

2. THE STORY OF MUTUALLY BENEFICIAL TRADE

The story of mutually beneficial trade rests on a number of quite distinct pieces of analysis, which are, on examination, incompatible with

each other. This is both unsatisfactory and paradoxical, in that the conditions for mutually beneficial trade do not seem particularly difficult to specify in a purely static analysis.

One would expect international trade to be mutually beneficial when it involves the products of localised natural resources, products for which the consumers of the two countries have different degrees of preference, products of localised skilled labour and products of manufacturing establishments which have achieved different economies of scale. Given the uneven distribution of metals, precious stones, oil and gas, soils and climate in relation to (often highly arbitrary) national boundaries, it would require very odd national consumption preference patterns for there to be no scope for mutually beneficial trade in minerals, foodstuffs and agricultural raw materials. Skills which cannot be quickly acquired, and differences in unit costs deriving from scale of operation, create scope for mutually beneficial trade in some industrial products and services.

The original variant of the story of mutually beneficial trade, the theory of comparative advantage, should not be seen as an explanation of how trade comes about. Rather it should be seen as a reminder that opportunities for mutually beneficial trade can exist, and that static welfare losses will be incurred if these opportunities are neglected. The reminder can be shown to retain its validity even when there are large absolute differences in productivity between the trading partners in all commodities traded. The benefit is mutual because both countries can increase the total volume of consumables at their disposal by shifting inputs into the production of the commodity for which the ratio of domestic input costs to foreign input costs is lower. What we have here, then, is the analysis of static welfare gains from trade, on the assumption that resources are fully mobile *within* a country and completely immobile *between* countries. But there is nothing in this argument to the effect that every country *must* have a comparative advantage in some product (since conceivably the relevant ratios could be identical for all tradeable products), or to indicate whether any existing comparative advantage is natural—arising from, say, climate or geology—or created historically—by the prior destruction of indigenous handicraft industries, or colonial development of mineral or agricultural monoproduct economies, for example. Thus there is the danger that, in joining the chorus of praise for the theory of comparative advantage ('beautiful', 'never...controverted', *Samuelson, 1970: 647; Johnson, 1974: 30*) one is persuaded to overlook its severe limitations, both as an explanation of how comparative advantages arise, are lost *or taken away*, and as a policy guide in a world in which resource mobility is low *within* poor countries and high *between* poor countries and rich ones.

The second variant of this story, the Heckscher—Ohlin theory, attempts to give a specific account of how comparative advantages arise by rooting them in international differences in what are called 'factor endowments', their stocks of capital and labour at a given point in time. But this involves a change in assumption from those that underlie comparative advantage theory. Whereas the latter depends on the assumption of different techniques of production (which account for the large differences in absolute productivity between rich and poor countries) for any given product, the Heckscher—Ohlin theory begins by reversing this assumption, so that each commodity is produced by the same technique in each country [*Robinson, 1974: 8*]. Differences in the factor-intensity of products, combined with stocks of capital and labour varying between countries, are then left to account for comparative advantages. It is on the strength of this reasoning that poor countries are recommended to specialise in labour-intensive products and trade their surplus of such products for imports of the rich countries' capital-intensive goods.

This reasoning has only to be set down for its weaknesses, both as an explanation of actual poor country/rich country trade and as a guide to which commodities ought to enter their trade, to become patent. Its persuasive force derives entirely from its exclusion by assumption of all the other relevant determinants of comparative advantage. Localised natural resources are excluded by restricting the meaning of 'factor endowments' to stocks of capital and labour. The cost advantages conferred by scale of operation are excluded by the assumptions of constant returns to scale, and of a level of technology that is independent of the average level of capital stock per man. Differential labour skills are excluded by assuming labour to be homogeneous. Differences in taste, which (leaving aside natural resources) heavily influence which commodities are produced domestically, and hence which are available for export, are excluded by the assumption of identical tastes.

Thus, even without introducing into the argument such substantial queries as whether prices in fact adjust in the way that the economists' model of perfect competition predicts, or the effects of monetary institutions in modifying the interactions of the underlying real variables, the Heckscher—Ohlin theory appears to be no more than an elaborate tautology. In fact, even stronger assumptions than those already mentioned are required to underwrite its validity. The possibility of factor-intensity reversals (i.e. changes in which good is the capital- or labour-intensive one as capital and labour prices change) has to be ruled out; the degree of variation in the capital and labour endowments of the two countries must be restricted; and the analysis must be confined to only two goods—a third good, let alone an intermediate product that does not enter final consumption, cannot be incorporated [*Johnson, 1958: 28–30*]. What was paradoxical about Leontief's finding that the United States' exports were labour-intensive was not that it contradicted the Heckscher—Ohlin theory, but that it was received as a test of a theory that was in principle untestable.

The third variant of the story of mutually beneficial trade, the idea of trade as a 'vent for surplus', again rests on different assumptions from those underlying comparative advantage analysis *or* the factor endowment theory. This time we revert to the assumption of differences in technology between the rich and the poor country, but combine this with the assumption that, before trade takes place, some productive resources in the poor country are unemployed. Trade is said to benefit the poor country because incomes are created thereby for the previously unemployed resources, incomes which must be more valuable than the leisure thereby sacrificed because the transition to exporting was made voluntarily . . . . Examination of the fine texture of the colonial history of Ghana and Nigeria seems to undermine the validity of the view that idle resources existed before trade, and that the switch towards agricultural export was a matter of voluntary choice rather than of the economic and political pressure of the colonial state.

The happy ending of the story of mutually beneficial trade would therefore need very considerable dilution. While there are static welfare gains from specialising according to comparative advantage when internal resources are fully mobile, the general presumption that poor countries have a comparative advantage in goods with low capital/labour ratios cannot be sustained. Therefore, general recommendations that poor economies should specialise in labour-intensive exports are simple-minded or mischievous. Further, when trade opportunities do bring unemployed resources into voluntary employment, static welfare is obviously increased thereby. But the existing trade patterns between rich and poor countries cannot be interpreted as merely a result of this pleasantly painless transition to full employment of resources in the poor country. Indeed, the best documented examples of vent-for-surplus trade are of a significantly different version from that mentioned above: the only idle resource in this version is a poor country's natural resource (e.g. Peruvian guano), which enters the poor country's exports only because of an inflow of both foreign capital and foreign labour, and it's exploitation creates nothing except the familiar export enclave [*Levin, 1960*]. Clearly this version of vent-for-surplus is not a story of mutually beneficial trade, but of structural biases in the gains from trade.

3. THE STORY OF STRUCTURALLY BIASED GAINS FROM TRADE

The theories of trade which suggest that the benefits of trade accrue disproportionately to rich countries not only recognise differences in technological level between rich and poor countries, but make these differences (and associated institutional dissimilarities) the pivot on which their arguments turn. In addition, they depart from the exclusive emphasis on static resource reallocation in order to consider dynamic or historical processes. For example, the natural resource version of the vent-for-surplus model cities institutional rigidities related to pre-capitalist technology to explain why domestic capital and labour fail to combine with particular natural resources in poor countries, and analyses the growth spurts of poor countries, export industries over the long run.

The best known exponent of the view that gains from trade are biased against poor countries is undoubtedly Prebisch. Prebisch argued that the bias operates through a secular decline in the terms of trade of primary producers *vis-à-vis* those of manufactured goods producers. Such a decline is equivalent to long-period transfers of income from less developed to developed countries and is a result of the former's failure to regulate trade in the right way. Empirically, the secular decline is not well established, but this failure results not so much from Prebisch's admittedly inadequate choice of indicators as from the general difficulty of gathering reliable relevant statistics over the hundred years or so which the theory requires [*Helleiner, 1972: 20–22; Yotopoulos and Nugent, 1976: 341–345*]. In these circumstances it would be over hasty to dismiss the theory simply because of its weak empirical basis. Rather, suppose that, on the most exacting of definitions, a deterioration of primary producers' terms of trade can be demonstrated, and accept that this would be equivalent to an international transfer of income. How far do the explanations of secular decline which Prebisch puts forward provide a plausible theory of the determinants of the terms of trade? Prebisch gives his views of the effect of technical change on the terms of trade in a concrete context. Policies to improve the productivity of primary producers' export industries are self-defeating, 'as some of the fruits of such technical advance will usually be transferred . . . to the outer world' in the form of lower primary product export prices; prices fall because labour in the LDCs is unable, because of population pressure, to take out its productivity gains in the form of higher wages—unlike labour in developed countries which benefits from strong unions and a monopolistic product market. As a remedy, protection of LDCs' domestic manufacturing industry permits wages there and in the primary export sector to rise, and thus prevents the latter's expansion beyond the point where marginal social benefit equals marginal social cost.

There is empirical evidence [*Salter, 1960: 114–160, 166–201*] to suggest that (at any rate, before the introduction of 'productivity agreements') productivity gains in developed countries were *not* appropriated by the labour in the industry where they arose, but were diffused throughout the economy in the form of price reduction or slower price rises than would otherwise have taken place. Nor is there any reason to distinguish between developed countries' export and non-export in-

dustries in this distributive process. It seems plausible that the developed countries are in fact distributing their productivity gains to their overseas customers, including the LDCs. If this is so, there is no longer any asymmetry between developed and LDCs, and the bias in the world economy that chronically worsens poor countries' terms of trade still awaits an explanation. What remains of the Prebisch thesis is a statement of the economic problems arising from a partially monetised labour market, from which is derived a familiar argument for tariffs. It is not correct, as both Prebisch and his critics (*e.g., Flanders, 1964*] suggest, that this argument rests on or is strengthened by the existence of overpopulation. The justification for intervention in trade, not necessarily by means of a tariff, is based on the premise of a primary products export sector which, if not checked, would tend to expand production beyond the point where marginal social benefit equals marginal social cost, because for social and institutional reasons labour in the primary products export sector is paid above its marginal social productivity. This is a situation which could arise no less in a sparsely than in a densely populated country. Moreover, although the analysis is cast in terms of a primary product export sector, the institutional arguments apply equally to any export sector which can draw on unlimited supplies of labour in the Lewis sense [*Lewis, 1954*].

The second important element which Prebisch introduced into the discussion were variables on the demand side, which may be labelled 'tastes'. It is another of the assumptions of the simplified Heckscher–Ohlin model that tastes do not alter. Prebisch maintains that increasing world income will alter tastes, and that the changing pattern of demand can be predicted from estimates of different products' income elasticities of demand. Since the income elasticities for poor economies' exports are consistently smaller than for their imports, poor economies cannot grow at the same rate as developed economies without running into foreign exchange crises at fixed exchange rates —and exchange depreciation turns the terms of trade against the depreciator. Is this the explanation which Prebisch requires?

The disparity between income elasticities of demand is said to be due to Engle's law of food consumption—that households with smaller incomes spend a larger proportion of their income on food, and that as their income increases a smaller share of each marginal increment is spent on food. The food demand arising within the poor economies themselves may slow down the deterioration of food producers' terms of trade, but will not arrest it altogether, because, even in Asia and the Far East, the income elasticity of demand for food does not equal, still less exceed, unity. Nonetheless, the quantitative importance of food should not be exaggerated: it forms only two-fifths of the poor economies' total exports of primary products. Apart from food, the rich countries' demand for raw materials is undermined by technical progress, which develops substitutes for the raw materials previously imported from primary producers. Thus the relative rate of growth of demand for imported raw cotton, natural rubber and cane sugar, for example, slackens as world economic activity expands.

However, is the switch to synthetics a pure demand factor, equivalent to other changes in tastes? This view only makes sense given Prebisch's very primitive concept of technical progress as a force both 'disembodied', i.e., not incorporated in any way in the only factor of production he allows, labour, and 'exogenous', i.e., not related to other economic variables such as costs, profits and output. Synthetics do not simply appear: they are substituted when market conditions make it profitable to do so. Nor are they immutable once introduced. Rising labour or other costs in their production may make the natural product again competitive.

Of course, developed countries do establish domestic production of substitutes that is inefficient judged by world market prices, and then protect them by tariffs—for example, the US or EEC beet sugar industry. But this is best regarded as an example of the deleterious effects of economic nationalism, and not as an inevitable result of the process of income expansion.

How will the demand for manufactures change as world income expands? There seem to be few reliable estimates of income elasticities for industrial goods as such. Intuitively, it seems likely that they are higher than those for food. Of more importance is the flexibility of the industrial production structure which allows switching away from those manufactures with low elasticities, which thus are long-run losers in the export market.

In general, one can agree that Prebisch has been rightly criticised for his crude identification of poor countries with primary production, and rich countries with industrial and manufacturing production. In the context of the structure of world trade, this is misleading. Developed countries contribute a larger share by value of world exports of primary products than do the less developed countries. In addition, they take up a very much larger share of developed countries' manufactured exports than do the poor economies. To regard a price fall for manufactures as a gain exclusive to poor economies involves an heroic simplification. It is immensely to Prebisch's credit that, by stressing the need to examine the world's real historical experience and dynamic factors like changes in technology and tastes, he attempts to escape from the pitfalls of simple static analysis. Yet he does not provide a proper dynamic analysis in its place. Too much of his thesis rests on institutional factors introduced without any look at their social and economic causation: technical change is introduced without its dynamic— e.g., the causes of its transmission, its countervailing and stabilising effects; and even in the most reasonable section, on demand influences, the equilibrating forces that would tend to arrest secular terms of trade decline are neglected.

Apart from vent-for-surplus in its natural resources version and Prebisch's analysis of the determinants of poor countries' terms of trade, a third strand of structuralist analysis is provided by so-called 'product cycle' theories of trade [*e.g., Vernon, 1966*]. These theories hinge on an assumed technological and institutional gulf between rich and poor countries, as a result of which product innovation can be done successfully only in the former. Trade patterns are therefore determined in the field of manufactures by the vintages of particular products, the oldest having become standardised in production and so exported from needing the technological equivalent of bespoke tailoring and so exported from rich poke tailoring and so exported from rich countries to poor. This sort of theory explicitly recognises poor countries' ability to export manufactures, unlike other structuralist theories which, in analysing the terms of trade, presume that they can export only natural resource or agricultural products, but it resembles these theories because, with the plausible assumption that bespoke manufactures carry a much higher profit margin than standardised products, it becomes another explanation of structurally biased gains from trade.

The policy prescriptions which follow from structuralist analyses of international trade cluster around the central issue of finding ways of intervening in markets that will improve the terms on which poor countries trade, as compensation for the structural disadvantages which they suffer in international exchange. The proposals currently being put forward by UNCTAD and being discussed in the continuing North-South dialogue on a new international economic order consist of a scheme for a Common Fund to finance price stabilisation of ten core primary commodities and eight others; agreeing a code of conduct for multinational companies operating in poor countries (including such matters as the transfer of technology); securing reductions in tariff and non-tariff barriers to poor countries' exports on a non-reciprocal basis, rather than by the agreed mutual reductions under the aegis of GATT; and increasing the volume of international finance available to mitigate the effects of balance-of-payments crises in poor countries.

The discussion and negotiation of these proposals has produced a wealth of fascinating empirical information on the specific characteristics of particular commodity markets, on the abundance and ingenuity of non-tariff barriers in rich countries and on the operating practices of multinational firms. The snail-like pace at which the *status quo* is changed is only partly a reflection of the very dull and detailed nature of the negotiations. The lack of progress in many areas is partly also a reflection of the fact that information and 'correct' arguments are insufficient as a means of changing the trade policies of advanced capitalist countries. As has been argued elsewhere [*Abdel-Fadil et al., 1977*], 'present arrangements reflects an existing balance of world power and give the third world as a bloc little opportunity for altering the balance of power at the international level. The bargaining position of third world countries depends also on a community of common interests which is not necessarily sustainable' (pp. 211–212). The notion of common interests among underdeveloped countries is important in structuralist analysis and policy, but rests on the doubtful conception that the principal economic division of the world is between rich and poor countries, and that this economic division is reflected in a political division. The determinants of political positions cannot, however, be 'read off' from levels of economic development in this way; for example, the regimes in Nicaragua, Central African Empire and Haiti have little in common politically with the regimes in Tanzania, Algeria, Mozambique and

Angola; we cannot expect this heterogeneous collection of nation states to have common political positions in relation to aspects of international capitalism.

On the other hand, two positive points may be made: first, the current negotiations for an NIEO may bring material improvements for certain groups within some underdeveloped countries, particularly for exporters of the core primary commodities; secondly, individual nation states have varying degrees of freedom of manoeuvre in relation to international trade and economic relations, both in isolation and as part of collectives; this freedom of manoeuvre cannot, however, be determined in the abstract.

4. THE STORY OF TRADE-INDUCED GLOBAL POLARITY

Marxist analyses of international trade, though analytically more heterogeneous than those in the comparative advantage tradition, tend to analyse trade within the context of world capitalism or imperialism. Samir Amin's recent effort in this tradition is discussed here, not because it is taken to be the 'best' Marxist analysis of trade, but because it illustrates sharply some fundamental problems of analyses conducted at this generalised level [Amin, 1974; 1976; 1977].

Amin's analysis of world capitalism is conducted in terms of two categories: centre and periphery [1977, ch. 5]. Capitalism at the centre developed on the basis of the expansion of the home market, whereas capitalism in the periphery was introduced from the outside: the economies of the periphery 'are without any internal dynamism of their own' [1976: 279]. Furthermore peripheral capitalism is 'distorted' in three main ways: the distortion towards export activities ('extraversion'); the 'hypertrophy' of the tertiary sector; and the distortion towards light branches of activity and the use of modern production techniques [1976, ch. 4]. As economic growth proceeds,

features of underdevelopment—such as disarticulation, domination by the centre, etc.— are accentuated; autocentric growth is impossible, since the periphery is 'complementary and dominated' [1976: 288].

According to Amin, economic relations between central and peripheral economies can be understood by means of the theory of unequal exchange [1977, Part IV]. Amin's version of the latter differs from that of Emmanuel [1972], with whom the theory is usually associated, in certain important respects. The essential elements of the theory, in Amin's view, are the preeminence of 'world values'; that is, in the world capitalist system, 'social labour is crystallised in goods which have an international character' [1977: 181]; and the universal character of capitalist commodity alienation, by means of the direct or indirect sale of labour power. Since capital is internationally mobile, the rate of profit tends to equality throughout the world, but since labour is internationally immobile, wages vary between countries. Hence the transformation of international values (the only meaningful ones) into international prices (again, the only meaningful ones) implies the transfer of value from some nations to others [1977: 187]. Simply stated, unequal exchange is the exchange of goods whose production involves wage differentials greater than those of productivity.

Brevity prevents examination here of many logical difficulties in these propositions, such as the use of the value-form, the glossing over of the problem of transforming values into prices and the assumption that identical production processes will generate equal organic compositions of capital despite variations in wages (and hence differences in variable capital). Even if a systematic relationship between prices and values could be established, however, many vital political and economic issues remain unilluminated by analysing trade exclusively in terms of unequal exchange.

More generally, the logical status of Amin's argument is unclear. Certain categories (centre and periphery) are defined as having certain characteristics; these characteristics are asserted to be determining; then it follows that all other characteristics are secondary, or results of membership of the category. Information presented by Amin, although impressive in its scope, is used to demonstrate the correctness of the theory; thus, the basis of selection of the information is given by the theory. In the event of information not demonstrating the correctness of the theory, resort is had to the 'appearances-essences' dichotomy, particularly the version which regards appearances of diversity as disguising an underlying unity [*e.g., Amin, 1977: 166–167*].

Neither advanced capitalist countries nor the underdeveloped countries can be regarded as facing similar problems in relation to world markets, world financial institutions, etc. The problems economies face depend upon the structure of these economies and their particular location within the international capitalist system. Within the framework of Amin's type of 'universal theory', discussion of particular economies takes the form of illustrations and exemplars of the validity of the universal theory itself, rather than advancing our understanding of those economies. Amin's analysis, therefore, cannot provide an understanding of any particular economy and its relationship to the international capitalist system, since it denies the need to do so [*cf. Cutler et al., 1977, II: 243–254*].

The policy implications of Amin's analysis can be summarised in two main points. First, underdeveloped countries have no freedom of manoeuvre in relation to world capitalism: 'so long as the underdeveloped country continues to be integrated in the world market, it remains helpless . . . the possibilities of local accumulation are nil' [*1974: 131*]. Second, as economic growth at the periphery occurs, so underdevelopment develops; therefore, only a radical and complete break with the world capitalist system will provide the conditions necessary for genuine development. To illustrate the style and strategy of Amin's argu-

ment, it is worth quoting at some length his views on the possibilities of national financial independence:

The creation of a national currency confers on the local authorities no power of effective control so long as a country's inclusion in the world market is not challenged: even control of the exchange and of transfers does not prevent the transmission to the periphery of fluctuations in the value of the dominant currencies of the centre, nor does it prevent transmission to the periphery of the centre's price structure. Money here, constitutes the outward form of an essential relation of dominance, but it is not responsible for this relation [*1974: 483*].

Thus economic policy at the national level in a peripheral capitalist economy is ineffective; the only solution is a revolutionary break with the world capitalist system.

Amin's policy conclusions are based on a denial of national economies as units of analysis, a denial of the significance of differences between peripheral economies, and a denial that national economic policy is a legitimate arena of debate, dispute and political struggle. Yet the level of a national economy is a level at which crucial issues are determined which affect the conditions of operation of capitalism; these conditions vary between economies and have important effects on economic, social and political organisation. Some examples of issues which affect the conditions of operation of capitalism are the nature of multinational activity and policies towards multinationals, e.g., requirements concerning localisation of labour and training; local content requirements concerning inputs; taxation policies; disclosure requirements with respect to information; the level of long-term indebtedness and hence the relationship of a national economy to institutions such as the IMF, which significantly affects the scope for independent national economic policies; policies towards trade unions and the distribution of income and wealth, which can significantly affect the structure of demand and the composition of output.

There are many 'peripheral' countries where the political forces for a socialist revolution are weak or nonexistent. Therefore areas of research, analysis and policy which concern the relationship of a particular national economy to the international capitalist system cannot be dismissed without disregarding the conditions of life for the majority in such countries in the short and medium term. There are some peripheral countries where the freedom of manoeuvre may be limited, others where it may be less limited, but this cannot be determined in the abstract. In any event, for socialists to dismiss such issues as irrelevant is irresponsible.

One is not belittling the tragic possibilities of the contemporary socioeconomic world by suggesting that international trade is not the stuff of tragedy. On the contrary, such possibilities are done less than justice by analyses which rely on 'aprioristic' reasoning at a high level of abstraction. It would be better, as others have already suggested, to redirect investigation towards the dynamic of innovation and accumulation within the core capitalist economies, and to the different forms which the expansion of capitalist social relations have taken on the periphery [*Brenner, 1977*]. This might elucidate the hypothesis that this expansion produces a variety of particular deformations of international trade—forced specialisation, vulnerability to foreign economic control—but that the causes of these deformations do not lie within the realm of international trade itself.

5. RESEARCH RELEVANT TO POOR COUNTRIES' TRADE PROBLEMS

The previous arguments imply that, while some variants of each type of theory suggest certain valuable insights into either the rationale for, or the historical determinants of, trade by poor countries, no one story preeminently compels rational assent. At the same time, a self-imposed and sceptical si-

lence need not follow. No logical objection arises if, for example, historical analysis in a Marxist conceptual tradition is introduced to explain the structural differences between rich and poor countries which the structuralists take as their point of departure; if technological and institutional gaps are used to explain internal and international maldistribution of the benefits from trade; and if Ricardian comparative advantage is accepted as one of the elements that should enter into the planning of a country's foreign trade, alongside long-run dynamic economic considerations and the objective requirements of national security. The prospects for intelligent eclecticism in trade theory are far from hopeless.

Intelligent eclecticism is, however, at a great discount, Perhaps from a mistaken understanding of intellectual purity, or perhaps for less laudable reasons, it is more popular to project from the partial insights of each type of theory a total view which vociferously excludes the insights of the other types of theory. This produces prolonged and noisy disputes between antagonists who entirely fail to connect with each other's arguments, plus a general tendency to assume that relevant empirical information is either already to hand or easily predictable from the chosen theoretical approach. In these circumstances, the appetite for new research into particular institutions, economies and processes gets blunted. By challenging the exclusivity of partial insights, one may hope to whet it again. . . .

Each story about trade and poor economies has a distinctive set of attitudes to the problems and policies just discussed. Proponents of mutually beneficial trade seem to quite overlook the existence of 'colonial' trade patterns, justifying actual trade patterns as a reflection of comparative advantage, except for the 'distortions' resulting from tariffs. Multinationals are seen as efficient and rational enterprises caught between the political pressures of their home and their host governments, whose chief defect is that their overindulgence in self-financed investment pre-empts the optimal allocation of funds that would be produced by the international capital market [*Penrose, 1971*]. Regional common markets and commodity stabilisation schemes are disapproved of as 'second best' solutions for export instability: the 'first best' solution is taken to be the total removal of trade barriers plus the increment to international liquidity needed to finance the short-term balance-of-payments deficits which instability creates for poor economies.

Theorists of asymmetric gains from trade originally argued as if the bias in trade benefits resulted from differences in the degree of modernisation between the rich and the poor economies. More recently it has been suggested the colonial relationships are the origin of rich countries' firms' market power in some poor economies, and that it is the abuse of this market power that biases the gains from trade—a line of reasoning given empirical support by a close study of French iron and steel exports to her ex-colonial territories in Africa [*Yeats, 1978: 167–180*]. Multi-nationals are seen not just as monopolists, but as creators and exploiters of their monopoly power, which needs to be curbed by the same kind of antimonopoly regulations as already exist at the national level [*Feld, 1978*]. The advocacy of economic intervention carries over to the positive encouragement of regional cooperation and commodity schemes, given a clear recognition that the conditions for 'global welfare maximisation' are politically unattainable in a divided world.

With theories of trade-induced polarisation, one has moved completely from Mancunian to Manichaean economics. Here, as has been noted, all reformist policies, indeed policies *tout court* are impotent. The determinism of the system can only be broken by a spontaneous revolution.

Those who thought that the structuralist approach failed to make all the necessary connections in theory, and condemned its supporters to a very innocent brand of political practice, may well quail at the crudity of some recent Marxist responses to the demand for a more comprehensive and realistic attack on the problems of international relations and world poverty. But one is free to dissent from the view that comprehensiveness and realism are indistinguishable from rigid determinism and radical despair. Socialists need not be forced back to the old structuralist positions, let alone to neoclassical versions of comparative advantage theory, by the weakness of many of the Marxist views which have been heard so far. We can still ask for the structuralist approach to be developed less economistically and more fully in relation to the history of world society and politics. We can still ask that the insights to be derived in this way be used to combat the naivety to many of the reforms paraded under the structuralist banner. We can also ask that the Marxist approach, based on historical analysis, and the setting of economic issues in their social and political context, be developed more in relation to the specificities of economies, institutions and agencies. There is another kind of story about trade and poor economies, which sooner or later should be able to be told.

REFERENCES

Abdel-Fadil, M., T. F. Cripps and J. Wells, 1977, 'A New International Economic Order?', *Cambridge Journal of Economics*, 1, 205–213.

Amin, S., 1974, *Accumulation on a World Scale*, New York, Monthly Review Press.

Amin, S., 1976, *Unequal Development*, Brighton, Harvester Press.

Amin, S., 1977, *Imperialism and Unequal Development*, New York, Monthly Review Press.

Brenner, R., 1977, 'The Origins of Capitalist Development: A Critique of neo-Smithian Marxism', *New Left Review*, No. 104.

Cutler, A., B. Hindess, P. Q. Hirst and A. Hussein, 1977, *Marx's Capital and Capitalism Today*, London, Routledge & Kegan Paul.

Emmanuel, A., 1972, *Unequal Exchange: the Imperialism of Trade*, London, New Left Books.

Feld, W. J., 1978, 'United Nations Proposals for a

Code of Conduct for Multinational Enterprises', in W. G. Tyler (ed.), *Issues and Prospects for the New International Economic Order*, Lexington, Massachusetts, D. C. Heath.

Flanders, J., 1964, 'Prebisch on Protectionism: an Evaluation', *Economic Journal*.

Helleiner, G. K., 1972, *International Trade and Economic Development*, London, Penguin Education.

Johnson, H. G., 1958, *International Trade and Economic Growth: Studies in Pure Theory*, London, Allen and Unwin.

Johnson, H. G., 1974, *Technology and Economic Interdependence*, London, Macmillan (for the Trade Policy Research Centre).

Levin, J. V., 1960, *The Export Economies*, Cambridge, Mass., Harvard University Press.

Lewis, W. A., 1954, 'Economic Development with Unlimited Supplies of Labour', *The Manchester School*, April.

Lewis, W. A., 1978, *The Evolution of the International Economic Order*, Princeton, N. J., Princeton University Press.

Little, I. M. D., T. Scitovsky and M. F. G. Scott, 1970, *Industry and Trade in Some Developing Countries: A Comparative Study*, Oxford, Oxford University Press (for the Organisation for Economic Cooperation and Development).

Morrison, T. K., 1976, *Manufactured Exports from Developing Countries*, New York, Praeger.

National Bureau of Economic Research, 1975, *Foreign Trade Regimes and Economic Development* (12 volumes; 10 country studies by various authors and two comparative studies by J. N. Bhagwati and A. C. Kreuger), New York and London, Columbia University Press.

Nayyar, D., 1978, 'Transnational Corporations and Manufactured Exports from Poor Countries', *Economic Journal*, March.

Penrose, E. T., 1971, 'Problems Associated with the Growth of International Firms', in *The Growth of Firms, Middle East Oil and Other Essays*, London, Frank Cass.

Prebisch, R., 1959, 'Commercial Policy in the Underdeveloped Countries', *American Economic Review*, May (AEA Proceedings).

Rangarajan, L. N., 1978, *Commodity Conflict*, London, Croom Helm.

Robinson, J. V., 1974, *Reflections on the Theory of International Trade*, Manchester, Manchester University Press.

Salter, W. E. G., 1960, *Productivity and Technical Change*, Cambridge, Cambridge University Press, second edition.

Samuelson, P., 1970, *Economics*, New York, McGraw-Hill, eighth edition.

Singer, H. W., 1950, 'The Distribution of Gains between Investing and Borrowing Countries', *American Economic Review*, May (AEA Proceedings).

Singer, H. W., 1974, 'The Distribution of Gains from Trade and Investment—Revisited', *Journal of Development Studies*, Vol. 11.

Singh, A., 1978, 'Basic Needs versus the New International Economic Order: the Significance of Third World Industrialisation', Cambridge, Department of Applied Economics (mimeo).

Tinker, H., 1974, *A New System of Slavery; Export of Indian Labour Overseas 1830–1920*, Oxford, Oxford University Press (for the Institute of Race Relations).

Vaitsos, C. V., 1978, 'Crisis in Regional Economic Cooperation (Integration) among Developing Countries: A Survey', *World Development*, June.

Vernon, R., 1966, 'International Investment and International Trade in the Product Cycle', *Quarterly Journal of Economics*, Vol. 80, May.

Yeats, A. J., 1978 'Monopoly Power, Barriers to Competition and the Pattern of Price Differentials in International Trade', *Journal of Development Economics*, Vol. 5, No. 2, June.

Yotopoulos, P. A., and J. B. Nugent, 1976, *Economics of Development: Empirical Investigations*, New York, Harper & Row.

27. Import Substitution and Industrialization in Latin America: Experiences and Interpretations*

Werner Baer

Throughout most of the Fifties and Sixties many Latin American governments adopted Import Substitution Industrialization (ISI) as their principal method to achieve economic growth and socio-economic modernization. By the opening of the Seventies, however, there was considerable doubt about ISI's success in solving the region's development problems. In many countries the possibilities for further import-substitution had disappeared. Industrial growth had slowed, job opportunities in industry for Latin America's rapidly growing urban population were scarce, income distribution had in many countries either remained unchanged or had become more concentrated than in the early post-World War II years, and most industrial goods produced within the region were priced so high that export possibilities were severely limited.

Considerable debate has taken place among economists and policymakers over the merits of ISI as a strategy for economic development, the performance of ISI in various countries, over the nature of post-ISI problems which these countries have faced, and over policies to deal with these post-ISI problems.

In this review article I shall first describe the nature of ISI in Latin America, its occurrence prior to World War II, and its development in the decades of the Fifties and Sixties. I shall then review the problems which developed as ISI reached maturity and review various analyses developed to explain these

problems. Finally, I shall examine various strategies which have been suggested for the post-ISI period.

THE NATURE OF ISI IN LATIN AMERICA

ISI is an attempt by economically less-developed countries to break out of the world division of labor which had emerged in the nineteenth century and the early part of the twentieth century. Under this division, Latin America (and most areas of Asia and Africa) specialized in the export of food and raw materials, while importing manufactured goods from Europe and the United States. Import substitution consists of establishing domestic production facilities to manufacture goods which were formerly imported. It follows that all countries which industrialized after Great Britain, went through a stage of ISI; that is, all passed through a stage where the larger part of investment in industries was undertaken to replace imports. ISI would come to a close when most investment was channeled towards the construction of capacity to produce for new incremental demand.

The ISI wave in Europe and the United States occurred in the middle and second half of the nineteenth century. It is a well-known fact that in this early ISI process governments played an active role in encouraging and protecting the development of infant industries. Another characteristic of nineteenth century ISI is its "national" character. Although in some countries finance for infrastructure investment was obtained from abroad, industries were for the most part in domestic hands, while the design of machines and skilled manpower to run them were often imported from England in the early industrialization period.

* From *Latin American Research Review*, 7, no. 1 (Spring 1972), pp. 95–111.

The author wishes to thank David Felix, Andrea Maneschi, Carlos M. Pelaez, William Steel, and William O. Thweatt for many useful suggestions.

Once Western Europe and the United States had undergone their initial industrializations, import substitution did not come entirely to an end. However, it ceased being mainly a mechanism of industrialization, and became in the twentieth century part of a continuing process of growth and of a changing pattern of industrial specialization among economically advanced countries.

There are various historical reasons why the countries of Africa, Asia and Latin America did not undergo ISI at the time of, or right after, the European ISI's. Colonial policies of European countries provide much of the explanation for the former two cases, while socio-economic structure helps explain the Latin American case. The presence of attractive external markets for the region's primary exports, which benefited the elites, meant that there was little political desire to change the structure of the economies. Also in the nineteenth century and early part of the twentieth century, Latin American countries did not have the entrepreneurial classes, labor force, infrastructure, market size, or administrative capacity to cope with an extensive industrialization process. Also in the case of some countries, like Brazil, European powers had enough leverage to force governments to maintain free trade policies, thus in effect blocking any possibility of ISI.

ISI BEFORE AND DURING THE SECOND WORLD WAR

Latin America was not completely devoid of manufacturing activities prior to World War I. It has by now been well documented that in the latter part of the nineteenth century workshops and small factories in textiles and food products industries had developed in some parts of Argentina, Brazil, Mexico and other larger countries. Also, machine tools and spare parts workshops developed to service railroads, sugar refining mills, etc. These activities were usually started by importers of equipment. There were some isolated attempts to raise tariffs both to protect incipient industries and to stimulate the creation of new ones. It would be mistaken, however, to speak of "industrialization" prior to World War I. The bulk of manufactured goods consumed in Latin America were either imported or produced by small domestic workshops, while exports consisted almost entirely of primary products. Except for Argentina, the population was primarily rural, and the primary export sector was the pacesetter of economic activity, while workshops and small industries were appendages to general economic activity.

It should be noted, however, that on the eve of World War I the primary export sector with its complementary activities in services (banking, merchandizing, government) and social infrastructure (communication, transportation, etc.) had in many Latin American countries created a fairly substantial middle class which consumed large quantities of imported manufactured consumer goods.

ISI INDUCED FROM ABROAD

World War I, the Great Depression of the Thirties and World War II induced pronounced spurts of ISI in most larger Latin American countries. The interruption of shipping and the decline of non-military production in Europe and the United States during World War I created severe shortages of imported manufactured goods in Latin America, raised relative prices of such goods, and increased profitability of ISI investment. Textiles, food products, and various other light consumer goods industries were the principal fields of ISI in that period. In the Twenties many of these newly created ISI industries stagnated because of renewed U.S. and European competition and the general refusal of policy makers to protect infant industries of recent vintage. It was generally thought that World War I had been an aberration from the natural order of things, which was reflected in the world division of labor of the nineteenth century. Hence policy makers were reluctant to tamper with a movement back to "normalcy."

The depression of the Thirties resulted in renewed shortages of imported goods. The fall of foreign exchange receipts from exports forced most countries of the region drastically to curtail imports. The decline resulted at first in increased use of productive capacity which had been underutilized in the Twenties, and later in the creation of new industrial capacity. As in World War I, the depression-induced ISI occurred primarily in light consumer goods industries, although in some cases, especially Brazil, steel and capital goods industries were developed on a relatively small scale.

World War II had a stimulating effect on ISI industries: shortages of foreign manufactured goods led to full utilization of industrial capacity; some investment in new capacity occurred when capital goods could be imported; and even some textile products were exported by Argentina, Brazil, and Mexico.

ISI IN THE FIFTIES AND SIXTIES

But it was only after World War II that ISI became a deliberate policy tool for economic development. Most of the larger countries of Latin America implicitly or explicitly accepted the ECLA analysis of the hopelessness of gearing their economies towards the traditional world division of labor. Continued reliance on the export of food and primary products was thought to be precarious because of the instability of such exports, which would not be conducive to long term development because of the relatively slow growth of world demand for such products. It was thought that ISI would introduce a dynamic element into the Latin American economies and increase their rates of growth. The latter were deemed essential to deal with the population explosion of the region and to meet the demands of the

increasingly urban population for the ways of life of the masses in more advanced countries. It was also thought that ISI would bring greater economic independence to Latin American countries: self-sufficiency in manufactured goods would place Latin American economies less at the mercy of the world economy.

The principal policy instruments used to promote and intensify ISI were: protective tariffs and/or exchange controls; special preferences for domestic and foreign firms importing capital goods for new industries; preferential import exchange rates for industrial raw materials, fuels and intermediate goods; cheap loans by government development banks for favored industries; the construction by governments of infrastructure especially designed to complement industries; and the direct participation of government in certain industries, especially the heavier industries, such as steel, where neither domestic nor foreign private capital was willing or able to invest.

The promotion of ISI industries was indiscriminate, that is, there were not attempts to concentrate on industrial sectors which might have had a potential comparative advantage. In some countries ISI occurred for considerable periods of time in consumer goods industries only. A concise summary is given by David Felix: "the initial industries are generally consumer goods or building materials producers with a relatively simple technology and a low capital requirement per worker and per unit of output. They are then followed by consumer goods industries requiring a more sophisticated technology and larger capital outlay, shading subsequently into industries producing relatively complex consumer durables, steel, engineering and chemical products."[1] This description is especially relevant in the cases of countries such as Argentina, Chile, Venezuela. In other countries, especially Brazil, the government was anxious to promote maximum vertical integration, i.e., to promote both final consumer goods industries and intermediate and capital goods sectors.

In some cases, where the initial thrust of ISI was on final consumer goods industries, a built-in resistance to backward vertical integration developed.[2] That is, firms which established themselves in the first ISI period pressured governments not to develop domestic intermediate and capital goods industries, since these would produce inputs at substantially higher prices than imported inputs. However, as the areas for further ISI declined, most countries pressed on with backward integration efforts.

An important feature of Latin American ISI in the Fifties and Sixties was the participation of foreign capital. Although its proportion of total savings was often substantially below 10 percent, it was instrumental in setting up key manufacturing industries by transferring know-how and organizational capabilities. This was also true in infrastructure investments and heavy industries owned by governments, which depended on foreign financing and technical aid.

THE RESULTS OF ISI

Tables 1 through 5 present a summary of the impact of ISI on the principal economies of the region and on the Latin American economy as a whole. In Table 1 we have various measures of the changes in the percentage distribution of the Gross Domestic Product. It should be noted that for countries where the data are available, industry already represented a significant proportion of GDP in the earlier decades of the century. However, as mentioned earlier, these industries consisted to a large extent of small workshops; in 1950 still over half of the work force in manufacturing was engaged in artisan-type of activities (see Table 2a). By the Sixties, industry had become the dominant sector in Argentina, Brazil, Mexico, and Chile. The annual rates of growth of various sectors shown in Table 1 indicate the extent to which industry was the pace setter in the post-World War II decades. We shall comment later on the other tables.

CRITIQUES OF ISI

Let us now turn to the various critiques which have been made of Latin American ISI. The critics can be divided into two groups which I shall designate as the "market critics" and the "structural critics." Although some arguments are common to both sets of critics, there is a certain philosophic-analytical similarity of the views within each camp which seem to justify the division I have made.

(a) The Market Critics

Many economists in this category view Latin America's ISI as an inefficient way of using resources to develop the region's countries. The more conservative economists believe that since world production can be best be maximized by having each country (or area of the world) specialize in the sectors where it has the greatest comparative advantage, Latin America should have continued to specialize in the production of primary products. This specialization would have maximized world output and made possible a higher income level in all parts of the world.

Because of the declining share of food and primary products in world trade, more moderate critics recognize the need for some ISI. But they criticize the indiscriminate way in which ISI was carried on, that is, by across-the-board promotion of industries without regard even to potential comparative advantage. The Latin American ISI strategies are seen as drives towards national self-sufficiency in total disregard of the advantages of an international division of labor along newer lines. This emphasis on autarky is seen as prejudicial to rapid economic growth for a number of reasons.

Given small markets, limited capital, and a dearth of skilled manpower, autarkic industrial growth leads to the development of inefficient and high-cost industries. The situation becomes especially pronounced in industries having high fixed costs. These industries require large-scale output in order to bring

TABLE 1. Changes in the Structure of the Economies of Selected Countries (Percentage Distribution of GDP According to Principal Sectors)

Argentina	1960 Prices		1937 Prices	
	1927–9	1963–5	1927–9	1963–5
Agriculture	27.4	17.1	30.5	18.4
Oil & Mining	0.3	1.5	0.6	3.5
Manufacturing	23.6	33.7	13.4	18.6
Construction	4.2	3.6	3.1	2.6

Source: Díaz-Alejandro, *Essays*.

Brazil		Current Prices				1953 Prices			
	1939	1947	1953	1960	1968	1947	1953	1960	1968
Agriculture	25.8	27.6	26.1	22.6	17.9	30.0	26.1	22.2	20.5
Industry	19.4	19.8	23.7	25.2	28.0	20.6	23.7	28.0	29.3
Other	54.8	52.6	50.2	52.2	54.1	49.4	50.2	49.8	50.2

Source: Fundação Getulio Vargas, Centro de Contas Nacionais.

Mexico	Current Prices					
	1900	1910	1930	1940	1950	1960
Rural	34.6	27.9	25.9	24.3	22.5	18.9
Extractive	6.4	9.1	13.5	8.5	5.7	5.4
Commerce & Transp.	23.4	23.4	23.4	28.5	31.0	30.6
Mfg., Construc. & Elec.	13.2	13.7	16.7	22.6	24.5	27.7

Source: Reynolds, *Mexican Economy*.

Latin America	Current Prices		Annual Rates of Growth		
	1950	1967	1950–60	1960–67	1950–67
Produc. of Goods	52.4	52.3	4.9	4.6	4.8
Agriculture	25.2	20.5	3.5	3.5	3.5
Mining	4.1	4.4	6.1	4.1	5.3
Manufacturing	19.6	24.1	6.2	5.8	6.0
Construction	3.5	3.3	4.6	4.1	4.4
Basic Services	7.2	8.3	5.5	5.7	5.6
Other Services	40.4	39.4	4.8	4.4	4.6
Commerce & Finance	18.0	18.8	5.1	4.9	5.0
Misc. Services	22.4	20.6	4.5	3.9	4.2
Total	100.0	100.0	4.9	4.6	4.8

Source: Naciones Unidas, CEPAL, *Estudio económico de América Latina, 1968* (New York, 1969), p. 18.

TABLE 2. **(a) Distribution of Economically Active Population (per cent distribution)**

Argentina			1925–9	1960–1
Rural Sector			35.7	21.7
Oil and Mining			0.3	0.6
Manufacturing			22.0	26.0
Construction			5.5	6.0
Public Utilities			0.5	0.8
Transport			4.6	5.7
Communications			0.5	1.0
Commerce, Finance and Housing			13.6	14.3
Government Services			4.6	10.4
Other Services			12.6	13.6

Source: Díaz-Alejandro, *Essay*.

Brazil		1940	1950	1960
Primary		71.0	64.4	58.5
Secondary		8.9	12.9	12.7
Tertiary		20.1	22.7	28.8
Total		100.0	100.0	100.0

Source: Various Brazilian demographic censuses.

Mexico	1910	1940	1950	1960
Agriculture	67.1	65.4	58.3	54.1
Mining	1.9	1.7	1.2	1.2
Mfg., Construc. & Power	13.1	11.0	14.8	17.7
Services	17.8	21.9	25.7	27.0
Total	100.0	100.0	100.0	100.0

Source: Reynolds, *Mexican Economy*.

Latin America	1950	1960	1965	1969
Agriculture	53.4	47.2	44.5	42.2
Mining	1.1	1.0	1.0	1.0
Manufacturing	14.4	14.4	14.0	13.8
(artisan)	(7.5)	(6.8)	(6.4)	(6.1)
Construction	3.8	4.1	3.9	4.5
Basic Services	4.2	5.1	5.3	5.5
Other Services	23.1	28.2	31.3	33.0
(commerce & finance)	(7.8)	(9.0)	(9.5)	(10.1)
Total	100.0	100.0	100.0	100.0

Source: CEPAL, 1969.

(b) Growth of Employment by Sectors and Population Growth (yearly rates of growth)

	Employment Growth			Population Growth	
	1950–60	1960–69		1950–60	1960–69
Agriculture	1.3	1.5	Total	2.8	2.9
Manufacturing	2.6	2.3	Urban	4.8	4.4
(artisan)	(1.5)	(1.6)	Rural	1.4	1.4
Mining	2.0	2.2			
Construction	3.2	4.0			
Basic Services	4.6	3.4			
Other Services	4.7	4.6			

Source: CEPAL, 1968.

TABLE 3 (a) Real Rate of Growth (Annual) by Sectors for Latin America and Selected Countries

| | 1955–60 | 1960–65 | 1955–60 | 1960–65 | 1955–60 | 1960–65 |
	Latin America		Argentina		Brazil	
Agriculture	2.7	4.8	−0.4	2.1	3.7	6.9
Manufacturing	6.6	5.6	3.8	4.1	10.3	4.9
Construction	4.2	5.9	4.3	2.0	7.2	2.8
	Chile		Mexico		Colombia	
Agriculture	2.3	3.1	3.0	3.9	3.5	3.0
Manufacturing	3.2	6.7	8.1	8.0	6.1	5.9
Construction	1.4	4.6	8.1	5.9	−0.2	1.9

Source: Naciones Unidas, *Estudio económico de América Latina, 1965.*

(b) Latin America: Growth Rates of the Total GDP and of Industrial Product (Annual Cumulative Rates)

	Total Product	Industrial Product
1940–50	5.0	6.8
1950–60	4.7	6.3
1960–68	4.5	5.4

Source: United Nations, *Economic Bulletin for Latin America*, second half of 1969.

TABLE 4 (a) Growth of Urban Population and Industrial Employment (Average Annual Rates of Growth: 1950–60)

	Urban Population	Industrial Employment
Argentina	3.0	1.7
Brazil	6.5	2.6
Mexico	5.6	4.8

Source: Table in Little, Scitovsky, and Scott, *Industry and Trade*, p. 84.

(b) Growth of Industrial Product and Industrial Employment (Annual Growth Rates: 1950–68)

	Industrial Product	Industrial Employment
Argentina	4.5	2.2
Brazil	7.3	2.2
Colombia	6.2	2.4
Chile	4.6	2.2
Peru	7.8	3.4
Mexico	6.7	4.7
Latin America	6.0	2.8

Source: Raúl Prebisch, *Transformación y desarrollo: La gran tarea de América Latina*, (Washington, D.C., 1970), p. 45.

TABLE 5. (a) Latin America's Participation in World Trade (Latin America's Exports as a Per Cent of World Exports)

1948–10.9%	1960–7.0%
1950–10.6%	1964–6.4%
1957–7.8%	1968–5.0%

Source: *Regional Integration and the Trade of Latin America*, Committee for Economic Development, Jan. 1968; and *International Trade, 1968*, GATT.

(b) Changes in Latin America's Import Coefficients (Value of Imports of Goods and Services as a Per Cent of GDP)

	1928	1938	1948–9	1957–8	1962	1960*	1967*
Argentina	17.8	12.1	11.2	5.8	7.1	8.0	6.6
Brazil	11.3	6.2	6.6	5.8	4.5	7.8	5.6
Chile	31.2	14.9	11.5	9.5	11.3	15.7	15.7
Colombia	18.0	11.0	10.6	8.2	8.8	12.2	8.8
Mexico	14.2	7.0	8.5	7.8	6.8	7.8	7.8
Peru			9.6	16.1	13.6	19.0	28.1
Latin America			10.2	9.9	8.7	10.0	9.9

Source: Joseph Grunwald and Philip Musgrove, *Natural Resources in Latin American Development* (Baltimore, 1970), p. 20.

* CEPAL, 1968.

(c) Imports as a Percentage of Total Supplies by Categories

	Consumers' Goods	Intermediate Goods	Capital Goods
Brazil			
1949	9.0	25.9	63.7
1955	2.9	17.9	43.2
1959	1.9	11.7	32.9
1964	1.3	6.6	9.8
Mexico			
1950	2.4	13.2	66.5
1955	2.3	n.a.	63.4
1960	1.3	10.4	54.9
1965	n.a.	9.9	59.8

Source: Little, Scitovsky, and Scott, *Industry and Trade*, p. 60.

costs down to levels prevailing in more advanced industrial countries. Outstanding examples are the steel and automobile industries which have been established in most of the larger Latin American countries. In the case of automobiles, the situation was worsened because a large number of these countries permitted the establishment of many firms, thus completely eliminating the possibilities of economies of large scale production. In the late Sixties, the annual output of cars and trucks in eight Latin American countries was 600,000, which was produced by ninety firms (an average of 6,700 per firm). The situation is well summarized by Scitovsky: "Protection usually confines the protected manufacturer to the domestic market and so inhibits the exploitation of economies of scale, especially in small countries and in industries where scale economies are important and call for very large-scale operations. Moreover governments anxious to secure the benefits of competition often encourage many firms to enter industry in order to create domestic competition where protectionist policies have suspended foreign competition." The result, however, is contrary to what is aimed for, since such government policy "restricts the scope for economies of scale yet further and often leads to the emergence of too many firms, each with too small an output capacity, and frequently with too small a market to utilize fully even that capacity."[3]

In the last few years the concept of "effective protection" has been used by numerous economists to analyze distortions which have arisen during the ISI process. Nominal tariff rates measure only the percentage by which prices of protected goods exceed their world prices. This amount is also the difference by which domestic substitutes can exceed the international price. The "effective" tariff or rate of protection "shows the percentage by which the value added at a stage of fabrication in domestic industry can exceed what this would be in the absence of protection; in other words, it shows by what percentage the sum of wages, profits, and depreciation allowances, payable by domestic firms can, thanks to protection, exceed what this sum would be if the same firms were fully exposed to foreign competition."[4] Thus, if a product uses a considerable amount of imported inputs on which there is no tariff or on which the tariff rate is lower than the tariff on the finished product, protection is higher than is indicated by the nominal tariff, since the margin available for domestic value added is larger than the difference indicated by the tariff. In a number of Latin American countries the effective tariff on consumer goods was found to be much higher than for intermediate or capital goods. Such high levels of effective protection eliminate incentives to increase production efficiency and make it difficult to bring the cost of production to international levels.

The stress on autarky—on maximizing internal vertical industrial integration (promoting not only final goods production, but also intermediate and capital goods)—impedes growth because resources are not used in sectors where they will produce the highest possible output. Had Latin American countries specialized in only a few products with the greatest potential comparative advantage, and exported a large surplus while importing other goods, total output available would have been higher and these nations would have grown more rapidly than they actually did. As it happened, autarky was practiced in each country, and no attempt was made until the late Sixties to at least promote ISI on a regional basis; in other words, to promote a complementary industrial structure within Latiin America.

A study by Baranson of automobile industries in developing countries (which includes information on Argentina, Brazil, and Mexico) illustrates many of the problems of autarkic development. He contrasts the proliferation of automobile firms in developing countries with the quest by European producers for increased exports and consolidation with competitors, both inside and outside their countries, in order to keep down unit cost. He finds that among the main deficiencies are "underdeveloped supplier capacities, inadequate quality control systems, and a dearth of qualified technicians and managers. By creating a 'sellers' market,' protection and import-substitution tend to undermine quality." Thus, Baranson found that many "basic materials that are considered standard stock in open economies often must be procured locally or specially ordered in small batches at considerably higher cost or at inferior quality. . . . Lack of uniformity in raw materials and semi-finished goods such as castings and forgings creates special problems in milling and machining to required specifications. In high-volume production, precision and uniformity are built into automated equipment. Developing countries with limited markets are much more dependent upon the very machine labor skills in which they are deficient." Also, considering the many parts which go into an automobile, Baranson found that outside plant procurement averages about 60 percent by value in advanced economies, while in countries like Mexico and Brazil this factor amounts to only 40 percent. Such a condition further reduces the possibility of economies of large scale production.[5] As a result, Baranson found that factory costs in Argentina, Brazil, and Mexico were about 60 percent to 150 percent higher than in the United States.

Similar problems were found in many other industries. A study of the manufacture of heavy electrical equipment in developing countries found that in Argentina "excessive diversification, unused capacity, large inventories because of import controls, and difficulties in obtaining outside finance explain the high price level."[6] ECLA has also provided numerous illustrations of the problems discussed above. It found that in 1964, "the paper industry (excluding newsprint) had 292 plants of which only 25 had a capacity of 100 tons daily, which is considered the minimum economic size. In the chemical industry, too, there are a great many instances in which there is a wide gap between the plant sizes most frequently found in the region and the sizes constructed in the industrialized countries."[7]

Some economists have been concerned about the domestic resource cost involved in the type of ISI which has been promoted in Latin America. They have stressed the need to calculate for various industries the value of domestic resources required to save a unit of foreign exchange. The rate of transformation between domestic and foreign resources thus obtained should be compared to the appropriate exchange rate. The higher the former is over the latter, the greater presumably is the "waste" of resources; that is, if domestic resources had been used for export purposes, the foreign exchange earned would have fetched more goods than the goods produced by using the resources domestically.

Policies employed to stimulate industries have often been prejudicial to the functioning of the more traditional agricultural sector. The allocation of investment resources (credit) to new industries has often meant that a few resources were available to increase agricultural efficiency. Overvalued exchange rates, which favored industries by providing cheap imported inputs, hurt agriculture by making its goods less competitive on the international market and/or by making it less profitable to export agricultural products. Finally, the combination of higher industrial prices caused by protection and by price control of agricultural goods, turned the internal terms of trade against agriculture. All these factors hurt agricultural production and exports. Argentina is probably the outstanding example of ISI occurring to the detriment of agriculture and agricultural exports.

Critics have also pointed to the detrimental results of neglecting exports during the heyday of ISI. Some stress the negative effects of ISI policies on the production and exportation of traditional goods, while others emphasize the failure to diversify the export structure in accordance with the changing internal economic structure which ISI brought about. While, as was mentioned earlier, the contribution of industry to GDP became dominant in the years after World War II, the commodity composition of Latin America's exports remained almost unchanged. For example, in the late Sixties, over 90 percent of Argentina and Brazil's exports still consisted of traditional primary and food products, while about three-quarters of Mexico's exports consisted of such products. Until the Sixties, little efforts were made by Latin American countries to stimulate non-traditional exports. And while in the early Sixties the development of the Latin American Common Market, the Central American Common Market, the introduction of drawbacks and rebates on domestic taxes for export efforts in some countries (Argentina, Mexico, Colombia) represented attempts to stimulate non-traditional exports, the net effects by the late Sixties were still slight.

The neglect of exports during the ISI period in Latin America, that is, the failure to stimulate traditional exports and to diversify the export structure, could have serious consequences. The original advocates of ISI had hoped that their policy would lead Latin

American countries to greater self-sufficiency and would make their economies more independent of the vicissitudes of international trade. It appears, however, that there is a lower limit to the import coefficient (import/GDP ratio) for most economies, as becomes clear by examining Table 5(b). While ISI was taking place, not only was the import coefficient reduced, but the commodity composition of imports changed. An increasingly larger proportion of imports consisted of raw materials, semi-finished products, and capital goods. These represented the inputs of the ISI industries which were not available domestically, and were thus the principal reason for the increasing downward stickiness of the import coefficient.

It is thus ironic that the net result of ISI has been to place Latin American countries in a new and more dangerous dependency relationship with the more advanced industrial countries than ever before. In former times, a decline in export receipts acted as a stimulus to ISI. Under the circumstances, a decline in export receipts not counterbalanced by capital inflows can result in forced import curtailments which, in turn, could cause an industrial recession. Such results have been experienced by Argentina and Colombia, and other countries face the same danger.

To guard against such a situation, Latin American countries would have to make increasing efforts to diversify exports. Such actions, however, assume that they are able to compete in the international market. Considering the high cost structure of many Latin American ISI industries, the many bureaucratic obstacles exporters have faced, and the lack of an adequate credit mechanism to export manufactured goods, export diversification is not an easy task.

(b) Structural Critics

Since World War II, most Latin American countries have experienced a population explosion. Annual population growth for the entire region increased from 1.9 percent to over 2.8 percent in the late Fifties and Sixties. During the same period, migration from the countryside to the cities increased dramatically. One may see in Table 2(b) that the urban population growth rate in the post-World War II period was over three times as large as the rural growth rate. The same table also shows that the rate of labor absorption in industry was substantially smaller than the rate of growth of urban population. In Table 2(a), it is clear that after two decades of industrialization, the proportion of the labor force employed in manufacturing industry in Latin America as a whole actually declined somewhat, and that almost half of these workers were still engaged in artisan workshops. In some of the individual countries shown, the proportion rose a few points, but very modestly compared to the changes in the contribution of industry to GDP. The failure of ISI to create direct employment opportunities has worried both "structural" and "market" critics.

The latter blame the low labor absorption rate on price distortions. Most countries used certain types of subsidies to capital in order to stimulate industrialization. In a number of countries, domestic and foreign firms were given special exchange rate privileges to import capital equipment. Development banks gave cheap credit (often at negative real rates of interest) to help finance investment in favored industries. At the same time, wages in industry were relatively high because of labor legislation which had been introduced in the Thirties and Forties in such countries as Argentina, Brazil, and Chile. Thus, there were no incentives to adopt labor-intensive techniques of production. On the contrary, the relative price structure of capital and labor was such as to actually stimulate the search for and adoption of capital-intensive techniques.

The structural critics of ISI worry about low labor absorption rates not only because of the services social problems of urban unemployment or underemployment which result, but also because of their implication for income distribution. With an unequal distribution of income, a fiscal system which does not redistribute income, and a leading growth sector (industry) whose incremental capital/labor ratio is high (usually substantially higher than the economy's average capital/labor ratio), the tendency will be for income to become even more concentrated than before. The evidence available for Latin American countries tends to confirm this trend.

Because of the concentration of income, the growth of demand for industrial products may not be sufficient to maintain the initial ISI momentum. What makes this situation worse is the lumpiness of many ISI industries. Because of indivisibilities, many industries were forced to build substantially ahead of demand. Thus, the existence of excess capacity which is not being rapidly filled by growing demand dampens the incentive to invest.

This situation could, of course, be avoided by various types of redistributive policies of governments—redistribution by income groups, by sectors of the economy, and by regions. Progressive tax measures and/or appropriate wage policies could be used to redistribute incomes among social groups; government credit and fiscal policies could redirect resources to neglected sectors (such as agriculture, housing, road building) and geographical regions.

Potential domestic demand for industrial products exists in most Latin American countries because the ISI process occurred in an unbalanced fashion. We have already mentioned the trends towards the concentration of income which could be reversed by appropriate policies and thus result in considerable demand expansion. However, there were other imbalances. As ISI proceeded, such sectors as agriculture, low income housing, transportation, and other infrastructure facilities were often neglected, threatening countries with severe bottlenecks. In the larger countries, ISI resulted in a strong regional concentration of industry and income, especially in Brazil, Mexico, and Argentina. Although such regional concentration made sense when taking into account external economies to firms set-

tling close to suppliers, to decent infrastructure facilities, and to skilled labor supplies, etc., it was of a self-reinforcing nature. Increasing regional concentration of wealth presented many countries with the political need to redistribute income on a regional basis. All these forces make it possible to generate new demand through government policies.

Georgescu-Roegen, however, called attention to a problem which might arise from post-ISI redistribution efforts. The profile of the productive structure which resulted from the ISI process reflects the demand profile which existed at the time when the process was started. This demand profile was based on a distribution of income which, in most cases, was quite unequal. Efforts to change the distribution of income in the post-ISI era in order to achieve greater social justice, increase aggregate demand, diminish intersectoral and/or inter-regional imbalances, will change the demand profile. Such changes could result in a substantial amount of imbalance or lack of synchronization between the country's productive and demand profiles. The degree of such imbalance depends, of course, on the flexibility of various productive sectors. For example, to what extent can the productive facilities of the consumer goods and capital goods industries be converted from producing luxury goods to producing mass consumption goods?

The greater the inflexibility of the country's productive structure, the greater the "structural-lock" dilemma of the country. Thus, the full use of the existing productive capacity would imply the necessity for the type of income distribution which would produce the requisite demand profile, i.e., a very unequal distribution of income. The alternative, a more egalitarian distribution of income, might imply considerable capacity in a number of industries.

This "structural lock" dilemma should be set off, however, against the import constraint problem. It has been claimed that high income inequality encourages a more import-intensive demand profile. That is, higher income groups consume technically more sophisticated goods which have relatively high direct and indirect import requirements. Thus, although a greater degree of income concentration could avoid a "structural lock" problem, it could lead to stagnation caused by import constraints.

EVALUATION AND OUTLOOK
FOR THE FUTURE

In my general attitude towards the critiques which I have summarized, I fully subscribe to the views of Bergsman and Candal in their evaluation of the Brazilian ISI experience: "Hindsight makes it easy to point out specific mistakes, even to suggest some modifications in policy that clearly would have avoided the greatest inefficiencies. It is much harder to compare actual results which those that might have come from some totally different policy that would not have included industrialization."

It is clear that in most, if not all, Latin American countries, industrialization was carried out on too wide a spectrum, given limited capital and human resources and very narrow markets. Also, excessively high effective production did not lead resources into fields which would have the highest possible potential comparative advantage, and protection gave a comfortable enough profit margin to all inside the market to neglect the search for greater efficiency. However, outright condemnation of inefficiencies has to be qualified. For political reasons, ISI within the context of a larger Latin American Common Market was not feasible in the immediate postwar period. A more specialized export-oriented ISI not only depended on the possibilities of Latin American economic integration, but also on the willingness of the United States and Europe to accept Latin American manufactured imports. If one admits that an international division of labor can no longer be based

on nineteenth century lines (given the relative decline of primary products in world trade), one has to expect structural changes in both the developing and the developed parts of the world. For example, one would expect the United States and Europe to accept a decline in the textile industry in order to make room for such imports from the Third World. Given the unwillingness to do this, one should temper one's condemnation of Latin American countries for not being more selective in their choice of industries. This does not excuse the proliferation of many firms in small markets (e.g., automobiles) which produced unnecessary high costs.

Many economists have the bad habit of generalizing from limited experience and evidence. This is especially true in the ISI discussions. The development of an integrated industrial structure might not make much sense in a small country like Chile, while it does make some sense in a country like Brazil. Although an elegant argument about industrialization having been promoted at the expense of agriculture can be made with empirical evidence from Argentina, it would be difficult to apply this argument to the Brazilian case. Coffee output was not sacrificed for the sake of industrialization.

The explanation of the labor-absorption problem in terms of factor price distortion is based on good deductive reasoning in economic theory, but there is little empirical evidence to back the explanation. In some industries the technological choices are limited. In most Latin American automobile industries the equipment installed was second hand and thus the assembly line operations are technologically substantially behind the more automated plants in Europe and the United States. The equipment in most of Latin America's textile industries is so old that various missions have recommended a thoroughgoing modernization in order to make these industries profitable and competitive. There exists, of course, the possibility of placing greater efforts in discovering more labor-intensive techniques, which might be achieved if Latin American countries would increase the resources earmarked for scientific and technological research. Only 0.5 percent of Latin America's GNP goes into such efforts, as compared to over 3 percent for the United States. It remains doubtful, however, whether price distortions explain Latin America's labor absorption problem.

Although the argument about the necessity for export diversification is well taken, the pontification of many economists concerning the past neglect of industrial exports is open to some criticisms. It seems that many forget that a large number of the key manufacturing industries of Latin America were constructed by or with the aid of foreign capital. The chief attraction of the latter was the promise of a growing protected market. It might have been rather difficult to convince firms to establish themselves in Brazil, Argentina, and other countries on the condition that from the beginning 40 to 50 percent of the output should be exported. Had there been a genuine interest by domestic and foreign firms to export manufactured goods, I suspect that the bureaucratic and exchange rate obstacles to such exports might have fallen earlier.

It could also be asserted that the high-cost structure of Latin America's industries makes export diversification difficult. Here, of course, there might be a dilemma. If the high-cost structure is in large part caused by the narrow market which raises unit costs, only increased sales could reduce the latter. And thus we might face an interesting chicken-egg problem. But even if this could be resolved through subsidies, exports of manufactured goods would still have to face non-price competitive factors such as credit terms, brand names, delivery terms, marketing organizations, etc. Since the importance of price vs. non-price competition in the international trade of manufactured and capital goods has never been firmly established, it is difficult to claim that the high cost structure is one of the principal barriers to export diversification. We have already mentioned the political problem of penetrating European and American markets.

Since most economists' intellectual energies in the last few decades have been spent worrying about the efficient allocation of resources, it is natural that those economists who have devoted their attention to developing countries should have spent most of their time examining and recommending how factors of production are or should be allocated. Relatively little thought was given to the fact that concern about development should include concern about the development of factors of production, not just their allocation. The many "inefficiencies" might prevent a developing country undergoing ISI from realizing its maximum crude growth rate in the short-run. This cost has to be weighed against the modernization or development which ISI brings about. Little work along these lines, that is, on the measurement of changes in the quality of factors of production, has been done in Latin America or in other parts of the developing world.

FUTURE POLICIES

By the late Sixties many Latin American countries were taking measures to eliminate some of the grosser distortions which ISI had brought along. In a number of countries the tariff level was brought down (e.g., Brazil, Argentina). This was not done to encourage more imports, but to decrease the level of effective protection and monopoly profits and thus give an incentive to firms to rationalize their operations. Measures were taken in such countries as Brazil, Argentina, and Peru to reduce the number of automobile firms and thus encourage lower cost production by scale economies.

There has been a constant effort by ECLA and the Inter-American Development Bank to push for greater economic integration via the Latin American Common Market. It is hoped that such integration would increase and diversify the exports of individual countries and that there would also result a rationalization of production throughout the continent by making the Latin American economies more complementary to each other. Besides trade in finished goods, attempts have been made to encourage "complementation agreements," in which there would be a division of labor along vertical lines (for example, the Chilean automobile industry specializing in the production of certain parts which would be assembled in Brazil). Unfortunately this process has not made as much progress as its advocates had hoped. It seems that a division of labor within Latin America would not necessarily result in national economic structures which would be to the liking of individual countries.

The problem of post-ISI stagnation, i.e., the finding of a new dynamic source of growth, has preoccupied many Latin American governments as the decade of the Seventies opened. In Brazil the government of President Emilio Medici has stated that its principal aim would be to develop a "program of social integration" which would increase the labor force participation in the national product, to develop the internal frontier of Amazonia, and to begin a gigantic road building program which would more effectively link various regions of the country and better link farming areas to markets. Peru is currently experiencing some drastic social reforms—land reform, programs of worker profit-sharing schemes, etc. The new Mexican president has also emphasized the need for income redistribution.

It remains to be seen if a redistribution of income and a growth of industrial exports will provide the same dynamism to the Latin American economies as the period of ISI. Turning from the demand to the supply side, one should also consider the effects of high population growth rates and social equity policies on the capital/output ratio. The latter will probably be much higher than in the past, which means that the growth produced by each unit of investment will be lower than in the past. Thus many economies in the future might have to balance the conflicting claims

arising from the need for higher saving to attain growth rates similar to those in the ISI days, and the pressures for more egalitarian socio-economic policies which tend to depress the capacity to save.

The employment problem will probably be the most difficult to cope with. At this writing it is doubtful that industry will be able to absorb a substantially larger proportion of the economically active population. Can the service sector effectively make use of the burgeoning urban masses? Can agrarian reforms be instituted in such a manner as to absorb manpower, or will agricultural modernization of necessity have to result in an increased expulsion of labor from the countryside? Even if there is no food problem, is there any possible economic structure in Latin America which will effectively employ all those who are employable? Or is the only solution to the dilemma the development of a population policy?

1. David Felix, "Monetarists, Structuralists, and Import-Substituting Industrialization: A Critical Appraisal," In: *Inflation and Growth in Latin America*, Werner Baer and Isaac Kerstenetzky, eds., 383 (Homewood, 1964; 2nd printing, New Haven, 1970).

2. Albert O. Hirschman, "The Political Economy of Import-Substituting Industrialization in Latin America," QJE, 82: 17–24 (1968).

3. Tibor Scitovsky, "Prospects for Latin American Industrialization Within the Framework of Economic Integration," In: *The Process of Industrialization in Latin America*, 43 (Washington, D.C., 1969), p. 42.

4. Little, Scitovsky, and Scott, *Industry and Trade in Some Developing Countries*, 39 (New York, 1970).

5. Jack Baranson, *Automotive Industries in Developing Countries*, 25–26 (Baltimore, 1969).

6. Ayhan Cilingiroglu, *Manufacture of Heavy Electrical Equipment in Developing Countries*, 31 (Baltimore, 1969).

7. "Industrial Development in Latin America," *Economic Bulletin for Latin America*, 13 (1969).

28. Trade Policy for Developing Countries*

Donald B. Keesing

THE ROLE OF INTERNATIONAL TRADE

International trade contributes to growth and development in a developing country in a number of ways. It expands output and provides additions to incomes through demand for local natural resources which, as the old phrase "vent for surplus" suggests, might otherwise go practically unused. More generally, it permits a developing economy to specialize, based on its relatively abundant resources, while importing goods and services that would be very expensive or impossible to produce locally. Thus, through trade, the country can potentially obtain more of each type of output than it could produce for itself.[1]

Benefits from trade are also based on economies of scale, i.e., advantages from large-scale production. The extent of the division of labor, and hence the output attainable per worker in any economy, are limited by the size of the market. Poor countries offer only tiny markets for most industrial products, so that a developing country will be impoverished by the high unit costs if it tries to produce a little of each product for its inadequate home market. Such a country stands to gain enormously by importing many or most of the goods that can be produced cheaply only on a large scale, and by building its manufacturing industries partly around exports, so that a larger scale of production can be attained.

By sharply raising incomes, trade expands demand, enlarging opportunities for learning, scale economies and a productive division of labor. At the same time it greatly expands the resources available for processes of savings, investment and accumulation that play a central role in development, including not only investment in physical capital, but also investment in intangible assets such as "human capital."[2]

Then, too, trade helps to create and demonstrate the existence of markets—initially for imports—that can eventually be made the basis for import substitution and industrialization around the domestic market.

It provides through imports, a supply of capital equipment, technical assistance, raw materials and other key inputs essential for industrial development, augmenting local supply capabilities where they are weakest or nonexistent.

It also brings with it new products, new technology, new standards and new ideas, and assistance in mastering them. Indeed, trade goes hand in hand with travel by businessmen and technical specialists, such as industrial engineers, through which a flow of information is set up and technology is transferred across international boundaries. Economists are just beginning to realize to what extent efforts, for example, to export manufactures bring forth advice and technical assistance from foreign buyers on matters ranging all the way from product design and production techniques to cost accounting. In any case, technology transfer seems to depend on having people travel abroad, study foreign plants, and engage in direct personal interchanges with specialists from other countries. To some extent this happens in industrial projects set up with imported equipment and advice, but it happens much more with a lot of trade than with little or none.

In addition, trade is a source of stimulus and pressures from international competition, which can be a major source of motivation for actually mastering the techniques and meeting

---

* From *Trade Policy for Developing Countries*. World Bank Staff Working Paper No. 353, August 1979, pp. 2–25.

the standards of foreign competitors. Learning to export and even trying to export manufactures is valuable partly for this reason. Competition from imports, too, can potentially motivate improved performance, especially since, in a developing country, many industries consist of only one or two or a very few enterprises, as a reflection of the small size of the local market. Unless subjected to foreign competition, these firms are more likely to collude than compete, and they will tend to raise prices, neglect quality, and perform poorly in terms of technology and efficiency. Import competition helps to weed out hopelessly inefficient local firms while driving others to greater efforts and higher performance standards.

Even though trade is valuable for all these reasons, this does not mean that more trade is desirable in all situations. Trade policy must not only pursue these advantages but also balance them against the gains from learning to produce goods and services that could be imported. There is also a need to limit disruptions and pains in the growth process as a result of the vicissitudes of trade and capital movements, and to tailor trade to the needs of growth and development. Trade policy is partly a matter of selecting and implementing a strategy and overall approach, to take full advantage of the potential benefits, limit the disruptions, and cultivate the learning opportunities, taking into account a country's particular situation and resources.

THE GOAL OF INDUSTRIAL DEVELOPMENT AND ITS RELATION TO ECONOMIC GROWTH

This paper is concerned especially with the use of trade policy to promote industrial development, defined here as the mastery and expansion of modern manufacturing industries.[3] This in turn can be viewed as part of a wider process of economic growth and development having two sides: one is economic

growth, raising earnings and income levels; while the other is economic development, transforming and expanding supply capabilities so that a wide range of output can be produced up to what might be called "high modern standards." Industrial development is part of this second process involving a transformation of supply capabilities in manufacturing industries. This involves:

- creating modern manufacturing industries;
- expanding their production and capacity;
- improving their technology, organization and efficiency;
- raising the quality of their output;
- widening their range and flexibility;
- building up their marketing and design and product-development capabilities;
- augmenting their capability for borrowing and adapting technology from abroad;
- shifting the mix and "structure" (eventually if not immediately) in directions deemed desirable in the long run;
- making locally owned industrial enterprises strong and competitive by the "best" international standards.

The wider task of economic development, of which industrial development is an important part, involves an analogous transformation of supply capabilities in the economy as a whole, not only in manufacturing but also in agriculture, construction, mining, transport and communications, finance, distribution of goods to consumers, foreign and wholesale trade, education, health and medical services, power and water supply, sewerage and sanitation, public administration, national defense, engineering and research, other service and professional activities, and cultural facilities and recreation, along with the mix of activities.

Successful development on practically all these fronts, and particularly in manufacturing is required to turn a country into an "industrialized" or "developed" nation, able to generate a high level of income per person based on its human resources and organizations and physical facilities, without having to rely on rents from natural resources or earnings from investment abroad, or from a narrow and vulnerable specialization at home. Of course, no national economy produces everything for itself, and a very small economy— one with less than, say, five million people— cannot expect to master the same wide range of modern industries and other activities as a larger economy; instead it must expect to remain somewhat specialized as part of a wider industrialized economy. But it can still reach for high standards in everything it does undertake, and it can strive for flexibility based on the quality of its human resources and infrastructure. In this light, development is concerned with earnings potential and vulnerability in the long run, while growth is concerned with actual output, earnings, living standards, and effective demand.

Economic growth has a huge impact on industrial (and overall) development, since effective demand on an adequate scale is required before an industry (or other economic activity) can be launched and mastered. Successful growth leads to a rising demand for consumer goods and indirectly for producer and investment goods. Systematic development efforts alongside this growth help to widen demand to include a broad range of producer goods that would not necessarily be needed in a narrowly-based process of economic growth. As part of this process of demand creation, government programs often play a large role in areas such as road building, electrification, irrigation, mass education, defense and many others, not to mention the impact of the public authorities in shaping incentives, financing major investments, and initiating specific projects. In some eras developing countries such as Turkey, Mexico and Brazil seem to owe much of their industrial vigor to government initiatives creating demand through public development programs.

In industry as in many areas, the objectives of growth and development sometimes con-flict—raising output rapidly conflicts with learning skills essential to build a modern nation, which sometimes must be learned at the cost of sacrifices in efficiency, or in programs with only very slow returns. But these objectives do not conflict much because growth is so essential to industrial development. Any development program that does not contribute to growth, or detracts seriously from growth, becomes self-defeating. A country can foster industrial development at a modest cost in growth, on highly selected fronts, but except perhaps if it is enormously rich in oil revenue, it cannot afford a massive concentration on development without carefully weighing growth effects of each measure and each investment. Lessons on this score abound in the past history of such different countries as India, Ghana, Chile, Argentina, Algeria and socialist Cuba, to mention only a few that have undertaken ambitious development programs with too little attention to growth. This point is fundamental in choosing trade policy in developing countries bent on industrial development.

IMPORTS, IMPORT SUBSTITUTION AND INDUSTRIAL DEVELOPMENT

Imports and import substitution play central roles in industrial and overall development under any sort of trade regime. Autarkic development is hardly feasible, even in the largest of economies: even China and the Soviet Union rely on strategically chosen imports of equipment, technology, raw materials and food. Smaller economies are even more dependent on imports at every stage in their development.

Industrial development, in particular, is highly dependent on imports, which supply some or all of the following:

- capital equipment to start production;
- spare parts and repair services required to keep production going;

- some of the construction materials required;
- fuel and raw materials;
- intermediate manufactured inputs (for example, special steels or parts for assembly) required in production;
- technical assistance and engineering, design and other services required to launch production;
- technology, which frequently must be paid for in one way or another (royalties, foreign enterprise profits or fees, search costs, etc.);
- consumer goods not locally produced which may be required as incentive goods or as inputs into health of the labor force;
- financial, insurance, transportation and other services indirectly required.

Over the course of time, successful development leads to mastery of production of many of these requisite goods and services that are at first imported. As a result, as a country's own output becomes more diversified and technically "sophisticated," the composition of imports shifts systematically toward goods, services, and technologies that are increasingly complex and require a larger and larger scale of production, along with raw materials that cannot be found locally.

By some broad definitions, within manufacturing, import substitution is nearly synonymous with industrial development—the exceptions would involve processing or labor-intensive manufacturing for export where the product was not first imported. After all, in any economy that starts out industrially behind the leaders, practically all modern industrial goods are at one stage only produced abroad in more advanced economies, and are imported before being produced locally. Usually the existence of a market for imports helps to show the feasibility of (and precedes) local production on an adequate scale. However, in a growing economy, local production soon exceeds the scale attained previously by imports. Eventually, restrictions

against imports can be relaxed. By a narrow definition, import substitution is only the initial production replacing imports, while the subsequent expansion is a product of domestic demand growth coupled with expanding supply capabilities. (When import constraints are relaxed, there may be more imports alongside local production than there ever were, before the local industry got started!)[4] Depending on which definition is used, industrial growth over a long span of development consists in any fairly large economy mainly of import substitution (based on a broad definition) or mainly of domestic demand and supply growth (where import substitution is defined narrowly).

By either a narrow or a broad definition, however, the amount of import substitution that takes place, and how fast, may depend on export success and overall growth even more than on direct efforts to accelerate and promote import substitution. This is because total purchases, including imports, are limited by effective demand, while import growth (paving the way to import substitution) is limited by import capacity, which is increased by export success. Exports and economic growth lead to increased imports and foster a "natural" process of import substitution, based on a combination of transport cost protection (most industries tend to locate near markets or raw material supplies for reasons of transport costs), scale economies, improved infrastructure, and growing capabilities of the labor force, making new industries profitable. This natural process can sometimes be hastened through protection, subsidies, or other incentives, and governments can sometimes improve the results through direct attention to the quality, scale and timing of the resulting industrial expansion. But by itself, such attention may be misplaced without major efforts to promote exports and growth at the same time.

Reliance on careful analysis and evaluation of projects and selection among alternatives through cost-benefit calculations (and, also, where industries are highly interdependent, through appropriate modeling), can help to avoid premature import substitution projects. These all too often turn out to have a negative value added at world prices—implying a negative effect on the balance of payments—and burden the growth of other industries and depress real incomes by the high prices they must charge, in order to make even a low rate of return. Often, too, the capital investment must be publicly subsidized, while the output is inferior compared to imports.[5]

Details apart, however, even a small developing country requires successful import substitution in a wide range of products, in order to emerge as a fully developed country. One of the challenges in trade policy is how to achieve this success.

THE IMPORTANCE OF EXPANDING EXPORTS

Export expansion, too, is an important feature of the growth and development process, to the point where a large expansion of exports is very nearly a necessary condition for sustained rapid growth and development over any lengthy period, at least in a market economy. (In regard to qualitative results this may well be true in any but the largest command economy as well.)

Exports make possible the benefits from trade, discussed already. They are required to pay for the imports required in development, both directly and by adding to the country's borrowing and debt-servicing capacity; they allow the country to gain the benefits of specialization, including economies of scale, and so on down the list.

Inter-country comparisons show strong positive associations between export growth and overall economic growth, beyond what can be explained by the fact that production for export is a part of output. This is almost certainly a reflection of the economic benefits from specialization, along with favorable effects associated with international competition and the other benefits already touched.

Alternatively, the relationship between exports and economic growth can show itself instead in a negative direction. When, for whatever reason, exports fail to expand, and especially when they decline, some of the links between trade and growth begin to operate in reverse, with the result that development tends to be slowed down by a lack of stimulus and dynamism, as well as by lack of imported inputs and market demand. These negative effects are likely to be especially acute in manufacturing, since it is highly dependent on trade in ways already mentioned.

As a result of these links, exports and import substitution are, on the whole, complementary. If exports do not grow and overall growth is sluggish, the process of import substitution is slowed sharply through difficulties on both the demand and supply sides. Feasible opportunities become exhausted because markets are too small to make new industries profitable, while the "import intensity of import substitution"—its heavy requirements for imports of equipment, intermediate inputs, fuel, etc.—adds to the obstacles.

Paradoxically, import substitution turns out to have been exceptionally rapid and successful in economies that have given unusually strong attention and incentives to industrial exports, such as Japan, Korea and Taiwan; in the period 1960–76 industrial growth rates averaged over 17 percent per year in Korea and over 15 percent in Taiwan, considerably higher than in any other developing country. By the early 1970's, despite their spectacular growth, exports only accounted for about 10 percent of the demand for manufactured goods in Japan, 24 percent in Korea and 28 percent in Taiwan. In the last two, some of the industries set up to substitute for imports have been sufficiently large and efficient from the start so that they have quickly been able to compete in export markets as well.

One of the least widely understood points about trade policy is that the need for exports, and the associated need for incentives to maintain or increase them, are not diminished, but may even increase when international conditions make exports difficult to achieve, for example, as a result of adverse trends in the world economy or increasing protection abroad. Of course, exports themselves are likely to decline, and investments in export-oriented capacity may have to be cut back, but paradoxically the value to the economy from successfully exporting becomes greater than ever, since exports are still needed just as much and are harder to get. This means that protection or poor demand conditions abroad do not change the need to pursue export promotion alongside import substitution as a central part of trade and industrial policy.

As noted already, however, there can be too much of a good thing: an export bonanza involving a high degree of specialization based on one or two natural-resource products brings major problems in its wake. In particular, there is a danger here that both industry and agriculture will be held back by import competition. In this case, development may well be promoted by policies that tax (in one way or another) leading export products, while giving special assistance to other sectors. However, in practice, superabundance of export earnings is rarely a problem except in economies rich in mineral exports, or in periods of exceptionally high primary product prices. Even in these cases it is exceptional for a developing country to be able to plan around a sustained growth of its primary export earnings. Much of the difficulty in trade policy comes from the need to expand exports without neglecting other objectives such as gaining valuable learning experience.

PROTECTION AND EXPORT TAXES

Among its advantages, the existence and growth of trade opens the possibility of using administratively easy-to-apply instruments for stimulating local production of products that start out being imported. Protection can be given through tariffs—taxing particular imports but not locally produced versions of the same products—or through quantitative restrictions on imports, such as quotas or outright embargoes, limiting the imported supply; or through both together. In each case, provided that protection can be enforced (despite smuggling, cheating and corruption), the effect will be to raise the prices and profits received by local producers of the product, while afflicting with higher prices the people who use or consume the product.

Protection is very nearly equivalent to a tax on all the unprotected industries, and particularly the export industries, as well as the users of the product, in order to help the protected industry. How much the protection is worth, to the industry protected, depends not only on the dimensions of its protection (e.g., the height of the tariff) but also on how many other industries are protected at the same time. If every industry is protected equally, the effect is simply a tax on all trade, and therefore on all exports, without favoring one import-competing industry over another. Because user industries are hurt, protection for an industry's final product can be cancelled out, wholly or in part, by protection of the industries that supply it with capital goods.

This point lies behind the notion of "effective protection," which in principle is a measure of the net effect of the system of protection on the value of a firm's (or industry's) "value added" after paying for inputs purchased from other firms or industries. Another point behind the notion of effective protection is that the effect of a tariff in raising value added depends on the share of the product's price that represents inputs purchased from other industries. Suppose, for example, that only two industries receive protection, each in the form of a 50 percent nominal tariff, while there continues to be no tariff at all on their inputs. In the first of these industries, before the tariff is imposed, inputs imported or purchased from other industries comprise 50 percent of the final price, while 50 percent represents value added ("in world prices"). In the second, these purchased inputs account for 90 percent of the product price and value added is only 10 percent. The effective tariff will be 100 percent in the first case but 500 percent in the second, meaning that the 50 percent nominal tariff doubles value added from 50 to 100 percent of the world price in the first case, but raises it to six times what it was (a 150 percent final price, minus the same 90 percent for input costs, raises value added from 10 to 60 percent of the world price) in the second.

A major disadvantage of widespread use of protection is that it discourages and decreases trade, thereby destroying or giving up many of the advantages from trade that were described in a previous section. Of course, for a developing country it may be extremely important to encourage the growth of new industries that could not initially compete with imports; but once these industries are well started their continued protection acts as a disincentive to other industries, and the existence of widespread protection acts as a disincentive to the growth and diversification of exports, including exports from the new industries initially created through protection.

In face of this dilemma it is important to keep in mind that export taxes have many of the same effects as tariffs (import taxes) and they also discourage trade, but with essential differences. Export taxes fall specifically on the particular exports taxed—which can be chosen to be the primary exports that can bear taxation most—while they indirectly encourage, to some extent, all forms of import substitution and all the exports that are not taxed. This sort of effect may be superior, for a developing country, to the effect of protection which is to discourage indirectly all exports however desirable, as well as all unprotected import-competing industries. By choosing which exports to tax, and how much, and by applying protection only selectively and temporarily, a developing country can achieve a trade regime that is equivalent to much higher ongoing protection both for industry and for other new and diversified economic activities, coupled with large export subsidies for all

these new industries and other new ventures. The selective use of protection then becomes equivalent to picking out a few industries for extra-high protection above all the rest.

A highly simplified arithmetical example may help to illustrate what is involved. Suppose that a primarily agricultural developing country wants to promote manufacturing and, secondarily, diversification of its agriculture and its exports. For this purpose it wants to discriminate against its traditional export agriculture, giving its manufacturing industries incentives at least twice as attractive. It also would like to give special incentives, not quite as strong, to new export crops, and exceptionally high incentives at least temporarily, to a carefully chosen group of high-priority industries. To implement this strategy, suppose that on a numerical scale, if one sets arbitrarily equal to 100 the incentive to be given to the traditional export crops, what is needed is incentives in the order of 160 for new export crops, 200 for most manufacturing, and 300 for the high-priority industries. If the complications caused by input-output relationships could be ignored, this structure of incentives could be achieved by setting the exchange rate to give 200 as the ordinary yield for foreign exchange saved or earned, and placing a 50 percent tax on traditional agricultural exports, a 20 percent tax on others, and a protective tariff of up to 50 percent in the special high-priority industries.[6] By contrast, with no export tax at all, and an exchange rate of 100, not only very high protection (100–200 percent in manufacturing) but also very high export subsidies would be needed to achieve anything like the same structure of incentives, if it were feasible at all.

Achieving such a result mainly through export taxes has some practical advantages. First, there will be a large tax revenue easily collected that can then be applied in part to development expenditures, including infrastructure and subsidies to new industries. Second, the tax on exports can be modulated and adjusted each year to take into account export performance and the need for foreign exchange earnings. If the more heavily taxed exports cease to grow, and lack of trade growth and import capacity begins to hold back the country's development, the taxes on principal exports can be reduced to speed up export growth; but if temporarily high prices of the product threaten to cause too strong a growth of import and purchasing power, hurting local industries while causing price inflation, the tax can be raised higher and some of the proceeds can be set aside to be spent in years of low prices. (Of course, depending on the product this effect may be achievable through public-sector purchasing and marketing schemes or through some other special institutional arrangement, which amounts to export taxation.) Not least important is the administrative feasibility of this approach. Export subsidies are practically impossible and massive protection is very difficult to implement well in a developing country, while a large tax on a country's main export products is relatively easy to administer. Finally, trading partners frown on export subsidies and may retaliate against them with countervailing duties or other pressures, but without these subsidies each new industry will be discouraged from exporting, despite the small size of the domestic market.

Another set of influences is also centrally important: the real value of protection depends on local cost levels and on actual competing imports. The degree of import competition, and the cost inflation, experienced by local industries (and agriculture and services) will depend on how the government spends the proceeds of the export tax, and indeed on the whole government budget along with aid and borrowing from abroad. To the extent that public spending goes for debt-service abroad or sophisticated equipment built abroad, this will have little effect in bidding up local prices or in generating competing imports. If the spending goes for local construction or government salaries, however, the added local demand will be likely to raise prices and spill over into imports, with or without protection.

Low levels of protection in a developing country, supplemented by export taxes and conservative government spending, tend to mean low local prices and costs—including wage costs, which are likely to reflect the cost of living—making industries competitive both in exporting and in competing against imports. An extreme case of export taxes holding down local wages and prices comes when, as in Thailand, these taxes fall mainly on the local food staple (in this case rice), since its low price reduces the cost of living. By contrast, high levels of protection characteristically result in high local prices and wages, as translated through the exchange rate, so that protection appears essential in order for local industries to compete against imports, and exporting nontraditional products without subsidies appears practically impossible.

A related point is that regardless of the degree and structure of protection in a country, or even its price level, the real intensity of competition from imports will be determined in a fundamental sense by the level and composition of imports; and in shaping this structure, protection is only one influence among many. The value of exports and other sources of foreign exchange is a more basic influence. Another powerful influence affecting the composition, if not the level, is the pattern of government expenditure, and in particular the public sector's foreign exchange expenditures; one study shows that 52 percent of U.S. exports to developing countries in 1976 went to governments and public sector agencies or enterprises.[7]

Massive reductions in the capacity to import have occurred historically in times of war, depression and export disasters. In some instances, notably in India and Latin America in World War I, the Great Depression, and World War II, local industrial production has received a major stimulus as a result. However, historical experience suggests that exposure to imports can also be very good for development, particularly in sharpening the competitive edge of the industries that survive. In this regard it is instructive that Hong Kong and Singapore share a background as free ports, subject to some of the most vigorous import competition on earth, while Korea and Taiwan spent several decades as colonies exposed to severe (sometimes unfair) Japanese competition, and then received a flood of U.S. aid followed by rising imports when exports expanded and foreign capital came in. Many of the best results in development are achieved, as already noted, in times of rapidly rising trade, perhaps not only because industries have access to means of production and growing markets, but also because they are subject to a process of losing their protection.

In any case, since protection and export taxes alike are powerless to achieve a growth in trade—they ordinarily have the opposite result, at least until the "infant industries" grow up and begin to export—they tend to work best where trade growth is ample and especially when it is so substantial as to cause difficulties from too much import competition and an excessive, narrow export specialization.

Export taxes have a special value, too, in the case where a developing country enjoys a degree of monopoly power at a worldwide level in the supply of a particular export commodity, since in this situation an export tax can help to improve the country's terms of trade, so that the foreign customer will actually pay part of the tax. In practice, this is an exceptional situation and is not likely to last long, if the country applies strong export taxes (and for that matter high protection, which has a general effect of raising local prices) to raise its price. Other suppliers will soon cut into its share of the world market.[8]

CENTRAL ROLE OF
THE EXCHANGE RATE

Quite apart from the use of protection, subsidies, export taxes, or other special measures at an industry level, a developing country has a powerful and simple instrument for promoting industrialization around the home market, and through exports at the same time, in the form of exchange rate policy.

On the export side, the extent to which exports of all kinds are promoted depends above all on the relationship between the exchange rate effectively applied to exports, and domestic prices and costs. If, in real terms, people are well rewarded for producing exports, they will be encouraged to produce more; if not, they will turn their attention in other directions.

The exchange rate, as it relates to domestic prices and costs, also determines the rewards for saving foreign exchange by producing import-competing goods and services. Here, as in exporting, there is often a choice between, on the one hand, saving or earning foreign exchange, and on the other, using the same local resources in alternative ways—for example, producing nontradeable goods and services, working less hard, seeking government favors, or holding factors of production idle. Import substitution is rewarded, side by side with exports, when the real rate of exchange is shifted so that imports are made expensive. Local production is discouraged, apart from special measures of government intervention, when imports are made cheap.

Of course, maintaining a favorable real exchange rate is no simple matter—the export incentive and price effects of protection and export taxes have already been touched, but in addition, pursuing this objective involves macro-level management of the economy, with difficulties and complications that will not be discussed until later, in connection with measures to foster exports. A developing nation's price level in terms of internationally used currencies is also determined to some extent by its geography and resources. Nonetheless, exchange rate policy is a central tool of trade policy, with far-reaching effects, which are often underrated.

Note, however, that the relationship between exchange rate incentives for earning or saving foreign exchange is not wholly symmetrical, because if exports are poorly rewarded through the exchange rate system, with the result that export earnings dwindle, ways must be found for reducing imports even when, on its face, the official exchange rate continues to encourage them. Thus, an overvalued exchange rate, one by which the price of foreign exchange is set too low so that exports and (seemingly) import substitution are discouraged, is likely to have to be roughly compensated by a massive use of quantitative import restrictions, exchange controls, tariffs and subsidies. Compared to the effects of maintaining an equilibrium or undervalued exchange rate, however, there will be costs and inefficiencies. For example, local industries will get a (probably false) impression that they are hopelessly incompetent and inefficient, compared to their foreign competition. Some import substitution activities will be overlooked and discouraged, others will not be started for lack of foreign exchange, some will be badly designed because the "wrong" prices are used, some will get undeserved windfall profits, etc. So the stimulus for import substitution will be very uneven.

In practice, the celebrated success of so-called "outward-looking" or "export-promoting" strategies of development is built largely around the use of "realistically" valued exchange rates. The leading purpose in most cases has been export expansion, but the success of this approach also comes in part from their use of superior means for promoting import substitution and production for the domestic market. Correcting the exchange rate shows local industries where and when they are efficient and how their costs really compare with those of foreign competition. Meanwhile, no import-competing activity is neglected, nor is special attention generally required. Everyone concerned is led automatically by the price system to achieve import substitution as well as exports. However, these positive effects cannot easily be disentangled from those of more exports and more capacity to import at the same time.

Use of exchange rates in this way can even be viewed as a development strategy—in extreme form, a "mercantilistic" one. Richard Cooper has argued that Japan, Italy, West Germany and a few other developed countries succeeded in accelerating industrialization, starting in the 1950's, by tipping their exchange rates in the direction of undervaluing their currencies. This generated a very heavy demand for their manufactured goods at home as well as abroad. Japan depreciated repeatedly in the 1930's for a similar effect. Obviously not all countries can do this at once, and it may only work well in a relatively small economy with a strong potential for exporting manufactures; but there are ample precedents for the use of such a strategy.[9]

1. This is the basic point of the theory of comparative advantage. Putting the point differently, the country has the opportunity of choosing among a much more attractive set of options than it would have without trade.

2. Meaning education, labor skills, health, etc. —investments that raise the productivity of people.

3. Mining, construction, electric power and water supply are often grouped with manufacturing as industrial activities. In this paper, however, inclusion of primary production and major "nontradeable" subsectors with industry would complicate the exposition to no advantage.

4. This is sometimes viewed, perhaps misleadingly, as negative import substitution.

5. Theoretically such a project might be justified if it served in effect as a training school. But this effect if weighed properly will seldom be sufficient to outweigh the negative features.

6. Taking input-output relationships into account, of course, such a structure of export taxes and tariffs would cause some high incentives for manufacturing based on exportable raw materials. However, the basic principle remains generally valid even if details must be adjusted.

7. In developed market economies this share was only 17 percent.

8. Unless all act as a cartel to raise their prices (by export taxes or other means such as export limits for each supplier), in which case there is still an incentive to cheat by cutting prices and exporting a larger share. This is one of the international

actions by developing countries that lie outside the scope of this study.

9. However, . . . it is not easy to achieve real depreciation side by side with large-scale public development expenditures since these will push up prices. Unless otherwise underutilized resources can be put to work producing tradeable goods, devaluation is likely to be cancelled out by price increases.

Further Readings

1. Trade and Exchange

Diaz-Alejandro, Carlos F. "International Markets for LDC's—The Old and the New." *American Economic Review* 68, no. 2 (May 1978).

Findlay, Ronald, "Economic Development and the Theory of International Trade." *American Economic Review* 69, no. 2 (May 1979).

Michaely, Michael. *Foreign Trade Regimes and Economic Development*. New York: Columbia University Press, 1975.

Morton, Kathryn, and Tulloch, Peter. *Trade and Developing Countries*. New York and Toronto: Wiley, 1977.

2. International Economics

Balogh, T., and Balacs, P. "Fact and Fancy in International Economic Relations." *World Development* 1, nos. 3–4 (March/April 1973).

Helleiner, G. K., ed. *A World Divided: The Less Developed Countries in the International Economy*. New York, Cambridge University Press, 1976.

Holsen, John A., and Waelbroeck, Jean L. "The Less Developed Countries and the International Monetary Mechanism." *American Economic Review* 66, no. 2 (May 1976).

United Nations. *The Future of the World Economy*. New York, 1976.

3. Trade Policies

Balassa, Bela, and associates. *The Structure of Protection in Developing Countries*. Baltimore and London: Johns Hopkins University Press, 1971.

Corden, W. M. *The Theory of Protection*. Oxford: Clarendon Press, 1971.

Johnson, Harry G., ed. *Trade Strategy for Rich and Poor Nations*. Toronto: University of Toronto Press, 1971.

Meier, Gerald M. *Problems of Trade Policy*. New York: Oxford University Press, 1973.

Streeten, Paul, ed. *Trade Strategies for Development: Papers of the Ninth Cambridge Conference on Development Problems, September 1972*. Cambridge University Overseas Studies Committee. New York: Wiley, 1973.

4. Debt

Aronson, Jonathan David, ed. *Debt and the Less Developed Countries*. Boulder, Colo.: Westview, 1979.

Goodman, Stephen H., ed. *Financing and Risk in Developing Countries*. New York: Praeger, 1978.

Smith, Gordon W. *The External Public Debt Prospects of the Non-Oil Exporting Developing Countries*. NIEO Series, no. 10. Washington, D.C.: Overseas Development Council, 1977.

5. Import Substitution

Hirshman, Albert C., "The Political Economy of Import-Substituting Industrialization in Latin America." *Quarterly Journal Economics*, (February 1968).

Little, I. M. D. "Import Controls and Exports in Developing Countries." *Finance and Development* 15, no. 3 (September 1978).

Maitra, P. "Import Substitution and Changing Import Structure in an Underdeveloped Country." *Economic Affairs* 15, no. 4 (April 1970).

6. Industrial Development

Cukor, Gyorgy. *Strategies for Industrialization in Developing Countries*. New York: St. Martin's Press, 1974.

Sutcliffe, R. B. *Industry and Underdevelopment Readings*. Reading Mass.: Addison-Wesley, 1971.

Teubal, M. "Heavy and Light Industry in Economic Development." *American Economic Review* 63, no. 4 (September 1973).

World Bank. *Industry*. Sector Working Paper. Washington, D.C., April 1972.

11

International Resource Transfers: Multinational Corporations and Foreign Aid

29. Multinational Corporations in World Development*

Department of Economic and Social Affairs, United Nations Secretariat

In the past quarter of a century the world has witnessed the dramatic development of the multinational corporation into a major phenomenon in international economic relations. Its size and geographical spread, the multiplicity of its activities, its command and generation of resources around the world and the use of such resources to further its own objectives, rival in terms of scope and implications traditional economic exchanges among nations.

The term "multinational corporation" is used here to cover all enterprises which control assets—factories, mines, sales offices and the like—in two or more countries. Effective control may be exercised not only with complete or majority ownership of affiliates by their parent companies but with a sufficient minority share. This broad definition permits maximum use to be made of existing data, which are variously defined and not generally amenable to reclassification to suit a more restricted definition. One implication of the definition is that multinational corporations are responsible for most foreign direct investment. Nevertheless, the most important questions to be asked in connection with multinational corporations are not limited to financial flows. They concern a host of other activities such as the transfer of technology as well as goods, the provision of managerial services and entrepreneurship and related business practices, including cooperative arrangements, marketing restrictions and transfer pricing. As the operations of multinational corporations have expanded and evolved, the elements not directly related to the provision of capital have become increasingly important. Moreover, these operations can only be understood as components of an international corporate system. Parent companies that own foreign-based enterprises typically control these enterprises' activities and determine the way in which financial, technical and managerial resources are allocated around the world and the resulting mix of the entire package.

* From United Nations Department of Economic and Social Affairs, *Multinational Corporations in World Development*. New York, 1973. Extracted and reprinted in *Development Digest*, 12, no. 1 (January 1974), pp. 67–80.

SIZE, PATTERNS AND TRENDS

A central characteristic of multinational corporations is the predominance of large-size firms. Both their absolute and relative size has grown dramatically, especially during the last decade. Typically, the amount of annual sales now runs into hundreds of millions of dollars. Each of the largest four multinational corporations has a sales volume in excess of $10 billion, and more than 200 multinational corporations have surpassed the one billion level. Indeed, for most practical purposes, those with less than $100 million in sales can safely be ignored. The very size of the larger corporations as compared with other economic entities, including the economies of many nations, suggests an important source of power. One form of economic power results from their predominantly oligopolistic market positions. Typically, the markets in which they operate are dominated by a few sellers or buyers. Frequently they are also characterized by the importance of new technologies, of special skills, or of product differentiation and heavy advertising, which sustain or reinforce their oligopolistic nature by making entry of competitors more difficult.

The very large multinational corporations have many foreign branches and affiliates. Although almost half of some 7,300 multinational corporations have affiliates in one country only, nearly 200 multinational corporations have affiliates in twenty or more countries. Almost all of the multinational corporations are the product of developed countries. Eight of the 10 largest multinational corporations are based in the United States. All in all, United States firms account for about a third of the total number of foreign affiliates; together with companies based in the United Kingdom, the Federal Republic of Germany and France, they account for over three-quarters of the total. Of a total estimated book value of foreign investment of about $165 billion, most of which is owned by multinational corporations, the United States accounts for more than half, and over four-fifths of the total is owned by the same four countries. Moreover, foreign direct investment of these countries tends to be concentrated in a relatively small number of firms within each home country. In the case of Japan, however, many small firms appear to have participated in foreign investment along with a few very large ones.

The dramatic growth of multinational corporations in the postwar period has been accompanied by unprecedented growth in the number of affiliates, the levels of capital flow and the stock of investment. Between 1950 and 1966, the number of United States affiliates increased three times, from 7,000 to 23,000. The more recent entry of Japan into the field has been marked by a particularly rapid rate of growth in the number of affiliates. Although no precise data exist, there are indications that the growth of French affiliates was somewhat higher than those of the United Kingdom, while affiliates of the Federal Republic of Germany are growing more rapidly than those of the United States. The growth in numbers of affiliates has been accompanied by an increase in the flow of direct foreign investment and in its accumulated value. During the last decade, the flow of direct investment from 13 countries of the Organization for Economic Cooperation and Development rose from $2.9 billion to $7.9 billion a year. Among the countries with an above-average rate of increase were Japan, the Federal Republic of Germany, Italy, the Netherlands and the Scandinavian countries. The stock of investment by country of origin is shown in Figure 1.

While the network of multinational corporations is world-wide, the bulk of their activities is located in the development market economies. Over two-thirds of the estimated book value of foreign direct investment is located in this area, where the advanced economic level and similarities in institutional and social structures have facilitated the spread of the multinational corporate system. Although the developing countries have received only about a third of this total, the presence of

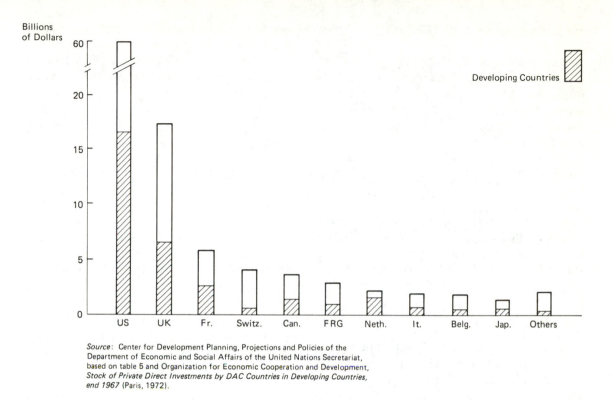

Figure 1. Developed market economies (DAC countries): Estimated stock of foreign direct investment by country of origin and area of investment, end 1967.

foreign multinational corporations in these countries is generally of much greater significance relative to the size of their economies. Among the developing countries, the western hemisphere has attracted an estimated 18 percent of the total stock of foreign direct investment, Africa 6 percent, and Asia and the Middle East 5 and 3 percent respectively.

Distribution by Sector

Historically, the activity of multinational corporations developed in the extractive and public utility areas before it became prominent in manufacturing. When manufacturing activities abroad began to grow, they appeared in the processing of raw materials or in the production of consumer goods. It appears that, initially, manufacturing operations increased faster in developed countries; later in develop-

ing countries; but in the last ten years their growth has again been more dynamic in developed countries, especially in western Europe. Industrial sectors involving high technical skills have witnessed the fastest growth.

Manufacturing is at present the major activity of multinational corporations. It represents a little more than 40 percent of the total estimated stock of foreign direct investment of the main developed market economies. Petroleum accounts for 29 percent, mining and smelting for 7 percent and other industries for 24 percent. Whereas is developing countries half of the estimated stock of investment is in extractive industries and a little more than a quarter in manufacturing, in developed market economies half of it is in manufacturing, and about 30 percent is in extractive industries (see Figure 2).

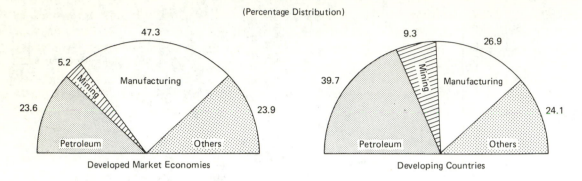

(Percentage Distribution)

47.3

5.2

Manufacturing

23.6

23.9

Petroleum   Others

Developed Market Economies

9.3   26.9

39.7   Manufacturing

24.1

Petroleum   Others

Developing Countries

Source: Center for Development Planning, Projection and Policies of the Department of Economic and Social Affairs of the United Nations Secretariat, based on Organization for Economic Cooperation and Development, as tabulated in Sidney E. Rolfe, *The International Corporation* (Paris, 1969).

Figure 2. Developed market economies (DAC countries): Estimated distribution of estimated stock of foreign direct investment by sector and area, end 1966.

Ownership Patterns

By and large, multinational corporations exercise effective control over their foreign affiliates through complete or majority ownership, although at times such control can be exercised from a minority position. At least 80 percent of United States affiliates and 75 percent of United Kingdom affiliates are either wholly-owned or majority-controlled. This desire for majority ownership and control appears to be a general characteristic of multinational corporations from other home countries, except in the case of Japanese multinational corporations, where a somewhat more sizeable proportion of affiliates (and of the investment in them) are minority-owned ventures. This difference in the ownership pattern is apparently influenced by differences in methods of control as well as in the industrial and the geographical distribution of foreign activities. The predominance of trading activities and light industries in the case of Japanese multinational corporations suggests that a relatively small share in their affiliates may be adequate in many cases. Moreover since a relatively high proportion of Japanese investment—made mostly in recent years—is located in developing countries, the ownership

pattern may also have been influenced by a tendency of some Japanese multinational corporations to maintain a relatively low profile in some of those countries.

Dimensions in Developing Countries

Generally speaking, the relative importance of the multinational corporation in developing countries is rising in the manufacturing and services sectors and declining in the primary industries, in particular those connected with agriculture (plantations). On balance, the over-all importance of the multinational corporation is growing. As a source of the net flow of resources to developing countries, private direct investment flows from such corporations represented about one-fifth of the total in the 1960s. During the decade, this flow increased at an average annual rate of 9 percent. In six out of the 12 developing countries for which data were available, the stock of foreign direct investment increased faster than the gross domestic product. In a few cases, decreases or slow growth resulted from the liquidation of foreign investment through nationalization.

The relative size of foreign investment varies by country and by industrial sector, and the share of foreign affiliates' activity in output, employment or exports varies accordingly. In some countries, the foreign content of the local economy is very high, and at times concentrated in one sector, while in others it is less significant or more diversified. In the Middle East, which accounts for 9.4 percent of the total foreign direct private investment in developing countries, petroleum accounts for approximately 90 percent of the total stock of foreign investment. In South America (36 percent of the total), on the other hand, 39 percent of foreign investment is in manufacturing, 28 percent in petroleum and 10 percent in public utilities. In Africa (20 percent of the total), 39 percent is in petroleum, 20 percent in mining and smelting and 19 percent in manufacturing. In Asia (15 percent), manufacturing has attracted 30 percent, petroleum 22 percent and agriculture 18 percent of the total foreign investment stock. In Central America (19 percent of the total), manufacturing has attracted 31 percent, petroleum 16 and trade 13 percent of the total.

Only a few developing countries have a stock of direct foreign investment of more than $1 billion: Argentina, Brazil, India, Mexico, Nigeria, Venezuela and five groupings of Caribbean islands. These account for 43 percent of the total stock of investment in developing countries, which is roughly the same proportion as that of their combined gross domestic product to the estimated total for all developing countries. In 12 countries in Africa, the Middle East and Latin America the investment in either petroleum or mining exceeds $200 million. More than $200 million is invested in manufacturing in Argentina, Brazil, India, Mexico and the Philippines. In India and Malaysia, investment in agriculture exceeds $200 million.

There is evidence of an increase in the exports of foreign affiliates, both as a share of total sales and as a share of total industrial exports in Latin America. Thus, exports of United States manufacturing affiliates in Central and South America accounted for 4 percent of their total sales in 1957, 7.5 percent in 1965 and 9.4 percent in 1968. Their share in the total exports of manufactures from these regions, which was 12 percent in 1957, reached 41 percent in 1966. In Argentina, between 1965 and 1968, exports of United States affiliates accounted for 14.5 percent of total exports; in Mexico, such affiliates accounted for 87 percent of exports of manufactures in 1966 and in Brazil they represented 42 percent.

THE NATURE OF MULTINATIONAL CORPORATIONS

Organizational Structure

An analysis of the organizational development of 170 United States-based multinational corporations suggests that they have adopted their formal structures of organization in several fairly discrete stages. From an initial period of uncontrolled experimentation which gave considerable autonomy to the subsidiaries, and the subsequent establishment of international divisions which curtailed this autonomy to some extent, many multinational corporations moved eventually to dismember their international divisions and create either world-wide product divisions or area divisions, depending on the firm's strategy of expansion. Other corporations found a mixed structure, with some world-wide product divisions and some area divisions, to be more appropriate for their particular strategy. The "world-wide" product division structure is related to a strategy having a wide diversity in products, while the "area division" is related more to a strategy based on taking a narrow line of products into more and more foreign countries.

These reorganizations have been accompanied by considerable changes in the attitudes of top management: assumptions that business abroad is fundamentally different from business at home have been replaced by a global perspective and a recognition of the need to integrate closely related domestic and foreign units. Coordination problems still persist, however, in these global structures, especially for those firms with widely diversified product lines and extensive geographical coverage. Many firms are relying increasingly on improved training procedures to maintain coordination. Such training helps to reduce the need for continuous consultation with the center and thus to reduce the costs of coordinating staff groups.

Whereas United States-based multinational corporations have developed carefully designed formal organizations, those of other national origins have tended to rely more on informal procedures. With increasing competition, however, and also increasing scale and complexity, the European-based multinational corporations have increasingly been forced to employ more formalized procedures of organization and control. This is most marked for those with integrated networks of specialized production abroad, because it is there that managerial tasks are most similar: a high degree of central planning and advance scheduling of product flow is essential if the economic gains from reduced costs are to be realized.

Control Procedures

In the early years, control of foreign subsidiaries is often minimal or restricted solely to the screening of capital projects. The need for greater centralization, set off by the creation of an international division or by some traumatic event such as a devaluation or the write-off of a capital project, leads to the establishment of a strong central finance and control group. This group introduces procedures for optimizing the cash flows of the entire global system. Decisions about hedging on foreign exchange, borrowing, declaring dividends and so on, are taken centrally. The effect is to subordinate the interests of the subsidiary to those of the corporation as a whole. Consequently, the profits reported for local tax purposes may be understated, and measures of performance may become

meaningless unless appropriate adjustments are made to allow for the distortions associated with global optimizing decisions. Sometimes the continued growth of foreign subsidiaries has been accompanied by a loosening of the financial reins, partly because of a realization that the system can be "overmanaged." However, few foreign subsidiaries are allowed to set their own financial policies.

Apart from direct control, the enterprise has developed a corps of trained men attuned to a common set of policy guidelines and standard procedures. Similarly, in other functions, common procedures are enforced. Product choices for the subsidiaries are almost always limited to those products manufactured in the home country, especially in the case of the United States. Marketing procedures, long considered to be the function immune above all others to efficient centralization, are in some firms becoming standardized. Manpower policies regarding key managerial positions are, as a result, being constantly adapted in order to select and train men of different nationalities who can work within this new style of management and at the same time provide an adequate response to governmental pressure for local representation.

Profit and Ownership Policies

Dividends and royalty payments are not the only means whereby multinational corporations withdraw profits from a foreign subsidiary. Profits can be recorded in other units of a global system, including holding companies located in tax havens, through control of the transfer prices for goods and services supplied by the parent company or exports to other affiliates.

The importance of these controls in influencing the net profit before local taxes depends largely on the proportion of total purchases and sales tied to other affiliates. Import purchases, which are usually tied in, are generally small relative to purchases from local sources. This percentage tends to decline as the local economy develops; but it increases as firms develop networks of specialized, interrelated production. Exports to other affiliates, subject to controls and allocations among all the affiliates, are becoming increasingly important, particularly as the networks are developed. Prices charged for tied imports have been shown in some instances to be far above prevailing world prices, and conversely those for exports have been below world prices. Overpricing, particularly for wholly-owned affiliates, has been used as an alternative to royalty payments. Considerable variation exists, however, in the amount of overpricing or underpricing and its over-all frequency is not known. There is some evidence to suggest that overpricing has been reduced, both by governmental pressures and by problems of internal control.

Another aspect of profit management that generates tension is the recorded profitability of foreign subsidiaries. The apparent high profitability of foreign affiliates of multinational corporations needs to be examined carefully: not only are the profit figures liable to distortion, but the capital base of the affiliate has many discretionary components. The capital structure of a newly established subsidiary generally has a large proportion of locally raised debt if it is a joint venture, but much less if it is wholly-owned. Studies of United States investment in Australia and Japan have shown that contributions of technology are likely to be capitalized in joint ventures, but not in wholly-owned subsidiaries. This difference may partly explain why wholly-owned subsidiaries have generally reported a higher return on book equity than joint ventures. Further, wholly-owned subsidiaries are provided with special support services at low or zero cost; royalty payments are temporarily forgiven; dividends are postponed. On the other hand, in later years, parent companies expect to be able to move funds between subsidiaries on demand. These qualifications should be kept in mind in analyzing data on the recorded profits of foreign affiliates.

The general trend towards centralization and tighter control leads to increased conflict with governments as they become more insistent upon a greater degree of local participation and influence. Although changes in the relationships between foreign investors and host governments are indicated, the nature of these changes is as yet uncertain. Increasingly, novel forms of ownership arrangement will come into being. Multinational corporations may be allowed unambiguous control for as long as they make a critical contribution that cannot be made by others. As that contribution diminishes, so local control will increase. Various "fade-out" arrangements have already been implemented, and more are appearing in the legislation of developing countries. There are many problems in identifying contributions with sufficient clarity for the purposes of writing a contract, but doubtless these will be overcome as the multinational corporations realize from experience that ownership for a limited time is not necessarily against their interests.

The use of management contracts is also likely to become more frequent. Here the multinational corporation can make a contribution and at the same time earn profits without having the tie of owning physical assets. Such contracts are already widely used by consortia of construction firms in developing countries. Some, particularly marketing contracts, are appearing in the manufacturing sector. Management contracts in production may be closely tied to new forms of royalty agreement.

THE MULTINATIONAL CORPORATION IN INTERNATIONAL RELATIONS

Given their world-wide spread and significant role in the world economy, multinational corporations are one of the main non-governmental participants in international relations. Yet, despite the fact that their activities cover many countries, that they participate in diverse economic and social systems, and that their interests extend around the globe, there are no "world citizens" by whom multinational corporations can be staffed. The equity of such corporations and the top management of their global operations tends to be in the hands of citizens of their home countries. At the same time, their corporate interests do not always coincide with those of their home country.

In developing countries multinational corporations can have an impact on international relations by contributing towards placing countries in interdependent or dependent positions from which governments may find it difficult to extricate themselves except at considerable cost. To a large extent this results from the fact that the operations of the multinational corporations are controlled from outside the territory of the host country, and that their policies are based on considerations which transcend those of host as well as home countries. Sometimes the reluctance of governments to pursue policies in respect of multinational corporations that would be desirable from their national point of view may be due to their concern about the repercussions which may result from the reactions of home governments. Such inhibitions may also stem from actions which multinational corporations might take to bring pressure to bear on a government by influencing foreign official or private lending and insurance agencies, customers, and other firms. The political aspect of the host country-multinational corporation relationship is assuming greater importance as multinational corporations continue to expand, as national independence in many countries has lent immediacy to the issue of sovereignty over natural resources and key industries, and as episodes of disguised or overt political interference have come to light.

Another source of tension lies in the introduction by multinational corporations of foreign cultural values and the dilution of the host country's heritage. For instance, the introduction of machine-made goods may contribute to net output but only at the expense of displacing handicraft products. Although this is a common phenomenon in the process of modernization, caused also by domestic enterprises, the ousting of local products by the output of multinational corporations and the displacement of indigenuous enterpreneurs by foreigners are highly visible and much resented. On the other hand, when a multinational corporation operates in a more or less self-contained fashion, especially in oil production or mining in remote places, without any significant change in the old order—as though an oasis had been created in a desert —the question arises as to whether much benefit can be derived from the "enclave." There may also be "industrial enclaves," when the structure of industries in the host country has become so lopsided as to hinder sustained development. This is most glaring in cases where activity is highly concentrated in sectors, such as luxury articles catering for the few, which have limited prospects of interaction with the rest of the economy.

It has long been recognized, however, that private direct investment through the multinational corporation is unique in providing from a single source a package of critical industrial inputs: capital, technology, managerial skills and other services required for production and distribution. The scale requirements of present research and development activity, the decrease of technological and commercial risks in the development of new products and processes through multiproduct and/or multinational operations, as well as the specific organizational requirements for the application of science and technology to economic needs, give a particular comparative advantage to the multinational corporation. Quite often this advantage has rested on its ability to combine for commercial use different developments in science and technology for which the basic research was undertaken elsewhere. When production of high technology products is desired, this may be the only way of initiating it.

In many developing host countries, the suspicion is often expressed that the multinational corporation serves as an alient agent to extend "imperialistic" domination and to perpetuate politico-economic *dependencia*. Even in developed host countries, foreign control of key sectors by multinational corporations is regarded in many quarters as a serious infringement upon political independence, and even sovereignty itself. In spite of such strong reservations, however, the majority of governments of host countries have, on the whole, encouraged foreign direct investment. Indeed, through their offers of generous incentives, governments at times appear to be bidding against each other in efforts to attract multinational corporations. In encouraging the entry of multinational corporations, host governments seem to look upon their contribution as positive, although at the same time they tacitly attempt to obtain an acceptable trade-off between political, economic and sociocultural costs and benefits.

In home countries, an old debate has recently been rekindled concerning the economic and political implications of investing abroad. The traditional view of its beneficial effects on employment and balance of payments have been disputed by various groups, particularly by organized labor. Governments of the home countries have also found, at times, that multinational corporation activities tend to circumvent or even disrupt their trade, fiscal or monetary policies. Political ramifications in home countries arising out of the operations of multinational corporations have also come under increasing scrutiny, as they can lead to conflict with other governments. Such tensions between governments arise from political confrontations in support of multinational corporations, and also from jurisdictional questions such as the problems of extraterritoriality, of tax loop-holes or of overlapping taxation.

In host and home countries the taxation of corporate income varies significantly from one country to another. Differences among countries are found not only in the tax rates—which usually range between 35 and 50 percent of profits—but also in the definitions of taxable income, in the principles that govern taxing jurisdiction and in practices in making allowances for foreign taxation. In the face of these differences, the problem of the allocation of a multinational corporation's worldwide income among the taxing jurisdictions of the countries in which it operates assumes particular importance. The allocation affects, on the one hand, the tax revenue of the corporation's home country and the various countries in which the subsidiaries are located, and on the other the corporation's over-all tax bill.

One of the most troublesome aspects of the allocation problem in the case of multinational corporations is that of "transfer pricing." The sale by a parent company to its foreign subsidiary, or by one subsidiary to another, of intermediate goods used as inputs by the purchaser is affected at an internal so-called "transfer price." Often there is no market price for the goods in question from which a "normal" cost for these goods could be estimated. The setting of transfer prices at unreasonable levels can not only serve to minimize a corporation's over-all tax bill, but can also be used to circumvent exchange restrictions, minimize customs duties, satisfy local partners of foreign subsidiaries and for a variety of other purposes.

The problems that surround the taxation of multinational corporation activities are further exacerbated by differences in the taxation principles followed by various countries. While every country claims the right to tax income arising within its borders ("territorial" principle), some also claim the right to tax income arising outside their borders when that income is received by a corporation incorporated, domiciled or with its center of control within the country ("world-wide" taxing principle). In these circumstances, a claim to tax income arising abroad implies double taxation. It also implies that competition among firms within a given host country will take place under different tax rates if the home countries of these firms follow different taxation principles. In fact, however, those countries which tax income arising beyond their borders grant tax credit on account of foreign taxes paid on income from foreign sources, usually up to the level of the domestic tax rate.

The International Economy

At the international level, the operations of multinational corporations have an important bearing on the functioning of the entire international monetary and trade system, both in the short and the long run. The recent currency crises have focused attention on "hot money" movements. Although such movements have been more a symptom of fundamental defects in the system than a basic cause, any reform of the monetary system will have to consider possible scrutiny of short-term capital movements as well as compensatory arrangements. The implications of the multinational corporations for the international trade regime are equally wide. In the general framework of decisions on the location of world-wide activities, capital flows may be partially substitutable for trade flows. Furthermore, the predominance of intra-corporation transactions in trade may render adjustment mechanisms less sensitive, and limit free market operations.

TOWARD A PROGRAM OF ACTION

The positive contributions of multinational corporations to the many facets of development have been readily recognized. At the same time the problems raised have become increasingly visible. The generally favorable reception given to multinational corporations in the host countries in the immediate postwar years, as vehicles for scarce capital, modern technological know-how and skills and as a link to the world market, has increasingly been tempered by skepticism and concern.

Even in some home countries, questions of possible conflicts in interest between multinational corporations and various social groups have been raised. In the search for solutions to these difficult problems, a strategy for action should be developed which would concentrate on the setting up of an appropriate machinery whereby many key issues can be dealt with flexibly and simultaneously. [*Note*: the proposals listed below include only some of those intended for international organizations.]

No matter how wisely the host and home countries deal with the multinational corporations, and how socially responsive the behavior of these corporations may be, tensions and conflicts will inevitably arise. International machinery and procedures must be devised for dealing with them.

(a) As a minimum, there should be a proper international forum in which views can be aired and problems discussed. The U.N. Economic and Social Council, aided by a committee under it, could assume the main function, drawing on the findings of other more specialized bodies on particular aspects. The objective of the forum would not be to adjudicate but to gather and publicize facts and, through public opinion, serve as a deterrent to abuses.

(b) International efforts can also be launched for the harmonization of national policies. A particularly urgent area is that of the taxation of profits of affiliates, which is also related to tax evasion and double taxation. Another urgent area is the harmonization of incentive measures for foreign investment. Although country variations cannot be eliminated, some definition of the rules of the game and of procedures for negotiation is possible. A further area for harmonization is anti-monopoly legislation. Current efforts by regional organizations should serve as a forerunner of broader international efforts. Lastly, the harmonization of environmental regulations would guard against the abuse of such regulations as an instrument for restricting trade.

(c) The various rules of conduct can, in due course, be gathered together and codified. This is implicit in proposals such as that for the establishment of a kind of GATT for international investment. Less ambitiously, a broad international code of conduct in respect of multinational corporations could be negotiated. Although such a code is unlikely to be enforceable without the GATT type of organization, the discussions leading to it could serve as an educational process. Such a code could also serve as a guide to the review and appraisal of the activities of host and home countries as well as of the multinational corporations. On a more limited

but still international scale, multinational corporations could be registered with an international organization under the auspices of the United Nations. A set of qualifying criteria, such as "multinationality" of ownership and management, and certain duties and obligations, such as minimum disclosures and periodic reports, could be specified.

(d) So long as international authority is lacking, there can be virtually no appropriate machinery for the settlement of disputes. More use, therefore, may be made of voluntary conciliation or arbitration procedures. While a number of governments may be unwilling to submit themselves to arbitration, some may find it convenient. Pre-arrangements may therefore be made for resort to such procedures.

30. Development Finance: Unmet Needs*

Brandt Commission

The developing countries obtain finance from a number of sources: government-to-government aid programmes and export credit agencies; international financial institutions, including the World Bank Group and Regional Development Banks, the IMF, the UN agencies and other multilateral funds; private investment, much of it by multinational corporations; and commercial banks. The creation and expansion of the system of financing development in recent decades amounts to a major change in international economic cooperation.

* From Brandt Commission Report, *North-South: A Program for Survival* MIT Press, Cambridge, Mass., 1980, pp. 221–229, 232–236.

The Third World will have enormous financial requirements in the next few decades. We have surveyed the large unmet needs, particularly in the poorer countries, in food production, industrialization, development of energy and minerals, transport and communications, education and health. The developing countries' economic growth has slowed down from 6 percent a year during 1967–72 to 5 percent in the mid-1970s, and probably below that in the last three years. However great their own efforts, huge sums will be needed to enable the countries of the South to regain their momentum, to provide the jobs and incomes to overcome poverty, and to enable them to become more self-sufficient and to take a fuller part in the world's trading system.

THE CHANNELS FOR AID

For the transfer of official funds there are two main channels: one flows directly between the countries concerned, and the other goes through the multilateral institutions. UN agencies receive their funds from donor governments. The World Bank gets some of its funds directly from governments, particularly those for its soft loans through the International Development Association (IDA) window; the rest of its money is borrowed on the world's capital markets, under guarantees provided by subscriptions of the member governments. The Regional Development Banks have a similar structure.

A very big change has occurred in the composition of the total flows to the developing countries. In 1960, 60 percent came from concessional aid or Official Development Assistance (ODA). By 1977, more than two-thirds was commercial, mainly from private bank loans, direct investment and export credits. The debt burdens of a number of countries have become extremely heavy. Both the amounts and types of available finance are now clearly inadequate. And the uncertainty of future flows threatens progress in development.

Most official assistance, whether bilateral or multilateral, covers the foreign exchange cost of specific investment projects: dams, power stations, railway and road systems, industrial projects, rural development schemes. Little is made available for 'programme lending', for national development programmes as a whole, which can support the entire set of projects and activities of a country in the face of low savings and fluctuating fiscal revenue and foreign exchange. The developing countries as well as many experts—including the Pearson Commission—have laid great stress on the need for this type of finance, which gives more flexibility and certainty to overall economic management. Similarly lacking is support for financing exports, particularly capital goods; and for economic integration between developing countries, through financing of payments arrangements. The issue of adequate finance for commodity price stabilization is still not fully settled; the refinancing of debts is handled in an *ad hoc* manner.

GROWING DEBTS

The better-off developing countries have been able to overcome a number of these problems with funds from commercial sources, mainly loans from banks and export credits. One of the most dramatic changes in recent years has been the increase in the loans of the international private market, which now account for nearly 40 percent of the outstanding debt of developing countries, compared to only 17 percent in 1970. Most of the private loans have gone to a few middle-income countries, helping them increase rapidly their investment, output and exports, giving these countries the freely usable foreign exchange which they need—not tied to individual projects, to orders from particular countries, or to any specific economic policy. But there are also drawbacks to these private loans as a method of financing. Their terms (though they improved in 1977 and 1978) have meant that the countries have to meet heavy debt-servicing burdens. In the three-year period 1979–81 the aggregate payments for servicing the debts of all developing countries excluding OPEC are estimated at $120 billion—on top of the sharply rising trade deficits. As we show below, the borrowing needs of these countries are likely to rise considerably further in the 1980s. As the loans fall due, they need to borrow more in order to repay and service them. The debtor economies and the entire international credit structure are now very vulnerable to any disruptions in the flows of capital, which can be caused by a greater demand for credit in the North, by a borrowing country being regarded as less creditworthy, by insufficient bank capital, or by the actions of regulatory authorities.

The heart of the debt problem is that a very large proportion of funds are lent on terms which are onerous for borrowers from the point of view of both the repayment capacity of the projects they finance and the time debtor countries need to correct structural imbalances in their external accounts. The debt servicing record of developing countries has been excellent on the whole and payments crises have been rare. But there are likely to be more difficulties with payments in the future. Already between 1974 and 1978 many more countries were in arrears on their current payments, or were renegotiating—or trying to renegotiate—their debts with private banks. These banks may be able to expand their credit still further; but the risks and constraints of the present unbalanced structure of debts will mean that developing countries must look for new sources of long-term finance.... with trade deficits rising sharply and with the leading banks already highly exposed, there is great concern that the international banking system, which has played a crucial role in channelling OPEC and other surpluses to the deficit countries in the last five years, should be able to perform the same role in the future.

RELATIONSHIPS

It is not only the volume and kinds of finance which are inadequate: it is also the relationships between borrowers and lenders. The developing countries do not have an adequate share of responsibility for decision-making, control and management of the existing international financial and monetary institutions. The latter have made significant contributions to development through their lending and technical assistance. At the same time, they have been hesitant to engage in some of the activities of critical importance to developing countries, as we shall describe. Many countries also have misgivings about the involvement of some of these institutions in the de-

termination of their domestic policies and priorities, which has in some cases gone beyond what could be justified by the need to protect current loans and guarantee their responsible use. Further, the major international financial institutions have not been able to secure universal membership. The USSR and most of the countries of Eastern Europe are not members, and the People's Republic of China has so far not taken its place in these institutions. The lack of universality, in addition to its political cost, deprives countries of the benefits of learning from each other's development experience and curtails the scope of international assistance.

OFFICIAL AID: A DISAPPOINTING RECORD

The poorer and weaker countries have not been able to raise much money on commercial terms. For them, Official Development Assistance or aid is the principal source of funds. While the needs for concessional finance have been growing, the actual flows have faltered. It was a decade ago that the United Nations resolved on the objective of one percent of the gross national product of developed countries for the net transfer of resources to developing countries, including private flows, and within it 0.7 percent as a target for official development assistance. The ratio between these two figures reflected the relative flows at that time and the ODA target was largely a political goal. At the time this target was discussed, most of the industrialized countries accepted it, some with a time frame (e.g. Belgium, the Netherlands, Sweden) and others in principle (e.g Federal Republic of Germany). But some others, most notably the United States, did not commit themselves to the target.

While the one-percent norm for overall net flows (including private investment and commercial lending) has been reached, the hopes aroused for the ODA target have been dashed. The average performance in this respect of the industrialized countries in the OECD was only 0.35 percent of GNP in 1978. This is a deeply disappointing record. At the same time, we must point out that a number of individual countries, such as the Scandinavian countries and the Netherlands, have exceeded the target. It is very encouraging that the OPEC countries have, with their increased oil revenues in recent years, contributed nearly 3 percent of their GNP. Their effort is specially noteworthy because, in their case, aid does not result in export orders to the donors. On the other hand, the United States contribution has fallen from 0.5 percent in 1960 to 0.27 percent. Japan at 0.23 percent and the Federal Republic of Germany at 0.38 percent also remain at low levels, although they had accepted the target in principle. Also disappointing is that the average performance of the Soviet Union and other CMEA countries, according to OECD estimates, has been only of the order of 0.04 percent of their GNP.

Relative performance between different countries in meeting this target is a matter on which hard and fast comparisons may not be in order. Some donors have argued that while their aid performance has been low, their trade policies are liberal; some who have shown better performance also include expenditures on overseas commitments which in a proper reckoning should not qualify as aid; some donors allocate their aid as far as possible on need-based criteria; others concentrate theirs on countries with whom they have special historical, commercial or other ties. Assistance from the eastern countries has been available for public sector, industrial and resource sectors for which aid from other sources has been unavailable and they take goods in repayment of debt. These clarifications are important but they do not contradict the position that the industrialized countries as a whole, and the major ones among them, have failed to fulfil expectations and commitments.

This failure points to a marked lack of political will. We must face this issue squarely. In the annual aid reviews in the Development Assistance Committee (DAC), governments with poor aid performance often plead budgetary constraints and balance of payments difficulties, but it is clear that these are not insuperable obstacles. When GNP in industrial countries increases by 3 to 4 percent a year, the allocation of one-fortieth to one-thirtieth of the annual *increase* in GNP to foreign aid would close the gap between 0.3 and 0.7 percent in only five years. The pressure on public funds is always intense, as our experience makes us well aware, but what the neglect of foreign aid expresses is ultimately the lack of political priority attached to it.

WHY MORE AID IS ESSENTIAL

We have been informed that in many countries the political climate is at present unfavourable to an increase in aid, with a range of serious domestic problems looming large. But this climate must be changed. Citizens of rich countries must be brought to understand that the problems of the world must be tackled too, and that a vigorous aid policy would in the end not be a burden but an investment in a healthier world economy as well as in a safer world community. International development issues must be given the attention at a high political level that their urgency entitles them to.

Public opinion in industrial countries has often been critical of aid. Some developing countries are highly inegalitarian, and there have been doubts whether aid was getting through to the poor. The mass media have given much publicity to cases of waste, corruption, and extravagance, and the resulting scepticism creates resistance to the aid-giving intentions of governments. There is no doubt that the use of aid can and should be made more effective. At the same time it would be wrong not to recognize that the overwhelming proportion of aid money is usefully spent on the purposes for which it is intended, and aid has already done much to diminish hardships in low-income countries and to help them provide a basis for progress in rural development, health and education. For the poorest countries, aid is essential to survival.

Fortunately there have recently been signs of a more favourable attitude to aid in some major countries as the importance of the Third World is slowly beginning to be more clearly perceived. Japan not long ago announced a doubling of its aid programme. The Federal Republic of Germany is increasing its aid. The French government is raising some parts of its multilateral assistance. A new and important source of aid in the 1970s has been the OPEC members which supplied about 20 percent of all Official Development Assistance in 1978. This represents an average of 1.59 percent of their GNP; but individual countries such as Saudi Arabia, Kuwait, the United Arab Emirates and Qatar have provided between 6 to 15 percent of their GNP in past years, and between 4 and 5 percent in 1978. Besides OPEC a number of other developing countries have in recent years provided assistance. So far most of this has taken the form of scholarships and the provision of technical assistance experts, but India, Yugoslavia and some Latin American countries are also extending financial assistance. The People's Republic of China although itself a developing country has also given significant aid to several other developing countries.

We argue below that an increase in total aid must remain a high priority for alleviating the worst deprivation in the developing world. The spreading practice of development aid makes us think the time has come to consider a universal system of contributions, based on present targets for the richest countries but also providing for contributions from all other countries, except the poorest, on a sliding scale related to income. This would be an expression of shared responsibility for international development....

GAPS IN FINANCING DEVELOPMENT

As we have suggested, there are a variety of shortcomings in the network of development finance which taken together show the need for a number of fundamental changes. The overall flow of finance must increase, in the interests both of the Third World and the world economy. The poorest countries urgently need more concessional aid; the middle-income countries need loans on longer maturities. Types of finance which are currently difficult or impossible to obtain must become available in significant volumes. Loans for development need to be in more flexible forms and on a longer-term basis. Developing countries need better access, if necessary through intermediaries, to capital markets. And relations between borrowers and lenders must be improved. Multilateral institutions need to be restructured to enable the Third World to participate effectively in their management and control.

It is also urgent to fill the serious gaps in the existing financial flows to the developing world. We analyse these gaps from three perspectives: the needs of different groups of countries; sectors of activity; types of lending. The Commission has taken into account reliable estimates that have been made by international institutions. These requirements do not all add up to a total. There is a considerable area of overlap between needs related to country-groups and those identified in sectoral terms. Types of lending are a separate dimension. Our main purpose in this review of gaps is essentially to illustrate the nature, magnitude and high priority of unmet needs and to argue that a massive global effort is necessary to meet them....

COUNTRY NEEDS

Least Developed, Low-income and Lower Middle-income Countries

The low-income countries, which contain most of the world's poor people, have a very limited capacity, as we have seen, to participate in the world economy. They depend on exports of primary commodities; their agriculture is frequently threatened by drought; they have a thin margin between income and consumption; and their domestic savings are necessarily low. Looking into the future, the prospects for their food supplies are alarming. They need massive investments in irrigation and agriculture to avoid dangerous food deficits towards the end of the decade; and large outlays for improving health, nutrition and literacy.

The poverty belts of Asia and Africa need long-gestation projects for such purposes as water management, hydropower, transport, mining, afforestation, the prevention of soil erosion and desertification, and the elimination of diseases. These tasks alone will require extra finance of at least $4 billion a year over at least twenty years.

Whatever criteria are used, existing assistance to the poorer countries is inadequate, in both investment and recurrent spending. If present levels of assistance are merely continued, there cannot be much progress in meeting essential needs, and an annual growth in income per head of only one percent in low-income Africa and only 2.8 percent in low-income Asia would be possible. This, according to the World Bank's 1979 *World Development Report*, would actually widen the gap in living standards between the poor and the rich countries (from 1:40 in 1975 to 1:47 by 1990) even if the poor countries were to increase their savings sharply—an unacceptable situation. The aggregate needs of all the least developed countries for external capital are estimated by UNCTAD at $11 billion annually during the 1980s, and $21 billion during the 1990s, to support a 6.5 percent rate of GDP growth (3.5 percent *per capita*). For the poorest countries the assistance should be highly concessional.

According to a study for the Overseas Development Council in Washington, countries with an income per head of below $520 (least developed, low-income and lower middle-income) will need annual aid in the 1980s in the range of $40–54 billion (in 1980 dollars), either for achieving a 3.5 to 4 percent growth in *per capita* income, or for obtaining resources equal to half the costs of meeting essential human needs, the other half being borne by the countries themselves. If 1980 aid were no higher in real terms than in 1977, it would fall short of adequacy for such objectives by $21–35 billion. If this shortfall could be met in the early 1980s low-income and lower middle-income developing countries could tackle the worst forms of poverty, and they could finance industrial and agricultural projects, imports of raw materials, fertilizers, equipment and spare parts. Such assistance will have to be concessional but it need not be all in the form of grants, except for the least developed countries. Depending on circumstances, the transfers can be a blend of different types of finance—soft loans like those provided by IDA, bilateral long-term low-interest development loans, interest-subsidized market loans, export credits. Food aid may also play an important part. Developing countries will need project loans, which where appropriate can finance local currency costs; and also programme loans, to complement project lending and to meet maintenance needs.

Middle-income and Higher-income Countries

The middle-income and higher-income developing countries need development loans on terms and in forms which suit their stage of development. Their total borrowing requirements will be affected by the growth and openness of markets for their exports. They need improvement in the maturity structure of their debts. They need longer-term programme finance. Some lower middle-income countries will also need interest subsidization.

According to World Bank projections (which assume annual inflation of 7.2 percent), borrowing by these countries from commercial banks and other private sources will be needed at a level of $155 billion in the year 1985 (in current dollars) compared to less than $40 billion annually in 1975–7. By 1990 it will be as much as $270 billion. Even this may turn out to be an underestimate: the projected rate of growth of exports in the 1980s (6.3 percent) may be too high in the light of the present prospects for the world economy, and oil prices have been assumed constant at their 1975 levels in real terms, although this assumption is already out of date. In any case, much more official lending is needed to reduce the pressure on the international credit structure and the associated risks; and to reduce the difficulties of the middle-income countries in servicing their debts. Their financing problems should also be tackled through other means, including better access to the bond markets of industrialized countries. Their debt service ratio (the proportion of their exports absorbed by servicing debts), which in 1977 averaged 9.2 percent and already exceeded 20 percent for a few countries, is now projected almost to double from 1975–7 to 1990. If these countries are to receive adequate funds, at the right time and on terms that they can reasonably repay, there can be no substitute for a major expansion of public lending, mostly in the form of programme loans. . . .

MISSING TYPES OF FINANCE

For reasons which are partly historical, partly based on the self-interest of donors and partly due to an inadequate understanding of the role of external resources in helping development, most of the official finance which developing countries get is earmarked for the purchase of capital goods from outside. In the initial stages aid was no more than an extension of credits which industrialized countries were providing to promote the export of their capital goods, taking the shape of additions to such credits and the improvement of credit terms. The popularity of monumental projects, both in donor and recipient countries, further strengthened the trend. What was overlooked was that the shortage of domestic capital which creates the need for external re-

sources is not identical with the gap in the capacity to pay for imported capital goods. The poorer developing countries need external finance to cover their local currency expenditure if they are to avoid inflationary pressures and balance of payments difficulties.

We now turn to the types of official finance which are lacking or difficult to obtain: programme loans, which provide long-term capital not specifically linked to projects and improve the structure of debt; export credits for capital goods; support of economic integration; finance for stabilizing commodity prices. They are the means of meeting some of the needs of countries and sectors which we have discussed. We discuss each type of finance below.

Programme Lending

The most serious gap is in programme lending—that is, providing flexibly usable funds which are not tied to specific investment projects. Most bilateral and multilateral financing is available only for projects, as we have said; but project loans on their own are inefficient in facilitating an adequate transfer of resources. They are disbursed very slowly. In the experience of the World Bank, there is almost a ten-year cycle on average from the first identification of a project to its completion.

An exclusive reliance on project lending also produces certain important biases: firstly, it favours large projects over small, since lending agencies have a minimum threshold size of operations, to keep down their administrative costs. Secondly, it favours new fixed investment, rather than using existing capacity more efficiently, since working capital (labour and raw materials) is not normally eligible for project finance. Thirdly, the specification of projects and the tying procedures of agencies may encourage capital-intensive processes, which may not suit the developing country. Fourthly, the industrialized countries and the lending agencies from time to time change their views on development priorities; this leads to changing preferences for the type of projects they want to finance, often irrespective of the developing countries' own priorities.

Project and programme lending are in fact complementary. Programme lending corrects some of the distortions which come from relying exclusively on project lending. Firstly, programme loans are disbursed quickly, normally over two or three years. When these loans finance imports which are sold on the domestic market, they generate local currency for the government. Thus they can help to finance the local costs of projects and accelerate their execution. Secondly, programme lending, by providing more flexible funds, can encourage self-reliance. A country may have its own industrial plants which may make it unnecessary to use scarce foreign funds on importing capital goods. Or a country may have a large excess industrial capacity from previous investments, which it cannot put into full production because it lacks foreign exchange; and this need cannot be met by project lending, which aims to create new capacity. In both cases, programme loans help to provide jobs and raise incomes throughout the economy. Thirdly, developing countries also need the long-term support of programme loans for undertaking changes which cannot be achieved through project lending alone— including building up their social infrastructure, administration and management, or diversifying economies which depend too heavily on a few commodities or minerals.

Expanded programme loans would help to lighten the debt burden especially if it involves the lengthening of maturities. Developing countries need foreign exchange to adjust to balance of payments difficulties which can arise from a variety of causes outside their control. These cannot be treated as projects; but if they are not adequately met, the whole development programme will be jeopardized. The distinction between temporary support for 'adjustment', which should normally be provided by the IMF, and longer-term borrowing is often blurred. In real life, a country's needs for short-, medium- and long-term external finance do not fall into tidy compartments; the line of demarcation is a shifting one. If finance for adjustment is available too little and too late, the only solution for a developing country is a quick correction, which curtails growth, lowers wages, reduces employment and worsens income distribution. It is particularly serious for the poorer and weaker countries who cannot borrow from commercial banks, and who need long-term programme lending. What is needed essentially is a bridge between the long-term project financing available from such institutions as the World Bank and the short-term adjustment finance available from the IMF. Without this kind of bridge, in the form of long-term programme lending developing countries have often slid back on their development programmes or have depended too heavily on commercial loans, jeopardizing their future capacity to borrow.

In highlighting these aspects of programme vis-à-vis project lending, we are not unaware that the industrialized countries of the North and the East have preferred to lend money to identifiable projects whose successful completion can be monitored and benefits from which can be clearly discerned. They have been apprehensive that general-purpose lending for balance of payments support might enable, if not encourage, diversion of foreign exchange to arms purchases, waste or misuse. They feel that the monitoring of the use of programme loans will raise very sensitive questions in borrower-creditor relationships, questions which both parties would prefer to avoid. The receiving countries, on the other hand, see the overwhelming emphasis on project loans as a constraint on their self-reliant development, and worse, as one more instance of lack of trust. We recognize this difference in perceptions but we believe that it should be possible to avoid this conflict. It should be feasible for programme lending to supplement and complement project lending, and for it to be related to well-conceived, clearly defined development programmes, the fulfilment of which can be monitored. In many developing countries, domestic public financing institutions such as industrial and agricultural development banks could be more extensively used as channels for external support to sectors and programmes. Later, we also deal with changes in international institutional structures that are necessary to build greater trust and confidence between borrowers and lenders.

Export Finance

The developing countries need support for providing export credits, particularly for capital goods. The market for capital goods is highly competitive: not only in the price, quality, aftersale service and speed of delivery of the goods, but also in the availability and cost of export credit finance. A number of developing countries are now exporting capital goods and others are developing the potential to do so. To sell them, the exporters have to extend medium-term credit for which, being deficit countries, they need refinancing. Some developing countries in recent years have provided export credit finance, but further rapid growth of their capital goods exports would strain their institutions.

There have been many initiatives for refinancing schemes, but they have not been followed up. Only the Inter-American Development Bank can refinance export credits for capital goods, mainly within Latin America; and a new Latin American Export Credit Bank, with a modest equity participation of the International Finance Corporation, plans to refinance short- and medium-term credit for non-traditional goods. One effect of giving broad support to export credit finance would be to stimulate trade among developing countries and their economic cooperation.

Economic Integration

Developing countries need financial support to increase trade among themselves. Economic integration has long been a principal

objective, intended to ensure closer cooperation and expansion of trade. But many integration schemes have achieved only slow progress, or have retrogressed. This has sometimes been due to political causes, but is also partly due to the balance of payments difficulties of the participants. Liberalizing trade under such schemes often creates payments deficits for one or more members *vis-à-vis* other partners. The difficulty can be overcome by expanding mutual credit through payments arrangements, but external assistance is needed when the partners, despite intragroup surpluses, have difficulty with overall payments and have individually little access to external finance. More generally, there is need for the periodic settlement of balances from intra-trade, and such payments will require outside finance. This can be provided by programme lending if it is on an adequate scale.

Commodity Stabilization

In the chapter on commodities we have argued the case for more commodity agreements and for financing national stocks. Finance is urgently needed to stabilize the prices of primary products of developing countries, and to assure a price floor. Without this they cannot improve their external economic situation, and stable commodity export prices for the poor countries would also help to sustain their demand for manufactured goods and promote assured supplies of raw materials. This need has been recognized for a long time but no decisive action has been taken and unstable prices and earnings still dislocate the world economy. The weak economies which are heavily dependent on a few primary exports are especially vulnerable. This will entail larger capital support to the Common Fund in the course of time, or increased programme lending.

RELATIONSHIPS AND INSTITUTIONS

We are not the first to have drawn attention to the missing elements in the structure of financing. Their common feature is that they involve difficult and sensitive policy issues in the economic and political relationships between North and South. Whether it is programme lending, or commodity stabilization, or promotion of developing countries' exports, or finance to enable them to cooperate with each other more effectively—all of these, in their several ways, singly and together, are forms of finance which would enable the poor countries to become more self-reliant and independent participants in a more equitable exchange with the rich countries. Thus they all call for a new approach to decision-making.

These gaps have persisted, partly because the governments of the North have been reluctant to change their practices adequately; partly because the developing countries have not been able to influence critical decisions in international institutions. The quality of the relations between borrowers and creditors is vitally important to the character of financial institutions, and their ability to provide for the needs of their clients; the inequality between borrowers and lenders has made it harder to reach joint agreement and to generate mutual trust. Greater equality and participation by the developing countries can help to overcome these difficulties.

Further Readings

1. Foreign Aid

Abbott, G. C. "Two Concepts of Foreign Aid." *World Development* 1, no. 9 (September 1973).

Centre for Development Planning, Projections and Policies, "Foreign Aid and Development Needs." *Journal of Development Planning*, no. 10 (1976).

Chenery, Hollis B., and Carter, Nicholas G. "Foreign Assistance and Development Performance, 1960–1970." *American Economic Review* 63, no. 2 (May 1973).

Goulet, Denis, and Hudson, Michael. *The Myth of Aid: The Hidden Agenda of the Development Reports*. Prepared by the Center for Development and Social Change, International Documentation on the Contemporary Church. New York: North America-Orbis Books, 1971.

Isenman, Paul J., and Singer, H. W. "Food Aid: Disincentive Effects and Their Policy Implications." *Economic Development and Cultural Change* 25, no. 2 (January 1977).

Pearson, Lester B. *Partners in Development: Report of the Commission on International Development*. New York, Washington, and London: Praeger, 1969.

Seers, Dudley. "Why Visiting Economists Fail." *Journal of Political Economy* 70, no. 4 (August 1962).

Williams, Maurice J. "The Aid Programs of the OPEC Countries." *Foreign Affairs* 54, no. 2 (January 1976).

2. Foreign Investment

Killick, T. "The Benefits of Foreign Direct Investment and its Alternatives: An Empirical Exploration." *Journal of Development Studies* 9, no. 2 (January 1973).

Lall, S. "Less Developed Countries and Private Foreign Direct Investment: A Review Article." *World Affairs* 2, nos. 4 and 5 (April/May 1974).

Reuber, Grant L. *Private Foreign Investment in Development*. Oxford, England: Oxford University Press, 1973.

Stamp, M. "Has Foreign Capital Still a Role to Play in Development?" *World Development* 2, no. 2 (February 1974).

3. Multinational Corporations

Agmon, Tamir, and Kindleberger, Charles P., eds. *Multinationals from Small Countries*. Cambridge, Mass., and London: MIT Press, 1977.

Barnet, Richard J., and Muller, Ronald E. *Global Reach: The Power of the Multinational Corporations*. New York: Simon & Schuster, 1974.

Bergsten, C. Fred; Hersh, Thomas; and Moran Theodore H. *American Multinationals and America Interests*. Washington, D.C.: Brookings Institution, 1978.

Drucker, Peter F., "Multinationals and Developing Countries: Myths and Realities." *Foreign Affairs* 2, no. 2 (February 1974).

Dunning, J. H. "Multinational Enterprises and Trade Flows of Less Developed Countries." *World Development* 2, no. 2 (February 1974).

Helleiner, Gerald K. "The Role of Multinational Corporations in the Less Developed Countries' Trade in Technology." *World Development* 3, no. 4 (April 1975).

ILO. *The Impact of Multinational Enterprises on Employment and Training*. Geneva, 1976.

Streeten P. "Policies towards Multinationals." *World Development 3, no. 6 (June 1975)*.

Vernon, Raymond. *Storm Over the Multinationals: The Real Issues*. Cambridge, Mass.: Harvard University Press, 1977.

Part IV

Possibilities and Prospects

In the last two chapters, we look first at the role and limitations of the public sector in the areas of development planning and economic stabilization policies and then at prospects for the world economy in the 1980s. Chapter 12 begins with a critical examination of both the economic planning process and the planning experience in an excellent paper by Tony Killick. Killick stresses both the manpower and the political limitations of planning and the many reasons why elegant paper plans often fail in practice. He calls for a more sensible and politically realistic approach by economists to the formulation of national plans. Killick's essay is followed by a highly relevant and timely paper by Alejandro Foxley on the experiences of economic stabilization policies and the movements toward a free market economy in Chile during the 1970s. The issues explored by Foxley—the interrelation between economic liberalism and political freedom, the relevance of monetarism, the search for new models of development and the allure of authoritarianism in conducting stabilization programs—are likely to be widely debated during the 1980s as more developing countries are forced to tighten their financial belts. Mexico and Argentina provide the most recent (1982) examples.

The final chapter of the volume, 13, focuses on the structure of and prospects for the world economy in the 1980s. Mahbub ul Haq sets forth both the reasons for, and the nature of, Third World demands for the creation of a new international economic order (NIEO). He argues that such changes are essential if less developed countries are to benefit in any significant way from their interactions with rich nations. Issues such as commodity pricing, commodity agreements, debt rescheduling, technology transfer, trade restrictions, multinational corporation investment, foreign assistance, and the activities of the World Bank and the International Monetary Fund (IMF) all come under the North-South NIEO debate.

In the final reading, John W. Sewell makes a compelling case for the degree to which the developed nations of the North need the economic development of the less developed countries of the South in order that they, the North, may continue to prosper. He argues that developed countries rely on less developed countries to an increasing degree not only in the area of raw material supplies but also for markets to sell their exports and investment opportunities for their surplus capital. This is an issue that is often overlooked when developed-nation politicians and citizens ask the question: "Why should we be concerned with the economic development of the poor nations of Africa, Asia and Latin America?"

12

Development Planning, Free Markets and the Role of the State

31. The Possibilities of Development Planning*

Tony Killick

The premise of this paper[1] is a belief that development planning in practice has achieved few of the benefits that its advocates expected from it. Most reasons given for this poor performance do not get to the source of the problem, which is the naïvety of the implicit model of governmental decision-making incorporated in the planning literature. More realistic views of politics and decision-making, familiar in other social sciences and even other branches of economics but largely ignored in development economics, pose the questions whether planning, as it has come to be understood, is feasible at all, and, even if feasible, whether it is an efficient instrument of economic policy.

THE NATURE OF DEVELOPMENT PLANNING

Although planning occurs in many types of decision-making units and is often defined to cover any attempt to select the best means to achieve desired ends,[2] this paper focuses more narrowly on comprehensive development planning in low-income countries (although

the discussion is also relevant to the 'special case' of industrial countries). Advocates of comprehensive development planning typically propose that plans should meet the following specifications:[3]

(a) Starting from the political views and goals of the government, the plan should define policy objectives, especially as they relate to the future development of the economy;

(b) It should set out a strategy by means of which it is intended to achieve the objectives, preferably translated into specific targets;

(c) It should present a centrally co-ordinated, internally consistent set of principles and policies, chosen as optimal means of implementing the strategy and achieving the targets, and intended to be used as a framework to guide subsequent day-to-day decisions;

(d) It should cover the whole economy (hence it is 'comprehensive' as against 'colonial' or 'public sector' planning);

(e) In order to secure optimality and consistency, it should employ a more-or-less formalized macro-economic model (which, however, may remain unpublished), em-

* From *Oxford Economic Papers*, 41, no. 4 (October 1976), pp. 161–84.

ployed to project the intended future performance of the economy;

(f) It typically covers a period of, say, five years and finds physical expression as a medium-term plan document, which may, however, incorporate a longer-term perspective plan and be supplemented by annual plans.

Most of the time, most low-income countries have development plans which apparently endeavour to meet all or most of these specifications; we are thus examining a highly significant aspect of applied economics, and the characteristics listed are chosen to identify what is common to most comprehensive development plans rather than to draw attention to any special features or eccentricities.

The economic case for development planning, while sometimes taken as axiomatic,[4] is generally made out in terms of the failings of an unregulated market economy.[5] Perhaps the chief of the arguments views planning as a superior means of arriving at investment and other decisions affecting the future, with the market seen as supplying information which is a poor guide for such decisions, leading to avoidable uncertainties and myopia.[6] Thus, Scitovsky and others drew attention to the interdependence of investment decisions and alleged that aggregate investment made up of atomistic decisions would be less than that which would result from 'centralised investment planning' providing more realistic signals of present plans and future conditions.[7] In other ways, too, planning is seen as a means for correcting discrepancies between private and social valuations, for example the market's tendency to over-value unskilled labour. Under the influence of the 'big push' school of thought, it has also been seen as the only way to mobilize resources on the scale necessary for a successful development effort, and as the only practical means of weaving the various threads of economic policy into a consistent whole.[8]

THE CRISIS IN PLANNING: EXPLANATIONS; SOLUTIONS

Although it is not a matter that can be reduced to any simple demonstration, there would probably be little disagreement today that the practice of planning has generally failed to bring many of the benefits expected from it. Waterston's study of the lessons of experience concluded that 'there have been many more failures than successes in the implementation of development plans';[9] Seers's keynote paper for a 1969 conference on 'The Crisis in Planning' was entitled 'The Prevalence of Pseudo-planning';[10] and Healey is surely accurate in claiming that the results 'have been sadly disillusioning for those who believed that planning was the only way'.[11]

The disillusionment seems to apply in most parts of the third world. Myrdal's 1968 Asian study stated that 'planning can be considered a going concern only in India and Pakistan'[12] and events since then have seen the disintegration of Pakistan as it then was and the publication in India of a new plan widely thought to be quite unrealistic.[13] The Organisation of American States has reported that it was 'repeatedly discovered that long-term plans were either not put into effect, or they were implemented officially for only a fraction of their time, or they were simply ignored at the moment of governmental decisions'.[14] In similar vein, the U.N. Economic Commission for Africa has stated that development plans 'had little, if any, impact on the overall development of [West African] countries, and can *at best* be taken as an expression of the desires of governments or the hopes of small groups of experts'.[15] Helleiner has written of a disillusionment in Africa with the potentialities of planning,[16] and I know of no African state which is currently engaged in a serious planning effort, in the sense of using its plan as a guide to day-to-day policy decisions and the preparation of its budgets.[17]

None of this, of course, is to deny individual successes nor some genuine benefits.

The creation of planning agencies and preparation of plan documents has surely had an educational effect among politicians and administrators, helping to define, and raise the understanding of, major policy issues. Planners do not spend all their time dressing windows and have certainly helped to raise the standard of policy decisions on matters such as project selection. Nevertheless, there has been a vast gap between the theoretical benefits and practical results of development planning. It is doubtful whether plans have generated more useful signals for the future than would otherwise have been forthcoming;[18] governments have rarely in practice, reconciled private and social valuations except in a piecemeal manner;[19] because they have seldom been operational documents, plans have probably had only limited success in mobilizing resources (although they probably have induced larger aid flows) or in co-ordinating economic policies.

The profession cannot be criticized for being unresponsive on this situation. Much thought has been given to the sources of poor plan performance, with the most commonly mentioned causes listed below.[20]

(a) Deficiencies in the plans: they tend to be over-ambitious, to be based upon inappropriately specified macro-models, to be insufficiently specific about policies and projects, to overlook important noneconomic considerations, to fail to incorporate adequate administrative provision for their own implementation.

(b) Inadequate resources: incomplete and unreliable data; too few economists and other planning personnel.

(c) Unanticipated dislocations to domestic economic activity: adverse movements in the terms of trade; irregular flows of development aid; unplanned changes in the private sector.

(d) Institutional weaknesses: failures to locate the planning agency appropriately in the machinery of government; failures of communication between planners, administrators, and their political masters; the importation of institutional arrangements unsuited to local circumstances.

(e) Failings on the part of the administrative civil service: cumbersome bureaucratic procedures; excessive caution and resistance to innovations; personal and departmental rivalries; lack of concern with economic considerations. (Finance Ministries are a particularly frequent target, often said to undermine the planning agency by resisting the co-ordination of plans and budgets.)

There is certainly ample evidence that each of these tendencies has contributed to the planning crisis, the precise combination varying over time and from country to country. But there seems to be a growing consensus among economists that yet another set of factors is the most important explanation: that 'lack of government support for the plans is the prime reason why most are never carried out successfully'.[21] Seers, while also finding fault with administrators and economists, argues that 'political forces encourage the production of pseudo-plans';[22] Tinbergen sees as one of the difficulties 'that among politicians, probably as a consequence of our educational system, a preference exists for thinking in qualitative terms only';[23] and Myrdal refers to 'rivalries between parties or ministers' as one of the major problems.[24]

In the face, presumably, of the futility of advocating reformed political systems, most proposals for improving plan performance tend to the administrative or organizational. Frisch, for example, has developed an administrative decision model intended to secure 'optimal implementation'.[25] Myrdal perhaps comes closest to advocating a political solution in arguing for 'democratic', or decentralized, planning.[26] Helleiner also tries to grasp the political nettle, with the prescription that 'those engaged in planning activities must be sufficiently close to the seat of political power to be relevant to the actual process of political decision making' but sees the practical application of this largely in terms of 'new institutions and personnel'.[27] Consistent with his views on the baneful influence of traditional education, a U.N. committee headed by Tinbergen advocates 'Intensified training of many persons involved';[28] and Waterston's proposal for an 'operational approach' to planning emphasizes the use of annual plans tied into budgetary procedures and supplemented by 'multi-annual sector programmes'.[29]

Some large questions have, however, gone unasked in these attempts to respond to the planning crisis, leaving some doubt whether the resulting prescriptions have been radical enough. The inclination to see politicians as the spoilers leaves one wondering why it would not be in their own interests to support their planners, if planning is viewed as a way of raising the rationality and effectiveness of public policies.[30] Might it be that the concept of development planning is one that could not, with the best will in the world, be built into the process of government because 'politics isn't like that'? Might it even be that a government really committted to the full execution of a plan could end up making worse rather than better decisions? It might similarly be asked of those advocating administrative-type reforms, what makes them think these solutions to be attainable through precisely those political processes which are blamed for past failings? Are not deficient institutions and procedures an expression of the political system itself, not to be remedied without first or simultaneously instituting political changes? For example, the respective roles of the planning agency and the finance ministry reflect, in substantial part, a distribution of political power; is it useful, then, to make proposals for raising the relative influence of the planning agency while remaining silent on the distribution of power?

Economists have generally failed to ask such questions and, significantly, it was a political scientist who, on reviewing explanations for plan failures similar to the list given above, was led to observe that it 'rather plainly adds up to the conclusion that planning is more or less bound to fail, given the probability that many of these factors will be present in any situation of underdevelopment', and to urge that 'Any useful conceptualisation of the planning process must start from a model of politics'.[31] The record of past performance suggests the possibility that effective planning may simply not be feasible, so the next step is to take up Leys's point and examine the model of politics upon which the notion of development planning appears to have been built.

A PLANNER'S MODEL OF POLITICS

This task, however, is one of combing the literature for hints and inferences, because the main characteristic of writings on development planning is the virtual absence of systematic discussion of the implications of planning for political systems, or vice versa, even though authors often insists that a plan is essentially a political document. Writers such as Lewis do have pithy things to say about politics but only at the level of shrewd common sense.[32] Virtually no attempt is made to use the analytical tools of the political scientist; economists seem to find it more comfortable to get rid of this problem by treating politics as creating 'boundary conditions' constraining the variation of targets and policy instruments.[33] The result is a largely unarticulated view of political processes, which appears to owe the greatest intellectual debt not to the study of government but to economists' own theories of the behaviour of individuals and firms.[34]

The starting-point is an implicit assumption that governments normally seek to act in the national interest. This follows from a theory which establishes the case for planning largely to correct for the social defects of the market mechanism. The problem of social choice, as Arrow has pointed out, is that it needs public officials whose 'one aim in life is to implement the values of other citizens as given by some rule of collective decision making.'[35] If ministers individually and collectively pursue personal or sectional, rather than national, interests they will merely be replacing the private valuations of the market by their own imposed *private* valuations, for we surely would not want to define as social *any* government valuation. So if plans are to reconcile private and social interests and if the objectives they incorporate are to provide a plausible proxy for a social welfare function then these objectives 'must always have been considered as some version of "the general interest" '.[36] Or as Heal has it, 'the objective function in a planning problem serves to represent, or make numerically explicit, social preferences'.[37]

The analogy with a social welfare function draws attention to further assumptions we must make about governments and the men that form them. It is a standard formulation that it is a primary responsibility of the government to formulate a set of objectives between which it will have priorities in situations of goal conflicts and trade-offs.[38] Note the implications: that governments collectively are clear about their economic objectives and are willing to have these articulated in a public document. We might also note that, while usually taking a properly positivist view that the formulation of objectives is a task for governments not planners, the idea of development planning rests upon the unstated presumption that development (however defined) will rank very high among the goals of economic policy. If development were to be subordinated to, say, price stability or the short-run maximization of consumption there may remain a case for some sort of planning but not planning which takes development as the first-order goal.

It follows from what has already been said that economists, if not explicitly, see ministers as role-oriented, as looking for the solution of problems through acts of policy. One of the merits often claimed for planning is that it enables problems to be anticipated and defined, and assists the selection of the most appropriate policy solutions.[39] So a rather high-minded view is taken: of politicians in power because of the good they can do, unafraid of problems, anxious to use their time and powers to solve them. The view is also taken that circumstances will be such that the government will be willing and able to undertake the large 'bunching' of decisions that is implicit in the conscientious adoption of a medium-term plan.

The influence of our models of economic man and the profit-maximizing firm are fairly evident in our (usually tacit) view of governments as single decision-making units and as optimizers, seeking the best possible policy response to a given set of problems, wishing always to be consistent (if A is preferred to B and B is preferred to C then . . .), at least in the medium term. This is indicated by the heavy emphasis in the literature on macro-modelling, input-output, mathematical programming, and other techniques for achieving optimization and internal consistency.[40] Even more tacit, perhaps, is a belief that politicians see problems essentially as economists see them (if a problem were perceived in some radically different way there is clearly little likelihood that the policy response recommended by the economist would meet the needs of the politician), of which an assumption that politicians' time-horizons are distant enough for perspective and medium-term planning to be appropriate is a case in point. Another influence on the planning literature is Tinbergen's sharp distinction between objectives and policy instruments, with its corollary that choices between alternative policy weapons are relatively value-neutral.

Economists' expectations that a government will have a clearly defined set of policy objectives in the medium term also suggests the inference that governments will maintain a relatively high degree of internal unity. Without it there would be little chance of formulating a consistent, relatively settled and operational set of objectives, or of imposing the discipline of the plan on subsequent decisions. In the absence of harmony, the prime task of political leadership would be to maintain an essential minimum of unity by continuous compromises, playing one group off against another, fudging contentious issues, reshuffling the cabinet, and so on. The dynamics of such a situation would reduce the utility of medium-term planning; political time-horizons would not be long enough. It is unsurprising, therefore, that lack of government agreement on objectives and lack of unity within cabinets are among the reasons given for plan failures.[41] This reasoning can be taken a little further to point out the obvious, but generally unstated, fact that the notion of medium-term planning presupposes the absence of chronic political instability or, at least, a clear national consensus on what the objectives of economic policy ought to be, so that governments may differ in personnel but not in intent. If these conditions are not satisfied a political document like a plan will survive only as long as the regime that spawned it. While essential to medium-term planning, the assumption of political stability or consensus is a strong but rarely articulated one.

The literature also has implications for the locus of power in society. The emphasis on the use of plans to produce a co-ordinated system of economic policies implies a relatively high degree of centralization. If planning functions are delegated over a number of separate agencies the practical task of co-ordination becomes much more difficult, with inconsistencies and conflicts between agencies becoming virtually inevitable.[42] It is true that writers on development planning have had a good deal to say in favour of regional planning but without being very clear about how to reconcile it with central co-ordination. In practice, as Waterston found, 'regional planning has proceeded independently of national planning, with the result that a series of unintegrated re-

gional plans has sometimes been produced, based on regional aspirations rather than available resources'.[43] The underlying philosophy is for *central* planning, which is why Myrdal's proposals for 'democratic' planning would represent a departure from the normal. The advocacy of central planning in which government objectives are taken to have been considered 'as some version of the general interest' presupposes adequate powers at the centre to ensure that the general interest prevails over special interests. Or perhaps we are making the even stronger assumption that interest groups will not pursue their own objectives when these are shown to be inconsistent with the general interest? Thus, Tinbergen advocates 'distributive meetings' between planners and others—which are most remarkably different from any inter-ministerial meetings I have ever attended—where[44]

the distribution of something—say, the building volume—over a number of interested groups—say the Ministries—is discussed and maybe even decided upon. This meeting tries to solve a number of equations—e.g. those representing the condition of equal marginal utility of various uses made of one product . . . a comparison of the marginal utilities of different groups is involved—the central problem of the structure of the social welfare or utility function.

Note the assumed subordination of the particular to the national interest, allowing utilities to be equalized at the margin.

The type of society that appears to be the most amenable to development planning, then, is a monistic one, as compared with a pluralistic society in which government policies respond to, and seek to adjudicate between, competing group pressures. As Leys puts it, if the central planners were given the powers needed to implement the plans 'the problem of political pluralism would have virtually disappeared'.[45] It is therefore no coincidence to find many of the weaknesses of Indian planning blamed upon competition between the rival pressure groups which were, however, but an expression of that country's erstwhile parliamentary democracy.[46] The implicit assumption of monism has another facet, in its implication of relatively simple control relationships, with the centre issuing commands (laws) and the periphery passively implementing them. A centralized structure of authority would help plan implementation but would contradict a view of political leadership in which there is a plurality of roles and a much more subtle interplay of responses between the leaders and the led. A similar contradiction would arise if we viewed government departments and other implementing agencies as having goals of their own not always coinciding with those of the ruling politicians.

This latter point and much that precedes it reveals a tendency in the literature to tacitly assume the state to be a highly efficacious agent of change and control. In fact, the derivation of a theory of planning from an analysis of market defects and failures rests upon the unstated presumption that when markets fail the state will do better. There is much talk of market failures; little, at least until recently, of government failures.[47]

Some adversaries of planning, of whom this writer is not one, oppose it on the grounds that they distrust the motives and efficacy of central governments.[48] But without taking this view one may still have serious doubts about the presumption of state efficacy because it requires some extraordinarily strong assumptions about information and uncertainty. It requires governments and their administrators to have a sufficient understanding of the behaviour of the economy to be able to make accurate diagnoses of its weaknesses and to know with reasonable accuracy how it will respond to given policy measures. There would seem to be little case for medium-term planning except on the grounds that governments are faced with manageable degrees of uncertainty and can be reasonably confident of the consequences of their policy actions (including

the absence of major unwanted second-order effects). This further implies an ample stock and flow of information and rather advanced capacity to process and interpret it.[49] It takes for granted (by failing to consider the opposite) that the costs of obtaining and processing the information would be exceeded by the benefits derived therefrom.

To sum up, economists have adopted a 'rational actor' model of politics.[50] This would have us see governments as composed of public-spirited, knowledgeable, and role-oriented politicians; clear and united in their objectives; choosing those policies which will achieve optimal results for the national interest; willing and able to go beyond a short-term point of view. Governments are stable, in largely undifferentiated societies; wielding a centralized concentration of power and a relatively unquestioned authority; generally capable of achieving the results they desire from a given policy decision. They are supported by public administrations with ready access to a very large volume of relevant information which can be processed efficiently. How political scientists might label such a regime is unclear but one is reminded of Wicksell's observation that 'much of the discussion in fiscal theory proceeds on the implicit and unrecognised assumption that the society is ruled by a benevolent despot'—a paradoxical result to emerge from the liberal-individualist tradition of western economics.

This view of politics invites major doubts about its realism and, therefore, its relevance. The next step, then, is to contrast the planner's model with the conclusions of political scientists, sociologists, and others who have studied governments and their decision processes. It would be contradictory to propose as an alternative a single *behavioural* model of government to cover the extreme diversity to be found among developing countries, and the intention is rather to offer a few generalizations which can plausibly be regarded as having fairly widespread application to these countries.

BEHAVIOURAL VIEWS OF POLITICS AND DECISIONS

The first generalization is that, far from being monistic, society is marked by considerable differentiation and severe social tensions, caused by differences of religion, caste, tribe, language, regional origin, education, and rather extreme inequalities of income and wealth.[51] Although pressure groups may not yet have achieved a high level of organization, politics will, in varying degrees, reflect competing interests within society, and conflict management will be a chief preoccupation of governments. Thus, governments will tend to be coalitions and their actions (and their development plans) will not so much be chosen, but rather be the resultants of bargaining between individuals, groups, and agencies.[52] Due, however, to limited institutional and other capacities to resolve these conflicts peaceably, there is a more frequent tendency than in industrial nations for social conflict to result in violence and other extra-legal actions, and thus for greater political instability. Politics may be competitive but not openly so, with competition often occurring despite the absence of a legal framework of electoral choice between opposed political parties. The pluralistic nature of society will tend to result in a diffusion of power, geographically and among institutions,[53] and the first concern of a government and its civil service is likely to be the maintenance of its own power.[54]

Non-industrial modernising societies . . . lack the powerful integrating thrust found in industrial societies. Social organisations are more chaotic and confused. Politics becomes the mechanism of integration, and authority is the critical problem confronting the leaders.

The 'arm of the law' is unlikely to stretch throughout society. For this reason and also because of bureaucratic resistances, there are likely to be rather large differences between the commands issued from the centre and the actual conduct of civil affairs. In other words, there will probably be rather severe limitations on governments' ability to achieve what they want.

The next generalization, one that scarcely needs elaboration, is that the planner's view of politicians as role-oriented and relatively disinterested is unlikely to be generally valid. If we view society as fragmented and its politics as an arena for competition between rival interests, it follows that many of its participants will seek to promote particular rather than general interests. However, politics may not primarily be seen as a means of achieving specific policy goals at all:[55]

Party members have as their chief motivation the desire to obtain the intrinsic rewards of holding office; therefore they formulate policies as means of holding office rather than seeking office in order to carry out preconceived policies.

Ministers may be at least as often concerned to evade issues as to confront them, and will often prefer to react to problems rather than anticipate them. Some would go further, viewing politics as aggrandizement, in which the chief concerns of those in power are 'first, the enrichment of the government itself (i.e. of the ruler, of Ministers, of party leaders, of top civil servants, and possibly of numerous subordinate ranks of public officers and party workers), and secondly the buying of political support which will enable the government to maintain itself in power'.[56] My point is not to advocate this position but rather to point out the unwisdom of taking an exclusively high-minded view of politicians.

Governments will, moreover, often be right in deferring action in the real world of imperfect knowledge and large uncertainties, especially in open economies highly susceptible to movements in trade and capital flows beyond their own control. Thus, Rawls has proposed a 'principle of postponement' which holds that, 'other things being equal, rational plans try to keep our hands free until we have a clear view of the relevant facts'.[57] Certainly, one generalization which can be offered with confidence is that knowledge will be very incomplete, the more so the further ahead the decision-maker is trying to look. The existing *stock* of knowledge, the current *flow* of information, the *capacity* to absorb and interpret information—all these are gravely deficient in developing, and all other, countries. Economists are well aware of this but have failed to recognize its uncomfortable implications for development planning.[58] In a hit-or-miss world where there is only the most approximate grasp of how an economy will respond to a given policy action and when that action will almost certainly generate unexpected second-order effects, it is by no means obvious that *medium-term* planning is helpful or fitting.[59] The standard answer would be that the remedy is to improve our knowledge rather than abandon planning, but are we entitled to assume that the benefits from acquiring the necessary additional knowledge (even if that were feasible) would exceed the costs of doing so? The recent growth of interest in the economics of information has not yet had much impact on the planning literature; there is little treatment in it of the often acute time constraints within which government decision makers normally operate and the large costs, therefore, of decision procedures which fail to economize on time. What is clear is that the often acute state of uncertainty in which policy has to be formulated will tend to shorten time horizons in a manner inimical to medium-term planning.

Acceptance as the general case of a society which is fragmented, in which the role-orientation of politicians cannot be taken for granted, and in which most policy decisions have to be made in the presence of large uncertainties, has a number of far-reaching implications for the way in which we can reasonably view governmental processes. One is that the notion of a national interest (and a social welfare function) tends not to be very useful. A fragmented society implies the division of influence and decision-making over numerous agencies, each with its own way of perceiving problems, its own preferences and priorities, inevitably giving rise to multiple and conflicting objectives.[60] In consequence, governments normally stick to a high and non-operational level of generality when stating their objectives and are most reluctant to specify with any precision what priorities they attach to each of these.[61] Indeed, one of their objectives may be to conceal what their true objectives are.[62] Moreover, the interplay of interest groups, agencies, and personalities will result in a constantly shifting balance of preferences,[63] giving the ideal of a long-term or even medium-term policy perspective a rather utopian quality—a tendency made all the stronger because the working-out of past policies will provide an input into the further definition of problems and goals. Hence, in so far as they are defined at all, the objectives of policy will only be revealed *ex post*, rather than being available *ex ante* for use in the preparation of medium-term plans. The existence of multiple objectives will also undermine the distinction between goals and policy instruments, for what is regarded simply as an instrument by some may be regarded by others as having at least some of the qualities of a goal (e.g., the question of public ownership, incomes policies, and the exchange rate).[64] This further obscures the concept of the social welfare function and complicates yet more the formulation of policy.

It is for reasons such as these that concepts like the national interest and the social welfare function quite fail to provide either a philosophical or an operational basis for the normative economics of planning. In this respect political philosophers, who have generally abandoned the use of such abstractions, are in advance of economists, still stuck with them. Quite apart from the problem of interpersonal comparisons or Arrow's impossibility theorem, the identification of interests, the conversion of these into a national interest, and its translation into policy actions present insuperable difficulties. The answer is not simply to be found in the preferences of the majority, for:[65]

We often think it right, for example, to tax the majority to relieve a needy minority; and we should condemn majority action if it took no account of suffering inflicted on the few, merely because they were a few.

It is, moreover, difficult to draw any but the most tentative conclusion about public attitudes to specific policy issues from the results of electoral voting, even in the relatively few developing countries which enjoy openly competitive politics. Indeed, many political theorists would deny the possibility altogether:[66]

The elcctors' will is limited to the single question decided at the poll: who shall govern? Nothing can be inferred beyond that. To say that a party programme has been endorsed by the electorate—or even by a majority of the electors—is highly misleading, for no-one can say how many voted for the party *despite* any given item, or even despite the entire programme. The mandate theory is capable of a negative application at best: one can say of any given proposal of a victorious party only that it was not so unpopular that it cost the party the election. That is scarcely an electoral authority to proceed.

How much more intransigent these problems become in the political systems of those developing countries which lack meaningful elections and institutional arrangements that 'encourage consultation, negotiation, the exploration of alternatives, and the search for mutually beneficial solutions'.[67]

All this, and the fact that governments' effective range of choice will be constrained by the capacities and preferences of public agencies, calls seriously into question the usefulness of the concept of optimization, for that ideal presumes the existence of a clearly defined objective function, awareness of the full range of possibilities, and also at least a large probability that a policy act will have the consequences it is anticipated to have. Decision making in the face of major social divisions becomes a balancing act rather than a search for optima; a process of conflict-resolution in which social tranquillity and the maintenance of power is a basic concern rather than the maximization of the rate of growth or some such. Indeed, one of the further implications of the foregoing is that economic objectives, including development, are likely to come lower on the pecking order of government concerns that the case for development planning implicitly assumes. The maintenance of government authority and social peace will tend to be the dominant themes, with adoption of a development objective conditional on the extent to which it furthers these higher-priority, 'non-economic' concerns. Yet another implication is that consistency is not necessarily to be taken as a norm of the rationality of government policies, for the maintenance of authority and the balancing of competing groups may well force governments to twist this way and that, simultaneously or sequentially pursuing apparently contradictory policies.[68]

To the dynamic tensions of conflict-resolution and the pervasive facts of ignorance and uncertainty, we might add the further consideration, familiar in other branches of economics, that man (and man-managed institutions) quite lacks the intellectual equipment to pursue the kind of optimizing rationality that is often assumed of him in economics (and of governments in development planning).[69] The reality is what Simon has called the 'principle of bounded rationality':[70]

The capacity of the human mind for formulating and solving complex problems is very small compared with the size of the problems whose solution is required for objectively rational behaviour in the real world—or even for a reasonable approximation to such objective rationality.

Man (including politicians and civil servants) responds by simplifying, by narrowing the range of alternatives considered, by economizing on information and its costs—in a word, by abandoning optimization:[71]

There is every evidence that in complex policy situations, so-called decision makers do not strive to optimise some value nor is the notion of optimisation a useful way of ordering and analysing their behaviour regardless of their intentions.

To borrow from the modern theory of the firm, we have to view governments as 'satisficers'—as pursuing solutions that are 'good enough', as being satisfied with any one of a range of possible outcomes, as placing a premium on risk-avoidance and flexibility—a point well conveyed by the cliché that politics is the art of the possible. Satisficing offers this flexibility by being defined in terms of aspiration levels which are adjusted in the light of past attainments and changing perceptions of future possibilities. It probably biases decisions in favour of incremental rather than structural change, for major transformations create new uncertainties and conflicts which are often difficult to anticipate.[72]

All in all, then, it seems that a behavioural view of politics and decision-making in developing countries conflicts at almost every point with the, largely implicit, 'rational actor' model of politics adopted by proponents of development planning, summarized at the end of the previous section. Governments will not have clear and stable objectives, but the resolution and avoidance of social conflicts and the maintenance of their own authority are likely to be among their main preoccupations, with a consequential demotion of the development objective. The fragmentation of power, the implementation gap, and the large uncertainties surrounding many decisions seriously devalue the notion of optimization; the uncertainties and the fact of political instability also make for shorter time horizons than would be compatible with medium-term planning. A view of policy formation as a process of continuous adaptation also subverts the idea of planning for the medium term. The role-

orientation of politicians cannot be taken for granted; nor are we entitled to assume that planning is, or could be, used to assert social values over market imperfections. The intention here is not to assert a monolithic model of politics in low-income countries in direct opposition to the planner's model; merely to suggest that the points made in this section are large parts of the scene of which we ought to take note.

If we do so, 'the prevalence of pseudo-planning' is no longer much of a mystery. Economists' conceptions of development planning are based on a view of politics so far removed from the realities as to vastly reduce the operational utility of the concept. For the most part, governments do not and *could not* function in the manner implied in the literature, and so that type of activity which has come to be called planning is inevitably rather unrelated to actual day-to-day decision making. As Paul Baran has complained, 'In our time . . . faith in the manipulative omnipotence of the State has all but displaced analysis of its social structure and understanding of its political and economic functions.'[73] Moreover, the foregoing provides no grounds for a Friedmanite defence of the planner's model, along the lines that its behavioural deficiencies do not matter because outcomes are *as if* the model were realistic: the planning crisis has emerged precisely because actual outcomes have differed so much from the planned intentions.

But besides questioning the practicability of development planning, it is also worth asking whether, if planning were feasible, it would be an efficient instrument of policy. The analysis has emphasized decision-making as a continuous and interactive process. Decisions are seen as inputs into ongoing controversies rather than as decisive conclusions of these controversies, as impinging upon our freedom to act in the future,[74] and whose consequences will likely throw up new problems. Ends are likely to be adjusted to means, in the light of past experience, just as means are tailored to ends. And we require a decision system flexible enough to accommodate uncertainties and to allow decisions to be postponed until uncertainty is reduced.[75] Although it seems a paradoxical criticism,[76] medium-term development planning is not well equipped to accommodate the dynamics of decision-making.[77] Cybernetics provides a better model, in which policies are continuously adjusted in the light of feedback information on the consequences of past actions.[78]

CONCLUSIONS

Apart from the last paragraph, the argument developed here has been directed at the practicability of planning and has left much of the theoretical case for it unscathed. There remains an obvious need for taking an over-all view of economic policy, for studying the interactions between policy instruments and for trying to co-ordinate them. There is still a need to try to anticipate problems and thus defuse them, and to try to understand the future implications of present actions. There remains a need for a vehicle, albeit a Trojan Horse, that will permit 'the economic point of view' to be represented in the councils of government and planning may be such a vehicle. The issue, then, is not whether planning is desirable but what can be rescued from medium-term development planning that is also feasible?

First, it would be more fruitful to think of planning as a continuous *input* into decision processes than as a discontinuous, once-every-five-years, *output* of the system. Among its chief functions would be the reduction of uncertainties, thus widening the scope for improved, more 'rational', decisions (always provided that the costs of doing so would be exceeded by the benefits): improving the flow of feedback information, monitoring progress, advising on the adjustments the feedback indicates to be desirable,[79] and suggesting what seems the best first move in any situation.[80]

This viewpoint is, however, likely to be unpopular. Many economists will surely resist the conclusion that optimization has limited practical meaning and, therefore, that sophisticated optimizing techniques, while they may be valuable for purposes of academic analysis, are of much less value as devices for influencing the future. Yet the attention bias induced by preoccupation with the use of planning models—and the elegance and internal consistency they offer—has surely harmed the cause of planning by contributing to a neglect of political realities and the mundane specifics of everyday policy. Of course, quantitative techniques remain important, but the economic adviser will be even better served by attending to policy issues and their solution within a politically realistic framework.

The argument of this article also throws doubt on the practical usefulness of a long-term development strategy, for all its attractiveness as a concept. In the fluxing kaleidoscope of social tensions, conflicting interests, and changing governments (to say nothing of the unpredictability of the outside world), it would seem that the concept could only be given practical meaning if there were a broad consensus on the desired long-term nature of society, but reasons have been given for believing that such a consensus rarely exists. We may have to be content with trying to devise strategies for particular aspects of socio-economic policy which virtually demand a long-term perspective, such as population, manpower, and educational planning.

Planning, then, is seen partly as a way of insinuating (or maintaining) a corps of economic advisers into day-to-day governmental decision-making, working in competition with other groups for influence within the system.[81] But considered as members of a pressure group economic advisers are not always effective[82] and would do well to attend more to the *resources* they can deploy and to identifying the key *leverage points* upon which to concentrate within the decision-making system. Their resources include possession of expertise and information valued by governments and their civil services; superior ability to produce certain kinds of outputs (briefings on the state of the economy, submissions to the World Bank and IMF); a greater facility in marshalling arguments on questions of economic policy; and power to provide or withhold legitimization for certain types of expenditure (e.g. as a result of project evaluations).

The profession, it is true, has given thought to be best status and location of planning agencies.[83] But there are actually likely to be a *number* of important leverage points where it would be valuable to have economic expertise, and one of the costs of development planning has been that it has often tied to a relatively unproductive agency economists who could have been better employed in budget bureaux, commerce ministries, finance corporations, and so on. In particular, the finance ministry offers itself as a natural leverage point for economists. The budget is of critical importance politically and for economic policies, and many of the resources of government are devoted to its implementation. It is thoroughly built into the decision process and provides obvious opportunities for economists to deploy the resources at their command. Thus, a practical illustration of the type of planning being advocated here would be the introduction of programme and performance budgeting.

Should planners still produce plans? The trend of the argument runs against it but the issue depends on how badly governments feel they need a plan. If a plan is wanted badly enough then ability to produce it becomes one of the economist's resources in seeking to influence policies. In such situations the best rules are (*a*) to keep plans flexible (which favours annual plans),[84] and (*b*) to avoid devoting such a concentration of expertise to their preparation that other leverage points are neglected.

Lastly, it is tempting to draw a more general lesson from the analysis of this article. The planner's model of politics presented earlier

had three major characteristics: (1) it was largely unarticulated, being derived mostly by inferences from the literature; (2) it was nevertheless normative in nature;[85] and (3) it incorporated a very high degree of abstraction from observed behaviour. That it should be so was convenient to the profession. It we had to articulate our model of politics and still be taken seriously as advisers we would surely have to narrow the gap between the model and observed behaviour. But reducing the level of abstraction would bring us face to face with the limited relevance of much of the planning literature and many of the techniques with which it is replete. For behavioural theory,

has no use for traditional basic concepts: optimisation has no usable meaning; economists' heavy investment in calculus becomes redundant; equilibrium is not defined; and there are no general analytical solutions.[86]

Thus, one can see the case of development planning as an illustration of a paradigm crisis that confronts economics on a wider front, in which the returns from our 'investment in calculus' are dependent on a level of abstraction from the real world, and with a disciplinary specialization, which threatens the social usefulness of our profession. I would urge that it is irresponsible to offer policy advice while abstracting in such high degree from political realities; that we would benefit from being more explicit in our assumptions about politics; that we should narrow the gap between our prescriptive view of politics and the real world; and that in so doing we should consider the possibility that other social scientists might have useful things to say.

1. I am grateful to Peter O. Steiner for helpful comments on an earlier draft.
2. Waterston, 1966, p. 8, for example, defines planning as 'an organised, intelligent attempt to select the best available alternatives to achieve specific goals'.
3. For examples of this type of formulation see

Tinbergen, 1964, pp. 42–3; Waterston, 1972, pp. 83–6; and Lewis, 1966, *passim*.

4. P. T. Bauer, 1971, chapter 2A.

5. Both early and recent writings on this subject start from this base. For examples see Lewis, 1951, chapter 1, and Griffin and Enos, 1970, chapter 2.

6. Meade, 1970, provides a sophisticated theory of planning along these lines, in which planning becomes a mimicry of comprehensive forward markets, although he is not specifically writing about low-income countries.

7. Scitovsky, 1954, pp. 305–6. See also Rosenstein-Rodan, 1943, p. 248, and Dobb, 1960, chapter 1.

8. Tinbergen, 1955, p. 68 and *passim*, is among those who emphasize the importance of seeing economic policies as a co-ordinated system.

9. Waterston, 1966, p. 293.

10. Seers, 1972.

11. Healey, 1972, p. 761.

12. Myrdal, 1968, p. 732. Not all would agree about the effectiveness of planning even in these cases, for Hanson's 1966 study of Indian planning drew attention to numerous failings and Gadgil complained at about the same time of a 'total absence of a policy frame' in Indian planning (quoted by Minhas, 1972, p. 23).

13. For evidence of a decline in the seriousness of Indian planning after 1964 see the report by Lipton, 1972.

14. From a report to a ministerial meeting of the Inter-American Economic and Social Council of May 1969; quoted and translated by Powelson, 1972, pp. 196–7.

15. U.N. Economic Commission for Africa, 1966, p. 73 (author's emphasis).

16. Helleiner, 1972, p. 333.

17. For an examination of the planning experience in Ghana see Killick, forthcoming, chapter 6. This arrives at preponderantly negative conclusions about plan effectiveness.

18. In ibid. I argue that Ghana's *Seven-year Plan* gave such misleading signals about the future as to induce substantial over-investment in manufacturing, with consequentially adverse effects on capacity utilization. Shen, 1975, shows for a large sample of African development plans that there is no significant correlation between plan sector targets and actual performance and that market forces remain the most important determinants of performance.

19. Little and Mirrlees, 1974, p. 86, note that while 'one of the main reasons why planning is required is that market prices are misleading. It is ironical that most planning at the project level has nevertheless been done in the light of market prices.'

20. To avoid a wearisome number of detailed references, the reader is referred for examples of the following points to Waterson, 1966, chapters VI to IX, and Faber and Seers (eds.), 1972, *passim*. See also Powelson, 1972; Tinbergen, 1964; and Myrdal, 1968, chapter 15.

21. Waterston, 1966, p. 340.

22. Seers, 1972, p. 24.

23. Tinbergen, 1964, p. 43.

24. Myrdal, 1968, p. 732.

25. Frisch, 1966, *passim*.

26. Myrdal, 1968, chapter 18 *passim*.

27. Helleiner, 1972, pp. 354 and 347.

28. Tinbergen, 1972, p. 160.

29. Waterston, 1972, *passim*.

30. For one Prime Minister who thinks planning politically advantageous see Williams, 1972, p. 40.

31. Leys, 1972, pp. 56 and 60. The discussion of his paper, summarized in the same volume, certainly seems to justify Leys's complaint about how difficult other social scientists find it to communicate with economists (p. 79).

32. See especially Lewis, 1965.

33. For example, in Tinbergen, 1967 (A), p. 59.

34. Simon, 1957, p. 241, represents economic man as being assumed to have 'knowledge of the relevant aspects of his environment which, if not completely absolute, is at least impressively clear and voluminous. He is assumed also to have a well-organised and stable system of preferences, and a skill in computation that enables him to calculate, for the alternative courses of action that are available to him, which of these will permit him to reach the highest attainable point on his preference scale'. The reader will recognize many similarities between this account and the following description of a planner's model of government. Simon goes to note a complete lack of evidence that individuals have the capacities economists assume them to have.

35. Arrow, 1963, p. 107, quoting Bergson with approval.

36. Tinbergen, 1955, p. 69.

37. Heal, 1973, p. 59.

38. See, for example, Griffin and Enos, 1970, pp. 31 ff.

39. See Tinbergen, 1964, pp. 42–3 for an illustration.

40. See especially Chenery (ed.), 1971, and Todaro, 1971. Also Lewis, 1966, Part III; Tinbergen, 1967 (B), chapters 5–9; and Heal, 1973 *passim*.

41. See Waterston, 1966, p. 318, for example. The same writer's study of planning in Morocco concluded that the besetting problem was 'the lack of basic agreement about what the national interest requires and the consequent absence of a consistent development policy' (Waterston, 1962, p. 49). Ghai, 1972, p. 130, relates a deterioration in plan implementation in Kenya to 'a weakening of the political unity, and factional bickering in the ruling party'.

42. For reasons of this type, the successful use of programme budgeting has been associated with increased centralization of decision-making powers (McNamara's tenure in the U.S. Department of Defence being the most celebrated illustration)— and has been attacked on the same grounds: see Burkhead and Miner, 1971, chapter 6.

43. Waterston, 1966, p. 407.

44. Tinbergen, 1964, p. 99.

45. Leys, 1972, p. 71.

46. See Hanson, 1966, pp. 526–7 and *passim*; also Prasad, 1972, pp. 82–6.

47. Not in writings specifically on planning, that is. Elsewhere, there is growing realization of the limited efficiency of governments in many low-income countries, of which Little *et al.*, 1970, and its companion volumes, are well-known examples.

48. P. T. Bauer (1971, pp. 69–95), for example, opposes planning because it tends to add to the power of the state.

49. Imagine, for example, the vast informational requirements of Tinbergen's scheme for the determination of an 'optimum policy':

 (i) the fixation of a collective preference indicator;

 (ii) the deduction, from this indicator, of the targets of economic policy generally;

 (iii) the choice of 'adequate' instruments, qualitative and quantitative;

 (iv) the determination of the quantitative values of the instrument variables, as far as such instruments are chosen and

 (v) the formulation of the connections between

(a) the relation between targets and quantitative values of instrument variables on the one hand and (b) the structure of the economy studied on the other hand.' (Tinbergen, 1955, p. 4.)

50. The term is from Allison, 1971

51. In support of the propositions in this paragraph see Dahl, 1970, chapter 6, and sources quoted there, and also Kuznets, 1966, Table 8.3 and commentary.

52. See Allison, 1971, p. 162, on government action as a resultant in the sense just used.

53. Although less than in industrial societies such as the United States, where it has been estimated that there are more than 100,000 governmental units (Lindblom, 1959, p. 175).

54. Apter, 1965, p. 42.

55. Downs, 1957, p. 296.

56. Rimmer, 1969, p. 201.

57. Rawls, 1971, p. 420.

58. Stolper, 1966, is an important exception but his work on 'planning without facts' does not appear to have received the attention it deserves.

59. Even in industrial countries, where conditions are much more favourable to accuracy, there are often large discrepancies between planned, or forecast, changes and actual events. Theil, 1961, chapter 3, for example, shows very large discrepancies between predicted and actual changes in macro-economic variables in the Dutch economy. In relation to the U.S. Federal government, Wildavsky, 1964, pp. 47–8, observes that 'budget officials soon discover that . . . possible consequences of a single policy are too numerous to describe, and that knowledge of the chain of consequences for other policies is but dimly perceived for most conceivable alternatives'.

60. See Pressman and Wildavsky, 1973, for an illuminating analysis of the way in which the intermediation of executing agencies alters and subverts the intentions of the central government.

61. Thus, Tinbergen summarized governmental responses to questionnaires that virtually all governments have as their economic goals 'to increase national income, to improve the employment situation, to achieve and maintain balance of payments equilibrium, to achieve and maintain price stability, to obtain a more equal distribution of income among individuals, and to obtain a balanced regional economic development' (Tinbergen, 1964, p. 36 and Table 7). All were on the side of the

angels but, needless to say, no indication was given of the relative weights that would be attached to these goals in face of the manifest certainty that they would come into conflict with each other. Governmental reluctance to specify operational objectives is notoriously the rule in the case of public enterprises, which generally have to operate with vague and potentially contradictory terms of reference. See Foster, 1971, p. 19, and Killick, forthcoming, chapter 9.

62. This is not necessarily to take a cynical view, for the use of stealth can be a legitimate weapon of politics. Consider, for example, the manner in which General de Gaulle was brought to power and his subsequent policies in Algeria.

63. To quote Wildavsky's study of the American Federal budget system again (1964, p. 47), 'budget officials soon discover that ends are rarely agreed upon and that they keep changing.'

64. See Streeten, 1972, chapter 4, for a critical discussion of the goals-instruments distinction.

65. Benn and Peters, 1959, p. 273.

66. Ibid., p. 345.

67. Dahl, 1970, p. 62. That circumstances such as these create particularly acute difficulties for the definition of the general interest may be inferred from Arrow's argument, 1963, p. 91, that 'we may expect that social welfare judgements can usually be made when there is both a widespread agreement on the decision process and a widespread agreement on the desirability of everyday decisions'.

68. 'To the extent that fragmentation achieves an aggregating of values, it does so by processes involving widespread conflict among various decision-making centres. The conflict often takes the form of conflicting or inconsistent government policies. It is therefore not appropriate to postulate as a norm that public policy be consistent, or to take inconsistency in public policy as symptomatic of irrationality . . . what is often called irrationality in government is sometimes to be desired' (Lindblom, 1959, p. 179). See also Cyert and March, 1963, p. 116, who argue that organizations achieve 'quasi resolutions' of conflicts among goals by attending to different goals at different times, solving one problem at a time.

69. 'A comparative examination of the models of adaptive behaviour employed in psychology (e.g. learning theories), and of the models of rational behaviour employed in economics, shows that in almost all respects the latter postulate a much greater complexity in the choice mechanisms, and a much larger capacity in the organism for obtaining information and performing computations, than do the former' (Simon, 1957, p. 261).

70. Ibid., p. 198.

71. R. Bauer, 1968, p. 2.

72. I particularly have in mind the 'strategy of decision' propounded in opposition to economists' optimization models by Lindblom, which he calls the 'strategy of disjointed incrementalism', although this is less applicable to developing countries than to the American case, by which it is strongly influenced. See especially Braybrooke and Lindblom, 1963, chapter 5.

73. Baran, 1958, p. 86.

74. 'Cabinet papers may apparently crystallise an apparent moment of choice, yet that choice may in a sense only register a minor option in an outcome which was broadly determined by "increments" of decision at other points in the system at earlier stages' (Leys, 1972, p. 60).

75. A point entirely missed by Waterston (1972, p. 89) when he regrets the 'preference of many political leaders for maintaining investment options in their own hands and for improvisation.'

76. Elliot, 1958, p. 67, for example, talks of economic planning as injecting 'the time factor and the problem of process into the centre of economic analysis'.

77. Thus, in an analysis of rural development projects in Kenya, Holmquist, 1970, p. 228, points out that 'There is a popular conception of planning which sees the acceptance of a plan as the "big" decision which in turn determines the policy outcome. But this . . . ignores that fact that fundamental policy decisions are made during, as well as prior to, implementation.'

78. Indeed, R. Bauer, 1966, pp. 7–8, has suggested in a different context that a 'cybernetice approach' to planning would not be very different, in its sensitivity to feedback, from muddling through. One indication of a movement in this direction is the tendency in more advanced economies for the determination of fiscal policy through annual budgets to give way to more frequent use of regulators and 'mini-budgets'.

79. This position is not far removed from Stolper's who, in the face of chronic uncertainty, advocates 'optimising as one goes along; as viewing the long run as a sequence of short runs; and as incor-

porating into present decisions only as much of the future as is reasonably known' (1966, p. 4). In fact, governments often do use their economists in the sort of way advocated here, as in Taiwan, where actual planning has been described as 'a process of correction and adjustment to the influences of an active environment' (Kade, Hujer, and Ipsen, 1969, p. 37).

80. I have borrowed this idea from Cohen and Cyert, 1965, p. 313.

81. Note, though, that the view of economists as one of a number of groups struggling to assert their points of view to the ultimate decision-makers is subversive of a positivist approach, which sees the economic adviser as disinterestedly presenting the costs and benefits of each possible policy option.

82. As Leys, 1972, pp. 61–2, points out, economists in government often fail as a group because they lack discrimination ('pursuing very ambitious goals in all sectors at all times'), because they are often poorly located within the system, and because of an attention bias which predisposes them to neglect political realism in the search for technically optimal solutions.

83. For example, see Waterston, 1966, chapter XIII.

84. Economists have generally argued against reliance on annual plans and it is interesting that its main advocates include an economic administrator (Waterston, 1972 passim) and a political scientist (Leys, 1972, pp. 66 ff.).

85. Thus, Tinbergen, 1955, pp. 74–6, takes a strongly moralistic view of 'Personal hobbies or aversions; animosities between various offices, directorates, ministries or countries' as among the influences that 'intervene wrongly' in the formation of policy. Recall also his assertion that government objectives 'must always have been considered as some version of "the general interest" '. Griffin and Enos, 1970, p. 185, provide a more recent example of the normative nature of economists' writings on politics, prefacing their discussion of plan implementation and organization with the statements that 'Government must assume a positive role in development. It cannot be content merely to hold the ring while others fight . . . if Government is to contribute to progress rather than retard it it must be properly organised.'

86. Loasby, 1971, p. 882, writing about theories of the firm.

BIBLIOGRAPHY

Agarwala, A. N., and Singh, S. P. (eds.), *The Economics of Underdevelopment*, Oxford U. P., Bombay, 1958.

Allison, Graham, T., *Essence of Decision: Explaining the Cuban Missile Crisis*, Little, Brown & Co., Boston, 1971.

Apter, David E., *The Politics of Modernization*, Chicago U. P., 1965.

Arrow, Kenneth J., *Social Choice and Individual Values*, Wiley & Sons, New York, 2nd edn., 1963.

Baran, Paul A., 'On the political economy of backwardness' reproduced in Agarwala and Singh, *The Economics of Underdevelopment*, Oxford U. P., Bombay, 1958.

Bauer, P. T., *Dissent on Development*, Weidenfeld and Nicolson, London, 1971.

Bauer, Raymond A., *Social Indicators*, MIT Press, Cambridge, Mass., 1966.

—— 'The study of policy formation: An introduction' in Bauer and Gergen (eds.), 1968, chapter 1.

—— and Gergen, Kenneth J. (eds.), *The Study of Policy Formation*, Free Press, New York, 1968.

Benn, S. I., and Peters, R. S., *Social Principles and Democratic State*, Allen & Unwin, London, 1959.

Braybrooke, David, and Lindblom, Charles E., *A Strategy of Decision*, Free Press, New York, 1963.

Burkhead, Jesse, and Miner, Jerry, *Public Expenditure*, Macmillan, London, 1971.

Chenery, Hollis B. (ed.), *Studies in Development Planning*, Harvard U. P., Cambridge, Mass., 1971.

Cohen, Kalman J., and Cyert, Richard M., *The Theory of the Firm*, Prentice-Hall, Englewood Cliffs, N. J., 1965.

Cyert, Richard M., and March, James, *A Behavioural Theory of the Firm*, Prentice-Hall, Englewood Cliffs, N. J., 1963.

Dahl, Robert A., *Modern Political Analysis*, Prentice-Hall, New Jersey, 1970 (2nd edn.).

Dobb, Maurice, *An Essay on Economic Growth and Planning*, Monthly Review Press, New York, 1960.

Downs, Antony, *An Economic Theory of Democracy*, Harper & Row, New York, 1957.

Elliot, John E., 'Economic planning reconsidered', *Quarterly Journal of Economics*, Feb. 1958.

Faber, Mike, and Seers, Dudley (eds.), *The Crisis in Planning*, Chatto and Windus, London, 1972 (2 vols.).

Foster, C. D., *Politics, Finance and the Role of Economics: An Essay on the Control of Public Enterprise*, Allen & Unwin, London, 1971.

Frisch, R., 'Optimal implementation', *Revista Internazionale di Scienze Economiche e Commerciali*, Milan, 1966, No. 1.

Ghai, Dharam, 'The machinery of planning in Kenya', in Faber and Seers, 1972, vol. 2, chapter 4.

Griffin, Keith B., and Enos, John L., *Planning Development*, Addison-Wesley, London, *ca.* 1970.

Hanson, A. H., *The Process of Planning: A Study of India's Five-year Plans, 1950–1964*, Oxford U. P., London 1966.

Heal, G. M., *The Theory of Economic Planning*, North-Holland, Amsterdam, 1973.

Healey, Derek T., 'Development policy: New thinking about an interpretation', *Journal of Economic Literature*, Sept. 1972.

Helleiner, G. K., 'Beyond growth rates and plan volumes—planning for Africa in the 1970's', *Journal of Modern African Studies*, Oct. 1972.

Holmquist, Frank, 'Implementing rural development projects', in Hyden Jackson, and Okumu, *Development Administration: The Kenyan Experience*, Oxford U. P., Nairobi, 1970.

Kade, G., Hujer, R., and Ipsen, D., 'Kybernetik und Wirtschafsplanung', *Zeitschrift für die gesamte Staatswissenschaft*, Tübingen, 1969, No. 1.

Killick, Tony, *Development Economics in Action: A Study of Economic Policies in Ghana* (forthcoming).

Kuznets, Simon, *Modern Economic Growth: Rate, Structure and Spread*, Yale U. P., New Haven, 1966.

Lewis, W. Arthur, *Principles of Economic Planning*, Public Affairs Press, Washington D. C., 1951.

—— *Politics in West Africa*, Allen & Unwin, London, 1965.

—— *Development Planning*, Allen & Unwin, London, 1966.

Leys, Collin, 'A new conception of planning?' in Faber and Seers (eds.), 1972, vol. 1, chapter 3.

Lindblom, Charles E., 'The handling of norms in policy analysis', in Abramovitz, M. *et al., The Allocation of Economic Resources*, Stanford U. P., 1959.

Lipton, Michael, 'Planning the improvement of planning in India and Pakistan', a group report in Faber and Seers (eds.), 1972, vol. 2, pp. 68–78.

Little, I. M. D., and Mirrlees, J. A., *Project Appraisal and Planning for Developing Countries*, Heinemann, London, 1974.

Little, Ian, Scitovsky, Tibor, and Scott, Maurice, *Industry and Trade in Some Developing Countries*, Oxford U. P., London, 1970.

Loasby, B. J., 'Hypothesis and paradigm in the theory of the firm', *Economic Journal*, Dec. 1971.

Meade, J. E., *The Theory of Indicative Planning*, Manchester U. P., 1970.

Minhas, B. S., 'Objectives and policy frame of the fourth Indian plan', in Faber and Seers (eds.), 1972, vol. 2, chapter 1.

Myrdal, Gunnar, *Asian Drama*, Twentieth Century Fund, New York, 1968.

Powelson, John P., *Institutions of Economic Growth*, Princeton U. P., Princeton, N. J., 1972.

Prasad, P. S. N., 'The lessons of experience', in Faber and Seers, 1972, vol. 2, chapter 2.

Pressman, Jeffrey L., and Wildavsky, Aaron, *Implementation*, California U. P., Berkeley, 1973.

Rawls, John, *A Theory of Justice*, Harvard U. P., Cambridge, Mass., 1971.

Rimmer, Douglas, 'The abstraction from politics', *Journal of Development Studies*, Apr. 1969.

Rosenstein-Rodan, P. N., 'Problems of industrialisation of eastern and southeastern Europe', *Economic Journal*, June–Sept. 1943.

Scitovsky, Tibor, 'Two concepts of external economies', *Journal of Political Economy*, Apr. 1954 (reproduced in Agarwala and Singh, 1958, and page numbers refer to their volume).

Seers, Dudley, 'The prevalence of pseudo-planning', in Faber and Seers (eds.), 1972, vol. 1, chapter 1.

Shen, T. Y., 'Sectoral development planning in tropical Africa', *Eastern Africa Economic Review*, June 1975.

Simon, Herbert, *Models of Man*, Wiley & Sons, New York, 1957.

Stolper, Wolfgang F., *Planning Without Facts*, Harvard U. P., Cambridge, Mass., 1966.

Streeten, Paul, *The Frontiers of Development Studies*, Macmillan, London, 1972.

Theil, H., *Economic Forecasts and Policy*, North-Holland, Amsterdam, 2nd edn., 1961.

Tinbergen, Jan, *On the Theory of Economic Policy*, North-Holland, Amsterdam, 1955 (2nd edn.).

—— *Central Planning*, Yale U.P., New Haven, 1964.

—— *Economic Policy: Principles and Design*,

North-Holland, Amsterdam, revised edition, 1967 (A).
—— Development Planning, Weidenfeld and Nicolson, London, 1967 (B).
—— 'The United Nations Development Planning Committee', in Faber and Seers (eds.), 1972, vol. 1, chapter 7.
Todaro, Michael P., *Development Planning: Models and Methods*, Oxford U. P., Nairobi, 1971.
United Nations Economic Commission for Africa, *Economic Survey of Africa. Vol. 1: Western Subregion*, Addis Ababa, 1966.

Waterston, Albert, *Planning in Morocco*, Johns Hopkins, University Press, Baltimore, 1962.
—— *Development Planning: Lessons of Experience*, Oxford U. P., London, 1966.
—— 'An operational approach to development planning', in Faber and Seers (eds.), 1972, vol. 1, chapter 4.
Wildavsky, Aaron, *The Politics of the Budgetary Process*, Little, Brown & Co., Boston, 1964.
Williams, Eric, 'The purpose of planning', in Faber and Seers (eds.), 1972, vol. 1, chapter 2.

32. Towards A Free Market Economy: Chile 1974–1979*

Alejandro Foxley

1. INTRODUCTION

The economic policy of Chile's military regime has attracted international attention, stirring up controversy in financial and academic circles far beyond its borders. The international press has dedicated long articles to analyzing what has come to be called the "Chicago experiment". At times the amount of attention paid to Chile seems exorbitant considering Chile's limited importance in the world economy. Why all the interest?

The reasons are many and varied. Some people see the "Chilean experiment" as a test of the consistent and sustained application of a monetarist strategy to the problems of economic instability and chronic inflation which have scourged many Western economies during the past decade. For others, the "experiment" is one of the "most important reforms in the underdeveloped world in recent history",[1] a viewpoint which implicitly validates the "Chilean model" as a credible framework to substitute for the type of economic policies which have been followed in many developing countries in the post-war years.

Given the authoritarian political system in which the Chilean "experiment" has been carried out and the "experiment's" high social cost, a third factor which arouses interest is a more general question. Chile's current economic and political situation concretely poses the much debated problem of the interrelation between economic liberalism and political freedom in the context of developing economies. One thesis, favorable to the authoritarian formula, maintains that establishing economic "freedom" is a prerequisite to attaining true political freedom.[2] An opposing theory claims that there is a fundamental contradiction in a developing economy between economic neoclassical liberalism and the true democratization of a society.[3]

The relevance of monetarism, the search for new models of development and the allure of authoritarianism as a political pattern for

* From *Journal of Development Economics*, 10, No. 1 (February 1982), pp. 3–29.

the process of economic stabilization are all themes which occupy an important place in discussions on modern economic policy. The economic policies of Chile's military government provide a case study which is particularly appropriate for illuminating these themes.

In this work we try to answer the most obvious questions raised by the Chilean case. Is the Chilean economic "experiment" a success or a failure? Are the policies which have been followed merely short-term stabilization policies or are they designed to change the pattern of development in the long run? How have those policies affected the structure of production and the patterns of income distribution and holdings of capital assets?

In the second section, we analyze some of the principal macroeconomic results of the policies, relating them to the various possible objectives of the model. In the third section, we discuss the underlying character of the policies followed, delineating the interrelations between short-run stabilization objectives and the long-run objectives of structural change. The fourth section describes the principal changes in the functioning of the Chilean economy during this period. This section is subdivided into three parts: the first deals with changes in individual economic factors (the State, the private business sector, workers); the second with the transfer of resources towards newly important participants in the economy made possible by the new policies; and the third with the changes in the economy as it moves from a 'closed' to an 'open' system. A fifth section outlines the structural changes which resulted from modifications in the way the economy operates. In this section, changes in the productive structure and in patterns of distribution are studied. The sixth section contains our conclusions.

2. SUCCESSES AND FAILURES OF AN ECONOMIC POLICY

Just as occurred in the Brazilian case, the economic policy of Chile in the period from 1974 to 1979 has been the object of a profound controversy. The economic results from that period are interpreted as a resounding success by some and as quite negative by others. As we will see, two different economic stories can be constructed depending on the indicators which are selected to evaluate the economy's performance.

Indicators which usually are cited as the basis for arguing the success of Chile's economic policy are presented in table 1. These indicators show: (1) a reduction in the inflation rate from 600 percent in 1973 to 39 percent in 1979, (2) the achievement of relatively high rates of growth for the gross domestic product (GDP) from 1977 to 1979 following the deep recession provoked by the "shock" treatment administered in 1975, (3) a significant reduction in the fiscal deficit so that the deficit was eliminated in 1979, (4) the dynamic growth of non-traditional exports which tripled between 1974 and 1979, (5) a growing surplus in the balance of payments by 1979 as a result of the accumulation of reserves after initial difficulties in stabilizing the balance of payments, and (6) an accelerating net inflow of foreign capital that reached more than thirteen hundred million dollars in 1978 and 1979, and was responsible for bolstering reserves.

This set of positive results indicates that the economy has been a success according to the performance standards usually considered by international credit organizations, particularly the International Monetary Fund. The results also neatly fit the criteria which international private banking circles regard as signs of health in an economy, as a recent study of private North American banks shows.[4]

A different story can be compiled by selecting other indicators, such as those which appear in table 2. These are the kind of variables generally used to argue that the Chilean economic policy has been far from successful. In summarized form, the critical argument contends that: (1) the Chilean economy has grown in the period from 1974 to 1979 at an average rate which is significantly below the

TABLE 1. Macroeconomic indicators.[a]

Year	GDP (1)	Consumer prices (2)	Fiscal deficit (3)	Non-traditional exports (4)	Net capital in-flows (5)	Balance of payments (6)	Gross reserves (7)
1970	3.5	36.1	2.9	225.9	531.3	226.1	917.3
1974	4.2	369.2	8.9	273.2	275.0	−54.2	317.7
1975	−16.6	343.3	2.9	401.9	323.6	−297.5	311.1
1976	5.0	197.9	2.0	510.3	253.0	485.7	732.7
1977	8.6	84.2	1.5	588.5	444.0	−7.0	685.5
1978	6.0	37.2	0.8	644.9	1,384.6	545.8	1,197.6
1979	7.2	38.9	−1.7	897.5	1,478.9	803.6	2,170.6

[a] Column (1) ODEPLAN (n.d.), annual rates of variation. The figures for 1978 and 1979 correspond to provisional estimates for GDP. (2) CPI, by Cortázar and Marshall (1980). (3) Treasury Department (1978) and ODEPLAN (n.d.). Percentages of GDP. (4) Central Bank of Chile, in Ffrench-Davis (1979). Figures in millions of dollars of 1977. (5) *Ibid.* (6) *Ibid.* (7) *Ibid.*

TABLE 2. Other macro results.[a]

	1960–1970	1970–1979	1974–1979
(1) GDP	4.5	2.6	2.5
(2) Production of goods	4.5	1.6	1.9
(3) Production of services	4.4	8.1	3.7
(4) GDP per capita	2.3	0.7	0.8
(5) Rate of investment	15.3	11.7	11.2
(6) Total employment	2.1	0.6	0.2
(7) Rate of unemployment	6.5	9.8	13.4

[a] Row (1) ODEPLAN *op. cit.* and estimates. *Gemines Report* no. 21 for 1979. Annual variation rates. (2) *Ibid.* The production of goods includes agriculture, fishing, mining, industry, and construction. (3) *Ibid.* The production of services includes electricity, gas and water, transportation, trade and other services. (4) *Ibid.* (5) *Ibid.* and 'Taller de Coyuntura' (1979). Investment in fixed capital over PBG. (6) Meller, Cortázar and Marshall (1979) and Treasury Department, *op. cit.*, Annual variation rates. (7) *Ibid.*

recent historical rate (as can be seen in table 2, in per capita terms this rate has not reached 1 percent per year), (2) economic growth has been even slower in sectors which produce goods as the modest growth which is seen at the aggregate level has been largely due to the expansion of services, (3) the potential for future growth is limited by low rates of investment which have scarcely surpassed 11 percent, (4) the employment level has stagnated in this period, during which there has also been a high rate of unemployment.

The figures [in table 2] are averages for the period. They do not reflect the annual trend of the indicators, particularly for the last years of the period. In fact the averages, which cover a period characterized by a strong recession which lasted until the middle of 1976, conceal a trend towards recuperation beginning in 1977 which, for some indicators such as GDP, is significant.

A more precise image of these trends can be seen in table 3, which includes figures to fill in the picture presented by the positive and negative indicators shown in tables 1 and 2. In table 3 it is apparent that the trend towards recovery of GDP just reached in 1978 the per capita level of 1970, and only in 1979 surpass-

TABLE 3. Economic and social indicators.[a]

	GDP per capita (1)	Balance in current account (2)	Debt service ratio over (3)	Investment rate (4)	Total employ-ment (5)	Employed in pop. of 12 years and over (6)	Unem-ployment rate (7)	Real salaries + wages (8)	Salaries and wages as share of national income (9)
1970	100.0	−159.9	33.5	15.0	100.0	42.9	6.1	100.0	44.3
1974	102.4	−254.3	18.6	13.0	104.6	40.4	9.2	65.1	34.6
1975	89.3	−532.3	40.0	10.7	99.0	37.4	13.4	62.9	34.7
1976	91.4	159.5	44.2	9.8	94.9	35.0	16.3	64.8	34.7
1977	97.6	−551.4	49.2	10.6	99.3	35.8	14.0	71.5	—
1978	101.7	−776.6	46.4	11.3	102.7	36.2	13.9	76.0	—
1979	107.4	−685.3	42.3	12.9	105.4	36.3	13.8	82.3	—

	Per capita consump-tion (10)	Consumption of the		Average pension (12)	Housing construc-tion, avg. per per-son (13)	Enrollment in pop. of 10–20 years of age (14)	Enrollment in 1st grade in corresponding population (15)	Hospital beds per person (16)	Health service per person (17)
		Poorer 20%	Richer 20% (11)						
1970	100.0	7.6	44.5	100.0	100.0	100.0	100.0	100.0	100.0
1974	102.7			59.3	85.3	113.1	106.3	94.4	89.3
1975	91.2			52.0	49.8	—	99.4	91.7	84.5
1976	87.3			56.4	38.4	—	94.3	88.9	90.3
1977	—			60.9	42.0	116.3	96.2	86.1	91.3
1978	—	5.2	51.0	67.0	44.2	115.2	—	83.3	94.2
1979	—			75.9	—	—	—	—	—

[a] Columns (1) ODEPLAN op. cit., see note (1) in table 1. (2) Central Bank of Chile, in Ffrench-Davis (1979), figures in millions of dollars of 1977, (3) Central Bank of Chile. (4) ODEPLAN op. cit., and Taller de Coyuntura op. cit., (5) Meller, Cortázar and Marshall (1979). (6) Ibid. (7) Ibid. (8) Taller de Coyuntura op. cit. (9) ODEPLAN op. cit. (10) Ibid. (11) INE (1969, 1978). (12) Superintendency of Social Security. (13) ODEPLAN op cit. and estimates for 1977 and 1979 based on Taller de Coyuntura op. cit. (14) INE (n.d.). (15) Schiefelbein and Grossi (1978). (16) INE (n.d.). (17) Ibid.

ed the per capita level of 1974.[5] Table 3 also shows a very slow recovery of the rate of investment beginning in 1977, as can be observed in the fourth column. This slow recovery suggests that the possibility of maintaining the high rate of growth of GDP observed in the last three years should be viewed very cautiously. On the other hand, the surplus in the balance of payments observed in table 1 has been accompanied by a marked trend towards a deficit in the current account (and also in the trade balance), which was compensated by an influx of financial assets from abroad. The debt service ratio

rose to over 40 percent of exports in 1975, and has stayed there until 1979.

One of the most striking aspects of the Chilean economic experience in the past six years has been the simultaneous deterioration of employment, wages, per capita consumption, and other social indicators which measure the population's access to housing, education, and health as well as the skewing of consumption by income strata. These figures are also shown in table 3.

The trend towards recovery reflected in the social welfare indicators is not very significant. The national unemployment rate has remained above 13 percent. Real wages and salaries in 1979 are still 18 percent below the 1970 level.[6]

In brief, the economic results of the 1974–1979 period give mixed signs: the rate of inflation decreases, after a deep recession GDP reaches pre-recession levels, the fiscal deficit is eliminated, there is an accumulation of reserves and nontraditional exports expand rapidly.

At the same time, a low investment rate, a significant deficit in the commercial balance, increasing external indebtedness, high unemployment, real wage reduction, and a deterioration in the distribution of consumption and basic social services are among the negative factors.

Can this be considered a successful result? Obviously the information given up to now is relatively aggregated. On the other hand, as is obvious, the evaluation of any economic policy depends on the objectives chosen.

Some of the objectives in Chile 1974–1979 were related to economic stabilization. Others had to do with an attempt at transforming the basis of functioning of the economy radically altering the ownership of property, the structure of production, and the development strategy. Thus, we must go beyond macroeconomic indicators to evaluate the degree of success in these other objectives.

3. NATURE OF THE ECONOMIC POLICIES IN CHILE, 1974–1979

The economic policies evaluated in this paper are an attempt to radically apply an orthodox stabilization approach which, under very different political conditions and with little success, had been put into practice in several countries at the end of the fifties and early sixties in Latin America.[7]

As in those experiences, the first aim of the policies is to balance the external accounts and reduce inflation. The principal tools are monetary control and elimination of the fiscal deficit. Together with these key policy measures, the orthodox policy seeks to gradually eliminate subsidies and exchange controls, free prices, including the interest rate, and gradually readjust the exchange rate. It also attempts to eliminate restrictions on the flow of foreign capital and to introduce severe norms of self-financing to public enterprises. At the same time, it strongly reduces real wages. This policy package is oriented to the elimination of market disequilibria resulting from the inflationary process.

But the policies applied in Chile after 1973 are not only short-term adjustment policies. As we have argued elsewhere, these policies have a strong component of structural change.[8] The diagnosis of inflation, although stressing its monetary origins, broadens to engulf a supposed generalized malfunctioning of the economy. Key factors would be the excessive size of the State including public enterprises, the inefficient allocation of investment due to the lack of a private capital market and the misallocation of resources resulting from high tariff barriers. This is the rationale behind the structural changes proposed in Chile after 1973. The implementation of structural reforms along these lines is given as high a priority as the economic stabilization program itself. When there is a tradeoff between the two, it is the long-term objectives that often prevail.[9] Therefore, it seems justified to define the character of the Chilean economic policy, as opposed to the monetarism of the fifties, as a new form of structuralism. Obviously the objectives and the instruments used differ radically from those proposed by the so-called Latin American structuralist school. Also the implications of the policies in terms of income distribution and changes in the power structure differ greatly. But in its reach and even its "revolutionary" fervor, it is not less ambitious than the most radical attempts at structural change from the left, as during the Allende period in Chile.

This new type of economic orthodoxy is not only a Chilean phenomenon. Similar policies are being applied in Argentina and

Uruguay.[10] It is not necessarily a coincidence that these "orthodox-structuralist" policies are being applied in these three countries by authoritarian governments. We will examine in the next two sections the nature of the structural changes brought about as part of Chile's orthodox-authoritarian experiment.

4. CHANGES IN THE FUNCTIONING OF THE ECONOMY

For clarity's sake we shall divide the subject in three different, although related, aspects: (1) changes in the role of economic agents, (2) mechanisms of transference of resources to "new" economic agents, (3) opening up of the economy to world trade.

4.1 Changes in the Role of Economic Agents: The State and the Privatization of the Economy

One of the basic elements of the new economic policy consisted in a drastic change in the role assigned to economic agents in Chile. The State gradually decreased in importance. This was attained by means of a reduction in public expenditures, and a more limited presence of the State as a producer and as a developmental agent. . . .

This withdrawal of the State from economic activity is accompanied by a substantial decrease in public employment . . . . Public sector employment fell nearly 20 percent between 1974 and 1978. Thus previous expansionary trends were drastically reversed.[11] The employment reductions are more important in development institutions (19 percent reduction per year) and in public enterprises (10.5 percent reduction per year). These figures clearly reflect the priorities in the new economic policy. Where the State left the field, the private sector, either domestic or foreign entered. Particularly important is the growth of private financial institutions. . . .

Organized labor is excluded from this picture. Not only wages are controlled and in fact drastically curtailed in real terms, but no collective bargaining is allowed, strikes are forbidden, and no mechanism exists for the participation of labor in economic decisions. Only in 1979 is a "labor plan" implemented which regulates, under conditions of subordination of workers to the employers, the functioning of labor unions and allows for a very restricted form of collective bargaining.

4.2. Mechanisms of Transference of Resources to the "New" Economic Agents

The change in the role of economic agents which we have just described (less State participation, privatization of economic activities, modifications in labor legislation), was initially posed only as an efficiency requirement of the model. It was supposedly neutral as to its distributive effects. In practice this was not so. In fact, the economy's adjustment process to the desired conditions implied a massive transfer of resources towards the private sector, particularly towards financial firms and large industrial enterprises. This transfer of resources was made possible because of the particular form taken by the processes of privatization, of market liberalization and of inflationary control.

Thus, privatization of State enterprises occurred in extremely advantageous conditions for the new owners. In table 4 we have estimated the implicit subsidy for those who bought these public assets. The subsidy turns out to be equivalent to 30 percent of the firms' net worth and up to 40 percent and 50 percent of the purchase value.[12] The low sale price was influenced by the State's urgency to sell and its doing so in a moment of deep recession and high interest rates, a point at which short-term profitability of the enterprises decreased. Given these circumstances, only those firms who had liquid resources or access to cheap foreign credit were in a position to buy the auctioned enterprises.

Something similar occurred in the agricultural sector, in which the policy was to return a

TABLE 4. Subsidy in the sale of state enterprises (millions of dollars of 1978).[a,b]

Discount rate		Sale value	Value of assets in 1978	Subsidy	Subsidy as percentage of asset value
1974–78	1979–83				
10	10	496.1	731.8	235.7	32.2
25	15	533.0	731.8	198.8	27.2

[a] The figures correspond to a sample of 41 enterprises and banks which represent around 60 percent of the firms auctioned. The value of the sale updated to 1978, assumes a 4 year payment period for the industrial firms and 8 quarters for banks, with interest rates of 10 percent and 8 percent respectively.

[b] Source: Dahse (1979) and CORFO (1980).

fraction of the lands expropriated during Agrarian Reform to their primitive owners. Another part was sub-divided into individual plots and handed over to peasants.... In April 1979, 30 percent of the expropriated land had been returned to the former owners and 35 percent had been assigned in individual plots to peasants and small farmers. Moreover, already in June 1978, nearly 40 percent of these lands had been sold or leased by peasants to third parties, as a consequence of the high cost of credit and reduced technical assistance.

As can be seen, the privatization of manufacturing firms, as well as that of the land reform sector, implied a transfer of assets, generally undervalued either to former owners, in the agricultural case, or to business groups in the industrial and financial sectors. The foregoing tendency was reinforced by the particular form taken by the process of market liberalization. Thus, the liberalization of the foreign credit market was only partial. A ceiling was imposed on foreign borrowing, as a percentage of the value of assets. Given that only large enterprises and the better established banks and financial institutions had access to cheap, rationed external credit, and that domestic interest rates were much higher, this constituted a source of large profits for banks and larger firms. Zahler [1979] has estimated the profit for the enterprises which had access to external credit in the period 1976–1979 to be in the order of 800 million dollars .... These profits arise from the high differen-

tial in interest rates, taking into account expected devaluation between the foreign rates (from 6 percent to 11 percent) and domestic interest rates in dollars (between 118 percent and 42 percent).

On the other hand, the process of market liberalization did not follow uniform rules with regard to factor and goods prices. Upon the drastic freeing up of prices followed by wage contraction, a strong bias against labor sets in, as can be seen in table 5. The drastic fall of the relative price of labor with respect to wholesale prices, export, and industrial prices is obvious when inspecting table 5. The relative reduction in wages reaches between 50 percent and 60 percent in 1976, and is still between 30–40 percent during 1978.

These sets of relative prices are extremely favorable to productive enterprises, particularly those in export activities. Undoubtedly it allowed them to absorb a good part of the greater costs associated with the severe 1975–1976 recession and it has provided a cushion that facilitates adjustment to increased external competition resulting from lower tariffs. The effect of changes in relative prices is reinforced when considering the reduction in the employer's contribution to social security. The accumulated effect of both factors on the cost of labor ... dropped from 15.8 percent of the gross value of production in 1970 to 10.2 percent in 1978.

Another important way in which resources were transferred to the economic "newcomers" came about as a by-product of the policy

TABLE 5. Prices and wages (1970 indexes = 100).[a]

	(1) Remunerations ÷ wholesale prices	(2) Remunerations ÷ export prices	(3) Industrial remunerations ÷ industrial prices
1970	100.0	100.0	100.0
1974	49.7	50.3	57.5
1975	40.0	36.3	46.7
1976	40.5	45.3	53.5
1977	52.2	60.7	67.2
1978	57.9	57.9	73.1

[a] *Sources*: (1) INE, *Indice de Sueldos y Salarios* (ISS) and *IPM*, national products. (2) INE, *ISS*, Exchange rate and Ffrench-Davis, *Indice de Precios Externos y Valor Real del Comercio Internacional de Chile, Notas Técnicas* no. 15, CIEPLAN, 1979. (3) INE, *ISS*, Industrial Sector and Industrial *IPM*.

of economic stabilization. This policy was characterized by a strict monetarist, closed economy approach. The policy sought stabilization through partial use of the instruments at its disposal: principally the reduction of money supply, real wages, and the fiscal deficit.

The approach was successful in producing a sharp drop in effective demand and in reducing real wages. Prices increased without any relation to demand since the impact of expectations and costs was difficult to gauge in a situation which passed rapidly from 'repressed' inflation to open inflation. Consequently, high inflation continued far longer than expected. The economy entered a prolonged phase of recession with high inflation, a period characterized by generalized market disequilibrium. Market imbalances surfaced in the form of sharp and intermittent movements in relative prices.

Anyone with enough liquidity to react quickly to these fluctuations in relative prices benefited from those movements. So did, obviously, anyone with special access to economic information which would allow him to correctly predict those movements or to know ahead of time of any corrective measures planned by the government.

The economic groups which controlled the country's large firms and financial sector took full advantage of these opportunities for speculation. Market disequilibria and high inflation lasted over five years, long enough for those groups to corner for themselves the speculative gains available in different markets.

In short, beginning in 1973, the operation of the Chilean economy fundamentally changed not only because the economic roles assigned to different participants changed, but also because the dynamic processes of adjustment to a new economic model made possible the real transfer of resources towards economic industrial-financial groups. These groups took advantage of this resource transfer, using it to acquire a dominant position in the country's productive apparatus, as will be shown below.

4.3. Transition from a Closed to an Open Economy

At the end of 1973, the average nominal tariff on imports to Chile was 94 percent. By June 1979, a gradual policy of tariff reductions brought nearly all tariffs down to a uniform 10 percent except for automotive vehicles. The process of tariff reduction, which took a little over five years, was part of a general liberalization of restrictions of foreign trade: elimination of non-tariff barriers; a reduction on limits to foreign investment, foreign credit, and foreign exchange transactions. At the same time, however, the government attempted to maintain an exchange rate which would favor Chilean exports. The government also sought to encourage exports by exempting exported goods from the across-the-board value added tax on all products sold in Chile and from export custom duties.

Policies designed to open the economy were resolutely put into effect from 1974 to 1978. By the end of six years, the Chilean economy was well on its way to becoming an "open" economy with few barriers to international trade. Below, we will briefly review the principal changes which have occurred as a result of the transition from a closed to an open economy.[13]

One of the objectives of liberalizing imports was to encourage the development of an export sector. Lower tariffs reduced the cost to the Chilean producer of intermediate goods. An increase in the volume of imports would raise the equilibrium exchange rate for the dollar, creating an exchange rate more favorable to export growth.

The policy of export stimulation was also helped by the low wage rates which prevailed during that period, as was shown in table 3, and by the special tax exemptions on exports which were mentioned above. The policy was also aided by excess capacity in the industrial sector which resulted from the anti-inflation program.

The growth of exports in the period was undoubtedly significant. Normalizing for the price of copper, total exports rose from 15 percent of GDP in 1970 to 18 percent in 1977. Nevertheless the greater success was obtained in the growth of non-traditional exports. . . . During the period 1974–1979, non-traditional exports tripled. This was accompanied by export diversification. If copper is excluded from total exports to avoid the effect of excessive price fluctuations, industrial exports rose from 59 percent of total exports in 1974 (excluding copper), to 65 percent in 1978.

As regards imports, they grow rapidly after 1978. The expansion is particularly significant for imports of non-food consumption goods, whose growth rate is over 100 percent be-

tween 1974 and 1979. On the other hand, imports of capital goods fall during the recession and only in 1978 do they recuperate 1970 levels. A similar behavior is observed when looking at intermediate imports. . . .

In brief, empirical evidence indicates that trade liberalization has caused: (a) significant export expansion, (b) a change in the composition of imports, in which the most rapid growth is observed in the imports of non-food consumption goods, (c) a differentiated impact of tariff reduction on the various branches of industry, (d) stagnation in industrial employment, accompanied by a slow recuperation in industrial output levels. Undoubtedly this adjustment process was helped by the remarkable fall in wages with respect to the exchange rate and to industrial prices . . . .

It is perhaps too early to make a definite assessment of the impact of trade liberalization in Chile. Although the process of tariff reduction ended in 1979, the appreciation of domestic currency that results from a fixed exchange rate established in June 1979 (given that domestic inflation more than doubles external inflation) is further reducing effective protection in the industrial sector. A final evaluation must wait until these effects have sorted themselves out.

5. CHANGES IN THE STRUCTURE OF THE ECONOMY

Up to this point, we have analyzed the main changes in the economy's operation which resulted from policy reforms begun in 1973. These changes, the new roles of participants in the economy, and greater degree of openness to foreign trade, no doubt have repercussions on the structure of production and on patterns of income and wealth distribution. But the effects are slow to take form. Given the short period of time which has passed, we can now only observe the merging outlines of some of the tendencies. . . .

Changes in Patterns of Distribution

An economy which undergoes profound changes such as Chile experienced beginning in 1973 will probably, in the long run, sustain changes not only in its production and trade structure, but also in its patterns of distribution.

In the long run, some of the important factors related to changes in income distribution are changes in patterns of property ownership, in the relative power of different participants in the economy, and in the importance of different productive sectors.

What has happened to the first two of these factors in the period which we are studying? As we have described in a previous section, the roles of the economic participants changed as a result of the reduction of the role of the State and of the rapid privatization of economic activities. We observed that this process and the government's general policy orientation favored privileged participation and access to resources by the business sector, particularly by large- and medium-sized firms and by the financial sector. These were the sectors which most benefited from the massive transfer of resources which accompanied the transition from high inflation and a closed economy to more moderate prices and an "open" economy.

A recent study identifies the groups that benefited from this process and describes the concentration of wealth which resulted from it. By the end of 1978, five economic conglomerates controlled 53 percent of the total assets of Chile's 250 largest private enterprises. Nine conglomerates, including those five, controlled 82 percent of the assets in the Chilean banking system. And the same nine groups also controlled 60 percent of total bank credits and 64 percent of loans made by financial institutions. The same study showed that in a sample of 100 enterprises, the assets of firms controlled by the five most important conglomerates seemed to grow 97 percent between 1969 and 1978, while assets of the remaining firms grew only 14 percent. This figure is indicative of the rapid expansion of conglomerates, a significative feature in the process of asset concentration, together with the privatizations, the reversion of Agrarian Reform, and the liberalization of prices accompanied by wage repression.

In the short term, that is until 1978, the distributive changes observed are strongly influenced by the high unemployment rates and the fall of real wages. In table 6, employment and unemployment figures are given. Employment at a national level, which had grown 2 percent per year in the '60s, shows a growth of only 0.3 percent per year between 1970 and 1979, and stagnation between 1974 and 1979.

The slow growth of employment together with an expansion of population of working age of nearly 10 percent between 1974 and 1978, explains the high unemployment rates observed, which are more than twice the historic rates. In 1979 unemployment reached 13.8 percent. Adding to this the so-called "Minimum Employment Program", the figure would rise to 17.8 percent. Unemployment rate for blue-collar workers reaches 28.4 percent if one includes the minimum employment program. High unemployment is accompanied by a fall in real wages that reaches 40 percent at the end of 1974 and early 1975.

The simultaneous reduction in employment and wages generates a regressive distribution of income, a proxy of which we consider household consumption expenditures by income brackets. The figures were given in table 2 and point to a concentration of consumption in the high income brackets.

On the other hand, empirical evidence shows a marked stratification in consumption. The consumption of non-essential imported consumption goods, which grows about 300 percent between 1970 and 1978, is highly concentrated in the highest 20 percent of the families. The families consume nearly 60 percent of the total. . . . The trickle-down in con-

TABLE 6.   Employment and unemployment (thousands of persons).[a]

	Labor force (1)	Employed (2)	Unemployed (3)	Unemployment rate (4)	PEM[b] (5)	Unemployment plus PEM on labor force (6)
1970	2,950.1	2,770.1	180.0	6.1	—	6.1
1974	3,189.6	2,896.2	293.4	9.2	—	9.2
1975	3,169.8	2,743.5	426.3	13.4	60.6	15.4
1976	3,139.8	2,628.0	511.8	16.3	157.8	21.3
1977	3,197.3	2,750.7	446.6	14.0	187.7	19.8
1978	3,307.2	2,845.8	461.4	13.9	145.8	18.4
1979	3,385.6	2,918.4	467.2	13.8	133.9	17.8

[a] *Sources*: Columns (1) to (4) Meller, Cortázar and Marshall (1979); column (5) INE, *Informativo Estadistico*; column (6) is obtained from columns (1), (3) and (5).

[b] PEM: Minimum Employment Program.

sumption to other income groups is scarce, being almost negligible for the lower 20 percent of the families.

Contrasting with the expansion of luxury consumption which concentrates in high income groups, essential food consumption per family for the poorer groups shows a reduction of 20 percent in real terms between 1969 and 1978. . . . Instead, the consumption per family of the same basic food products for the high income groups grows slightly. This marked dualism in consumption seems to be an essential characteristic of the model. It is in agreement with the patrimonial changes and with the income distribution patterns previously discussed.

6. CONCLUSIONS

The Chilean economy, in the period 1974–1979, has simultaneously been subject to a process of economic stabilization and of transition towards a free market economy.

In the first aspect a substantial decrease of the rate of inflation was attained; the Balance of Payments was adjusted, accumulating international reserves; and, after passing through a deep recession, the economy shows signs of recuperating the levels of production of 1970.

Other indicators, however, show negative results: high unemployment persists in the seventh year of application of the policy, distribution of income and household expenditures is regressive, investment levels are low, and the deficit in the current account of the Balance of Payments is growing, as is external debt. These indicators cast a shadow on the growth potential of the model, as has been applied in Chile, and in its capacity to absorb labor in productive activities.

But macroeconomic indicators are only the more visible, but perhaps less important part, of the revolutionary process of change in the Chilean economy in this period. The process of transition to a free market economy implied that, simultaneously with the anti-inflationary policy, deep structural reforms were carried out: a drastic privatization of the economy; a quick opening of the economy to world markets; a massive transfer of resources to the modern sector of industry and finance. As a consequence of the latter, powerful conglomerates with ample economic and political influence emerge. This is one of the outstanding traits of the industrial organization scheme which arises from the experiment.

The conglomerates or "economic groups" are in fact the new actors in the process of development. They increasingly control industrial assets, as well as that of banks and financial institutions. Besides, they are the dynamic agents in the process of industrial adjustment to face foreign competition. These conglomerates are the ones that relate to international private banks and control the larger proportion in the flow of external loans.

The other basic modification in the functioning of the Chilean economy refers to the radical opening up to world markets. This process does not result in as deep a breakdown of the industrial sector as could have occurred. Although several industrial branches suffer significant losses in markets and industrial employment goes down, other activities seem to adapt successfully.

The financial opening, which goes together with the commercial opening, helps to overcome the problems derived from the recession and the transition to the open economy. Nevertheless, it has distorting effects on other aspects. It prolongs the price stabilization period as it becomes the most important source of monetary expansion. At the same time, it reinforces the tendency towards asset concentration as it gives differentiated access to cheap external credit (in comparison to domestic credit) mainly to large enterprises of the modern sector; and makes it possible to keep an undervalued exchange rate that coexists with large deficits in trade flows.

Production adjustment, as a result of the opening up of the economy, is just beginning to show. As expected, new production patterns are oriented towards expanding primary producing activities (mainly copper mining and agricultural and forestry products) and exports.

However, the most dynamic sectors are commerce, financial activities, and personal services. The first two are stimulated by expanded foreign trade and by the development of the capital market. Demand for personal services grows as a consequence of the rapid expansion in income for high income groups. At the same time that the productive structure changes, a higher degree of asset and income concentration is observed.

What type of economy emerges from the deep structural changes undertaken in Chile after 1973? Certainly what we have is an open economy, with more specialization and potentially higher incentives for efficiency in domestic production. It is also an economy that is more vulnerable with respect to changes, shock, and fluctuations in the international economy. It is, on the other hand, highly dependent on the availability of private external credit in order to balance the current account deficit.

A salient feature of the model is the wide dispersion of income and consumption patterns between the rich and the rest of the population. With respect to consumption, a marked stratification is produced. The 'deprivation horizon' is a reality for low income groups, as is 'the opulent consumer society' for the higher income sectors.

This is only one of the unsolved problems. Other persistent problems are extremely high unemployment and low investment. In the political sphere the model has not been able to solve the inherent contradiction between economic freedom, a basic objective of the model and of the Friedmanian "ideary", and the political authoritarianism which accompanies it. After all, facing the dilemma, it seems that the Chilean model has certainly chosen capitalism, but has forgotten all about freedom.

1. Harberger (1979).
2. Cauas and Saieh (1979).
3. Prebisch (1978). 'Even if orthodox neoclassical principles are followed with intelligent virtuosism, the great objectives of economic efficacy, social efficiency and respect for human rights cannot be reached simultaneously.'
4. Friedman (1981).
5. It has to be noted that the National Accounts have been published until 1976 only. There are estimates for some global indicators prepared by ODEPLAN, which cover the years 1977 and 1978, and which have been repeatedly modified by ODE-PLAN. These have to be considered as provisional figures. The estimation of the 1979 growth rate was

made by GEMINES, a private firm. It is not an official estimate.

6. The Wages and Salaries Index in nominal terms has been deflated by the Consumer Price Index as corrected by Cortázar and Marshall (1980). The corrected CPI shows that actual price increases in 1978 were 52.8 percent over the official CPI published by the National Statistical Institute (INE) and 27.5 percent over the CPI corrected by the University of Chile, the latter being the most commonly used until the Cortázar–Marshall study.

7. Foxley (1981).

8. Foxley (1981).

9. Some examples are given in Foxley (1980).

10. Díaz-Alejandro (1981).

11. With regard to 1973, public employment dropped 25 percent and represents a decrease of 100,000 persons.

12. The calculation was made based on the figures of Dahse (1979), for a sample of 41 enterprises, as explained in the note of table 4.

13. What follows is based on studies by Ffrench-Davis (1979) and Vergara (1980).

REFERENCES

Cauas, J. and A. Saieh, 1979, Politica economica 1973–1979, Boletin del Banco Central, no. 621, Nov.

CORFO, 1980, Gerencia de normalización, and El Mercurio, Feb. 27.

Cartázar, R., 1979, Remuneraciones, empleo y distribucón del ingreso en Chile 1970–1978, Mimeo. (CIEPLAN, Santiago).

Cortázar, R. and J. Marshall, 1980.

Dahse, F., 1979, Mapa de la extrema riqueza (Editorial Aconcagua, Santiago).

Departamento de Economia, U. Chile, 1978, Comentarios sobre la situación económica, 2nd semester.

Diaz-Alejandro, C., 1981, Southern cone stabilization plans, in: W. Cline and S. Weintraub, eds., Economic stabilization in developing countries (Brookings Institution, Washington, DC).

Ffrench-Davis, R., 1979, Politicas de comercio exterior en Chile: 1973–78, Mimeo., Nov. (CIEPLAN, Santiago).

Ffrench-Davis, R., 1980, Liberalización de importaciones: La experiencia Chilena en 1973–1979, Collección Estudios CIEPLAN, no. 4. Dec. (CIEPLAN, Santiago).

Foxley, A., 1980, Stabilization policies and stagflation: The cases of Brazil and Chile, in: A. Foxley and L. Whitehead, eds., World development, Special Issue, Economic stabilization in Latin America: Political dimensions, Nov. (Oxford).

Foxley, A., 1981, Stabilization policies and their effects on employment and income distribution, in: W. Cline and S. Weintraub, eds., Economic stabilization in developing countries (Brookings Institution, Washington, DC).

Friedman, I., 1981, The role of private banks in stabilization programs, in: W. Cline and S. Weintraub, eds., Economic stabilization in developing countries (Brookings Institution, Washington, DC).

Harberger, A., 1979, Declarations, The Wall Street Journal, Oct. 5.

INE, 1969, Encuesta de presupuestos familiares.

INE, 1977, Encuesta nacional del empleo.

INE, 1978, Encuesta de presupeustos familiares.

INE, 1979, Ill Encuesta de presupuestos familiares, Vol. III, May.

INE, n.d., Compendio estadistico.

Meller, P., R. Cortázar and J. Marshall, 1979, La evolución del empleo en Chile 1974–1978, Colección Estudios CIEPLAN, no. 2.

ODEPLAN, n.d., Cuentas Nacionales de Chile.

Prebisch, R., 1978, Estructura socioeconómica y crisis del sistema. Revista de la CEPAL, 2nd. semester.

Schiefelbein, E. and M. L. Grossi, 1978, Análisis de la matricula escolar en Chile (CIDE).

Treasury Department, 1978, Exposición sobre el estado de la hacienda pública, Jan.

Vergara, P., 1980, Apertura externa y desarrollo industrial en Chile: 1974–1978, Colección Estudios CIEPLAN, no. 4, Dec. (CIEPLAN, Santiago).

Further Readings

1. Development Planning

Blitzner, Charles R., Clark, P., and Taylor, L., eds. *Economy-Wide Models and Development Planning*. London: Oxford University Press, 1975.

Chenery, Hollis B., et al., eds. *Studies in Development Planning*. Harvard Economic Studies, vol. 136. Cambridge, Mass.: Harvard University Press, 1971.

Khalid, R. O. "Planning and the Budget Process: An Introduction." *Finance and Development* 15, no. 2 (June 1978).

Lewis, W. Arthur. *Development Planning: The Essentials of Economic Policy*. New York: Harper & Row, 1966.

Mirrlees, J. A. "Social Benefit-Cost Analysis and the Distribution of Income." *World Development* 6, no. 2 (February 1978).

Roemer, Michael. "Planning by 'Revealed Preference': An Improvement upon the Traditional Method." *World Development* 4, no. 9 (September 1976).

Tinbergen, Jan. *Development Planning*. Translated from the Dutch by N. D. Smith. New York and Toronto: McGraw-Hill, 1967.

Todaro, Michael P. *Development Planning: Models and Methods*. New York: Oxford University Press, 1971.

Waterston, Albert. *Development Planning: Lessons of Experience*. Baltimore: Johns Hopkins University Press, 1972.

2. Project Analysis

Bhatt, V. V. "On a Development Bank's Selection Criteria for Industrial Projects." *Economic Development and Cultural Change* 25, no. 4 (July 1977).

Harberger, Arnold C. *Project Evaluation: Collected Papers*. Markham Economics Series. Chicago: Markham, 1973.

Lal, Deepak. *Methods of Project Analysis: A Review*. Baltimore and London: Johns Hopkins University Press, 1974.

Little, I. M. D., and Mirrlees, James A. *Project Appraisal and Planning for Developing Countries*. New York: Basic Books, 1974.

Little, I. M. D., and Scott, M. F. G. *Using Shadow Prices*. New York: Holmes & Meier, 1976.

Misham, E. J. *Cost-Benefit Analysis*. New York: Praeger, 1976.

OECD. *Manual of Industrial Project Analysis in Developing Countries*, vol. 1, *Methodology and Case Studies*. Paris: Development Centre of the Organization for Economic Cooperation and Development, 1968.

Squire, Lyn, and van der Tak, Herman C. *Economic Analysis of Projects*. A World Bank Research Publication. Baltimore: Johns Hopkins University Press for the World Bank, 1975.

United Nations. *A Guide to Practical Project Appraisal: Social Benefit: Cost Analysis in Developing Countries*. New York: United Nations Industrial Development Organization, 1978.

3. Fiscal Policy and Inflation

Aghevli, Bijan B., and Khan, Mohsin S. "Government Deficits and the Inflationary Process in Developing Countries." *IMF Staff Papers*, September 1978.

Bird, Richard, and Oldman, Oliver. *Readings on Taxation in Developing Countries*. Baltimore: Johns Hopkins University Press, 1964.

Heller, Peter S. "A Model of Fiscal Behavior in Developing Countries: Aid, Investment and Taxation." *American Economic Review* 65, no. 3 (June 1975).

Kaldor, Nicholas. "Will Underdeveloped Countries learn to Tax?" *Foreign Affairs* (January 1963).

Rothstein, Robert L. "Politics and Policy-Making in the Third World: Does a Reform Strategy Make Sense?" *World Development* 4, no. 8 (August 1976).

Toye, J. F. J., ed. *Taxation and Economic Development*. London: Frank Cass, 1979.

Wang, T. N., ed. Taxation and Development. New York: Praeger, 1976.

4. Banking and Finance

Bhatt, V. V., and Meerman, J. "Resource Mobilization in Developing Countries: Financial Institutions and Policies." *World Development*; 6, no. 1 (January 1978).

Cairncross, Alex. *Inflation, Growth and International Finance*. Albany: State University of New York Press, 1975.

Desai, V. "Role of Banks in Economic Growth." *Economic Affifairs* 21, no. 6 (June 1976).

Friedman, Irving S., and Costanzo, G. A. *The Emerging Role of Private Banks in the Developing World*. New York: Citicorp, 1977.

Newlyn, W. T. *The Financing of Economic De-velopment*. Oxford, England: Oxford University Press, 1977.

World Bank. *Development Finance Companies*. Sector Policy Paper. Washington, D.C., April 1976.

13

The World Economy of the 1980s

33. A View from the South: The Second Phase of the North-South Dialogue*

Mahbub ul Haq

If we review the formal agenda of the North-South negotiations, this is a time for great despair. There is no visible progress on the issues being negotiated within the UNCTAD framework—whether the establishment of a Common Fund, or debt relief, or codes of conduct for technology transfer. The bitter memory of the CIEC negotiations in Paris is slowly fading away, along with its meager accomplishments. The U.N. General Assembly's Committee of the Whole ran into serious problems before it even got going—although efforts are currently being made to revive its mandate. The Joint Bank-Fund Development Committee is still drifting in search of a meaningful agenda for action.

But I do not believe that such a summary judgment on North-South negotiations is either fair or helpful. Restructuring the international order so as to make it more equitable and more responsive to the needs of the poor nations is a long-term *process*, not an event. It will require patient work on both sides if negotiations are to succeed.

* From Martin M. McLaughlin (ed.), *The United States and World Development: Agenda 1979.* Published for the Overseas Development Council by Praeger, New York, 1979, pp. 115–124.

Note: The paper expresses the personal views of the author.

The real disappointment of the first phase of these negotiations is not that the North has not accepted the specific proposals put forward by the South. The real disappointment has been that the North has not put forward any counterproposals that it considered more reasonable. The North has been content to remain frozen in an essentially defensive posture—finding fault with the agenda presented by the South, and bargaining for more time by readily agreeing to formal negotiating machinery and then frustrating all attempts to reach some meaningful conclusions. In other words, the North has not taken these negotiations too seriously: they are not at the top of its priority agenda. The North-South dialogue has not become a shared responsibility: the North, perhaps unconsciously, has assumed the role of the judge and the jury before which the South, as plaintiff, is presenting its "inadequate" case.

A continuation of these attitudes will not lead to any productive negotiations. If the second phase of the North-South dialogue is to make real progress, changes are required on *both* sides. The North must make up its mind as to the priority it is going to give to the call for a restructured international order and whether it will take active initiatives in thinking about and in negotiating a new order—initiatives that accommodate the legitimate interests and aspirations of poor nations along with its own concerns. This is an item that the North should seriously discuss within its own quiet summits if the second phase of the negotiations is not to lead to further frustrations and recriminations. The South, for its part, has to calmly review the experience so far to determine for itself the order of priority it should give to the various items on the negotiating agenda, the substantive work that should be organized to back up its proposals, the mistakes that have been made in the negotiating process so far, and the negotiating forums and tactics that are most appropriate for the future. This calm analysis can best proceed in small South-South dialogues in order to prepare for the second phase of the negotiations.

I do believe that the first phase of the North-South dialogue is coming to an end. This phase was used by the Third World primarily to establish the need for a major change in the existing world order. The poor nations have argued vehemently that they cannot get an equitable deal from the present international economic structures, just as the poorest people within national orders fail to get equitable treatment. Once there are major disparities in income distribution within a country, the market mechanism ceases to function either efficiently or equitably, since it is weighted heavily in favor of the purchasing power in the hands of the rich. Those who have the money can make the market bend to their own will. This is even more true at the international level than at the national, since there is no world government, and since there is no international equivalent of the mechanisms that exist within countries to create political pressures for the re-distribution of income and wealth.

EVIDENCE OF INEQUITIES IN THE PRESENT ORDER

While major controversies still surround this whole subject, analysts in the developing na-

tions—as well as some in the developed—have pointed to impressive and growing evidence showing that the poor nations are getting a raw deal from existing market structures. To cite just a few examples:

1. There is a tremendous imbalance today in the distribution of international reserves. The poor nations, with 70 per cent of the world population, received less than 4 per cent of the international reserves of $131 billion during 1970–1974, simply because the rich nations controlled the creation and distribution of international reserves through the expansion of their own national reserve currencies (mainly dollars) and through their decisive control over the International Monetary Fund.

2. The distribution of the value added of the products traded between the developing and the developed countries is heavily weighted in favor of the latter. The developing countries, unlike the developed, receive back only a small fraction of the final price that the consumers in the international market are already paying for their products—simply because many of them are too poor or too weak to exercise any meaningful control over the processing, shipping, and marketing of their primary exports.

3. The rich nations have raised a formidable protective wall around their life-styles, through tariff and non-tariff barriers and restrictive immigration practices, while paying handsome tributes at the same time to the "free" working of the international market mechanism. The developing countries contend that most markets are already managed to a large extent: the only question is who manages them and for whose benefit.

4. Most of the contracts, leases, and concessions that the multinational corporations have negotiated in the past with the developing countries reflect a fairly inequitable sharing of benefits. In many cases, the host government is getting only a frac-

tion of the benefits from the exploitation of its own natural resources by the multinational corporations.

5. The poor nations have only a pro forma participation in the economic decision making of the world. Their advice is hardly solicited when the big industrialized nations get together to take key decisions on the future of the world economy; their voting strength in the Bretton Woods institutions (World Bank and International Monetary Fund) is less than one third of the total; and their numerical majority in the U.N. General Assembly has meant no real influence so far on international economic decisions.

6. An unequal relationship pervades the intellectual world and the mass media as a whole. The developing countries often have been subjected to concepts of development and value systems that were largely fashioned abroad.

THE SECOND PHASE OF THE DIALOGUE: FIVE PROPOSALS

A lot has been said about the inequities of the present world order—sometimes with a good deal of bitterness. This is not unusual in the first phase of any major movement, such as trade unionism, civil rights, or women's liberation. By those standards, the first phase of the North-South dialogue has been conducted with remarkable dignity and sophistication, with few smashed windows and no burnt bridges. I disagree with those who believe that nothing concrete has been achieved in this first phase. What has been achieved is a high degree of visibility for the concern for a new order and a reluctant acceptance by the rich nations that these issues must be faced after all.

We are now reaching the threshold of the second phase of the North-South dialogue, when serious negotiations can, and must, begin. It is not necessary to settle all the argu-

ments on which considerable emotion already has been spent in the first phase. It is not possible to establish complete unanimity before the process of hard bargaining begins. And it may even be counterproductive to keep rehearsing the partisan arguments of yesterday when the challenge of finding some agreed solutions is already upon us.

I believe that we must now prepare for the second phase of the dialogue. This process of preparation requires the kinds of changes in attitudes by both North and South that I have already mentioned. But, supposing that such attitudinal changes can be achieved on both sides, how can we then best proceed? Let me take the liberty of making five specific proposals.

1. Toward a Statement of Principles

First, it is unfortunate that the North-South dialogue is still proceeding without a framework of principles agreed to by both sides. Concrete negotiations are always facilitated if a broad consensus on objectives and principles is established first. Let me be rash enough to suggest some premises on which a consensus needs to be established before serious negotiations really can begin:

(a) A new order is required by the entire international community, not only by the developing countries, in view of the growing interdependence between rich and poor nations;

(b) Both sides must eventually gain from any new arrangement that is devised if it is not to degenerate into either exploitation or dependency;

(c) The new order must be based firmly on the concept of equality of opportunity both within and among nations;

(d) The main economic objective of the new order should be to restore orderly growth in an equitable global system;

(e) The attainment of these goals will require long-term structural changes, not short-term financial concessions;

(f) These changes can be negotiated only over time and in gradual stages by establishing an agreed framework for dialogue.

I offer these suggestions only illustratively. It is hard enough to negotiate fundamental changes. It can only become harder if there is not even a minimum of consensus on the overall objectives and direction of these changes. For instance, in many quarters in the developed countries, the demand for a new order is still regarded as a vain effort by the Third World to hijack the accumulated wealth of the rich nations. It is insufficiently recognized that the old order is not serving the interests of the developed countries either—whether in the field of energy, inflationary pressures, recessionary cycles, or an increasingly hostile environment for multinationals abroad. Nor is it fully appreciated that the increasing independence of the rich and poor nations and the graduation of many Third World countries from a state of dependency to greater self-reliance requires the evolution of new international understandings and arrangements in any case. On the other hand, the developing countries, in the initial excitement of the battle, have sometimes confused short-term concessions with structural changes. It has not been clear at times whether their demand is for a little more foreign assistance, or a few more trade preferences, or a quick dose of debt relief—or whether it is for the elimination of those biases within the international market system that prevent full and self-reliant development of their national economies. A clarification of objectives on both sides is vital for serious negotiations.

One of the key issues in this debate is the "biases" or "imperfections" of the international system. Developing countries contend that many market structures are biased against their interests. If this is not so, they argue, then why do they receive back only 10–15 per cent of the final price paid by consumers for their internationally traded commodities?

Why only a 4 per cent share in new international reserve creation over the last twenty-five years? Why so little participation in international economic decision making?

The developed countries argue that they are not manipulating the market system, but they conveniently fail to explain why anyone should expect international market structures to work any better than national market structures, which also bypass the interests of the poor. It is amazing that despite the central importance of this issue, there are so few objective studies available on it.[1] I believe that one of the major tasks for the international intellectual community is to document objectively how the existing international market structures actually work in each field—commodities, manufactures, services, credit, technology, decision making, etc.—and whether or not they really are working either efficiently or equitably. In the last analysis, nothing is more convincing than the facts.

2. Ends or Means?

Second, I have the uneasy impression that the North-South dialogue presently is far too concerned with means rather than with ends. There is a preoccupation at present with negotiations regarding commodity price stabilization, debt relief, an increase in official development assistance, and so on. It is not sufficiently clear in each case what objectives will be served by each of these proposals, what the total cost of the package will be, who will really benefit, and how priorities should be chosen from among the various contending proposals on the international agenda.

Is it possible to reverse the order of the present dialogue and to derive means from ultimate ends rather than the other way around? Until recently, ends and means were hopelessly mixed up in the national development debate as well. There was a fascination with GNP growth until it was recognized that growth was a necessary, but not a sufficient, condition for meeting the ultimate objectives of the society, particularly for alleviating poverty. In the national development dialogue, therefore, the focus has recently been shifting from intermediate means to the real objectives of development. A similar refocusing is needed in the international dialogue.

The challenge before the international community is to prepare a coherent international development strategy for the next few decades —a strategy that ensures accelerated growth in the developing countries, meeting of basic human needs as a priority item, elimination of the worst forms of absolute poverty before the end of the century, and orderly growth— uninterrupted by excessive inflation or unemployment—in the industrialized countries. It would then be necessary to identify the means needed to achieve these objectives. The next step would then be to cost out each of the means, add up the total bill, determine priorities in the total package, consider how benefits are distributed among developing nations, and suggest a politically feasible agenda for international action.

This is a formidable task, but I also believe that it is an essential one. Without such an overall framework, it is impossible to pass summary judgments on the current items on the North-South agenda. The relative priority of each item can best be clarified, to both sides, if it is related to an indicative global plan, aimed at accelerated and equitable growth.

3. Areas of Common Interest

My third proposal is that the international community should focus its primary attention on exploring areas of common interest between developing and developed countries. I suggest this for two reasons. For one thing, we are now entering that second phase of negotiations where practical compromises can only be reached by identifying the middle ground that unites the two sides rather than by concentrating on the extreme edges that divide them. And the second reason is that the area of interdependence between developing and developed countries is increasing very rapidly.

It is insufficiently recognized today that the rich nations have become more and more dependent on the poor nations, for their markets as well as for their supplies, and that this trend is going to accelerate dramatically over the next few decades. As an aside, let me add that it would be a real service if relevant studies were undertaken to find out how the situation has changed over the last few decades, and how the "reverse dependency" of the rich nations on the poor nations is likely to emerge as a major development in the next few decades. An objective analysis of current trends regarding interdependence will bring home to the rich nations the plain truth, generally ignored so far, that the Third World is going to become increasingly important in their economic and political affairs.

In redrawing the rules of the international order so that they reflect a fairer distribution of gains, some interests are bound to be hurt. But a system of rules generally accepted as fair is preferable, in the long run, to a system that leads to conflicts and confrontations. A world in which every nation exercises its power to attain its short-term national interests is bound to end up as a world in which we are all worse off—possibly substantially worse off. A world order based on equitable principles and worldwide solidarity, on the other hand, is one in which we all can prosper.

There are many areas of common interest where the long-term objectives of both developed and developing countries can be served by changes in present structures. Let me mention just a few.

Major rethinking must be done today regarding the existing geographical distribution of industries. The comparative advantage of the developed countries in some industries is being eroded by the rising cost of labor, energy, transportation, environmental pollution, urban congestion, and other economic and social factors. Some of the developed countries are already beginning to take a far-sighted view about future industrial patterns and to plan a systematic change in the location of industry. On the other hand, the developing countries need to specialize in industries where their comparative advantage is the greatest instead of establishing costly and un-economic capital-intensive industries each time they are frustrated in expanding their labor-intensive industries. In fact, both sides suffer at present through a misallocation of resources. And neither the objectives of world efficiency nor those of world equity are served by some of the present distribution of industries. We live in a strange Alice in Wonderland situation where each side plays by the wrong rules.

Take the related area of trade in manufactured goods. The developing countries could earn an additional $24 billion a year if all present tariff and non-tariff barriers were dismantled by the industrialized countries. It is not much of a gain for the developed countries to frustrate the exports of textiles and footwear from the developing world, only to see these countries establish uneconomic steel mills instead, which could have been set up more efficiently by the developed countries in the first instance. And it is counterproductive to insist that debts must be repaid as contractual obligations and then to deny the developing world the means with which to repay them. We are back again to Alice's Wonderland. More liberal trade can benefit both sides. Liberalization of trade barriers, rather than trade preferences, is the real issue.

The developed countries have shown a good deal of intolerance for even limited immigration of *unskilled* labor from the developing world, even while they have readily accommodated the flow of highly *skilled* manpower (the "brain drain"). It is remarkable indeed that, despite formidable obstacles, the limited immigration that has taken place has enabled the developing world to obtain about $10 billion a year of remittances from their own nationals. Here again, if we go back to the fundamentals of economics that we learned from Adam Smith, we see that a somewhat freer flow of labor across national frontiers is the best guarantee for increasing world efficiency as well as for equalizing economic opportunities.

Access to knowledge and technology is restricted at present by the establishment of patents. Greater sharing of this knowledge and technology can obviously accelerate worldwide development. Can we not think of international arrangements whereby these patents should become outmoded and invalid after the first few years in which the innovators can recover their investment costs and profits?

Let me take a final example: the current tension between multinationals and the developing world. Both sides have a lot to gain if they only extend their time horizon and search for a mutually beneficial "social contract." The multinationals should not seek to maximize profits over a short period of a few years, which can only result in indiscriminate exploitation and their final ejection. They should take a fairly long-term view and subject their profit maximization to the longer-term development needs of the country they are dealing with. Profit maximization is not a sin. It is the time horizon over which it is done that is critical. On the other side, the developing countries can legitimately insist on a predominant share in the exploitation of their own natural resources, but they must also provide a legally stable framework within which multinationals can operate without undue uncertainty. Some degree of accommodation on both sides is badly needed if the flow of foreign private investment is to continue. Let me recall the famous dictum of the great socialist economist, Joan Robinson, who said that there is only one thing worse than being exploited by a capitalist, and that is not to be exploited at all.

Let me also state quite frankly that it is going to be extremely difficult to establish any international agreement even in these areas of common interest. In each of these proposals, while there are long-term benefits to both sides, there are always short-term costs to some sections of the global community and a necessity for a painful adjustment to change. Normally, those who are hurt are concentrated and well-organized, for instance, industries seeking protection in the developed countries. Those who are to gain are sometimes unconscious of their own gains and are generally dispersed and disorganized: for instance, consumers in the developed countries and producers in the developing world. Since the ruling administrations are often worried about the next election rather than the next generation, it becomes very difficult for politicians to resist pressure groups and lobbyists who seek to advance their sectional interests at the cost of national and global interests.

All acts of great leadership like the Marshall Plan for the reconstruction of Europe or the New Deal in the United States—involved a certain cost to some sections of society though they led to tremendous long-term, mutual benefits. We have moved into an era where the need for long-term structural changes has greatly increased but where it has become increasingly difficult—particularly in the Western world—to find the necessary agents and allies for long-term change. One of the major challenges for the international community today is to devise new mechanisms to influence public opinion and to create a climate of ideas that facilitates long-term changes by preparing for them systematically in advance to ease the pains of transition.

4. Institutional Changes

This brings me to my fourth suggestion. I believe that the future relations between North and South must be viewed in a long-term historical perspective. Fundamental changes are inevitable. In fact, the evolution of international institutions and structures closely parallels that of national institutions, although over a considerably longer time interval. I am personally convinced that the evolution of three international institutions is inevitable in the long run: a system of international taxation, an international central bank, and a global planning system. This may take several decades, but I cannot conceive of a future world order where these three institutions will not take shape, in one form or another, in a global community that is becoming so very interdependent, and where the allocation of world resources and distribution of benefits of growth is going to continue to be a central issue.

These developments will not come simultaneously or without preparation. In fact, the three institutions that I just mentioned were already implicit in the proposals of restructuring the world order that Lord Keynes advanced in the 1940s in connection with the Bretton Woods Conference. It would be a major advance if we by now could accept that such an institutional framework is bound to emerge over the long run and start to identify some of the intermediate steps needed to smoothe the transitional period. One lesson we all have learned from history is that change is inevitable. A few decades from now, the only tribute we might be able to pay to human ingenuity and international maturity would be that such change was orderly and deliberate rather than chaotic and forced.

5. Crossing the Threshold

Finally, let me advance two specific action proposals for crossing the threshold to the second phase of the dialogue:

First, I believe that one of the foremost challenges for the international community today is how to meet the basic human needs of over a billion people living in absolute poverty in the developing world. As several eminent persons have already proposed, a specific plan of action should be prepared to meet these basic human needs substantially by the year 2000. This plan should identify the respective responsibilities of developing and developed countries in achieving such a goal. It should cover not only financial transfers of resources from the rich to the poor nations, but all other forms in which the restructuring of the world economic order would enable the developing countries to meet these needs in a self-reliant manner—by increasing the productivity of their poorest people, by adequate provision of relevant public services to them, and by a comprehensive social and economic transformation of their systems. Such a plan is not a technocratic proposition; it is basically a political proposition. It would perhaps require *a summit at the highest level to agree on the objectives and dimensions of a global enterprise to meet basic needs substantially by the year 2000*.

Second, we need to graduate from discussion forums to decision-making forums at some stage of the North-South dialogue. To go back to a historical precedent, the Bretton Woods Conference was convened in the 1940s to consider the reconstruction of Europe and to provide an institutional framework for an orderly development of the world. Today, the issues have become more complex and span a wide field, from food to energy to technology to multinationals and to the entire gamut of human development. I believe that when the intellectual groundwork has been laid, and when a suitable political climate has been prepared for restructuring the world order—when areas of common interest have been identified, and when specific plans of action have been prepared in a number of fields—it will be necessary to have *another conference such as Bretton Woods to re-examine and establish the basic premises for a new world order*. It is true that the agenda may have to be made fairly selective and manageable, that the entire international community must participate on the basis of some form of representation, that the issues may have to be elevated to the highest political level, and that this ambitious enterprise may require a series of action-oriented decision-making conferences rather than just one. But these are all matters of serious consideration.

As I said in the beginning, it is in the interest of all sides that we should by now graduate into the second phase of the North-South dialogue, where reasoned analysis replaces initial heated arguments. This is not going to be an easy transition. Nor can we always separate passion from reason. But if there is one contribution that reasoned analysis can make, I believe it lies in making the international community conscious that it is possible to combine the legitimate aspirations of the developing countries with the enlightened self-interests of the developed countries and that a new international economic order can work to the long-term benefit of all nations.

1. One of the notable studies in this connection is Gerald K. Helleiner's *World Market Imperfections and the Developing Countries*, Occasional Paper No. 11, NIEO Series (Washington, D.C.: Overseas Development Council, 1978).

34. Can the North Prosper Without Growth and Progress in the South?*

John W. Sewell

This chapter examines the proposition that the economic progress of developing countries now affects the economic performance of industrialized countries to a greater degree than at any time in the past and that this impact will continue to grow. The impact of the developing countries on the industrialized countries can be either positive or negative. Prosperous economic partners will reinforce U.S. growth and progress; conversely, the economic problems of others are likely to have an adverse effect on the well-being of the United States.

The United States participates in a world economy that is still dominated by the industrialized nations, but the activities of new economic actors, particularly the developing countries, are already measurable and will be of increasing importance to the well-being of the U.S. economy over the next two decades. The image of all the developing countries as needy recipients of foreign assistance has been overtaken by events as the impact of the developing countries collectively (and in some cases individually) on the international economy has become more significant. The relationship between rich and poor countries now is increasingly commercial. While this does not mean that economic relations with the South have become more important to the developed nations than their own domestic economic transactions or their economic relations

with one another, it does have profound implications for a range of policy choices to be made by the United States and other developed nations in the coming years.

This chapter concentrates on the mutual benefits to be gained from the implementation of policies aimed at supporting progress in the developing countries. The analysis presented here is still tentative and needs to be extended and refined. By highlighting some of the major aspects of the growing eonomic stake of the United States and other industrial countries in the development of the Third World, this chapter seeks (a) to prompt additional analysis by economists and foreign policy specialists of how the existing international economic order can be redesigned to work more efficiently and more beneficially for both the industrial and the developing countries, (b) to increase public understanding and discussion of these key questions, and (c) to stimulate concrete policy proposals by governments and private institutions.

A NEW PERCEPTION OF GLOBAL INTERDEPENDENCE

International "interdependence" is hardly a new notion. Almost two hundred years ago, Adam Smith and David Ricardo analyzed the gains to be made from international trade, and the development of the United States itself was largely funded by capital from foreign banks and governments.

In this century, the economic links among industrial countries have grown rapidly, particularly in the post-World War II period, during which initial dependence on the United States has evolved into a true interdependence among *developed* countries. The linkages be-

* From Martin M. McLaughlin (ed.), *The United States and World Development: Agenda 1979.* Published for the Overseas Development Council by Praeger, New York, 1979, pp. 45–63, 71–76.

Note: This chapter was prepared with the assistance of Dorothy K. Seavey, ODC Staff Associate, and John Mathieson, ODC Fellow.

tween the economies of the United States, the European countries, and Japan—and the fact that the achievement of each of these countries' domestic economic objectives requires a large degree of international cooperation—are well recognized today. But the perception that the economies of the North and the South are also more closely integrated than at any time in the past has not yet permeated the awareness or decision making of most policymakers and planners. While it is widely agreed that the developing countries' prospects for improved market access, higher aid levels, and increased development financing are not good without continued growth in the developed countries, little analysis has been devoted to the possibility that continued economic growth in the industrialized world may itself be strongly affected by economic progress or stagnation in the developing world as well as by the quality and degree of North-South cooperation. Far more attention needs to be paid to the growing likelihood that, over the next two decades, the growth and progress of the poor countries will have an impact on economic growth and employment levels in the industrialized countries—both through stimulating demand for the products of the North and through dampening inflationary pressures that constrain measures to stimulate growth in the North.

Major economic problems currently confront national policymakers in the developed and developing countries. Industrial countries are struggling to stimulate growth and regain the high employment and low inflation rates of the last decade. Middle-income countries are attempting to maintain the remarkable growth patterns they achieved during the 1960s and early 1970s in the hope of meeting the needs of their populations over the next several decades. The low-income countries are trying to improve their development prospects and the outlook for their poor majorities. Several decades ago these problems would have been viewed as largely domestic concerns. Now there is a wide consensus that they are international in scope and that they are much more interrelated than in the past.

What is the long-run outlook for world growth and income levels? Table 1 illustrates the economic prospects of three sets of countries for the year 2000 under two sets of assumptions about growth rates.

The higher figures for the year 1985 are based on World Bank projections for the 1975–1985 period. The annual per capita growth rate forecasts for this period are 2.7 percent for the low-income countries, 3.3 percent for the middle-income countries, and 3.5 percent for the developed countries. The lower figures, which project growth rates that are

TABLE 1. Per Capita Income Prospects Under Various Growth Rate Assumptions, by Groups of Countries (constant 1975 $)

	1950	1975	1985[1]	2000[2]
Low-Income Countries	104	150	171–195	220–327
Middle-Income Countries	454	957	1,128–1,327	1,453–2,223
Developed Countries	2,614	5,883	7,004–8,316	9,019–13,932

[1] The higher figures are World Bank projections based on 1975–1985 annual per capita growth rates of 2.7 percent for the low-income countries, 3.3 percent for the middle-income countries, and 3.5 percent for the developed countries. The lower figures are ODC estimates based on growth rates only half that high.

[2] The higher figures assume a 3.5 percent annual growth rate for all countries between 1985 and 2000. The lower figures assume a 1.7 percent annual growth rate between 1985 and 2000. Both sets of figures are ODC estimates.

only half as high, are presented mainly to show what might happen if growth performance were to fall short of current expectations.

The differences between the high and low projections for 1985 are significant enough, but what might the figures look like in the year 2000? If the per capita growth rate for all countries from 1985 to 2000 were 3.5 percent, which is the recent historic growth rate of the industrial countries, as well as the internationally set target rate for per capita growth in the low- and middle-income countries for the U.N. Second Development Decade of the 1970s, per capita income could amount to nearly $14,000 for developed countries and to $327 for low-income countries by the year 2000. However, if the lower growth rates for each group of countries were to prevail through 1985 and a 1.7 per cent annual growth rate were to prevail in all countries thereafter, then per capita income in the year 2000 would be only $9,019 (or about $5,000 lower) for developed countries and only $220 (or over $100 lower) for the low-income countries.

Projections of outcomes two decades ahead are of course highly conjectural and should be viewed as possibilities rather than predictions. Growth rates might also exceed those which generated the higher per capita income levels suggested by Table 1; on the other hand, in the absence of major changes in global economic trends and policies, the lower projections for per capita income in Table 1 would become increasingly likely. If the lower estimates are at all accurate, then the stake of both developed and developing nations in improved cooperation is very high. This chapter asserts that the economic prospects of the developed and the developing worlds are in fact linked and that attention must now be paid to the possibility that, for the balance of this century, improved cooperation between the North and South could mean the difference between global progress and prosperity on the one hand, and an uncertain and uncomfortable future for the rich countries and in-

creasingly dismal prospects for the developing world on the other. . . .

THE GROWING ROLE OF DEVELOPING COUNTRIES

The developing countries are playing an increasingly stronger role in the international economy. The oil-exporting states offer the most obvious example, but a number of other developing countries are also exerting a stronger influence on other parts of the international economic system. The developing countries produce many of the minerals as well as other raw materials necessary to support high standards of living in the industrial world. They constitute large and growing markets for goods made in industrial countries. Since 1970, for example, the non-OPEC developing countries have more than doubled their imports. In 1977 they purchased $176 billion of world imports, or 16 percent of the world's total; the industrial countries supplied 60 percent of these imports.[1] The developing countries also manufacture and export growing amounts of lower-cost consumer goods to the developed world and offer important investment opportunities for multinational corporations. In addition, the developing countries now are playing a considerable role in international finance, as private banks derive higher proportions of their earnings from international operations.

In the political arena, the developing countries also are playing an increasingly important role in a number of international forums. Since 1974, these countries have been pursuing a series of demands for changes in the economic and political systems created after World War II. Their aim is the creation of a "new international economic order" in which they have a fairer share both in decision making and in the benefits that flow from that order. The result, to date, has been a stalemate, with neither North nor South achieving what it sees as a satisfactory result from the current negotiations. However, the fact that the industrial countries have felt it is important enough to participate in such discussions in itself provides evidence of the growing power of the developing countries to determine at least part of the agenda for international negotiations.

The increased impact of the developing countries is the natural result of their unprecedented economic growth in the postwar period, as well as of the fact that many areas previously under colonial rule are now independent states. The process of international economic development has already reached a point where a substantial number of developing countries represent new frontiers of economic growth. Despite the widespread poverty at their base, their economic role is substantial.

The assertion that developing-country growth can directly affect developed-country well-being is supported by a report prepared for the U.N. Conference on Trade and Development by economists at the University of Pennsylvania.[2] This report concludes that a 3 percent increase in the growth rates of the non-oil-exporting developing countries could result in an annual increase of 1 percent in the growth rates of the OECD countries. That 1 percent increase would, for the industrialized countries, amount to the equivalent of about $45 billion, which in turn would result in a large increase in jobs. The secondary gains might be even higher. These findings are based on econometric modeling and are not definitive, but they do indicate that the developing countries are now important to the economic well-being of the developed countries. This has been borne out by a study of the actual effects of the actions of the developing countries on the industrial economies during the 1974–75 recession. The fact that the developing countries continued to finance a high level of imports from the industrial countries by borrowing funds from private and official sources and drawing down reserves had "a perceptible impact on business trends in the developed countries. Their balance of payments deficit has sustained demand as much as, say, a vigorous German demand expansion."[3]

The issues of trade, commodities, debt and development financing, food, energy, and population discussed below illustrate areas where developments in the South have a direct economic impact on the North. Most of the discussion in the sections that follow is cast in terms of the U.S. relationship with the Third World. The arguments, however, are also applicable to other developed countries and their concerns. Particular issues may have greater or lesser importance for individual countries, but the principle that the economic and political well-being of the developed world will be affected to a growing degree by progress in the developing countries toward meeting their own development goals holds for all.

MEDIUM-TERM GAINS FROM MUTUALLY BENEFICIAL ECONOMIC RELATIONSHIPS

Over the next decade, the value to the industrial countries of progress in the developing countries is particularly marked in connection with the problems of inflation and unemployment, slower growth of trade, rising protectionism, fluctuating prices and supplies of commodities, and growing debt and financing problems. The causes of and solutions to these problems are highly interrelated. Trade, commodities, and debt and development financing are all areas in which economic gains can be realized by the North and South through mutually beneficial changes in existing arrangements and institutions. The industrial countries must ensure that a growing amount of financial resources from a *variety* of sources is available to the developing countries. Particularly for the middle-income countries, trade measures and stable commodity prices will be important in providing these resources—as will continued access to credit from a number of private and governmental sources. Equally important, especially for the poorest developing countries, will be continued support from the international financial institutions and increases in both bilateral and multilateral concessional development assistance to support economic and social development.

Trade. The arguments stressing the direct developed-country interest in Third World development usually focus first on trade. Given an appropriate mix of cooperative policies, the developing countries can, over the next decade, offer growing markets for exports from the North (thereby creating jobs in export industries), act increasingly as suppliers of low-cost consumer goods, and reduce inflationary pressures that restrict national growth policies. These benefits will continue to increase over the long run.

American exports of goods and services now equal nearly 10 percent of U.S. GNP (as compared with 5 percent in 1960); until the onset of the current global recession, they had been growing rapidly. Exports are now about equal to business fixed investment and are 2.5 times the amount spent on residential construction, both of which are considered to be important indicators of the health of the American economy. Exports are estimated to account for one of every eight jobs in the manufacturing sector and for the production of one third of the farm acreage in the United States.

While the figures noted above refer to overall U.S. trade, a significant portion of that trade is with developing countries. In 1977, American merchandise exports to the non-OPEC developing countries were about 27 percent of total U.S. exports—more than were purchased by the European Community, Eastern Europe, the Soviet Union, and China combined. Twenty-five percent of U.S. imports came from these same developing countries. Since U.S. export growth depends on the ability of purchasers to buy goods, de-

velopment in the poor countries has direct economic importance for the United States.

The developing countries have increased their exports of manufactured products at a remarkable rate over the past fifteen years. Their exports of manufactured goods rose from $3.8 billion in 1960 to $35.3 billion in 1975, or nearly tenfold. U.S. imports of manufactured goods from non-OPEC developing countries have exhibited a similar pattern, increasing from $1.7 billion in 1965 to $18.2 billion in 1977.

Lower developed-country trade barriers clearly improve the economic situation of the developing countries and are essential to their progress in the future. Although many in the North now feel threatened by increased imports of manufactures from the developing countries and are pressing for protectionist measures, Table 2 shows that the developing countries' exports of *manufactured* goods have not been the overall cause of the current U.S. trade deficit (or of the loss of jobs within the United States on an overall basis), even though individual industries may have been hit particularly hard by import competition. The United States had a surplus of over $3 billion in 1977 in its trade in manufactured goods with the non-OPEC developing countries (and Japan and the European Community had even larger favorable balances).

Table 2 underscores the importance of the developing countries as markets for the exports of the United States (as well as of other industrial countries). As indicated earlier, more American goods and services are purchased by the developing countries than by many countries and areas that traditionally have been among the major markets for American goods. In fact, for most of the recent past, American exports to developing countries grew at a faster rate than its exports to developed countries. In the period 1970 to 1975, U.S. exports to non-OPEC developing countries grew at an average annual rate of nearly 21 percent, compared with an average annual rate of growth of under 17 percent in

TABLE 2. U.S. Manufactures Trade Balance with Non-OPEC Developing Market Economies, 1965, 1970, 1975, 1977 ($ millions)

	Manufactures Exports	Manufactures Imports	Manufactures Balance	Overall Balance[1]
1965	5,271	1,729	+ 3,542	+2,706
1970	8,140	3,813	+ 4,327	+2,946
1975	21,215	10,464	+10,750	+7,954
1977	21,548	18,205	+ 3,343	−4,290

[1] These figures include trade in primary commodities, in which the United States historically has recorded deficits vis-à-vis non-OPEC developing countries. They also include commodities not classified according to kind.

Source: Based on data from U.S. Department of Commerce, *Highlights of U.S. Export and Import Trade*, Document No. FT 990, December 1977, Table E–6 and 1–78, and microfilm series EM 450 and JM 135, December 1977.

U.S. exports to the developed countries over the same period. These exports not only benefited firms in the export sector but also provided jobs for many Americans. There is much potential for continued growth in U.S. exports, since demand in the developing countries is far from satiated and indeed could expand rapidly as these countries advance economically. As long as the purchasing power of the developing countries is at least maintained (and preferably expanded), trade between the North and the South is likely to increase at a rapid rate.

However, trade with the developing countries is a two-way street. Unless the developing countries can export to the United States and the other industrial countries, they will not be able to earn the foreign exchange that will in turn allow them to purchase the goods and commodities produced in the industrial countries (or to repay their growing debts, as will be discussed below). The direct interrelationship between the development progress of the developing countries and their ability to purchase goods produced in the developed countries—and ultimately the impact of this demand on jobs and economic growth in the industrial world—is rather dramatically evidenced by trends since 1975. The high rate of growth of U.S. exports to developing countries declined sharply during 1976 and 1977. In fact, while U.S. exports to developed coun-

tries grew by 7 percent, U.S. exports to non-OPEC developing countries virtually remained stagnant between 1975 and 1977. This decrease is particularly striking in view of the fact that in the immediately preceding years, exports to developing countries had grown at a faster rate than exports to developed countries. Indeed, U.S. exports to some of the middle-income developing countries that until recently were among the major markets for U.S. products seem to be slowing down even more dramatically, a development that is now contributing to the trade deficit of the United States. For instance, after several years of rapid growth, American exports to Brazil decreased from over $3 billion in 1975 to less than $2.5 billion in 1977—a decline of nearly 17 percent. Similarly, U.S. exports to Mexico (the United States' fourth largest export market) dropped from $5.1 billion in 1975 to $4.8 billion in 1977, a decline of almost 6 percent. The result in the manufacturing sector is underlined by the shrinkage between 1975 and 1977 in the favorable trade balance shown in Table 2

The decrease in non-OPEC developing-country imports from the United States is one characteristic of a period in which world trade has been growing very slowly due to the recession in the industrial countries. The developing countries have had to cut back their imports from industrial countries because of the worldwide inflation that has drastically increased the prices they have to pay for imported energy, food, and manufactured goods.[4] Reductions in developing-country purchases of industrial-country goods contribute to stagnation in the industrial countries, which in turn leads to further protectionist pressures and decreased market access and demand for the exports of developing countries.

The ability of the developing countries to purchase the goods produced by the industrial countries thus has an important impact on the economic progress of both groups of countries. Cutting off the access of the developing countries to developed-country markets ultimately may be self-defeating, therefore, since it ignores the benefits that *developed* countries will derive from liberalized trade. In a recent Brookings Institution study, William Cline suggests that the overall welfare gains from trade liberalization with all countries could be about five times as large as the direct trade benefits normally cited by economists. The present discounted value of the total welfare benefits that could result from tariff cuts of 60 percent, for instance, is approximately $170 billion, of which $50 billion would accrue to the United States.[5] Thus there are important indirect economic benefits to be realized from trade liberalization: (a) larger markets encourage greater economies of scale, (b) increased exports stimulate investment and encourage faster growth rates, (c) import competition encourages cost-cutting technological change, which increases the overall efficiency of the economy, and (d) domestic price inflation is inhibited by greater competition from abroad.

The Brookings Institution study also indicates that a worldwide reduction in existing tariffs of 60 percent could lower the consumer price index in the United States by approximately 0.23 percent. This is not a negligible amount, given the current high level of concern in this country about any increase in prices. The secondary effects, moreover, would be much larger. The same study concludes that the welfare gains to the United States from the anti-inflationary impact of such a tariff cut alone (in the form of prevented unemployment) could translate into an increase in GNP of about 1 percent.[6]

Lower-priced imports from the developing countries have particular and direct importance for consumers in the developed countries because of their impact on retail prices. Imports usually provide items at the bottom of the price range of any particular line of merchandise and yet have a high profit margin for retailers. Without such goods, retailers would tend to increase their prices on domestically produced items in order to maintain profit margins. Richard Anderson, president of a large American retail shoe chain, the Kinney Shoe Corporation, recently indicated that prices of shoes in that chain's stores might increase by 40 percent if it could purchase only domestically produced shoes.[7] A recent World Bank report points out that wholesale prices for apparel and consumer electronics—two product categories in which a large portion of U.S. imports comes from the developing countries—rose much more slowly than those of other goods: "The wholesale prices of apparel rose by only 26 percent in the United States during 1970–76, while other wholesale prices rose by 66 percent. Over the same period, prices of consumer electronics fell by 2.5 percent."[8]

Lower-priced imports also reduce inflation in importing countries by providing direct competition for domestic producers and thus stimulating increased domestic efficiency. On the basis of the counter-inflationary impact of rapidly growing trade among the industrial countries in the 1960s, the McCracken Committee concluded that an expansion of imports from developing countries could "make a useful contribution to stimulating growth and holding inflation in check."

In the short run, trade liberalization would also have a small, positive *direct* effect on employment in the United States, since more jobs would be gained from the resulting increased employment in the export sector than would be lost as a result of increased imports. Furthermore, over the long run, the dynamic effects of trade liberalization would eventually result in a much greater expansion of employment as freer trade stimulated economic growth. This conclusion runs counter to the widespread belief among the public—and labor—that trade liberalization only destroys jobs. The Brookings study indicates the opposite. Simulating the effects of different tariff-cutting formulas, that analysis shows that under the current working formula of the Tokyo Round—the "Swiss" formula, which provides for an average tariff cut of 44 percent—a balance of 30,000 U.S. jobs would be created and U.S. exports would increase by about $3 billion. (These gains come from expanded trade with all countries; the gains specifically attributable to trade with the developing countries would be less.)

The fact that some jobs *will* be lost while others are created underlines the importance of adjustment programs, particularly for hard-hit industries such as footwear and leather. The Cline study estimates that the labor adjustment costs would range up to $611 million annually for the United States. For both political and moral reasons, trade liberalization should not be an area where the overall gains for the many are paid for by a few individuals, unions, firms, and regions. But traditional programs of adjustment assistance, which have directed benefits to individual workers and firms already seriously affected by imports no longer will be sufficient for the kinds of shifts in industrial production that will be necessary in the future if the developed countries are to accommodate to and benefit from the development of the developing countries. Instead, some form of *anticipatory* planning is needed to deal with economic dislocation. An International Labour Organisation study suggests that such policies should have two elements: (1) the encouragement of technological innovation in those industries that can adapt to changing conditions,

and (2) dynamic policies to transfer capital and labor from sectors that cannot make such transitions to those that can compete internationally.[9] Such policies are much more easily undertaken in a period of economic growth and high employment than during a recession. This fact, in turn, underlines the interrelated nature of these problems. Developing-country growth can act as a stimulus to industrial-country progress, but only if the shifts necessary to accommodate increased developing-country exports are undertaken.

Those who want to restrict the growth in trade between the industrial and developing countries ignore the possibility that tremendous changes are taking place in the patterns of world production as well as trade. A recent World Bank report concludes:

The international pattern of comparative advantage is changing rapidly, and developing countries are becoming suppliers of a growing range of manufactures.... Simultaneously, output is stagnating and employment is declining in corresponding sectors in the industrialized countries. This is the process which economic history and theory would lead one to expect. But it is occurring at an unprecedented speed; not surprisingly this vast restructuring of the world economy is leading to frictions and defensive responses. The potential for a considerable expansion of international specialization is evident, although the rate at which the opportunities are taken will largely be determined by the economic policies both of the industrialized countries and of the newly industrializing ones.[10]

If this conclusion is correct, the industrial countries should make the shifts necessary to adjust to growing developing-country exports not only to maintain demand for their own exports and to decrease inflation but also to maintain the long-run competitiveness of their economic positions. As Robert Baldwin has argued persuasively, "Unless the industrialized countries are willing to shift resources from sectors where they lose their comparative advantage into new lines of comparative efficiency, it will become more and more difficult not only to maintain adequate growth rates, but their economies may be plagued by chronic unemployment and inflation."[11]

Commodities. The prices of various commodities and raw materials have been of great concern to the rich countries since the 1950s, particularly since the price shocks of the early 1970s. For the poor countries, of course, they have been important for a considerably longer period. These countries have objected for many years to the prices they receive for their raw materials in comparison to the prices they pay for the manufactured goods they import from the industrialized countries. For the developed countries, the main recent issues are access to supplies of imported raw materials and the impact of widely fluctuating raw material prices on inflation and employment within their own economies. In addition, both rich and poor countries are concerned about timely investments in the new sources of production that both groups of countries will need in the years ahead.

The concern among industrial-country leaders about sufficiency of supply is well founded. The United States, for instance, is dependent on the outside world for over half its consumption of materials such as columbium, manganese, cobalt, platinum, chromium, aluminum, tin, fluorspar, nickel, mercury, zinc, and tungsten. Other industrial countries have an even higher degree of dependence. Developing countries are important suppliers of many of these raw materials.

Both sides have come to understand that effective commodity agreements could be of substantial benefit to industrial as well as developing countries. If properly designed, price stabilization agreements could both prevent excessive fluctuations in prices and provide the certainty that would stimulate increased investment and exploration for new sources of raw materials (as well as expanded exploitation of existing sources). Developed-country officials now acknowledge that while increases in commodity prices tend to produce an over-

all increase in prices, subsequent declines in commodity prices are not fully reflected (for a variety of reasons) in the final prices of finished products. This "ratchet effect" means that although prices usually rise, they rarely decline. As a result, inflation becomes institutionalized. Developed countries are also concerned about commodity prices because (a) rapidly rising commodity prices can result in substantial losses in output and employment, and (b) wide fluctuations in commodity prices often result in a lack of investment in new capacity at both the primary and production stages. Without such investment, supplies become inadequate to meet the demand from resumed growth in subsequent years, again pushing prices higher.

Two recent ODC studies quantify the benefits that might flow from commodity price stabilization. Jere Behrman has simulated what would have happened if a group of eight "core" commodities (coffee, cocoa, tea, rubber, jute, sisal, copper, and tin) and five other products (wheat, rice, wool, bauxite, and iron ore) had been covered by price stabilization agreements and buffer stocking arrangements during the period 1963 to 1972.[12] This study concludes that developing-country revenues would have risen by about $5 billion in present discounted value for the entire decade. Economic gains to the United States alone— in the form of unemployment prevented and GNP loss avoided—that would have resulted from the reduction of inflationary pressures would have amounted to $15 billion over the decade. In addition, both the developing and developed countries would have benefited from reduced planning uncertainties, higher rates of investment for producers because of the reduction of risk, and larger supplies for consumers attributable to increased investment.

Another quantitative study, directed by Lance Taylor, concludes that the net welfare gain for all countries over a twenty-year period from a 15-million-ton wheat buffer stock, including both foreign trade and domestic effects, would amount to $2.5 billion.[13] This modest figure does not take into account any macroeconomic output gains that might be achieved because of reduced difficulties in managing inflation and the resulting increase in employment. For instance, a global food reserve could avoid repetition of the experience of 1973–74, when a 3 percent shortfall in grain production led to more than a 300 percent rise in grain prices—an increase that contributed importantly to worldwide inflation.

The lead time required to increase the production of many raw materials is steadily lengthening; unless steps are taken in the near future to increase investment in these industries, there are likely to be sharp price rises in the 1980s. The World Bank estimates that gross investment in the developing countries in nine major non-fuel minerals (bauxite, copper, iron ore, nickel, lead, manganese ore, phosphate rock, tin, and zinc) will have to total $95 billion between 1976 and 1986 to meet relatively moderate growth in world demand.[14] Unfortunately, exploration for minerals in the developing countries has declined in recent years in the face of increased investment uncertainties and political risks. This situation places a premium not only on buffer stock agreements but also on new arrangements that provide greater assurance against increased political uncertainties.

Development Financing and Debt. If growth and demand in the developing countries are limited by financial constraints, many of the positive effects of the North's relations with the South will be diminished. The industrial countries thus have an interest in ensuring that sufficient capital and credit are available to the developing countries to finance effective development efforts and to service their public and private debt.

Prior to 1973, the amount of debt owed by the developing countries was not a matter of general concern—especially since the exports of many of the borrowing countries were

growing at a rapid rate. After the price increases of the early 1970s, however, the situation changed rapidly as developing countries borrowed increasing amounts of resources to maintain their development progress and as banks had to recycle the OPEC surpluses.

The external public debt (including undisbursed debt) owed by the non-OPEC developing countries grew by 54 percent between 1972 and 1976, reaching an estimated level of nearly $166 billion by the end of 1976. Private debt not guaranteed by developing-country governments could add as much as another $25–$30 billion to this amount, bringing the total debt owed by the non-oil-exporting developing countries to almost $200 billion. This debt burden falls unevenly on various countries; most of it, particularly that owed to private banks, is held by the middle-income developing countries. For some countries, service payments already amount to more than 20 percent of their export earnings. In contrast, the poorest countries together owe a smaller amount, mainly the repayment of past development assistance loans.

The costs to the industrialized economies of a series of defaults (which now seem unlikely) by major developing-country borrowers cannot be accurately calculated. Indeed, estimates vary widely. However one calculates the particular prospects, though, it is clear that the continued financial well-being of the developing countries will be an important factor in the stability of the international financial system and thus of prime importance to the United States and other industrial economies. The private banking sector has an important stake in the financial well-being of many developing countries; indeed, the role of private banks in recycling the funds of oil-producing countries was essentially a creative response to a difficult situation. Although the extent of the commercial banks' exposure in the developing world has been exaggerated (in fact, private banks have a better repayment record on their loans to developing countries than on their domestic loans), the shock—

psychological and economic—that would result from default by a major developing country, due to an inability to service past loans or
to qualify for additional credits, would be considerable. Therefore all parties have an interest in maintaining the ability of the developing countries to service past loans and to
continue to borrow in order to regain and/or
maintain their development momentum. . . .

CAN THE SOUTH BECOME PART OF THE "ENGINE OF GROWTH" FOR THE NORTH?

The key assertion of this analysis is that the
North has a substantial economic stake in the
present and future prosperity of the South and
that there are fruitful areas for cooperation
that can be mutually beneficial. If these preliminary observations are correct, a continuation of present policies aimed at marginal
changes in existing institutions and approaches
no longer will be adequate if the world's economic and political systems are to work
efficiently and equitably for the rich countries,
let alone for the poor. Serious attention needs
to be given to assuring that the developing
countries become an integral part of the "engine" of future world economic growth, just
as the establishment after World War II of the
Bretton Woods system of financial institutions
and the planned recovery of the European
countries became the "engine" of the unprecedented global economic progress that took
place in the 1950s and 1960s.

On the basis of the evidence presented in
this paper, the choice between the continuation of present global policies and a more far-
reaching effort to make policies and institutions congruent with the needs of the world
for the next twenty-five years might mean a
difference in rates of economic growth of as
much as 1 or 2 percent annually in some of the
developed countries. (In the case of the developed countries, a difference between an
annual per capita GNP growth rate of 1.7 percent and 3.5 percent over the remaining years

of this century would result in a per capita income by the year 2000 that was nearly $5,000
higher.) Such a stepped-up effort could mean
a development pattern in the United States
and the other industrial countries that more
closely resembled the relatively low inflation
and high employment of the 1960s in contrast
to constantly recurring periods of high inflation and high unemployment of the mid-
1970s.

Stressing the importance of U.S. international economic policy toward the developing
countries and the benefits that could be derived from more far-reaching policy changes
does not imply that domestic economic policies in the industrial countries are not important or that the costs of adjusting to a changed
international economic environment will be
marginal. The coordination of fiscal and
monetary policies in the OECD countries in
order to revive economic growth, control and
reduce inflation, and correct current-account
imbalances and trade deficits are critical
domestic economic goals that will also benefit
the developing countries. It will be very difficult, however, for the industrial countries to
achieve these objectives unless an appropriate
international economic environment exists.
The United States, for example, cannot continue to grow if the rest of the world is stagnant. In short, healthy economic conditions in
the developing countries will support healthy
economic conditions in the industrial countries.

Increasing prosperity and world economic
growth will bring costs and adjustments as
well as benefits. The current economic situation in the United States, for example, height-
ens considerably the initial concerns of many
Americans about the apparent economic, political, and social costs of responding to the
proposals of the South for a new international
economic order. There is a genuine—and justified—feeling that domestic problems should
have top priority. As a result, it is extremely
difficult to persuade the American public that
North-South reforms should be undertaken

at a time when domestic conditions are so unsatisfactory.

However, there are no easy solutions to global problems that will not entail short-term costs to some sectors. Increasing developing-country access to markets in the developed countries will affect jobs and firms in certain industries. The financing needed by the developing countries to service their debts and to maintain development programs entails budgetary costs, as do any additional capital transfers to the developing countries in the form of aid or loans. While these and other costs will have to be borne, they should be viewed as investments in the future. Political vision and will are required to establish the basis for long-term progress while at the same time addressing short-term costs.

Leaders in both the North and the South urgently need to develop a new program of global cooperation that gives priority to broad reforms of existing international structures and policies in order to increase both the efficiency and equity of the existing international economic order and to enable the South to help fuel world economic growth. Even discussing such a program, let alone negotiating and implementing it, will be difficult until perceptions about the costs of not cooperating become clear to leaders in the rich and poor countries.

If the North-South dialogue is to move beyond its current stalemate, there must be general agreement on a set of perceptions about the world, among them a recognition of the fundamental changes in the world economy that have overtaken the institutions and policies designed for the world of the 1950s, awareness of the need to devise new mechanisms for managing the global economy, acceptance of the fact that the industrial countries as well as the developing countries require a new international economic order, and finally a sense of urgency and vision about the very different world of the 1980s and beyond that is likely to confront policy-makers.

The "mutual gains" thesis of this chapter has important implications for the perceptions of both the developed and developing countries. The industrial countries must come to grips with the fact that the old international economic order is not working well for them and that the nations of the South already are important to the North's own progress and well-being, and will become increasingly so in the future. Trade liberalization, commodity price stabilization, and concessional resource transfers are in the interest of the industrial countries as well as the developing countries. For their part, the developing countries should take into account the legitimate concerns of the industrial countries when formulating their proposals. This was not done, for example, when the developing countries refused to discuss the global energy supply in the context of the North-South dialogue.

Progress toward a new international order will not necessarily come smoothly and harmoniously. The choices are not easy, and one should not underestimate the possible adjustments and costs in the short run within and among the developed countries. However, the costs of not pursuing a mutually beneficial world order will be high. The world economy has changed rapidly in the last decade, and adjustment is required by the industrial and developing countries alike.

The long-run benefits of accommodating to the changed global circumstances could be great. An expanded cooperative effort that gave priority to reforming the world's economic system and to addressing essential human needs could eventually make the world more efficient, equitable, and just. There is no doubt that the world's greatest reservoir of economic potential is the still underdeveloped and underutilized human and physical resources of the developing countries. By raising the purchasing power of the people of these countries, releasing new resources, and developing new markets for both the poor and rich countries, higher levels of economic activity can be created within and between all countries. In effect, the developing countries of the South could over the next two decades become an important part of the engine of growth and resumed progress of the world.

POLICY IMPLICATIONS

The key conclusion of the argument presented here—that the industrial economies can gain from developing-country progress—suggests four general objectives, the attainment of each of which in turn implies the need for actions in several areas of policy implementation. (Due to the interrelated nature of the objectives, many of the general policy initiatives enumerated below would meet more than one objective.)

I. *The industrial countries should increase efforts to enhance economic progress in the developing countries. The North has a growing economic stake in the progress of the South, and mutual benefits imply mutual resposibilities.* Five sets of Northern policy initiatives fall under this broad objective:

1. Policies to expand the access of the developing countries to developed-country markets through reductions in tariff and non-tariff barriers. The outcome of the current "Tokyo Round" of trade negotiations will be particularly important in this regard.
2. Policies to improve developing-country access to international capital and credit markets. The immediate need is to increase the capacity of both the World Bank and the International Monetary Fund to supply resources to the developing countries. In addition, more imaginative methods should be developed to link public and private institutions in co-financing arrangements.
3. Policies to increase productive investment in developing countries concentrating on increased production of food, energy, and raw materials. In each case, significant underutilized capacity and resources exist in the developing countries.

4. Policies to meet the basic needs of the world's poorest people, who require adequate nutrition, health services, basic education, and, above all, employment and a chance to earn a decent living. A serious commitment on the part of the North to increase concessional transfers will be necessary if there are to be increased commitments by developing-country governments to meeting basic human needs. Exploration of forms of international taxation or "automatic" transfers of resources will be important in this regard.
5. Policies to increase the stability of the revenues from raw material exports earned by developing countries.

II. *The industrial countries should take steps to increase the benefits and minimize the costs of their economic and commercial relations with the developing countries.* A number of new policy initiatives are needed in this area:

1. Policies to coordinate and plan for structural trade adjustments over the longer term and to improve already existing adjustment assistance programs dramatically in order to accommodate *in advance* to economic dislocation stemming from trade with the developing countries.
2. Policies to improve the export orientation of both private firms and government in the United States. If the United States is to respond to a more competitive international environment, its export performance must be considerably better than in the past. Such a policy must be implemented in a way that avoids the use of export subsidies and should take the development goals of the importing countries into account.
3. Policies aimed at stabilizing commodity prices in order to lessen the impact that price fluctuations have within the industrialized countries. The negotiation of in-

dividual commodity agreements and of the Common Fund should be pursued.

4. Policies to increase and publicize the gains to consumers resulting from the availability of imported consumer goods. Few Americans realize the favorable impact that these goods have on consumer prices and inflation in this country.

III. *The developing countries, without jeopardizing their own progress, should also consider the economic needs and problems of the North.* The actions of developing countries have an increasing impact on other countries, both developed and developing, and the policymakers of the latter also need to accept the premise that mutual benefits imply mutual responsibilities. Several policy recommendations flow from this assertion:

1. Leaders of the more economically advanced developing countries should assume their share of the responsibility for increasing the efficiency and equity of the international economic system by opening up their own markets to both rich and poor countries and by extending assistance and preferences to poorer developing countries. Several advanced developing countries are reaching a threshold similar to that of Japan in the 1950s. They are now in a position to make reciprocal concessions in trade negotiations and to lower their often high levels of protectionism. They should now assume full responsibility as members of the international system.

2. The main exporting developing countries need to weigh carefully the impact of the pace of change in their policies on rich-country importers. Too rapid an expansion of exports often leads to a backlash detrimental to both sides. Rich and poor countries should jointly search out ways to gradually increase nondisruptive market access for the exports of manufactures from developing countries.

3. Policy proposals aimed at the North should include suggestions for relationships that benefit both sides. The South needs to acknowledge that the new international economic order that eventually emerges from these negotiations should reflect the concerns of the North as well as the South and should include benefits for developed as well as developing countries.

4. Policies to expand both (a) domestic markets and (b) trade cooperation *among* developing countries will be particularly important. There is a potential limit on the rate at which Northern economies can absorb increased developing-country exports. Increasing trade among developing countries will have the double virtue of expanding Southern markets and lowering pressures on Northern economies.

5. Developing-country leaders need to emphasize programs to meet the basic human needs of their poorest people and undertake programs to improve the distribution of income within their own countries. Such policies are necessary both for their own sake and to meet the concerns of those in the North who see the need for equity *within* as well as *among* states.

IV. *Both developed and developing countries need to establish new institutions and procedures for international decision making that will facilitate the establishment of mutually beneficial changes in the existing international economic systems.* Currently, discussions between North and South are hampered by the fact that institutions are dominated either by the rich countries (as in the International Monetary Fund) or by the poor countries (as in UNCTAD) or are so completely representative (the U.N. General Assembly is the most obvious example) as to make serious negotiation extremely difficult, if not completely impossible. Consequently, there is a need for developed and developing countries jointly to consider and bring about changes in institutions and procedures to facilitate North-South discussions and negotiations. Improvements of this type that merit consideration include the following:

1. Changing the membership and voting structure within institutions such as the IMF and World Bank in order to increase the participation of the developing countries. Over the longer period, the IMF hopefully can begin to assume more of the functions of a global central bank. In the trade field, where both the GATT and UNCTAD already exist, there may be need for some overall coordinating mechanism.

2. Seeking ways to create smaller subgroups, particularly within the United Nations system of organizations, so that those governments most deeply involved in any particular issue come to the center of the negotiations.

3. Creating, where necessary, new institutions to deal with new problems. The establishment of the International Fund for Agricultural Development is a pertinent example of an institution that has come into being in the last few years in which voting power is shared more equitably between donors and recipients and between developed and developing countries. A particularly urgent need is for some new international institutional structure to deal globally with the energy problem.

4. Finally, there is a need to agree on some new forum where both industrial and developing countries can meet to establish broad policy guidelines and periodically assess the progress in reforming and restructuring the international economic order. It now is increasingly unlikely that a "new international economic order" will be created in some grand negotiation analogous to the Congress of Vienna. Rather, it will take long, tough negotiations in a

series of separate and often technical forums. Therefore, some overview and assessment process will be needed. The design of such a forum has now been made much more difficult both by the demise of the Conference on International Economic Cooperation and by the uncertain start of its successor, the Committee of the Whole of the U.N. General Assembly. The crucial element in any new process or institution, however, will be the *political* commitment of leaders in both North and South to participate in such a process.

1. United Nations. *Monthly Bulletin of Statistics*, Vol. 32, No. 6, March 1978, Special Table C; and Vol. 31, No. 5, May 1977, Special Table C.

2. U.N. Conference on Trade and Development, "Trade Prospects and Capital Needs of Developing Countries, 1976–1978," Doc. No. TD/B/C.3/ 134, Geneva, April 15, 1976.

3. John A. Holsen and Jean L. Waelbroeck, "The Less Developed Countries and the International Monetary Mechanism," *American Economic Review*, Vol. 66, No. 2 (May 1976), p. 175.

4. Some observers also attribute part of the slowdown to the fact that the United States is losing its share of the markets in many developing countries. Frank A. Weil, Assistant Secretary of Commerce for Industry and Trade, estimates that the exports of America's major competitors in 1977 grew three to five times faster than the U.S. rate of 4.6 percent. (Testimony to the Subcommittee on International Finance, Senate Committee on Banking, Housing, and Urban Affairs, February 23, 1978, p. 16.)

5. William R. Cline, Noboru Kawanabe, T.O.M. Kronsjo, and Thomas Williams, *Trade Negotiations in the Tokyo Round: A Quantitative Assessment* (Washington, D.C.: Brookings Institution, 1978), p. 79.

6. Ibid., pp. 81–82.

7. *Consumer Reports* (January 1978), p. 19.

8. *World Development Report, 1978*, op. cit., p. 16.

9. ILO International Labour Office, *Employment, Growth and Basic Needs: A One-World Problem*, published for the Overseas Development Council in cooperation with the International

Labour Office (New York: Praeger Publishers, Inc., 1977), Chapter 7.

10. Development Policy Staff, *Prospects for Developing Countries, 1978–85* (Washington, D.C.: World Bank, 1977), p. 44.

11. Robert E. Baldwin, "Trade Policies and Protectionist Pressures in the United States" (Paper delivered at a conference on Challenges to a Liberal International Order, sponsored by American Enterprise Institute, Washington, D.C., December 1–2, 1977), mimeographed, p. 17.

12. Jere R. Behrman, *International Commodity Agreements: An Evaluation of the UNCTAD Integrated Commodity Programme*, Monograph No. 9, NIEO Series (Washington, D.C.: Overseas Development Council, 1977).

13. Lance Taylor, Alexander H. Sarris, and Phillip C. Abbott, "Grain Reserves, Emergency Relief, and Food Aid," NIEO Series, prepublication edition (Washington, D.C.: Overseas Development Council, 1977), mimeographed, p. iv.

14. Cited in Helen B. Junz, "The Bargain Must Be Balanced," *Foreign Policy*, No. 30 (Spring 1978), pp. 167–68.

Further Readings

1. The New International Economic Order

Al-khalat, Nazar. "OPEC Members and The New International Economic Order." *Journal of Energy and Development* 2, no. 2 (Spring 1977).

Amuzegar, Jahangir. "The North South Dialogue: From Conflict to Compromise." *Foreign Affairs* 54, no. 3 (April 1976).

Bauer, P. T., and Yamey, B. S. "Against the New Economic Order." *Commentary*, (April 1977).

Bhagwati, Jagdish N. *The New International Economic Order: The North-South Debate.* Cambridge, Mass.: MIT Press, 1977.

Green, R. H. and Singer, H. W. "Toward a Rational and Equitable New International Economic Order: A Case For Negotiated Structural Changes." *World Development* 3, no. 6 (June 1975).

Leontief, Wassily, et al. *The Future of the World Economy: A United Nations Study.* New York: Oxford University Press, 1977.

Lewis, W. Arthur. *The Evolution of the International Economic Order.* Princeton: Princeton, University Press, 1978.

Singh, Jyoti Shankar. *A New International Economic Order: Toward a Fair Redistribution of the World's Resources.* Praeger Special Studies in International Economics and Development. New York: Praeger, 1977.

Tinbergen. Jan, coordinator. *RIO: Reshaping the International Order.* A Report to the Club of Rome. New York: Dutton, 1978.

Ul Haq, Muhbub. *The Poverty Curtain: Choices for the Third World.* New York: Columbia University Press, 1976.

UNESCO. "Towards a New International Economic and Social Order." *International Social Science Journal* 28, no. 4 (1976).

United Nations. *Declaration on the Establishment of a New International Economic Order, Resolutions of the General Assembly at its Sixth Special Session, April 9– May 2, 1974.* New York, 1974.

Contributors

1. Werner Baer is Professor of Economics at the University of Illinois at Urbana-Champaign.
2. Assefa Bequela is with the International Labour Office, Geneva.
3. Nancy Birdsall is an economist at the World Bank, Washington, D.C.
4. Brandt Comission is more formally known as the Independent Commission on International Development Issues under the Chairmanship of Willy Brandt. Its Executive Secretary was Goran Ohlin and its staff included Liaqat Ali, Robert Cassen, S. Guhan, Jafad K. Halitzadeh-Sirazi, Martha Loutfi, Justinian Reveyemamu and Gerhard Thiebach.
5. Gilbert T. Brown is an economist with the World Bank, Washington D.C.
6. Hollis Chenery was Vice President, Development Policy, at the World Bank and is now Professor of Economics at Harvard University.
7. Theotonio Dos Santos is at the Center for Economic Studies, University of Chile.
8. Charles R. Frank is a Vice President, Salomon Brothers, and formerly Deputy Assistant Secretary, U.S. Department of State. Dr. Frank is an economist.
9. David H. Freedman is with the International Labour Office, Geneva.
10. Alejandro Foxley is an economist at CIEPLAN, a social science research unit in Santiago, Chile.
11. Denis Goulet, a philosopher/political scientist, is O'Neil Professor, Education for Justice, at the University of Notre Dame.
12. John Harris is Professor of Economics and Director, African Studies Center, Boston University.
13. Peter J. Henriot, a political scientist, is Director of the Center for Concern, Washington, D.C.
14. Norman Hicks is a Senior Economist in the Policy Planning and Program Review Department of the World Bank, Washington, D.C.
15. Jean-Pierre Jallade is an economist with the Institute of Education, European Cultural Foundation, Paris.
16. Donald Keesing is an economist with the World Bank, Washinton, D.C.
17. Tony Killick is an economist with the Overseas Development Institute in London.
18. Simon Kuznets is Professor of Economics, Harvard University.
19. Franklyn Lisk is an economist with the International Labour Office, Geneva.
20. Geoffrey McNicoll, an economist/demographer, is Deputy Director and Senior Associate, Center for Policy Studies, Population Council.
21. Moni Nag, an anthropologist, is a Senior Associate, Center for Policy Studies, Population Council.
22. Howard Pack is Professor of Economics, Swarthmore College.
23. Gustav Papanek is Professor of Economics, Boston University.
24. John W. Sewell is President of the Overseas Development Council, Washington, D.C.
25. Alan B. Simmons is a sociologist/demographer with the International Development Research Center, Ottawa, Canada.
26. John Simmons was an educational economist at the World Bank, Washington, D.C. He is currently Professor of Labor-Management Relations, University of Massachusetts.
27. Sheila Smith is a Fellow of Girton College, Cambridge, and Assistant Director of Development Studies, University of Cambridge.
28. Frances Stewart is a Fellow of Sommerville College, Oxford University and

Senior Research Officer at the Institute of Commonwealth Studies in Oxford University.

29. Paul Streeten is Professor of Economics and Director of the Center for Asian Development Studies at Boston University.

30. John Toye is a Fellow of Wolfson College, Cambridge and Assistant Director of Development Studies, University of Cambridge.

31. Mahbub ul Haq is Director of the Policy Planning and Program Review Department of the World Bank, Washington, D.C. He was previously Chief Economic Advisor of the Pakistan Planning Commission.

32. Richard Webb is an economist with the World Bank, Washington, D.C. and was formerly Chairman of the Department of Economics, Catholic University of Lima.

33. Clifton R. Wharton is Chancellor of the State University of New York. Dr. Wharton is an agricultural economist.